"Matthew Harmon's *Galatians* offers rich fare for students, pastors, and scholars alike. Building on the flurry of recent scholarship on the letter, Harmon provides a sure path through the interpretive hotspots. Two features of this commentary especially stand out. Harmon builds on his own prior scholarly labors in identifying and analyzing Paul's use of Scripture. That foundation serves the reader well when Harmon turns to the biblical and theological motifs in the letter. Harmon does not leave matters in the first century but shows how Paul continues to speak to us today."

—**A. Andrew Das,** *professor of religious studies, assistant dean of the faculty, Elmhurst University*

"Matthew S. Harmon offers a detailed and rigorous analysis of Paul's letter to the Galatians, mindful of exegetical detail as well as wider theological themes. An excellent treatment of the text that will benefit students and pastors alike."

—**Michael F. Bird,** *academic dean and lecturer in theology, Ridley College, Melbourne, Australia*

"Matt Harmon has written a fine commentary that helps pastors and students alike to understand Paul's succinct formulations of central aspects of his theology. Readers who look for assistance on Greek formulations, on historical matters, on the structure of Paul's argumentation, on exegetical details, and on theological emphases will find it all in this compact volume. As is always the case in a commentary, there are places where readers will beg to differ with some detail or conclusion, but Harmon's always-fair discussion will force dissenters to reevaluate their position. The *Bridge* sections contain helpful material for personal and pastoral application."

—**Eckhard J. Schnabel,** *Mary F. Rockefeller Distinguished Professor of New Testament, Gordon-Conwell Theological Seminary*

"Matthew Harmon strikes a fine balance between introductory issues, exegesis, and thematic discussion covering nine different topics ranging from God to justification and righteousness to Paul's use of the Old Testament in Galatians. In other words, this is a feast, featuring up-to-date interaction with a foundational Pauline epistle viewed within the context of the best current scholarship. The volume richly fulfills the aims of a biblical theology commentary, in that the exegesis is faithful to the text ('biblical'), while the exposition does justice to Paul's towering awareness of God, Jesus, the Messiah, and the human plight ('theological'). A great commentary for this cultural moment and far beyond!"

—**Robert W. Yarbrough,** *professor of New Testament, Covenant Theological Seminary*

"Whereas most New Testament commentaries miss the theological wood for the exegetical trees, Harmon's *Galatians* commentary keeps both firmly in view. A rich and rewarding exposition of Paul's most passionate epistle, the book offers not only insightful treatments of faith, justification and the law, but also salvation history, humanity, Christology and the doctrine of God, all set within the context of Paul's use of the Old Testament. A model of theological interpretation and biblical theology, and a gift to preachers."

—**Brian S. Rosner,** *principal, Ridley College, Australia*

Matthew S. Harmon has written a well-researched commentary that both judiciously weighs the interpretive options without overwhelming the reader with minutiae and sagaciously guides the reader in opening up the truth of the gospel that Paul conveys in this letter. What is most valuable is the extensive section on biblical and theological themes with its rich fund of theological insights. Having read through the analysis of the text, one can better appreciate how Galatians fits theologically in the larger canon and notably contributes to it. This commentary will amply reward preachers, teachers, and students of Galatians who purchase it and use it.

—**David E. Garland,** *professor of Christian Scriptures, George W. Truett Theological Seminary, Baylor University*

"Dr. Harmon's important commentary will help readers understand Paul's letter to the Galatians in light of the most recent research on the letter and recent debates about Paul and his theology. This commentary also reflects the insights that come when a scholar seeks to understand not only what Paul is saying, but also why Paul thinks and argues the way that he does. That is, Harmon pays close attention, as we all should, to the way that Paul's interpretation of the Old Testament and that his own type of biblical theology grounds and informs the apostle's thought and arguments. While providing strong arguments for his own interpretive decisions, Harmon does not neglect to mention alternative proposals where appropriate. This commentary will enrich the understanding of students, pastors, and scholars!"

—**Roy E. Ciampa,** *S. Louis and Ann W. Armstrong Professor of Religion; chair of the department of biblical and religious studies, Samford University*

"Commentaries on Galatians are a dime a dozen, but few Galatians commentaries excel in clarity and robust biblical-theological insight. Galatians, too, is a difficult book to understand, but Harmon wisely guides his readers through the thicket of grammatical, theological, and historical issues. I'm eager for the church to put this excellent commentary to use. Pastors and scholars will not be disappointed."

—**Benjamin L. Gladd,** *associate professor of New Testament, Reformed Theological Seminary*

GALATIANS

GALATIANS

Evangelical Biblical Theology Commentary

General Editors

T. Desmond Alexander, Thomas R. Schreiner,
Andreas J. Köstenberger

Assistant Editors

James M. Hamilton, Kenneth A. Mathews,
Terry L. Wilder

Matthew S. Harmon

 LEXHAM
ACADEMIC

Galatians
Evangelical Biblical Theology Commentary

Copyright 2021 Matthew S. Harmon

Lexham Academic, an imprint of Lexham Press
1313 Commercial St., Bellingham, WA 98225
LexhamPress.com

Print ISBN 9781683595632
Library of Congress Control Number 2021940551

General Editors: T. Desmond Alexander, Thomas R. Schreiner, Andreas J. Köstenberger
Assistant Editors: James M. Hamilton, Kenneth A. Mathews, Terry L. Wilder
Lexham Editorial: Derek Brown, Elizabeth Vince, Abigail Salinger, Jessi Strong,
    Mandi Newell, Abigail Stocker, Danielle Thevenaz
Cover Design: Joshua Hunt
Typesetting: Justin Marr

CONTENTS

GENERAL EDITORS' PREFACE

I n recent years biblical theology has seen a remarkable resurgence. Whereas, in 1970, Brevard Childs wrote *Biblical Theology in Crisis*, the quest for the Bible's own theology has witnessed increasing vitality since Childs prematurely decried the demise of the movement. Nowhere has this been truer than in evangelical circles. It could be argued that evangelicals, with their commitment to biblical inerrancy and inspiration, are perfectly positioned to explore the Bible's unified message. At the same time, as D. A. Carson has aptly noted, perhaps the greatest challenge faced by biblical theologians is how to handle the Bible's manifest diversity and how to navigate the tension between its unity and diversity in a way that does justice to both.[1]

What is biblical theology? And how is biblical theology different from related disciplines such as systematic theology? These two exceedingly important questions must be answered by anyone who would make a significant contribution to the discipline. Regarding the first question, the most basic answer might assert that biblical theology, in essence, is *the theology of the Bible*, that is, the theology expressed by the respective writers of the various biblical books *on their own terms* and *in their own historical contexts*. Biblical theology is the attempt to understand and embrace *the interpretive perspective of the biblical authors*. What is more, biblical theology is the theology of the *entire* Bible, an exercise in *whole-Bible theology*. For this reason biblical theology is not just a modern academic discipline; its roots are found already in the use of earlier Old Testament portions

---

[1] D. A. Carson, "New Testament Theology," in *DLNT* 810.

in later Old Testament writings and in the use of the Old Testament in the New.

Biblical theology thus involves a close study of *the use of the Old Testament in the Old Testament* (that is, the use of, say, Deuteronomy by Jeremiah, or of the Pentateuch by Isaiah). Biblical theology also entails the investigation of *the use of the Old Testament in the New*, both in terms of individual passages and in terms of larger Christological or soteriological themes. Biblical theology may proceed *book by book*, trace *central themes* in Scripture, or seek to place the contributions of individual biblical writers within the framework of the Bible's larger overarching *metanarrative*, that is, the Bible's developing story from Genesis through Revelation at whose core is *salvation* or *redemptive history*, the account of God's dealings with humanity and his people Israel and the church from creation to new creation.

In this quest for the Bible's own theology, we will be helped by the inquiries of those who have gone before us in the *history of the church*. While we can profitably study the efforts of interpreters over the entire sweep of the history of biblical interpretation since patristic times, we can also benefit from the labors of scholars since J. P. Gabler, whose programmatic inaugural address at the University of Altdorf, Germany, in 1787 marks the inception of the discipline in modern times. Gabler's address bore the title "On the Correct Distinction between Dogmatic and Biblical Theology and the Right Definition of Their Goals."[2] While few (if any) within evangelicalism would fully identify with Gabler's program, the proper distinction between dogmatic and biblical theology (that is, between biblical and systematic theology) continues to be an important issue to be adjudicated by practitioners of both disciplines, and especially biblical theology. We have already defined biblical theology as whole-Bible theology, describing the theology of the various biblical books *on their own terms* and *in their own historical contexts*. Systematic theology, by contrast, is more topically oriented and focused on contemporary contextualization. While there are different ways in which the relationship between biblical and systematic theology can be construed, maintaining a proper distinction between the two disciplines arguably continues to be vital if both are to achieve their objectives.

---

[2] The original Latin title was *Oratio de iusto discrimine theologiae biblicae et dogmaticae regundisque recte utriusque finibus.*

The present set of volumes constitutes an ambitious project, seeking to explore the theology of the Bible in considerable depth, spanning both Testaments. Authors come from a variety of backgrounds and perspectives, though all affirm the inerrancy and inspiration of Scripture. United in their high view of Scripture and in their belief in the underlying unity of Scripture, which is ultimately grounded in the unity of God himself, each author explores the contribution of a given book or group of books to the theology of Scripture as a whole. While conceived as stand-alone volumes, each volume thus also makes a contribution to the larger whole. All volumes provide a discussion of introductory matters, including the historical setting and the literary structure of a given book of Scripture. Also included is an exegetical treatment of all the relevant passages in succinct commentary-style format. The biblical theology approach of the series will also inform and play a role in the commentary proper. The commentator permits a discussion between the commentary proper and the biblical theology it reflects by a series of cross-references.

The major contribution of each volume, however, is a thorough discussion of the most important themes of the biblical book in relation to the canon as a whole. This format allows each contributor to ground biblical theology, as is proper, in an appropriate appraisal of the relevant historical and literary features of a particular book in Scripture while at the same time focusing on its major theological contribution to the entire Christian canon in the context of the larger salvation-historical metanarrative of Scripture. Within this overall format, there will be room for each individual contributor to explore the major themes of his or her particular corpus in the way he or she sees most appropriate for the material under consideration. For some books of the Bible, it may be best to have these theological themes set out in advance of the exegetical commentary. For other books it may be better to explain the theological themes after the commentary. Consequently, each contributor has the freedom to order these sections as best suits the biblical material under consideration so that the discussion of biblical-theological themes may precede or follow the exegetical commentary.

This format, in itself, would already be a valuable contribution to biblical theology. But other series try to accomplish a survey of the Bible's theology as well. What distinguishes the present series is its orientation toward Christian proclamation. This is the Evangelical Biblical Theology Commentary series! As a result, the ultimate purpose of this set of volumes is not exclusively, or even primarily, academic. Rather, we seek to relate biblical theology to our own lives and to the life of the church. Our desire is to equip those in Christian ministry who are called by God to preach and teach the precious truths of Scripture to their congregations, both in North America and in a global context.

The base translation for the Evangelical Biblical Theology Commentary series is the Christian Standard Bible (csb). The csb places equal value on faithfulness to the original languages and readability for a modern audience. The contributors, however, have the liberty to differ with the csb as they comment on the biblical text. Note that, in the csb, Old Testament passages that are quoted in the New Testament are set in boldface type.

We hope and pray that the forty volumes of this series, once completed, will bear witness to the unity in diversity of the canon of Scripture as they probe the individual contributions of each of its sixty-six books. The authors and editors are united in their desire that in so doing the series will magnify the name of Christ and bring glory to the triune God who revealed himself in Scripture so that everyone who calls on the name of the Lord will be saved—to the glory of God the Father and his Son, the Lord Jesus Christ, under the illumination of the Holy Spirit, and for the good of his church. To God alone be the glory: *soli Deo gloria*.

LIST OF ABBREVIATIONS

AB	Anchor Bible
AnBib	Analecta Biblica
AcBib	Academia Biblica
ASV	American Standard Version
BDAG	Danker, Frederick W., Walter Bauer, William F. Aarndt, and F. Wilbur Gingrich. *Greek-English Lexicon of the New Testament and Other Early Christian Literature.* 3rd ed. Chicago: University of Chicago Press, 2000 (Danker-Bauer-Arndt-Gingrich)
BDF	Blass, Friedrich, Albert Debrunner, and Robert W. Funk. *A Greek Grammar of the New Testament and Other Early Christian Literature.* Chicago: University of Chicago Press, 1961
BECNT	Baker Exegetical Commentary on the New Testament
BHGNT	Baylor Handbook on the Greek New Testament
BHT	Beiträge zur historischen Theologie
Bib	*Biblica*
BJRL	Bulletin of the John Rylands University Library of Manchester
BLG	Biblical Languages: Greek
BNTC	Black's New Testament Commentary Series
BrillDAG	The Brill Dictionary of Ancient Greek
BSac	*Bibliotheca Sacra*
BZNW	Beihefte zur Zeitschrift für die neutestamentliche Wissenchaft
CBQ	*Catholic Biblical Quarterly*

CSB	Christian Standard Bible (2017)
CurBR	*Currents in Biblical Research (formerly Currents in Research: Biblical Studies)*
CurTM	*Currents in Theology and Mission*
CTR	*Criswell Theological Review*
CTJ	*Calvin Theological Journal*
DBI	*Dictionary of Biblical Interpretation.* Edited by John Hays. 2 vols. Nashville: Abingdon, 1999
DLNT	Dictionary of the Later New Testament and Its Developments
DNTB	*Dictionary of New Testament Background.* Edited by Craig A. Evans and Stanley E. Porter. Downers Grove, IL: InterVarsity Press, 2000.
DNTUOT	*Dictionary of the New Testament Use of the Old Testament.* Edited by G. K. Beale and D. A. Carson. Grand Rapids: Baker, forthcoming
EDNT	*Exegetical Dictionary of the New Testament.* Edited by Horst Balz and Gerhard Scheider. ET. 3 vols. Grand Rapids: Eerdmans, 1990–1993
ESBT	Essential Studies in Biblical Theology
ESEC	Emory Studies in Early Christianity
ESV	English Standard Version (2001)
ET	*English Translation*
EvQ	*Evangelical Quarterly*
FRLANT	Forschungen zur Religion und Literatur des Alten und Neuen Testaments
ITC	International Theological Commentary
HALOT	*The Hebrew and Aramaic Lexicon of the Old Testament.* Ludwig Koehler, Walter Baumgartner, and Hohan J. Stamm. Translated and edited under the supervision of Mervyn E. J. Richardson. 4 vols. Leiden: Brill, 1994–1999
HCSB	Holman Christian Standard Bible (2009)
HTR	*Harvard Theological Review*
KJV	King James Version
NKJV	New King James Version (1982)
JBL	*Journal of Biblical Literature*
JETS	*Journal of the Evangelical Theological Society*
JGRChJ	*Journal of Greco-Roman Chrstianity and Judaism*
JSJ	*Journal for the Study of Judaism in the Persian, Hellenistic, and Roman Periods*

JSNT	*Journal for the Study of the New Testament*
JSOT	*Journal for the Study of the Old Testament*
LD	Lectio Divina
LD Commentaries	Commentaire biblique: Nouveau Testament
LNTS	The Library of New Testament Studies
LSJM	*Liddell and Scott Greek-English Lexicon with Revised Supplement*
LXX	Septuagint (early Greek translation of the Old Testament)
MM	Moulton, James H., and George Milligan. *The Vocabulary of the Greek Testament.* London, 1930. Prepr., Peabody, MA: Henderson, 1997
NAC	The New American Commentary
NASB	New American Standard Bible (2020)
NET	New English Translation (2017)
NETS	A New English Translation of the Septuagint (2007)
NICNT	The New International Commentary on the New Testament
NICOT	New International Commentary on the Old Testament
NIDNTT	*New International Dictionary of New Testament Theology*
NIDNTTE	*New International Dictionary of New Testament Theology and Exegesis*
NIGTC	The New International Greek Testament Commentary
NIV	New International Version (2011)
NIV1984	New International Version (1984)
NLT	New Living Translation (2015)
NovT	*Novum Testamentum*
NovTSup	Supplements to Novum Testamentum
NSBT	New Studies in Biblical Theology
NT	New Testament
NTL	The New Testament Library
NTS	New Testament Studies
OT	Old Testament
OTL	Old Testament Library
PRSt	*Perspectives in Religious Studies*
RSV	Revised Standard Version (1971)
NRSV	New Revised Standard Version (1989)

SBJT	*The Southern Baptist Journal of Theology*
SBLDS	*Society of Biblical Literature Dissertation Series*
SNTSMS	Society for New Testament Studies Monograph Series
TDNT	*Theological Dictionary of the New Testament.* Edited by Gerhard Kittel and Gerhard Friedrich. Translated by Geoffrey W. Bromiley. 10 vols. Grand Rapids: Eerdmans, 1964–1976
Tg	Targum
TLZ	*Theologische Literaturzeitung*
TRENT	Traditions of the Rabbis from the Era of the New Testament
TWOT	*Theological Workbook of the Old Testament.* Edited by R. Laird Harris, Gleason L. Archer Jr., and Bruce K. Waltke. 2 vols. Chicago: Moody Press, 1980
TynBul	*Tyndale Bulletin*
VT	*Vetus Testamentum*
WBC	Word Biblical Commentary
WTJ	*Westminster Theological Journal*
WUNT	Wissenschaftliche Untersuchungen zum Neuen Testament
ZECNT	Zondervan Exegetical Commentary on the New Testament
ZNW	*Zeitschrift für die neutestamentliche Wissenchaft und die Kunde der älteren Kirche*
ZPEB	*Zondervan Pictorial Encyclopedia of the Bible.* Edited by Merrill C. Tenney. 5 vols. Grand Rapids: Zondervan, 1975
ZTK	*Zeitschrift für Theologie und Kirche*

INTRODUCTION

" G alatians is my favorite epistle, the one in which I place all my trust. It is my Katie von Bora."[1] Martin Luther could think of no higher praise for Paul's Letter to the Galatians than to compare it to his beloved wife. Few books of the Bible have had as much historical impact on the church as Galatians.

I. Author

The opening line of the letter unambiguously identifies the apostle Paul as the author of the letter, and even the most critical scholars rarely if ever challenge this.[2] Paul almost certainly wrote this letter through an amanuensis—a person trained in taking dictation for letters. In 6:11 Paul confirms that he used this common custom in the ancient world by noting: "Look at what large letters I use as I write to you in my own handwriting." At this point Paul signals he has taken the pen from the scribe and is writing the final paragraph himself. Even when using an amanuensis, authors in the ancient world would often write the final lines of a letter in their own handwriting to authenticate the genuineness of the letter.[3] Second Thessalonians 3:17 confirms that Paul did this: "I, Paul,

---

[1] Martin Luther, *Off the Record with Martin Luther: An Original Translation of the Table Talks*, trans. Charles Daudert (Kalamazoo, MI: Hansa-Hewlett, 2009), 311.

[2] A notable twist on this consensus may be found in J. C. O'Neill, *The Recovery of Paul's Letter to the Galatians* (London: SPCK, 1972), 1–15, 73–83; he concludes that Paul only wrote two-thirds of Galatians.

[3] See E. Randolph Richards, *Paul and First-Century Letter Writing: Secretaries, Composition, and Collection* (Downers Grove, IL: IVP, 2004), 171–75.

am writing this greeting with my own hand, which is an authenticating mark in every letter; this is how I write."

II. Recipients & Date

Because the questions surrounding the date and recipients of Galatians are so intertwined, they must be treated together. There are at least three key issues that must be addressed to determine who the Galatians were and when Paul wrote this letter to them: (1) how the terms "Galatia" and "Galatians" are used; (2) the relationship between the events in Acts (esp. the Jerusalem Council in Acts 15:1–35) and the events recorded in Galatians (especially 2:1–14); and (3) proposed verbal and theological similarities between this letter and other Pauline Epistles (especially Romans).

Before we explore these issues, it should be emphasized that one's conclusions on these matters do not necessarily result in radically different interpretations of the meaning of Galatians as a whole. But they do affect one's understanding of specific passages (esp. Gal 2:1–14), the circumstances that form the historical context of the letter, and the effort to reconstruct the early history of the church. So to that end we will look at each of these issues individually before attempting a synthesis.

A. The Meaning of the Terms "Galatia" and "Galatians"

In Galatians 1:2 Paul indicates that he is writing to "the churches of Galatia" (ταῖς ἐκκλησίαις τῆς Γαλατίας). The noun Γαλατία was used in two primary ways.[4] First, it could refer to an ethnic or tribal group from Gaul who migrated to the central plains of Asia Minor (modern-day Turkey) during the third century BC. They eventually settled in the towns of Tavium, Pessinus, and Ancyra, and were allowed to govern themselves even after the Romans gained control of the area in 189 BC.[5] Known as the North Galatian theory, it was the virtual consensus of scholars until the nineteenth century and is still held by many today.[6]

---

[4] The same is true of the adjective Γαλατικός (Acts 16:6; 18:23) and the noun Γαλάτης (Gal 3:1).

[5] For a concise summary of the history of Galatia, see Eckhard J. Schnabel, *Early Christian Mission* (Downers Grove, IL: IVP, 2004), 2:1094–96.

[6] Among the more recent commentaries, advocates of North Galatia include Hans Dieter Betz, *Galatians: A Commentary on Paul's Letter to the Churches in Galatia* (Philadelphia: Fortress, 1979), 1–5; James D. G. Dunn, *The Epistle to the Galatians*, BNTC (Peabody, MA: Hendrickson,

But, secondly, Galatia could refer to the Roman province created in 25 BC, which, in addition to the area where ethnic Galatians lived, included the area of Lycaonia, Isauria, and parts of Phrygia and Pisidia. As such it included the cities of Pisidian Antioch, Iconium, Lystra, and Derbe, where Paul planted churches during his first missionary journey (Acts 13:1–14:28). This view is known as the South Galatian theory and is held by a number of scholars.[7] So which sense does Γαλατία have here in Galatians 1:2?

From the internal evidence of Galatians itself, the most one can say is that evidence supporting both views yet not decisively excluding either may be found within Galatians itself. Advocates of North Galatia sometimes suggest that the lack of reference to persecution in Paul's description of his own preaching of the gospel when founding the Galatian churches cannot be easily squared with the mention of persecution Paul faced in Pisidian Antioch, Iconium, Derbe and Lystra recorded in

---

1993), 5–7; J. Louis Martyn, *Galatians: A New Translation with Introduction and Commentary*, AB 33 (New York: Doubleday, 1997), 15–17; Martinus C. de Boer, *Galatians: A Commentary* (NTL; Louisville: Westminster John Knox, 2011), 3–5; in addition to the commentaries, see Colin J. Hemer, *The Book of Acts in the Setting of Hellenistic History* (Winona Lake, IN: Eisenbrauns, 1990), 277–307; Raymond E. Brown, *An Introduction to the New Testament* (New York: Doubleday, 1997), 468–77.

[7] For the South Galatian view, see Ernest De Witt Burton, *A Critical and Exegetical Commentary on the Epistle to the Galatians*, ICC (Edinburgh: T&T Clark, 1920), xxi–xliv; F. F. Bruce, *The Epistle to the Galatians: A Commentary on the Greek Text*, NIGTC (Grand Rapids: Eerdmans, 1982), 3–18; Ronald Y. K. Fung, *The Epistle to the Galatians*, NICNT (Grand Rapids: Eerdmans, 1988), 1–3; Richard N. Longenecker, *Galatians*, WBC 41 (Dallas: Word, 1990), lxi–lxxii; Timothy George, *Galatians*, NAC (Nashville: B&H, 1994), 40–46; Ben Witherington, *Grace in Galatia: A Commentary on St. Paul's Letter to the Galatians* (Grand Rapids: Eerdmans, 1998), 2–20; Simon Légasse, *L'épître De Paul Aux Galates*, LD 9 (Paris: Cerf, 2000), 28–30; Thomas R. Schreiner, *Galatians*, ZECNT (Grand Rapids: Zondervan, 2010), 22–31; Douglas J. Moo, *Galatians*, BECNT (Grand Rapids: Baker, 2013), 2–18; A. Andrew Das, *Galatians*, ConcC (St. Louis: Concordia, 2014), 20–30; David A. DeSilva, *The Letter to the Galatians*, NICNT (Grand Rapids: Eerdmans, 2018), 39–48; Craig S. Keener, *Galatians: A Commentary* (Grand Rapids: Baker, 2019), 16–22. Also noteworthy is James M. Scott, *Paul and the Nations: The Old Testament and Jewish Background of Paul's Mission to the Nations with Special Reference to the Destination of Galatians*, WUNT 84 (Tübingen: J. C. B. Mohr, 1995). After an extensive survey of the table of nations in the OT, Jewish tradition, and in Paul, Scott turns to consider how this tradition might inform the destination of Galatians. He concludes that from this Jewish perspective Paul is "most likely sending his letter ... to the churches of Phrygia-Galatica, which he founded on his First Missionary Journey and then visited again on his Second Missionary Journey" (215). Although one may question the pervasiveness within Second Temple Judaism of viewing the world through the lens of the Table of Nations, Scott is to be applauded for approaching the issue from a unique angle, and his contribution deserves serious consideration.

Acts 13–14.[8] South Galatia proponents note that the three references to Barnabas (Gal 2:1, 9, 13) suggest that he was known to the Galatian churches, which indicates that Barnabas was part of founding the Galatian churches. According to Acts, however, Barnabas only accompanied Paul during his first missionary journey, during which the churches in the South Galatia hypothesis were planted.[9] But in both cases the arguments hinge upon the testimony of Acts and not the internal evidence of Galatians alone.

The other two occurrences of the noun Γαλατία in Paul's letter do not settle the debate. Both 1 Corinthians 16:1 ("Do the same as I instructed the Galatian churches") and 2 Timothy 4:10 ("Crescens has gone to Galatia") could be understood in either an ethnic or provincial sense. When Peter addresses his first letter to those "living as exiles dispersed abroad in Pontus, Galatia, Cappadocia, Asia, and Bithynia" (1 Pet 1:1), he most likely refers to the province of Galatia. But even if that is so, it does not settle how Paul is using the term.

More significant is the evidence from Acts, where Luke twice uses the adjective Γαλατικός. After adding Timothy to his ministry team in Lystra (Acts 16:1–5), Paul and Timothy "went through the region of Phrygia and Galatia" (τὴν Φρυγίαν καὶ Γαλατικὴν χώραν) (Acts 16:6). Although the grammar of this expression is debated, the reference here is most likely to the southern portion of the province of Galatia, where Paul had planted churches during his first missionary journey.[10] Geographical considerations further support a South Galatia view, as the territory represented by the North Galatia view was not as populous, had cities that generally lacked any Jewish population, and presented language barriers.[11]

---

[8] See, e.g., James Moffatt, *An Introduction to the Literature of the New Testament* (3rd ed.; New York: Scribner's Sons, 1915), 99.

[9] See Richard Bauckham, "Barnabas in Galatians," *JSNT* 2 (1979): 61–70.

[10] Burton (*Galatians*, xxxi–xxxii) notes that geographical names ending in -ια (such as Φρυγία) were regularly used as adjectives, strongly suggesting that Φρυγία here functions as an adjective modifying the noun χώραν. By bracketing Φρυγίαν καὶ Γαλατικὴν with the definite article and the singular noun χώραν, Luke signals he means one region instead of two. The expression "distinguishes the part of Galatia that is Phrygian (much of the southern region of the province of Galatia) from Galatian territory that is not" (Craig S. Keener, *Acts: An Exegetical Commentary*, 4 vols. [Grand Rapids: Baker Academic, 2012–2015], 3:2324–25).

[11] For discussion of the geographical data, see Rainer Riesner, *Paul's Early Period: Chronology, Mission Strategy, Theology* (Grand Rapids: Eerdmans, 1998), 281–86; Stephen Mitchell, *Anatolia: Land, Men, and Gods in Asia Minor*, 2 vols. (Oxford: Clarendon, 1993), 2:3–4; Cilliers Breytenbach, "Probable Reasons for Paul's Unfruitful Missionary Attempts in Asia Minor (a Note on Acts

Furthermore, even if one concludes that North Galatia is intended here, the text merely notes that Paul passed through the region and gives no indication that he engaged in ministry there, much less that he planted churches. At most Acts 16:6 allows for the *possibility* that Paul engaged in ministry in the northern regions of provincial Galatia, but given the importance of the issues addressed in Galatians, it seems strange that Luke would not mention the planting of these churches if the recipients of Galatians were churches in North Galatia.

Several years later, after spending some time in Antioch, Paul "set out, traveling through one place after another in the region of Galatia and Phrygia [τὴν Γαλατικὴν χώραν καὶ Φρυγίαν], strengthening all the disciples" (Acts 18:23). Although the grammar of this expression is slightly different from that in Acts 16:6,[12] on the whole it seems most likely that Luke refers to the province of Galatia where Paul planted churches during the first missionary journey, and Phrygia refers to the part of that region located in the province in Asia toward Ephesus.[13]

Thus, although the use of the noun Γαλατία in the New Testament cannot determine decisively whether it is being used ethnically or provincially, the use of the related adjective Γαλατικός in Acts favors a provincial reference to South Galatia, where Paul and Barnabas planted churches in Pisidian Antioch, Iconium, Lystra, and Derbe. Given the fact that ethnic Galatians were in Paul's time only a small minority in any region of the province of Galatia, Oakes concludes that the apostle addressing them "would be such an unusual proceeding for Paul that, if

16:6–7)," in *Die Apostelgeschichte und die hellenistiche Geschichtsschreibung: Festschrift für Eckhard Plümacher zu seinem 65. Geburtstag*, ed. Cilliers Breytenbach and Jens Schroter (Leiden: Brill, 2004), 157–69. Some advocates of North Galatia object that South Galatia cannot be referred to in Acts 16:6 because that area has already been mentioned in 16:4–5. But 16:5 could be understood parenthetically, with 16:6 repeating the action of 16:4, removing this difficulty; see Moo, *Galatians*, 7 and Keener, *Acts*, 3:2325.

[12] Whereas the grammar of 16:6 (τὴν Φρυγίαν καὶ Γαλατικὴν χώραν) suggests that Paul refers to one region yet specifies a specific portion of it (i.e., the Phrygian area of Galatia, referring to the southern portion), the grammar of Acts 18:23 (τὴν Γαλατικὴν χώραν καὶ Φρυγίαν) seems to distinguish between Galatia and Phrygia as distinct regions. The difference is that in Acts 16:6 Luke places the noun Φρυγίαν and the adjective Γαλατικὴν (joined by καί) between the definite article and the one noun (χώραν) they both modify. Here the adjective Γαλατικὴν is placed between the definite article and the noun χώραν but is followed by καί and the noun Φρυγίαν.

[13] See the discussions in Hemer, *The Book of Acts in the Setting of Hellenistic History*, 120; Riesner, *Paul's Early Period*, 285–86; Schnabel, *Early Christian Mission*, 2:1199–200.

he were doing it, we would expect to see much more obvious signs why his mission proceeded here along such *ethnically* specific lines—something radically at odds with his general religious ideas."[14] While some have objected that Paul would not have called people living in Lyconia and Pisidia "Galatians,"[15] Das is correct that if Paul writes to the churches in Pisidian Antioch, Iconium, Lystra, and Derbe, "the only term he could use that would include the entirety of his audience would be 'Galatians.' "[16]

B. THE RELATIONSHIP BETWEEN ACTS AND GALATIANS

Once we accept that Acts provides historically reliable information about Paul's ministry, we have another asset in determining the date and recipients.[17] Unfortunately, the evidence from Acts is not clear cut and can be interpreted in different ways. The central issue is the number of post-conversion visits that Paul makes to Jerusalem. In Galatians Paul mentions two visits: three years after his conversion (1:18) and then "after fourteen years" (2:1). Acts mentions at least four visits: a post-conversion visit (9:26–30), the famine relief visit (11:27–30), the Jerusalem council (15:1–29), and the visit during which he was arrested in the temple (21:15–23:22). This last visit can safely be ruled out as too late in Paul's life, leaving three visits in Acts to line up with the two in Galatians.[18]

---

[14] Peter Oakes, *Galatians*, Paideia (Grand Rapids: Baker, 2015), 18.

[15] So de Boer, *Galatians*, 4.

[16] Das, *Galatians*, 28

[17] The historical reliability and value of Acts in reconstructing the early Christian movement in general and Paul's life in particular remain hotly disputed issues that cannot be resolved here. I am persuaded that Acts contains independent and reliable information about Paul and his ministry, and will accordingly draw upon it when pertinent. For a defense of the historical reliability of Acts in general, see Martin Hengel, *Acts and the History of Earliest Christianity* (Philadelphia: Fortress, 1980); W. Ward Gasque, *A History of the Interpretation of the Acts of the Apostles* (Peabody, MA: Hendrickson, 1989); Hemer, *The Book of Acts in the Setting of Hellenistic History*; Bruce W. Winter, ed., *The Book of Acts in Its First Century Setting*, 6 vols. (Grand Rapids: Eerdmans, 1993–1996); and Keener, *Acts*, 1:90–220. With specific reference to the value of Acts for reliable information on Paul, see F. F. Bruce, "Is the Paul of Acts the Real Paul?," *BJRL* 58 (1975): 282–305; Joseph A. Fitzmyer, *The Acts of the Apostles*, AB 31 (New York: Doubleday, 1998), 129–41; Ben Witherington, *The Acts of the Apostles: A Socio-Rhetorical Commentary* (Grand Rapids: Eerdmans, 1998), 430–38; Stanley E. Porter, *Paul in Acts* (Peabody, MA: Hendrickson, 2001), 205–6; Keener, *Acts*, 1:221–57. For an excellent survey of research on the use of the Acts material in constructing a Pauline chronology, see Riesner, *Paul's Early Period*, 1–28.

[18] It is, of course, possible that neither Paul nor Acts mentions every trip that Paul made to Jerusalem. But it seems unlikely that in Galatians Paul would omit a visit to Jerusalem,

Since there is widespread agreement that the post-conversion visit Paul
mentions in Galatians 1:17 corresponds to Acts 9:26–30, the main question is which visit mentioned in Acts corresponds to the one described
in Galatians 2:1–10. Here is the first possibility:[19]

Table 1:

Option I		
Date (approx.)	Acts	Galatians
33–35	Paul's conversion (9:1–25)	"God ... was pleased to reveal his Son in me" (1:15–16)
35–38	Post-conversion visit (9:26–30)	"Then after three years..." (1:18)
44–47	Famine relief visit (11:27–30)	"Then after fourteen years..." (2:1–10)
Shortly before 48/49	PAUL WRITES GALATIANS	PAUL WRITES GALATIANS
48/49	The Jerusalem Council (15:1–29)	

In this scenario, Paul heard about the situation in Galatia sometime after
he returned to Antioch from his first missionary journey (Acts 14:24–28),
yet before the Jerusalem Council (Acts 15:1–35).[20]

Here is the second possible scenario:

---

since it would potentially undermine his argument that his authority comes directly from
the risen Christ and not the Jerusalem church or its apostles. For a helpful discussion of
the issue, see David Wenham, "Acts and the Pauline Corpus II: The Evidence of Pauline
Parallels," in *The Book of Acts in Its Ancient Literary Setting*, ed. Andrew D. Clarke and Bruce
W. Winter (Grand Rapids: Eerdmans, 1993), 215–58, esp. 226–243.

[19] For helpful comparisons of Gal 2:1–10 with both Acts 11:27–30 and 15:1–35, see
Longenecker, *Galatians*, lxii–lxxxiii; Wenham, "Acts and the Pauline Corpus," 226–43;
Witherington, *Grace in Galatia*, 13–20; Moo, *Galatians*, 10–13. The dates in Table 1 are approx-
imate, as it is difficult to determine fixed points in Paul's life due to the lack of data. On the
challenges, see Riesner, *Paul's Early Period*, 29–32; Jack Finegan, *Handbook of Biblical Chronology:
Principles of Time Reckoning in the Ancient World and Problems of Chronology in the Bible*, rev. ed.
(Peabody, MA: Hendrickson, 1998), 390–402; Martin Hengel and Anna Maria Schwemer, *Paul
between Damascus and Antioch: The Unknown Years* (Louisville: Westminster John Knox, 1997),
1–23; Andrew Steinmann, *From Abraham to Paul: A Biblical Chronology* (St. Louis: Concordia,
2011), 322–45. Arguably the only fixed point in a Pauline chronology is that he appeared
before Gallio the proconsul of Achaia in the city of Corinth, who ruled from July 51 to July
52 AD. Yet even this "fixed point" allows for differing opinions regarding the dating of other
events in Paul's life.

[20] See, e.g., Bruce, *Galatians*, 43–56; Fung, *Galatians*, 9–28; Schreiner, *Galatians*, 22–31; Moo,
Galatians, 2–18; Das, *Galatians*, 36–42.

Table 2:

Date (approx.)	Acts	Galatians
	Option 2	
33–35	Paul's conversion (9:1–25)	"God ... was pleased to reveal his Son in me" (1:15–16)
35–38	Post-conversion visit (9:26–30)	"Then after three years..." (1:18)
44–47	Famine relief visit (11:27–30)	
48/49	The Jerusalem Council (15:1–29)	"Then after fourteen years..." (2:1–10)
Sometime after 48/49	PAUL WRITES GALATIANS	PAUL WRITES GALATIANS

Understood this way, Paul could have written the Galatians sometime in the 50s, perhaps as late as around the time he wrote Romans (ca. AD 57).[21]

So which is more likely? The place to begin is by identifying the similarities and differences between Paul's visit to Jerusalem described in Galatians 2:1–10 with the possible parallels in Acts 11:27–30 and Acts 15:1–35. Table 3 lays out a summary.[22]

As the data from this chart indicates, the evidence is not clear cut for either view. The main factor in favor of Galatians 2 = Acts 15 is the overlap in the "primary" issue discussed: whether or not gentile believers must be circumcised and required to observe the Mosaic law. Yet there are subtle differences as well. According to Galatians 2:1, Paul and Barnabas went up to Jerusalem "according to a revelation," whereas in Acts 15:1 it was men from Judea arriving in Antioch teaching that circumcision was necessary for salvation. Galatians 2:1–10 describes a private meeting between Paul and the "pillars" (Peter, James, and John), while Acts 15 describes a meeting involving the apostles, elders, Paul, Barnabas, and the "whole assembly."

Other factors favor identifying Galatians 2 with Acts 11:27–30. Paul going to Jerusalem "according to a revelation" (Gal 2:2) aligns well with Paul and Barnabas taking famine relief to Jerusalem because the prophet Agabus foretold a severe famine (Acts 11:27–28). The apostle's comment that the "pillars" asked Paul and Barnabas to continue to remember the

---

[21] See, e.g., Burton, *Galatians*, xliv–liii; Betz, *Galatians*, 9–12; de Boer, *Galatians*, 5–11; Oakes, *Galatians*, 19–22; Keener, *Galatians*, 7–13.

[22] Adapted from Moo, *Galatians*, 13.

Table 3:

	Acts 11:27–30	Galatians 2:1–10	Acts 15:1–35
Location(s)	Antioch and Jerusalem	Antioch and Jerusalem	Antioch and Jerusalem
Immediate Occasion	Prophets foretold a famine	"according to a revelation"	Men from Judea teaching that circumcision is necessary to be saved
Participants	Paul and Barnabas; elders mentioned but their role is unclear	Paul, Barnabas, Titus, James, Cephas (Peter), John	Paul, Barnabas, "other" believers; Peter, James, "apostles and elders"; "the whole church"
Nature of the "meeting"	None specified	Private	Whole congregation led by the apostles and elders (specifically Peter and James)
Primary Issue	Famine relief	Circumcision of gentile believers	Circumcision and obedience to the Mosaic law for gentile believers
Format	No meeting mentioned	Paul sets forth his gospel message	Paul reports on his gentile mission; Peter confirms; James issues the decision
Result	Paul and Barnabas deliver the famine relief from the church in Antioch and then return to Antioch	The "pillars" extend the right hand of fellowship, recognizing different spheres of ministry. They ask that Paul and Barnabas continue to remember the poor	James decides not to require gentile believers to be circumcised or keep the Mosaic law, but asks them to avoid certain practices offensive to Jews. A letter is sent from the apostles, elders, and the whole church announcing the decision

poor makes good sense if the reason for their visit was to provide famine relief (Acts 11:27–30). But differences are all too apparent as well. Acts 11:27–30 says nothing at all about circumcision, let alone any efforts to force Titus to be circumcised. Nor does Acts 11:27–30 refer to any meeting at all between Paul and the Jerusalem apostles; it simply states that Paul and Barnabas delivered the aid to the elders.

Since neither the famine relief visit (Acts 11:27–30) nor the Jerusalem Council (Acts 15:1–21) lines up exactly with Galatians 2:1–10, a decision between the two is difficult. Although arguments from silence are not decisive and must be used with caution, one striking omission favors identifying Galatians 2 with Acts 11:27–30. If Galatians 2 = Acts 15, it is difficult to understand why Paul would not have mentioned the agreement reached during the Jerusalem Council.[23] Such an agreement would have undercut the opponents' two key arguments: (1) circumcision is required for justification: and (2) Paul is out of step with the leaders of the Jerusalem church. Furthermore, if Galatians 2 = Acts 15, then Paul does not mention the famine relief visit at all in Galatians. While it is true that Paul is under no obligation to mention every trip to Jerusalem, such an omission would seem to open Paul to the charge that he is withholding key information about his interaction with the Jerusalem church by not mentioning a visit to Jerusalem. In light of this consideration it seems more likely that Galatians 2:1–10 recounts a private meeting that Paul had with the "pillars" during the famine relief visit recorded in Acts 11:27–30.

C. Verbal and Theological Similarities to Other Pauline Epistles

Another consideration that some scholars use to date Galatians are parallels to other Pauline Letters.[24] Romans, written sometime between AD 55–57, covers similar subjects, including: justification by faith, circumcision, Abraham, the role of the Mosaic law in the life of the Christian, gentile inclusion, the relationship between Jew and gentile in the people of God, and the adoption of believers into God's family, etc. Yet even with such similarities, there are also noteworthy differences between Galatians and Romans. Similarities in language and subject are hardly a firm foundation for establishing a date for Galatians, as there are several other possible explanations for such similarities. Consequently, similarities with other Pauline Letters are not helpful in dating Galatians.

---

[23] For a helpful discussion of this issue, see F. F. Bruce, "Galatian Problems. 2. North or South Galatians?," *BJRL* 52 (1970): 243–66.

[24] See the lengthy list in Joseph Barber Lightfoot, *St. Paul's Epistle to the Galatians. A Revised Text with Introduction, Notes, and Dissertations*, 4th ed. (Grand Rapids: Zondervan, 1957), 45–48 and the summary in Moo, *Galatians*, 17–18.

D. CONCLUSION

Based on the evidence laid out above regarding the potential recipients of the letter and the date, there are three main possibilities. If Paul is writing to churches in North Galatia, he writes after the Jerusalem Council, sometime during the 50s. If South Galatia is the destination, the date could either be shortly before the Jerusalem Council (if Gal 2 = Acts 11:27–30) or any time after the Jerusalem Council (if Gal 2 = Acts 15:1–21), likely sometime in the 50s.[25]

While we cannot be definitive, the overall weight of the evidence favors the South Galatia theory. Paul is writing to the churches in Pisidian Antioch, Iconium, Lystra, and Derbe—planted during his first missionary journey with his ministry partner Barnabas (Acts 13:1–14:28). Paul writes sometime after returning to Antioch (Acts 14:26–28) and before the Jerusalem Council (Acts 15:1–21). Since the Jerusalem Council occurred in AD 48 or 49, a date shortly before that seems most likely.[26]

E. THE CHURCHES OF SOUTH GALATIA

Working with the assumption that Paul is writing to the churches he and Barnabas planted on his first missionary journey, some brief discussion of the province of Galatia and these churches is necessary. By the time of Paul, the Roman province of Galatia had expanded from its origins consisting of Celtic tribes to a diverse region with a variety of ethnicities that was the product of Roman administrative convenience rather than natural geographical or ethnic boundaries. According to Breytenbach, Galatia "was inhabited by Paphlagonians, Galatians, Phrygians, Pisidians, Isaurians, Lycaonians, and Pamphylians, as well as Roman colonists." Therefore, what follows is a brief summary of Paul's experience planting churches in these communities based on Acts and supplemented by historical research.

Luke devotes the most attention to Paul's time in Pisidian Antioch (Acts 13:13–52), recording a lengthy summary of Paul's synagogue sermon and the response. Originally established by Greek colonists sometime

---

[25] The latter possibility is a more modern development; for an extended defense of a South Galatia destination but a date after the Jerusalem Council, see Moisés Silva, *Interpreting Galatians: Explorations in Exegetical Method*, 2nd ed. (Grand Rapids: Baker, 2001), 129–39 and Keener, *Galatians*, 7–13.

[26] So also Longenecker, *Galatians*, lxii–lxxxiii; Schreiner, *Galatians*, 22–31; Moo, *Galatians*, 8–18; Das, *Galatians*, 20–47.

in the fourth or third century BC, the city was reconstituted as a Roman military colony by the emperor Augustus.[27] As the original starting point of the Via Sebaste—a major Roman road that ran south to Perga (Acts 13:13–14) and was then extended east from Pisidian Antioch through Iconium and Lystra—the city was an important commercial center that attracted merchants. Although agriculture was central to the economy, inscriptions indicate the presence of a wide range of professions. In addition to the large temple to the emperor Augustus erected in the center of the city, a number of deities were worshiped, such as Zeus/Jupiter, Asclepius, Demeter/Ceres, and Dionysius. The Jewish population was apparently large enough and influential enough to stir up trouble for Paul and Barnabas.

Upon arriving in Pisidian Antioch, Paul was invited to preach in the synagogue. The initial response was encouraging: "As they were leaving, the people urged them to speak about these matters the following Sabbath. After the synagogue had been dismissed, many of the Jews and devout converts to Judaism followed Paul and Barnabas, who were speaking with them and urging them to continue in the grace of God" (Acts 13:42–43). But when they returned the following week the response was different. Because some of the Jews began to contradict Paul's message, the apostle announced that he and Barnabas were turning their focus to preaching the gospel to the gentiles (Acts 13:44–49).[28] In the weeks that followed, the Jews continued to stir up trouble for Paul and Barnabas, even persuading some of the leading men of the city to make life difficult for them (Acts 13:50). Despite this persecution, the gospel spread throughout the region (Acts 13:49), and the disciples in Pisidian Antioch were "filled with joy and the Holy Spirit" (Acts 13:52).

After traveling about ninety miles southeast along the Via Sebaste, Paul and Barnabas arrived in Iconium.[29] A major crossroads, Iconium had strong links to the emperor Claudius and was the most famous city of a fourteen-community tetrarchy. Although originally a Phrygian city, in

---

[27] Information on Pisidian Antioch in this paragraph is taken from Schnabel, *Early Christian Mission*, 2:1098–1103.

[28] It is worth noting that in Acts 13:47 Paul justifies this focus on the gentiles by quoting Isa 49:6, a text that he alludes to in Gal 1:15–16 when describing his conversion and commissioning as an apostle to the gentiles (see notes at 1:15–16).

[29] Information on Iconium in this paragraph is summarized from Schnabel, *Early Christian Mission*, 2:1111.

25 BC the emperor Augustus had granted the city the status of a full Roman colony. According to Schnabel, "the citizens of Iconium were divided into four tribes that were named after the deities worshiped in the city."[30] The worship of a wide range of Roman, Greek, and Phrygian deities has been attested, along with the presence of the imperial cult. There was also a synagogue in Iconium, which is where Paul and Barnabas began their ministry in the city. As a result of their preaching, "a great number of both Jews and Greeks believed" (Acts 14:1). Once again, unbelieving Jews stirred up trouble for them among the gentiles, eventually leading to a division in the city (Acts 14:2–4). Learning of a conspiracy between Jews, gentiles, and even the rulers of the city to mistreat and stone them, Paul and Barnabas fled the city (Acts 14:5–7).

Their next stop along the Via Sebaste was Lystra, a city about twenty miles southwest of Iconium.[31] Before Augustus established it as a Roman colony in 25 BC, all that existed on the site was a small town. By the time Paul visited, the city had become much larger, housing a significant military veteran population. As with the other cities in the region, various gods and individuals were worshiped and venerated. The account in Acts 14:8–18 specifically highlights two deities that resulted in trouble for Paul and Barnabas. After healing a man who had been crippled from birth, the crowd exclaimed "The gods have come down to us in human form!" (Acts 14:11). The people began calling Barnabas Zeus, and Paul they called Hermes because he was the chief speaker (Acts 14:12). Such a reaction may have been prompted by a local legend that Zeus and Hermes had taken on human form and wandered through the region.[32] According to this legend, no one showed them hospitality except an old couple, whom Zeus and Hermes richly rewarded while bringing judgment on the rest of the people. Perhaps not wanting to risk the wrath of the gods, the local priest of Zeus begins to make preparations to offer sacrifices to them (Acts 14:13). Paul and Barnabas tear their clothes in horror, explaining that it is the living God who has healed the crippled man (Acts 14:14–17). Even with this denunciation they barely prevented the crowds from offering them sacrifices (Acts 14:18). But when Jews from Pisidian

---

[30] Schnabel, *Early Christian Mission*, 2:1111.

[31] Information on Lystra in this paragraph is summarized from Schnabel, *Early Christian Mission*, 2:1111–12.

[32] For a helpful discussion of the possible mythical backgrounds to this story, see Keener, *Acts*, 2:2145–53.

Antioch and Iconium arrived in Lystra, they turned the crowds against Paul and Barnabas, leading to Paul being stoned and left for dead (Acts 14:19). Paul managed to survive but left with Barnabas the next day for Derbe (Acts 14:20).

Derbe was located about eighty miles southeast of Lystra and, perhaps more significantly, about eighteen miles from the main highway between Iconium and the Cilician Gates.[33] Paul may have chosen this city slightly off the beaten path to prevent the Jews who stirred up trouble for him from following him.[34] Not much is known about the city. Although originally a Hellenistic city, it came under Roman rule in 129 BC. Because of its close association with the emperor Claudius, the city received the honorary title "Claudioderbe." Luke gives virtually no detail about Paul and Barnabas' time in Derbe; he merely notes that "After they had preached the gospel in that town and made many disciples, they returned to Lystra, to Iconium, and to Antioch" (Acts 14:21).

As this brief summary shows, Paul and Barnabas planted the churches in Galatia in the face of challenging circumstances. They faced opposition everywhere they went from both Jews and gentiles. When they passed through these same cities on the way back to their home base in Syrian Antioch, they appointed elders in every church (Acts 14:23). But given how young these churches were, it should have been no surprise that they were vulnerable to threats from both outside and inside the church.

III. The Circumstances Surrounding the Letter

So what happened between the time Paul left the Galatian congregations and the writing of the Letter to the Galatians? Determining those circumstances is no simple matter, and certainty is illusive. Further complicating matters is that we must attempt to reconstruct what happened using the information that Paul provides in this letter, a process that scholars refer to as mirror-reading.[35] As a result, the conclusions that different scholars

---

[33] Information on Derbe in this paragraph is adapted from Mark Wilson, "Galatia," in *The World of the New Testament: Cultural, Social, and Historical Contexts*, ed. Joel B. Green and Lee Martin McDonald (Grand Rapids: Baker, 2013), 529–30.

[34] Another possibility is that someone in Lystra referred Paul and Barnabas to a contact/ friend in Derbe (so Wilson, "Galatia," 530).

[35] For helpful discussions of mirror-reading, see the following: John M. G. Barclay, "Mirror-Reading a Polemical Letter: Galatians as a Test Case," *JSNT* 31 (1987): 73–96; Silva, *Interpreting Galatians*, 103–12; Nijay Gupta, "Mirror-Reading Moral Issues in Paul's Letters,"

draw based on the data can vary greatly. Yet the goal when evaluating different reconstructions based on mirror-reading should be to "seek out those that listen sympathetically to the greatest number of texts and that 'fit' these texts as closely and plausibly as possible."[36] With that in mind, what follows is our best effort to reconstruct the circumstances that led Paul to write this letter.

A. THE ARRIVAL OF THE OPPONENTS[37]

Sometime after Paul left the churches in Galatia, a group of outsiders began to cause trouble in these congregations.[38] Paul portrays them as cutting in front of the Galatians in their efforts to run the race of the Christian life (Gal 5:7). These Jewish Christian teachers appear to have

---

JSNT 34 (2012): 361–81; D. A. Carson, "Mirror-Reading with Paul and against Paul: Galatians 2:11–14 as a Test Case," in *Studies in the Pauline Epistles: Essays in Honor of Douglas J. Moo*, ed. Matthew S. Harmon and Jay E. Smith (Grand Rapids: Zondervan, 2014), 99–112. For an alternative view that questions the need and value of such reconstructions based on mirror-reading, see Justin K. Hardin, "Galatians 1–2 without a Mirror: Reflections on Paul's Conflict with the Agitators," *TynBul* 65 (2014): 275–303.

[36] Carson, "Mirror-Reading," 112.

[37] Scholars continue to debate the best term or terms to use when referring to these opponents. The traditional label has been Judaizers, which reflects their efforts to "judaize" (i.e., compel gentiles to live as Jews; see 2:14) the Galatians. Many scholars, however, have abandoned this term because it gives the impression that Paul's problem with them was Judaism itself. Alternative terms include teachers (Martyn), influencers (Nanos), missionaries (Dunn), and rivals (Das), among others. For a sampling of the recent discussion on Paul's opponents in Galatia, see the essays in Mark D. Nanos, ed., *The Galatians Debate: Contemporary Issues in Rhetorical and Historical Interpretation* (Peabody, MA: Hendrickson, 2002), 321–433. For discussion of the drawbacks of each term with a plea for the superiority of "influencers," see Nanos, *Galatians Debate*, 400–1. While it is certainly important to understand and portray Paul's opponents fairly, we must also recognize that Paul regarded them as false teachers who were preaching a different gospel than the true gospel that he proclaimed (1:6–9). He even wishes they would mutilate themselves (5:12). So if we regard Paul's letter as the inspired word of God, we should embrace Paul's assessment of his opponents as accurate.

[38] Although the vast majority of scholars conclude the opponents are outsiders, Justin Hardin, building on the work of Bruce Winter, argues that they are local Jewish believers who promoted circumcision for gentile believers as a means of avoiding persecution from local civic authorities because the Galatian believers had stopped participating in the imperial cult. By taking on circumcision, these gentile believers would appear to the authorities to be Jews; see Bruce W. Winter, "Civic Obligations: Galatians 6.11–18," in *Seek the Welfare of the City: Christians as Benefactors and Citizens*, ed. Bruce W. Winter (Grand Rapids: Eerdmans, 1994), 123–44 and Justin K. Hardin, *Galatians and the Imperial Cult: A Critical Analysis of the First-Century Social Context of Paul's Letter*, WUNT 2/237 (Tübingen: Mohr Siebeck, 2008), 85–115. For a helpful response to Hardin, see Schreiner, *Galatians*, 35–39.

argued their case on three fronts: theological, ethical, and ecclesiological.[39] Theologically, they argued that in addition to believing in Christ it was necessary to be circumcised in order to be justified before God as a true descendant of Abraham (2:16–5:1).[40] Thus their basic message appears to have been faith in Christ plus works of the law equals justification. They may have argued that Paul had not told the Galatians the "full" gospel message, perhaps out of fear that they would not respond positively to his preaching if he had told them about the necessity of keeping the Mosaic law (Gal 1:10). In addition to promoting circumcision, these teachers may have also pressed for keeping the dietary laws and perhaps even the observance of the Jewish calendar (Sabbath, festivals, etc.).[41]

The opponents likely grounded their arguments in the story of Abraham. As part of the covenant that God made with Abraham, the Lord required Abraham and his male descendants to be circumcised as a sign of this covenant (Gen 17:9–14). This requirement extended even to the foreigner (Gen 17:12, 27). This textual argument was likely supplemented by the Jewish tradition that Abraham kept the requirements of the Mosaic law before it was even given.[42] The opponents may also have

---

[39] Some have objected to referring to the opponents as Jewish Christians, regarding such a phrase as anachronistic; see esp. Mark D. Nanos, *The Irony of Galatians: Paul's Letter in First-Century Context* (Minneapolis: Fortress, 2002), 129–43. Instead, Nanos argues that these "influencers" (as he terms them) were local Jews who sought to bring the gentile Christians within the protective sphere of the synagogue as proselytes, where they would be regarded from a Roman perspective as adherents to the protected religion of Judaism. But, as Das (*Galatians*, 11–13) rightly notes, Paul nowhere in Galatians mentions governing authorities; the "influencers" are clearly afraid of persecution from other Jews because of their belief in Jesus as Messiah.

[40] Reconstructions of the opponents' teaching run the spectrum from those who despair of determining with any confidence the nature of their teaching (minimalist) to those who confidently provide detailed reconstructions on numerous points (maximalist); for the minimalist perspective, see, e.g., Heinrich Schlier, *Der Brief an die Galater*, 14th ed. (Göttingen: Vandenhoeck & Ruprecht, 1971), 19–24. A good example of the maximalist view can be found in J. Louis Martyn, "A Law-Observant Mission to Gentiles," in *The Galatians Debate: Contemporary Issues in Rhetorical and Historical Interpretation*, ed. Mark D. Nanos (Peabody, MA: Hendrickson, 2002), 348–61.

[41] Galatians 2:11–14 recounts an incident in Antioch where Jewish Christians attempted to compel gentile believers to observe the Jewish food laws. While Paul may simply use this incident as an example of an effort to "judaize" gentile believers, it could also suggest a similar push by the opponents in Galatia to promote Jewish dietary restrictions. When Paul laments that the Galatians "are observing special days, months, seasons, and years" (Gal 4:10), this may suggest they have begun to observe the Jewish calendar, perhaps including Sabbaths and festivals.

[42] See discussion in Biblical Theology §1.1.2.

argued that without being circumcised, the gentile Galatian believers would be analogous to Ishmael, who although he was a physical descendant of Abraham was not part of the line of promise and therefore did not share in the inheritance promised to Abraham. The way to remedy that was to be circumcised—in essence, to convert to being a Jew who also happened to believe in Jesus as the Messiah.

Ethically, the opponents may have argued that adopting the Mosaic law was necessary to provide guidelines for living the Christian life. As gentile converts, the Galatians lacked a clear set of ethical guidelines for living a life that was honoring to the one true God. Where better for these gentile believers to turn for such guidance than the Mosaic law? By surrendering to the yoke of the Mosaic law, the Galatians would find a reliable guide for ordering their lives.

On the ecclesiological front, the opponents appear to have challenged Paul's authority and status as an apostle. Central to their claims was Paul's relationship with the Jerusalem church, and in particular with key leaders such as Peter, James, and John. The specifics of their argument are not clear. The false teachers may have claimed to be acting under the authority of the Jerusalem church in promoting the necessity of circumcision, meaning that Paul was out of step with or flat out disobedient to them. Or, the opponents may have argued that Paul and the Jerusalem church were not on the same page theologically, and when push came to shove the Jerusalem leaders had greater authority than Paul. In any case, the extent to which Paul explains his interactions with the Jerusalem church and its pillars strongly suggests his opponents were making an issue of Paul's relationship to the Jerusalem church.[43]

B. PAUL'S RESPONSE

Paul addresses the ecclesiological issue first, beginning in the first line of the letter. After referring to himself as an apostle, he quickly adds "not from men or by man, but by Jesus Christ and God the Father who raised him from the dead" (1:1). In expressing his astonishment that the Galatians are in danger of departing from the true gospel, Paul states unequivocally that "If anyone is preaching to you a gospel contrary to what you received, a curse be on him!" (1:9). It is the gospel message

---

[43] For the dissenting view that the opponents did not question Paul's apostolic authority or his relationship with the Jerusalem church, see Witherington, *Grace in Galatia*, 25 and throughout his exposition of 1:13–2:14.

itself that has authority, not the status of the person who proclaims it. Far from being inferior to the Jerusalem leaders, Paul explains that God revealed the risen Jesus to him directly and commissioned him to preach the good news to the gentiles (1:15–17). After his conversion, Paul's interactions with the Jerusalem church and its leaders were limited. He made a brief visit to Jerusalem about three years after his conversion, but among the leaders he only saw Cephas (Peter) and James the brother of Jesus while there (1:18–19). Paul insists that during this time period the churches in Judea only knew him by reputation as the persecutor turned preacher (1:20–24).

Paul then recounts a visit to Jerusalem fourteen years later (2:1–10), which, as noted above, likely corresponds to the famine visit recounted in Acts 11:27–30. During this visit he privately laid out before key leaders in the Jerusalem church the gospel he preached (2:2). Despite the efforts of some "false brothers" to compel Titus (a gentile believer) to be circumcised, Paul and Barnabas did not yield to them for a moment (2:3–5). The Jerusalem leaders not only added nothing to what Paul preached (2:6), but they readily acknowledged the grace of God at work through Paul's ministry among the gentiles (2:7–10). By extending to them the "right hand of fellowship" (2:9), the Jerusalem leaders affirmed that they were on the same page as Paul when it came to their understanding of the gospel.

The apostle describes one more incident relevant to his relationship with the Jerusalem leaders (2:11–14). While Paul was ministering in Antioch, it was customary for Jewish and gentile believers to eat meals together. But when "certain men came from James" (2:12), Cephas and the rest of the Jews (including even Barnabas!) stopped eating with the gentile believers because they "feared those from the circumcision party" (2:12–13). Paul confronted the issue in front of the entire congregation, calling out Cephas for "deviating from the truth of the gospel" (2:14).

Paul's response, then, to the ecclesiological challenge from his opponents in Galatia can be summarized in three basic points. First, authority in gospel ministry rests ultimately in God and the gospel, not the reputation, status, or position of an individual or individuals. Paul goes so far as to place himself under a curse if he preaches a different gospel than the one the Galatians received from him initially. Second, Paul insists that he and the leaders of the Jerusalem church preach the same gospel. While their respective spheres of ministry may differ, the content of their message does not. Third, even a leader in the church as respected as Cephas can be wrong, and when that is the case, he is accountable to others in the church for that error. Again, one's status or reputation does not guarantee infallibility.

In response to the theological attacks of his opponents, Paul's response is lengthy and intricate, so it can only be summarized here. The starting point is justification, by which Paul means God's act of declaring a person not guilty in his court of law.[44] He insists that justification is based on faith in Christ and not works of the law (2:15–16).[45] Works of the law (including, but not limited to, circumcision, food laws, and Sabbath keeping) cannot make a person right before God. Indeed, if a right standing were possible through the law, then Christ's death on the cross was for nothing (2:21). By trusting in Christ, believers die to the law because they share in Christ's crucifixion; the new life the believer lives is now lived by faith in the Son of God who loved and gave himself for his people (2:18–20). To return to observing the Mosaic law would be an effort to rebuild what was destroyed at the cross (2:17–18). Faith rather than works of the law is also the basis for their initial reception and ongoing experience of the Holy Spirit (3:1–5).

To prove his point about justification by faith, Paul brings forward his key witness—Abraham. He was justified by faith, and all—regardless of their ethnicity—who have faith like Abraham receive the blessing promised to Abraham (3:6–9). Relying on works of the law brings a curse because no one can perfectly obey its terms, but Christ has redeemed his people by suffering the curse of the law and unleashing the blessing of Abraham and the promised Spirit on Jew and gentile alike who believe (3:10–14). Christ is the promised seed of Abraham, and the giving of the Mosaic law 430 years after God made that promise to Abraham does not change the reality that the inheritance promised to Abraham comes on the basis of faith and not the law (3:15–18). God gave the Mosaic law covenant as a temporary institution to reveal and expose sin until the coming of Jesus, the promised seed of Abraham (3:19–25). It was never intended to bring eschatological life, but rather serve as a guardian until Christ came. Now that Christ has come, all who are united to

---

[44] For further discussion of justification in Galatians, see Biblical Theology §6.0.
[45] For further discussion of the disputed phrase πίστεως Χριστοῦ (either "faith in Christ" or "faithfulness of Christ"), see Biblical Theology §8.2.

Christ by faith—regardless of their ethnicity, socioeconomic status, or
gender—are sons of God, offspring of Abraham who share in Christ's
inheritance (3:26–29). Before Christ came, humanity was under slavery to
the elements of the world, but through his death and resurrection Christ
has redeemed his people and enabled them to be adopted as sons who
have God's eschatological Spirit dwelling in them (4:1–7). In light of these
staggering realities, Paul wonders how the Galatians can even consider
returning to a form of slavery under the elementals (4:8–11) and reminds
them of the joy they experienced when he first preached the good news to
them (4:12–20). Paul concludes his main argument with a retelling of the
Abraham story mediated through his reading of Isaiah (4:21–5:1). Those
who rely on the law are children of the flesh like Ishmael, still enslaved
under the Mosaic law covenant. But all who trust in Christ are children of
the promise like Isaac and citizens of the heavenly Jerusalem that Christ
inaugurated through his death and resurrection. In Christ they are free
from the powers of sin, death, the law, and the elements of the world.

At the foundation of Paul's theological response to his opponents are
two further distinct but closely related differences with them; one is
hermeneutical, the other is redemptive-historical. At the hermeneutical
level Paul reads Scripture differently than his opponents, using two key
lenses to guide his interpretation. First and foremost is the gospel itself,
centering on the death and resurrection of Jesus as the fulfillment of the
Old Testament hope. Everything, including the story of Abraham and the
role of the Mosaic law covenant, is reexamined in light of this. The second
lens is using later Scripture to interpret previous Scripture. Although
this was a widely practiced Jewish interpretive method, Paul's use of this
approach to interpret the Abraham story through the lens of Isaiah 49–54
helps explain how the apostle can seemingly flip the story of Abraham on
its head from how his opponents appear to have interpreted it.

On the redemptive-historical level,[46] Paul sees elements of both continuity and discontinuity between the pre-Christ period of human history
and the post-Christ period, whereas his opponents seem to see significant continuity and little if any discontinuity. For the opponents, the
death and resurrection of Jesus appear to be simply the final piece in the

---

[46] For discussion of the role that salvation history plays in Galatians, see Biblical
Theology §1.0.

unfolding work of God in human history, with little changing because of it. Paul, on the other hand, while affirming continuity in arguing that Christ is the promised seed of Abraham who inherits what was promised to him, sees the arrival of Christ as a decisive shift in the ages. Through Christ the new creation has broken into this present evil age that is under slavery to the elements of this world and created the eschatological people of God who live in the power of the long-awaited Holy Spirit. With the dawn of this new age, the Mosaic law covenant—along with its distinctive practices of circumcision, food laws, and Sabbath observance—has been done away with, since the fulfillment of the Abrahamic promise has come in the person and work of Christ.

In response to the ethical argument that the Mosaic law is necessary to govern the Christian life, Paul warns the Galatians that choosing the law as the means to relate to God is necessarily a rejection of Christ (5:2–6) and openly wishes that his opponents would mutilate themselves (5:7–12). Because of their freedom in Christ, believers are now able to serve one another through love and thus fulfill the goal of the law (5:13–15). They do this by walking in the power of the Spirit and fighting against the flesh and its deeds (5:16–26). Rather than being under the Mosaic law, believers are under the law of Christ, which they fulfill by bearing one another's burdens (6:1–5) and seeking to do good to everyone, but especially fellow believers (6:6–10). The work of Christ has brought into existence the eschatological people of God (i.e., the children of the heavenly Jerusalem) who are free from the powers of sin, the flesh, and the law, and it has inaugurated the new creation reign of Christ through the Spirit, who empowers God's people to live transformed lives and serve others through love (6:11–18).

IV. Structure

Since the groundbreaking work of Hans Deiter-Betz, discussions of the structure of Galatians have been largely dominated by the potential role that ancient rhetorical forms and practices play in shaping the letter.[47]

---

[47] See Betz, *Galatians*, 14–25. Among the key studies since then are G. Walter Hansen, *Abraham in Galatians: Epistolary and Rhetorical Contexts* (Sheffield: JSOT Press, 1989); Philip H. Kern, *Rhetoric and Galatians: Assessing an Approach to Paul's Epistle*, SNTSMS (Cambridge:

This approach seeks to analyze the letter within the various forms of rhetoric that were used in the ancient world. In the Greco-Roman world there were three distinct kinds of rhetoric. *Forensic/judicial rhetoric,* often associated with the courtroom, sought to determine guilt or innocence in the context of defense and accusation. *Deliberative rhetoric* looks to the future and calls the audience to make a decision about a course of action. *Epideictic rhetoric* offers praise or blame with respect to a person or situation. While Betz argued that Galatians falls into the forensic category, other scholars—even some who share Betz's affinity for rhetorical criticism—have identified a number of ways that Galatians does not fit neatly in the forensic category.

Other scholars, stressing that Galatians is in fact a letter, have turned to the ancient handbooks of epistolary theory for assistance in determining the structure of Galatians.[48] Usually Galatians is classified as a "rebuke-request" letter, designed to rebuke the Galatians for their departure from the true gospel and request that they live in accordance with that true gospel. Yet these epistolary approaches, like the rhetorical ones mentioned above, fail to explain a number of features in Galatians.[49] In light of these shortcomings, the conclusion of David Aune seems apt:

> Early Christian letters tend to resist rigid classification, either in terms of the three main types of oratory or in terms of the many categories listed by the epistolary theorists ... Attempts to classify one or another of Paul's letters as *either* judicial *or* deliberative *or* epideictic (or one of their subtypes) run the risk

---

Cambridge University Press, 1998); Robert A. Bryant, *The Risen Crucified Christ in Galatians,* SBLDS (Atlanta: Society of Biblical Literature, 2001), 1–109; D. F. Tolmie, *Persuading the Galatians: A Text-Centred Rhetorical Analysis of a Pauline Letter,* WUNT 2/190 (Tübingen: Mohr Siebeck, 2005). For commentaries in addition to Betz that take some form of this approach, see Longenecker, *Galatians,* c–cxix; Witherington, *Grace in Galatia,* 25–41; DeSilva, *Galatians,* 62–91. For helpful discussions of the shortcomings of these approaches when it comes to the structure of Galatians, see Schreiner, *Galatians,* 52–58; Das, *Galatians,* 48–68; and Keener, *Galatians,* 37–41.

    [48] See, e.g., Hansen, *Abraham in Galatians,* 21–54; Nils A. Dahl, "Paul's Letter to the Galatians: Epistolary Genre, Content, and Structure," in *The Galatians Debate: Contemporary Issues in Rhetorical and Historical Interpretation,* ed. Mark D. Nanos (Peabody, Mass: Hendrickson, 2002), 117–42; G. Walter Hansen, "A Paradigm of the Apocalypse: The Gospel in Light of Espistolary Analysis," in *The Galatians Debate: Contemporary Issues in Rhetorical and Historical Interpretation,* ed. Mark D. Nanos (Peabody, MA: Hendrickson, 2002), 143–54.

    [49] See further Keener, *Galatians,* 41–43.

of imposing external categories on Paul and thereby obscuring the real purpose and structure of his letters.[50]

Yet the inability of either rhetorical or epistolary analysis to produce a satisfactory and widely accepted structural layout of Galatians does not mean that various rhetorical and epistolary devices are entirely absent from the letter. Paul uses a wide variety of literary and rhetorical devices in Galatians, and identifying them can be valuable for interpreting his message to the Galatians. Furthermore, Paul's Letters follow the general pattern of: (1) opening; (2) letter body; (3) closing. The opening sections within Paul's Letters usually follow a set pattern: (1) author/sender; (2) recipients; (3) greeting/ salutation; (4) thanksgiving and or prayer. Yet in Galatians, the thanksgiving section is noticeably absent, as Paul moves straight from the salutation to a statement of astonishment at the Galatians' departure from the true gospel. Such an omission likely signals Paul's deep concern for these congregations.

So in light of this discussion, my approach to the structure of Galatians is based on an effort to follow the flow of the letter based on both structural and thematic elements in the text.[51] Scholars, of course, often differ on the specifics of where certain literary sections begin and end, as well as the divisions of even major sections of Galatians.[52]

Therefore, the structural outline that follows should be considered a modest attempt to capture the major movements of the epistle and the relationship between the parts and the whole.

---

[50] David Edward Aune, *The New Testament in Its Literary Environment* (Philadelphia: Westminster, 1987), 203, cited in Das, *Galatians*, 53.

[51] Throughout the commentary I have incorporated various elements of what has come to be called discourse analysis. Although scholars use this expression in multiple ways, I am using it in the very general sense of "studying larger units of speech and writing above the sentence level, especially regarding how units of discourse relate to each other" (Andrew David Naselli, *How to Understand and Apply the New Testament: Twelve Steps from Exegesis to Theology* [Phillipsburg: P&R Publishing, 2017], 129). At the heart of my approach is determining the logical relationship between clauses, often relying especially on Steven E. Runge, *Discourse Grammar of the Greek New Testament: A Practical Introduction for Teaching and Exegesis* (Peabody, MA: Hendrickson, 2010) and G. K. Beale, William A. Ross, and Daniel J. Brendsel, *An Interpretive Lexicon of New Testament Greek: Analysis of Prepositions, Adverbs, Particles, Relative Pronouns, and Conjunctions* (Grand Rapids: Zondervan, 2014).

[52] One of the major points of disagreement is where the argument that begins in 3:1 ends, with scholars proposing 4:7 (de Boer, *Galatians*, 11–15), 4:12 (Longenecker, *Galatians*, c–cxviii; Schreiner, *Galatians*, 52–59), 4:31/5:1 (Betz, *Galatians*, 14–28), and 5:12 (Dunn, *Galatians*, 20–22; Moo, *Galatians*, 62–64).

V. Outline

EXPOSITION

I. Greetings and Astonishment (1:1–10)

Paul uses a broadly consistent format to begin his letters that he has adapted from his broader Greco-Roman culture: self-identification, identification of the recipients, a greeting, and a prayer of thanksgiving. The opening paragraph (1:1–5) contains the first three of these elements. Even within these opening lines several key themes of the letter are introduced: the divine origin of Paul's status as an apostle, the centrality of the death and resurrection of Christ, and the dawning of the Messianic age that resulted from it. All of this was according to the will of God the Father, who deserves eternal glory.

But instead of the expected prayer of thanksgiving, Paul launches straight into a rebuke of the Galatians (1:6–10). The apostle expresses his astonishment that they are turning away from the God who called them through the true gospel for another so-called gospel. Paul reminds them that if anyone, regardless of who they are, preaches a different gospel, they are under God's curse. Final authority within the church rests in the one true gospel that God revealed to Paul, who rather than being a people pleaser is a servant of Christ. As with the previous paragraph, several key themes are introduced: the centrality of God's grace in calling people to himself, the incompatibility of the one true gospel with the message of the opponents, and Paul's identity as a servant of Christ.

A. Greetings in the Gospel (1:1–5)

> [1] Paul, an apostle—not from men or by man, but by Jesus Christ and God the Father who raised him from the dead— [2] and all the brothers who are with me: To the churches of Galatia. [3] Grace to you and peace from God the Father and our Lord Jesus Christ, [4] who gave himself for our sins to rescue us from this present evil age, according to the will of our God and Father. [5] To him be the glory forever and ever. Amen.

Context

The opening lines of New Testament letters usually introduce key themes and issues that are unpacked in the letter body, and Galatians is no exception. Paul's emphasis on the divine origin of his apostleship (1:1) anticipates the lengthy account of his conversion and commissioning as an apostle to the gentiles, a status that his opponents appear to have challenged (1:11–2:14). The central elements of the gospel are also highlighted: the self-sacrificial death of Jesus to rescue his people from this present evil age (1:3–4), and God the Father as the one who raised Jesus from the dead (1:1), planned this great work of redemption (1:4), and deserves eternal glory for it all (1:5). Each of these elements will be further explained in the lengthy argument at the center of the letter (3:1–5:1).

Structure

This opening paragraph contains several key elements of a typical Greco-Roman letter.[1] Paul begins the letter by identifying himself as the author (1:1–2a). Using three prepositional phrases, Paul describes himself as an apostle whose status and authority are not of human origin but divine, anticipating the extended defense of his apostolic status later in the letter. Both Jesus and the Father who raised him from the dead conferred this status upon him, and he is joined by an unspecified group of believers who are with Paul in sending this letter. Next Paul identifies the recipients, who are by contrast described simply as the churches of Galatia (1:2b). Finally,

---

[1] For helpful summary of these features in Greco-Roman letters, see William G. Doty, *Letters in Primitive Christianity* (Philadelphia: Fortress Press, 1973), 1–48; and Hans-Josef Klauck, *Ancient Letters and the New Testament: A Guide to Context and Exegesis*, trans. Daniel P. Bailey (Waco, TX: Baylor University Press, 2006), 17–27. On these elements in Paul's letters, see Thomas R. Schreiner, *Interpreting the Pauline Epistles*, Guides to New Testament Exegesis 5 (Grand Rapids: Baker, 1990), 25–29; and Jeffrey A. D. Weima, *Paul the Ancient Letter Writer: An Introduction to Epistolary Analysis* (Grand Rapids: Baker Academic, 2016), 11–50.

the apostle greets them (1:3–5). He wishes them grace and peace that comes from both God the Father and the Lord Jesus Christ (1:3). Just as God the Father was further described in 1:1, Paul now further describes Christ as the one who gave himself for the sins of his people to deliver them from this present evil age, an act that was carried out in accordance with the will of the Father (1:4). The introduction culminates in a doxology of praise to the Father (1:5), which has the effect of setting Paul's greeting within the context of worship.[2]

1:1. As is customary in first-century letters, Paul begins by identifying himself as the author. He refers to himself as an apostle (ἀπόστολος). Although this term can refer to a messenger in general, as Paul uses it here it has the sense of an authoritative witness of Jesus' resurrection commissioned by Christ himself (Luke 6:13; Acts 1:15–26).[3] Paul uses three prepositional phrases to stress the divine origin of his status as an apostle. He is an apostle "not from men" (οὐκ ἀπ' ἀνθρώπων), meaning that the origin of his call was not from human beings. Nor is he an apostle "by man" (οὐδὲ δι' ἀνθρώπου), indicating that his call to be an apostle did not come through the agency of another man. By shifting from the plural "men" to the singular "man" in these two phrases, Paul moves from the generic category (an apostleship that has human origins) to the specific (his apostleship did not come through any particular person, including the pillars in the Jerusalem church).[4]

Instead, Paul is an apostle "by Jesus Christ and God the Father" (διὰ Ἰησοῦ Χριστοῦ καὶ θεοῦ πατρὸς). In other words, his commission to be an apostle was given to him directly by Jesus Christ and God the Father working together. Paul may be drawing here on Old Testament texts such as 2 Samuel 7:12–17 and Psalms 2:7–9 and 89:26 that refer to the promised

---

[2] Martyn, *Galatians*, 87.

[3] According to Longenecker (*Galatians*, 2), "Classical Greek writers usually used the term in an impersonal way, most often to refer to a naval expedition for military purposes—even, at times, of the boat used to transport such an expedition." He goes on to note the common suggestion that the rabbinic concept of the *shaliach* lies behind this term, before rightly concluding that it cannot adequately account for all the features of a NT apostle (Longenecker, *Galatians*, 3). Martyn (*Galatians*, 93) suggests that both concepts may be rooted in the kings of Israel sending out servants for a task that he and he alone defined.

[4] Similarly Moo, *Galatians*, 67–68. Betz (*Galatians*, 38) notes possible parallels with Amos 7:14–15 and Jer 1:5–6, as well as the self-descriptions of Greek poets (Hesiod, *Theog.* 21–34; *Erga* 1–10). Witherington (*Grace in Galatia*, 73) goes so far as to suggest Paul is in fact echoing Amos 7:14–15.

Messiah as God's Son.[5] To emphasize the close relationship between the
Father and the Son, Paul further describes the Father as the one "who
raised him from the dead" (τοῦ ἐγείραντος αὐτὸν ἐκ νεκρῶν).[6] Whereas
in the Old Testament God is often identified as the one "who brought you
out of the land of Egypt, out of the place of slavery" (Exod 20:2), he is
now identified as the one "who raised [Christ] from the dead" to restore
his people from exile through the promised new exodus (Jer 16:14–15;
23:7–8; Ezek 37:1–14).[7] At the heart of Paul's gospel was the resurrection
of Christ; without it our faith is worthless and we as believers "should be
pitied more than anyone" (1 Cor 15:17b–19). The resurrection of Jesus
signaled that the last days had begun (Acts 2:14–40). Regardless, it was as
a result of his resurrection that Christ commissioned apostles, including
Paul (Acts 9:1–18), to proclaim the good news to the ends of the earth.

By emphasizing the divine origin of his apostolic calling, Paul appears
to be responding to criticism by his opponents in Galatia. Perhaps they
argued that his apostolic calling originated with human beings (whether
the apostolic circle in Jerusalem or the sending church of Antioch) and
was mediated through a human being (again, perhaps the Jerusalem apostles, or Peter in particular). As such, Paul's authority was not on the same
level as that of Peter and the rest of the Jerusalem apostles. But as Paul
will further explain in 1:15–16, his apostolic calling came directly from
Jesus Christ, whom the Father raised from the dead.

Paul's self-description reminds us that every believer's identity is ultimately determined by God, not ourselves. Although we are not apostles,
God has shaped our identity by raising Christ from the dead and uniting
us with his risen Son by faith. Regardless of who we were before we knew
Christ, because we have been crucified and raised with Christ, we have
a new identity (Gal 2:19–20; compare Rom 6:1–11).

1:2. Before identifying the recipients, Paul mentions "all the brothers who are with me" (οἱ σὺν ἐμοὶ πάντες ἀδελφοί). Since Paul is not

---

[5] de Boer, *Galatians*, 25.

[6] Das (*Galatians*, 78) notes the similarity of this phrase to a set of Jewish prayers known as
the *Amidah* (also known as the *Eighteen Benedictions*), dating from the first century, which in
part reads: "Thou art mighty ... that liveth for ever, that raiseth the dead ... that quickeneth
the dead ... Blessed art Thou, O Lord, who quickenest the dead!"

[7] Roy E. Ciampa, *The Presence and Function of Scripture in Galatians 1 and 2*, WUNT 102
(Tübingen: Mohr Siebeck, 1998), 46. Thus the mention of the resurrection here may fore-
shadow the return from exile and second exodus motifs that appear later in the letter; see
further Biblical Theology §1.2.

more specific, we can only guess to whom he refers. If he writes this letter before the Jerusalem Council (Acts 15:6–29), Paul may be referring to "Barnabas and some others" who went with him from Antioch to Jerusalem (Acts 15:2). If so, however, why not specifically mention Barnabas, whom the Galatians clearly know (Gal 2:2)?[8] In light of the uncertainty, it seems best to see a general reference to other believers who share Paul's understanding of the gospel and acknowledge his apostolic authority. Describing these believers as "brothers" (ἀδελφοί) also reminds the Galatians that they are part of the same spiritual family regardless of their physical proximity, a theme that is central to the letter.

Paul identifies the recipients as "the churches of Galatia" (ταῖς ἐκκλησίαις τῆς Γαλατίας). As used in Greco-Roman literature, ἐκκλησία referred to an assembly, or more specifically "a regularly summoned legislative body."[9] More importantly, the LXX often uses it to refer to the assembled people of God, especially when they are gathered for worship (e.g., Deut 4:10; 23:2–9; 2 Chr 1:2–5; 6:3–13).[10] In the New Testament ἐκκλησία consistently refers to a specific group of believers in a particular location, though there are places where it has the broader sense of the people of God more universally considered (e.g., Eph 1:22; 3:10; Col 1:18, 24).[11] The plural here in 1:2 clearly indicates that specific congregations are in view.

The specific congregations that make up "the churches of Galatia" are those Paul and Barnabas established during their so-called first missionary journey in the towns of Pisidian Antioch, Iconium, Lystra, and Derbe (Acts 13:1–14:28).[12] As the accounts in Acts make clear, Paul faced persecution of some kind at every stop. In Pisidian Antioch the Jews incited leading people of the city to drive Paul and his team out (13:50).

---

[8] Longenecker (*Galatians*, 5–6) suggests that the brothers mentioned here are leaders of the church in Antioch. The reason that Paul doesn't mention Barnabas is because of his failure during the Antioch incident (2:11–13); see further Bauckham, "Barnabas in Galatians," 61–72.

[9] BDAG s.v. ἐκκλησία 1.

[10] In the LXX ἐκκλησία consistently translates קָהָל, which often refers to the congregation of Israel assembled for divine worship (*HALOT* s.v. 1 קָהָל.g).

[11] For more on the people of God in Galatians, see Biblical Theology §7.2.

[12] On the identity of these churches, see the Introduction, 2–6. The possibility that additional churches are included cannot be ruled out, since Acts is likely not comprehensive. Furthermore, since Paul's practice was to proclaim the gospel in urban areas and then send out associates to smaller localities within the region, it is possible that additional cities may have been reached with the gospel.

Jews and gentiles joined together in Iconium to try to stone them, but Paul and his team fled before they could (14:5–6). In Lystra they managed to stone Paul and drag him out of the city, leaving him for dead (14:19). No wonder Paul told the disciples in these various cities when he passed back through that "it is necessary to go through many hardships to enter the kingdom of God" (Acts 14:22)! The resurrection of Jesus has not only brought in the last days, but created the eschatological people of God as well. Every local congregation is a particular expression of that larger people, strategically placed by God to be an outpost of his kingdom in this fallen world called to live worthy of the gospel (Phil 1:27).

1:3. Now that the author and the recipients have been identified, Paul proceeds to the greeting. In Greek the standard greeting was χαίρειν (compare Acts 15:23; Jas 1:1), and Paul appears to have adapted this when he consistently uses χάρις ("grace") in the greeting of his letters.[13] Grace is one of the key motifs in Paul's theology, as it encompasses God's kindness shown to us in Christ despite our persistent rebellion against him. Not only have we been saved by grace, but God intends to display the riches of his grace to us for all eternity (Eph 2:4–7). Because the grace of God has appeared in Jesus Christ, we are empowered to obey God as we await the return of "our great God and Savior, Jesus Christ" (Titus 2:11–13). Thus God's grace is no mere static disposition of his character, but a dynamic power that achieves God's purposes for his people.[14] From first to last and every point in between, the Christian life is immersed based entirely on the grace of God shown to us in the gospel. Thus when Paul writes "grace to you" he is not only affirming that grace has already come to the Galatians but he is indirectly praying for them to experience fresh outpourings of grace in their lives as individuals and as a body.

Not only does Paul indirectly pray for fresh measures of grace, but peace (εἰρήνη) as well. This in turn may be an adaptation of the standard Jewish greeting "shalom" (שָׁלוֹם). Far more than a subjective feeling of calm, peace refers to the restored relationship that believers have with God because we have been justified by faith (Rom 5:1). Understood against

---

[13] If, as I believe, Galatians is Paul's first extant letter, it is worth noting that his standard salutation is established at the outset (see the other similar salutations in Rom 1:7; 1 Cor 1:3; 2 Cor 1:2; Eph 1:2; Phil 1:2; Col 1:2; 1 Thess 1:1; 2 Thess 1:2; 1 Tim 1:2; 2 Tim 1:2; Titus 1:4; Phlm 1:3).

[14] Dunn, *Galatians*, 31.

its Old Testament background, peace is a one-word theological shorthand for the final state of well-being that will result from Yahweh's promised salvation. In particular, Isaiah 40–66 stands out as a significant framework for Paul's understanding of peace.[15] The heralds sent out to preach the gospel proclaim peace (Isa 52:7), which is accomplished by the suffering of the Servant (Isa 53:5). The result of the Servant's work is a covenant of peace (Isa 54:10) that produces peace for God's people (Isa 54:13). When God consummates his purposes for human history, he will make peace flow like a river (Isa 66:12). Now that the suffering servant Jesus Christ has become our peace, we not only have peace with God but with fellow believers regardless of their ethnicity (Eph 2:11–22).[16] Peace is the fruit of the Spirit in our lives (Rom 8:6; Gal 5:22) and yet something that we should actively pursue (Rom 12:18; 14:19). Thus peace has an already/not-yet dynamic—it is something that God has already given to us, yet we still await its full consummation in a new heavens and new earth.

This combination of grace and peace may have it roots in another Old Testament passage: Numbers 6:25–26 (LXX).[17] As part of the blessing that Aaron was to pronounce over the people of Israel, he was instructed to say, "May the Lord make his face shine on you and be gracious to you, may the Lord look with favor on you and give you peace." The grace that God has shown us in Jesus Christ has changed us from rebels to sons and daughters who are at peace with God and each other. Together these two words form "a prayer which recognizes God as the source of the enabling ('grace') to live in mutually productive and beneficial harmony ('peace')."[18]

This grace and peace is "from God the Father and our Lord Jesus Christ" (ἀπὸ θεοῦ πατρὸς ἡμῶν καὶ κυρίου Ἰησοῦ Χριστοῦ).[19] In other words, God the Father and the Lord Jesus Christ work together to provide us with the

---

[15] See further Matthew S. Harmon, *She Must and Shall Go Free: Paul's Isaianic Gospel in Galatians*, BZNW 168 (Berlin: de Gruyter, 2010), 52–55.

[16] Note that in this passage Paul combines citations of Isa 57:19 and Isa 52:7; see the discussion in Thorsten Moritz, *A Profound Mystery: The Use of the Old Testament in Ephesians* (New York: Brill, 1996), 23–55.

[17] Ciampa, *Presence and Function*, 48.

[18] Dunn, *Galatians*, 32.

[19] Here the csb departs from the NA[28], which reads "from God our Father and the Lord Jesus Christ" (cf. esv). Both readings are well supported, and a definitive decision is difficult. For a helpful summary of the textual witnesses, see Moo, *Galatians*, 74. The difference in meaning is negligible.

grace and peace we so desperately need.[20] Our familiarity with passages like this often blinds us to the profound statement Paul is making. Central to Judaism was the confession known as the *Shema*: "Listen, Israel: The Lᴏʀᴅ our God, the Lᴏʀᴅ is one" (Deut 6:4). Yet in 1 Corinthians 8:6 Paul reinterprets this confession in light of Christ: "Yet for us there is one God, the Father. All things are from him, and we exist for him. And there is one Lord, Jesus Christ. All things are through him, and we exist through him." As Bauckham observes, "Thus, in Paul's quite unprecedented reformulation of the Shema', the unique identity of the one God *consists* of the one God, the Father, *and* the one Lord, his Messiah."[21] The Father and Son work in concert to extend grace to God's covenant people. By identifying Jesus as Lord, Paul is both affirming his identity as Yahweh and asserting Jesus' universal dominion over all creation originally intended for Adam.[22]

Regardless of our circumstances, as believers we can live in the joy that comes from knowing that God's grace and peace rest upon us. Yet we also live with the eager anticipation of the full realization of that grace and peace when God consummates the new creation (Rom 8:19–25).

1:4. Having concluded the previous verse by mentioning "our Lord Jesus Christ," Paul now describes what he did. Christ "gave himself for our sins" (τοῦ δόντος ἑαυτὸν ὑπὲρ τῶν ἁμαρτιῶν ἡμῶν).[23] Paul uses the language of Isaiah 53 to describe the sacrificial death of Jesus for the sins of his people, probably with verse 10 particularly in view: "Yet the Lᴏʀᴅ was pleased to crush him severely. When you make him a guilt offering, he will see his seed, he will prolong his days, and by his hand, the Lᴏʀᴅ's pleasure will be accomplished."[24] Within its original context, the

---

[20] The preposition ἀπό here indicates "the originator of the action" referred to (BDAG s.v. ἀπό 5.d).

[21] Richard Bauckham, *Jesus and the God of Israel: God Crucified and Other Studies on the New Testament's Christology of Divine Identity* (Grand Rapids: Eerdmans, 2008), 28.

[22] So Dunn, *Galatians*, 33. He suggests that the frequent allusions to Psa 8:6 and Psa 110:1 in the NT link the title Lord to Adam's dominion over creation (compare 1 Cor 15:25–27).

[23] Instead of ὑπὲρ τῶν ἁμαρτιῶν ἡμῶν some manuscripts read περὶ τῶν ἁμαρτιῶν ἡμῶν. Although the external evidence is fairly even, the internal evidence favors ὑπὲρ as the original text; see further Harmon, *She Must and Shall Go Free*, 61n58.

[24] For more on this allusion, see Harmon, *She Must and Shall Go Free*, 56–66. The key phrase is "when you make him a guilt offering," which in the LXX shares similar language to Galatians 1:4. Others have suggested different verses from Isaiah 53 as the source of Paul's language. But the larger point of an allusion to Isaiah 53 is widely recognized even if scholars disagree on the particular verse. Oakes (*Galatians*, 40) suggests that the Day of Atonement (Lev 16) may also be in the background here. Another possibility is that Paul draws from an

fourth Servant Song (Isa 52:13–53:12) explains the way in which God will accomplish the new exodus—through the death and resurrection of the suffering servant.[25] By suffering for the sins of his people, the Servant will justify them (Isa 53:11), restore the marriage between God and his people (Isa 54:4–8), and establish a new covenant with them (Isa 54:10; compare Jer 31:31–34). By using the language of Isaiah 53, Paul presents Jesus Christ as the promised suffering servant who has accomplished the new exodus through his death and resurrection. As such he anticipates his argument in Galatians 4:1–7, where new exodus language takes center stage in his argument.

This is not the only place Paul borrows language from Isaiah 53 to explain that Christ suffered the punishment that we deserved for our sins. By describing the work of Jesus in the language of the suffering servant here in the opening of the letter, Paul anticipates the key role that the crucifixion of Jesus plays at various points later in Galatians, several of which allude to Isaiah 53 as well.[26] Elsewhere in his letters Paul uses a form of either δίδωμι ("to give") or παραδίδωμι ("to hand over") to describe the self-sacrificial nature of Christ several times (e.g., Rom 4:25; 8:32; Eph 5:2, 25; 1 Tim 2:6; Titus 2:14), which likely stems from his understanding of Isaiah 53. This language emphasizes that, far from being a tragic accident (compare Acts 2:2–24), Christ as the Good Shepherd freely and willingly laid down his life for the sins of his people and took it up again (John 10:14–18). Without this glorious reality, there is no gospel (1 Cor 15:1–19).

In claiming that Christ gave himself for our sins (τῶν ἁμαρτιῶν ἡμῶν), Paul highlights two things. First, our rebellion against God is so heinous that it required the horrific death of Jesus to reconcile us to him. Throughout Galatians Paul uses several different words to describe our alienation from God, many of which overlap in meaning.[27] The noun ἁμαρτία is a general term that refers to an offense against God, something that violates his character or his revealed will. By using the plural, Paul

---

early Jewish-Christian Christological confession; see Richard B. Hays, "Galatians," in *New Interpreters Bible* (Nashville: Abingdon, 2000), 203.

[25] See Rikki E. Watts, "Consolation or Confrontation? Isaiah 40–55 and the Delay of the New Exodus," *TynBul* 41 (1990): 31–59.

[26] See, e.g., Gal 1:10; 2:20; 3:2, 5, 13, 16; 4:1–7. For a helpful discussion of how Paul develops this theme of Jesus' crucifixion in Galatians, see Robert A. Bryant, *The Risen Crucified Christ in Galatians*, SBLDS (Atlanta: Society of Biblical Literature, 2001), 163–94.

[27] For more on the ways that Paul describes humanity apart from Christ in Galatians, see Biblical Theology §7.1.

may have in view particular acts of sin that subject us to God's righteous judgment.[28] Second, by using the pronoun "our" (ἡμῶν), Paul captures both our personal responsibility for our rebellion against God, as well as the specific nature of Christ's work. In other words, Christ died for my sins as an individual believer, and our sins as the eschatological people of God, not merely for sin in general.

The purpose of Christ's self-sacrificial death for our sins comes in the next clause: "to rescue us from this present evil age" (ὅπως ἐξέληται ἡμᾶς ἐκ τοῦ αἰῶνος τοῦ ἐνεστῶτος πονηροῦ).[29] Although the verb Paul uses here (ἐξαιρέω) can have the generic sense of "rescue," it is also used with specific reference to the exodus (Exod 3:8; 18:4, 8, 9, 10; Judg 6:9; Acts 7:9, 34) and eschatological salvation (Isa 31:5; 60:16; Ezek 34:27).[30] In Isaiah 40–66 this verb often highlights the contrast between impotent idols and Yahweh as the only one who can truly deliver God's people in a new exodus from their bondage to sin (Isa 42:22; 43:13; 44:17, 20; 47:14; 48:10; 50:2; 57:13; 60:16). Just as the original exodus was the definitive act of redemption in the Old Testament, so the cross (which, as we will see later in Gal 4:1–7, is portrayed as a new exodus) is the definitive act of redemption in the New Testament. The "us" that are rescued are believers, Jew and gentile alike.

The realm from which believers are rescued is "this present evil age" (τοῦ αἰῶνος τοῦ ἐνεστῶτος πονηροῦ). The present evil age was a Jewish way of referring to the current time period that was dominated by sin, death, and the devil as a result of the fall. On the day of the LORD the Messiah would come and bring about the age to come (compare Eph 2:7), when God would consummate all his promises to his people through his Messiah and usher in a new heavens and new earth where all remnants of sin, death, and the curse were gone forever. The defining mark of this age to come would be the gift of the Holy Spirit to all of God's people.

---

[28] Alternatively, Paul may have in view the sins of the community considered as a whole; see Ciampa, *Presence and Function*, 60n100.

[29] When used with a subjunctive verb, the conjunction ὅπως indicates purpose (BDAG 2.a.α).

[30] On this verb, see François Bovon, "Une formule prépaulinienne dans l'épître aux Galates (Ga 1, 4–5)," in *Paganisme, judaïsme, christianisme: Influences et affrontements dans le monde antique: Mélanges offerts à Marcel Simon*, ed. F. F. Bruce (Paris: Éditions E. de Boccard, 1978), 97–105.

The advent of Jesus Christ inaugurated the age to come but did not consummate the end of the present evil age. Thus believers participate in the age to come while still living in a world under the present evil age. So when Paul says that Christ rescued us from this present evil age, he means that believers are no longer slaves to the powers that dominated the present evil age.[31] This rescue from the present evil age was accomplished "according to the will of our God and Father" (κατὰ τὸ θέλημα τοῦ θεοῦ καὶ πατρὸς ἡμῶν). The preposition κατά indicates that the will of God the Father was the norm/standard that governed Christ's redemption of his people.[32] By mentioning the will of God, Paul reinforces that the self-sacrificial death of Jesus the suffering servant was the predetermined plan of God long before it happened (Isa 53:10; Acts 2:22–24).

This is now the third time in these opening verses that God has been identified as "Father." By using this title Paul may be drawing on Old Testament passages that consistently link the fatherhood of God to either the original exodus from Egypt or the promise of a second exodus.[33] Consider, for example, Jeremiah 31:9: "They will come weeping, but I will bring them back with consolation. I will lead them to wadis filled with water, by a smooth way where they will not stumble, for I am Israel's Father, and Ephraim is my firstborn." An additional possibility is that Paul is drawing on Jewish traditions stemming from 2 Samuel 7:14 that anticipated God "adopting" the Messiah and his people in the age of restoration.[34] In any case, the association between God as Father and the redemption of his people likely serves as the background of Paul's emphasis on the fatherhood of God in 1:1–5.

By mentioning both the resurrection (1:1) and crucifixion (1:4) of Jesus, Paul is highlighting the redemptive work of Jesus as the long promised new exodus and the inauguration of the age to come. The suffering

<hr>

[31] For more on the present evil age, see Biblical Theology §1.3.1.
[32] See BDAG s.v. κατά 5.a.a. This is the first of several occurrences of κατά with this sense in Galatians (e.g., 2:2; 3:29; 4:23, 28–29).
[33] Ciampa, *Presence and Function*, 40–44. In addition to Jer 31:9, see Exod 4:22; Deut 32:5–20, 36–43; Isa 1:2; 63:16; 64:4–12; Jer 3:12–19; Hos 11:1–11.
[34] James M. Scott, Adoption as Sons of God: An Exegetical Investigation into the Background of Υιοθεσια in the Pauline Corpus, WUNT 48 (Tübingen: J. C. B. Mohr, 1992), 96–117.

servant has come at last to lead his people out of their bondage to the powers of this present evil age into the eschatological grace and peace foretold in the Old Testament.

1:5. The only appropriate response to Christ giving himself for the sins of his people is worship, so it should not be surprising that Paul erupts in doxology: "To him be the glory forever and ever. Amen" (ᾧ ἡ δόξα εἰς τοὺς αἰῶνας τῶν αἰώνων, ἀμήν).[35] In Greek this sentence has no verb; woodenly it reads "to him glory"; so in English a verb must be supplied. Although it makes little difference in meaning, on the whole it seems more likely that it should be rendered "to him is the glory" rather than "to him be the glory" based on the parallel expression in 1 Peter 4:11.[36] Glory (δόξα) refers to the visible display of God's character and fame. All that God does is ultimately motivated by his commitment to displaying his glory (Rom 11:33–36).

Such glory is to be ascribed to God "forever and ever" or, more woodenly, "into the ages of ages" (εἰς τοὺς αἰῶνας τῶν αἰώνων). Although it is understandable why nearly all English translations render it "forever and ever," doing so prevents the English reader from connecting this expression (εἰς τοὺς αἰῶνας τῶν αἰώνων) to the "present evil age" (τοῦ αἰῶνος τοῦ ἐνεστῶτος πονηροῦ) in the previous verse. The point is that God's glory will be recognized in every age, regardless of how many ages there are! Adding "amen" to the end of this clause adds a final solemn note of "let it be so." It invites the reader to echo this resolve to see God glorified for all eternity.

The display and recognition of God's glory is the ultimate goal of all that God has done in creation and redemption. God is working all things toward the day when every knee will bow and tongue confess that Jesus Christ is Lord "to the glory of God the Father" (Phil 2:11). As we await that day, God commands us that whatever we do, "in word or in deed, do everything in the name of the Lord Jesus, giving thanks to God the Father through him" (Col 3:17). But he does not leave us to our own strength; God provides the Spirit to empower us to "put to death the deeds of the body" (Rom 8:13). Yet when we inevitably sin, God displays his unique glory by forgiving our sin without compromising his justice (Exod 34:6–7;

---

[35] That this doxology is found word for word also in 4 Macc 18:24; 2 Tim 4:18; and Heb 13:21 may suggest this was "a well-known liturgical formula in the ancient Jewish and Christian communities" (Ciampa, *Presence and Function*, 63–64).

[36] See BDF 128.5. Moo (*Galatians*, 74) suggests that Paul may have had both in mind.

Rom 3:21–26). No wonder Paul exclaims in Romans 11:36 that "from him and through him and to him are all things. To him be the glory forever. Amen." By inviting the Galatians to say "amen," Paul displays "his conviction that his own words can and will become the active word of God, because God will be present as the letter is read to the Galatians in their services of worship."[37]

Bridge

"Who am I?" is one of the fundamental questions in life. The world around us seeks to define who we are based on status, wealth, privilege, and pedigree. Our sinful hearts tempt us to seek our identity in these and other dead ends. But as believers, our identity is determined by God himself. Through the death and resurrection of Jesus Christ we are brothers and sisters in the family of God, recipients of God's grace and peace. Jesus Christ the suffering servant has delivered us from our slavery to sin and the powers of this present evil age and led us in the new exodus the Old Testament prophets had foretold. As a result, we are the eschatological people of God who live to glorify God in all that we say, think, do, and feel. That is our identity as believers. Is that how you think of yourself? Is that how you view your fellow believers? The extent to which we embrace this identity in large part determines our experience of the joy that comes from knowing the crucified and risen Lord Jesus Christ.

B. PAUL'S ASTONISHMENT AND THE DANGER OF DEPARTING FROM THE TRUE GOSPEL (1:6–10)

> [6] I am amazed that you are so quickly turning away from him who called you by the grace of Christ and are turning to a different gospel— [7] not that there is another gospel, but there are some who are troubling you and want to distort the gospel of Christ. [8] But even if we or an angel from heaven should preach to you a gospel contrary to what we have preached to you, a curse be on him! [9] As we have said before, I now say again: If anyone is preaching to you a gospel contrary to what you received, a curse be on him! [10] For am I now trying to persuade people, or God? Or am I striving to please people? If I were still trying to please people, I would not be a servant of Christ.

---

[37] Martyn, *Galatians*, 106.

Context

Instead of the customary thanksgiving section that normally follows the Pauline greeting, the apostle expresses his deep concern for the Galatians. For the first time Paul mentions the opponents stirring up trouble in Galatia who are distorting the true gospel the apostle preached to them. This tension between the true gospel preached by Paul and the distorted "gospel" (which is in fact no gospel at all!) proclaimed by the opponents establishes the larger context for the letter. It prompts Paul to explain how the gospel he received through a revelation of Jesus Christ is the fulfillment of the promise to Abraham, the means by which a person is declared righteous before God, the end of the Mosaic law covenant, and the inauguration of the promised new creation in which the eschatological people of God (composed of Jew and gentile) are indwelled and empowered by the Holy Spirit (2:14–6:10). Any who depart from this one true gospel—regardless of who they are—stand under God's curse. And it is this one true gospel that has made Paul a servant of Jesus Christ, the suffering servant.

Structure

There are three smaller units within this paragraph.[38] First, Paul begins with a statement of astonishment that the Galatians are so quickly abandoning the one true gospel for a different gospel that is in fact no gospel at all (1:6–7). Second, using two conditional clauses, Paul then explains that anyone (even if it is he or an angel from heaven!) who preaches a different gospel is under God's curse (1:8–9). Finally, the apostle concludes the paragraph with an assertion that he is not a people-pleaser but a servant of Christ (1:10). The sharp tone of this paragraph establishes the dire situation in Galatia and prepares the reader for Paul's robust defense of the true gospel in contrast to the false teaching of his opponents.

1:6. After greeting the recipients of the letter, Paul typically moves to a section where he thanks God for the fruit that the gospel has produced in them.[39] But he is so concerned about the situation in the Galatian

---

[38] See similarly de Boer, *Galatians*, 37–38.

[39] Every other Pauline Letter except for Titus contains a section where Paul thanks God (Rom 1:8–15; 1 Cor 1:4–9; Eph 1:15–23; Phil 1:3–8; Col 1:3–8; 1 Thess 1:2–10; 2 Thess 1:3–10; 1 Tim 1:12–17; 2 Tim 1:3–7; Phlm 4–7) or praises God (2 Cor 1:3–14) near the beginning, usually with a form of the verb εὐχαριστέω. By itself the absence of a thanksgiving section

churches that he suddenly launches right into a rebuke.⁴⁰ Paul begins by stating "I am amazed that you are so quickly turning away" (Θαυμάζω ὅτι οὕτως ταχέως μετατίθεσθε). By itself the verb rendered "I am amazed" (θαυμάζω) is neutral; only the context can determine whether the amazement or wonder is in a good or bad sense. Thus in the Gospels it often expresses the wonder of the disciples or the crowds at the words or works of Jesus (e.g., Matt 8:27; 9:33; 22:22; Luke 9:43; John 7:15, 21). Here in 1:6, however, the context clearly shows that Paul's amazement expresses his shock, frustration, and disappointment with the Galatians.⁴¹

That amazement is rooted in the fact that "you are so quickly turning away" (οὕτως ταχέως μετατίθεσθε). In this context the verb "turn away" (μετατίθημι) has the sense of "to have a change of mind in allegiance."⁴² It was sometimes used in philosophical discussions to refer to someone who turned away from one philosopher/philosophy to another. For example, the third-century author Diogenes Laërtius used this verb to refer to "one who runs from one philosophical school to another."⁴³ Closer to Paul's day, 2 Maccabees 7:24 recounts the efforts of the Seleucid king Antiochus IV to persuade a Jewish man to "turn from the ways of his fathers [μεταθέμενον ἀπὸ τῶν πατρίων]" and embrace Greek life, culture, and thought.⁴⁴ The present tense of the verb, along with the larger context here in 1:6, suggest that the "turning away" is an ongoing process. Thus, from Paul's perspective, the Galatians are not merely tweaking or improving Paul's gospel message, but they are in the process of turning away from the gospel to another system of thought and way of life altogether.

---

does not necessarily signal Paul's consternation, but replacing it with a stinging rebuke certainly does!

⁴⁰ Betz (*Galatians*, 46–47) suggests that Paul uses here a rhetorical device common in law courts and politics, designed to rebut and attack the actions of an opposition party. The suddenness of the rebuke is further intensified by the lack of a particle or conjunction that connects this sentence with the previous one, a feature known as *asyndeton*. Besides signaling emphasis, asyndeton can be used to indicate a sudden change in topic as it does here; see Daniel B. Wallace, *Greek Grammar Beyond the Basics: An Exegetical Syntax of the New Testament* (Grand Rapids: Zondervan, 1996), 658.

⁴¹ Paul may be drawing from rebuke letters of his day, in which authors often used the verb θαυμάζω "to shame the recipients into adopting a new course of action" (Das, *Galatians*, 99).

⁴² BDAG s.v. μετατίθημι 3.

⁴³ Christian Maurer, "μετατίθημι, μετάθεσις" in *TDNT* 8:161.

⁴⁴ It would be quite ironic if Paul had this text in mind, since the Galatians are turning away from the gospel to embrace "the ways of the fathers" (i.e., distinctively Jewish markers such as circumcision, food laws, etc.)!

From Paul's perspective this turning away has happened "so quickly" (οὕτως ταχέως).⁴⁵ The adverb rendered "quickly" (ταχέως) refers to "a very brief extent of time, with focus on speed of action."⁴⁶ If indeed Paul is writing to the churches planted during his first missionary journey (Acts 13:6–14:28)—in cities such as Pisidian Antioch, Iconium, Lystra, and Derbe—shortly before the Jerusalem Council (Acts 15:1–21), less than a year had passed between the time he left these churches and received news of their turning away.⁴⁷ So quickly indeed!

The remainder of the verse specifies who/what the Galatians are turning from and what they are turning to. They are turning away "from him who called you by the grace of Christ" (ἀπὸ τοῦ καλέσαντος ὑμᾶς ἐν χάριτι [Χριστοῦ]). By turning away from the gospel that Paul preached, the Galatians were in fact turning away from the living God himself. It was through the true gospel that God "called" (καλέσαντος) the Galatians to himself. Paul regularly uses the verb καλέω (along with it cognate noun κλῆσις and adjective κλητός) to describe the effectual summons of God, whether to a relationship with him or to a task to be accomplished.⁴⁸ He may have drawn this theological sense of the word from its use in Isaiah 40–66 (LXX), "where it becomes closely equivalent to 'choose' (and commission) [Isa 41:8–9; 42:6; 43:1; 45:3–4; 48:12; 49:1; 51:2]."⁴⁹

This calling took place "by the grace of Christ" (ἐν χάριτι [Χριστοῦ]), or perhaps more likely "in the grace of Christ."⁵⁰ The realm in which God's call took place is that of "grace" (χάρις), God's undeserved goodness and kindness. Although the term occurs just seven times in Galatians, grace is

---

⁴⁵ The first adverb (οὕτως, "so") intensifies the force of the second (ταχέως, "quickly").
⁴⁶ BDAG s.v. ταχέως 1.a.β.
⁴⁷ For discussion of the dates and timetable, see Introduction, 2–10.
⁴⁸ See, e.g., Rom 8:30; 9:11, 24; 1 Cor 1:9; Gal 1:15; Eph 4:1, 4; 1 Thess 2:12; 2 Thess 2:13–14. This is no mere invitation, but an act of God in which he provides the recipient with the desire and ability to respond. See further NIDNTT 1:275.
⁴⁹ Dunn, Galatians, 40. For more on the Isaianic background of καλέω, see TDNT 3:490. Ciampa (Presence and Function, 78–79) suggests that in light of the exodus overtones present in Galatians, Hosea 11:1–2 may serve as background here as well.
⁵⁰ The prepositional phrase ἐν χάριτι [Χριστοῦ] can be understood in at least three different ways: (1) adverbially, "graciously" (BDAG s.v. ἐν, 11); (2) instrumental, "by the grace of Christ" (Longenecker, Galatians, 15; CSB) or (3) sphere/realm "in the sphere/realm of the grace of Christ" (e.g., Betz, Galatians, 48; Das, Galatians, 102). In a twist on this final option, Moo (Galatians, 77, 85–86) translates this expression "to live in the grace of Christ," arguing that "Paul's point here is to remind the Galatians that God has called them to continue to live and to remain in the grace associated with the decisive, epoch-changing Christ event."

an important theme in this letter written to counteract the false teaching that insists individuals must add works to what God has done for us in Christ. Paul makes this clear by referring to this as the grace "of Christ" (Χριστοῦ).[51] Writing to the Corinthians, Paul states, "For you know the grace of our Lord Jesus Christ: Though he was rich, for your sake he became poor, so that by his poverty you might become rich" (2 Cor 8:9). All of God's blessings come to his people through the grace of the Lord Jesus Christ and his work on our behalf.

In turning away from the God who called them in the grace of Christ, the Galatians are turning "to a different gospel" (εἰς ἕτερον εὐαγγέλιον). The Greek noun for "gospel" (εὐαγγέλιον) and the cognate verb "preach the gospel" (εὐαγγελίζω) are key terms in the letter, appearing a combined fourteen times.[52] The early Christians used this word family as a summary term for the message of what God had done for his people in Christ and the proclamation of that message. Paul seems especially dependent on the use of this word family in Isaiah 40–66, where it refers to God establishing his reign over all the nations through the redemptive work of the servant of Yahweh.[53] According to Paul, the message of the false teachers is fundamentally "different" (ἕτερος) from the gospel he proclaimed. It is not even a distant cousin of his gospel, but rather from another family entirely.[54]

---

[51] The word Χριστοῦ is missing from a few of the earliest manuscripts of Galatians (𝔓46vid Fvid G H) and references in some of the early church fathers (Tertullian, Cyprian, Ambrosiaster, Pelagius). But its presence in other early witnesses (P51 ℵ A B Fc Ψ) as well as a number of later manuscripts tips the scales of the external evidence in favor of its inclusion. The internal evidence further supports Χριστοῦ as the original text, since every other place in Paul's letters where χάρις is modified by a reference to Christ in the genitive reads either "Lord Jesus Christ" or "Lord Jesus" (1 Cor 16:23; 2 Cor 8:9; 13:13; Gal 6:18; Phil 4:23; 1 Thess 5:28; 2 Thess 3:18; 1 Tim 1:14; Phlm 25). The uniqueness of the expression here ("grace of Christ") makes it unlikely that a scribe added Χριστοῦ but possible that some scribes omitted it because it was unprecedented elsewhere in Paul (so Moo, Galatians, 86). See also the discussion in Bruce M. Metzger, A Textual Commentary on the Greek New Testament (2nd ed.; Stuttgart: Deutsche Bibelgesellschaft, 2002), 520–21.

[52] For εὐαγγέλιον, see 1:6, 7, 11; 2:2, 5, 7, 14; εὐαγγελίζω occurs in 1:8 (2x), 9, 11, 16, 23; 4:13; and προευαγγελίζομαι in 3:8.

[53] On the Isaianic background to εὐαγγέλιον/εὐαγγελίζω, see Harmon, She Must and Shall Go Free, 67–70. Bruce (Galatians, 81–82) singles out Isa 61:1 (LXX) as especially important for the NT background.

[54] Not only does the context suggest this, but the use of the adjective ἕτερος may also. In some contexts, ἕτερος has the sense of "being dissimilar in kind or class from all other

Paul's language here suggests the possibility that the events in Galatia remind him of the golden calf incident in Exodus 32–34.[55] Not long after God sealed his covenant with the Israelites at Mount Sinai (Exod 24:1–11), the Israelites "turned aside quickly out of the way" that Yahweh commanded them and made a golden calf to worship (Exod 32:8 ESV; compare Deut 9:16). Just as the Israelites' departure from the way of Yahweh jeopardized their status as the people of God, so now, if the Galatians depart from the God who called them in the grace of Christ, their status as the new covenant people of God is jeopardized.

As believers today, we are just as susceptible to turning away from the God who called us. Even though we have been born again and have the Holy Spirit dwelling inside us, the sinful inclination to turn away from God to other things remains until Christ returns or we die. As long as we cling to the person and work of Jesus Christ as our only hope to stand before a holy God, we can be confident that despite our being prone to wander, God will bring us safely home to his heavenly courts.

1:7. Lest his reference to "another gospel" in the previous verse be misunderstood, Paul hastens to qualify "not that there is another gospel" (ὃ οὐκ ἔστιν ἄλλο).[56] Regardless of what the false teachers claimed, their message of faith in Christ plus keeping the Mosaic law was not good news at all.[57] Paul makes it clear from this opening salvo that the issue in Galatia

---

entities" (BDAG 2). Thus, for example, Paul uses this adjective in 1 Cor 15:40 to distinguish between the splendor of heavenly bodies and that of earthly ones.

[55] See especially Ciampa, *Presence and Function*, 71–78. According to Exodus 32:8 (LXX), the Israelites turned away "quickly" (ταχὺ) from the way God commanded them. Longenecker (*Galatians*, 14) notes a possible link to Judges 2:17 (LXX), which notes that during the period of the judges the Israelites "quickly" (ταχὺ) turned away from the way of their fathers.

[56] Some (e.g., Burton, *Galatians*, 420–22; Bruce, *Galatians*, 80–81; Longenecker, *Galatians*, 15; George, *Galatians*, 93) have argued that Paul draws a subtle but important distinction by his choice of vocabulary in 1:6–7. In 1:6 he refers to a "different" (ἕτερον) gospel, whereas in 1:7 he speaks of "another" (ἄλλο) gospel. In some contexts, ἕτερος has the sense of "another of a different kind," whereas ἄλλος can mean "another of the same kind"; for examples, see MM, *Vocabulary of the Greek Testament* (London: Hodder and Stoughton, 1930), 257. But in several places Paul uses ἕτερος and ἄλλος interchangeably (see, e.g., 1 Cor 12:8–10; 2 Cor 11:4), making a hard and fast distinction unlikely here in Gal 1:6–7. After a helpful survey of the data, Moo (*Galatians*, 86–87) rightly concludes: "The difference in vv. 6 and 7 is not 'different in kind' versus 'another of the same kind,' but 'a gospel in contrast to the true gospel' or 'a competing gospel' versus simply 'another.'"

[57] For a summary of the false teachers' message, see Introduction, 15–21. That Paul uses the word "some" (τινές) may indicate his uncertainty as to the identity of these false teachers.

is not one on which believers can reasonably disagree; the very nature of the Christian faith is at stake.

At this point Paul makes his first specific reference to the false teachers, and he describes them in two ways.[58] First, he refers to them as the ones "who are troubling you" (οἱ ταράσσοντες ὑμᾶς). Although the verb ταράσσω can mean literally to stir or shake something (e.g., John 5:7), the figurative meaning of "cause inward turmoil" is far more common in the New Testament.[59] These opponents are doing more than merely confusing the Galatians; "they are frightening them out of their wits, intimidating them with the threat of damnation" if they do not follow their teachings.[60] Notably this is the same verb used in Acts 15:24. To communicate their decision that gentiles did not need to keep the Mosaic law in order to be saved (cf. Acts 15:1), the Jerusalem apostles in their letter to the gentile churches identify the problem as people who "went out from us and troubled [ἐτάραξαν] you with their words" (Acts 15:24). No doubt Paul would have agreed with the words of Sirach 28:9: "a sinful man will disturb [ταράξει] friends and inject enmity among those who are at peace."

More intriguing is the possibility that Paul is echoing the story of Achan, who in 1 Chronicles 2:7 is referred to as the one "who brought trouble on Israel when he was unfaithful by taking the things set apart for destruction."[61] While it is legitimate to wonder whether the Galatians would have noticed such a subtle echo, there should be little question that, as a man steeped in the Jewish Scriptures, Paul may have seen the false teachers in Galatia as modern-day Achans who, through their departure from the gospel, threatened to bring the Galatians under God's curse (see Gal 1:8–9).

Second, these false teachers "want to distort the gospel of Christ" (θέλοντες μεταστρέψαι τὸ εὐαγγέλιον τοῦ Χριστοῦ).[62] While it appears

---

[58] Paul signals the close relationship between these two descriptions by using one definite article to govern these two present active participles (οἱ ταράσσοντες ... καὶ θέλοντες).

[59] BDAG 2. In some secular writings the term can refer to political unrest (LSJM).

[60] Martyn, *Galatians*, 112.

[61] See Ciampa, *Presence and Function*, 79–82. While it is true that neither 1 Chr 2:7 nor the account of Achan's sin in Joshua 7 use the verb ταράσσω, Ciampa demonstrates how pervasive the association between Achan and trouble was within the Jewish tradition, as well as the typological connection between exodus and conquest within Jewish literature. Furthermore, it should be noted that 1 Chr 2:7 does use the word ἀνάθεμα, which is prominent in Gal 1:8–9.

[62] The genitive τοῦ Χριστοῦ is probably objective; i.e., the gospel about Christ.

that the false teachers presented themselves as adding to or completing what Paul taught, the apostle sees it as an attempt to "distort" (μεταστρέφω) the gospel. The only other New Testament occurrence of μεταστρέφω is in Acts 2:20, where in quoting from Joel 3:4 (ET=2:31) the apostle refers to sun being "turned into darkness." In the LXX the verb is often used in contexts where the change is sudden, unexpected, or even dramatic. Consider, for example, Deuteronomy 23:5: "Yet the LORD your God would not listen to Balaam, but he turned the curse into a blessing for you because the LORD your God loves you."[63] Far from improving Paul's message, the false teachers were distorting it into something entirely different.

False teachers troubling God's people by distorting the gospel are just as dangerous today as they were in Paul's day. Regardless of whether it is the more obvious errors of cults such as the Mormons and Jehovah's Witnesses or the more subtle lures of the prosperity gospel, every generation faces the danger of troublemakers who distort the gospel for their own ends. Jesus himself promised that this present evil age would be characterized by false teachers (Matt 24:10), so we must remain vigilant to protect the purity of the true gospel.

1:8. To make it clear that his attack on the false teachers is not personal, Paul poses a hypothetical situation in the form of an "if … then" statement to illustrate the final authority of the gospel itself rather than any person or angel.[64] At issue is anyone who "should preach to you a gospel contrary to what we have preached to you" (εὐαγγελίζηται [ὑμῖν] παρ᾽ ὃ εὐηγγελισάμεθα ὑμῖν).[65] Thus Paul has in view any message that contradicts the gospel he originally preached to the Galatians.

It does not matter whether "we" (i.e., Paul and his ministry associates) or "an angel from heaven" (ἄγγελος ἐξ οὐρανοῦ) proclaim this different gospel.[66] As Dunn notes, "the angelic interpreter was a standard element

---

[63] See further examples in Exod 14:5; 1 Sam 10:9; 1 Macc 9:41; 3 Macc 5:8; Pss 65:6 (ET=66:6); 77:44 (ET=78:44); 104:29 (ET=105:29); Amos 8:10.

[64] Paul uses a third-class conditional statement, which raises a hypothetical for consideration without indicating how likely the hypothetical actually is. The ἀλλά that introduce this verse introduces additional information for further consideration; see David Arthur DeSilva, *Galatians: A Handbook on the Greek Text*, BHGNT (Waco, TX: Baylor University Press, 2014), 8.

[65] The textual evidence for the presence (ℵ² A 81. 104. 326. 1241 d; Tert^pt Ambst) and absence (ℵ* F G Ψ ar b g; Mcion^t Tert^pt Lcf Cyp) of ὑμῖν in this clause is evenly split; see the discussion in Metzger, *Textual Commentary*, 121.

[66] Some see the "we" here as a stylistic device ("editorial we") Paul uses to refer to himself alone (so Wallace, *Greek Grammar*, 396). But the use of the emphatic pronoun ἡμεῖς

in Jewish apocalypses—the heavenly messenger (the word is the same in the Greek) who gave the stamp of heavenly authority to the message he delivered [Ezek 8:2ff.; Dan 10:5ff.; 1 Enoch 1:2ff.; 2 Enoch 1:4ff.; Apoc. Zeph. 2:1ff.; 4 Ezra 2:44ff.; 4:1ff.]."[67] Whether the false teachers were actually claiming angelic revelation is beside the point, and Paul's language should not be pressed beyond its limits.[68] Perhaps all that Paul intends is a bit of hyperbole to emphasize that the gospel they first received from Paul is the final arbiter of what is true, and everything—even the subsequent preaching/teaching of Paul himself—was to be evaluated by it. Anything contrary to the gospel "that was delivered to the saints once for all" (Jude 3), regardless of its source, is to be rejected.

As for anyone who does preach a contrary gospel, Paul writes "a curse be on him!" (ἀνάθεμα ἔστω). The severity of departing from the gospel is reinforced by Paul's use of the word ἀνάθεμα. While this word was used in Greco-Roman literature with a variety of senses,[69] there is little doubt that the LXX provided the backdrop for his use of it here. Of the twenty-six occurrences of ἀνάθεμα in the LXX, twenty-two of them translate a form of the root חרם.[70] Although this root can refer to something devoted to the service of the Lord (Lev 27:28), it most often refers to "a ban for utter destruction, the compulsory dedication of something which impedes or resists God's work, which is considered to be accursed before God."[71] The paradigmatic example is Joshua 7, where Achan "took some of what was set apart [LXX τοῦ ἀναθέματος], and the LORD's anger burned against the Israelites" (7:1). As a result, God's anger burned against the Israelites,

---

along with the reference in 1:9 to a similar warning issued previously suggest Paul has his ministry team (especially Barnabas) and perhaps even "all the brothers who are with me" (1:2) in view.

[67] Dunn, *Galatians*, 45.

[68] See, e.g., Martyn (*Galatians*, 113), who suggests the false teachers claimed angelic authority. Longenecker (*Galatians*, 17) reads too much into the language here when he suggests that Paul has in view the Judaizers' claim of approval from the Jerusalem apostles.

[69] It could have the generic sense of anything devoted to the gods, the more specific sense of something that was under the curse of the gods, or even the curse itself (LSJM; NIDNTT 1:413). For examples of its use in Greco-Roman literature, see MM, 33 and Adolf Deissmann, *Light from the Ancient East: The New Testament Illustrated by Recently Discovered Texts of the Graeco-Roman World*, trans. Lionel Richard Mortimer Strachan (London: Hodder & Stoughton, 1910), 95–96.

[70] Of the four that do not render a form of חרם, three are not translations of Hebrew texts (Jdt 16:19; 2 Macc 2:13; 9:16). The fourth (Num 21:3) translates the name of the city of Hormah, which does come from the Hebrew root חרם.

[71] TWOT 324–25.

and they were defeated in their next battle (7:2-5). When Joshua asks the Lord why they were defeated (7:6-9), God explains that the Israelites have broken the covenant by keeping for themselves objects set apart for destruction (7:10-15). Once Achan is revealed as the guilty party, he and his entire family are burned and stoned (7:16-26). As noted in the previous verse, Paul may have this very event in mind as he thinks of the false teachers troubling the Galatians. Like Achan before them, the false teachers were endangering God's covenant people by departing from the one true gospel.

Paul may also have in mind the covenant curses pronounced on those who try to lead God's people to worship other gods (Deut 13:1-18).[72] As he reflects on the false teachers, Paul classifies them as false prophets who are trying to lead the Galatian churches to worship other gods through their different so-called gospel. Under the Mosaic covenant, the divinely appointed punishment for false prophets was to be placed under God's ἀνάθεμα (Deut 13:12-18). Just as the Israelites faced the danger of being led away from the God who delivered them from their slavery in Egypt to worship other gods, so now the Galatians face the threat of being led away from the God who delivered them from this present evil age (Gal 1:4) to embrace another gospel.[73] Thus when Paul invokes "a curse" (ἀνάθεμα) on anyone proclaiming a gospel contrary to the one he first preached to the Galatians, he is asking for God's judicial wrath to be executed.[74] While modern readers might be quick to scoff at the notion of curses, the Galatians would not have done so. They lived in a culture where curses "were regarded as an evil, poisonous substance which occupies humans, destroys them from the inside, and makes them a threat to their environments."[75] It was even common to wear amulets or other objects believed

---

[72] Karl Olav Sandnes, *Paul - One of the Prophets? A Contribution to the Apostle's Self-Understanding*, WUNT 43 (Tübingen: J. C. B. Mohr, 1991), 71-73.

[73] Ciampa, *Presence and Function*, 83n45.

[74] The NET captures this well: "let him be condemned to hell!" As an alternative to this view, Betz (*Galatians*, 54) argues that Paul refers to excommunication from the church. But several factors mitigate against limiting Paul's words to excommunication from the church: (1) the use of ἀνάθεμα elsewhere in Paul with this meaning (e.g., Rom 9:3; 1 Cor 12:3; 16:22); (2) the context here in Galatians; (3) the possible echo of the Achan story; and (4) possible echoes of OT covenant curse texts.

[75] Kjell Arne Morland, *The Rhetoric of Curse in Galatians: Paul Confronts Another Gospel*, ESEC 5 (Atlanta: Scholars Press, 1995), 158, cited in Das, *Galatians*, 107. For a helpful discussion of inscriptions that shed light on the religious environment of Galatia and curses, see Clinton

to ward off the efforts of others to curse them. Paul's pronouncement of a curse on those proclaiming a different gospel would not have been dismissed lightly.

In an age that prizes "tolerance" above all things, Paul's words of condemnation may sound harsh. But when the truth of the gospel and people's eternal destinies are at stake, the apostle has no room for niceties. Those who seek to teach must pay careful attention to their life and doctrine (1 Tim 4:16), since teachers "will receive a stricter judgment" (Jas 3:1).

1:9. To emphasize the gravity of what he is saying, Paul repeats his sober warning, though not without some subtle changes. He begins "as we have said before" (ὡς προειρήκαμεν). While the verb προλέγω can refer to something that has been stated earlier in the same letter (e.g., 2 Cor 7:3), here it likely refers to a warning "we" issued on a previous occasion when Paul was with the Galatians.[76] Just as in the previous verse, Paul uses the first-person plural to remind the Galatians of what he and Barnabas said when with them.[77] Acts 14:22 notes that when Paul and Barnabas were passing back through these Galatian churches, they were "strengthening the disciples by encouraging them to continue in the faith and by telling them, 'It is necessary to go through many hardships to enter the kingdom of God.'" It is this previous warning that Paul has in mind when he writes "I now say again" (ἄρτι πάλιν λέγω).

Paul now repeats the content of the warning from 1:8, but in a slightly different form:

E. Arnold, "'I Am Astonished That You Are So Quickly Turning Away' (Gal 1.6): Paul and Anatolian Folk Belief," *NTS* 51 (2005): 429–49.

[76] For the view that Paul refers back to the warning of 1:8, see D. J. Armitage, "An Exploration of Conditional Clause Exegesis with Reference to Galatians 1, 8–9," *Bib* 88 (2007): 381. Paul uses προλέγω nine times (Rom 9:29; 2 Cor 7:3; 13:2 [2x]; Gal 1:9; 5:21 [2x]; 1 Thess 3:4; 4:6). The expression "now again" (ἄρτι πάλιν) that follows stresses the temporal focus (Moo, *Galatians*, 82). The two occurrences in Gal 5:21 also confirm that Paul speaks of warning them on a previous occasion. After his list of the works of the flesh, he writes: "I tell you about these things in advance [προλέγω]—as I told you before [προεῖπον]" (HCSB). Paul uses the present tense to refer to the current warning in 5:19–21, and the aorist tense to indicate the warning he gave while with them. The perfect tense of προλέγω here in 1:9 likely stresses the abiding significance of that previous warning.

[77] So also Dunn, *Galatians*, 44. Some have argued that the first-person plural here is simply an "editorial we" that Paul uses for effect; see, e.g., Martyn, *Galatians*, 114–15 and Moo, *Galatians*, 81. But if indeed Paul is referring to something he communicated to the Galatians on a previous occasion (as the verb seems to suggest), it makes sense that Paul would (indirectly) include Barnabas.

Table 4:

1:8	ἐὰν	ἡμεῖς ἢ ἄγγελος ἐξ οὐρανοῦ	εὐαγγελίζηται [ὑμῖν]	παρ᾽ ὃ εὐηγγελισάμεθα ὑμῖν	ἀνάθεμα ἔστω.
	if	we or an angel from heaven	should preach to you	a gospel other than what we have preached to you	a curse be on him!
1:9	εἴ	τις	ὑμᾶς εὐαγγελίζεται	παρ᾽ ὃ παρελάβετε	ἀνάθεμα ἔστω.
	if	anyone	is preaching to you	a gospel contrary to what you received	a curse be on him!

There are three noteworthy differences. First, there is a shift from the specific ("we or an angel from heaven") to the general ("anyone"). Thus the warning in 1:8 is a specific application of the more general warning Paul issued when with the Galatians. Second, the gospel that was "preached" (εὐηγγελισάμεθα) in 1:8 becomes the gospel that "you received" (παρελάβετε) here in 1:9. The verb παραλαμβάνω was often used in both Greek and Jewish literature to refer to the receiving of tradition, whether from a philosopher, the mystery religions, or the rabbis.[78] Paul uses it to refer to passing along the theological content of the gospel and its related ethical and ecclesiological entailments (1 Cor 11:23; 15:1–3; Phil 4:9; Col 2:6; 1 Thess 2:13; 4:1). The interplay between the gospel being preached and received is also found in 1 Corinthians 15:1: " Now I want to make clear for you, brothers and sisters, the gospel I preached [εὐηγγελισάμην] to you, which you received [παρελάβετε], on which you have taken your stand." Once Paul and his team preached the gospel to the Galatians, it became something that they received and were now responsible for safeguarding.

The third difference is likely the most significant yet the hardest for the English reader to see. Whereas in 1:8 Paul used a third class conditional statement (a hypothetical for consideration), here in 1:9 he uses a first class conditional statement (a situation presented as true for the sake of argument).[79] Thus Paul moves from the (unlikely) hypothetical situation of he or an angel from heaven preaching a different gospel to

---

[78] See BDAG s.v. παραλαμβάνω 2.γ and *NIDNTT* 3:748.

[79] For helpful discussions of conditional clauses, see Stanley E. Porter, *Idioms of the Greek New Testament*, BLG 2 2 (Sheffield: JSOT Press, 1992), 254–67 and Wallace, *Greek Grammar*, 679–712. Moo (*Galatians*, 82) cautions against making a sharp distinction between the third

the very real present situation of someone (i.e., the ones "troubling" the Galatians, 1:7) preaching "a gospel contrary to what you received."[80] In both cases, the result is the same: "a curse be on him!" (ἀνάθεμα ἔστω). Paul's words here in 1:8–9 make it clear that final authority in the church does not rest in any person (or angel for that matter!) but in the truth of the gospel revealed in the person and work of Christ. Not even an apostle or those who have "credentials" from trusted church leaders have the authority to alter or "improve" the message, no matter how well-intentioned they may be. Consider how Paul describes himself in 1 Corinthians 4:1–2: "A person should think of us in this way: as servants of Christ and managers of the mysteries of God. In this regard, it is required that managers be found faithful." All who proclaim the gospel will one day answer to God for their stewardship of the mysteries of God (1 Cor 4:1–5); the question is, Will we be found faithful (compare Matt 25:14–30)?

1:10. Paul now brings this section (1:6–10) to a close by applying the principle of the ultimate authority of the gospel (1:8–9) to himself.[81] The main thrust of this verse is to emphatically state that he is in no way motivated in his life and ministry by a desire to be a "people-pleaser." He shows this by asking two questions and offering a conditional statement.

The first question is, "For am I now trying to persuade people, or God?" (Ἄρτι γὰρ ἀνθρώπους πείθω ἢ τὸν θεόν).[82] While the verb translated "persuade" (πείθω) usually has the sense of "persuade, convince" in the New Testament, the context here makes such a meaning unlikely.[83] Instead,

---

and first class conditionals here yet agrees that the difference in view is the move from a general warning to a specific one.

[80] The present tense of the verb "preaches" (εὐαγγελίζεται) suggests the action is ongoing.

[81] The γάρ that links this verse to the previous verses can be understood in various ways: (1) cause/reason (Burton, *Galatians*, 31; Dunn, *Galatians*, 48; DeSilva, *Handbook*, 10); (2) clarification/explanatory (Das, *Galatians*, 110); or (3) inferential (Longenecker, *Galatians*, 18; Martyn, *Galatians*, 141; Schreiner, *Galatians*, 88–89). On the whole, inferential stating a conclusion seems most likely.

[82] The context makes it clear that the present tense verb πείθω is conative, indicating an action that is attempted but unsuccessful. For a helpful discussion of the difficulties of this clause, see Das, *Galatians*, 111–12.

[83] BDAG s.v. πείθω 2.c. It is true that elsewhere Paul uses πείθω to refer to persuading people to believe the gospel (2 Cor 5:11). But nowhere else in the LXX or NT does θεός occur as the direct object of πείθω. There are two occurrences in Josephus (*Ant.* 4:123; 8:256), and they clearly have the sense of trying to "persuade God" to do something. Betz (*Galatians*, 55) argues that the expression "persuade God" was "a polemical definition of magic and

as the next question shows, Paul refers here to gaining approval from either people or God.[84] The adverb "now" (ἄρτι) may suggest that Paul is (perhaps sarcastically) responding to a charge by the false teachers that he was seeking the approval of people (especially gentiles) by preaching his Torah-free gospel. Calling down God's curse on any (including himself!) who preach a different gospel than the one he first preached to the Galatians is clear evidence that Paul is far more concerned about pleasing God than he is about pleasing people.

The second question clarifies the first: "Or am I striving to please people?" (ἢ ζητῶ ἀνθρώποις ἀρέσκειν). The verb rendered "striving" (ζητέω) means "to devote serious effort to realize one's desire or objective."[85] By itself the verb "please" (ἀρέσκω) has a neutral meaning, and it can even refer to pleasing God in a good sense (Ps 68:32 [ET=69:31]; Rom 8:8; 15:3; 1 Thess 4:1). But the context here clearly indicates the negative sense of "act[ing] in a fawning manner" in an attempt to win someone's approval.[86] Dunn is probably correct when he suggests that Paul's devout Jewish opponents in Galatia drew the conclusion that "someone who was preaching faith in the Jewish Messiah Jesus, to Gentiles, but without making clear the covenant obligations of that faith, was guilty of softening or cheapening the gospel."[87] Paul draws a similar contrast between pleasing people or God in 1 Thessalonians 2:4: "Instead, just as we have been approved by God to be entrusted with the gospel, so we speak, not to please [ἀρέσκοντες] people, but rather God, who examines our hearts." Thus the expected answer to Paul's question of whether he is striving to please people is an emphatic "Absolutely not!"

To highlight the absurdity of the claim that he is a people pleaser, Paul uses a conditional statement that makes it clear he is not: "If I were still trying to please people, I would not be a servant of Christ" (εἰ ἔτι ἀνθρώποις ἤρεσκον, Χριστοῦ δοῦλος οὐκ ἂν ἤμην).[88] In effect Paul says, "If I were really motivated in my gospel ministry by a desire to please

---

religious quackery." Thus Paul would be denying that he was a religious charlatan. But the clauses that follow suggest that πείθω is parallel in meaning to ἀρέσκω ("please").

[84] Similarly Moo, *Galatians*, 84.

[85] BDAG s.v. ζητέω 3.d.

[86] BDAG s.v. ἀρέσκω 1.

[87] Dunn, *Galatians*, 49.

[88] Paul uses a second class conditional statement, which assumes that the protasis (the "if" part) is not true for the sake of the argument; see further Wallace, *Greek Grammar*, 694–96.

people (and it is obvious that I am not!), I definitely would not be a servant of Christ!" In referring to himself as a "servant of Christ" (Χριστοῦ δοῦλος), Paul uses imagery that would have been familiar to everyone in the first century. Slavery was an integral part of Greco-Roman culture; according to some estimates nearly two-thirds of the population of the Roman Empire were slaves in the first century.[89] To be a slave is to be under the ownership and authority of another person—in Paul's case, Jesus Christ.[90]

But there is likely more to the expression "servant of Christ" than its first-century cultural significance. In several other places Paul identifies himself as a slave/servant of Christ (Rom 1:1; Phil 1:1; Titus 1:1); indeed, it appears to be one of his favorite self-designations.[91] He likely drew this title from the Old Testament, where it can refer to someone (such as Abraham, Moses, David, etc.) who has a special relationship with God and/ or a special task to perform for him.[92] This title is especially prominent in Isaiah 40–55, where, among other things, it refers to an unspecified figure called by God to accomplish his purposes. Since Paul draws upon the servant language from Isaiah 49 in Galatians 1:15–16 and again in 1:24 to portray his apostolic calling and ministry, it is likely that here in 1:10 he refers to himself as a "servant of Christ" (Χριστοῦ δοῦλος) to anticipate that description.[93]

One need not look far to find those in ministry who are more concerned about pleasing people than they are about pleasing God. Indeed, every minister of the gospel faces the temptation to alter the message to tickle people's ears (cf. 2 Tim 4:3). But as servants of Christ we have no authority to do so. We serve at the pleasure of our Lord Jesus Christ, who himself took the form of a servant to free us from our slavery to sin and death (Rom 6:1–11; Phil 2:6–8; Heb 2:14–16).

---

[89] For a helpful summary of slavery in the Greco-Roman world, see James S. Jeffers, *The Greco-Roman World of the New Testament Era: Exploring the Background of Early Christianity* (Downers Grove, IL: IVP, 1999), 220–36.

[90] On this theme, see Murray J. Harris, *Slave of Christ: A New Testament Metaphor for Total Devotion to Christ*, NSBT 8 (Downers Grove, IL: IVP, 2001), 107–25.

[91] See Harris, *Slave of Christ,* 54–61, 139–56.

[92] See further Ciampa, *Presence and Function,* 93–95 and especially Harmon, *She Must and Shall Go Free,* 70–75, 103–15. The Hebrew word most frequently used is עֶבֶד, which is rendered by several different terms in the LXX, including δοῦλος (e.g., Isa 49:3).

[93] On this important theme in Galatians, see Biblical Theology §3.0.

Bridge

From this paragraph three points of application warrant careful reflection. First, the tendency of the human heart to wander away from God and the true gospel does not disappear when a person professes faith in Christ. The eighteenth-century hymnist Robert Robinson captured this reality well in the fourth verse of his hymn "Come Thou Fount of Every Blessing":[94]

> O to grace how great a debtor
> Daily I'm constrained to be!
> Let Thy goodness, like a fetter,
> Bind my wandering heart to Thee.
> Prone to wander, Lord I feel it,
> Prone to leave the God I love;
> Here's my heart, O take and seal it,
> Seal it for Thy courts above

Even though we have been born again and have the Holy Spirit dwelling inside us, the sinful inclination to turn away from God to other things remains until Christ returns or we die. No wonder that in the next verse of the hymn Robertson pointed to that very reality:

> O that day when freed from sinning,
> I shall see Thy lovely face;
> Clothed then in blood washed linen
> How I'll sing Thy sovereign grace;
> Come, my Lord, no longer tarry,
> Take my ransomed soul away;
> Send thine angels now to carry
> Me to realms of endless day

Our hope does not rest in our determination but in the hope of seeing Christ face to face on the last day and his power to bring us safely home to his heavenly courts.

Second, persevering in the true gospel is not without its challenges. Just as in Paul's day, there are many varieties of false teachers leading people astray from the true gospel today. Such false teachers and their

---

[94] Robert Robinson, "Come Thou Fount of Every Blessing," *Indelible Grace Hymn Book*, accessed March 11, 2021, http://hymnbook.igracemusic.com/hymns/come-thou-fount-of-every-blessing.

errors must be clearly identified and condemned. In an age when "toler-ance" is prized as the ultimate virtue, such clear condemnation will often be resisted. But when people's eternal destinies are at stake, ministers of the gospel must speak with boldness and clarity. For the gospel itself is the final authority for the life of the individual believer and the church as a body. The status or reputation of the person proclaiming error ulti-mately does not matter.

Third, those who serve in gospel ministry will inevitably face the temptation to be a people pleaser. For some the temptation takes the form of refusing to preach/teach hard truths that may offend certain people; for others it may look like saying or doing certain things to win the approval of certain key people. Regardless of the form, however, people-pleasing not only undermines the advance of the gospel but enslaves a person to what others think of us. The solution is to embrace our identity as servants of Christ and make our ambition to please him, knowing that we must one day appear before him to give an account of our life and ministry (2 Cor 5:9–10).

II. Paul's Conversion and Apostolic Commission (1:11–2:21)

The first major section of Galatians focuses on the divine origin of the gospel Paul preaches and his commission as an apostle to the gentiles. It begins with a thesis statement about the divine origin of Paul's gospel message (1:11–12). The apostle is at pains to emphasize that he received it directly through a revelation of Jesus Christ, rather than receiving it or being taught it by another person. To bolster his claim that he received the gospel directly through a revelation of Jesus Christ, Paul recounts four events/periods from his life and concludes with a summary of that divine gospel message.

The first event is Paul's conversion and commission as an apostle to the gentiles (1:13–17). Whereas his life in Judaism was characterized by his persecution of the church and zealous commitment to the traditions of his ancestors (1:13–14), that all changed when God revealed his Son Jesus in Paul to commission him to preach the gospel to the gentiles (1:15–16a). In response, Paul did not consult with anyone, including the Jerusalem apostles (1:16b–17).

The second event/period is the early years of his ministry (1:18–24). Again, the focus is on his interactions (or lack thereof) with the Jerusalem church. Three years after his conversion/commission, Paul visited Jerusalem for fifteen days, staying with Cephas and seeing no other apostle except James the brother of Jesus (1:18–19). After a brief oath swearing to the veracity of his account (1:20), Paul recounts his departure into Syria and Cilicia (1:21) and asserts that he was known to the churches in Judea by reputation only (1:22–23). The result was those same Judean churches glorifying God at work in and through Paul (1:24).

The third event/period is his second visit to Jerusalem (2:1–10). Paul now fast-forwards another fourteen years to a trip to Jerusalem with Barnabas and Titus (2:1). During this visit he presented the gospel to the leaders of the Jerusalem church to ensure his vision of a church consisting of Jew and gentile together (2:2–3). Paul remained steadfast despite the efforts of false brothers to compel circumcision for gentile believers (2:4–5). Yet despite their efforts, the leaders of the Jerusalem church and Paul agreed on the content of the gospel while acknowledging different broad spheres of ministry: Peter among the Jews and Paul among the gentiles (2:6–9). All the Jerusalem leaders asked was for Paul to remain committed to remembering the poor (2:10).

The fourth and final event is a confrontation with Cephas in Antioch (2:11–14). At first Cephas was eating with gentile believers, but out of fear he stopped doing so when certain men from James arrived (2:11–12). As a result, the rest of the Jewish believers followed his lead, including even Barnabas (2:13). Seeing that Cephas and the rest of the Jewish believers were behaving in a way that was out of step with the gospel, Paul confronted Peter in front of the entire church (2:14)

Paul concludes this lengthy section with a summary of his gospel message (2:15–21). Central to the gospel is how one is justified. Paul asserts that regardless of ethnicity, no one is justified by works of the law; instead justification comes by faith in Christ (2:15–16). In light of this fundamental truth, Paul responds to the claim of the opponents that justification requires observing the Mosaic law (2:17–20). Since justification by faith in Christ eliminates the distinction between Jew and gentile, Christ is the one responsible for the "sin" of failing to keep the Mosaic law regulations (i.e., circumcision, food laws, Sabbath) that distinguish Jew from gentile (2:17). Indeed, any effort to reestablish these regulations would make Paul a transgressor of the new covenant (2:18). Presenting his own experience as a paradigm for all believers, Paul asserts that he died to the law when he was crucified with Christ (2:19–20a). As a result, Christ now lives inside of him to empower a life of obedience based on faith (2:20b). Therefore, Paul refuses to nullify the grace of God revealed in the gospel because Christ's death demonstrates that justification could not come through the law.

A. THESIS (1:11–12)

> [11] For I want you to know, brothers and sisters, that the gospel preached by me is not of human origin. [12] For I did not receive it from a human source and I was not taught it, but it came by a revelation of Jesus Christ.

Context

This brief paragraph introduces the thesis of the long argument that spans 1:11–2:21. Paul's basic point is simple: the gospel he preaches has a divine origin. To support this thesis Paul recounts: (1) his conversion and calling to be an apostle to the gentiles (1:13–17); (2) his early ministry (1:18–24); (3) his second visit to Jerusalem (2:1–10); (4) his confrontation with Peter in Antioch (2:11–14); and (5) a summary of the gospel message (2:15–21). A central motif in this section is Paul's relationship to the Jerusalem church. It appears the opponents in Galatia claimed that Paul was out of step with the leadership of the Jerusalem gospel and had in effect "gone rogue" from them. In this section then Paul walks a fine line between asserting that his status as an apostle of the true gospel message comes directly from the risen Christ (just like that of the Jerusalem apostles), while at the same time acknowledging the apostolic status of the Jerusalem apostles.

Structure

This thesis statement consists of a statement introduced with a disclosure formula ("I want you to know") about the divine origin of Paul's gospel message (1:11), followed by an explanatory statement denying its human origins and asserting its divine origin (1:12). As such it closely parallels 1:1, where Paul made similar denials and assertions about the origin of his status as an apostle.[95]

---

[95] Longenecker (*Galatians*, 23) notes that the "οὐκ ... οὐδὲ ... οὔτε ... ἀλλὰ construction of vv. 11–12 corresponds to the οὐκ ... οὐδὲ ... ἀλλὰ construction of v 1, which necessitates

1:11. Now that Paul has established the final authority of the gospel and his identity as a slave of Christ who strives to please God rather than people, he moves to explain the heavenly origin of the gospel.[96] In doing so he addresses the Galatians as "brothers and sisters" (ἀδελφοί), a term that reminds believers that we are members of God's family, adopted sons and daughters who have God's Spirit (see 4:4–7).

When Paul writes "I want you to know," he uses a verb (γνωρίζω) that was common in Greek letters to introduce the disclosure of important information.[97] As he does elsewhere (e.g., 1 Cor 12:3; 15:1; 2 Cor 8:1), Paul uses this verb to introduce a key statement that he will subsequently unpack: "the gospel preached by me is not of human origin" (τὸ εὐαγγέλιον τὸ εὐαγγελισθὲν ὑπ᾽ ἐμοῦ ὅτι οὐκ ἔστιν κατὰ ἄνθρωπον), or, perhaps better, "not based on human thought" (compare HCSB). If so, Paul stresses that the gospel is not bound by human ideals or governed by human standards,[98] and as such it transcends human wisdom (compare 1 Cor 1:18–31). As such, there is "a relation of misfit, even contradiction, between the 'good news' and the typical structures of human thought and behavior. The good news stands askance to human norms because its origin lies outside the human sphere."[99] Just as Paul's status as an apostle is "not from men" (οὐκ ἀπ᾽ ἀνθρώπων) nor "by man" (οὐδὲ δι᾽ ἀνθρώπου; 1:1), so too his gospel is "not governed by human standards" (οὐκ … κατὰ ἄνθρωπον). This repeated emphasis on the divine origin of the gospel and Paul's status as an apostle suggests that his opponents were questioning the legitimacy of Paul's message and status.

---

that we interpret the two sets of statements in similar fashion."

[96] Deciding whether γάρ or δέ is the original reading is not easy. Despite the NA[28] rendering, the textual evidence for δέ is both early and impressive ($\mathfrak{P}^{46\ 2.*}$א A D[1] K L P Ψ). Despite the fact that Longenecker (*Galatians*, 22) and Witherington (*Grace in Galatia*, 90) both favor δέ, I (along with the majority of commentators) think γάρ is more likely. It seems probable that a scribe may have changed γάρ to δέ to conform it to 1 Cor 15:1 (Γνωρίζω δὲ ὑμῖν, ἀδελφοί, τὸ εὐαγγέλιον ὃ εὐηγγελισάμην ὑμῖν) and 2 Cor 8:1 (Γνωρίζομεν δὲ ὑμῖν, ἀδελφοί). See the discussions in Metzger, *Textual Commentary*, 521 and Silva, *Interpreting Galatians*, 44–49. Instead of seeing the γάρ as explanatory, Moo (*Galatians*, 92) understands it as simply a narrative marker expressing continuation.

[97] See Longenecker, *Galatians*, 22.

[98] The preposition κατά with the accusative here is best understood as indicating "the norm that governs something" (BDAG B.5.a.α). Paul uses the expression κατὰ ἄνθρωπον six other places (Rom 3:5; 7:22; 1 Cor 3:3; 9:8; 15:32; Gal 3:15; Eph 4:22), and in most cases it expresses a contrast between something human and something divine or spiritual. Perhaps the closest parallel is 1 Cor 9:8: "Am I saying this from a human perspective [κατὰ ἄνθρωπον]? Doesn't the law also say the same thing?" See similarly Moo, *Galatians*, 93.

[99] John M. G. Barclay, *Paul and the Gift* (Grand Rapids: Eerdmans, 2015), 355–56.

Since the gospel transcends human wisdom, we should not be surprised when people reject it as foolishness. But it is precisely through the preaching of the gospel that God's wisdom is revealed and so-called human wisdom is exposed as folly (1 Cor 1:18–31).

1:12. Paul further explains the thesis stated in 1:11 with two negative statements followed by a positive one. First, Paul "did not receive it from a human source" (οὐδὲ γὰρ ἐγὼ παρὰ ἀνθρώπου παρέλαβον αὐτὸ). As elsewhere in Paul's letters (1 Cor 15:3; Col 2:6; 1 Thess 2:13; 2 Thess 3:6), the verb translated "receive" (παραλαμβάνω) refers to the receiving of tradition.[100] Paul is not denying the value of receiving specific traditions related to the content of the gospel, since elsewhere he affirms and uses them (compare 1 Cor 15:3–8).[101] Rather, he is stressing that his initial reception of the gospel did not come through this means. Whereas during his days as a Pharisee he based his life on the traditions handed down by generations of men before him, his new life is based on something far grander—a revelation of Jesus Christ (see below).[102] Second, Paul asserts "I was not taught it" (οὔτε ἐδιδάχθην). The gospel was not like the rabbinic traditions that he learned at the feet of Gamaliel in Jerusalem (Acts 22:3). Again, Paul is not denying the value of being taught the gospel and its implications through another person, as he himself engages in this very activity (see Col 2:6–7)! The point is that Paul's initial reception of the gospel did not come through human agency. As Hays notes, "Even though he can pass on traditional kerygmatic and liturgical formulas to his churches, these formulas must be understood as particular 'performances' of an underlying story that Paul has learned directly from God."[103] The combination of these two phrases recalls Paul's assertion in 1:1 that his status as an apostle was "not from men or by man" (οὐκ ἀπ᾽ ἀνθρώπων οὐδὲ δι᾽ ἀνθρώπου), and signals that he is now further unpacking that opening line.[104]

---

[100] When παραλαμβάνω has this meaning, it is often followed by the preposition παρά to indicate the source (BDAG A.3.a.β), as it does here (see also 1 Thess 2:13; 4:1; 2 Thess 3:6).

[101] Whereas in Gal 1:12 the point is that Paul received the gospel directly from God, in 1 Cor 15:1–8 Paul stresses that his gospel summary is the common and accepted teaching of the church (so Moo, *Galatians*, 93–94).

[102] Similarly Das, *Galatians*, 121.

[103] Richard B. Hays, "The Letter to the Galatians: Introduction, Commentary, and Reflection," in *The New Interpreter's Bible*, ed. Leander E. Keck (Nashville: Abingdon, 2000), 211.

[104] Moo (*Galatians*, 94) notes that "Paul imitates the sequence of 1:1 by following a pair of denials with a positive affirmation."

Instead, as the third and positive statement indicates, Paul claims the gospel "came by a revelation from Jesus Christ" (ἀλλὰ δι᾽ ἀποκαλύψεως Ἰησοῦ Χριστοῦ).[105] The means that God used to confront Paul with the gospel was a "revelation" (ἀποκάλυψις) of Jesus Christ.[106] The noun ἀποκάλυψις refers to a revelation or disclosure, whether of hidden truths (Rom 16:25; Eph 3:3) or a person (here; 2 Cor 12:1, 7; Rev 1:1), often of an eschatological nature.[107] The emphasis of this word falls on divine agency; although God the Father is not specifically named, he is in fact the agent of revelation. Thus although the expression ἀποκαλύψεως Ἰησοῦ Χριστοῦ could mean that Jesus Christ is the source or the agent of the revelation, it seems better to see Jesus Christ as the object of God's revelation.[108] Paul's point, then, could be summarized as "I received the gospel through God revealing Jesus Christ in me." As we will see below, that is essentially what Paul will say in 1:15–16 when he uses the cognate verb ἀποκαλύπτω: "God ... was pleased to reveal his Son in me, so that I could preach him among the Gentiles." Again, we should note the parallels to 1:1, where Paul argues that his status as an apostle does not come through the agency of any human being. Paul did not receive his gospel from detailed study of Torah, nor elaborate human reasoning, but directly from God himself in his encounter with Jesus Christ on the Damascus road (see 1:15–16 below).

In our fallen world it is common to hear people suggest that we should look inside of ourselves for the solutions to our problems. But the gospel makes it clear that the only true solution to our problems is what God has revealed to us through his Son Jesus Christ. No amount of internal navel-gazing will solve what is wrong with us.

---

[105] Strictly speaking there is no subject or verb in this Greek clause, so the reader needs to supply them. The most natural option is usually to keep the subject ("I") and the verbs ("received" and "was taught") from the previous clause: "but [I received and was taught] through a revelation of Jesus Christ." But since that does not make the best sense, most English translations keep "I" as the subject and supply the verb "received."

[106] While the preposition διά can indicate personal agency, it is better to take it as indicating means (BDAG A.3.a) in light of our understanding of the genitive Ἰησοῦ Χριστοῦ and the language of 1:15–16.

[107] See similarly Dunn, *Galatians*, 53.

[108] While a number of commentators see the genitive here as subjective (e.g., Longenecker, *Galatians*, 24), the parallel language in 1:16 indicates this is an objective genitive (so also Silva, *Interpreting Galatians*, 65–68; Schreiner, *Galatians*, 97; Moo, *Galatians*, 95).

Bridge

We live in a world that offers many so-called gospels—stories and claims about what will bring meaning, satisfaction, joy, comfort, etc. All of them are based on some form of human wisdom. But the true gospel centers on the revelation of the crucified and risen Jesus Christ; as such it is the foundation of the life and ministry of the individual believer and the local church. Paul makes this point clear in 1 Corinthians 3:10–11, when he writes "According to God's grace that was given to me, I have laid a foundation as a skilled master builder, and another builds on it. But each one is to be careful how he builds on it. For no one can lay any foundation other than what has been laid down. That foundation is Jesus Christ." Is that gospel the foundation of your life, your church, your ministry?

B. PAUL'S CONVERSION (1:13–17)

> [13] For you have heard about my former way of life in Judaism: I intensely persecuted God's church and tried to destroy it. [14] I advanced in Judaism beyond many contemporaries among my people, because I was extremely zealous for the traditions of my ancestors. [15] But when God, who from my mother's womb set me apart and called me by his grace, was pleased [16] to reveal his Son in me, so that I could preach him among the Gentiles, I did not immediately consult with anyone. [17] I did not go up to Jerusalem to those who had become apostles before me; instead I went to Arabia and came back to Damascus.

Context

This paragraph is the first of several that narrate a specific event or time period from Paul's life in support of his thesis that the gospel he preaches came from a revelation of Jesus Christ (1:11–12). In one respect it is arguably the most important of the events/time periods Paul mentions because it centers on the actual revelation of Christ to Paul that transformed him from a persecutor of the church to a preacher of the gospel.

Structure

This paragraph divides into two sections. In 1:13–14, Paul describes his life in Judaism before he became a follower of Jesus. He characterizes this period of his life with three statements using imperfect tense verbs: (1) he persecuted the church; (2) he tried to destroy the church; and (3) he was advancing in Judaism beyond his peers. All of that changed, however, when God delighted to reveal his Son Jesus in Paul (1:15–17). This gracious act was planned before Paul was born (1:15), and the purpose of this revelation was to commission Paul to proclaim the gospel to the gentiles (1:16b). In response to this revelation, Paul stresses that he did not consult with anyone (1:16c), not even the apostles in Jerusalem (1:17a), but instead went off to Arabia and then back to Damascus (1:17b).

1:13. The word "For" (γάρ) marks what follows as an explanation of Paul's thesis that the gospel came to him as a revelation of Jesus Christ.[109] He says that the Galatians "have heard about my former way of life in Judaism" (τὴν ἐμὴν ἀναστροφήν ποτε ἐν τῷ Ἰουδαϊσμῷ). By "way of life" (ἀναστροφή) Paul refers to how he lived, thought, spoke, believed, felt, and acted. He uses this same noun to describe how the Ephesians lived before their conversion (Eph 4:22), as well as how Timothy should live as an example of godliness (1 Tim 4:12). Peter frequently uses this same noun to refer to both the kind of life believers should live (1 Pet 1:15; 2:12; 3:1–2, 16; 2 Pet 3:11) as well as the way unbelievers live (1 Pet 1:18; 2 Pet 2:7). Paul classifies his former way of life as being "in Judaism" (ἐν τῷ Ἰουδαϊσμῷ), an expression that identifies Judaism as the governing sphere and controlling influence.[110] After his conversion Paul was still ethnically a Jew (Rom 9:1–5; 11:1–2). But when Paul refers here to "Judaism" (Ἰουδαϊσμός) he has in mind the entire network of traditions, practices, and beliefs associated with the Jewish way of life, with particular emphasis on the Mosaic law and the traditions associated with it.[111]

---

[109] Moo (*Galatians*, 99) suggests that the γάρ introduces 1:13–2:14.

[110] While the preposition ἐν can be understood several ways, it is best to see it as indicating "a close personal relation in which the referent of the ἐν-term is viewed as the controlling influence" (BDAG 4.c).

[111] So similarly Schreiner, *Galatians*, 98. Here in Gal 1:13–14 are the only two NT occurrences of the noun Ἰουδαϊσμός. It does not occur in the canonical books of the LXX, Josephus, or Philo. It does occur in 2 Macc 2:21; 8:1; 14:38 [2x]; 4 Macc 4:26, where in each case it refers to the practices and beliefs that distinguish Jews from gentiles. The early church father Ignatius uses Ἰουδαϊσμός five times in his letters (Ign. *Magn* 8:1; 10:3 [2x]; Ing. *Eph* 6:1 [2x]), and he contrasts it with grace, "Christianity/Christian doctrine" (Χριστιανισμός). Of course, Ignatius' use of the term Ἰουδαϊσμός comes at a much different period in the history of the early church and cannot automatically be imported back into Paul's use in Galatians. Dunn (*Galatians*, 56) argues that "Judaism ... as a description of the religion of Jews, only emerged in the Maccabean revolt, a fact which stamped its character as fiercely nationalistic and loyal to the law, in reaction to those who attempted to eliminate its distinctiveness." But this narrow understanding of the term does not account for the contrast between "the present Jerusalem" in 4:25 and the "Jerusalem above" in 4:26 (see commentary there).

That he calls this his "former" way of life signals that Judaism is no longer the governing sphere and controlling influence of his life.

Paul explains the nature of his former life in Judaism with three imperfect tense verbs in 1:13–14.[112] First, Paul writes, "I intensely persecuted God's church" (καθ᾽ ὑπερβολὴν ἐδίωκον τὴν ἐκκλησίαν τοῦ θεοῦ). In 1:2, Paul refers to the individual congregations of believers when he refers to the "churches of Galatia"; here the singular reference to the "church of God" has in view the universal church, consisting of all true believers everywhere. As noted in 1:2, the LXX often uses ἐκκλησία to refer to the assembled people of God, especially when they are gathered for worship (e.g., Deut 4:10; 23:2–9; 2 Chr 1:2–5; 6:3–13). Note the irony: in his zeal for the purity of the people of God, Paul was in fact persecuting them!

As a Pharisee, Paul likely considered the Christians a threat because they were leading people to trust in a crucified "messiah." After all, Deuteronomy 21:23 made it clear that "anyone hung on a tree is under God's curse." Not content merely to drive Christians from Jerusalem (Acts 8:1–4), Paul sought and received permission from the high priest to hunt down believers in Damascus (Acts 9:1–2). But in doing so he was attacking "God's church," the people whom God "purchased with his own blood" (Acts 20:28). Second, Paul "tried to destroy" God's church. This verb (πορθέω) sometimes occurs in military contexts to portray a decisive victory.[113] Paul would not rest until this threat to Judaism was wiped out entirely.

Everyone has regrets from their past; something we said or did, or perhaps something we failed to say or do. But when viewed in light of the grace of God experienced through the gospel, even these regrets can be seen as part of God's larger purposes to draw us to himself.

1:14. Whereas verse 13 focused on Paul's actions directed toward the church, verse 14 shifts attention to his relationship with his peers. Paul states the third aspect of his life in Judaism: "I advanced in Judaism beyond many contemporaries among my people" (προέκοπτον ἐν τῷ Ἰουδαϊσμῷ ὑπὲρ πολλοὺς συνηλικιώτας ἐν τῷ γένει μου). The verb

---

[112] The first (ἐδίωκον) and third (προέκοπτον; v. 14) imperfects are customary, indicating a regularly recurring activity in the past, while the second (ἐπόρθουν) is conative, portraying an action that was attempted; see Wallace, *Greek Grammar*, 548–51.

[113] In addition to 4 Macc 4:23, see the several occurrences in Josephus (*Ant.* 5:31; 9:253; 13:338; *War* 4:534) and Philo (*Conf.* 1:159). For examples from Greek literature, see BrillDAG s.v. πορθέω.

"advanced" (προκόπτω) has the sense of making progress in something; thus, "Jesus increased [προέκοπτεν] in wisdom and stature" (Luke 2:52). In certain Stoic writings the verb can refer to growth in the moral and spiritual development of a person.[114] But for Paul the realm of progress was Judaism, within which Paul had a stellar resume: "circumcised the eighth day; of the nation of Israel, of the tribe of Benjamin, a Hebrew born of Hebrews; regarding the law, a Pharisee; regarding zeal, persecuting the church; regarding the righteousness that is in the law, blameless" (Phil 3:5–6). Given his obvious abilities, Paul's claim is no idle boast.

The reason Paul surpassed his contemporaries was because he was "extremely zealous for the traditions of my ancestors" (περισσοτέρως ζηλωτὴς ὑπάρχων τῶν πατρικῶν μου παραδόσεων; Gal 1:14).[115] He demonstrated a passionate commitment not only to the doctrines and practices of the Scriptures, but the additional distinctives of the Pharisees and their extrabiblical oral and written traditions.[116] In the first century the Pharisees were well-known for the scrupulous and exact observance of the Mosaic law and their own traditions (see Acts 22:3; 26:5 and Josephus, *War* 1:110; *Ant.* 17:41).[117] Paul learned these traditions as a student under Gamaliel (Acts 22:3), a well-known first-century rabbi and prominent Pharisee.[118]

Paul may have seen himself following in the footsteps of his ancestor Phinehas. While in the wilderness, the Israelites "began to prostitute themselves with the women of Moab. The women invited them to the sacrifices for their gods, and the people ate and bowed in worship to

---

[114] Gustav Stählin, "προκοπή, προκόπτω" in *TDNT* 6:705.

[115] The adverbial participle ὑπάρχων (which the csb renders "I was") is probably causal (so also DeSilva, *Handbook*, 16), though it could have a more general sense of attendant circumstances.

[116] For a helpful survey of zeal in Second Temple Judaism, see Dane C. Ortlund, *Zeal without Knowledge: The Concept of Zeal in Romans 10, Galatians 1, and Philippians 3*, LNTS (London: T&T Clark, 2012), 62–114. Longenecker (*Galatians*, 30) suggests that, as used here, "traditions of my fathers" includes: (1) the teachings and practices developed by the Pharisees, some of which were eventually recorded in rabbinic literature, and (2) various interpretations common in the synagogues, some of which were eventually recorded in the Targums.

[117] Helpfully noted by Dunn, *Galatians*, 60. However, Dunn too narrowly focuses the nature of Paul's zeal on a commitment to preserve the ethnic distinctiveness of the Jewish people. By contrast, Ortlund (*Zeal without Knowledge*, 137–50) is correct to see this zeal as primarily vertically oriented and more holistically encompassing the entirety of Paul's pre-conversion efforts to live a life pleasing to God.

[118] On Paul as a student of Gamaliel, see Keener, *Acts*, 4:3215–21.

their gods" (Num 25:1b–2). Phinehas, the grandson of Aaron the priest, discovered an Israelite man and Midianite woman in the act and thrust his spear through the two of them (Num 25:6–9). By his actions "Phinehas ... turned back my wrath from the Israelites because he was zealous among them with my zeal, so that I did not destroy the Israelites in my zeal" (Num 25:11).

Phinehas's zeal for Yahweh, his law, and the purity of God's people became a model for later Jews, often in the context of relating to gentiles. Mattathias, the instigator of the Maccabean rebellion, "burned with zeal for the law, as Phinehas did against Zimri the son of Salu" (1 Macc 2:26 RSV). Sirach 45:23–24 remembers Phinehas as one who was "zealous in the fear of the Lord and ... stood firm in the turning of the people ... he also made atonement for Israel" (NETS). Philo holds Phinehas up as model of bold zeal and virtue overcoming pleasure (*Leg.* 3:242; *Post.* 1:182; *Conf.* 1:57; *Mut.* 1:108; *Mos.* 1:301–14). It seems likely that before his conversion Paul saw himself acting within this tradition of zeal to preserve the purity of God's people in view of dangers from the surrounding gentile culture.[119]

Zeal itself is a neutral thing. When directed toward the wrong person or object it can lead to disaster. For Paul that wrong object was the Jewish traditions surrounding the Mosaic law covenant that led him to persecute the church. Today some may pursue a similar zeal for religious traditions that are far removed from the gospel itself, and in doing so ironically move away from the truth of the gospel. The kind of zeal that God calls us to have is one that is based on the knowledge of the gospel (Rom 10:2) and has Christ as its object.

1:15–17. The trajectory of Paul's life completely changed, however, "when God ... was pleased to reveal his Son in me" (Ὅτε δὲ εὐδόκησεν [ὁ θεὸς] ... ἀποκαλύψαι τὸν υἱὸν αὐτοῦ ἐν ἐμοί).[120] God took great pleasure

---

[119] Ciampa (*Presence and Function*, 110–11) notes that Psalm 105:31 (LXX) "ties together Phinehas' action with justification language which echoes Gen 15:6." Thus Paul may be anticipating his own citation of Gen 15:6 later in Gal 3:6.

[120] The combination of "but when" (Ὅτε δὲ) introduces the sharp contrast between Paul's former life in Judaism and what God did to change his life. Paul is fond of drawing such sharp contrast between one's life before Christ and one's life as a believer (see, e.g., Eph 2:4). The brackets surrounding ὁ θεὸς reflect the uncertainty of whether it was in the original text. It is absent in some early witnesses (𝔓46 B), though it is present in a wide range of witnesses, including some relatively early ones (א A D). On the whole, it seems most likely that this is a scribal addition to make the subject of εὐδόκησεν explicit; see Metzger, *Textual Commentary*, 521–22.

in choosing to do what he did; this was no begrudging act. That act was "to reveal his Son" (ἀποκαλύψαι τὸν υἱὸν αὐτοῦ), language that echoes his statement in 1:12 that he received the gospel "by a revelation of Jesus Christ" (δι᾽ ἀποκαλύψεως Ἰησοῦ Χριστοῦ). The verb ἀποκαλύπτω depicts making something known that was previously hidden, sometimes in the context of revealing divine secrets (Dan 2:19, 22 [THB]; Matt 11:25; 1 Cor 2:10; Eph 3:5; 1 Pet 1:12). Yet in this case the revelation was not the content of a message—it was God's Son himself.[121] While traveling to Damascus to arrest Christ-followers, Paul encountered the risen Jesus Christ and was struck blind (Acts 9:1–9). This revelation of Jesus Christ takes place "in" Paul, a phrase that indicates the sphere in which the revelation takes place.[122] In other words, God's intention in revealing Jesus Christ in Paul is to demonstrate Jesus Christ in the life and ministry of Paul in such a way that Jesus Christ becomes the focus of everything that Paul is and does (cf. Gal 2:20–21).

Paul further describes God in two ways. First, he is one "who from my mother's womb set me apart" (ὁ ἀφορίσας με ἐκ κοιλίας μητρός μου). Paul uses this same verb (ἀφορίζω) in Romans 1:1 to claim that he was "set apart for the gospel of God" as an apostle. Here, however, he goes further, claiming that God set him apart before he was even born.[123] Like Jacob (Rom 9:10–12), the Isaianic servant (Isa 49:1; see further below), and Jeremiah (Jer 1:5), God chose Paul for a specific role in his redemptive plan before Paul took his first breath. Second, Paul says that God "called me by his grace" (καλέσας διὰ τῆς χάριτος αὐτοῦ). As noted in 1:6, the

---

[121] Paul likely uses sonship language here to anticipate the long argument of 3:1–5:1, which in large part centers on who the true "sons of Abraham" are.

[122] While most English versions translate "to me," the csв more accurately has "in me." In the eight other occurrences of the construction ἀποκαλύπτω + ἐν in the LXX/NT, not once does ἐν indicate the recipient of revelation. Instead it marks (1) the time when something is revealed (Num 24:4, 16; Dan 2:19; 1 Pet 1:5); (2) the sphere/location of a revelation (Judg 5:2; 1 Sam 2:27; Prov 11:13); or (3) the actions or being by which something is revealed (Ezek 16:36; 22:10); see further Harmon, *She Must and Shall Go Free*, 82. Murray Harris regards the use of ἐν here as an "example of the basic locative sense" of this preposition; see Murray J. Harris, *Prepositions and Theology in the Greek New Testament* (Grand Rapids: Zondervan, 2011), 118–19 and also Moo, *Galatians*, 104–5.

[123] Strictly speaking the expression ἐκ κοιλίας μητρός μου can be understood as "from the time of my birth" or "before my birth." Moo (*Galatians*, 103) notes that while most LXX and occurrences have the former sense, the latter is more consistent with the allusion to Isa 49:1 and is thus to be preferred.

verb καλέω has the force here of an effectual summons, not merely an invitation. The instrument God used to call Paul was his grace, which here is a shorthand for what Christ has done for his people. Paul did nothing to deserve such a calling; in fact, he did everything to deserve God's judgment.

The purpose of God calling Paul was "so that I could preach him among the Gentiles" (ἵνα εὐαγγελίζωμαι αὐτὸν ἐν τοῖς ἔθνεσιν), or perhaps more strictly "preach the good news about him among the Gentiles."[124] Although Paul's focus here is on his calling as an apostle, it is mistaken to conclude that the apostle does not also have his conversion in view.[125] By referring to his "former way of life in Judaism" (1:13), Paul implies he has a new way of life. His claim in 2:19–20 that he no longer lives but Christ lives in him further confirms that this experience was both a conversion and a calling.

The content of the good news Paul was called to preach was not the Mosaic law, the traditions of the fathers, or even helpful principles for a happy and satisfied life. It was "Jesus Christ and him crucified" (1 Cor 2:2). Such preaching was to take place "among the Gentiles" (ἐν τοῖς ἔθνεσιν). The one who had devoted himself to maintaining the purity and distinctness of the Jewish people from the gentiles had now been commissioned by God to proclaim the good news about the one he once regarded as a false messiah.

Paul shapes the description of his conversion and call with language from the Isaianic Servant Songs, and especially from Isaiah 49 (LXX).[126] Like the Isaianic servant, Paul was called from his mother's womb (Isa 49:1 // Gal 1:15). Just as God delighted to reveal his Son in Paul, God says to the servant "You are my servant, Israel, in whom I will be glorified"

---

[124] Translating this way helps preserve the link between Paul's claim that he received the gospel (εὐαγγέλιον) he preached from a revelation of Jesus Christ (1:11–12) and God's commission to preach the good news (εὐαγγελίζω) about Christ (1:16).

[125] For the claim that Paul was not converted but merely called, see especially James D. G. Dunn, "Paul's Conversion—a Light to Twentieth Century Disputes," in *Evangelium, Schriftauslegung, Kirche*, ed. Jostein Adna, Scott J. Hafemann, and Otfried Hofius (Göttingen: Vandenhoeck & Ruprecht, 1997), 77–93. For a thorough rebuttal of Dunn's view, see Peter T. O'Brien, "Was Paul Converted?," in *Justification and Variegated Nomism: Volume 2: The Paradoxes of Paul*, ed. D. A. Carson, Peter T. O'Brien, and Mark Seifrid (Grand Rapids: Baker, 2004), 361–91.

[126] What follows is a summary of the longer treatment in Harmon, *She Must and Shall Go Free*, 78–86. Similar language is also found in Jeremiah 1:5, but the number of additional echoes of Isaiah 49 indicate that the latter is the primary text in view.

(Isa 49:3 // Gal 1:15–16).[127] Isaiah 52:10 foresaw a day when "the LORD has displayed his holy arm in the sight of all the nations; all the ends of the earth will see the salvation of our God" (compare Gal 1:15–16). Those who announce Yahweh's salvation are described as those "who [bring] good news" (Isa 52:7 // Gal 1:16). God promises to make the servant "a light for the nations, to be my salvation to the ends of the earth" (Isa 49:6 // Gal 1:16). Paul saw his life and ministry as the fulfillment of God's promise to raise up a servant through whom eschatological salvation would reach to the ends of the earth and incorporate the gentiles within the people of God.[128]

In the aftermath of this life-altering encounter with the risen Christ, Paul states two things he did not do and one thing he did do (1:16b–17). First, Paul "did not immediately consult with anyone" (εὐθέως οὐ προσανεθέμην σαρκὶ καὶ αἵματι).[129] The verb rendered "consult" (προσανατίθημι) has the sense here of "confer or communicate with for the purpose of obtaining or giving instruction."[130] The Greek historian Diodorus Siculus uses this verb to describe Alexander the Great seeking counsel from seers on the interpretation of an omen (17.116.4). Thus Paul's point here is that he was not dependent on any human authority for the meaning of God's revelation to him or the content of his gospel message; he received it as a direct revelation from God (1:11–12).[131] Further support for this conclusion is found in noting that the phrase translated "anyone" is literally "flesh and blood" (σαρκὶ καὶ αἵματι), an expression that often highlights human weakness in contrast to divine or spiritual realities (John 1:12; 1 Cor 15:50; Eph 6:12). The second thing Paul did not do is "go up to Jerusalem to those who had become apostles before me" (ἀνῆλθον εἰς Ἱεροσόλυμα πρὸς τοὺς πρὸ ἐμοῦ ἀποστόλους). Paul's insistence here on his independence from the Jerusalem church

---

[127] Although not an exact verbal match, the conceptual link is strong; see Carey C. Newman, *Paul's Glory-Christology: Tradition and Rhetoric* (Leiden: Brill, 1992), 205–7.

[128] See Biblical Theology §3.1.

[129] While it is possible that εὐθέως could modify the clause "I went away to Arabia," the emphasis in the context on Paul's independence makes it more likely that εὐθέως modifies "I did not consult" (Moo, *Galatians*, 105).

[130] MM, 546

[131] Thus there is no contradiction with Acts 9:10–24, which describes Paul's interactions with Ananias and other believers in Damascus in days and weeks after his conversion. Paul's point here is that he did not consult with anyone about the legitimacy, meaning, or significance of his encounter with the risen Christ.

and the account of one of his later visits to Jerusalem in 2:1–10 suggests that his opponents in Galatia criticized him on this front.[132] Moo is probably correct when he suggests "the agitators were arguing that Paul was an unlearned or perhaps disobedient disciple of the Jerusalem apostles."[133]

So instead of consulting with anyone or immediately heading to Jerusalem, Paul "went to Arabia" (ἀπῆλθον εἰς Ἀραβίαν). Arabia could refer in general to the vast area east of the Jordan River spanning Israel from the northeast to the southeast, including the northern portion of the Arabian Peninsula. Where exactly in that vast expanse Paul went and why he went there is unclear. Some suggest that he sought solitude in the wilderness to reflect on the meaning and significance of the revelation he received, perhaps even traveling to Mount Sinai.[134] But on the whole it seems slightly more likely that Paul went to the Nabatean kingdom south of Damascus and east of the Jordan River and began preaching the gospel.[135] In 2 Corinthians 11:32–33 Paul recounts being run out of Damascus by an official of King Aretas of Nabatea, indicating at some point he actively engaged in ministry. While we cannot be sure why Paul chose this area, he may have been motivated by its geographical proximity, the close ethnic relationship between Arab Nabateans and the Jews, and/or even his understanding of prophetic promises in Isaiah.[136] Whatever the

---

[132] See further the Introduction, 15–17.

[133] Moo, *Galatians*, 106.

[134] See, e.g., Burton, *Galatians*, 55–58; Joachim Rohde, *Der Brief des Paulus an die Galater* (Berlin: Evangelische Verlagsanstalt, 1989), 62–63; Longenecker, *Galatians*, 34–35; Riesner, *Paul's Early Period*, 258–60. One of the more extensive arguments is found in N. T. Wright, "Paul, Arabia, and Elijah (Galatians 1:17)," *JBL* 115 (1996): 683–92. Wright argues that Paul regarded himself as zealous for Yahweh in the tradition of Phinehas (Num 25:7–13) and, more importantly, Elijah (1 Kgs 19:14). After Elijah's confrontation with Ahab and Jezebel, he fled to Mount Horeb "to resign his prophetic commission" (685). Just as Paul followed Elijah's example in his pre-conversion zeal, according to Wright, so too Paul followed Elijah by going to Mount Sinai (= Arabia; cf. Gal 4:25) and then returning to Damascus (compare 1 Kgs 19:15 with Gal 1:17). When combined with the fact that Paul describes his call in prophetic terms, Wright concludes that Paul's purpose in going to Arabia must have been for communion with God, whether to attempt to resign his prophetic commission or at least complain of his inadequacy.

[135] It is also possible that Paul initially began preaching in Nabatea because of its proximity and then went to Mount Sinai to reflect on this revelation; see Hengel and Schwemer, *Paul between Damascus and Antioch: The Unknown Years*, 109–19.

[136] See especially Hengel and Schwemer, *Paul between Damascus and Antioch*, 106–26. They cite Isa 60:6–7 and the associated Targumic traditions that link those geographical regions to Nabatea. Seyoon Kim contends that Paul was motivated by his understanding of Isa 42:11 and 60:17, which he contends links "Keder" with Nabatea; see further Seyoon Kim, *Paul and*

reason, Paul eventually "came back to Damascus" (πάλιν ὑπέστρεψα εἰς Δαμασκόν), likely to continue his missionary activities.

God has a way of interrupting our lives to accomplish his purposes. He does so for several reasons, such as turning us away from the path of disaster and making us more like Christ. But his ultimate objective is to magnify his own glory in and through our lives so that his kingdom advances here on this earth. Only when we embrace this reality will we experience the depths of joy that God has for us in knowing his Son Jesus and following him no matter the cost.

Bridge

The past is a powerful thing. If we are not careful, though, we can allow it to be seemingly all-powerful. Far too many people allow their past to define who they are today. There is no denying that our past has a profound role in shaping who we are. But it does not determine who we are. It is wise for us to understand our past and recognize how it has shaped who we are today, but we make a terrible mistake when we think that our past determines who we are. One encounter with Jesus is enough to change the entire direction of a person's life. With that confidence, we can boldly share the gospel, knowing that if God chooses to reveal his Son to that person through the proclamation of the gospel, he or she will be transformed from spiritual death to spiritual life.

C. PAUL'S EARLY MINISTRY (1:18–24)

> [18] Then after three years I did go up to Jerusalem to get to know Cephas, and I stayed with him fifteen days. [19] But I didn't see any of the other apostles except James, the Lord's brother. [20] I declare in the sight of God: I am not lying in what I write to you. [21] Afterward, I went to the regions of Syria and Cilicia. [22] I remained personally unknown to the Judean churches that are in Christ; [23] they simply kept hearing: "He who formerly persecuted us now preaches the faith he once tried to destroy." [24] And they glorified God because of me.

Context

This is the second time period that Paul describes in support of his thesis that the gospel he preaches came from a revelation of Jesus Christ

---

the New Perspective: Second Thoughts on the Origins of Paul's Gospel (Grand Rapids: Eerdmans, 2002), 103–4 and discussion in Harmon, She Must and Shall Go Free, 86–87.

(1:11–12). After the events surrounding his encounter with the risen Christ (1:13–17), Paul now turns to his first post-conversion visit to Jerusalem and the years of ministry in Syria and Cilicia immediately following it. He recounts these events to validate his own apostolic status and independence from the leadership of the Jerusalem church.

Structure

With his conversion and calling described (1:15–17), Paul now moves to recount his early ministry in the period following his conversion (1:18–24). This section divides into two smaller units.[137] Paul begins by describing his first post-conversion visit to Jerusalem (1:18–20). He continues to emphasize his independence from the Jerusalem church by noting this visit: (1) was three years after his conversion; (2) lasted only fifteen days; and (3) only included encounters with two of the apostles (Cephas and James the brother of the Lord). Paul even swears an oath before God to affirm the truthfulness of what he is saying. In the second half of this passage Paul summarizes his ministry activity in the regions of Syria and Cilicia (1:21–24). He emphasizes that during this period of his life he remained unknown to the churches in Judea, while acknowledging that they glorified God at work in him because they knew of his transformation from persecutor of the church to preacher of the gospel. So not only was Paul's conversion and commission the direct result of God revealing his Son in him apart from any involvement of the Jerusalem church and its leaders, but his earliest ministry was carried out independently of them as well.

1:18. Although Paul did not immediately consult with anyone in the aftermath of his conversion, he acknowledges that "Then after three years I did go up to Jerusalem to get to know Cephas" (Ἔπειτα μετὰ ἔτη τρία ἀνῆλθον εἰς Ἱεροσόλυμα ἱστορῆσαι Κηφᾶν).[138] Acts 9:26–30 records this visit, noting the disciples' hesitancy to embrace Paul until Barnabas

---

[137] Paul uses the Greek adverb ἔπειτα ("then") in 1:18 and 1:21 to mark these two smaller units.

[138] Moo (*Galatians*, 108–9) notes that in Greek the phrase "after three years" (μετὰ ἔτη τρία) can refer to a time period of two to three years depending on whether Paul is counting inclusively or exclusively. It makes the most sense that the three years counts from Paul's conversion rather than his return to Damascus, since his point is that he did not immediately consult with anyone about the content of his gospel message, including the Jerusalem apostles. Thus if Paul's conversion took place in AD 31/32, this visit took place AD 33/34; if he was converted in AD 33/34, the visit occurred AD 36/37. The specifics of the date do not alter Paul's point here either way; see similarly Schreiner, *Galatians*, 109.

vouched for him. But instead of focusing on his preaching ministry and
the threats to his life during this visit to Jerusalem, Paul focuses on his
interaction with Cephas (Peter's Aramaic name).[139] The fact that Paul
sees no need to explain who Cephas is indicates the Galatians already
knew about Cephas, at least in general terms. Paul's purpose was "to get
to know" him,[140] not learn the content of the gospel message. During this
visit Paul "stayed with him fifteen days" (ἐπέμεινα πρὸς αὐτὸν ἡμέρας
δεκαπέντε), which could suggest, but does not demand, that Paul was
Peter's houseguest.[141] The contrast between the three years between
conversion and the first visit to Jerusalem with the fifteen-day duration
of that trip to Jerusalem suggests "how impossible it is to conceive of
Paul as a disciple of Peter."[142] It is certainly possible that Paul learned
further detail about Jesus' life and ministry during this time, but that is
a far cry from being dependent on Peter for the content of his gospel. As
C. H. Dodd has famously said, "We may presume they did not spend all
the time talking about the weather."[143]

1:19. During this fifteen-day visit, Paul further explains that he "didn't
see any of the other apostles except James, the Lord's brother" (ἕτερον
δὲ τῶν ἀποστόλων οὐκ εἶδον εἰ μὴ Ἰάκωβον τὸν ἀδελφὸν τοῦ κυρίου).
Further stressing his independence from the key leaders of the Jerusalem
church, Paul explains that the only apostle he met with other than Peter
was James the brother of the Lord.[144] Although not one of the original
twelve, James the brother of Jesus became the leader of the Jerusalem

---

[139] Like its Greek counterpart Peter (Πέτρος), Cephas (Κηφᾶς) means rock in Aramaic.
In addition to its four occurrences here in Galatians (1:18; 2:9, 11, 14), it appears four times
in 1 Corinthians (1:12; 3:22; 9:5; 15:5) and once in John 1:42. There is no obvious reason why
Paul uses Cephas rather than Peter.

[140] Although the verb Paul uses here (ἱστορέω) can mean to inquire of someone for
information (LSJM 2), such a sense is the exact opposite of the point Paul is making in the
context. Instead, here it means to "visit in order to get to know" (TDNT 3:396). See further
Otfried Hofius, "Gal 1:18: Ἱστορῆσαι Κηφᾶν," ZNW 75 (1984): 73–85.

[141] As argued by Martyn, *Galatians*, 173.

[142] Longenecker, *Galatians*, 37.

[143] C. H. Dodd, *The Apostolic Preaching and Its Developments* (London: Hodder & Stoughton,
1936), 16.

[144] It is possible to understand the underlying grammar as excluding James from the
apostles, as the NIV seems to suggest: "I saw none of the other apostles—only James, the
Lord's brother." But this requires taking the expression εἰ μὴ ("except") as referring in gen-
eral to important people rather than specifically to the apostles, which is unlikely; see Moo,
Galatians, 110. Betz's claim that Paul mentions Cephas and James because the opposition in
Galatia derives its authority from them is without basis (*Galatians*, 78).

church in the aftermath of Herod Agrippa I (AD 41–44) persecuting the church (Acts 12:1–17). Although James and the rest of his brothers were not among Jesus' followers early in his ministry, by the time of Jesus' final visit to Jerusalem he had likely become a follower.[145] James was among those to whom the risen Jesus appeared (1 Cor 15:7). Even outside the church James had a reputation for piety, yet as a result of his faith in Jesus he was stoned to death by the Jewish leaders in AD 62 (Josephus, *Ant.* 20:200). As noted in the previous verse, this visit appears to correspond to Acts 9:26–30.[146]

1:20. At this point Paul inserts a parenthetical comment attesting the veracity of his account: "I declare in the sight of God: I am not lying in what I write to you" (ἃ δὲ γράφω ὑμῖν, ἰδοὺ ἐνώπιον τοῦ θεοῦ ὅτι οὐ ψεύδομαι).[147] Paul's opponents may have suggested that he was out of step with the authorities in the Jerusalem church or perhaps directly disobeying them. Stressing his independence from them, Paul insists what he writes is true and goes so far as to swear an oath by invoking God as his witness.[148] In both the Greco-Roman and Jewish world, oaths were a common way to assert the truthfulness of a statement,[149] though Jesus warned about their abuse (Matt 5:33–37). Paul uses similar language elsewhere to highlight the importance and truthfulness of statements, even if there is no obvious reason to doubt it (Rom 1:9; 9:1; 10:2; 2 Cor 1:23; 8:3; 11:10; Gal 4:15; 1 Tim 2:7). Paul places himself under oath to insist his account in 1:13–2:10 is truthful, regardless of what his opponents might claim. In

---

[145] See Richard Bauckham, *Jude and the Relatives of Jesus in the Early Church* (New York: T&T Clark, 2004), 56–57.

[146] The difficulty with this identification is that Paul mentions meeting only with Peter and James, whereas Acts 9:27 says that Barnabas brought Paul to the apostles. Schreiner (*Galatians*, 111) suggests that either Luke is using the plural loosely in Acts 9:27 or that Paul saw all the apostles but only had significant interaction with Peter and James.

[147] In Greek this verse is introduced with δέ, which signals a new development in the argument. Here that development is a parenthetical remark; see further Runge, *Discourse Grammar*, 31–32.

[148] A wooden translation of the Greek would be "now the things I write to you, behold before God that I am not lying." Thus, a verb must be supplied, and the most natural choice is μαρτυρέω ("I testify") or the related compound διαμαρτύρομαι ("I testify"); see Moo, *Galatians*, 110–11.

[149] Oaths were used in the OT to bind someone to fulfill a promise made or assert the truthfulness of a statement (Exod 22:10–11; Num 5:19–20). Within Roman legal practice, oaths could be used to affirm the truthfulness of a statement or even indicate one's willingness to go to court to prove the claim; see J. Paul Sampley, "Before God, I Do Not Lie (Gal 1:20): Paul's Self-Defence in the Light of Roman Legal Praxis," *NTS* 23 (1977): 477–82.

a world that traffics in half-truths and deception, believers should stand out for their honesty and commitment to the truth

1:21. The travelogue continues, as Paul states that after his fifteen-day visit to Jerusalem, "I went to the regions of Syria and Cilicia" (ἦλθον εἰς τὰ κλίματα τῆς Συρίας καὶ τῆς Κιλικίας). In Paul's day Syria and Cilicia were one Roman province, so when he refers to the "regions" (κλίματα) of Syria and Cilicia he is speaking in geographical rather than political terms. In other words, he speaks of distinct geographical regions within one Roman province.[150] This appears to be what Acts 9:30 describes; according to Luke, Paul left Jerusalem and went away to Tarsus (located in Cilicia). Paul does not specify what he did in Syria and Cilicia because his purpose is not to give an extended account of his life and ministry.[151] Paul mentions this time in Syria and Cilicia to again highlight his independence from the Jerusalem church and its leaders. Yet it seems safe to conclude that Paul engaged in evangelistic ministry, likely with a particular emphasis on the gentiles. Such gaps in our knowledge of Paul's ministry remind us that God's work through Paul and the rest of the early church was far broader than what we often realize.[152]

1:22. During his time in the regions of Syria and Cilicia, Paul asserts, "I remained personally unknown to the Judean churches that are in Christ" (ἤμην δὲ ἀγνοούμενος τῷ προσώπῳ ταῖς ἐκκλησίαις τῆς Ἰουδαίας ταῖς ἐν Χριστῷ).[153] Far from deriving his gospel or his ministry from the Jerusalem church, Paul remained personally unknown to the churches throughout the region of Judea.[154] They had not even seen his face![155] These churches

---

[150] Das, *Galatians*, 143.

[151] According to Acts 9:30, at the end of Paul's time in Jerusalem, believers learned of a plot to kill Paul and therefore "took him down to Caesarea and sent him off to Tarsus" (Acts 9:30). Riesner (*Paul's Early Period*, 245–68) argues that Paul headed to Tarsus (located in Cilicia) because he equated Tarsus with Tarshish in the eschatological prophecy of Isa 66:18–19. Schnabel (*Early Christian Mission*, 1046–69) contends that Paul engaged in an extensive evangelistic mission throughout these regions. Moo (*Galatians*, 112) suggests that Paul has in view his ministry in Tarsus (Cilicia) and Antioch (Syria), but reverses the chronological order to emphasize the more important area.

[152] Longenecker (*Galatians*, 41) suggests that it was during this time that Paul endured some of the hardships listed in 2 Cor 11:23–29.

[153] The δέ that introduces this verse marks a further development in Paul's personal narrative.

[154] Paul uses an imperfect passive periphrastic phrase (ἤμην ... ἀγνοούμενος) to reflect "the ongoing state of Paul's absence from Judea (such that he should remain 'unknown' by face)"; see DeSilva, *Handbook*, 22.

[155] A wooden translation of the Greek would be "I was unknown to the face." The face was a common biblical metaphor indicating someone's personal presence (Moo, *Galatians*, 113).

are further described as being "in Christ" (ἐν Χριστῷ), an expression that acts as "a label defining the sort of gatherings in mind: they are Christian gatherings in Judea."[156] Their identity as assemblies was determined by their union with Christ through faith,[157] not their ethnicity or even the requirements of the Mosaic law.[158] Union with Christ is not just something for the individual Christian. As local congregations, believers have union with Christ on a corporate level.

1:23. Even though Paul was personally unknown to the Judean churches, word was spreading that the persecutor had become the preacher: "they simply kept hearing: 'He who formerly persecuted us now preaches the faith he once tried to destroy'" (μόνον δὲ ἀκούοντες ἦσαν ὅτι ὁ διώκων ἡμᾶς ποτε νῦν εὐαγγελίζεται τὴν πίστιν ἥν ποτε ἐπόρθει).[159] Paul uses a periphrastic construction (ἀκούοντες ἦσαν) that suggests these churches regularly heard reports and rumors of his ministry activities.[160] In these reports Paul was referred to as one "who formerly persecuted us" (ὁ διώκων ἡμᾶς ποτε), suggesting that before his conversion Paul was a well-known opponent of the church. Now, however, this notorious opponent of the gospel "preaches the faith he once tried to destroy'" (νῦν εὐαγγελίζεται τὴν πίστιν ἥν ποτε ἐπόρθε). The verb rendered "preaches" (εὐαγγελίζεται) is the same verb used in 1:8–9, 11, 16 to refer to preaching the gospel; thus the expression here could be rendered "preaches the good news about the faith." As used here, "faith" refers to the content of the gospel and the way of life that it entails. It was these beliefs/practices and those who held them that Paul "once tried to destroy" (ποτε ἐπόρθει). The imperfect tense of this verb portrays an action that was attempted but ultimately unsuccessful. Just as in 1:13, Paul combines the verbs "persecute" (διώκω) and "destroy" (πορθέω) to describe his pre-conversion life; such repetition forms an inclusio that marks off 1:13–24 as a literary unit. The Judean churches did not know Paul personally, but they were well aware of his radical conversion and call to ministry.

---

[156] Constantine R. Campbell, *Paul and Union with Christ: An Exegetical and Theological Study* (Grand Rapids: Zondervan, 2012), 124–27.

[157] Schreiner, *Galatians*, 112.

[158] Similarly Dunn, *Galatians*, 82.

[159] Again, the δέ introduces the next development in the narrative.

[160] The combination of an imperfect form (ἦσαν) with a present participle (ἀκούοντες) has the force of an imperfect indicative verb; see Wallace, *Greek Grammar*, 648.

A personal testimony can be a powerful tool for demonstrating the power of Christ to transform us. Even if it is not as "dramatic" as the apostle Paul's experience, a personal testimony can put flesh and bones on the truth of the gospel. For unbelievers it can show them the hope of real-life transformation; for believers it can encourage them afresh with the power of God. With whom can you share your personal testimony?

1:24. As a result of what the Judean churches were hearing,[161] "they glorified God because of me" (ἐδόξαζον τὸν θεόν). To "glorify" (δοξάζω) means to express the greatness and praiseworthiness of someone. It is especially prominent in John (16x), where it regularly refers to the Father bringing honor and praise to the Son and vice versa (11:4; 12:16, 23, 28; 13:31–32; 14:13; 15:8; 16:14; 17:1, 4–5, 10). For Paul the ultimate goal of his ministry was that Jew and gentile together would "glorify the God and Father of our Lord Jesus Christ with one mind and one voice" (Rom 15:6).

Strictly speaking, Paul says they were glorifying God "in me" (ἐν ἐμοί) rather than "because of me."[162] This distinction is important because Paul again echoes language from Isaiah 49:3 (LXX, my translation), where God says to his servant, "in you I will be glorified" (ἐν σοὶ δοξασθήσομαι).[163] Paul has already alluded to Isaiah 49:1 (Gal 1:15), Isaiah 49:3 (Gal 1:16), and Isaiah 49:6 (Gal 1:16) in this section, so it should come as no surprise he does so here. God's purpose of revealing his Son "in" Paul (1:16) has resulted in the Judean churches glorifying God "in" Paul because, as Paul will explain later in 2:20, Christ lives "in" Paul. The apostle understood his life and ministry as a fulfillment of the servant's commission to display God's glory by being a light of salvation for the nations.[164] Even though the Judean churches did not know Paul personally, the reports they heard

---

[161] Even though this clause is introduced with καί, the context suggests it indicates result; on this use of καί, see Beale, Ross, and Brendsel, *Interpretive Lexicon*, 56–57.

[162] While it is possible to translate ἐν ἐμοί as "because of me," several factors make "in me" preferable: (1) Since in 1:16 Paul referred to God revealing his son "in me" (ἐν ἐμοί), he likely intends a parallel thought here in 1:24 about the Judean churches glorifying God "in me" (ἐν ἐμοί); (2) There are several other ways to communicate the idea "because of me" (e.g., διά + accusative, ἀπό + genitive, ἐκ + genitive, ἐπί + genitive or dative) that are much more common and direct; (3) The parallels in John 13:31–32 and 17:10 clearly have a similar meaning; (4) Later in 2:20 Paul will assert that "Christ lives in me" (ζῇ δὲ ἐν ἐμοὶ Χριστός), suggesting that Paul intends to link the ideas of God revealing his son "in me" (1:16), the Judean churches glorifying God "in me" (1:24), and Christ living "in me."

[163] See further Ciampa, *Presence and Function*, 124–25, and Harmon, *She Must and Shall Go Free*, 87–88.

[164] See Biblical Theology §3.1.

about God at work in and through Paul's life and ministry led them to erupt in praise to God. The Galatians could learn a thing or two from these Judean churches and their response to Paul's ministry![165]

God intends our lives to be the sphere in which he displays his glory. We do not have to be an apostle, a pastor, a missionary, or someone in vocational ministry for God to display his glory in and through our lives. Even in the seemingly ordinary parts of our lives God intends to display his character and beauty to the world around us.

Bridge

Regardless of whether our conversion story is as dramatic as Paul's or not, God still intends the entirety of our lives to be the sphere in which he displays his beauty and his glory. Yet part of the way that God shows his glory in our lives is through our faithful testimony to who God is and what he has done. We must not assume that as people see our transformed lives they will conclude God is the one responsible for the change. As believers we should be quick to speak clearly about what God is doing in our lives so that others can see his power at work, and as a result glorify God.

D. PAUL'S SECOND VISIT TO JERUSALEM (2:1–10)

[1] Then after fourteen years I went up again to Jerusalem with Barnabas, taking Titus along also. [2] I went up according to a revelation and presented to them the gospel I preach among the Gentiles, but privately to those recognized as leaders. I wanted to be sure I was not running, and had not been running, in vain. [3] But not even Titus, who was with me, was compelled to be circumcised, even though he was a Greek. [4] This matter arose because some false brothers had infiltrated our ranks to spy on the freedom we have in Christ Jesus in order to enslave us. [5] But we did not give up and submit to these people for even a moment, so that the truth of the gospel would be preserved for you. [6]

Now from those recognized as important (what they once were makes no difference to me; God does not show favoritism)— they added nothing to me. [7] On the contrary, they saw that I had been entrusted with the gospel for the uncircumcised, just as Peter was for the circumcised, [8] since the one at work in Peter for an apostleship to the circumcised was also at work in me for the Gentiles. [9] When James, Cephas, and John—those recognized as pillars—acknowledged the grace that had been given to me, they gave the right hand of fellowship to me and

---

[165] Das, *Galatians*, 146.

Barnabas, agreeing that we should go to the Gentiles and they to the
circumcised. [10] They asked only that we would remember the poor,
which I had made every effort to do.

Context

Whereas in 1:11–24 Paul stresses that his apostolic status is independent
of the Jerusalem church and its apostles, the focus of 2:1–10 is the agreement between Paul and the Jerusalem leaders on the content of the gospel
itself.[166] He fast-forwards fourteen years to his second post-conversion
visit to Jerusalem. This is the third time period that Paul describes in
support of his thesis that the gospel he preaches came from a revelation
of Jesus Christ (1:11–12).

Structure

The account divides into two broad sections. In 2:1–5 Paul sets the scene
and identifies the opposition he faced while in Jerusalem. In response to
a revelation from God, Paul and Barnabas traveled to Jerusalem, bringing
with them an uncircumcised Greek believer named Titus (2:1). While
there Paul laid out before the leaders of the Jerusalem church in a private
meeting the gospel he preached, seeking to ensure that his vision of a
united people of God (consisting of Jewish and gentile believers in one
body) would not be thwarted (2:2). While he was there, "false brothers"
infiltrated this meeting and forcefully argued that Titus should be circumcised, a demand which Paul, Barnabas, and Titus just as forcefully
rejected (2:3–5).

The second half of this passage shifts the focus to how the leadership
of the Jerusalem church responded to this disagreement (2:6–10). While
the underlying syntax and logic of 2:6–10 is difficult, the general thrust
is clear enough.[167] Paul insists that in this private meeting the leaders of the Jerusalem church added nothing to his gospel (2:6). Instead,

---

[166] Similarly Schreiner, *Galatians*, 130.

[167] Moo (*Galatians*, 119–20) suggests that these syntactical and logical difficulties stem
from "the tightrope that Paul walks in this paragraph. On the one hand, he acknowledges
the legitimate authority and significance of the Jerusalem apostles and recognizes that
their agreement with his understanding of the law-free gospel is important ... But on the
other hand, he also wants to reduce the overly slavish regard for these 'pillars' among the
agitators and especially to deny that his law-free gospel depends for its truthfulness on
their attestation."

they extended the right hand of fellowship to Paul and encouraged his ongoing ministry to the gentiles (2:9b) because they recognized: (1) that God was working through Paul among the gentiles just as he was working through Peter among the Jews (2:7–8), and (2) that Paul's ministry among the gentiles was a manifestation of God's grace (2:9a).[168] The purpose/result of the Jerusalem leaders extending the right hand of fellowship was that Paul would focus his ministry among the gentiles, while the Jerusalem leaders would focus their ministry among the Jews. Paul closes the paragraph by noting that the only thing the Jerusalem leadership asked was that Paul and Barnabas continue to remember the poor, which Paul was in fact eager to do (2:10).

2:1. Paul now jumps ahead fourteen years to the next time he "went up again to Jerusalem."[169] The continued focus on his visits to Jerusalem confirms that his opponents in Galatians had raised questions about the apostle's relationship with the Jerusalem church. This is the same visit Acts 11:27–30 records,[170] and Paul notes here that he had two companions on this trip.[171] The first is Barnabas, a Levite from Cyprus who was a key member of the early church in Jerusalem (Acts 4:36). Known for his generosity (Acts 4:37), he vouched for Paul to the Jerusalem apostles during Paul's initial post-conversion visit to Jerusalem (Acts 9:26–28). When the Jerusalem church heard that the gospel had made inroads among the gentiles in Antioch, they sent Barnabas to investigate (Acts 11:19–22). Barnabas was so encouraged by what he saw that he traveled to Tarsus to find Paul and bring him back to Antioch to participate in the ministry there (Acts 11:23–26). Several years later the Antioch church sent out Paul and Barnabas on the missionary journey during which the Galatian

---

[168] These two reasons are expressed by two aorist adverbial participles: ἰδόντες ("seeing") in 2:7 and γνόντες ("knowing") in 2:9.

[169] It is unclear whether Paul's starting point for the fourteen years is his conversion (1:15–16), his first visit to Jerusalem (1:18), or his entry into Syria and Cilicia (1:21). Adding to the difficulty is whether Paul is counting "inclusively" (in which case fourteen years could be as short a period as twelve years and a few months) or "exclusively" (covering a period up to fourteen years and several months). For further discussion, see the Introduction, 2–14.

[170] Other scholars align the visit described here in 2:1–10 with the Jerusalem Council recorded in Acts 15:1–29. See further the discussion in the Introduction, 2–10.

[171] By stating that he went "with Barnabas" (μετὰ Βαρναβᾶ) and then adding "taking Titus along also" (συμπαραλαβὼν καὶ Τίτον) Paul signals the key role Titus will play in this visit (2:4–5).

churches were planted (Acts 13:1–14:28). So the Galatians would have been very familiar with Barnabas, and their experience with him would have made his hypocrisy in the Antioch incident all the more surprising (2:11–14).

During this visit to Jerusalem, Paul was "taking Titus along also" (συμπαραλαβὼν καὶ Τίτον).[172] Although he is not mentioned in Acts, Titus appears at several points in Paul's letters, including being the recipient of one. He appears to have been converted under Paul's ministry (Titus 1:4), perhaps in Syrian Antioch.[173] Paul sent Titus to Corinth as part of his relief collection for Jewish believers in Jerusalem (2 Cor 7:5–8:24). Paul left Titus in Crete to appoint elders in the churches on that island and correct the false teaching that was threatening the church (Titus 1:5; 2:1, 15). Near the end of Paul's life, he sent Titus to Dalmatia (2 Tim 4:10), presumably for ministry purposes. But all these events took place several years after Paul wrote to the Galatians. While it has been suggested that Paul specifically brought Titus to Jerusalem as a test case to force the issue with the Jerusalem church,[174] this cannot be convincingly shown and remains speculative. It is just as likely (if not more) that the false brothers (2:4) raised the issue. In any case, Paul's example shows that a spiritual leader must be ready and willing to confront issues lurking below the surface in the interest of promoting the health of the church.

2:2. Paul now explains the reason for this trip to Jerusalem:[175] "I went up according to a revelation" (κατὰ ἀποκάλυψιν).[176] Just as Paul received his gospel "by a revelation [ἀποκαλύψεως] of Jesus Christ" (1:12) and God "was pleased to reveal [ἀποκαλύψαι] his Son in me" (1:15–16), so now this trip to Jerusalem was because of God's direction. The apostle is stressing his dependence upon divine instruction and leading rather than human authorities even in his ministry itinerary. According to Acts 11:27–28 God revealed to the Antioch church through a prophet named

---

[172] The verb Paul uses here (συμπαραλαμβάνω) can have the sense of "take along with one, take in as an adjunct or assistant" (LSJM s.v. συμπαρακομίζω). It seems to have this sense in Acts 12:25; 15:37–38 where it refers to Paul and Barnabas taking along John Mark as part of their ministry team.

[173] So Longenecker, Galatians, 46.

[174] So, e.g., Betz, Galatians, 85; Hays, "Galatians," 222; Oakes, Galatians, 66–67.

[175] The δέ that begins this sentence marks a new development in the narrative.

[176] The expression κατὰ ἀποκάλυψιν expresses both the norm that governs the action as well as the reason for it (BDAG s.v. κατά 5.a.δ).

Agabus that a famine was coming.[177] In response the Antioch church sent Paul and Barnabas with gifts to alleviate their hardship (Acts 11:29–30).[178]

Paul says that, while in Jerusalem, he "presented to them the gospel I preach among the Gentiles" (ἀνεθέμην αὐτοῖς τὸ εὐαγγέλιον ὃ κηρύσσω ἐν τοῖς ἔθνεσιν). The verb "presented" (ἀνατίθημι) means "to lay something before someone for consideration."[179] Choosing this particular verb "implies that Paul counted their opinion on the matter referred as something he valued ... but not as something which determined the truth or otherwise of his gospel."[180] Thus Paul explained the content of his gospel proclamation "among the Gentiles" (ἐν τοῖς ἔθνεσιν), repeating the same phrase from 1:16 describing his apostolic call. Why Paul did this is not clear, since the purpose of the visit was to deliver famine relief. Perhaps rumors about Paul's message had reached key figures in the Jerusalem church and this visit provided a natural opportunity to set the record straight.

This conversation took place "privately to those recognized as leaders" (κατ᾽ ἰδίαν δὲ τοῖς δοκοῦσιν). That it took place "privately" (κατ᾽ ἰδίαν)[181] suggests a desire to avoid a larger public discussion that could be contentious.[182] Although the expression rendered "those recognized as leaders" (τοῖς δοκοῦσιν) can have a pejorative sense of people with a reputation that does not match the reality of who they are, in other places it speaks of those whose reputation is based on substance.[183] It reappears later in this passage as well (2:6, 9). Paul may be using this particular expression

---

[177] A number of regional famines during the mid- to late 40s are attested in ancient sources; see the discussion in Craig S. Keener, *Acts: An Exegetical Commentary*, 4 vols. (Grand Rapids: Baker, 2012), 2:1853–60.

[178] Schreiner (*Galatians*, 120–21) suggests that the prophetic revelation given through Agabus included instruction to send Paul and Barnabas to Jerusalem with the financial gift.

[179] BDAG s.v. ἀνατίθημι 2. The only other NT occurrence is Acts 25:14, where Festus discusses Paul's case with King Agrippa. In 2 Macc 3:9 the verb is used to describe an emissary communicating information to the high priest. Moulton and Milligan (MM, 38) note two examples in the papyri with the sense of "communicate," though they are from the third century AD.

[180] Dunn, *Galatians*, 92.

[181] This expression occurs frequently in the Gospels (e.g., Matt 14:13, 23; 17:1, 19; 20:17; 24:3; Mark 4:34; 6:31; 7:33; 9:2, 28; 13:3; Luke 9:10; 10:23) to describe Jesus separating himself from the crowds.

[182] It also suggests that this visit cannot be the Jerusalem Council of Acts 15; see further the discussion in the Introduction, 2–11.

[183] See the discussion in *TDNT* 2:232–33. For examples of positive uses of this expression, see Josephus *Ant.* 19:307; *War* 4:141, 159; Epictetus, *Enchiridion* 33:12; Euripides, *Hecuba*

because his Galatian opponents used it positively to refer to the Jerusalem apostles. Thus it allowed Paul to show appropriate respect for the leaders of the Jerusalem church while at the same time maintaining his independence. "Paul did not doubt the stature and position of these leaders. Nevertheless, he cautioned against overestimating their authority."[184]

Paul discussed his gospel preaching with the leaders of the Jerusalem church "to be sure that I was not running, and had not been running, in vain."[185] The apostle was not fearful that the content of his gospel message was wrong, but that his vision of Jew and gentile united together in the one eschatological people of God might collapse (Rom 15:8–13; Eph 3:2–12).[186] As Moo notes, "Cutting Gentiles off from the spiritual root that nourishes them (Rom. 11:17–24) would endanger their continuing experience of God's blessing and favor. And a split between Jewish and Gentile Christians could lead, Paul fears, to just such a situation."[187]

Paul again echoes the language of Isaiah 49, this time verse 4, where the servant laments, "I have labored vainly" (my translation, LXX: κενῶς ἐκοπίασα).[188] He regularly uses similar language to express concerns about his apostolic ministry bearing the kind of fruit he desires (2 Cor 6:1; Gal 4:11; Phil 2:16; 1 Thess 3:5). Paul was also fond of running imagery, using it frequently in his letters to portray the Christian life (Gal 5:7; Phil 3:14–15) or his own ministry (1 Cor 9:24–27; Gal 2:2; Phil 2:16). While this imagery is drawn from the popular athletic competitions of the Greco-Roman world, Habakkuk 2:2–3 may also have influenced Paul's usage.[189] There Yahweh instructs the prophet to "Write the vision; make it plain on tablets, so he may run who reads it" (Hab 2:2 ESV). Given that Paul cites Habakkuk 2:4 in Galatians 3:11, he may have seen his own apostolic ministry prefigured in the runner described in Habakkuk 2:2.[190]

---

295. Longenecker (*Galatians*, 48) notes the expression "was part of the political rhetoric of the day, being used both positively and derogatorily or ironically."

[184] Schreiner, *Galatians*, 121. He helpfully suggests that in using this term Paul is not criticizing the apostles themselves, but those who overstate the Jerusalem apostles' importance.

[185] On the difficult grammar of this clause using both a present subjunctive and aorist indicative with μή πως, see A. T. Robertson, *A Grammar of the Greek New Testament in the Light of Historical Research* (New York: Hodder & Stoughton, 1915), 988.

[186] So also Hays, "Galatians," 223.

[187] Moo, *Galatians*, 125.

[188] See further Harmon, *She Must and Shall Go Free*, 89–90.

[189] J. Duncan M. Derrett, "'Running' in Paul: The Midrashic Potential of Hab 2:2," *Bib* 66 (1985): 562–65.

[190] Ciampa (*Presence and Function*, 131–32) sees further evidence for this echo in the parallelism in Jer 23:21 between running (LXX: ἔτρεχον) and prophesying (LXX: ἐπροφήτευον).

Everyone who spends extended time in ministry has moments where they wonder if they have labored in vain. Challenges such as relational conflict, differing visions of ministry, disagreements over best practices in ministry, and betrayal from those you once trusted can lead anyone in ministry to question whether the struggle is worth it. In those moments, the truth of the gospel, the beauty of the Savior we serve, and the faithful encouragement of God's people must be our anchor points.

2:3. Paul now relates an incident that happened during this visit: "But not even Titus, who was with me ... was compelled to be circumcised" (ἀλλ᾽ οὐδὲ Τίτος ὁ σὺν ἐμοί ... ἠναγκάσθη περιτμηθῆναι). The sense of what Paul says here seems to be "If anyone might have been expected to be compelled to be circumcised, it would have been Titus; but even he was not compelled to be circumcised."[191] By describing Titus as the one "who was with me," Paul stresses that his interaction with the Jerusalem authorities did not remain hypothetical but involved a real-life case example in front of them. The verb "compel" (ἀναγκάζω) has the sense of forcing someone to act in a certain way, sometimes even under threat of violence (Acts 26:11).[192] It occurs frequently in the Maccabean literature to describe the efforts of the Seleucids to force the Jews to offer sacrifices to pagan gods and abandon their adherence to the food laws, circumcision, and the Sabbath.[193] Ironically, here it is now Jewish Christians who, through social and theological pressure, were trying to compel gentile Christians to be circumcised. Paul will use this verb again in 2:14 to describe Peter's efforts in Antioch to observe kosher requirements, as well as in 6:12 to describe the efforts of the false teachers in Galatia to force the gentile believers to be circumcised. Titus resisted this pressure "even though he was a Greek."[194] In this context, "Greek"

---

[191] Paul introduces this clause with the expression ἀλλ᾽ οὐδὲ, which here indicates a "thematic addition"—information that confirms that Paul had not been running in vain in his gospel ministry; see further Runge, *Discourse Grammar*, 337–48. For similar usage of this expression, see Luke 23:15; 1 Cor 3:2; 4:3.

[192] The text doesn't specify who attempted to compel Titus to be circumcised, though it was likely the "false brothers" who are mentioned in the following verse. Yet Dunn (*Galatians*, 96) goes well beyond what the text implies when he claims that "the Jerusalem apostles had tried to persuade Paul to accede to the demand, but did not insist; they were sympathetic to the demand but recognized the force of the reasons Paul gave for refusing and did not press the point." Nothing in the context indicates the Jerusalem apostles agreed that Titus should be circumcised; that would run counter to Paul's point in bringing up the incident in the first place.

[193] 1 Macc 2:25; 2 Macc 6:1, 7, 18; 7:1; 4 Macc 4:26; 5:2, 27; 8:2, 9.

[194] Thus the participle here is concessive.

(Ἕλλην) is essentially synonymous with "gentile"—someone who was not a Jew. Such pressure is not surprising since most first-century Jews considered circumcision necessary for gentiles converting to Judaism.[195] This belief is likely at the heart of Paul's dispute with his opponents, and in the course of the letter he will forcefully argue that gentiles do not need to become "Jews" in order to be justified before God.

This is the first reference to circumcision in Galatians, an issue that grows more significant as the letter continues. Although other ancient Near Eastern cultures practiced circumcision,[196] God gave the act special significance when he commanded Abraham to circumcise his male descendants as a sign of the covenant (Gen 17:1–27). By marking the male sexual organ through which the promise of countless descendants would be fulfilled, God reminded his people of this covenant promise. Circumcision came to be a definitive sign that one belonged to the people of God, and Israelite parents were commanded to circumcise their sons on the eighth day after birth (Lev 12:3). Yet the Old Testament also refers to "circumcision of the heart" as a picture of complete devotion to the Lord and a separation from sinful rebellion against him (Deut 10:16; Jer 4:4). As part of restoring his people and inaugurating a new covenant, God promised to circumcise the hearts of his people to enable wholehearted devotion to him (Deut 30:6; Jer 31:31–34; Ezek 11:19–20; 36:26–27). During the intertestamental period, circumcision became one of the defining identity markers for Jews, to the point that many continued to practice circumcision even under threat of losing their lives for doing so.[197] The prevailing expectation among first-century Jews was that gentile male converts should in fact be circumcised to complete their conversion.[198] Given the presence of internal Jewish debate over the necessity of circumcision for gentile converts, it is not surprising, then, that circumcision became a flashpoint of controversy within the early church.[199]

---

[195] See John Nolland, "Uncircumcised Proselytes," *JSJ* 12 (1981): 173–94 and Shaye J. D. Cohen, "Crossing the Boundary and Becoming a Jew," *HTR* 82 (1989): 26–30. For a helpful summary of circumcision within the first-century context of Judaism, see Keener, *Acts*, 3:2215–22.

[196] See G. E. Farley, "Circumcision," in *ZPEB* 1:904–6.

[197] See further Biblical Theology §5.3.1.

[198] Keener, *Acts*, 3:2215–22.

[199] Compare the conclusion of Betz (*Galatians*, 89): "Thus the internal Jewish debate became an internal Christian conflict."

Debates about theology and practices in the church that stay in the theoretical are one thing; it is an entirely different matter when there are real live people in the middle of the issue. But that is precisely the point where theology and faithful practices that flow out of it are most necessary.

2:4. Lest the Galatians think it was the Jerusalem leaders who tried to compel Titus to be circumcised, Paul identifies the true culprits.[200] It was "because some false brothers had infiltrated our ranks" (τοὺς παρεισάκτους ψευδαδέλφους); they were the ones who pressed for Titus' circumcision.[201] Perhaps they were members of the Jerusalem church who were suspicious of the increasing number of gentiles professing faith in Jesus and worried that Jewish distinctives were endangered by this development.[202] In any case, although they claimed to be Jesus followers, their behavior and beliefs reveal that they are not in fact believers.[203] Paul wants the Galatians to see their Mosaic-law-promoting opponents in the same light as these false brothers and learn from the apostle's response to them. The adjective (παρείσακτος) Paul uses to describe the actions of these false brothers stresses the secretive nature of their entry. Polybius uses this same term to describe soldiers secretly entering a besieged city (*Hist.* 2.7.8) and the ancients introducing various beliefs about the gods among the common people (*Hist.* 6.56.12). The extent to which these false brothers acted on their own initiative or were aided by others is unclear. While the verb rendered "infiltrated" (παρεισέρχομαι) by itself

---

[200] The δέ that begins this initial clause marks a further development in the narrative.

[201] The Greek of verses 4–5 is quite awkward. It begins with a prepositional phrase that gives the reason for an action that is never explicitly stated. It is followed by an extended relative clause that further describes the false brothers mentioned at the end of the initial clause. The relative clause is followed by a ἵνα clause that states the purpose of an unspecified action. This ἵνα clause is followed by a relative clause that further describes the false brothers to whom Paul did not yield, who were seeking to enslave believers. The purpose of not yielding to these false brothers is then stated in the ἵνα clause that follows, which ends the sentence. So despite the numerous subordinate clauses, Paul never provides the main clause of the sentence! Perhaps in the heat of dictating the letter Paul's train of thought got away from him. Das (*Galatians*, 172) suggests the broken syntax is a rhetorical ploy to grab the attention of the reader and highlight what follows.

[202] As suggested by Dunn, *Galatians*, 98.

[203] The only other NT occurrence of ψευδάδελφος is in 2 Cor 11:26, where Paul lists them as one of the many dangers he faced in ministry.

does not carry the notion of secrecy, the context here strongly suggests
the element of stealth.[204]

Paul continues his use of stealth language in stating that their purpose
was "to spy on the freedom that we have in Christ Jesus" (κατασκοπῆσαι
τὴν ἐλευθερίαν ἡμῶν ἣν ἔχομεν ἐν Χριστῷ Ἰησοῦ).[205] Like secret agents
gathering intelligence, these false brothers sought to gain an advantage
in their quest to require gentiles to be circumcised. This is the first occurrence of "freedom" (ἐλευθερία) in Galatians, a key theme whose importance transcends the three uses of the word (5:1, 13).[206] Indeed, when Paul
comes to the climax of his main argument (2:14–5:1), he summarizes: "For
freedom, Christ set us free. Stand firm, then, and don't submit again to
a yoke of slavery" (5:1). This is not freedom to do as we wish, but rather
the opportunity to "serve one another through love" (5:13). We have this
freedom because, as believers, we are "in Christ Jesus" (ἐν Χριστῷ Ἰησοῦ);
in other words, we are under the sphere of his control rather than the elemental forces of this world such as sin, death, Satan, and even the Mosaic
law.[207] The result the false brothers sought was "to enslave us" (ἵνα ἡμᾶς
καταδουλώσουσιν).[208] The slavery in view is a return to the controlling
authority of the Mosaic law, which inevitably leads to coming under its
curse (3:10). Paul uses a rare verb for "enslave" (καταδουλόω) that may
stress the intensity of the slavery.[209] The contrast between slavery and
freedom may subtly indicate that the promised Isaianic new exodus has

---

[204] The element of secrecy is absent in the only other NT occurrence (Rom 5:20), where it
describes the entry of the Mosaic law into the world. Polybius (*Hist.* 1.7.3) uses it to describe
people who entered a city under the pretense of friendship only to put the inhabitants to
the sword.

[205] The verb rendered "spy out" (κατασκοπέω) occurs just two other places in the LXX/
NT. In both 2 Sam 10:3 and 1 Chr 19:3 it describes the fear that David was sending his servants to spy on the Ammonites. The closely related verb κατασκοπεύω appears twelve times
in the LXX, where it describes those whom Joshua sent to survey the promised land (Josh
2:1–3; 6:22–25). Another cognate verb (κατασκέπτομαι) occurs twenty-nine times, thirteen
of which are in the account of Moses sending spies into the promised land (Num 13–14).

[206] On the themes of freedom and slavery in Galatians, see Biblical Theology §1.3.2.

[207] Thus ἐν Χριστῷ Ἰησοῦ has a locative force; so also Campbell, *Paul and Union with
Christ*, 80–81.

[208] Instead of the usual ἵνα + subjunctive to indicate purpose/result, Paul uses the less
common ἵνα with the future indicative (see BDF §369.2). There is no difference in meaning.

[209] This verb occurs only one other place in the NT (2 Cor 11:20) but ten times in the
LXX. It describes Pharaoh enslaving the Israelites (Exod 1:14; 6:5), the slavery that exile will
bring (Jer 15:14; Ezek 34:27), and the results of being captured in battle (1 Macc 8:10, 18).

now been inaugurated through Christ,[210] an argument that Paul will make in 3:1–5:1.

False teachers regularly work on the principle of stealth and deceit. They hide their true agenda behind a façade of concern for others when their true concern is for themselves. Satan hates the freedom the gospel brings and actively uses false teachers to convince believers to return to their former chains of slavery.

2:5. Despite the intense efforts of the false brothers, Paul and his ministry teammates "did not give up and submit to these people for even a moment" (οὐδὲ πρὸς ὥραν εἴξαμεν τῇ ὑποταγῇ).[211] Even in the face of theological and social pressure to have Titus circumcised, Paul stood firm in his conviction that such an act was not only unnecessary, but flat out wrong. The rare verb rendered "give up" (εἴκω) has the sense of "give way before [an] expression of force or argument."[212] In Jewish literature it can have the sense of surrendering oneself to God or his will (Josephus, *Ant.* 1:115), but it can also refer to yielding to or giving in to sin (Josephus, *Ant.* 2:46; 4:143). Philo uses it regularly to explain the inner workings of a person, especially in terms of the relationship between the mind and the passions (*Leg.* 3:128, 186; *Ebr.* 1:16; *Conf.* 1:48; *Ios.* 1:173; *Spe.* 3:201). Paul's language is even more intense than the English translation suggests; it could be woodenly rendered "we did not yield in submission."[213] They refused to yield "for even a moment," a phrase which in English idiom we might render as "not even for one second."

The reason they refused to yield was "so that the truth of the gospel would be preserved for you" (ἵνα ἡ ἀλήθεια τοῦ εὐαγγελίου διαμείνῃ πρὸς ὑμᾶς). The truth of the gospel is a summary phrase encompassing what Paul will argue in 2:14–5:1—that God justifies Jew and gentile alike based on faith in Christ and not on the basis of any works (including

---

[210] So Schreiner, *Galatians*, 125, following Ciampa, *Presence and Function*, 138–42.

[211] A number of manuscripts (e.g., D* b) omit οὐδέ, which flips the meaning of the clause to indicate that Paul did yield to these false brothers for the sake of the gospel. But both the context and the manuscript evidence indicate the phrase is in fact original; see the discussion in Moo, *Galatians*, 139.

[212] BDAG s.v. εἴκω. Although this verb occurs nowhere else in the NT, it occurs regularly in Josephus (40x) and Philo (21x). Ciampa (*Presence and Function*, 143) suggests a possible echo of Deut 13:8 (9 LXX), where Moses instructs the people not to yield to a prophet calling Israel to worship other gods, though it should be noted the LXX uses a different verb.

[213] Thus the dative expression τῇ ὑποταγῇ that follows the verb εἴκω indicates either manner (DeSilva, *Handbook*, 28) or is in apposition to the verb (Burton, *Galatians*, 84).

circumcision) that a person does. In contrast to the "different gospel" his opponents preached (1:6–9). Paul labored so that this true gospel "would be preserved for you." The verb rendered "preserved" (διαμένω) means "to remain continually."[214] Thus, in contrast to the current heavens and earth which will perish, the Son remains/endures forever (Heb 1:11, quoting Ps 102:26). The same is true of God's word, which remains forever (Ps 119:89). Paul held his ground because he wanted to preserve the true gospel for people like the Galatians and all others who would hear the good news of what God has done in Christ.

Preserving the truth of the gospel for both the current and future generations is a central task of pastors/elders. That is why, as part of the qualifications for an elder, Paul writes that he must be one who is "holding to the faithful message as taught, so that he will be able both to encourage with sound teaching and to refute those who contradict it" (Titus 1:9). If you are a pastor/elder, what measures are you taking to preserve the truth of the gospel for future generations?

2:6. In Greek, verses 6–10 are one long, complicated sentence introduced by the particle δέ to signal a continuation of the narrative from verse 3.[215] The main thought of this sentence is that leading figures in the Jerusalem church added nothing to Paul's gospel (2:6), but rather extended the right hand of fellowship to Paul and Barnabas (2:7–10).

Paul now shifts his focus from the false brothers back to "those recognized as important" (τῶν δοκούντων εἶναί τι), who were first mentioned in 2:2. In 2:9 it becomes clear this phrase refers to James, Cephas (i.e., Peter), and John. At the mention of these leading figures Paul interrupts his train of thought to qualify that designation with two further comments. First, "what they once were makes no difference to me" (ὁποῖοί ποτε ἦσαν οὐδέν μοι διαφέρει).[216] When it comes to discussing the truth

---

[214] BDAG s.v. διαμένω.

[215] For a helpful discussion of the particulars, see Moo, *Galatians*, 131 and Das, *Galatians*, 177. On δέ having a continuative force, see Longenecker, *Galatians*, 53.

[216] The Greek phrase ὁποῖοί ποτε ἦσαν can be understood several different ways. The key issue is the force of the particle ποτε, which usually has a temporal sense of "at some time or other," often in reference to the past ("formerly, previously"), though sometimes with a present or future force (BDAG s.v. ποτε 1). If ποτε is temporal here, Paul is either referring to their modest background as Galilean fishermen before rising to leadership within the early church ("what sort of ones they were formerly") or their status as leaders in the Jerusalem church at the time of this meeting ("what sort of ones they were at the time"). But ποτε can also have a generalizing force ("ever") when following a correlative or relative

of the gospel, personal status or pedigree are not relevant factors. This conclusion is rooted in a common biblical maxim: "God does not show favoritism" (πρόσωπον [ὁ] θεὸς ἀνθρώπου οὐ λαμβάνει).²¹⁷ Although the specific wording varies, this and similar expressions occur throughout Scripture to assert that God does not take status, appearance, or outward credentials into account in his treatment of people and nations (Deut 10:17; 2 Chr 19:7; Luke 20:21; 1 Pet 1:17). Paul uses this language to stress the impartial nature of God's judgment, regardless of one's ethnicity (Rom 2:11) or social status (Eph 6:9; Col 3:25). As applied to the present situation, the apostle's use of this proverb reinforces the truth that "one cannot be unduly influenced in the present theological discussions by past relationships or physical proximities, whatever they may have been."²¹⁸ What matters is the truth of the gospel. In a culture built on honor and shame dynamics, Paul's words here are an attempt "to subvert and replace those conventions with a value system centered on Christ and his cross."²¹⁹

Resuming the thought that began the sentence,²²⁰ Paul insists that the leading figures in the Jerusalem church "added nothing to me" (ἐμοὶ γὰρ οἱ δοκοῦντες οὐδὲν προσανέθεντο).²²¹ Paul uses the same Greek verb (προσανατίθημι) as in 1:16, where he asserts that he did not consult with anyone in Jerusalem in the immediate aftermath of his encounter with Christ. His point is that these important figures did not add anything to

---

pronoun (BDAG s.v. ποτε 3; BDF §303; Robertson, *Grammar*, 732). While both the temporal and generalizing sense could fit the context here, on the whole the generalizing force seems more natural. For a helpful discussion of the grammar here, see Moo, *Galatians*, 132.

²¹⁷ Woodenly the expression is "God does not receive the face." The Semitic expression "to receive the face" meant to show partiality or favoritism toward someone based on their appearance, status, ethnicity, or some other factor; see Moises Silva, "πρόσωπον," *NIDNTTE* 4:158.

²¹⁸ Longenecker, *Galatians*, 54.

²¹⁹ Das, *Galatians*, 180–81.

²²⁰ The γάρ that connects this clause continues the thought of the first clause of the verse, which was interrupted by Paul's aside about God's impartiality (see BDAG s.v. γάρ 2); see similarly Longenecker, *Galatians*, 54. By contrast DeSilva (*Handbook*, 30) sees the γάρ giving the grounds for Paul's refusal to give in to the demands of the false brothers (2:5). But this seems unlikely given the amount of intervening text. The awkward syntax here is an example of anacoluthon, where an author interrupts a sentence with a new thought and then fails to complete the sentence in a manner grammatically consistent with the original sentence; see further Robertson, *Grammar*, 435–38.

²²¹ Placing the pronoun ἐμοί ("to me") at the beginning of the clause may indicate emphasis: "to me they added nothing."

the gospel he preached, nor did they embrace the demands of the "false brothers smuggled in" (2:4 HCSB) to circumcise Titus.

Our natural inclination is to weigh the opinions and views of influential people more than those who lack such reputation or influence. But when it comes to the truth of the gospel, reputation and status cannot be the deciding factors. Leaders in the church can be tempted to make decisions based on how influential people might respond rather than how a decision conforms to the gospel. But pursuing a ministry based on people-pleasing will ultimately collapse under the weight of other people's opinions.

2:7. Verses 7–10 are the second part of the compound sentence comprising 2:6–10. The main thought of 2:7–10 is that the Jerusalem church leaders extended the right hand of fellowship to Paul and Barnabas. This main thought is further modified by two aorist adverbial participles that express why the Jerusalem leaders extended the right hand of fellowship to them (2:7, 9). Their purpose in extending the right hand of fellowship to Paul and Barnabas is expressed in 2:9c, followed by a final statement of apposition in 2:10.

The leaders of the Jerusalem church did not add to Paul's gospel; "On the contrary, they saw that I had been entrusted with the gospel for the uncircumcised" (ἀλλὰ τοὐναντίον ἰδόντες ὅτι πεπίστευμαι τὸ εὐαγγέλιον τῆς ἀκροβυστίας).[222] As used here, the verb rendered "entrusted" (πιστεύω) has the sense of giving something valuable to someone with the expectation that it will be preserved, protected, and/or promoted.[223] The perfect tense of the verb highlights Paul's status as one entrusted with the gospel. Paul frequently uses this word to describe his God-given calling as a minister of the gospel (1 Cor 9:17; 1 Thess 2:4; 1 Tim 1:11; Titus 1:3). Just as the Jewish people were "entrusted with the very words of God" (Rom 3:2), so too Paul has been entrusted with the gospel "for the uncircumcised." The word rendered "uncircumcision" (ἀκροβυστία) literally refers to the foreskin, making Paul's usage here an example of double metonymy, since it is being used "figuratively for

---

[222] The phrase "on the contrary" translates the Greek phrase ἀλλὰ τοὐναντίον, which is a strong adversative that "introduces an emphatic statement of contrast" (DeSilva, *Handbook*, 31).

[223] This verb was "frequently invoked in the context of patronage and friendship relations, particularly to speak of one party entrusting another with some task or deposit, or with some request" (DeSilva, *Handbook*, 31).

being in such a state as retains the foreskin ('uncircumcision'), thence for the group of people characterized by this state ('Gentiles')."[224]

God had called him to preach the gospel among the gentiles (1:16), so Paul understood that the primary focus of his ministry would be reaching gentiles with the gospel, "just as Peter was [entrusted with the gospel] for the circumcised" (καθὼς Πέτρος τῆς περιτομῆς).[225] This does not mean Paul would not preach to Jews and that Peter would not preach to gentiles. Paul regularly began his ministry in a new city by preaching in the synagogue; in fact, that is where many of these gentile Galatians would have first heard the gospel (Acts 13:13–52; 14:1–7)! God used Peter to preach the gospel to a Roman centurion and his family (Acts 10:1–48). Thus Paul is merely indicating their primary spheres of ministry. Paul's unique role was to focus on the gentile mission, while Peter was to focus on the Jewish mission.[226]

Referring to the gentiles as "the uncircumcised" and the Jews as "the circumcised" is an intentional way of connecting ethnicity and circumcision as the defining sign of the Mosaic covenant. As such, both are part of this present evil age that Christ has rescued believers from through his sacrificial death on the cross (1:4).

While all of us as believers have been entrusted with the gospel, there is a particular sense in which pastors/elders have been entrusted with the preservation and faithful proclamation of the gospel. As we grow in our understanding of what it means to be stewards of the gospel (1 Cor 4:1), the more we will seek to draw attention to the risen Lord who gave the gospel rather than ourselves.

2:8. The Jerusalem church leaders affirmed Paul's commission to preach the gospel among the gentiles because they recognized the one true God who was at work "in Peter for an apostleship to the circumcised

---

[224] DeSilva, *Handbook*, 31. Metonymy is "a figure of speech in which one term is used in place of another with which it is associated" (DeSilva, *Handbook*, 151).

[225] The two genitive expressions τῆς ἀκροβυστίας ("for the uncircumcised") and τῆς περιτομῆς ("for the circumcised") are best understood as indicating purpose or destination; see Wallace, *Greek Grammar*, 101. Like uncircumcision (ἀκροβυστία), the word circumcision (περιτομή) is a metonym in which "the procedure undergone [stands] for the person who underwent the procedure" (DeSilva, *Handbook*, 31).

[226] See similarly Das, *Galatians*, 184. Ciampa (*Presence and Function*, 145–47) suggests the possibility that this distinction of ministry spheres may have come from Isa 49:6, where the servant of Yahweh is called to raise up "the tribes of Jacob" and restore "the protected ones of Israel" while at the same time being "a light for the nations."

was also at work in me for the Gentiles" (Πέτρῳ εἰς ἀποστολὴν τῆς περιτομῆς ἐνήργησεν καὶ ἐμοὶ εἰς τὰ ἔθνη).[227] The verb rendered "work in" (ἐνεργέω) seems to emphasize God's work both in and through his appointed servants Peter and Paul.[228] This fits well with Paul's insistence in 1:16 that God revealed his Son "in me [ἐν ἐμοί] so that I could preach him among the Gentiles" and that as a result of Paul's ministry the churches in Judea "glorified God in me [ἐν ἐμοί]" (1:24 NKJV). By referring to God as "the one at work" (ὁ ... ἐνεργήσας), Paul likely makes an indirect reference to the Holy Spirit. He uses this same verb to describe the Spirit's work in believers through spiritual gifts (1 Cor 12:6, 11), and his reference to the "power that works in us" (Eph 3:20) as believers is likely another indirect reference to the Holy Spirit.[229] Later in 3:5 Paul again connects this verb with the Spirit. In effect, then, Paul is saying that the same Holy Spirit that empowers Peter's ministry empowers his as well.[230]

The purpose of God's work in both Peter and Paul is "apostleship" (ἀποστολή), a word that refers to the specific office of being an authoritative witness of Jesus' resurrection, commissioned by Christ himself (Luke 6:13; Acts 1:15–26). His apostleship was a gift from God (Rom 1:5) and confirmed by God's work in and through him (1 Cor 9:1–2). As an apostle (Gal 1:1), Paul's authority and status are equal to that of Peter; what distinguishes them is their different spheres of ministry focus. Those ministry spheres are repeated from 2:7, though with a slight twist. Paul uses the same word ("the circumcised [τῆς περιτομῆς]") for Peter's ministry focus but switches from "the uncircumcised" (τῆς ἀκροβυστίας) in 2:7 to "the Gentiles" (τὰ ἔθνη) here in 2:8. The change is likely stylistic, though it may also be driven by a desire to use language more consistent with Paul's understanding of his apostolic commission (compare 1:15; 2:2).[231]

---

[227] The γάρ that introduces the verse could either be explanatory or causal.

[228] The datives Πέτρῳ and ἐμοὶ are clearly parallel and should be understood as having the same force. They could be locative, indicating God's sphere of activity (so DeSilva, *Handbook*, 32) or means, stressing that both Peter and Paul are God's instruments (so Wallace, *Greek Grammar*, 163; Moo, *Galatians*, 135). A decision is difficult and perhaps unnecessary since both fit the context and result in a similar idea. Burton (*Galatians*, 94) suggests they are dative of advantage, which seems less likely.

[229] On this indirect reference to the Holy Spirit in Eph 3:20–21, see Gordon D. Fee, *God's Empowering Presence: The Holy Spirit in the Letters of Paul* (Peabody, MA: Hendrickson, 1994), 697–98. Other indirect references to the Spirit's work with this verb include Phil 2:13 and Col 1:29.

[230] On the work of the Spirit in Galatians, see Biblical Theology §2.3.

[231] In both 1:16 and 2:2 the expression is "among the Gentiles" (ἐν τοῖς ἔθνεσιν) whereas here it is "for the Gentiles" (εἰς τὰ ἔθνη). The difference is one of emphasis. The former

A mark of Christian maturity is the ability to recognize that the same God is at work even in the most diverse ministries. The God who empowers the preaching of the gospel is the same God who empowers the crisis counselor to lead a drug addict to find freedom in Christ. The God who empowers a missionary to take the gospel to an unreached people group is the same God who empowers the widow who knits scarves and mittens for those in need. The sooner we recognize the various ways that the one God works, the greater our joy and wonder will be.

2:9. With the parenthetical comment of 2:8 complete, Paul now resumes the train of thought begun in 2:7. The first reason the Jerusalem church leaders extended the right hand of fellowship to Paul (2:9c) was that they saw he had been entrusted with the gospel (2:7). He now gives the second reason: they "acknowledged the grace that had been given to me" (γνόντες τὴν χάριν τὴν δοθεῖσάν μοι). The verb rendered "acknowledge" (γινώσκω) here likely has the sense of "to grasp the significance or meaning of something."[232] The "grace" (χάρις) Paul has in mind here is not a generic reference to God's saving work in Christ, but the gift of apostleship. This conclusion is not only confirmed by the context, but also by a parallel in Romans 1:5, where Paul says that through Christ he received "grace and apostleship [χάριν καὶ ἀποστολὴν] to bring about the obedience of faith for the sake of his name among all the Gentiles." Even closer to Paul's language here is Ephesians 3:7, where he refers to his ministry as "the gift of God's grace that was given to me by the working of his power."[233] By referring to his apostolic ministry as grace given to him, Paul further emphasizes the divine origin of this calling, in contrast to the claims of human authority offered by his opponents.

At last Paul identifies the leaders of the Jerusalem church as James, Cephas, and John.[234] He has already mentioned Cephas (1:18) and James

---

designates the sphere of Paul's ministry, while the latter indicates the beneficiary (see BDAG s.v. εἰς 4.g).

[232] BDAG s.v. γινώσκω 3.

[233] See similar language in Rom 12:3; 15:15; 1 Cor 3:10; 15:10; Eph 3:2; see BDAG s.v. χάρις 4.

[234] Whereas in 1:18–19 Paul mentions Cephas first and then James, here James is listed first, followed by Peter and then John. Martyn (*Galatians*, 204) suggests that Paul moves James to the front of the list to reflect the "organization of affairs in the Jerusalem church. James was the chief leader, or was in the process of becoming that (2:12). It may also be, however, that Paul has placed James's name in the position of emphasis in order to say that even the leader known to be a strict adherent of the Law came to see that God was at work in Paul's circumcision-free mission to Gentiles." Some manuscripts (e.g., D F G) reverse

the brother of Jesus (1:19), but this is the first and only reference to John. Although there are several men named John in the New Testament, this likely refers to John the son of Zebedee. He and his brother James, along with Peter, formed the inner circle of Jesus' disciples (Matt 17:2; 26:37; Mark 5:37). He was a key leader in the early church (Acts 3:1–4:31) and the eventual author of the Gospel of John and 1–3 John. Paul says these three men are "those recognized as pillars" (οἱ δοκοῦντες στῦλοι εἶναι).[235] Although rare in the New Testament,[236] the term "pillar" (στῦλος) is common in the LXX. During the exodus God led his people by "a pillar of cloud" during the day and "a pillar of fire" at night (Exod 12:21–22; 14:19). This word appears repeatedly in Exodus describing the tabernacle and its construction, as well as in 1 Kings in connection with the building of the temple. The word was also used figuratively to depict strength, stability, or support. Wisdom, for example, is portrayed as building her house on seven pillars (Prov 9:1).[237] Jewish literature displays similar usage. God tells Jeremiah that his prayers "are as a firm pillar" in the midst of Jerusalem (4 Bar 1:2). The Jewish mother who watched her seven sons martyred before her eyes is described as "a roof nobly set upon the pillars of your boys, you endured, unmoved, the earthquake of the tortures" (4 Macc 17:3 NETS). Philo prays that the mind would function in the soul like a pillar in the house, providing stability (Migr. 1:124).

Referring to James, Cephas, and John as pillars has been understood primarily in two different ways. Some argue that this language is rooted in the Jewish expectation of a new Jerusalem and a new temple, with the apostles viewed as pillars for their foundational role.[238] Others suggest that the mention of three pillars "is due to a deliberate selection by the Aramaic-speaking Jerusalem church of three disciples/apostles as

---

the order of the names, likely in view of the order of 1:18–19, but the order of "James and Cephas" has strong manuscript support (א B C K L P) and is to be preferred as original.

[235] On the Greek expression behind the word "recognized" (οἱ δοκοῦντες), see 2:2.

[236] There are just three other NT occurrences. In 1 Tim 3:15 the church is described as "the pillar and foundation of the truth." Christ will make the one who overcomes tribulation "a pillar in the temple of my God" (Rev 3:12). Revelation 10:1 describes an angel descending from heaven as having legs "like pillars of fire."

[237] See further Moises Silva, "στῦλος," NIDNTTE 4:390.

[238] See C. K. Barrett, "Paul and the 'Pillar' Apostles," in Studia Paulina : In Honorem Johannis De Zwaan Septuagenarii, ed. W. C. van Unnik and Sevenster Jan Nicolaas (Haarlem: De Ervem F. Bohn N.V., 1953), 1–19; Richard Bauckham, "James and the Jerusalem Church," in The Book of Acts in Its First Century Setting, ed. Richard Bauckham (Grand Rapids: Eerdmans, 1995), 442–46; Keener, Galatians, 128–29.

community leaders on the basis of the model of the three patriarchs, Abraham, Isaac and Jacob, thought of in rabbinic sources as the three pillars of Israel, indeed, of the entire world."[239] While both are possible, the evidence in rabbinic sources suggests that this latter tradition extends back into the first century and better explains the unusual terminology here. Thus just as "God once 'established the world,' the covenant community Israel, on the basis of the three Patriarchs, so in the messianic period, inaugurated by the resurrection of Jesus from the dead, God was thought of by Jewish Christians as having 'established the world' anew, the new covenant community, the 'Israel of God,' to employ Paul's phrase from Gal 6,16, on the basis of three new pillars."[240]

Regardless of which view (if either is in fact in view) we accept, Paul is likely borrowing the language of his opponents in calling these men pillars. Yet without denying the title, Paul seems to distance himself from its significance by saying they are "recognized as pillars." Perhaps Paul's opponents were using "pillar" language to relegate Paul's own apostolic commission and authority to a secondary status in comparison to the leaders of the Jerusalem church. Thus Paul recognizes their role as leaders in the church without for one second diminishing his own status as an apostle.

Because these "pillars" recognized God's grace at work, they "gave the right hand of fellowship to me and Barnabas" (δεξιὰς ἔδωκαν ἐμοὶ καὶ Βαρναβᾷ κοινωνίας). The expression "right hand of fellowship" in this context signals a formal agreement that depends on the honor and integrity of the parties involved.[241] This and similar expressions occur in both Jewish and Greco-Roman sources with various forms of the power relationships between parties.[242] Here in 2:9, however, the expression

---

[239] Roger D. Aus, "Three Pillars and Three Patriarchs," ZNW 70 (1979): 252–61, quote from 255; see also Longenecker, Galatians, 57–58; Ciampa, Presence and Function, 149–50. Perhaps the clearest example is Exod. Rab. 15:7, which refers to Abraham, Isaac, and Jacob as the three pillars upon whom rest both the nation and the world.

[240] Aus, "Three Pillars and Three Patriarchs," 256–57. However, Aus is wrong to assume that the "merit of the fathers" ideology he sees so tightly bound to these pillar traditions in rabbinic sources was embraced by these Jewish Christians.

[241] See Craig S. Keener, "The Pillars and the Right Hand of Fellowship in Galatians 2.9," JGRChJ 7 (2010): 51–58.

[242] Old Testament examples include 2 Kgs 10:15; 1 Chr 29:24; 2 Chr 30:8; Ezra 10:19; Ezek 17:18; for LXX examples see 1 Macc 6:58; 11:50, 62, 66; 13:45, 50; 2 Macc 4:34; 11:26; 12:11–12; 13:22; 14:19; 15:15. For further discussion see NIDNTTE 1:664–67 and Ciampa, Presence and Function, 150–52.

denotes a mutuality rather than one party being more powerful than the other. Both the purpose and result of this act was "that we should go to the Gentiles and they to the circumcised" (ἵνα ἡμεῖς εἰς τὰ ἔθνη, αὐτοὶ δὲ εἰς τὴν περιτομήν). Just as in 2:8, there is a recognition of the respective ministry spheres where each would focus their efforts, while not indicating a rigid division of labor.[243]

Fellowship in the gospel is more than simply being in the same place at the same time with fellow believers. It is common participation in the benefits of the gospel. When we unite with fellow believers for the display of God's glory and the advancement of the gospel, we make the truth of the gospel visible for the world to see.

2:10. Paul adds one final outcome from this meeting with the Jerusalem church leaders: "They asked only that we would remember the poor" (μόνον τῶν πτωχῶν ἵνα μνημονεύωμεν).[244] While in the context of that original meeting in Jerusalem the "poor" had specific reference to Jewish Christians (Acts 11:27–30), it is unlikely the reference can be limited to Jewish Christians.[245] Paul introduces this request with the word "only" (μόνος) both to emphasize that the pillars added nothing to his gospel and to highlight its importance.[246] The present tense of the verb "remember" (μνημονεύω) portrays continuous concern overflowing into action. Concern for the poor was a staple of Jewish piety rooted in Scripture. The Israelites were commanded to allow their fields to remain fallow every seventh year so that the poor would be able to gather food (Exod 23:11), and even when they harvested their fields they were to leave

---

[243] Burton (*Galatians*, 97–98) suggests that the use of the preposition εἰς here indicates that the distinction between Paul and Peter's ministries would be one of geography—Peter focusing on predominantly Jewish areas and Paul focusing on predominantly gentile ones. Betz (*Galatians*, 100), however, disagrees, claiming the preposition points to ethnic rather than geographic divisions. Longenecker (*Galatians*, 59) proposes a mediating position, claiming that ethnicity and race would not have been so sharply distinguished in the ancient world as they may be today; they should instead be regarded as overlapping realities.

[244] In Greek this clause is woodenly: "only that we might remember the poor." The reader must therefore supply a main verb such as "they asked." Thus the ἵνα plus a subjunctive verb functions like an imperative (see BDAG s.v. ἵνα 2.g; BDF §387.3).

[245] As Schreiner (*Galatians*, 131) does. While acknowledging the parallel expression in Rom 15:26 where Paul refers to "the poor among the saints in Jerusalem" (τοὺς πτωχοὺς τῶν ἁγίων τῶν ἐν Ἰερουσαλήμ), Moo (*Galatians*, 138–39) is likely right in seeing a broader, more general reference. See further Bruce W. Longenecker, *Remember the Poor: Paul, Poverty, and the Greco-Roman World* (Grand Rapids: Eerdmans, 2010), 157–206.

[246] Thus 2:10 is an exception clause to the final clause of 2:6; so DeSilva, *Handbook*, 34.

the corners of their property unharvested for the poor to be able to gather food as well (Lev 23:22). The prophet Amos (among others) sternly rebukes the wealthy who oppress the poor (4:1; 5:11; 8:4, 6). The early Christians showed regular concern for the poor as well. Jesus embraces the practice of giving alms (Matt 6:2–4), and the early church pooled its resources to ensure that the poor had the necessities (Act 4:32–35; 6:1–7; 11:28–30). Hays suggests the possibility that such a request was rooted in the expectation that the nations would one day bring tribute to Israel's God on Mount Zion (Isa 2:2–3; 60:1–16).[247]

At first such a request might seem unexpected, but it makes sense if this visit to Jerusalem is the famine-relief visit recounted in Acts 11:27–30.[248] Witherington notes that conditions in Judea were difficult in light of a combination of factors including famine, food shortages, and a Sabbatical Year.[249] In any case, Paul affirms his wholehearted agreement with this request, saying it is something "I had made every effort to do" (ὃ καὶ ἐσπούδασα αὐτὸ τοῦτο ποιῆσαι).[250] The verb rendered "make every effort" (σπουδάζω) means "to be especially conscientious in discharging an obligation."[251] Less than a decade later Paul would show his commitment to remembering the poor by collecting money from his gentile congregations to alleviate the suffering of believers in Judea (Rom 15:22–29; 2 Cor 8:1–9:15).

A distinguishing mark of the early Christians was their care for the poor (Acts 2:45). When we as believers are willing to sacrifice our own material comforts to help meet the needs of others, we tangibly demonstrate that we treasure Jesus and his people more than the fleeting pleasures of this world.

Bridge

Threats to the gospel are present in every generation. Often the most dangerous are those that arise within the church. When those advocating false doctrine cannot win the day through persuasion and biblical argument, they often resort to leveraging influence with key people in the

---

[247] Hays, "Galatians," 227.

[248] See Introduction, 2–10 for further discussion.

[249] Witherington, *Grace in Galatia*, 144–45.

[250] Paul's language is rather emphatic; woodenly he says, "which also I was eager to do this very thing."

[251] BDAG s.v. σπουδάζω 3.

church. But in the midst of such efforts what matters is the truth of the gospel, and it is the responsibility of the pastor(s)/elders to preserve that truth for God's people both present and future. Those who strive toward this lofty goal can move forward knowing that their labors in the gospel will not be in vain on the last day, as they will be able to say with Paul, "I have fought the good fight, I have finished the race, I have kept the faith. There is reserved for me the crown of righteousness, which the Lord, the righteous Judge, will give me on that day, and not only to me, but to all those who have loved his appearing" (2 Tim 4:7–8).

E. THE INCIDENT IN ANTIOCH (2:11–14)

> [11] But when Cephas came to Antioch, I opposed him to his face because he stood condemned. [12] For he regularly ate with the Gentiles before certain men came from James. However, when they came, he withdrew and separated himself, because he feared those from the circumcision party. [13] Then the rest of the Jews joined his hypocrisy, so that even Barnabas was led astray by their hypocrisy. [14] But when I saw that they were deviating from the truth of the gospel, I told Cephas in front of everyone, "If you, who are a Jew, live like a Gentile and not like a Jew, how can you compel Gentiles to live like Jews?"

Context

This incident in Antioch serves as the last event in the narrative stretching from 1:11–2:21 that Paul uses to defend his status as an apostle of Christ who is independent from the leaders of the Jerusalem church (1:18–24) while simultaneously on the same page with them regarding the law-free nature of the gospel (2:1–10). This confrontation with Cephas further demonstrates Paul's independence from the Jerusalem leaders and at the same time shows that even a "pillar" like Peter could be wrong when it comes to living in step with the truth of the law-free gospel. The final verse of this paragraph is transitional in nature, both stating Paul's rebuke of Cephas in Antioch and introducing the theological exposition that follows in 2:15–21.

Although to contemporary Christians this incident may seem like much ado about nothing, for Paul the truth of the gospel was at stake. And the extensive reflections on this event in the early church demonstrates its importance for understanding the implications of the gospel.[252]

---

[252] For a helpful summary of this engagement, see Longenecker, *Galatians*, 64–65.

At stake was whether or not one had to become Jewish (i.e., observe Jewish requirements such as food laws, circumcision, and Sabbath observance) in order to be a Christian, or whether faith in Christ was sufficient for one's standing before God and standing within the church.[253] Paul does not say that Peter changed his mind, which may indicate that at the time he wrote the matter was still in dispute. But it seems almost certain that eventually Peter and Barnabas both came to see things Paul's way, given that Paul speaks favorably of both in later letters (1 Cor 3:22; 9:5–6) and Peter speaks favorably of Paul (2 Pet 3:15–16).

Structure

Departing from the more specific temporal markers with specific numbers of years in 1:18 and 2:1, Paul introduces this incident with a more generic "but when" (2:11). The basic summary of the incident is stated in the opening verse. Paul opposed Cephas when he came to Antioch because Cephas "stood condemned" (2:11). Verse 12 introduces the reason Cephas stood condemned: Cephas withdrew from eating with gentile believers when "men ... from James" arrived in Antioch, motivated by fear of "the circumcision party" (2:12). This move by Cephas resulted in the rest of the Jews in Antioch (including even Barnabas!) joining him in this hypocritical act (2:13). Paul responded by confronting Cephas in front of the church, calling him out for the inconsistency between the law-free gospel he believed and the separation from table fellowship with gentile believers that he was now practicing (2:14).

2:11. In contrast to the mutual agreement described in 2:6–10, Paul now recounts a situation where one of the pillars (Cephas/Peter) acted inconsistently.[254] It took place "when Cephas came to Antioch" (Ὅτε δὲ ἦλθεν Κηφᾶς εἰς Ἀντιόχειαν), an event that is not recorded in Acts.[255] Antioch of Syria (not to be confused with Pisidian Antioch, one of the cities Paul visited on his first missionary journey) was the third largest city

---

[253] For a helpful discussion of the issues involved in the Antioch incident, including thoughtful interaction with various scholarly views, see Das, *Galatians*, 216–32.

[254] This contrast may be partially signaled by the δέ that introduces this clause (so Moo, *Galatians*, 144; DeSilva, *Handbook*, 35), or the conjunction could simply have a continuative force.

[255] Moo (*Galatians*, 145) suggests that "Peter may have made this trip to Antioch just after Paul's first missionary journey. It may have functioned as an 'inspection' trip in which one of the Jerusalem apostles checks out the nature of the Christian movement in cities of the Diaspora (see Acts 8:14; 9:32)."

in the first-century Roman Empire, trailing only Rome and Alexandria.[256] Located on the Orontes River, it was capital of the Roman province of Syria and had a substantial Jewish population.[257] Because of persecution in Jerusalem, a number of early Christians fled to Antioch and established a church (Acts 11:19–21). When the Jerusalem church sent Barnabas to see what was happening, he was so encouraged that he retrieved Paul from Tarsus to continue the work in Antioch (Acts 11:22–26). Peter's visit to Antioch took place sometime after the famine-relief visit described in Galatians 2:1–10 (compare Acts 11:27–30).

During this visit Paul "opposed him to his face because he stood condemned" (κατὰ πρόσωπον αὐτῷ ἀντέστην, ὅτι κατεγνωσμένος ἦν). In Greek the phrase "to his face" (κατὰ πρόσωπον) occurs first for emphasis. This expression highlights the personal nature of the confrontation and the seriousness of the issue.[258] Because God does not "receive the face" (πρόσωπον [ὁ] θεὸς ἀνθρώπου οὐ λαμβάνει)—that is, show favoritism—when it comes to evaluating a person (2:6), Paul is not afraid to oppose Cephas "to the face" when he is out of step with the truth of the gospel. The verb "oppose" (ἀνθίστημι) is used elsewhere of opponents of the gospel (Acts 13:8; 2 Tim 3:8), and in this particular situation Paul considered Peter's actions to be contrary to the gospel and perhaps even a violation of the agreement recounted in 2:1–10.[259] As a result, Peter "stood condemned" (κατεγνωσμένος ἦν), an expression that has judicial overtones.[260] God commands judges to justify the righteous and "condemn

---

[256] On Antioch, see Schnabel, *Early Christian Mission*, 782–86.

[257] Scholarly estimates range between 20,000–65,000. If the total population of Antioch was approximately 250,000, that would mean Jews constituted anywhere from eight to twenty five percent of the city's inhabitants; see further Schnabel, *Early Christian Mission*, 784–85.

[258] See BDAG s.v. πρόσωπον 1.b.β.d. Compare its use in Acts 25:16, where Festus states that it is against Roman custom to hand over a prisoner "before the accused confronts the accusers face to face [κατὰ πρόσωπον]." DeSilva (*Handbook*, 35–36) suggests the equivalent English idiom would be "I got in his face."

[259] The expression ἀνθίστημι plus the prepositional phrase κατὰ πρόσωπον occurs several times in the LXX to express the idea of standing in the face of enemies. Sometimes it refers to nations not being able to stand in opposition to Israel (Deut 7:24; 11:25; 2 Chr 13:7-8), while other times it speaks of Israel's inability to stand in the face of its enemies (Deut 9:2; Judg 2:14).

[260] Paul uses a periphrastic construction consisting of the imperfect form of εἰμί (ἦν) plus a perfect tense participle (κατεγνωσμένος). Such a construction has the force of a pluperfect verb, and here it "stresses the condition Peter was in at the time of the confrontation itself"; see Stanley E. Porter, *Verbal Aspect in the Greek of the New Testament: With Reference to Tense and Mood* (New York: Lang, 1989), 470.

the wicked [καταγνῶσιν τοῦ ἀσεβοῦς]" (Deut 25:1 LXX).[261] By his actions Peter demonstrated that he was in the wrong, and the wrong was of such a nature that Paul had to confront him.

Although it can be uncomfortable, confrontation is sometimes a necessary part of life. It is especially necessary when an influential person acts in a way that is contrary to the gospel. Some people avoid confrontation by nature; others seek it out in unhealthy ways. Knowing our own personal tendencies can help us pursue faithfulness and wisdom in knowing when confrontation is necessary.

2:12. Paul now explains why Peter was in the wrong, contrasting Peter's initial actions with his latter ones: "For he regularly ate with the Gentiles before certain men came from James" (πρὸ τοῦ γὰρ ἐλθεῖν τινας ἀπὸ Ἰακώβου μετὰ τῶν ἐθνῶν συνήσθιεν).[262] Apparently when Peter was first in Antioch, "he regularly ate with the Gentiles" (μετὰ τῶν ἐθνῶν συνήσθιεν). This was his consistent practice,[263] likely as a result of his experience with Cornelius (Acts 10:1–48). Whether Peter personally continued to keep the Jewish food laws is not clear,[264] but in any event he willingly ate with gentile believers. The church in Antioch, consisting of Jews and gentiles, appears to have reached some kind of understanding whereby they could share in table fellowship without causing division.

All that changed when "certain men came from James" (πρὸ τοῦ γὰρ ἐλθεῖν τινας ἀπὸ Ἰακώβου). Beyond this brief description we do not know much about them. They are not to be identified with "the circumcision party" mentioned later in this verse (see below). These men from James were likely emissaries sent by the leader of the Jerusalem church.[265] Paul does not recount what these men from James said, which has led to a number of different proposals.[266] In my view the most likely scenario is that James sent them with news of a recent outbreak of violent persecution

---

[261] For additional examples in Greco-Roman literature, see LSJM s.v. καταγιγνώσκω.

[262] On the significance of table fellowship, see Biblical Theology §5.3.2.

[263] Paul's use of the imperfect tense (συνήσθιεν) portrays this as his customary practice.

[264] Dunn (*Galatians*, 121–22) argues that even after the Cornelius event Peter continued to observe the Jewish food laws. But others are likely correct that Peter gave up observance to Jewish dietary restrictions; see the helpful excursus in Schreiner, *Galatians*, 141–42.

[265] Some argue that these men from James overstepped whatever authority they had from James as a way of trying to establish authority for their own message; see, e.g., J. B. Lightfoot, *St. Paul's Epistle to the Galatians: A Revised Text with Introduction, Notes, and Dissertations*, 4th ed. (Grand Rapids: Zondervan, 1957), 112.

[266] For a helpful survey, see Carson, "Mirror-Reading," 99–112.

by the Jewish authorities, intensified by reports that Peter regularly broke the kosher laws and ate with gentiles.[267] Through these emissaries James asked Peter to exercise restraint in his association with gentiles and perhaps even to resume observance of the kosher laws as a way of easing the intense persecution the Jerusalem church was experiencing,[268] and perhaps out of concern for the effectiveness of ongoing outreach to Jews, of which Peter was a key leader. Das suggests that "Peter would have been implicated by mere association in the idolatry so common at gentile meals with the characteristic meat sacrificed to the gods and the wine of libation—even though the charge was entirely unjustified among gentile Christians with similar qualms about such meat and drink (cf. Rom 14:13–15:3; 1 Cor 8:7–13)."[269]

As a result of whatever these men from James said, Peter "withdrew and separated himself" (ὑπέστελλεν καὶ ἀφώριζεν ἑαυτὸν). Paul does not describe a single event, but a pattern of behavior.[270] In some Greco-Roman writings the verb rendered "withdrew" (ὑποστέλλω) can describe "military and political maneuvers of retreating to an inconspicuous or sheltered position."[271] Whether it has that same meaning here is unclear. In the LXX the verb rendered "separated" (ἀφορίζω) sometimes has the sense of separation for the sake of cultic purity (e.g., Lev 13:11; 20:25–26),[272] which would fit the context here. Together these two verbs suggest that at a minimum Peter stopped eating with gentile believers; perhaps he withdrew from any kind of fellowship with gentiles at all. Peter did this

---

[267] Here I am in large measure following Carson, "Mirror-Reading," 108–12. In essence this is a development of the proposal of Robert Jewett, "Agitators and the Galatian Congregation," *NTS* 17 (1971): 198–212, though Jewett is likely wrong to see the pressure coming exclusively or even mainly from the Zealots. Bruce (*Galatians*, 130) notes that the mid-40s saw a spike in Jewish revolutionaries fighting against Roman rule, requiring action by the Roman procurator to suppress it (Josephus *War* 2:118; *Ant.* 20:102). He suggests that some of this tension resulted in these Jewish militants viewing any Jews who associated with gentiles as traitors.

[268] Schreiner (*Galatians*, 140) contends that it is going beyond the evidence "to conclude that James demanded that Peter cease eating with Gentiles since Paul does not criticize James here but only Peter." This is probably correct, though it is also going beyond the evidence to assume that Paul would have criticized James if he had made such a suggestion.

[269] Das, *Galatians*, 209.

[270] The verbs "withdrew" (ὑπέστελλεν) and "separated" (ἀφώριζεν) are both in the imperfect tense, portraying repeated behavior.

[271] Betz, *Galatians*, 108.

[272] See NIDNTTE 3:544. Paul uses this verb to call believers to a life of moral purity when he quotes Isa 52:11 in 2 Cor 6:17.

"because he feared those from the circumcision party" (φοβούμενος
τοὺς ἐκ περιτομῆς). The identity of the "circumcision party" (τοὺς ἐκ
περιτομῆς) is not immediately clear.[273] While some equate them with
the men who came from James, on the whole it seems best to see them
as the non-believing Jews in Jerusalem who were persecuting the church
there.[274] Thus Peter feared that if he continued his table fellowship with
gentile believers in Antioch, the persecution of the Jerusalem church
by the Jewish authorities would continue to intensify. Perhaps James
had sent word through these messengers that Peter (because he was a
high-profile Jewish Christian) should temporarily return to observing the
food laws, but the rest of the Jews followed his lead.[275] In any case, note
the contrast between Paul's action in Jerusalem and Peter's actions here
in Antioch; Paul refused to submit for even a moment to those demanding
Titus be circumcised (2:4-5), while Peter caved to the pressure from the
circumcision party.[276]

Fear is one of the most powerful motivators. If it was powerful enough
to sway the actions of one of the so-called pillar apostles, we would be
foolish to think we are immune to its influence. Are there any areas of
your life where you are allowing fear rather than faith to determine
your actions?

2:13. The change in practice was not limited to Peter: "the rest of
the Jews joined his hypocrisy" (συνυπεκρίθησαν αὐτῷ [καὶ] οἱ λοιποὶ
Ἰουδαῖοι). Taking their cues from Peter, the rest of the Jewish Christians
in Antioch stopped engaging in table fellowship with gentile Christians.

---

[273] In Greek the expression is "the ones from the circumcision." The preposition ἐκ here
indicates their origin (BDAG s.v. ἐκ 3.b), while the word "circumcision" (περιτομή) is used
as metonymy for a Jewish person (DeSilva, *Handbook*, 37). By itself the expression is neutral.
In Col 4:11 Paul refers to Jewish Christian coworkers as those "of the circumcision" (οἱ ὄντες
ἐκ περιτομῆς), while in Titus 1:10 (esv) he refers to opponents of the gospel as "those of the
circumcision party" (οἱ ἐκ τῆς περιτομῆς).

[274] Again following Carson, "Mirror-Reading," 108-12. Witherington (*Grace in Galatia*,
155-56) provides further support for tensions in Judea being high around this time, noting
that according to Josephus (*War* 2:224-27; *Ant.* 20:112) thousands of Jews were killed at
the Passover festival in AD 49 because of unrest provoked by Zealots. Those who identify
the men from James with the circumcision party (thus making them Jewish Christians)
usually conclude that Peter and Paul disagreed theologically on the necessity of observing the law (see, e.g., Betz, *Galatians*, 108-10) or that Peter suffered a temporary lapse in
judgment to accommodate the concerns of these stricter Jewish Christians (see, e.g., Moo,
Galatians, 142-44).

[275] As suggested by Witherington, *Grace in Galatia*, 160.

[276] Helpfully noted by Betz, *Galatians*, 111.

While they likely viewed this as a temporary and strategic accommoda-
tion to ease the persecution of Jewish believers in Judea, Paul sees this
as an act of "hypocrisy." The verb Paul uses (συνυποκρίνομαι) has the
sense of "to join in playing a part or pretending."[277] Every New Testament
occurrence of this word family has the sense of outward behavior or
appearance that is out of step with an inward reality. In Greek literature
the word was often associated with orators or actors in a drama.[278] But
perhaps more analogous to its use here is Polybius, who writes that a
general named Fabius "pretended to agree with eager and adventurous
spirits" (*Hist.* 3.92.5) about going to battle when he had no intention of
doing so.[279] By using this language Paul portrays the withdrawal and separation of Peter and the rest of the Jewish Christians as inconsistent with
their theological conviction that the work of Jesus had united believing
Jews and gentiles into one body "by abolishing the law of commandments
expressed in ordinances, that he might create in himself one new man
in place of the two, so making peace" (Eph 2:15 ESV).

Most disappointing to Paul was that "even Barnabas was led astray by
their hypocrisy" (καὶ Βαρναβᾶς συναπήχθη αὐτῶν τῇ ὑποκρίσει). Paul's
wording suggests that Barnabas' decision was a direct result of seeing
Peter and the other Jewish Christians withdraw from table fellowship;[280]
perhaps he was even the last one on board. The verb rendered "carried
away" (συναπάγω) means "to cause someone in conjunction with others
to go astray in belief."[281] Peter uses this same verb when warning his readers to "be on your guard, so that you are not led away [συναπαχθέντες]
by the error of lawless people and fall from your own stable position"
(2 Pet 3:17). The same Barnabas who was instrumental in leading Jewish

---

[277] BDAG s.v. συνυποκρίνομαι. There are 31 total occurrences of this word family in the
NT: ὑποκριτής (17x), ἀνυπόκριτος (6x), ὑπόκρισις (6x), συνυποκρίνομαι (1x), ὑποκρίνομαι
(1x). The highest concentration of occurrences is in Matthew (14x), half of which occur in
Jesus' denunciation of the scribes and Pharisees in Matthew 23.

[278] See the many examples listed in LSJM s.v. ὑποκρίνω II and the discussion in U. Wilckens,
"ὑποκρίνομαι, συνυποκρίνομαι, ὑπόκρισις, ὑποκριτής, ἀνυπόκριτος," in *TDNT* 8:559–71.

[279] Cited in MM, 615. The occurrences in Josephus (41x) and Philo (35x) usually have
this broader sense of pretending to be something one is not rather than the more specific
sense of performing as an orator or an actor in a play.

[280] In Greek this clause is introduced with the conjunction."ὥστε, indicating result (BDAG
s.v. ὥστε 2.a.α).

[281] BDAG s.v. συναπάγω 1.

and gentile believers to live as one body was now acting in a way that threatened to undermine all that he and Paul had labored to achieve.

Hypocrisy is one of the most common charges leveled against Christians. While in this life our lives will never perfectly match what we know the Bible teaches, as believers that must be our goal. And when we inevitably fall short, we must be quick to confess, repent, and pursue growth in those areas.

2:14. Paul's response when he saw these events unfolding was swift and decisive, since his vision of a united church of Jew and gentile alike was in serious danger.[282] He describes the hypocrisy of Peter, Barnabas, and the rest of the Jewish Christians in Antioch as "deviating from the truth of the gospel" (οὐκ ὀρθοποδοῦσιν πρὸς τὴν ἀλήθειαν τοῦ εὐαγγελίου). The verb rendered "deviating from" (ὀρθοποδέω) has the sense of walking straight or upright, but by extension came to refer to acting in a right or straightforward manner.[283] Depending on how one understands the metaphor, the expression "truth of the gospel" (πρὸς τὴν ἀλήθειαν τοῦ εὐαγγελίου) could be either the standard that governs the walking or the destination toward which one walks.[284] Keeping with walking as a metaphor for the Christian life, perhaps the latter is best. Thus Peter, Barnabas, and the other Jewish Christians who stopped table fellowship with gentile Christians had left the path that expresses the truth of the gospel. Their actions were inconsistent with what they claimed to believe. The specific truth of the gospel in view here is likely that "a person is not justified by the works of the law but by faith in Jesus Christ" (2:16; see notes at 2:5).

---

[282] Moo (*Galatians*, 149) contends that Paul's wording ("but when I saw") implies that Paul was away from Antioch when the men from James arrived and that by the time he did return the damage had already been done; see similarly Das, *Galatians*, 212. This conclusion seems the most likely, though Burton (*Galatians*, 110) suggests that Paul's language indicates that it was not until this situation arose that the apostle "saw clearly that the only position consistent with the gospel" was that the law could not be binding on either gentile or Jew now that Christ has come.

[283] BDAG s.v. ὀρθοποδέω; see also the discussion in *NIDNTTE* 3:541. This verb is a compound of the words for "straight" (ὀρθός) and "foot" (πούς), from which our English word "orthopedic" eventually came.

[284] The issue is whether πρός indicates the standard (BDAG s.v. πρός 3.e.δ) or goal/destination (BDAG s.v. πρός 3.c). Paul far more regularly uses κατά to indicate standard, so goal/destination is probably preferable here; see further G. D. Kilpatrick, "Gal 2:14 Ὀρθοποδοῦσιν," in *Neutestamentliche Studien für Rudolf Bultmann zu seinem 70. Geburtstag am 20. August 1954*, ed. Walther Eltester (Berlin: Töpelmann, 1954), 269–74.

Because of this deviation from the truth of the gospel, Paul confronted
Cephas "in front of everyone" (ἔμπροσθεν πάντων). The "everyone" in
view extends not just to Barnabas and the rest of the Jewish believers,
but likely includes all believers in Antioch. Although Paul does not say, it
seems likely that he had made repeated efforts to change Cephas' mind
privately without success. When that failed, he had no choice but to
confront Cephas in the presence of the congregation. Public sin requires
public confrontation when private efforts fail to produce repentance.

Paul began his confrontation of Cephas with a complex question that is
structured as an "if ... then" construction.[285] The effect is to highlight the
disconnect between how Cephas has been living and what he is essentially
expecting the gentile Christians in Antioch to do. He asks: "If you, who are
a Jew, live like a Gentile and not like a Jew, how can you compel Gentiles
to live like Jews?" (εἰ σὺ Ἰουδαῖος ὑπάρχων ἐθνικῶς καὶ οὐχὶ Ἰουδαϊκῶς
ζῇς, πῶς τὰ ἔθνη ἀναγκάζεις ἰουδαΐζειν). Paul points out that even though
Peter was Jewish he was living "like a Gentile."[286] In this context to live
like a gentile means not to observe the food laws or other practices that
distinguished Jews from gentiles.[287] In other words, Peter was not living
"like a Jew" (Ἰουδαϊκῶς). Given the fact that as a Jewish man Peter was not
living like (an observant) Jew, Paul asks how he can possibly try to "compel"
gentile Christians to live as observant Jews (i.e., keeping the food laws).
This verb "compel" (ἀναγκάζω) is the same one used in 2:3 to describe the
efforts of some in Jerusalem to force Titus to be circumcised.

By withdrawing from table fellowship with gentile Christians unless
they followed the Jewish food laws, Peter and the other Jewish Christians
were trying to force gentile believers "to live like Jews."[288] But given Paul's

---

[285] Paul uses a first class conditional statement, in which the "if" part is assumed true
for the sake of the argument. It is difficult to know where Paul's actual words to Cephas
end. Many English versions end the quote here at the end of 2:14 (RSV, ESV, NRSV, HCSB, NET),
while others include all of 2:14–21 (NIV, NASB, NKJV). On the whole, Moo (Galatians, 153) is likely
correct when he argues that the use of the first person plural pronouns in 2:15–17 and the
tight logical connection between 2:18–21 and 2:17 "makes it likely that Paul continues to
'quote' his speech at Antioch right up to the end of verse 21."

[286] Thus the participle ὑπάρχων is concessive (so also DeSilva, Handbook, 39).

[287] Paul uses an adverb here (ἐθνικῶς) that occurs nowhere else in the NT or LXX. There
is an interesting occurrence in the third-century (AD) biographer Diogenes Laërtes, who uses
it to distinguish between a Greek (ἑλληνικῶς) and non-Greek way (ἐθνικῶς) of speaking
(Lives of Eminent Philosophers 7.56).

[288] Instead of the verb "live" (ζάω) plus the adverb "like a Jew" (Ἰουδαϊκῶς), in this
clause Paul uses a verb (ἰουδαΐζω) that means to "live as one bound by Mosaic ordinances or

language here, it seems unlikely the effort to make the gentile Christians "live like Jews" was limited to observing the food laws. It would only have seemed logical to extend this to circumcision. A further complication of their withdrawal from table fellowship with gentiles is that it likely precluded them from celebrating the Lord's Supper together. As such the withdrawal of the Jewish believers from table fellowship sent the not-so-subtle message that in order for gentile Christians to be accepted, they had to in essence become Jewish. "Ironically ... by attempting to preserve the integrity of the Jewish Christians as Jews, Cephas destroys the integrity of the Gentile Christians as believers in Christ."[289]

The gospel is not merely the way we begin the Christian life; it is the means by which we continue to live the Christian life. It sets out a path for us as believers to walk. And when we inevitably step off the path set out by the gospel, it is essential that other believers confront us with the goal of getting us back on the right path. Are there fellow believers in your life who feel the freedom to call you out when you deviate from living a life consistent with the gospel?

Bridge

Reputation and status do not guarantee that a person is right. Even the best of spiritual leaders can be swayed into a wrong course of action based on fear. But when the truth of the gospel is at stake, other believers must step forward and confront with a blend of boldness, humility, and love. Our actions must match what the gospel teaches about not only how we as individuals are right with God, but also what it teaches about living with fellow believers in love. When that becomes a reality we will avoid the hypocrisy that too often discredits our proclamation of the gospel.

---

traditions" (BDAG s.v. ἰουδαΐζω). Although this verb occurs nowhere else in the NT, it does occur in Esther 8:17 (LXX), where in response to fear of the Jews "many of the gentiles were circumcised and lived as Jews [ἰουδάιζον] because of the fear of the Jews" (my translation). In Josephus the only two occurrences refer to gentiles who had converted to Judaism or at least lived as Jews (*War* 2:454, 463). In the Jewish work *Theodotus* (second or first century BC) this verb refers to Shechemites "becoming Jews by being circumcised [περιτεμνομένους Ἰουδαῖσαι]." Perhaps dependent on Gal 2:14, Ignatius (early second century AD) warns the Magnesians, "It is absurd to profess Christ Jesus, and to Judaize [ἰουδαΐζειν]" (Ign. *Magn.* 10:3). In this context there is sharp contrast between living as a Christian and living in accordance with Jewish practices/customs, a contrast that Paul likely would not have expressed so starkly. The Greek writer Plutarch (c. AD 46–120) uses the verb to refer to a man who was "suspected of Jewish practices" (ἔνοχος τῷ ἰουδαΐζειν).

[289] Betz, *Galatians*, 112.

F. The Gospel Defined (2:15–21)

> [15] We are Jews by birth and not "Gentile sinners," [16] and yet because
> we know that a person is not justified by the works of the law but by
> faith in Jesus Christ, even we ourselves have believed in Christ Jesus.
> This was so that we might be justified by faith in Christ and not by
> the works of the law, because by the works of the law no human being
> will be justified. [17] But if we ourselves are also found to be "sinners"
> while seeking to be justified by Christ, is Christ then a promoter of
> sin? Absolutely not! [18] If I rebuild those things that I tore down, I show
> myself to be a lawbreaker. [19] For through the law I died to the law, so
> that I might live for God. [20] I have been crucified with Christ, and I no
> longer live, but Christ lives in me. The life I now live in the body, I live
> by faith in the Son of God, who loved me and gave himself for me. [21] I
> do not set aside the grace of God, for if righteousness comes through
> the law, then Christ died for nothing.

Context

At one level this paragraph is the conclusion of Paul's argument that
began in 1:11–12 with the assertion that he received his gospel through
a revelation of Jesus Christ. At the same time, this paragraph summarizes
the apostle's understanding of justification by faith apart from works of
the law, which lays the foundation for the extended argument of 3:1–5:1.
The language and argument of this paragraph are dense but the central
argument about justification by faith apart from the works of the law is
clear enough.

Beyond the significance of this paragraph for Galatians, it should
be noted that many of the most debated issues in Pauline theology are
addressed in 2:15–21. Indeed, Andrew Das goes so far as to say that "This
paragraph is the nexus of almost every major debate in Pauline theology."[290] Given its importance, the reader must proceed both carefully and
prayerfully to gain a better understanding of the nature of the gospel
and its implications for the life of the individual believer as well as the
corporate life of the church.

Structure

The thesis for the paragraph is straightforward; no one (whether Jew or
gentile) is justified by works of the law, but rather on the basis of faith

---

[290] Das, *Galatians*, 239.

in Christ (2:15–16). Paul then responds to the charge that justification is incomplete without observing the Mosaic law (2:17–20). The response has three components: (1) if being justified by faith in Christ apart from works of the law eliminates the distinction between Jew and gentile, then Christ is a servant of sin (according to the terms of the Mosaic law covenant) for leading Jews and gentiles to share table fellowship (2:17); (2) instead, reestablishing the Mosaic law covenant which Christ did away with would establish Paul as a transgressor (2:18); (3) since Paul (who presents himself as a paradigm for all believers) died to the law when he was crucified with Christ, Christ now lives in him to empower a life based on faith in Christ (2:19–20). The paragraph concludes with a summary reason for rejecting obedience to the Mosaic law as necessary for justification: returning to the Mosaic law would nullify the grace of God, since Christ's death demonstrates that justification/righteousness cannot come through the Mosaic law covenant (2:21).

2:15. Although this verse continues Paul's summary of what he said to Peter in front of the church at Antioch, it also begins a paragraph that defines Paul's gospel message and lays the foundation for his central argument in 3:1–5:1. Paul begins by taking up language that the men from James may have used to make their case. He affirms that "we are Jews by birth" (Ἡμεῖς φύσει Ἰουδαῖοι), or perhaps better, "we ourselves are Jews by birth" (ESV).[291] Paul uses the emphatic pronoun "we" (Ἡμεῖς) to refer to Peter, Barnabas, the other Jewish believers, and himself. They are Jews "by birth" (φύσει),[292] descendants in the line of promise that began with Abraham and continued through Isaac, Jacob, and his twelve sons. Paul recognized that his Jewish ancestry was in fact a blessing (Rom 3:2; Phil 3:5) but also a potential way that one might put "confidence in the flesh" (Phil 3:4). John the Baptist warned those who came to see him in the wilderness, "Don't presume to say to yourselves, 'We have Abraham as our father.' For I tell you that God is able to raise up children for Abraham from these stones" (Matt 3:9).

---

[291] There is no connecting particle to begin this clause, which makes it stand out in the argument. The absence of a verb in this clause requires the reader to supply one, with a form of "to be" (εἰμί) being the most natural choice.

[292] This is a dative of reference/respect ("with respect to nature"; see BDF §197 and DeSilva, *Handbook*, 41) or possibly a dative of manner ("naturally"; see Robertson, *Grammar*, 530). Here φύσις refers to one's "condition or circumstance as determined by birth" (BDAG s.v. φύσις 1).

From the perspective of those who still see the world within the dichotomy of Jew and gentile, the opposite of being Jews by birth is "Gentile sinners" (ἐξ ἐθνῶν ἁμαρτωλοί).[293] The csb rightly places this phrase in quotation marks to signal that this phrase was a derogatory slur used by Jews to distinguish themselves from the nations. Although the term "sinner" (ἁμαρτωλός) can have a generic meaning of anyone whose behavior does not meet God's standards, in this context it has the more specific sense of outsiders "who did not observe the Law in detail and therefore were shunned by observers of traditional precepts."[294] This use is especially prominent in the Synoptic Gospels and occurs regularly in connection with "tax collectors" (e.g., Matt 9:13; 11:19; Mark 2:15–17; Luke 15:1–2). In Jewish literature the term often had this more specific sense. Over time "the word ἁμαρτωλός, destined in the Jewish sphere to describe a radical or practical alienation from the Jewish Law as a declaration of the will of the one holy God, inevitably became a technical term for the Gentile. The Gentile was a ἁμαρτωλός in virtue of his not being a Jew and his failure to regulate his conduct according to the Torah."[295] By definition, then, to be a gentile was to be a sinner, and the immoral lives of many gentiles only reinforced this Jewish perception. This term was also used polemically by Jewish sects to distinguish themselves as righteous in contrast to other factions who were sinners for their failure to observe the law properly.[296]

Such language coming from Paul's pen is shocking until one realizes that he is taking his opponents' words as a starting point for dismantling their position. In the argument that follows, Paul will make clear that a simple identification between "gentile" and "sinner" ignores the more fundamental reality that all human beings—Jew and gentile alike—have

---

[293] Woodenly this Greek phrase (ἐξ ἐθνῶν ἁμαρτωλοί) could be rendered "sinners from among the gentiles." As such the preposition ἐξ indicates origin (BDAG s.v. ἐκ 3.b), though there could be an element of qualitative character expressed as well; see Don B. Garlington, "Paul's 'Partisan ἐκ' and the Question of Justification in Galatians," JBL 127 (2008): 570–73.

[294] BDAG s.v. ἁμαρτωλός b.β.

[295] K. H. Rengstorf, "ἁμαρτωλός, ἀναμάρτητος," TDNT 1:325–26. See texts such as Ps 9:15–17; 1 Macc 1:34; 2:44, 48; Tob 13:6; Pss. Sol. 1:1; 2:1–2; 17:22–25; 4 Ezra 3:28–36; 4:2 and the discussions in James D. G. Dunn, "Echoes of Intra-Jewish Polemic in Paul's Letter to the Galatians," JBL 112 (1993): 462–65 and Garlington, "Paul's 'Partisan ἐκ,' " 571–72.

[296] See Dunn, "Echoes of Intra-Jewish Polemic," 462–65. He notes texts such as 1 Macc 1:34; 2:44, 48; 1 Enoch 5:4–7; 82:4–5; 1QHᵃ 2:8–12; 1QpHab 5:4–8; Pss. Sol. 4:8; 13:6–12.

failed to live a life of obedience to God and are therefore in need of redemption.

It is easy to view the sin of others as worse than our own, or to somehow think that our own sin is not really that bad. Yet the apostle Paul regarded himself as the chief of sinners (1 Tim 1:15), and we would be wise to follow his example. As we grow in our awareness of the depth and extent of our sinfulness, we would be wise to remember the words of the Puritan Thomas Watson, who famously wrote, "'Til sin be bitter, Christ will not be sweet."[297]

2:16. Having taken the language of his opponents as his starting point, Paul is now ready to dismantle the ethnic privilege it rests upon. He begins with a statement that those involved in the dispute agree upon: "yet because we know that a person is not justified by the works of the law but by faith in Jesus Christ" (εἰδότες [δὲ] ὅτι οὐ δικαιοῦται ἄνθρωπος ἐξ ἔργων νόμου ἐὰν μὴ διὰ πίστεως Ἰησοῦ Χριστοῦ).[298] This statement provides the reason for the main clause of the sentence that follows.[299] That reason is a theological conviction about how a person is justified. As used here the verb rendered "justified" (δικαιόω) has the sense of "be acquitted, be pronounced and treated as righteous."[300] Thus justification refers to God declaring a person not guilty before him in his court of law. Jewish eschatology looked forward to this verdict being announced on the last day, when God would vindicate his people and condemn his enemies. But what Jews had seen as happening exclusively on the last day Paul saw as having an "already/not yet" dynamic. While he firmly believed that

---

[297] Thomas Watson, *The Doctrine of Repentance* (Carlisle, PA: Banner of Truth Trust, 1987), 61

[298] As the brackets around δέ indicate, it is unclear whether it is original or not. Several manuscripts (A D² Ψ 0278. 33. 1739. 1881) do not have it, including our earliest copy of Galatians (𝔓⁴⁶). Yet a number of significant manuscripts, including early ones, do have it (א C D * F G H 0278ᶜ. 81. 104. 1175. 1241ˢ. 2464), and on the whole it seems more likely to be original. As such, it could either signal progression in the argument or perhaps a slightly adversative sense.

[299] Thus the adverbial participle εἰδότες is causal (compare DeSilva, *Handbook*, 41; Moo, *Galatians*, 157), modifying the main verb of the clause "we ... have believed in Christ Jesus" here in 2:16. Other scholars, however, see it as concessive, modifying verse 15 (e.g., Schreiner, *Galatians*, 154n12) or attendant circumstances (Longenecker, *Galatians*, 83). The perfect tense of this participle may highlight the state of knowing. De Boer (*Galatians*, 143) suggests that Paul is quoting the content of 2:16a from "known material"—perhaps even formulated by the "new preachers in Galatia"—but this goes well beyond the evidence.

[300] BDAG s.v. δικαιόω 2.b.β. On justification and righteousness language, see Biblical Theology §6.0.

justification would happen on the last day ("not yet"), Paul also believed that it was possible to be justified now on the basis of faith ("already").

Paul contrasts two alternative paths to be justified, and this contrast forms a central theme in Galatians. On the first path one is justified "by works of the law" (ἐξ ἔργων νόμου), a phrase that expresses the means or the reason of justification.[301] The meaning of the phrase rendered "works of the law" is highly disputed.[302] While there is broad agreement that the phrase refers to doing what the Mosaic law commands, there is considerable discussion regarding why these "works of the law" cannot justify a person. While it has traditionally been understood to mean doing what the Mosaic law requires, in recent years a number of scholars have challenged this interpretation. Rather than see "works of the law" as a general statement of obedience, scholars such as James D. G. Dunn have argued that works of the law refer to those requirements of the law that specifically mark the person as a member of the Jewish nation. As such the focus of the phrase is not obedience to the law in general but specifically those obligations that distinguish Jews from gentiles, such as circumcision, food laws, and keeping the Sabbath. Understood this way, Paul is not describing an effort to earn God's favor through obedience to the law, but an effort to maintain the distinction between Jew and gentile. But while it is certainly true that the flash point in the Galatian crisis was circumcision (though it is possible Sabbath observance was

---

[301] See BDAG s.v. ἐκ 3.e.

[302] On a grammatical level, there is debate over what kind of genitive νόμου is. The three main possibilities seem to be subjective ("works the law commands"), objective ("works done to obey the law"), or attributive ("law-works"). On the whole it seems best to see the genitive as objective, though the practical difference between the options is admittedly negligible. The scholar who arguably has written the most on this phrase is James D. G. Dunn; see, e.g., James D. G. Dunn, "Works of the Law and the Curse of the Law (Galatians 3:10–14)," *NTS* 31 (1985): 523–42; James D. G. Dunn, "Yet Once More—'the Works of the Law': A Response," *JSNT* 46 (1992): 99–117; James D. G. Dunn, "4qmmt and Galatians," *NTS* 43 (1997): 147–53. In his earlier writings Dunn appears to claim that the phrase referred exclusively to the "boundary markers" of circumcision, food laws, and Sabbath observance that distinguished Jews from gentiles. In his later writings, however, he has clarified that he believes "works of the law" refers to doing what the law commands, though in the context of Gal 2:11–17 he states that doing the law "meant 'separating from Gentile sinners' and 'living the (distinctively) Jewish way of life' "; see James D. G. Dunn, *Beginning from Jerusalem*, vol. 2 (Grand Rapids: Eerdmans, 2008), 475–76. Burton (*Galatians*, 120) has a slightly different take, arguing that the phrase refers to acts of obedience to the Mosaic law done in a legalistic spirit in an effort to gain favor before God. But Paul's issue with works of the law cannot be reduced completely to the spirit in which they are done.

also in play at some level as well; see 4:10), Paul makes it clear later in
the letter that "every man who gets himself circumcised ... is obligated
to do the entire law" (Gal 5:3). And while the social function of the law to
separate Jew and gentile is a crucial part of the Galatian crisis, Paul sees
a more fundamental issue beneath it. The foundational issue is that it is
impossible for any human being to be declared right before God on the
basis of any kind of works, not even those commanded by the Mosaic law.[303]

By contrast,[304] it is possible to be justified "by faith in Jesus Christ"
(διὰ πίστεως Ἰησοῦ Χριστοῦ).[305] Like the expression "works of the law,"
this seemingly straightforward expression has occasioned significant
debate. The expression "faith in Jesus Christ" could instead be translated
as "faithfulness of Jesus Christ."[306] The former expresses the divinely
appointed human response that is the only way anyone can be justified before God. The latter identifies the path of justification as Christ's
faithful obedience in fulfilling the obligations of God's covenant. So if
the phrase means "faith in Jesus Christ," the contrast is between two
possible human responses (doing what the law says versus believing in
Jesus Christ). But if the phrase means "faithfulness of Jesus Christ," the
contrast is between the human response of doing what the law commands
and the divine provision of Jesus Christ's faithfulness/obedience on behalf
of his people. Although a good case can be made for "faithfulness of Jesus
Christ," on the whole, "faith in Jesus Christ" is preferable.[307] Paul's point,
then, is to juxtapose the effort to be justified on the last day by doing

---

[303] By contrast, some advocates of the New Perspective often argue that "works of the
law" cannot justify a person because they are rooted in the Mosaic law, which by its very
nature sharply distinguished Jew from gentile and has been abolished with the coming of
Christ; see, e.g., John M. G. Barclay, *Obeying the Truth: Paul's Ethics in Galatians* (Minneapolis:
Fortress, 1991), 235–41; Dunn, *Galatians*, 134–41; Donald B. Garlington, "'Even We Have
Believed': Galatians 2:15–16 Revisited," *CTR* 7 (2009): 3–28.

[304] Instead of seeing the phrase ἐὰν μὴ as indicating contrast (translated "but rather"),
some scholars argue it indicates exception ("except by"); see, e.g., Dunn, *Galatians*, 137–40
and DeSilva, *Handbook*, 42–43. But Schreiner (*Galatians*, 162–63) is certainly correct that the
larger context strongly favors the contrastive sense.

[305] From the English translations it is not immediately obvious that the phrases "by
the works of the law" (ἐξ ἔργων νόμου) and "by faith in Jesus Christ" (διὰ πίστεως Ἰησοῦ
Χριστοῦ) use different prepositions in Greek. Despite the difference, both appear to have
the same sense of means or basis.

[306] The literature on this subject is immense; for a helpful discussion of the various issues
involved, see the essays in Michael F. Bird and Preston M. Sprinkle, *The Faith of Jesus Christ:
Exegetical, Biblical, and Theological Studies* (Peabody, MA: Hendrickson, 2009).

[307] See the discussion in Biblical Theology §8.2.

what the Mosaic law commands and being justified by trusting in what
Jesus Christ has done through his life of perfect obedience, sacrificial
death on the cross, and resurrection from the dead.

Therefore, it is because Paul and his Jewish Christians know that justification is not by works of the law but by faith in Jesus Christ that Paul
says, "We ourselves have believed in Christ Jesus" (καὶ ἡμεῖς εἰς Χριστὸν
Ἰησοῦν ἐπιστεύσαμεν). Thus "we" refers to Jewish believers (i.e., Paul
and the Jewish Christians he is arguing with), and the sense of the Greek
here could also be translated "we ourselves also" or "we ourselves as
well."[308] When it comes to the basis of justification, Paul and the Jewish
Christians were in full agreement. That basic point of agreement on a
central plank of the gospel is what makes requiring gentile believers to
be circumcised or observe the food laws so incomprehensible to Paul,
regardless of their motives in doing so.

The purpose of believing in Christ is "so that we might be justified
by faith in Christ and not by the works of the law" (ἵνα δικαιωθῶμεν ἐκ
πίστεως Χριστοῦ καὶ οὐκ ἐξ ἔργων νόμου). Paul continues to press the
common ground with the Jewish Christians he is arguing with. The fact
that they had believed in Christ in order to be justified shows that justification comes by faith and not by works of the law.[309]

The final line of verse 16 gives the reason why justification is by
faith in Christ and not by works of the law, using a loose quotation
from Psalm 143:2. In verse 1 David prays for the Lord to hear his prayer
for mercy, pleading that he would answer him "in your righteousness"
(בְּצִדְקָתֶךָ / ἐν τῇ δικαιοσύνῃ σου). David then asks that God would not enter
into judgment against him, "for no one alive is righteous in your sight"
(כִּי לֹא־יִצְדַּק לְפָנֶיךָ כָל־חָי / ὅτι οὐ δικαιωθήσεται ἐνώπιόν σου πᾶς ζῶν).
David recognizes that on his own merits he has no hope of being vindicated before God, so he must rely on the mercy, faithfulness, and righteousness of God to be justified. Paul sees in this expression a universal
principle about the impossibility of anyone being justified before God
and adapts it to the situation in Galatia. Justification must be by faith
in Christ and not works of the law "because by the works of the law no

---

[308] The καί that begins this clause is best understood adverbially, perhaps with an intensive force (BDAG s.v. καί 2.b). The personal pronoun ἡμεῖς has an emphatic force here ("we
ourselves").
[309] Instead of διὰ πίστεως Ἰησοῦ Χριστοῦ, Paul here writes ἐκ πίστεως Χριστου. There
appears to be no difference in meaning between the two.

human being will be justified" (ὅτι ἐξ ἔργων νόμου οὐ δικαιωθήσεται πᾶσα σάρξ).[310] Or, more precisely, "no flesh" will be justified. In place of the LXX reading "no one living" (οὐ ... πᾶς ζῶν), Paul has substituted "no flesh" (οὐ ... πᾶσα σάρξ). By doing so Paul likely makes a subtle play on the act of circumcision (i.e., the cutting away of the flesh), as well as highlights humanity in its weakness, propensity toward sin, and corruptibility.[311] This modification also anticipates the key role that flesh (linked to both efforts to keep the Mosaic law's requirements as means of justification [3:3] and a self-directed life of indulgence in rebellion against God [5:19-21]) plays in the rest of the letter in contrast to both faith and the Spirit (see, e.g., 3:3; 4:29; 5:16-26). The Mosaic law was a good gift from God (Rom 7:12), but not even doing what it commands is sufficient to be justified before God on the last day.[312]

In such a long complex verse filled with exegetical and theological complexities, it can be easy to lose sight of the big picture. The chiastic structure of the verse highlights Paul's claim that justification is based on faith in Christ and not works of the law:

> because we know that a person is not justified by works of the law but by faith in Jesus Christ we ourselves also have believed in Christ Jesus, so that we may be justified by faith in Christ and not by works of the law because by works of the law no flesh will be justified.

Thus the point of disagreement between Paul and Peter is not on the basis of justification; it is whether requiring gentiles to keep the Mosaic law is consistent with justification by faith.

One key reason the gospel is offensive to people is that it stresses there is nothing a person can do to earn a right standing before a holy God. The only hope anyone—regardless of their ethnicity, gender, or socioeconomic status—has of being declared not guilty before God on the last day is faith in Jesus Christ. Faith is the means by which a person receives what Christ has done on the cross for his people.

---

[310] Paul makes a similar allusion to Ps 143:2 in Rom 3:20 ("For no one will be justified in his sight by the works of the law, because the knowledge of sin comes through the law").

[311] Similarly Dunn, *Galatians*, 140.

[312] The future tense of the verb "will be justified" (δικαιωθήσεται) is significant here. It demonstrates that Paul has in mind the believer's future justification (similarly Schreiner, *Galatians*, 167; Moo, *Galatians*, 162); see further Biblical Theology §6.3.3.

2:17. From this common ground on the basis of justification, Paul offers two conditional statements (2:17–18) designed to show the inconsistency between what the Jewish Christians believe about justification and their efforts to require gentile Christians to observe the Mosaic law. The implicit claim of their actions is that final justification is incomplete without works of the law.

The first implication of requiring works of the law is that "we ourselves are also found to be 'sinners' " (εὑρέθημεν καὶ αὐτοὶ ἁμαρτωλοί). Once again "we ourselves" refers to Jewish believers, and Paul repeats his language of "sinners" from verse 15. As used here, the verb "found" (εὑρίσκω) has the sense of discovering something intellectually through reflection or observation.[313] As Jewish believers who had ceased observing the food laws, they are found to be sinners (i.e., those who fail to observe the law and thus preserve the distinction between Jew and gentile) by those who combined their faith in Jesus with the conviction that obedience to the Mosaic law was still mandatory for all believers. This discovery occurs "while seeking to be justified by Christ" (ζητοῦντες δικαιωθῆναι ἐν Χριστῷ).[314] Paul portrays the pursuit of final justification as ongoing, using a verb (ζητέω) that expresses serious and intentional effort toward an objective.[315] The phrase translated "by Christ" (ἐν Χριστῷ) could also be rendered "in Christ." A decision is difficult, but on the whole "by Christ" seems more likely.[316] Thus Christ is the one who accomplishes the justification of the believer.

---

[313] BDAG s.v. εὑρίσκω 2.

[314] This clause, which actually occurs first in the Greek text, is introduced with a δέ that indicates progression in the argument.

[315] BDAG s.v. ζητέω 3.d. The present participle here is thus temporal and portrays the seeking as continual in nature.

[316] If "by Christ" is the correct translation, this could indicate either that Christ is the one who justifies the believer through his faithfulness (e.g., Longenecker, *Galatians*, 89), or it could be a shorthand for "by faith in Christ" (e.g., Burton, *Galatians*, 124). If "in Christ" is correct, the phrase explains that justification takes place in the sphere/realm of Christ; i.e., through the believer's union with Christ and/or his body (so Betz, *Galatians*, 119–20). While "in Christ" is a prominent Pauline motif, a survey of δικαιόω + ἐν indicates that this construction more often expresses agency or instrument than location/sphere. A good example is Gal 3:11, where Paul states that "no one is justified before God by the law" (ἐν νόμῳ οὐδεὶς δικαιοῦται παρὰ τῷ θεῷ); see also Acts 13:38–39; Rom 5:9; 1 Cor 4:4; 6:11; Gal 5:4. The fact that Paul goes on later in the verse to ask whether Christ is a promoter of sin implies that Christ is the agent of justification; see Campbell, *Paul and Union with Christ*, 114–15. For the locative view, see Schreiner, *Galatians*, 168; Moo, *Galatians*, 165.

The "if" part of the conditional statement can thus be summarized as follows. Paul in effect states, "Let's assume for a minute that as we Jewish believers pursue justification by Christ, we are found to be sinners—people who violate the Mosaic law by not keeping the regulations distinguishing the Jew from gentile (such as food laws, circumcision, Sabbath)." The "then" part of the conditional expresses the logical outcome if that premise were true, but in the form of a question: "is Christ then a promoter of sin?" (ἄρα Χριστὸς ἁμαρτίας διάκονος). The word rendered "promoter" (διάκονος) refers to "one who serves as an intermediary in a transaction."[317] This, then, is Paul's logic: if justification by Christ results in Jewish believers becoming "sinners" in the loaded sense of the term, then would it not follow that Christ is the promoter of sin?

The apostle's answer is succinct and emphatic: "Absolutely not!" (μὴ γένοιτο). This is Paul's favorite response to a claim that he finds almost inconceivable (Rom 3:4, 6, 31; 6:2; 15; 7:7; 9:14; 11:1, 11; 1 Cor 6:15; Gal 6:14). The thought that Christ would in effect be a promoter of sin is laughable, and by asking this question he expects his fellow Jewish believers to see the logical fallacy at the heart of their insistence that observing the "works of the law" is necessary for justification.

Paul's underlying logic in this verse seems to be along the following lines. Justification comes by faith in Jesus Christ, regardless of whether a person is Jew or gentile. As a result, Jew and gentile stand before God on equal ground and are part of the same covenant family. However, by associating with gentile believers, Jewish Christians are regarded as "sinners" because they disregard the requirements of the Mosaic law that specifically distinguish between Jews and gentiles. Yet it was being justified by Christ that led them to disregard these laws, so in that case Christ actually becomes an agent who causes or brings about sin (according to the logic of the Jewish Christians now advocating the practice of those requirements). Since we know that Christ could never be an agent of sin,

---

[317] BDAG s.v. διάκονος 1. Paul regularly uses this word in the sense of "servant" or "minister" to describe himself and others involved in gospel ministry (e.g., 1 Cor 3:5; 2 Cor 6:4; 11:23; Eph 3:7; 6:21; Col 1:7, 23–25; 1 Tim 4:6). Dunn (*Galatians*, 141–42) notes that this word could also have the sense of "table-waiter" and suggests a link to the use of the word in Mark 10:42–45 as well as Jesus' own table-fellowship with "sinners." He then pointedly summarizes: "Who could deny that Jesus would have been ready to 'wait upon' the meal tables of Jewish and Gentile disciples as Antioch? If such table-fellowship made Jewish believers 'sinners', it also made Christ a 'servant of sin', one who was at sin's beck and call."

Jewish Christians who disregard the purity laws and have close fellowship with gentile Christians cannot therefore be regarded as "sinners"
in that sense.

Whenever the freedom that Jesus accomplished for his people is lived
out, there will be those who say the gospel leads to sin. Paul seems to be
responding to just such a charge when he writes in Romans 6:1, "What
should we say then? Should we continue in sin so that grace may multiply?" Those who make such claims show they do not truly understand
the grace of God revealed in the gospel.

2:18. Paul now uses a second conditional statement to explain why
Christ cannot be a promoter of sin,[318] and he does so by indicating what
would make him a violator of God's will. The "if" part of the conditional is
as follows: "If I rebuild those things that I tore down" (εἰ γὰρ ἃ κατέλυσα
ταῦτα πάλιν οἰκοδομῶ). Within the larger context the "things that I tore
down" refers to the structures of the Mosaic covenant, though likely
with particular emphasis on the regulations that distinguished Jews
from gentiles (e.g., food laws, circumcision, Sabbath). These issues were
the point of contention between Paul and his fellow Jewish Christians.
From his perspective the actions of the Jewish Christians were implicitly
rebuilding the entire system of the Mosaic covenant that distinguished
Jews from gentiles, something that, through the work of Jesus Christ,
God had torn down.

The Old Testament prophets (and especially Jeremiah) often used
the combined language of "building" and "destroying" to describe what
God was either doing or about to do.[319] In his commission to Jeremiah
God says, "See, I have appointed you today over nations and kingdoms
to uproot and tear down, to destroy and demolish, to build and plant"
(Jer 1:10). God promises to build up and not tear down his people when
he brings them back from exile and institutes a new covenant with
them (Jer 24:6–7; 31:27–34). Through the new covenant inaugurated in
Jesus Christ, God has torn down the old covenant structures that distinguished Jews from gentiles. Paul says that were he to seek requiring

---

[318] Thus the γάρ that introduces this verse is explanatory (so also Longenecker, *Galatians*,
90; Schreiner, *Galatians*, 169). Another possibility is to see it as adversative, thus having the
sense "but"; see Jan Lambrecht, "Transgressor by Nullifying God's Grace. A Study of Gal
2,18–21," *Bib* 72 (1991): 219. Like the verse before, this is a first class conditional statement
in which the "if" part is assumed true for the sake of the argument.

[319] See especially Ciampa, *Presence and Function*, 203–7.

gentile Christians to observe the Mosaic law, only then would "I show myself to be a lawbreaker" (παραβάτην ἐμαυτὸν συνιστάνω). As used here, the verb rendered "show" (συνίστημι) means "to provide evidence of a personal characteristic or claim through action";[320] the present tense suggests ongoing action. A "lawbreaker" (παραβάτης) refers to one who violates a norm or a standard, but since the standard in view here is not the law, perhaps a better translation would be "transgressor" or perhaps "violator." The standard Paul would be violating is the new covenant.[321] By reestablishing the Mosaic regulations that Christ destroyed, Paul would be violating God's standards of righteousness as revealed in the new covenant. It would be a step backward in redemptive history to go back to the Mosaic covenant that God tore down when he built the new covenant in Christ.

For those who come from religious backgrounds where one's performance determined one's standing before God, it can be tempting to revert back to old, familiar patterns of relating to God and others. But Christ gave his life so that we might escape the bondage of performance, never to return to it again.

2:19–20. In verses 19–20 Paul now moves to justify his implicit claim that reestablishing the Mosaic regulations would in fact show him to be a violator of God's new covenant (2:17–18).[322] Returning to observance of the Mosaic law is unthinkable for Paul, since, he says, "through the law I died to the law" (ἐγὼ γὰρ διὰ νόμου νόμῳ ἀπέθανον). When Paul says "I," he is not only referring to his own personal experience, or even his experience as a Jewish Christian, but his experience as a representative human being regardless of ethnicity.[323] As such his experience is at root

---

[320] BDAG s.v. συνίστημι A.3. A good example of this usage is Romans 5:8: "But God proves his own love for us in that while we were still sinners, Christ died for us."

[321] While it is possible the "standard" in view here is "God's will" (see, e.g., Schreiner, *Galatians*, 170), a more specific reference to the new covenant is likely, since that is what is violated when anyone promotes a return to the Mosaic regulations. Ciampa (*Presence and Function*, 206–7) argues that what is torn down is the old covenant community, with the new covenant community being built up in its place. While there is obviously a close relationship between the Mosaic covenant and the old covenant people of God, the focus in the context here is the regulations and covenantal structures, not the people.

[322] See similarly Moo, *Galatians*, 167. Thus the γὰρ that begins this clause gives the grounds for the claim made in 2:18, which in turn supported 2:17 (DeSilva, *Handbook*, 47).

[323] Though as Moo (*Galatians*, 168) notes, "the experience that Paul refers to in verses 19–20 is broadly applicable (though perhaps in somewhat different ways) to all believers."

the same as every believer. As he will go on to explain later in verse 20, Paul died to the law when he was "crucified with Christ." To die to the law is to be set free from its power and authority. In Romans 7:1–3 Paul compares a person's relationship to the law to a marriage. If a woman gives herself to another man while her husband is alive, she commits adultery. But if her husband has died, she is free from the law of marriage and able to be joined to another man. Paul continues: "Therefore, my brothers and sisters, you also were put to death in relation to the law through the body of Christ so that you may belong to another. You belong to him who was raised from the dead in order that we may bear fruit for God" (Rom 7:4). Paul, just like all believers, died to the law by being crucified with Christ (see below).

But how did Paul's death to the law happen "through the law" (διὰ νόμου)? How is the law the means by which Paul died to the law? While it is possible that the law was the means God used to show him his sin and his spiritually dead state (which led him to trust in Christ), this does not match what Paul says elsewhere about his pre-conversion experience.[324] The underlying logic seems to depend on later passages in the letter. As he will argue in 3:10–14, the law brought him under a curse for his failure to obey it, sentencing him to death. But Christ redeemed him from that curse by taking the curse upon himself through his death and resurrection. As the Son of God he was "born of a woman, born under the law, to redeem those under the law" (4:4–5). Jesus fulfilled the demands of the law perfectly and took upon himself our curse for failing to obey God's requirements. Through his fulfillment of the law Jesus brought the era of the law to an end, inaugurating the new covenant. By believing in the one who fulfilled the law, Paul has died to the law. Returning to something he has died to therefore would make no sense.

Paul says that the purpose/result of dying to the law is "so that I might live for God" (ἵνα θεῷ ζήσω), or possibly "live to God."[325] Just as he died with reference to the law, Paul now lives with reference to God. Similar language occurs in 4 Maccabees 16:25, where those who were martyred

---

[324] Earlier in Gal 1:13–14 Paul asserts that before he encountered Christ he was surpassing his Jewish contemporaries in zeal for the Jewish way of life. In Phil 3:5–6 Paul describes his mentality before coming to know Christ as "blameless."

[325] The dative θεῷ probably indicates reference (similarly DeSilva, *Handbook*, 47; BDF §188.2 and Robertson, *Grammar*, 539 label this a dative of advantage), which is an intentionally broad category.

for refusing to break God's covenant are said to know "that those who die for the sake of God live unto God, as do Abraham and Isaac and Jacob and all the patriarchs" (compare 4 Macc 7:19).[326] This is resurrection language, and that fits Paul's train of thought here. Whereas before his life was oriented to and directed by the law, now his life is oriented to and by God through his Son Jesus Christ (see below). Just as God tore down the Mosaic law with its regulations and built the new covenant through Jesus Christ, so God tore down the old Paul and built a new Paul.

The way that he died to the law, Paul says, is that "I have been crucified with Christ" (Χριστῷ συνεσταύρωμαι). That is Paul's current status.[327] Before he encountered Christ, Paul's life was defined by his progress in Judaism; now his identity is defined by his union with the crucified Christ. By faith Paul was joined to Jesus Christ such that what happened to Christ happened to him. By using the language of crucifixion to refer to his union with Christ, Paul draws out the radical break between the old life and the new. The former life, centered on Torah observance and zeal for its protection, was nailed to the cross. By his sharing in the death of Christ, Paul died to the law and its claim upon his life as the organizing center of his existence.

For Paul, to be crucified with Christ means that "I no longer live, but Christ lives in me" (ζῶ δὲ οὐκέτι ἐγώ, ζῇ δὲ ἐν ἐμοὶ Χριστός).[328] When Paul says that he no longer lives, he means that he is no longer the one directing and controlling his life. The old Paul who oriented his life around meticulously observing the Mosaic law and promoting the sharp distinction between Jews and gentiles no longer lives. Instead, Jesus Christ is the one who directs, animates, and controls Paul's life. The risen Jesus Christ dwells inside of Paul, by the Holy Spirit, to empower Paul to live as God calls him to live. Although Paul does not explicitly mention the Spirit here, the apostle can speak almost interchangeably about the Spirit and Christ dwelling inside the believer. For example, in Romans 8:9–10 Paul refers to

---

[326] Noted by DeSilva, *Handbook*, 47.

[327] Paul uses the perfect tense here, which stresses his state or condition. By itself the perfect tense does not indicate whether a previous event is alluded to (see Porter, *Verbal Aspect*, 245–59), but the context here may suggest an ongoing state that is the result of a past action (perhaps either Jesus' crucifixion or the moment Paul was converted).

[328] The δέ that begins this first clause is continuative, marking progression in the argument (BDAG s.v. δέ 2), while the δέ that begins the second clause marks a sharp contrast (BDAG s.v. δέ 4.a).

the Spirit of God dwelling in believers, believers having the Spirit of Christ, and Christ being in believers. In Colossians 1:27 Paul speaks of "Christ in you" as a mystery at the heart of the gospel.[329] Paul even prays for the Ephesians that "Christ may dwell in your hearts through faith (Eph 3:17).

Paul further unpacks the underlying theological framework of Galatians 2:19–20 in Romans 6:1–11. As believers "we were buried with him by baptism into death, in order that, just as Christ was raised from the dead by the glory of the Father, so we too may walk in newness of life. For if we have been joined with him in the likeness of his death, we will certainly also be in the likeness of his resurrection" (Rom 6:4–5). Our "old self was crucified" with Christ so we are no longer "enslaved to sin" (Rom 6:6). Because believers have "died with Christ, we believe that we will also live with him" (Rom 6:8). This parallel passage makes it clear that although Paul uses the first singular pronoun in Galatians 2:19–20, he is presenting his own experience as paradigmatic for all believers, Jew and gentile alike. Through faith (see below) the believer is joined to Christ, the last Adam and the firstborn of the new creation. The death and resurrection of Jesus was the end of the old creation and the beginning of the new creation. Everything that defined a person before conversion is now subsumed under the more fundamental identity of being a new creation in Christ. Believers participate in this new creation by faith, which unites them to Christ who is the embodiment of the new creation.

The statement "Christ lives in me" (ζῇ δὲ ἐν ἐμοὶ Χριστός) should also be understood in light of Paul's other "in me" statements in the letter. Paul says that God delighted "to reveal his Son in me [ἐν ἐμοὶ]" (1:16), and that believers in Judea, because of Paul's proclamation of the gospel he once persecuted, "glorified God in me [ἐν ἐμοὶ]" (1:24 NKJV). In both of those verses Paul has echoed Isaiah 49:3, so an additional echo here seems likely.[330] Considered together, these three "in me" passages present a progression: (1) God delights to reveal his Son "in Paul" (1:16); (2) the Judean churches glorify God "in Paul" as a result of this divine purpose (1:24); and (3) the divine purpose of revealing Christ "in Paul" is realized to such an extent that Paul can claim he no longer lives, but Christ lives "in me" (2:20).

---

[329] On the nature of the mystery in Col 1:27, see G. K. Beale and Benjamin L. Gladd, *Hidden But Now Revealed: A Biblical Theology of Mystery* (Downers Grove, IL: IVP, 2014), 200–7.

[330] See further Harmon, *She Must and Shall Go Free*, 100–101.

As if to correct a possible misunderstanding of what he has said, Paul explains that "The life I now live in the body, I live by faith in the Son of God" (ὃ δὲ νῦν ζῶ ἐν σαρκί, ἐν πίστει ζῶ τῇ τοῦ υἱοῦ τοῦ θεου).[331] When he says that he no longer lives but Christ lives in him, Paul does not mean that his unique personhood has disappeared. He continues to live life "in the body" or, perhaps better, "in the flesh" (ἐν σαρκί). Even here when the word σάρξ has the more neutral sense of body, it often (as it likely does here) retains a sense of weakness or limitation.[332] This present evil age is dominated by sin and the flesh, and although in Christ believers have been delivered from its power (1:4), they still live in a world where those powers are active. So Paul lives "by faith in the Son of God." Faith is not only the basis of our justification, but the means by which believers continue to live the Christian life. Whereas earlier Paul spoke of faith in Christ (2:16), here it is faith in the Son of God. The change in titles for Jesus likely anticipates Paul's argument in 3:1–5:1 that through Jesus the Son of God, believers become not only sons of Abraham but sons of God as well.

The combination of the verb "live" (ζάω) and the noun "faith" (πίστις) may signal an allusion to Habakkuk 2:4, where God's people are told that "the righteous one will live by his faith."[333] We have already noted a possible allusion to Habakkuk 2:2–3 in Galatians 2:2, and Paul will directly quote Habakkuk 2:4 later in Galatians 3:11. Paul may use this subtle allusion to stress that he experiences the messianic age—while still living in this fallen world—by faith in the Son of God. As Ciampa notes, "the allusion to Hab 2:4 would fit neatly into the prior statements regarding tearing down and building, death and (resurrection) life, reinforcing the idea that Paul (and all believers in Christ) now lives in the eschatological world of redemption that is on the other side of the death-resurrection divide where the norms of Mosaic law no longer continue to play the same role as they did previously."[334]

Paul further describes the Son of God with two substantival participles that describe what he did for Paul. First, he "loved me" (τοῦ ἀγαπήσαντός με). While Paul frequently writes about Christ's love for his people (e.g., Rom 8:35–39; Eph 5:2; 2 Thess 2:13), what is unusual here

---

[331] This clause is introduced by δέ, which here marks progression in the argument.

[332] See BDAG s.v. σάρξ 2.b. On "flesh" in Galatians, see further Biblical Theology §7.1.2.1.

[333] See Ciampa, Presence and Function, 210–12. He notes that Hab 2:4 is the only place in the LXX where these two terms occur in "close syntactic relationship" (210).

[334] Ciampa, Presence and Function, 212.

is that he personalizes it. Christ's love for Paul is not a generalized love for humanity but a personal love for Paul himself. Yet since Paul is using himself as a paradigm for what is true of all believers (Jew and gentile alike), every believer can say with the apostle Paul that "Christ loved me." Second, Paul says the Son of God "gave himself for me" (παραδόντος ἑαυτὸν ὑπὲρ ἐμοῦ). Paul has already used similar language in 1:4, where he describes Christ as the one "who gave himself for our sins" (τοῦ δόντος ἑαυτὸν ὑπὲρ τῶν ἁμαρτιῶν ἡμῶν). Just as in 1:4, Paul describes the work of Christ in the language of the suffering servant of Isaiah 52:13–53:12.[335] Jesus willingly laid down his life not just in a generalized sense for humanity but specifically for Paul the individual. When combined with Paul's earlier description of his apostolic ministry in language borrowed from Isaiah 49 (see Gal 1:15–16), the picture that emerges is that Jesus Christ the suffering servant of Isaiah 53 dwells in Paul to fulfill the mission of the servant described in Isaiah 49.[336]

So for Paul, what it means to be crucified with Christ is that the old Paul, whose life was ordered and directed by the Mosaic law, no longer lives. Instead, it is the risen Jesus Christ who lives in Paul to empower and animate his new life. His union with the crucified and risen Christ also enables Paul to understand his own suffering as Christ carries forward the mission of the servant in and through him.[337] Paul experiences this reality by faith in Jesus Christ. This is the experience of every believer, not merely the apostle Paul. Our union with Christ is so profound that the moment we are joined to him by faith we die to our old way of life and are raised to a new way of life empowered by the risen Christ through his Spirit dwelling in us.

2:21. Paul now draws to a close his statement to Peter and the Jewish Christians in Antioch with an assertion followed by an explanation in the form of a conditional statement. The assertion is simple and to the point: "I do not set aside the grace of God" (Οὐκ ἀθετῶ τὴν χάριν τοῦ θεοῦ).[338] The verb rendered "set aside" (ἀθετέω) has the sense of rejecting

---

[335] See the notes at 1:4 and further discussion in Harmon, *She Must and Shall Go Free*, 101–2.

[336] See further Biblical Theology §3.0 and Harmon, *She Must and Shall Go Free*, 103–21.

[337] Helpfully noted in John Anthony Dunne, *Persecution and Participation in Galatians*, WUNT 2/454 (Tübingen: Mohr Siebeck, 2017), 148–49.

[338] The lack of a connecting particle in Greek (asyndeton) makes this climactic statement stand out as the conclusion of the argument of 2:15–21.

something as invalid.[339] Thus Jesus rebukes the Pharisees for "invalidating God's command in order to set up your own tradition" (Mark 7:9). Hebrews 10:28 notes that "Anyone who has set aside the law of Moses dies without mercy on the evidence of two or three witnesses" (ESV). Paul will use this same verb later in 3:15 in reference to human covenants not being "set aside" once ratified. By returning to observing the laws that distinguished Jews from gentiles under the Mosaic covenant, Paul would be rejecting the grace of God shown in the new covenant inaugurated by Christ through his death and resurrection.[340]

To further explain how returning to the Mosaic covenant's regulations would nullify the grace of God in the new covenant, Paul uses a first class conditional statement: "if righteousness comes through the law, then Christ died for nothing" (εἰ γὰρ διὰ νόμου δικαιοσύνη, ἄρα Χριστὸς δωρεὰν ἀπέθανεν). The word "righteousness" (δικαιοσύνη) comes from the same word family as the verb "justify" (δικαιόω), used repeatedly in 2:16–17 to refer to God declaring a person not guilty in his court of law.[341] Thus the noun refers to the status that comes from God's declaration. Returning to the law as the governing agent of the Christian life would in effect be claiming that righteousness comes through the law. But as Paul has already argued, "a person is not justified by the works of the law but by faith in Jesus Christ" (2:16). However, if righteousness did in fact come through the law, "Christ died for nothing." Although here the adverb translated "for nothing" (δωρεάν) clearly has the sense of without purpose or in vain, it can also mean freely given.[342] As such there may be a subtle but ironic wordplay between Christ as the one who gave (παραδίδωμι) himself, summarized as the grace of God (a free gift), and Christ dying in vain (δωρεάν).

Paul has pushed the logic of Peter and the Jewish believers in Antioch to its breaking point. If righteousness comes through obeying the Mosaic law (which is what requiring believers to observe the food laws implies),

---

[339] BDAG s.v. ἀθετέω 1.

[340] Another possible way of understanding Paul's claim is that he was being accused of setting aside the grace of God revealed in the Mosaic law. His opponents claimed that, by preaching a "law-free" gospel, Paul was rejecting God's gracious gift of the law (see, e.g., Burton, *Galatians*, 140; Longenecker, *Galatians*, 94; Martyn, *Galatians*, 259–60). Dunn (*Galatians*, 147–48) argues that the grace of God here refers to Paul's apostolic calling; thus Paul is saying that he does not reject God's gracious call on his life to preach the gospel to the gentiles.

[341] On justification and righteousness language, see further Biblical Theology §6.0.

[342] BDAG s.v. δωρεάν 1–3. For use similar to here, see Job 1:9 (LXX) and Ps 35:7 (34:7 LXX).

then God sending his Son to die on the cross was completely unnecessary. How could anyone who claims to be a believer ever think such a thing?

Yet every time we as believers think or act as if there is something that we can do to earn more of God's favor, we are in effect nullifying the grace of God shown through the cross. What Jesus has done through his life, death, and resurrection is not only necessary for our salvation, it is entirely sufficient.

Bridge

The gospel is offensive to human pride because it announces there is nothing a person can do to earn God's favor. By nature, we enter this world dead in our sin (Eph 2:1–3) and as enemies of God (Rom 5:10). But the gospel announces the good news that we can be declared not guilty in God's court of law by virtue of trusting in Jesus Christ and his work on the cross. When we trust in Christ, we share in Christ's death to sin, the law, and the powers of this present evil age. Because we also share in his resurrection, we experience the new creation life as the risen Christ lives in us. Through us the risen Christ continues the mission of the Isaianic servant to bring salvation to the ends of the earth. What an unbelievable blessing it is to have the Son of God who loved us and gave himself for us living inside of us to empower us to please God!

III. Seed of Abraham and Sons of Promise (3:1–5:1)

Satisfied that he has established both that (1) he is an apostle (on the same level as the Jerusalem apostles) who received the gospel directly from Jesus Christ and that (2) he and the Jerusalem leaders agree on justification by faith and not by works of the law, Paul now moves to the central argument of the letter. He must refute the opponents' claim that keeping the Mosaic law is necessary to be a son of Abraham who is justified before God and receives the inheritance God promised to him. The apostle's response is at one level quite simple: those who believe in Christ, regardless of their ethnicity, socioeconomic status, or gender are united to Christ and therefore receive his inheritance as the promised seed of Abraham. But along the way Paul must anticipate and respond to a number of potential objections from his opponents that can seem strange or complicated to modern readers nearly two thousand years removed from the situation. Therefore a summary of the argument will prove helpful.

The argument begins with a sharp contrast between hearing by faith and works of the law (3:1–5). Paul uses this contrast to ask the Galatians both how the Christian life begins and how it continues. For the first time in the letter, the Spirit takes center stage, and Paul summons the Galatians to reflect on their experience of him both at their initial conversion and in their ongoing Christian life. In one sense the remainder of 3:6–5:1 answers this question through an Isaianic and gospel-centered reading of the Abraham story. Paul begins with his thesis: According to the gospel preached to Abraham, Abraham was justified by faith, and those who share his faith (whether Jew or gentile) receive the blessing promised to Abraham, thus becoming his sons (3:6–9). From this thesis Paul explains two corollaries. In the first one (3:10–14), Paul asserts that a curse rests upon all who rely on (works of) the law because no one can fulfill its demands. However, Christ redeemed Jews and gentiles from the curse of the law by becoming a curse, so that those who are "in Christ Jesus" live by faith and receive the promised Spirit by faith. In the second corollary (3:15–18), Paul explains that since the promises made to Abraham came 430 years before the law, they cannot be altered by the law. Christ is the promised seed, and all those who are united to him inherit the promised blessing.

In light of these corollaries that seem to paint the Mosaic law in a negative light, Paul then moves to address a series of objections that he anticipates (3:19–25). God added the law as a temporary institution to deal with/provoke sin until the promised seed of Abraham came, something the Mosaic law was never intended to produce (3:19–20). The Mosaic law is not contrary to God's promises, since it was never intended to give eschatological life, and righteousness has always been based on faith not the law (3:21–22). The law acted as Israel's custodian until Christ came and the promise to Abraham's seed could be given through faith in Christ. Now that Christ has come, the law no longer functions as a custodian (3:23–25). With these potential objections answered, Paul states a provisional summary of his argument to this point (3:26–29). All (whether Jew or gentile, slave or free, male or female) are sons of God by virtue of faith and are incorporated into one body through baptism. Therefore, all who belong to Christ are by default Abraham's descendants, and as a result share in the blessing promised to him.

Paul extends his argument by discussing a third corollary (4:1–7) from his thesis: before we were sons, we were in bondage to the elementals, but Christ redeemed those under the law to inherit sonship and possess the

Spirit. From this corollary the apostle offers two sections of application: (1) why go back to slavery under the elementals by taking up the Mosaic law (4:8–11), and (2) imitate Paul in his freedom from the law and recall their initial love for each other (4:12–20).

The climax of the argument occurs in 4:21–5:1. The fulfillment of the Abrahamic covenant has come in Christ, the promised seed and the suffering servant; through his resurrection the new/heavenly Jerusalem is now bringing forth children (all who belong to Christ by faith) who live in freedom, something the law could never do. In this way the gospel promise made to Abraham that "all the nations will be blessed through you" (Gal 3:8 = Gen 12:3) is being fulfilled.

Paul's central point in this section of the letter, then, is that all (regardless of ethnicity, gender, or socioeconomic status) who believe in Christ, the seed of Abraham and the suffering servant, are justified sons of Abraham who receive the promised inheritance and live in the freedom of the Spirit. As such they should not observe the Mosaic law as a means of regulating their relationship with God or others.

A. A Sharp Contrast: Hearing by Faith or Works of the Law (3:1–5)

> [1] You foolish Galatians! Who has cast a spell on you, before whose eyes Jesus Christ was publicly portrayed as crucified? [2] I only want to learn this from you: Did you receive the Spirit by the works of the law or by believing what you heard? [3] Are you so foolish? After beginning by the Spirit, are you now finishing by the flesh? [4] Did you experience so much for nothing—if in fact it was for nothing? [5] So then, does God give you the Spirit and work miracles among you by your doing the works of the law? Or is it by believing what you heard—

Context

This paragraph marks the beginning of the central theological argument of the letter (3:1–5:1). Paul now begins to unpack the key themes of justification by faith apart from the works of the law that he emphasized in his rebuke of Cephas (2:14–21). The fundamental contrast of hearing with faith or works of the law introduced in this opening paragraph sets the stage for Paul's larger argument regarding the relationship between the promise made to Abraham and Mosaic law covenant. Along the way Paul introduces several key themes that run throughout the argument of 3:1–5:1, such as: (1) the centrality of Jesus' death; (2) the gift of the Spirit as the definitive evidence that a person has been saved; (3) the inadequacy of the law to either establish or maintain a right standing with God; (4) the centrality of faith in Christ for one's initial conversion and ongoing growth in godliness; and (5) the sharp antithesis between the flesh and the Spirit.

Structure

This section is dominated by a series of questions that invite the Galatians to reflect on both their initial conversion and their ongoing experience of the Christian life. The fundamental contrast in this paragraph is between doing the works of the law and believing the gospel message. After an initial rebuke, Paul reminds the Galatians of their vivid encounter with Jesus Christ through Paul's powerful preaching of the gospel (3:1). Paul then asks about their initial reception of the Spirit when they were initially converted—did that come through doing the works of the law or by believing the gospel (3:2)? The remainder of the paragraph focuses on the Galatians' ongoing experience of the Spirit with respect to: (1) their growth in godliness (3:3); (2) their experience of suffering (3:4); and (3) ongoing manifestations of the Spirit, including miracles (3:5). For each of these areas Paul asks whether it is based on doing the works of the law or believing the gospel message. Paul assumes the answer is obvious—believing the gospel message. The central point that Paul makes throughout this introductory paragraph is that both conversion and the ongoing experience of the Christian life is based on believing the gospel message rather than doing what the Mosaic law commands.

3:1. Paul signals his shift from summarizing what he said to Peter and the Jewish Christians in Antioch back to the situation in Galatia by addressing them directly with a stinging rebuke: "You foolish Galatians!" (Ὦ ἀνόητοι Γαλάται).[343] To be foolish (ἀνόητος) is the opposite of being wise (compare Rom 1:14) and highlights a person's lack of true understanding of a situation or matter. Thus Jesus rebukes the disciples on the road to Emmaus for failing to understand the need for the Messiah to suffer by saying, "How foolish [ἀνόητοι] and slow you are to believe all

---

[343] In Greek this expression could more woodenly be rendered "O foolish Galatians" (compare ESV). The use of the word "O" (Ὦ) should "be interpreted against the background of Semitic exclamatory interjections which introduce forceful or impassioned statements, often in the form of questions" (BDF §146.2).

that the prophets have spoken!" (Luke 24:25). Paul is convinced that the
Galatians should know better than to be enticed by the smooth words
of those demanding that obeying the law is necessary for justification
before God.

Paul's astonishment at the situation comes out in the question he
asks: "Who has cast a spell on you?" (τίς ὑμᾶς ἐβάσκανεν).[344] This is the
only occurrence of the verb translated "cast a spell" (βασκαίνω) in the
New Testament, but the concept is present elsewhere. It means "to exert
an evil influence through the eye."[345] Thus it can have the more general
sense of envy (e.g., Deut 28:54–56; Josephus, *Ant.* 10:250, 257; Philo *Flacc.*
1:143). In the ancient world there was widespread fear of the "evil eye,"
the belief that "certain individuals, animals, demons, or gods have the
power of casting an evil spell or causing some malignant effect upon every
object, animate or inanimate, upon which their eye or glance may fall.
Through the power of their eye, which may operate involuntarily as well
as intentionally, such Evil Eye possessors were thought capable of injuring
or destroying the life and health of others, their means of sustenance
and livelihood, their honor and personal fortune."[346] It was common for
people to take measures to protect themselves from the dangers of the
evil eye through various devices (such as amulets) or practices. The departure from Paul's gospel message by the Galatians is so unexpected and
shocking—and so clearly evidence of evil spiritual influence—that he says
it is as if someone has cast the evil eye upon the Galatians.[347]

---

[344] After the question "who hypnotized you?" some manuscripts (C D² K L P Ψ 0278.
33ᶜ. 104. 365. 1175. 1241. 1505. 1881. 2464) also include the phrase "to not obey the truth"
(τῇ ἀληθείᾳ μὴ πείθεσθαι). But Metzger (*Textual Commentary*, 524) is likely correct that this
phrase was copied from 5:7 where it also occurs.

[345] BDAG s.v. βασκαίνω 1.

[346] John H. Elliott, "Paul, Galatians, and the Evil Eye," *CurTM* 17 (1990): 264. Elliott, however, significantly over reads the extent and significance of the "evil eye" background here
in Galatians. By contrast, both Betz (*Galatians*, 131) and Witherington (*Grace in Galatia*, 204)
see in this language a reference to the sophistic rhetoric of the Galatian opponents, but
this seems less likely.

[347] See similarly Moo, *Galatians*, 181. There may also be an echo of Deut 28:53–57, the
only place where βασκαίνω occurs in the canonical books of the LXX; see Susan Eastman,
"The Evil Eye and the Curse of the Law: Galatians 3.1 Revisited," *JSNT* 24 (2001): 69–87. That
passage explains that one of the curses that will fall on the Israelites for disobedience is
that enemies will besiege them to the point that they will eat the flesh of their children.
Eastman links this background to the explicit mention of the curse of the law in 3:10, 14,
arguing that this language portrays Paul's Galatian opponents as those under the curse
of the law trying to inflict a similar curse on their "children in the faith," the Galatians.

Paul's astonishment is all the greater because the Galatians are people "before whose eyes Jesus Christ was publicly portrayed as crucified" (οἷς κατ' ὀφθαλμοὺς Ἰησοῦς Χριστὸς προεγράφη ἐσταυρωμένος).[348] Although the verb rendered "publicly portrayed" (προγράφω) normally has the sense of "written beforehand," here it has the sense of "to set forth for public notice."[349] Through Paul's powerful preaching, Jesus Christ was portrayed as "crucified."[350] Chrysostom notes that in saying "publicly portrayed as crucified," Paul is "showing that with the eyes of faith they saw more accurately than those who were there and witnessed the events."[351] Because God revealed his Son in Paul (1:15–16) and because the risen Christ lives inside of Paul (2:20), Paul is able to preach the crucifixion in such a compelling, beautiful, and glorious way that those who saw him preach in effect saw Christ crucified before their very eyes.[352]

By mentioning the crucifixion, Paul points back to the foundation of the gospel. The inadequacy of the Mosaic law to produce righteousness/ justification is demonstrated by the need for Christ to suffer such a humiliating death for our sins. While Paul has already indirectly referred to the cross (1:4; 2:20), this explicit reference to it anticipates 3:13, where Paul identifies the cross as the means by which Christ bears the curse that our disobedience to God warranted.

Paul's focus on the cross is not surprising. As he writes to the Corinthians, "I decided to know nothing among you except Jesus Christ and him crucified" (1 Cor 2:2). This does not mean that Paul refused to talk about anything except the crucifixion of Jesus. As elsewhere, Paul uses crucifixion as synecdoche for the totality of Christ's redemptive work. But it does mean that everything Paul did proclaim was grounded

---

[348] Eastman ("Evil Eye," 72), based on seeing Paul alluding to Deut 28:53–57, argues that "Christ crucified is presented here not merely as the antidote to the evil eye, but as the antidote to the curse of which the evil eye is but one manifestation. Just as amulets absorb the harmful power of the eye's hostile gaze, so Christ on the cross absorbs the harmful power of the curse."

[349] BDAG s.v. προγράφω 2. The other three NT occurrences have the sense of "written beforehand" (Rom 15:4; Eph 3:3; Jude 4). But the sense of "publicly displayed or proclaimed" is well attested in Greek literature; see the examples noted in *TDNT* 1:771 and *MM* 538.

[350] The perfect tense of the participle (ἐσταυρωμένος) draws out the stative force; through his preaching, Paul portrayed Jesus Christ as the crucified one. For all eternity he is and will be the crucified one.

[351] Cited from Mark J. Edwards, *Galatians, Ephesians, Philippians*, ACCS 8 (Downers Grove, IL: IVP, 2005), 34.

[352] See similarly Das, *Galatians*, 287.

in the cross of Christ: what Christians should believe, think, feel, and do. As followers of Christ, we should be no different today.

3:2. In an effort to set up the argument that follows, Paul states: "I only want to learn this from you" (τοῦτο μόνον θέλω μαθεῖν ἀφ' ὑμῶν). The apostle cuts through the fog created by his opponents in Galatia and invites the Galatians to consider the following question: "Did you receive the Spirit by the works of the law or by believing what you heard?" (ἐξ ἔργων νόμου τὸ πνεῦμα ἐλάβετε ἢ ἐξ ἀκοῆς πίστεως). Notice that Paul does not question whether the Galatians received the Spirit. He witnessed firsthand the evidence of the Spirit's work in and among the Galatians. As a result of Paul's preaching in Pisidian Antioch, "the disciples were filled with joy and the Holy Spirit" (Acts 13:52). For Paul, the Spirit was the definitive evidence that a person had come to know Christ (Rom 8:9–11) and the defining blessing of the messianic age (Eph 1:13–14; see Isa 32:15–20; 44:3–5; Ezek 36:26–27). As James Dunn aptly notes, "Since God had thus united them to his eschatological people, on whom the Spirit had been poured (e.g., Isa 32:15; Ezek 37:4–14; Joel 2:28–29), nothing more than that common participation in the Spirit was necessary for them formally to be recognized as part of that people (cf. Acts 2:47–48)."[353] Given the focus on justification in the previous section (2:15–21), it may seem unexpected to refer to receiving the Spirit. But Paul mentions the Holy Spirit at key points in the argument that stretches from 3:1–5:1, which eventually leads into a more specific discussion of the work of the Spirit in 5:16–26.[354]

In his question, Paul contrasts two proposed human means or grounds for receiving the Spirit.[355] The first is "by works of the law" (ἐξ ἔργων νόμου), an expression repeated from 2:16; as noted there, the phrase means doing what the Mosaic law commands. Just as the works of the law

---

[353] Dunn, *Galatians*, 153–54.

[354] On the person and work of the Holy Spirit in Galatians, see further Biblical Theology §2.3.

[355] In Greek, both "by works of the law" (ἐξ ἔργων νόμου) and "by believing what you heard" (ἐξ ἀκοῆς πίστεως) are introduced with the preposition ἐκ, which can express either how one does something or the basis for doing it (BDAG s.v. ἐκ 3.e). In this case, the difference is negligible at best. Instead of seeing a contrast between two different human responses, some commentators argue for a contrast between a human and a divine action; see, e.g., Betz, *Galatians*, 132; Richard B. Hays, *The Faith of Jesus Christ: The Narrative Substructure of Galatians 3:1–4:11*, 2nd ed. (Grand Rapids: Eerdmans, 2002), 124–32; Martyn, *Galatians*, 286–89. But this conclusion depends on interpreting the expression ἀκοῆς πίστεως along the lines of "proclamation that produces faith," which in our view is unlikely (see discussion above).

were not the basis for justification, Paul implies here that they are also inadequate for receiving the Spirit. The opponents may have been making an argument similar to that found in *Jubilees* 1:23–24, which connects the gift of the Holy Spirit with a renewed obedience to the law (likely echoing Ezek 11:19–20).[356] The problem with such an argument is assuming that the law in view is the Mosaic law; for Paul, the law that governs the Christian life is the law of Christ (Gal 6:2).

The other possible means/grounds is "believing what you heard" (ἐξ ἀκοῆς πίστεως). The underlying Greek expression can be translated a variety of different ways, depending on whether ἀκοή and/or πίστις are understood as active or passive in meaning and the kind of genitive relationship between the two words.[357] Thus ἀκοή can refer to the act of hearing or the content (i.e., message) of what is heard, while πίστις can mean faith/trust in something or that which is believed. But based on a likely allusion to Isaiah 53:1 and a parallel usage in Romans 10:14–17, this difficult phrase should be understood as "hearing with faith" or "believing what you heard."

In Isaiah 53:1, the prophet asks, "Who has believed what we have heard?" in response to the people's rejection of the message God has spoken through Isaiah.[358] That message centers on the suffering servant who bears the sins of his people by offering his life as a sacrifice, is vindicated by God, and justifies the many (Isa 53:4–12). Reflecting on people's rejection of the gospel message, Paul asks Isaiah's question in Romans 10:16. In response, Paul writes in Romans 10:17, "So faith [πίστις] comes from hearing [ἐξ ἀκοῆς], and hearing [ἀκοή] through the word of Christ" (ESV). Together the allusion to Isaiah 53:1 and the parallel in Romans 10:16–17 suggest that the phrase is best understood as "on the basis of hearing accompanied by faith." Thus, "Paul has transformed Isaiah's question into an affirmation of the proper way to respond to God's self-revelation in Christ."[359]

---

[356] Helpfully noted by de Boer, *Galatians*, 181 and Das, *Galatians*, 281.

[357] For a fuller discussion, see Harmon, *She Must and Shall Go Free*, 127–32 and the concise summary in DeSilva, *Handbook*, 53–54.

[358] In the LXX the verb rendered "believed" is πιστεύω (which is part of the same word family as πίστις), while the phrase "what we have heard" renders the noun ἀκοή. There are no occurrences of ἀκοή and πίστις together in the LXX, and this is the only occurrence of πιστεύω and ἀκοή together.

[359] Harmon, *She Must and Shall Go Free*, 132. This allusion also anticipates Paul's sustained engagement with Isaiah 51–54 in Galatians 3:1–5:1.

The way that Paul frames the question makes it clear that the correct answer to his question of how the Galatians received the Spirit is "by hearing with faith."[360] But the hearing in view is not merely the physiological process of sound entering the ears; it "conveys something of the connotation of the equivalent Hebrew word: faithful receptivity, an 'attentiveness' to the word of God that includes both trust in its content and giver and the disposition to obey."[361] Just as their justification came through believing in Jesus Christ, so too their receiving of God's Spirit came through hearing the gospel message and believing in Christ.

As present-day Christians, it can be easy for us to lose the wonder of God sending his Spirit to dwell inside us. Before the arrival of Christ and the inauguration of the new covenant, the Spirit only came upon key individuals within redemptive history such as kings, prophets, and priests.[362] But under the new covenant—just as God had promised (Ezek 36:27)—every believer experiences the indwelling of the Holy Spirit. What an inestimable gift!

3:3. Paul now repeats his initial rebuke by asking, "Are you so foolish?" (οὕτως ἀνόητοί ἐστε).[363] The question that follows reveals how the Galatians are being foolish: "After beginning by the Spirit, are you now finishing by the flesh?" (ἐναρξάμενοι πνεύματι νῦν σαρκὶ ἐπιτελεῖσθε). Andrew Das notes the chiastic structure of this question:[364]

A   After beginning [ἐναρξάμενοι]
   B   by the Spirit [πνεύματι]
      C   now [νῦν]
   B′   by the flesh [σαρκὶ]
A′   are you finishing [ἐπιτελεῖσθε]

The expression "beginning by the Spirit" points to the believer's conversion. The Christian life begins when the Spirit makes a person spiritually

---

[360] So similarly Schreiner, *Galatians*, 183 and Moo (*Galatians*, 183), who notes this conclusion is confirmed by the close connection Paul makes between the believer's faith and Abraham's faith.

[361] Moo, *Galatians*, 183.

[362] For a helpful study on this subject, see James M. Hamilton Jr., *God's Indwelling Presence: The Holy Spirit in the Old & New Testaments* (Nashville: B&H, 2006), 1–56.

[363] Although most English translations render this as a question, this initial clause could also be understood as a statement ("This is how you are foolish"), with the remainder of the sentence understood as a question.

[364] Das, *Galatians*, 293–94; see similarly DeSilva (*Handbook*, 55).

alive (Titus 3:4–7); thus the Spirit is the agent/means by which believers begin the Christian life.[365] After this promising start, however, Paul charges the Galatians with now "finishing by the flesh" (νῦν σαρκὶ ἐπιτελεῖσθε). As used here the verb rendered "finishing" (ἐπιτελέω) has the sense of completing a task, process, or goal.[366] The present tense of the verb portrays the action as ongoing.[367] The means by which they are trying to complete the Christian life is the flesh, a term that here has the negative sense of human nature under the power and control of sin and subject to the spiritual forces of evil in this fallen world.[368] The contrast between the Spirit and the flesh also anticipates later points in the letter (4:29; 5:16–26). The problem with works of the law is not merely that they are rooted in a period of redemptive history that has now ended (i.e., the Mosaic law covenant), but that they are rooted in doing rather than believing (see 3:10–14).[369]

Thus, by pursuing growth in the Christian life through observing the Mosaic regulations regarding circumcision and dietary restrictions, the Galatians are turning their backs on the only one able to empower them for the Christian life—the Holy Spirit. Paul makes a similar point in Philippians 1:6, when he expresses his confidence that "he who started [ἐναρξάμενος] a good work in you will carry it on to completion [ἐπιτελέσει] until the day of Christ Jesus." The Christian life is not something that God simply begins and then expects people to live in their own power and strength. Both the believer's justification and sanctification

---

[365] While Wallace (*Greek Grammar*, 165–66) argues for a distinction between dative of means and dative of agency, Porter (*Idioms of the Greek New Testament*, 98–99) is likely correct that "it is difficult to establish a specific difference in most instances. They all label a relationship by which (normally) a thing (and occasionally a person) brings about or enters into an action with respect to something else."

[366] BDAG s.v. ἐπιτελέω 1. Seven of the ten NT occurrences are in Paul (Rom 15:28; 2 Cor 7:1; 8:6, 11–12; Gal 3:3; Phil 1:6; Heb 8:5; 9:6; 1 Pet 5:9).

[367] By form, the verb ἐπιτελεῖσθε could either be middle or passive. If it is middle the sense could be "are you now going to make yourself complete by the flesh." If instead it is passive, the sense is "are you now going to be completed by the flesh." The difference is that the middle voice might suggest more active participation by the subject, while the passive would highlight the subject being acted upon. On the whole the middle seems slightly more likely (similarly Moo, *Galatians*, 184).

[368] Given that circumcision is the cutting away of the flesh, Paul may again be engaging in a subtle play on words here. This possibility is furthered by the fact that some Jewish authors (see, e.g., 1QS 5:4–5) in Paul's day viewed circumcision "as the antidote to the evil inclination" (Das, *Galatians*, 294).

[369] As rightly noted by Moo, *Galatians*, 185.

are based on faith in Christ and enabled by the Spirit. Does your life reflect that reality? Or does your everyday life subtly reflect that your growth in godliness depends on your performance?

3:4. Paul now appeals to the experience of the Galatian believers since their profession of faith and their reception of the Spirit: "Did you experience so much for nothing—if in fact it was for nothing?" (τοσαῦτα ἐπάθετε εἰκῇ; εἴ γε καὶ εἰκῇ). Other translations, however, render the first part of this verse "Have you suffered so much in vain?" (NIV1984). At issue is how to translate the verb πάσχω, which usually has the sense of suffer.[370] But the lack of references to suffering in the rest of the letter and the immediate context of discussing the Galatians' experience of the Holy Spirit lead some scholars to understand the verb in the neutral sense of experience—a sense that is well attested in Greek literature outside the LXX/New Testament.[371] But all things considered, suffer makes better sense.[372] First, Paul at least hints in 4:29 that just as Ishmael ("born as a result of the flesh") persecuted Isaac ("born as a result of the Spirit"), so also the Galatians are experiencing persecution. Second, the universal use of πάσχω elsewhere in the New Testament (42 times!) with the meaning "suffer" makes it likely to have the same meaning here. Third, Paul elsewhere connects the believer's experience of the Spirit (Rom 8:12–17) and suffering (Rom 8:18–25) as we await the consummation of God's promises.[373] Fourth, Paul has just made two references in the immediate context to the crucifixion of Christ (2:20; 3:1), the ultimate act of suffering, and used it

---

[370] See BDAG s.v. πάσχω 3, which notes that, with the possible exceptions of here and Matthew 17:15, this verb "in all other places, as always in LXX, in an unfavorable sense suffer, endure." For a helpful overview of the history of interpretation, see John Anthony Dunne, "Suffering in Vain: A Study of the Interpretation of Πάσχω in Galatians 3.4," *JSNT* 36 (2013): 3–16.

[371] For this view see, e.g., Fee, *God's Empowering Presence*, 386–87. For examples of the neutral meaning of experience in Greek literature, see the examples in BDAG s.v. πάσχω 1 and LSJM s.v. πάσχω. One of the stronger arguments for this neutral sense is the observation by Betz (*Galatians*, 134) that πάσχω was used in tandem with μανθάνω (cf. 3:2) in Greek thought to refer to learning and experiencing. But Witherington (*Grace in Galatia*, 215) notes that this same pair occurs in Heb 5:8 (the only other NT occurrence), and πάσχω clearly has the sense of suffer there.

[372] This is a change from what I concluded in Harmon, *She Must and Shall Go Free*, 132–33. What follows is adapted largely from Dunne, "Suffering in Vain," 7–10; for a subsequent expansion of these arguments, see Dunne, *Persecution and Participation*, 69–78.

[373] Note that the Spirit crying "Abba, Father!" appears in both Rom 8:15 and Gal 4:6, which further cements the connection.

as a paradigm for the Christian life.[374] Finally, Paul experienced suffering as he established the Galatian churches (Acts 14:5–6, 19), and he even warned these believers, "It is necessary to go through many hardships to enter the kingdom of God" (Acts 14:22).

So Paul asks the Galatians whether their suffering for the sake of Christ has been "for nothing—if in fact it was for nothing?" If they abandon dependence on the Spirit and instead rely on the flesh (by trying to keep the Mosaic law), the Galatians' suffering for the sake of Christ will have been pointless. Paul expects the Galatians to answer, "Of course not!"

As believers, instead of considering suffering unusual, we should expect it. Elsewhere Paul wrote that "all who want to live a godly life in Christ Jesus will be persecuted" (2 Tim 3:12). He even goes so far as to call suffering for the sake of Christ a gift (Phil 1:29). Part of the role of a ministry leader is to prepare believers to suffer in a way that shows that Jesus is our greatest treasure.

3:5. Paul draws a logical inference from his line of questioning with one final question.[375] But instead of focusing on the Galatians' reception of the Spirit, Paul shifts to the identity of the one who gave them the Spirit. He uses two substantival participles to describe God. First, he is the one "who supplies the Spirit to you" (ESV) (ὁ οὖν ἐπιχορηγῶν ὑμῖν τὸ πνεῦμα). The verb "supply" (ἐπιχορηγέω) highlights the act of supplying as a gift, and in the larger Greco-Roman world it was often used in the context of generous public service.[376] Although the verb is rare in the New Testament (2 Cor 9:10; Gal 3:5; Col 2:19; 2 Pet 1:5, 11), Paul uses a related noun (ἐπιχορηγία) in Philippians 1:19 to refer to God supplying Paul with the Spirit to enable him to endure his present suffering. The present tense of the verb here suggests a continual provision of the Spirit. God's generosity to his people is seen in his generous and ongoing provision of his Spirit. Second, God is the one who "works miracles among you" (ESV) (ἐνεργῶν δυνάμεις ἐν ὑμῖν). Paul uses the same verb (ἐνεργέω) as in 2:8, where it referred to God working powerfully through both Peter and Paul in their respective apostolic ministries. Here God is working "miracles" (δύναμις) among the Galatians; although the noun has the general sense of power, here (like many places in the Gospels) it refers to miracles or

---

[374] Oakes, *Galatians*, 104.

[375] That is the force of the particle οὖν (so also DeSilva, *Handbook*, 56).

[376] BDAG s.v. ἐπιχορηγέω. The verb is also found in marriage contracts describing the husband's responsibility to provide for his wife (*MM*, 251).

wonders. While Paul does not specify the exact nature of these miracles, they were sufficient to demonstrate their divine origin.[377]

Paul's question, then, is whether God supplies the Spirit to his people and works his miracles "by your doing the works of the law" or "by believing what you heard" (ἐξ ἔργων νόμου ἢ ἐξ ἀκοῆς πίστεως). Whereas in 3:2 Paul used this contrast to ask on what grounds one receives the Spirit, here he uses it to ask on what basis the Galatians continue to experience the powerful work of the Spirit in their lives. His implied point is that believers continue to experience the Holy Spirit on the same basis as they received him—hearing the gospel message with faith, and not works of the law. Since that is the case, why would one want or need to obey the Mosaic law?

How gracious of God to not only give the Spirit to his people, but to continually supply fresh measures of his Spirit. What a comfort to know that no matter what challenges we face as believers, God is eager to meet our needs through his Spirit working in and through us.

Bridge

Today's church is awash in books and seminars that promise the key to the Christian life is found in three keys, five steps, or seven principles. And while there may be helpful elements of such books, they can easily give the impression that ongoing faith in Christ and walking in the power of the Spirit are insufficient. But Paul makes it clear that faith in Christ not only initiates the Christian life but is also the ongoing means by which we live the Christian life.

B. The Gospel Preached Beforehand to Abraham (3:6–9)

⁶just like Abraham who believed God, and it was credited to him for righteousness?

⁷You know, then, that those who have faith, these are Abraham's sons. ⁸Now the Scripture saw in advance that God would justify the Gentiles by faith and proclaimed the gospel ahead of time to Abraham, saying,

---

[377] In light of the echoes of Isa 53:1 within the context, William Wilder suggests that Paul views these miracles as evidence that the promised Isaianic new exodus has taken place through Christ; see William N. Wilder, "'To Whom Has the Arm of the Lord Been Revealed?' Signs and Wonders in Paul's Isaianic Mission to the Gentiles (Romans 15:18–21 and Galatians 3:1–5)," in *The Crucified Apostle: Essays on Peter and Paul*, ed. Todd A. Wilson and Paul R. House (Tübingen: Mohr Siebeck, 2017), 239–44.

All the nations will be blessed through you. ⁹ Consequently those who have faith are blessed with Abraham, who had faith.

Context

This paragraph introduces and summarizes the thesis statement of the argument of 3:1–5:1. The main themes of that argument (3:1–5:1) are now laid out: one's status as a true son of Abraham rests on faith, and all who have the same kind of faith in God and his promises receive the blessing that God promised to Abraham. Each of the key terms in this thesis—faith/believe, sons of Abraham, justification/righteousness, inclusion of the gentiles within God's plan, blessing, and Scripture announcing these realities in advance—are unpacked in the course of the argument.

Structure

Although in one sense verse 6 continues the thought of the previous paragraph, its central role introducing the thesis statement (3:6–9) for the entire argument (3:1–5:1) warrants grouping it with this paragraph. Paul begins by citing Genesis 15:6, a text that establishes the centrality of Abraham's faith as the basis for his right standing before God (3:6). The apostle then draws a conclusion from Genesis 15:6—those who believe like Abraham did are the true sons of Abraham (3:7). Paul explains that this truth was foreseen in Scripture, which announced the good news of justification by faith in the promise (found in Gen 12:3) that in Abraham God would bless all the nations (3:8). The paragraph ends with a restatement of the conclusion of 3:7, but in the language of the promise from Genesis 12:3 stated in the previous verse: all who believe are blessed along with Abraham (3:9).

3:6. This verse is a hinge that connects Paul's assertion that believers received and continue to experience the Holy Spirit not on the basis of obeying the Mosaic law but rather by hearing the gospel with faith (3:1–5) with his extended argument about who the true sons of Abraham are (3:6–5:1). "Just like" (Καθὼς)[378] believers receive and experience the

---

[378] The force of καθώς as used here is debated. Some conclude that it is an abbreviation of Paul's frequently used expression καθὼς γέγραπται to introduce scriptural citations (Rom 1:17; 2:24; 3:4, 10; 4:17; 8:36; 9:13, 33; 10:15; 11:8, 26; 15:3, 9, 21; 1 Cor 1:31; 2:9; 10:7; 2 Cor 8:15; 9:3); see, e.g., Longenecker, *Galatians*, 112; Dunn, *Galatians*, 160; Hays, *Faith of Jesus*, 169–70. But the usual comparative force makes more sense here, linking the experience of the Galatians with Abraham (so also Moo, *Galatians*, 187).

Spirit on the basis of faith, "Abraham ... believed God, and it was credited to him for righteousness" (Ἀβραὰμ ἐπίστευσεν τῷ θεῷ, καὶ ἐλογίσθη αὐτῷ εἰς δικαιοσύνην).[379] This quote from Genesis 15:6 sets the stage for what follows, so a good grasp of the original context is important for understanding why Paul quotes it and what it means in the context of Galatians 3:6–5:1.

While Abram was living in Ur of the Chaldeans, God promised to bless him and eventually through him bless all the nations of the earth (Gen 12:1–3). That blessing would come through making Abram and his descendants into a great nation. But as the years passed, Sarai his wife remained barren, calling the promise into question. One day when Yahweh appeared to Abram, Abram complained that because he was childless, one of his servants was his heir (Gen 15:1–3). Yahweh responded by assuring Abram that his heir would come from his own body (Gen 15:4), and then directed Abram's attention to the sky, promising that his descendants would be as numerous as the stars (Gen 15:5). In response Abraham "believed the Lord, and he credited it to him as righteousness." Yahweh then affirmed his covenant with Abram by promising to give the land to his descendants, though only after they were afflicted for four hundred years (Gen 15:7–21). Thus God declared Abram righteous on the basis of his faith in the Lord and his trust that the Lord would fulfill his promise.

This statement that God declared Abram righteous on the basis of his faith was a fundamental tenet in Paul's understanding of God's plan for human history. Within the Old Testament itself, the promises that God made to Abram set the trajectory for the entire history of Israel and established a reference point for what God promised to do for all humanity. As a result, Second Temple Jewish writers often referred back to these promises as a sure foundation for their continued hope that God would restore the fortunes of his people.[380] One of the fundamental disagreements between Paul and his opponents in Galatia was the proper way to understand the relationship between what God had promised Abram and what Jesus Christ had accomplished through his life, death, and resurrection. Therefore in 3:6–5:1 Paul lays out his understanding

---

[379] For a helpful summary of the textual issues involved with this citation and its relationship to the LXX and MT, see Moo, *Galatians*, 189–91.

[380] For a summary of how Abraham was discussed within Second Temple Judaism, see Biblical Theology §1.1.2.

of how Jesus has fulfilled the Abrahamic covenant and the ramifications
of that fulfillment in Christ for Jew and gentile alike.[381]

So when Paul quotes Genesis 15:6, he is establishing the foundation for
his extended argument (3:6–5:1). He picks up language from 2:16, where
the relationship between righteousness/justification and faith was set
out. Besides introducing Abraham into the discussion, the other new
wrinkle is the language of faith/believing being "credited" to Abraham
as righteousness. The verb Paul uses (λογίζομαι) comes from the financial
realm, where one thing (in this case "faith") is credited to someone as
something else (in this case "righteousness").[382] His regular use of this
verb in discussing faith and righteousness (eleven times in Romans 4
alone!) may stem from Isaiah 53:11–12, where the suffering servant justifies (LXX δικαιόω) many and yet is numbered (LXX λογίζομαι) among
transgressors. This possibility is further strengthened by Paul's repeated
use of Isaiah in Galatians, and especially Isaiah 51–54 in Galatians 3:1–5:1.

Abraham believed God would fulfill his promise even though on a
human level it seemed impossible. Despite his old age and his wife's barrenness, "He did not waver in unbelief at God's promise but was strengthened in his faith and gave glory to God, because he was fully convinced
that what God had promised, he was also able to do" (Rom 4:20–21). As
a result, he is not only a model of initial saving faith, but ongoing persevering faith that sustains us in the midst of life's difficulties.

3:7. From his citation of Genesis 15:6, Paul draws an initial conclusion: "You know, then, that those who have faith, these are Abraham's
sons" (γινώσκετε ἄρα ὅτι οἱ ἐκ πίστεως, οὗτοι υἱοί εἰσιν Ἀβραάμ).[383] The
expression "those who have faith" (οἱ ἐκ πίστεως) is worded to parallel the expressions "by faith in Jesus Christ" (ἐκ πίστεως Χριστοῦ) in

---

[381] For more on Paul's understanding of the Abrahamic covenant, see further Biblical Theology §1.1.3.

[382] See examples in Moises Silva, "λογίζομαι," *NIDNTTE* 3:123–24.

[383] This clause is introduced with ἄρα, which indicates "an inference made on the basis of what precedes" (BDAG s.v. ἄρα 1.a). By form the verb rendered "you know" (γινώσκετε) could either be indicative or imperative. If it is indicative, Paul is stating something he believes the Galatians already know/understand. As an imperative, Paul would be command-ing the Galatians to understand his point, leaving open whether he believed the Galatians already knew the point or not. A decision is difficult and makes almost no difference in the argument, but an imperative makes slightly better sense (so also Moo, *Galatians*, 196–97). Longenecker (*Galatians*, 114) disagrees, claiming that "γινώσκετε ἄρα ὅτι is a typical dis-closure formula in ancient Hellenistic letters that serves more to remind readers of what is known than to exhort."

2:16 and "by believing what you heard" (ἐξ ἀκοῆς πίστεως) in 3:2, 5. By "those who have faith" Paul means those whose lives are characterized and directed by faith in Jesus Christ, not works of the law performed in the flesh. These are the ones whom Paul has already said are justified (2:16), have received the Holy Spirit (3:2), and continue to experience his miracle-working power in their lives (3:5).

It is these "by faith" people who are Abraham's sons.[384] On one level Paul appears to be using the common Semitic idiom whereby a person is referred to as a son of someone or something to indicate that the person shares a characteristic of that person, idea, or thing to a significant degree.[385] But the sonship language goes well beyond that here in Galatians. In fact, the entire argument of 3:6–5:1 could be summarized as answering the question "who are the true sons of Abraham?" The starting point for Paul's answer is that those who believe as Abraham did receive the same response from God: they are justified and regarded as true sons of Abraham. Although we cannot be certain, it seems likely that Paul's opponents in Galatians claimed that in order for gentile believers to be considered true sons of Abraham, they needed to be circumcised and observe the requirements of the Mosaic law. In response to this claim, Paul asserts that faith in Christ is sufficient to be granted the status of "sons of Abraham."

The defining mark of a true Christian is not attending church, reading the Bible, praying, or helping the poor. All these good things can be done by an unbeliever. What ultimately makes a person a son of Abraham is faith—faith in Christ and his promises. From that foundation everything proceeds.

3:8. Establishing that being a son of Abraham rests on faith in Christ is not enough for Paul; he must also establish that one's identity as a true son of Abraham does not depend on ethnicity. After all, John the Baptist rebuked Jews who believed they were sons of Abraham simply because

---

[384] The title "son of Abraham" refers to male and female believers alike, so some translations (e.g., NIV, NLT) render the phrase "children of Abraham." But such a translation obscures the "sonship" theme that runs throughout Galatians and prevents the English reader from connecting the believers' status as sons of Abraham (3:7; 4:21–5:1) and sons of God (3:26; 4:6–7) with Jesus' identity as the Son of God (1:16; 2:20; 4:4–6); see further Biblical Theology §7.2.1.1.

[385] Cf. BDAG s.v. υἱός 3.c.α and Maximilian Zerwick, *Biblical Greek: Illustrated by Examples* (Roma: Pontifical Biblical Institute, 1963), 15.

of their ethnicity when he said, "And don't presume to say to yourselves, 'We have Abraham as our father.' For I tell you that God is able to raise up children for Abraham from these stones!" (Matt 3:9). Jesus also rejected the Jewish leaders' claim to be sons of Abraham while at the same time rejecting him (John 8:53–58). Therefore, Paul must establish that one's status as a son of Abraham transcends ethnicity, and that this has been God's purpose from the very beginning. So Paul advances the argument by asserting that "Scripture saw in advance that God would justify the Gentiles by faith" (προϊδοῦσα δὲ ἡ γραφὴ ὅτι ἐκ πίστεως δικαιοῖ τὰ ἔθνη ὁ θεός).[386] Paul calls Scripture as his star witness in his case to prove that gentiles who trust in Jesus Christ are full-blooded sons of Abraham. The verb rendered "saw in advance" (προοράω) also occurs in Acts 2:31 to describe David as a prophet who saw in advance the resurrection of Jesus. Paul personifies Scripture as gazing down the corridors of the future envisioning what God would do in Paul's day.[387] What Scripture saw in advance was that "God would justify the Gentiles by faith."

Because it saw in advance that God would justify gentiles by faith,[388] Scripture "proclaimed the gospel ahead of time to Abraham" (προευηγγελίσατο τῷ Ἀβραὰμ). Paul uses another word from the "gospel" word group (προευαγγελίζομαι) to link what Scripture says with his own apostolic ministry of preaching the gospel to the gentiles (1:12–17; 2:2, 7–9) and contrast it with the "other gospel" that his opponents are preaching (1:6–9).[389] By choosing this verb, Paul "signal[s] simultaneously the *historical* priority of the announcement to Abraham and the

---

[386] Thus the δέ that begins this verse signals a further development in the argument, marking "a new stage in the argument" (Moo, *Galatians*, 198). Moo goes on to note that γραφή in this first clause is a general reference to the broad teaching of the OT, with the citation of Gen 12:3 offered as one specific example.

[387] Betz (*Galatians*, 143n42) notes several Second Temple Jewish texts that personify Scripture, such as Philo, *Leg.* 3:118 and *Contempl.* 1:78.

[388] In Greek the clause translated "Now the Scripture saw in advance that God would justify the Gentiles by faith" begins with an adverbial participle (προϊδοῦσα) that is best understood as causal (so also DeSilva, *Handbook*, 58). Thus this phrase gives the reason Scripture "told the good news ahead of time to Abraham." By contrast, Moo (*Galatians*, 198–99) sees the participial indicating identical action, meaning that it repeats the action of the main clause. The difference in meaning is insignificant.

[389] This is the only occurrence of προευαγγελίζομαι in the NT or LXX. This rare verb does occur three times in Philo (*Opif.* 1:34; *Mut.* 1:158; *Abr.* 1:153), and there are a handful of examples in Greek literature (see examples in BDAG s.v. προευαγγελίζομαι and LSJM s.v. προευαγγελίζομαι).

hermeneutical priority of the Christ-event."[390] Paul summarizes the gospel message that Scripture proclaimed in advance as God's words to Abraham: "All the nations will be blessed through you" (ἐνευλογηθήσονται ἐν σοὶ πάντα τὰ ἔθνη).[391] Paul appears to combine language from three texts in Genesis (12:3; 18:18; 22:18) to summarize Scripture's advanced proclamation of the gospel.[392] A brief look at these three texts will shed light on the apostle's argument here in Galatians.

Genesis 12:1–3 is the initial and foundational promise that God made to Abram. These promises can be grouped into the three broad categories of people, place, and presence.[393] God will bless Abram with land and a line of descendants to possess that land. After promising to bless those who bless Abram and curse those who curse him, God concludes by saying: "all the peoples on earth will be blessed through you" (Gen 12:3). God blessing Abram is not an end to itself, but a means to bless the world. Genesis 18:18 is one of several restatements of God's initial promise; this one occurs in

---

[390] Barclay, *Paul and the Gift*, 415.

[391] Or, "all the nations will be blessed in you" (compare ESV, NASB, KJV, NKJV, NET). The question is whether the prepositional phrase ἐν σοὶ has an associative sense ("with"), locative force ("in"), or an instrumental sense ("by, through"). The underlying Hebrew expression (בְּךָ) allows for all three senses, but the context here in Galatians seems to eliminate the instrumental sense. In favor of the associative sense is the following verse, where Paul seems to interpret the "in you" (ἐν σοὶ) from Gen 12:3 with the phrase "with you" (σὺν ... Ἀβραάμ). But the locative sense should not be ruled out, as later in Gal 3:14 Paul speaks of the blessing of Abraham coming to the gentiles "in Christ Jesus" (ἐν Χριστῷ Ἰησοῦ), though the CSB renders this phrase "by Christ Jesus" (see discussion at 3:14). Richard Hays (*Faith of Jesus*, 173–77) argues that Paul has in view here Abraham's faithfulness to Yahweh as the grounds of God's blessing of justification coming to the gentiles. But Schreiner (*Galatians*, 194) notes that the verb πιστεύω in 3:6 emphasizes Abraham's trust/faith, not his faithfulness, and Paul seems to clearly interpret "in you" (ἐν σοὶ) from Gen 12:3 with the phrase "with you" (σὺν ... Ἀβραάμ) in the next verse.

[392] These three texts each state God's promise, though with slightly different language. Genesis 12:3 (LXX) reads ἐνευλογηθήσονται ἐν σοὶ πᾶσαι αἱ φυλαὶ τῆς γῆς ("in you all the tribes of the earth will be blessed"), while Genesis 18:18 (LXX) states ἐνευλογηθήσονται ἐν αὐτῷ πάντα τὰ ἔθνη τῆς γῆς ("in him all the nations of the earth will be blessed"). Genesis 22:18 (LXX) reads καὶ ἐνευλογηθήσονται ἐν τῷ σπέρματί σου πάντα τὰ ἔθνη τῆς γῆς ("in your offspring all the nations of the earth will be blessed"). It appears that Paul is largely following Genesis 12:3 but has borrowed the phrase "all the nations" (πάντα τὰ ἔθνη) from either Gen 18:18 or 22:18 to include the word ἔθνος, which can mean either nation or gentile. For a helpful comparison of the possible texts in view, see Moo, *Galatians*, 218.

[393] This is a modified version of the helpful summary in Stephen G. Dempster, *Dominion and Dynasty: A Biblical Theology of the Hebrew Bible*, NSBT 15 (Downers Grove, IL: IVP, 2003), 75–85. See further Matthew S. Harmon, *Rebels and Exiles: A Biblical Theology of Sin and Restoration*, ESBT (Downers Grove, IL: IVP Academic, 2020).

the context of God's judgment on Sodom and Gomorrah (Gen 18:1–19:29). As Abraham journeys with his visitors toward Sodom, Yahweh wonders aloud whether to inform him what he is about to do, since "Abraham is to become a great and powerful nation, and all the nations of the earth will be blessed through him" (Gen 18:18). As the conduit through whom all the nations will be blessed, God eventually does reveal to Abraham his purposes. Genesis 22 records God testing Abraham by asking him to offer the promised offspring Isaac as a sacrifice. After intervening to stop Abraham, the angel of the Lord reiterates the promise to multiply Abraham's offspring and that his offspring will possess the gates of his enemies.[394] The angel of the Lord concludes: "And all the nations of the earth will be blessed by your offspring because you have obeyed my command" (Gen 22:18).

Thus Paul sees in God's promise to bless all the nations through Abraham the gospel in a nutshell. From this seed blessing will sprout the mature gospel of the life, death, resurrection, and ascension of Jesus Christ. The gospel is not something completely new and without precedent, as if God tried one thing in the Old Testament and then decided to go a new direction when he saw it was not working. With the coming of Christ, believers are now able to more clearly see that this has been God's plan all along. Just how that works out is what Paul will unpack in the remainder of his argument that runs through 5:1.

As believers, we should adopt the same method of reading Scripture as Paul models here—a gospel-centered, Christ-focused approach. These are the glasses we put on when reading the Bible, for that is what Jesus himself instructed his followers to do (Luke 24:44–49).

3:9. Paul now draws a conclusion from God's gospel proclamation that in Abraham all the nations will be blessed: "Consequently, those who have faith are blessed with Abraham, who had faith" (ὥστε οἱ ἐκ πίστεως εὐλογοῦνται σὺν τῷ πιστῷ Ἀβραάμ). He repeats the phrase "those who have faith" (οἱ ἐκ πίστεως) from 3:7, where it defined who the "sons of Abraham" were. Here they are "blessed" (εὐλογέω), picking up the verb

---

[394] While most English translations read "their enemies," the underlying Hebrew expression אֹיְבָיו is in fact "his enemies." Thus Gen 22:17 refers to an individual offspring; see T. Desmond Alexander, "Further Observations on the Term 'Seed' in Genesis," *TynBul* 48 (1997): 363–67 and Paul R. Williamson, *Abraham, Israel, and the Nations: The Patriarchal Promise and Its Covenantal Development in Genesis*, JSOTSup 315 (Sheffield: Sheffield Academic, 2000), 248–50. This distinction will be especially important; see below at 3:16.

from the quotation of Genesis 12:3/18:18 in the previous verse. The verb itself has a very general sense of God showing favor or kindness to a person, with the context often specifying the nature of the blessing. While clearly the blessing in view includes justification, it cannot be reduced to that, as Paul will go on to connect the "blessing of Abraham" with receiving the promised Spirit (3:14). Those who believe are blessed "with Abraham" (σὺν ... Ἀβραάμ), an expression that puts believers on the same level with the patriarch because they are blessed on the same basis: faith.

In describing Abraham as one "who had faith" Paul uses an adjective (πιστός) that could either refer to Abraham's faithfulness or his faith/trust. Given Paul's emphasis on Abraham's faith and that of the Christian in 3:6–8, Paul clearly has in view Abraham's active trust in God and his promises. This same adjective is applied to Abraham in Nehemiah 9:8 (LXX), where Nehemiah says to God, "you found his heart faithful before you and made a covenant with him to give him and his seed the land" (NETS). This refers back to Genesis 15:6 in the larger context of that chapter.[395] According to both Nehemiah and Paul, Abraham's defining characteristic was his faith in God and his promises.

But this was not how all Jews in Paul's day read the Abraham story.[396] In 1 Maccabees 2:52, Mattathias (the patriarch of the family who starts the rebellion against their pagan oppressors) exhorts his sons from his death bed to be zealous for Torah, even to the point of death if necessary, just as their ancestors had done. He then clinches the argument by asking: "Was not Abraham found faithful [πιστός] when tested, and it was reckoned to him as righteousness?" Sirach 44:20 strikes a similar note, where the author states that Abraham "kept the law of the Most High, and was taken into covenant with him; he established the covenant in his flesh, and when he was tested he was found faithful [πιστός]." In both cases it is the obedience of Abraham (whether keeping God's law or remaining true to Yahweh when tested) that leads to his status as righteous and the establishment of the covenant. Such an interpretation reads Abraham's

---

[395] In the Hebrew text of Neh 9:8, the word rendered "faithful" (נֶאֱמָן) is a participle form of the verb translated "believed" in the expression Abram "believed the Lord" (וְהֶאֱמִן בַּיהוָה) in Gen 15:6. That is the only place in the Abraham narrative (Gen 11:27–25:11) where this verb occurs. Furthermore, Neh 9:8 goes on to list the inhabitants of the land when God promised it to Abram, just as Gen 15:18–19 does (though admittedly the lists are not identical).

[396] For a helpful (albeit now somewhat dated) summary, see Hansen, *Abraham in Galatians*, 175–99.

life of faithfulness back into God's declaration that Abraham was righteous. While we cannot be certain that Paul's opponents in Galatia read the Abraham traditions this way, this perspective is certainly consistent with what they appear to have been arguing.

Since 3:6–9 functions as a thesis statement for the argument that runs through 5:1, a summary of the apostle's point in these verses is important. Abraham believed that God was who he said he was and would do what he had promised to do. As a result, God counted Abraham's faith as righteousness—a status of being not guilty in God's court of law. In other words, God justified Abraham on the basis of his faith. Everyone who trusts in Jesus Christ in the same way that Abraham believed God is a true son of Abraham and receives the blessing that God promised to bring to all the nations through Abraham. This blessing comes solely on the basis of faith, regardless of one's ethnicity. Scripture announced this good news (i.e., "the gospel") in advance because it foresaw that God would justify the gentiles by faith (and thus not by works of the law).

The combination of the themes of faith, justification/righteousness, the promise to Abraham, blessing to the gentiles, and the advance proclamation of the gospel may originate in Paul's reading of Isaiah 51:1–8.[397] Isaiah addresses those "who pursue righteousness ... who seek the Lord" to look to Abraham their rock and Sarah their quarry (51:1–2a). Although Abraham was just one man when God called him, God blessed and multiplied him (51:2b). So too the Lord will comfort Zion by transforming creation itself (51:3). All peoples are called to listen because instruction will go out from Yahweh, and his justice will be a light to the nations (51:4). God promises that his righteousness and salvation are both near and eternal (51:5–8). Thus Isaiah calls God's people to await the day when God will reveal his saving righteousness by trusting in God to fulfill his promise to bless Abraham. This saving righteousness will extend to all the nations, a message that is later described in Isaiah 52:7–10 as a proclamation of good news. By drawing on this Isaianic background, Paul indicates that this day has come—God has revealed his saving righteousness by fulfilling his promise to Abraham to bless all the nations. Thus all who share the faith of Abraham share in the blessings promised to him, regardless of their ethnicity.

---

[397] See further Harmon, *She Must and Shall Go Free*, 136–40.

While in one sense the word blessing can refer to even the smallest kindness that God shows us, we must never lose sight of the foundational blessings that God gives us through the gospel. These profound spiritual realities determine our identity, feed our souls, and sustain our perseverance in a fallen world. As a supplement to the blessings Paul describes here in Galatians, consider reflecting on the string of blessings he lists in Ephesians 1:3–14.

Bridge

"Scripture is like a river again, broad and deep, shallow enough for the lamb to go wading, but deep enough there for the elephant to swim."[398] The same is true of the gospel. On one level it is very simple: "Christ died for our sins according to the Scriptures, that he was buried, that he was raised on the third day according to the Scriptures, and that he appeared to Cephas, then to the Twelve" (1 Cor 15:3–5). Yet that irreducible core is set within a larger story that stretches from Genesis to Revelation. As believers, knowing that story is essential not only because it is the true story of the world, but it is our story, the story that should shape the way that we live in this world as God's redeemed people. An essential step in knowing that story is learning to read the Bible the way that Jesus and the apostles did (Luke 24:44–49). The Bible is like a television series with numerous seasons, with each individual story or passage similar to a single episode of that television series. If we do not have a good grasp of the entire series, we may understand the individual episodes at a basic level, but likely miss the larger significance of characters and events. Here in Galatians Paul provides us with an example of how to read Scripture with gospel-centered, Christ-focused lenses that reveal the central message of the Bible.

C. The Curse and the Christ (3:10–14)

[10] For all who rely on the works of the law are under a curse, because it is written, Everyone who does not do everything written in the book of the law is cursed. [11] Now it is clear that no one is justified before God by the law, because the righteous will live by faith. [12] But the law is not based on faith; instead, the one who does these things will live by them.

---

[398] Gregory the Great, *Moral.* inscr. 4. Cf. Andrew Naselli, "On Swimming Elephants," April 3, 2009, https://andynaselli.com/on-swimming-elephants.

[13] Christ redeemed us from the curse of the law by becoming a curse for us, because it is written, Cursed is everyone who is hung on a tree. [14] The purpose was that the blessing of Abraham would come to the Gentiles by Christ Jesus, so that we could receive the promised Spirit through faith.

Context

With his thesis stated that justification by faith and the status of being sons of Abraham are based on faith in God and his promises (3:6–9), this paragraph addresses a corollary that flows from that thesis regarding the Mosaic law (3:10–14). Paul must now explain why the Mosaic law cannot bring eschatological life, which is what Paul's opponents imply by insisting on the necessity of keeping the Mosaic law in order to be justified, full-blooded sons of Abraham.

Structure

Rather than bring the blessing promised to Abraham, the Mosaic law covenant brings a curse upon all who rely upon it because no one is able to keep its requirements (3:10). Paul then elaborates why the law cannot bring blessing and justification: the Old Testament itself announces that those who are righteous by faith will live (3:11), and the law operates on the fundamental principle of doing rather than believing (3:12). But what the law could not do, Christ has done; through his sacrificial death he became a curse to redeem us from the curse the law brings for disobedience (3:13). As a result of his death, the blessing of Abraham (epitomized by the gift of the Spirit) comes to both Jew and gentile alike (3:14).

The basic structure of this paragraph is a recurring pattern of an assertion related to the Mosaic law followed by a supporting citation from the Old Testament. Only in the final verse of the paragraph does the pattern break down; there Paul states two purposes/results of Christ redeeming us from the law. A chiastic pattern is present in 3:10–13,[399] with 3:10 and 3:13 focusing on the curse of the law and 3:11–12 giving two parallel reasons those who rely on works of the law are under a curse: (1) no one is justified by faith, and (2) the law is not of faith.

---

[399] For discussion of possible chiastic structures in this section, see Ardel B. Caneday, "The Curse of the Law and the Cross: Works of the Law and Faith in Galatians 3:1–14," Ph.D. diss. (Trinity Evangelical Divinity School, 1992), 283 and Andrew H. Wakefield, *Where to Live: The Hermeneutical Significance of Paul's Citations from Scripture in Galatians 3:1–14*, AcBib 14 (Boston: Brill, 2003), 132–45.

3:10a Those who rely on works of the law are under a curse
3:10b Deuteronomy 27:26 and 28:58
    3:11a It is evident that no one is justified
    by the law
        3:11b Habakkuk 2:4
        3:12a The law is not of faith
        3:12b Leviticus 18:5
3:13a Christ redeemed us from the curse of the law by becoming a curse for us
    3:13b Deuteronomy 21:23
3:14a Purpose 1: the blessing of Abraham might come to
the gentiles by faith
3:14b Purpose 2: we might receive the promise of the Spirit

Even with the prominence of Old Testament citations, allusions, and
echoes throughout the letter, Galatians 3:10–14 has the densest concentration of them. In addition to the clear citations noted above, there
are allusions/echoes from several Old Testament texts: Isaiah 53 (3:13a);
Genesis 12:3 (3:14a); Isaiah 44:3–5 (3:14b). Paul engages in such deep
and sustained engagement with Scripture not only because his opponents use it in their false teaching, but also because he is dealing with
biblical-theological structures and motifs that are fundamental to the
gospel and the biblical storyline.

3:10. With his thesis statement in place (3:6–9), Paul now develops his
argument by explaining why works of the law cannot justify or be the
basis on which one receives or experiences the Holy Spirit: "For all who
rely on the works of the law are under a curse" (Ὅσοι γὰρ ἐξ ἔργων νόμου
εἰσίν, ὑπὸ κατάραν εἰσίν). No matter who it is—Jew or gentile—who places
confidence or trust in the works of the law, the result is being "under
a curse" (ὑπὸ κατάραν).[400] This is the first of several key expressions in

---

[400] Hays ("Galatians," 258) argues that the expression "all who rely on the works of the
law" refers to the people of Israel in general; thus Paul is not stating a general principle
but rather making a historical observation that Israel experienced the curse for breaking
God's covenant. But this conclusion does not go far enough, as Paul is addressing gentile
believers who are on the verge of adding observance of the Mosaic law to their faith in
Christ. His point is not merely to describe Israel's failure under the law (as true as that
observation is!), but to insist that *all* (Ὅσοι)—regardless of ethnicity—who rely on the Mosaic
law for their standing before God are under a curse (see discussion below). Dunn (*Galatians*,
172–73) contends that those who rely on works of the law refers to those who put too

Galatians that use the preposition "under" (ὑπό) to express being under someone or something's power, control, or influence, always in a negative sense in this letter.[401] In God's initial promise to Abram, Yahweh said, "I will bless those who bless you, I will curse anyone who treats you with contempt" (Gen 12:3). To be under a curse is to experience God's displeasure and eventual judgment. According to this promise, what determines whether a person is blessed or cursed by God is their relationship to Abram. Within the context of Galatians 3:6–5:1, Paul is making a similar point, only now the key is one's relationship to Christ the seed of Abraham.

This contrast between blessing and curse runs as a thread throughout the Old Testament.[402] Here in 3:10 Paul is drawing on a particular example of this thread. In Deuteronomy 27–28, as the Israelites prepare to enter the promised land, God lays out blessings they will experience if they obey and the curses that will come if they do not. Paul draws from this section to support his assertion that all who rely on works of the law are under a curse. He cites Deuteronomy 27:26: "Everyone who does not do everything written in the book of the law is cursed."[403] This is the final curse in the first of two curse sections (27:9–26 and 28:15–68) separated by a passage announcing the blessings of the covenant (28:1–14). The scene culminates in 30:11–30, where Moses states that he has set before the people "life and death, blessing and curse. Choose life so that you and your descendants may live" (30:19). If they obey, Yahweh "will prolong

---

much emphasis on the distinctiveness of Jews from gentiles and the specific requirements of the law that reinforced that distinction such as circumcision, food laws, and Sabbath observance. But this conclusion does not go far enough, as part of Paul's critique of those who rely on works of the law is that the law and faith operate on completely different principles (doing vs. trusting).

[401] For this use of ὑπό, see discussion in Harris, *Prepositions and Theology*, 220–21. The other examples are: under sin (3:22); under law (3:23; 4:4–5, 21; 5:18); under a guardian (3:25); under guardians and stewards (4:2); and under the elemental forces (4:3).

[402] For more on this important theme, see further Biblical Theology §1.3.5.

[403] Paul's wording does not strictly follow the LXX or the MT; for a summary of the differences, see Moo, *Galatians*, 218–19 and Das, *Galatians*, 312–13. The most noteworthy variation from the LXX is that where it has "all the words of this law" (πᾶσιν τοῖς λόγοις τοῦ νόμου τούτου) Paul has written here "all the things written in the book of the law" (πᾶσιν τοῖς γεγραμμένοις ἐν τῷ βιβλίῳ τοῦ νόμου). Variations of this latter phrase occur several other places in Deuteronomy (28:58, 61; 29:27; 30:10). In those contexts, the phrase has a summative function, stressing the violation of the whole Mosaic covenant, not merely individual commandments. The Galatians cannot pick and choose elements of the Mosaic law; it is a package deal (cf. Gal 5:3). As Das (*Galatians*, 313) notes, "The Galatians must do either the *whole* Law or none of it. A piecemeal approach will not do! They must 'abide' by the Law as a comprehensive way of life without failure."

your days as you live in the land the Lord swore to give to your ancestors Abraham, Isaac, and Jacob" (30:20).

Thus in its original context Deuteronomy 27:26 calls Israel to avoid experiencing God's curse by doing everything that God commanded in the covenant. Yet Paul uses this verse to explain why all who rely on works of the law are under a curse. The unstated premise that bridges these two statements is that no one is able to keep everything written in the law. Thus Paul's argument can be laid out like this:[404]

1. Those who do not do everything written in the law are under a curse (3:10b).
2. No one is able to do everything written in the law (unstated premise).
3. Therefore, everyone who relies on works of the law for salvation is under a curse (3:10a).

While some have disputed that the Jews of Paul's day believed that God required perfect obedience, there is evidence that at least some Jews besides Paul concluded that it was both required and almost never achieved.[405] Thus it was reasonable for Paul to assume this middle premise without stating it explicitly.

N.T. Wright understands the logic of this citation from Deuteronomy 27:26 in a slightly different manner.[406] He contends that Paul is making a point about Israel's historical experience with the Torah. All who rely on works of the law are embracing Israel's national way of life, a way of life that historically speaking led to Israel's exile. Therefore, all who take upon themselves the Torah place themselves under this same curse. Thus, according to Wright, Paul is not assuming the implied premise that no one can keep the law perfectly. He is making a historical statement about Israel's corporate experience under the law.

---

[404] Although similar forms of this argument can be found in many scholars, this one is adapted from Thomas R. Schreiner, *The Law and Its Fulfillment: A Pauline Theology of Law* (Grand Rapids: Baker, 1993), 44. For discussion of other ways to understand Paul's logic and the underlying scriptural foundation, see further Biblical Theology §5.3.4.

[405] On the need for and impossibility of perfect obedience to the law in Jewish thought, see further Biblical Theology §5.3.4.

[406] See especially N. T. Wright, *The Climax of the Covenant: Christ and the Law in Pauline Theology* (Minneapolis: Fortress, 1992), 137–56.

While Wright is correct that the curse mentioned in Deuteronomy 27:26 and its larger context was pronounced over the nation of Israel, Paul says here in Galatians 3:10 that this curse applies to "all who rely on works of the law." The apostle intentionally broadens out a curse originally directed toward Israel—one which had historically been fulfilled in the culminating curse of exile—and applies it to anyone, Jew or gentile, who relies upon the works of the law to be justified (2:16), receive and continue to experience the Spirit (3:3, 5), or inherit the blessing promised to Abraham (3:6–9). The theological principle (validated by Israel's historical experience) that all who rely on works of the law are under a curse remains true for any who seek to relate to God on the basis of observing the Mosaic law.

Relying on what we do to be right with God or earn his blessing is a dead-end path. Yet even as believers, we can subtly fall into the trap of thinking that our performance earns us favor with God. The gospel reminds us that God's blessing and favor rest upon us not because of what we have done or will do, but because of what Christ has already done for us.

3:11. Paul now further develops his argument that those who rely on works of the law are under a curse by stating a claim that he regards as obvious: "Now it is clear that no one is justified before God by the law" (ὅτι δὲ ἐν νόμῳ οὐδεὶς δικαιοῦται παρὰ τῷ θεῷ δῆλον).[407] The adjective rendered "clear" (δῆλος) refers to something that is clearly visible to the point of being obvious.[408] Paul expects no one to dispute his claim.

---

[407] Again, the δέ that begins this clause has a continuative force, though Witherington (*Grace in Galatia*, 234) contends it is adversative.

[408] BDAG s.v. δῆλος. It is relatively rare in the NT (Matt 26:73; 1 Cor 15:27; Gal 3:11) and similarly uncommon in the LXX (just nine occurrences: Num 27:21; Deut 33:8; 1 Sam 14:41; 28:6; 1 Macc 15:23; 4 Macc 2:7; Sir 33:3; 45:10; Hos 3:4). Philo, however, uses it often (84x) to refer to things that are visible to the eye or concepts/ideas that are obvious. This adjective regularly occurs with ὅτι to indicate what is clear/evident; the challenge here in 3:11 is that there are two ὅτι statements. The first occurs at the beginning of the verse and introduces the clause "by the law no one is justified before God" (my translation), while the second immediately follows δῆλος and introduces the citation of Hab 2:4, "the righteous will live by faith." Because the second ὅτι statement immediately follows δῆλος, some scholars argue that it indicates what is clear, resulting in a translation like "because by the law no one is justified before God, it is evident that 'the righteous will live by faith'" (my translation). Based on comparable constructions in Greek literature where ὅτι occurs both before and after δῆλος, the grammatical evidence seems to favor taking the second ὅτι with δῆλος; see especially Wakefield, *Where to Live*, 207–14, as well as Frank Thielman, *Paul and the Law: A Contextual Approach* (Downers Grove, IL: IVP, 1994), 127–28; de Boer, *Galatians*, 202; and Das,

Although the content of this claim is similar to what Paul has already said in 2:16, the wording is slightly different. First, Paul adds the phrase "before God" (παρὰ τῷ θεῷ) to the verb justify (δικαιόω), perhaps as a subtle reminder that the issue at hand is God's declaration of righteousness, not man's.[409] Second, rather than rejecting justification "by the works of the law" (ἐξ ἔργων νόμου), Paul here dismisses justification "by the law" (ἐν νόμῳ). But given that Paul has used the former phrase in verse 10, it seems that this second phrase is stylistic variation that also expresses means.[410] The Mosaic law simply cannot make one right before a holy God.

The reason that the Mosaic law cannot be the means of justification, according to Paul, is that "the righteous will live by faith" (ὁ δίκαιος ἐκ πίστεως ζήσεται).[411] What on the surface seems like a straightforward citation of Habakkuk 2:4 is in fact a tangled web of interpretive issues. Habakkuk is structured around a series of "complaints" where the prophet wrestles with Judah's wickedness and God's use of the Babylonians to judge them. After God's announcement that he will use the Babylonians as his instrument of judgment (1:5–11), Habakkuk wonders how a pure and holy God like Yahweh can possibly use the wicked Babylonians—a people

---

Galatians, 317. But there are exceptions (as Wakefield admits), including an example in Philo (*Plant.* 1:123). Furthermore, Paul's pattern in this chapter is to make a theological claim and then introduce the ground for that claim with a Scripture citation, usually introduced with ὅτι (3:8, 10, 12, 13). Finally, the flow of Paul's argument makes better sense if the citation of Hab 2:4 is the ground for the claim that no one is justified by the law, which itself is an extension of the claim in 3:10 that all who rely on works of the law are under a curse; see similarly Moo, *Galatians*, 205.

[409] Although there is no other place where the prepositional phrase "before God" (παρὰ τῷ θεῷ) modifies the verb justify (δικαιόω), Paul does use it in connection with the related adjective (δίκαιος) in Rom 2:13—"For the hearers of the law are not righteous before God (δίκαιοι παρὰ [τῷ] θεῷ), but the doers of the law will be justified (δικαιωθήσονται)." Paul also uses this phrase in connection with God's justice or judgment in Rom 2:11; 9:14; 2 Thess 1:6. One should not overlook the possibility that Paul still has Ps 143:2 in mind from citing it earlier in 2:16; in the LXX the relevant line reads "no one living will be justified before you [ἐνώπιόν σου]" (my translation). Although not an exact verbal match, the conceptual overlap is clear.

[410] Another possibility is that the phrase ἐν νόμῳ has a locative sense; thus one cannot be justified "in the sphere/realm of the law"; see Witherington, *Grace in Galatia*, 234.

[411] It is also possible that the prepositional phrase "by faith" (ἐκ πίστεως) modifies "righteous" (ὁ δίκαιος) instead of "live" (ζήσεται), resulting in the following translation: "the righteous by faith will live" (so Das, *Galatians*, 320–21); for a helpful discussion of the arguments for both options and a convincing argument that "by faith" modifies the verb, see Caneday, "Curse of the Law," 281–84. This conclusion makes better sense as a parallel to the citation of Lev 18:5 in the next verse, where the prepositional phrase "by them" (ἐν αὐτοῖς) clearly modifies the verb "live" (ζήσεται); see discussion below.

more wicked than Judah—to judge his people (1:12–17), and then waits for a reply (2:1). God instructs Habakkuk to write the vision down and wait for its fulfillment (2:2–3). Verse 4 lays out two contrasting postures toward God and his promises: "Look, his ego is inflated; he is without integrity. But the righteous one will live by his faith."[412] In other words, those who are righteous will live (i.e., experience eschatological deliverance) by their ongoing trust in Yahweh and his promises. As Schreiner notes, "The many allusions to the exodus in Hab 3 indicate the promise of a new exodus, a new deliverance for the people of God. Hence, Habakkuk functions as a paradigm for the people of God. He will continue to trust the Lord even if the fig tree does not blossom and vines are lacking fruit (Hab 3:17–18)."[413]

Therefore, Paul sees in Habakkuk 2:4 a generalized statement of what Abraham experienced in Genesis 15:6.[414] Just as Abraham believed God and was counted righteous (Gen 15:6), so too all who are righteous by faith, like Abraham, will experience eschatological life through faith in God and his promises.[415] Psalm 143:1–2 also appears to be part of this scriptural matrix on justification by faith. Paul has already alluded to Psalm

---

[412] The Hebrew text (MT) could also be read as "the righteous one will live by his faithfulness" (i.e., his faithfulness in keeping the stipulations of God's covenant). Either way, however, the faith/faithfulness is that of the righteous person. By contrast, in the Greek textual tradition the phrase "his soul" (נַפְשׁוֹ) becomes "my soul" (ἡ ψυχή μου), which leads to a corresponding change in the final line. Codex Alexandrinus (A) has "my righteous one will live by faith" (ὁ ... δίκαιος μου ἐκ πίστεώς ζήσεται), while Codex Vaticanus (B) has "the righteous one will live by my faith/faithfulness" (ὁ ... δίκαιος ἐκ πίστεώς μου ζήσεται). Both Aquila ("the righteous by his faith will live [ὁ ... δίκαιος ἐν πίστει αὐτοῦ ζήσεται]") and Symmachus ("the righteous by his own faith will live" [ὁ ... δίκαιος τῇ ἑαυτοῦ πίστει ζήσεται]) differ from those texts as well. Paul's wording does not match any textual tradition of the LXX exactly, as he does not include any personal pronoun. In fact, his wording is closer to the MT, making it unclear whether Paul offers his own rendering of the MT (omitting any equivalent to the 3ms pronominal suffix "his") or simply omits any form of a first person pronoun ("my") to make it clear that the individual's faith is in view and not God's faithfulness. For a helpful discussion of the textual situation, see Moo, *Galatians*, 219–20.

[413] Schreiner, *Galatians*, 208.

[414] This connection is rooted in the Hebrew text of both verses. There are seventeen verses in the MT where a word from the צדק family and a word from the אמן family occur: Gen 15:6; Deut 32:4; 1 Sam 26:23; Neh 9:8; Job 9:2; Pss 40:11; 58:2; 96:13; 119:75, 138; 143:1; Prov 12:17; Isa 1:21, 26; 11:5; 59:4; Hab 2:4. In most of these occurrences it is the righteousness and faithfulness of God in view, often placed in poetic parallelism. But Gen 15:6 and Hab 2:4 are the only places where a person's righteousness is related to that person's faith/faithfulness.

[415] That Paul has in view eschatological life is broadly held by most commentators, though a notable exception is de Boer (*Galatians*, 207–8), who contends that the life in view is non-eschatological (i.e., focused on everyday living in the present). But for Paul, everyday life for the believer is inherently eschatological, so that "eschatological life" is

143:2 in Galatians 2:16 to ground his assertion that people are justified by faith in Christ and not by works of the law by alluding to Psalm 143:2, "no one alive is righteous in your sight." The preceding verse may also inform Paul's thought here, as Psalm 143:1 records David praying, "In your faithfulness [בֶּאֱמֻנָתְךָ / ἐν τῇ ἀληθείᾳ σου] listen to my plea, and in your righteousness [בְּצִדְקָתֶךָ / ἐν τῇ δικαιοσύνῃ σου] answer me." Paul appears to have seen in these texts (Gen 15:6; Ps 143:1–2; Hab 2:4) an underlying theme connecting faith in God and his promises with God's declaration that a person is righteous/justified. When writing to the Romans, Paul draws on these same texts to make similar points. Paul cites Habakkuk 2:4 to ground his central claim that in the gospel the righteousness of God is revealed "from faith to faith" (Rom 1:17). His assertion that "no one will be justified in his sight by the works of the law" (Rom 3:20) clearly alludes to Psalm 143:2. And he quotes Genesis 15:6 to argue that Abraham was justified by faith and not by works. Thus Paul sees in Habakkuk 2:4 a fundamental principle: the person who is righteous will experience eschatological life based on trusting in God and his promises.[416] Since this principle is true, it is evident that no one can be justified by the law.

God is not content with merely declaring us not guilty in his court of law on the last day. He wants to give us eschatological life. Not merely life that never ends, but a quality of life in which we experience the fullness of God's presence through his Spirit dwelling in us. Through the gospel, God has given us that eschatological life now through the Spirit indwelling us while we await the full consummation of that life in a new creation.

3:12. Using language from the citation of Habakkuk 2:4, Paul advances his argument further by explaining that the law operates on a completely different principle than faith:[417] "But the law is not based on faith" (ὁ δὲ

---

what the believer experiences now (in part) through the Spirit and what he or she will experience in full at the consummation of the new creation.

[416] Instead of seeing "the righteous" (ὁ ... δίκαιος) as a generic reference, some have argued that Paul here refers to Christ; see, e.g., de Boer, *Galatians*, 201–6. But as noted at 2:16, πίστις refers to the believer's trust/faith throughout Galatians. A hybrid position is taken by Hays (Hays, *Faith of Jesus*, 138–41), who argues that Paul refers to both Christ's faithfulness and the believer's faith. In 1QpHab 6:11–8:3 the Qumran community interprets Hab 2:4 as referring to loyalty to their Teacher of Righteousness and observance of the law; see discussion in Francis Watson, *Paul and the Hermeneutics of Faith* (New York: T&T Clark, 2004), 112–26.

[417] The δέ that begins this verse extends Paul's argument but does so by drawing a contrast (similarly Witherington, *Grace in Galatia*, 235; DeSilva, *Handbook*, 62). However, Schreiner

νόμος οὐκ ἔστιν ἐκ πίστεως). The phrase "based on faith" renders the same prepositional phrase (ἐκ πίστεως) that occurs at several key points in Galatians.[418] In 2:16 one is justified "by faith in Christ" (ἐκ πίστεως Χριστοῦ). According to 3:8, Scripture saw in advance that God would justify the gentiles "by faith" (ἐκ πίστεως). It is "those who have faith" (οἱ ἐκ πίστεως) who are blessed with Abraham (3:9). And in 3:11 Paul has just cited Habakkuk 2:4, "the righteous will live by faith" (ὁ δίκαιος ἐκ πίστεως ζήσεται). Indeed, Paul's use of this phrase throughout Galatians may derive from Habakkuk 2:4. Paul's point is that the law does not operate on the principle of believing or trusting.

Instead, it operates on a different principle, drawn from Leviticus 18:5: "the one who does these things will live by them" (ὁ ποιήσας αὐτὰ ζήσεται ἐν αὐτοῖς).[419] Within its original context, Leviticus 18:5 concludes a paragraph (18:1–5) that introduces a series of commands regulating sexual relationships (18:6–23), which is followed by a concluding paragraph that describes the consequences for disobedience and the blessings for obedience (18:24–30). The opening paragraph (18:1–5) reminds the Israelites not to engage in the practices of the Egyptians and the Canaanites or "walk in their statutes" (18:3 ESV). Instead, Yahweh commands "You shall therefore keep my statutes and my rules; if a person does them, he shall live by them" (18:5 ESV). In other words, God's people will experience his covenant blessings as a result of obeying what God commands.[420] Variations of this expression occur several times in Ezekiel

---

(*Galatians*, 210) argues for a continuative sense, seeing a succession of three arguments in 3:10–12 explaining why the law cannot save.

[418] As in those other cases, it expresses means or basis. Some (e.g., Martyn, *Galatians*, 315) have argued that here it communicates source—the law does not come from faith. But as Moo (*Galatians*, 207–8) rightly notes, this prepositional phrase is essentially a technical expression throughout the letter that expresses means or basis.

[419] Paul's citation largely follows the LXX, with two exceptions. First, Paul has changed the participle ποιήσας from an adverbial participle used conditionally to a substantival participle by placing a definite article before it. This move resulted in the second change: eliminating the word ἄνθρωπος from the citation, which in the LXX functions as the subject of the clause (a role now played by the substantival participle). Paul may have made these changes to align this citation with the other scriptural citations in this section: Deut 27:26 (πᾶς ὃς οὐκ ἐμμένει); Hab 2:4 (ὁ δίκαιος); and Deut 21:23 (πᾶς ὁ κρεμάμενος). See further discussion in Dietrich-Alex Koch, *Die Schrift als Zeuge des Evangeliums: Untersuchungen zur Verwendung und zum Verständnis der Schrift bei Paulus*, BHT (Tübingen: Mohr, 1986), 120.

[420] Thus in its original context, life refers to living in the promised land rather than eschatological life. But Paul has likely made the move from life in the land to eschatological life based on a typological connection between the two, such that life in the land was

as part of the prophet's call for the Israelites to obey God's covenant stipulations and condemnation of their failure to do so (Ezek 18:9, 17, 19, 21; 20:11, 13, 21, 25; 33:19), and they set up the contrast with oracles of restoration that promise a day when God will reverse his people's disobedience with covenant faithfulness empowered by the Spirit (Ezek 36–37).[421] Several Second Temple Jewish texts also allude to Leviticus 18:5, usually in a positive light to stress that obedience to God's commands is the pathway to eternal life.[422] Some later rabbinic texts even interpreted Leviticus 18:5 as indicating any man (including a gentile) could be righteous through obeying the Mosaic law (b. Sanh. 59a; b. B. Qam. 38a; m. 'Aboth).[423] The connection between doing the law and experiencing life (both in this life in the land and also in the age to come) was well established in the Judaism of Paul's day,[424] and Paul's opponents appear to be arguing from that perspective.

Whether or not Paul's opponents in Galatia were using Leviticus 18:5 to validate their claim that keeping the Mosaic law was necessary to be justified is unclear; what is clear is Paul's strenuous disagreement with the premise that obeying the Mosaic law is the path to eschatological life. Yet Paul insists that in contrast to faith in God and his promises (a principle summarized by citing Hab 2:4), the law operates on the principle

a type/shadow of the greater eschatological life that God's people experience in the new covenant and the new creation; on this see especially Simon J. Gathercole, "Torah, Life, and Salvation: Leviticus 18:5 in Early Judaism and the New Testament," in *From Prophecy to Testament: The Function of the Old Testament in the New*, ed. Craig A. Evans (Peabody, MA: Hendrickson, 2004), 126–45.

[421] See Preston M. Sprinkle, *Law and Life: The Interpretation of Leviticus 18:5 in Early Judaism and in Paul*, WUNT 241 (Tübingen: Mohr Siebeck, 2007), 34–40. He also notes an allusion to Lev 18:5 in Neh 9:29.

[422] See the helpful survey in Sprinkle, *Law and Life*, 55–130. He examines texts from Qumran (CD 3.15–16; 4QD266; 4Q504), *Pss. Sol.* 14:2–3, Philo (*Congr.* 86–87), and Pseudo-Philo (*L.A.B.* 23:10).

[423] See Das, *Galatians*, 322. He notes that the rabbis seized on the word "man" (הָאָדָם / ἄνθρωπος) to broaden the interpretation beyond Jews out to gentiles. It may be noteworthy that when Paul cites this verse, he omits this word, perhaps seeking to avoid this interpretation that would have fit well with his opponents' teaching. But it should be noted that we cannot be certain this interpretive tradition reaches back to Paul's day.

[424] See the helpful summary in Das, *Galatians*, 322–23, and the extended discussions in Gathercole, "Torah, Life, and Salvation," 126–45; Sprinkle, *Law and Life*, 53–130; and Douglas C. Mohrmann, "Of 'Doing' and 'Living': The Intertextual Semantics of Leviticus 18:5 in Galatians and Romans," in *Jesus and Paul: Global Perspectives in Honor of James D. G. Dunn for His 70th Birthday*, ed. B. J. Oropeza, C. K. Robertson, and Douglas C. Mohrmann (New York: T&T Clark, 2009), 152–66.

of performance: the one who does them will live by them (citing Lev 18:5). Indeed, Paul may have even derived the key phrase "works of the law" (2:16; 3:2, 5, 10) from the principle derived from Leviticus 18:5.[425]

Considered together, 3:10–12 teaches that attempting to gain life by doing the law is a dead end for at least three reasons. First, without doing "everything written in the book of the law" (and no one is able to perfectly obey everything written in the law), one experiences a curse rather than blessing and life (3:10). Second, rather than come on the basis of performance (i.e., doing the law), faith has always been the means by which one experiences eschatological life. A third reason, although it is not directly stated, can be implied from the larger context of Galatians and the larger context of the Old Testament citations. The law cannot bring eschatological life because it was part of a covenant that has been done away with now that Christ has come (Gal 3:15–29).

Even those who have come to faith in Christ can be lured back to relating to God on the basis of doing rather than believing. Doing is attractive because it is something tangible that we think we can control, while believing puts us in the position of relying on the Lord. Yet it is in relying on the Lord that God is most glorified and we are most satisfied.

3:13. Unlike each of the previous verses in this paragraph (3:10–14), the sentence that begins this verse does not begin with any connecting particle in Greek. In such a tightly crafted paragraph it has the effect of making this statement stand out.[426] Paul matches the syntax to the sudden, decisive intervention of God in human history to break the stranglehold of sin, death, and the curse. Where human ability to keep the law failed, God acted: "Christ redeemed us from the curse of the law" (Χριστὸς ἡμᾶς ἐξηγόρασεν ἐκ τῆς κατάρας τοῦ νόμου). This is the first explicit mention of Jesus Christ since 3:1, and it comes at a strategic point in the argument. The verb rendered "redeemed" (ἐξαγοράζω) is part of a family that has its origins in the commercial realm, where it could have the more general sense of buy or purchase.[427] But this verb was also used to refer to

---

[425] So also Watson, *Paul and the Hermeneutics of Faith*, 331–36.

[426] The technical term for the lack of a connecting particle is asyndeton, which as Longenecker (*Galatians*, 121) notes, further highlights the change in subject from the previous verses to Christ as the subject of 3:13.

[427] See BDAG s.v. ἐξαγοράζω and Friedrich Büchsel, "ἀγοράζω, ἐξαγοράζω" in *TDNT* 1:124–28.

delivering or redeeming slaves.[428] This backdrop of freedom from slavery suggests that Paul is evoking new exodus imagery to portray the work of Christ. Two additional lines of evidence (in addition to the use of this verb) support this conclusion.

First, the mention of being redeemed from "the curse of the law" (τῆς κατάρας τοῦ νόμου) picks up language from 3:10, where Paul has asserted that "all who rely on the works of the law are under a curse." That claim was grounded in a citation of Deuteronomy 27:26. As noted in 3:10, Deuteronomy 27–30 is a section that lays out the blessings and curses of the covenant. The culminating curse is exile from the land (Deut 28:64–68), which God tells Moses will certainly happen to Israel (Deut 31:16–29). Yet God also promises to bring them back from exile, circumcise their hearts to make them love Yahweh with all their hearts, and bless them so they may live (Deut 30:1–10).

Second, the prophets pick up this hope and regularly describe it in terms of a new or second exodus. This theme is especially prominent in Isaiah (41:17–20; 43:14–21; 51:9–11), and it culminates in the description of the suffering servant, which Paul alludes to here in 3:13.[429] Note the similarities between Galatians 1:4 (which echoes Isa 53) and Galatians 3:13:

Table 5:

	Christ	Redemptive Action	Object	Realm
1:3–4	our Lord Jesus Christ κυρίου Ἰησοῦ Χριστοῦ	to rescue ἐξέληται	us ἡμᾶς	from this present evil age ἐκ τοῦ αἰῶνος τοῦ ἐνεστῶτος πονηροῦ
3:13	Christ Χριστὸς	redeemed ἐξηγόρασεν	us ἡμᾶς	from the curse of the law ἐκ τῆς κατάρας τοῦ νόμου

The parallels are clear. Christ performs a redemptive act on "us" that removes "us" from a dangerous realm. But the parallels between the two verses do not stop there:

---

[428] The first century BC Greek historian Diodorus Siculus describes how a group of philosophers "purchased the freedom" (ἐξηγόρασαν) of a slave (*Lib.* 15.7.1).

[429] See further Harmon, *She Must and Shall Go Free*, 142–46.

Table 6:

	Christ	Reflexive Action	Beneficiary
1:3–4	our Lord Jesus Christ κυρίου Ἰησοῦ Χριστοῦ	gave himself δόντος ἑαυτὸν	for our sins ὑπὲρ τῶν ἁμαρτιῶν ἡμῶν
3:13	Christ Χριστὸς	becoming a curse γενόμενος ... κατάρα	for us ὑπὲρ ἡμῶν

These additional parallels suggest that the echo of Isaiah 53 in Galatians 1:4 applies here in Galatians 3:10. Christ redeems "us" from the curse of the law. Isaiah 52:13–53:12 presents the work of the suffering servant as experiencing the curses of the law promised in Deuteronomy 27–30 for breaking the covenant.[430]

Therefore, saying that Christ redeemed "us" from the curse of the law is an indirect way of claiming that the promised new exodus has taken place through the work of the suffering servant.[431] But the question remains: who is the "us" redeemed from the curse of the law? Based on the Old Testament background, a number of scholars argue that the "us" refers to Jewish Christians.[432] But despite strong arguments in its favor, the evidence favors the view that "us" here in 3:13 includes all believers, Jew and gentile alike.[433] Paul has stressed that *all* who rely on works of the law are under a curse (3:10), not merely Jews. While it is true that the Mosaic law was only given to the Jews, it is evident that gentiles are also under condemnation for their failure to obey God (Rom 2:12–16). The curse that the Israelites experienced for breaking the Mosaic covenant is in a sense a particular expression of the larger curse that fell

---

[430] There are a number of linguistic connections in Hebrew between the curses in Deut 27–29 and Isa 53; see Harmon, *She Must and Shall Go Free*,144–45 and Biblical Theology §1.2.2.

[431] Compare the conclusion of Hays ("Galatians," 261), who concludes that 3:13–14 indicates that "at last through Christ's death the curse has been lifted, Israel has been set free, the exile has ended, so that the ingathering of the Gentiles can now begin."

[432] See, e.g., Wright, *Climax of the Covenant*, 151–53 and Colin G. Kruse, *Paul, the Law, and Justification* (Peabody, MA: Hendrickson, 1997), 86–89. Those who argue for this view often note the following: (1) How can one say that gentiles were under the curse of the law? (2) Paul uses first person pronouns in 2:15–17 to distinguish Jewish believers from gentile believers and seems to do so again in 3:23–25; (3) Paul seems to distinguish between the "us" that Christ redeems in 3:13 and the gentiles in 3:14 to whom the blessing of Abraham comes; (4) From a redemptive-historical perspective, it makes sense to see a progression from God redeeming the Jewish people in fulfillment of his promises as logically prior to that redemption being extended to the gentiles (compare Rom 1:16).

[433] See similarly Fung, *Galatians*, 148–49; Moo, *Galatians*, 211–13; Das, *Galatians*, 331.

on all creation when Adam sinned (Gen 3:14–19). But most convincing
is the parallel train of thought between 3:13–14 and 4:4–5, as seen in the
following chart:[434]

Table 7:

Galatians 3:13–14	Galatians 4:4–6
	God sent His Son
Christ redeemed (ἐξηγόρασεν) us from the curse of the law	to redeem (ἐξαγοράσῃ) those under the law
by becoming (γενόμενος) a curse for us	born (γενόμενον) of woman, born (γενόμενον) under the law
The purpose was that the blessing of Abraham would come to the Gentiles by Christ Jesus	
	so that we might receive adoption as sons
so that we could receive the promised Spirit through faith	And because you are sons, God sent the Spirit of his Son into our hearts, crying, "*Abba*, Father!"

In 4:4–6 it is evident that the plural pronouns refer to Jewish and gentile
Christians alike, since the "we" who receive adoption (4:5) are equated with
the "you" (clearly the Galatian believers, who are predominantly gentile)
who are sons in 4:6.

A final reason for taking the "us" inclusively is the larger context of the
allusion to Isaiah 53 in this verse. Anticipating the work of the suffering
servant, Isaiah 52:10 asserts that "The LORD has displayed his holy arm in
the sight of all the nations; all the ends of the earth will see the salvation
of our God." The servant will "sprinkle many nations" (Isa 52:15), and as
a result of the servant's work, God's people will "inherit the nations" (Isa
54:3 LXX). God will make this descendant of David "a witness to the peoples"
(Isa 55:4), and a nation that the Israelites did not know will run to them
because Yahweh has glorified his people (Isa 55:5). Thus the universal scope
of the servant's work further suggests that "us" in Galatians 3:13 should be
understood to include both Jewish and gentile believers.

The means by which Christ redeemed believers from the curse of the law
is "by becoming a curse for us" (γενόμενος ὑπὲρ ἡμῶν κατάρα).[435] Whereas

---

[434] Adapted from Moo, *Galatians*, 212. These parallels are strengthened by the fact that
Gal 3:13 and 4:5 are the only places in the NT where the verb ἐξαγοράζω occurs.

[435] Thus the participle γενόμενος is best understood as indicating means, though it could
also be understood as temporal ("after becoming a curse") or causal ("because he became

all who rely on the works of the law are under a curse (3:10), those who have trusted in Jesus Christ have had the curse removed from them. Through his death on the cross Jesus experienced the curse that Jew and gentile alike deserved for their disobedience to God. As proof that Christ became a curse for his people, Paul cites Deuteronomy 21:23: "Cursed is everyone who is hung on a tree" (ἐπικατάρατος πᾶς ὁ κρεμάμενος ἐπὶ ξύλου).[436] In its original context, Deuteronomy 21:22–23 explains what to do with a man convicted of murder who is executed by hanging him on a tree. His body must not remain on the tree all night, but he is to be buried that same day, "for anyone hung on a tree is under God's curse." Were they to leave the body hanging on the tree, it would defile the land.

By the time of the New Testament period, at least some Jews applied this verse to crucifixion,[437] and there are several allusions to Deuteronomy 21:23 in the New Testament that do so as well. Peter says to the Jewish council, "The God of our ancestors raised up Jesus, whom you had murdered by hanging him on a tree" (Acts 5:30; see also 10:39). In his first letter this same apostle states that Jesus "bore our sins in his body on the tree"

---

a curse"). In the expression "for us," Paul uses the preposition ὑπέρ, which although it often has the sense of "on behalf of" can also take on the stronger substitutionary sense "in place of" (BDAG s.v. ὑπέρ A.1.c); see further Wallace, *Greek Grammar*, 383–89 and Harris, *Prepositions and Theology*, 211–15.

[436] Paul's exact wording does not match the LXX. First, Paul replaces the word for "curse" (κεκατηραμένος) with a different word for "curse" (ἐπικατάρατος) from Deut 27:26, which he quoted in 3:10. Second, and more importantly, Paul omits the phrase "by God" (ὑπὸ θεοῦ) that occurs after the word "cursed" in Deut 21:23. Some have suggested that this omission indicates Paul is distinguishing between the curse of the law and the curse of God; see, e.g., Koch, *Die Schrift als Zeuge des Evangeliums*, 124–25. A simple grammatical explanation seems more likely, however. The change from the perfect passive participle (κεκατηραμένος), which is naturally followed by the preposition ὑπό indicating the agent of the verb, to an adjective (κατάρα) likely necessitated dropping the prepositional phrase, since "An adjective with the prepositional phrase ('by God') is, grammatically, without parallel in the LXX and NT" (Das, *Galatians*, 327).

[437] For a helpful survey, see David W. Chapman, *Ancient Jewish and Christian Perceptions of Crucifixion*, WUNT 2/244 (Tübingen: Mohr Siebeck, 2008), 117–49. Note especially 4QpNah (4Q169) frags. 3–4 and 1.5–8 (which alludes to Deut 21:23 in connection with Alexander Jannaeus crucifying thousands of Pharisees) and 11QTemple (11Q19) 64.6–13 (where it is clear that hanging a person on the tree is the means of execution). After the NT period, the second-century church father Justin Martyr, in his Dialogue with Trypho, quotes the Jewish Trypho as citing Deut 21:23 to "prove" that Jesus cannot be the Messiah. What is especially noteworthy is that in his response, Justin draws on Isa 53; see Daniel P. Bailey, "'Our Suffering and Crucified Messiah' (*Dial*, 111.2): Justin Martyr's Allusions to Isaiah 53 in His *Dialogue with Trypho* with Special Reference to the New Edition of M. Markovich," in *The Suffering Servant: Isaiah 53 in Jewish and Christian Sources*, ed. Bernd Janowski and Peter Stuhlmacher (Grand Rapids: Eerdmans, 2004), 389–406.

(1 Pet 2:24). While we cannot be certain, it is possible that some early Jews used Deuteronomy 21:23 as proof that Jesus could not have been the Messiah.[438] But perhaps a better explanation for Paul connecting Deuteronomy 21:23 with Jesus' crucifixion is the application of this text in Numbers 25:4, where God instructs Moses what to do with those leaders who led the people into sexual immorality and idolatry: "Take all the chiefs of the people and hang them in the sun before the Lord, that the fierce anger of the Lord may turn away from Israel" (esv).[439] The death of these covenant-breakers by hanging them turns away God's wrath, and perhaps it is this connection that underlies Paul's use of Deuteronomy 21:23.

The underlying logic of Paul's thought here in Galatians 3:13 can perhaps best be summarized by what the apostle writes in Romans 8:3: "What the law could not do since it was weakened by the flesh, God did. He condemned sin in the flesh by sending his own Son in the likeness of sinful flesh as a sin offering." The curse that falls on all who rely on obeying God's commands to experience blessing, justification, and the Spirit has been experienced by Jesus Christ on the cross. Through his death, he absorbed the curse that all who disobey God deserve, and all who are united to him by faith are freed from the curse of the law.

No wonder that Christians through the ages have sung the wonders of our redemption, such as in the classic hymn "Redeemed—How I Love to Proclaim It"

> Redeemed—how I love to proclaim it!
> Redeemed by the blood of the Lamb;
> Redeemed through His infinite mercy,
> His child, and forever, I am.[440]

3:14. Paul concludes this section of his argument by stating two purposes/results of Christ redeeming us from the curse of the law by becoming a curse for us.[441] The first is that "the blessing of Abraham would come

---

[438] See Peter Stuhlmacher, *Biblische Theologie des Neuen Testaments*, 2 vols. (Göttingen: Vandenhoeck & Ruprecht, 1992), 1:154–55 and Seyoon Kim, *The Origin of Paul's Gospel* (Grand Rapids: Eerdmans, 1982), 46. Kim suggests that the early Christians turned this charge into a "weapon of counter-attack" to explain what Jesus accomplished on the cross.

[439] Caneday, "Curse of the Law," 321–25.

[440] Fanny Crosby, "Redeemed, How I Love to Proclaim It," *Hymnal.net*, accessed March 19, 2021, https://www.hymnal.net/en/hymn/h/301.

[441] This verse contains two ἵνα clauses, but it is not immediately clear whether they are coordinate (i.e., parallel to each other and thus indicating two purposes/results that

to the Gentiles by Christ Jesus" (ἵνα εἰς τὰ ἔθνη ἡ εὐλογία τοῦ Ἀβραὰμ γένηται ἐν Χριστῷ Ἰησοῦ).[442] Paul returns to language from 3:8, where he claimed that "Scripture saw in advance that God would justify the Gentiles by faith and proclaimed the gospel ahead of time to Abraham, saying, All the nations will be blessed through you." In the immediate context of 3:8, the content of that blessing includes at a minimum justification (3:6), status as a son of Abraham (3:7), and likely includes experience of the Spirit as well (3:2–5). This blessing comes "to the Gentiles" because Christ became a curse for all believers through his death on the cross (3:13). The phrase translated "by Christ" (ἐν Χριστῷ) is likely better rendered "in Christ."[443] Just as God had promised that "In you [ἐν σοὶ] shall all the nations be blessed" (Gal 3:8 ESV, quoting Gen 12:3/18:18), so now the blessing of Abraham comes to the gentiles "in Christ Jesus" (ἐν Χριστῷ Ἰησοῦ). Furthermore, Paul will proceed in the next section (3:15–18) to

---

flow from verse 13) or whether the second is subordinate to the first (i.e., the first clause indicates the purpose/result of 3:13, while the second clause gives the purpose/result of the first). Grammar alone cannot answer the question, for, as Moo (*Galatians*, 214–15n22) notes, there are examples in Paul's letters of two ἵνα clauses being used as coordinate (2 Cor 9:3; 12:7; Col 4:3–4) and others subordinate (Rom 15:31–32; 1 Cor 4:6; 2 Cor 11:12). So the decision hangs on how one understands: (1) the flow of the larger argument running from 3:6–14; (2) who "us" in v. 13 and "we" in v. 14 refer to; (3) the relationship between the blessing of Abraham and the promised Spirit. For those who argue the second clause is subordinate to the first, see, e.g., Betz, *Galatians*, 152; Chee-Chiew Lee, *Blessing of Abraham, the Spirit, and Justification in Galatians: Their Relationship and Significance for Understanding Paul's Theolgy* (Eugene, OR: Wipf and Stock, 2013), 53–59. But on the whole it seems better to understand the relationship as coordinate. First, the overall flow of the argument is to argue that one's identity as a son of Abraham depends on faith rather than obedience to the law or ethnicity. Second, if the "us" in 3:13 refers inclusively to all believers, then it makes sense to see the "we" here in 3:14 as inclusive of all believers as well. Third, as we will argue below, the echo of Isa 44:3–5, which connects blessing and the gift of the Spirit, suggests a coordinate rather than subordinate relationship. See similarly, e.g., Burton, *Galatians*, 176; Bruce, *Galatians*, 167; Longenecker, *Galatians*, 123; Schreiner, *Galatians*, 218–19; Moo, *Galatians*, 214–15; Das, *Galatians*, 334.

[442] Martyn (*Galatians*, 321) notes that the expression "blessing of Abraham" is found in Genesis 28:3–4, but there is nothing in the context of Galatians 3:14 that suggests Paul's use of the phrase necessarily depends on that passage. In Genesis 28:3–4 the specifics of the blessing of Abraham include being fruitful and multiplying, becoming a company of peoples, and taking possession of the land. Yet in the context of Galatians, the blessing of Abraham clearly includes justification by faith and the gift of the Spirit.

[443] DeSilva (*Handbook*, 64) concludes that "by Christ" here has a causal force and thus recapitulates the sense of 3:13, summarizing the sense as "by means of Christ Jesus becoming a curse on our behalf, thus releasing the blessing." Yet his admission of how well the locative sense fits the context makes one wonder why he did not opt for that view. Campbell (*Paul and Union with Christ*, 81–82) sees here a combination of agency and instrumentality.

identify Jesus as the singular seed to whom the blessing of Abraham was promised, then state that believers, regardless of ethnicity, status, or gender, "are all one in Christ Jesus [ἐν Χριστῷ Ἰησοῦ]. And if you belong to Christ, then you are Abraham's seed, heirs according to the promise" (Gal 3:28–29). Paul's point is that the blessing of Abraham comes to the gentiles in the realm/sphere of Christ, rather than the realm/sphere of the law.[444]

The second purpose clause further elaborates on the first: "so that we could receive the promised Spirit through faith" (ἵνα τὴν ἐπαγγελίαν τοῦ πνεύματος λάβωμεν διὰ τῆς πίστεως). Just as the "us" in 3:13 and the "we" in the first clause of 3:14 refer inclusively to all Christians, so too the "we" in this clause refers to all believers.[445] While not identical to the "blessing of Abraham" from the previous clause, the "promised Spirit" (τὴν ἐπαγγελίαν τοῦ πνεύματος)[446] is the definitive blessing that believers experience as a result of God fulfilling the promise made to Abraham in his promised descendant Jesus Christ (3:15–18).[447] Although nowhere in Genesis is the gift of the Spirit linked to the promise made to Abraham, that connection is developed in the Prophets.[448] Especially important is Isaiah 44:1–5, which connects the themes of blessing, Spirit, and seed.[449] God reassures "Jacob my servant, Israel whom I have chosen" not to fear (44:1–2) because he promises that "I will pour water on the thirsty land and streams on the dry ground; I will pour out my Spirit on your descendants and my blessing on your offspring" (44:3). The future hope of God's people rests on God pouring out his Spirit on the

---

[444] Some scholars have suggested that Paul here paraphrases the words of the angel of the Lord to Abraham in Gen 22:18, which in the LXX reads "and in your offspring shall all the nations of the earth be blessed, because you have obeyed my voice" (NETS); see most recently Caroline E. Johnson Hodge, *If Sons, Then Heirs: A Study of Kinship and Ethnicity in the Letters of Paul* (Oxford: Oxford University Press, 2007), 104. If so, Paul has essentially substituted "Christ Jesus" for "seed," which does fit the context of Galatians here quite well.

[445] A notable dissenting voice is Wright (*Climax of the Covenant*, 154–55), who maintains that even this first person plural pronoun refers exclusively to Jewish Christians.

[446] Woodenly the expression is "the promise of the Spirit," but the genitive expression here is likely epexegetical (i.e., the promise that is the Spirit = the promised Spirit).

[447] This is preferable to the conclusion of Moo (*Galatians*, 216), who regards the blessing of Abraham (which in the context he equates with justification) and the promise of the Spirit as "related but separate gifts of the new covenant."

[448] On this see especially Lee, *Blessing of Abraham*, 95–135.

[449] See further Harmon, *She Must and Shall Go Free*, 146–50 and Rodrigo Jose Morales, "The Words of the Luminaries, the Curse of the Law, and the Outpouring of the Spirit in Gal 3,10–14," *ZNW* 100 (2009): 269–77.

servant's descendants, which results in those descendants multiplying (44:4) and Jew and gentile alike identifying themselves as belonging to Yahweh (44:5). As the suffering servant, Christ died to enable the blessing of Abraham to come to the gentiles, which Isaiah sees as culminating in the gift of the Spirit to both Jew and gentile alike.

The gift of the Spirit is received "through faith" (διὰ τῆς πίστεως).[450] The connection between the believer's faith and experience of the Spirit harkens back to 3:2–5, where Paul emphasized that both the initial reception and ongoing experience of the Spirit is based on "hearing with faith" rather than works of the law or the flesh. This phrase also looks back to 2:16, where Paul insists that "a person is not justified by the works of the law but by faith in Jesus Christ [διὰ πίστεως Ἰησοῦ Χριστοῦ]." The blessing of Abraham, which includes but is not limited to justification and the gift of the Spirit, comes on the basis of faith in Jesus Christ. Or as Paul put it earlier: "those who have faith are blessed with Abraham, who had faith" (3:9).

From the very beginning, God's purpose in human history was to redeem people from among the nations. As those who have experienced the blessing of Abraham and the gift of the Spirit through faith in the curse-bearing Christ, we should seek to invite those around us to enjoy those very same blessings through the redemption found in Christ.

Bridge

Many in our culture think God grades on a curve; as long as the good works outweigh the bad, God will accept them. But the Bible makes it clear that, as a holy and just God, he demands perfection. The good news of the gospel is that Jesus has taken upon himself the curse that our disobedience deserves through his death and resurrection. Through faith in him we can experience eschatological life in the present through the promised Spirit that comes to us in fulfillment of God's promise to Abraham. Take a moment to thank God in prayer for the staggering nature of the blessings he has given us in Christ.

D. CHRIST THE SINGULAR SEED (3:15–18)

[15] Brothers and sisters, I'm using a human illustration. No one sets aside or makes additions to a validated human will. [16] Now the promises were

---

[450] Consistent with his larger argument, Hays (*Faith of Jesus*, 102–11) argues that this is a reference to the faithfulness of Christ, not the faith of the believer.

spoken to Abraham and to his seed. He does not say "and to seeds," as though referring to many, but referring to one, and to your seed, who is Christ. [17] My point is this: The law, which came 430 years later, does not invalidate a covenant previously established by God and thus cancel the promise. [18] For if the inheritance is based on the law, it is no longer based on the promise; but God has graciously given it to Abraham through the promise.

Context

In this paragraph Paul lays out a second corollary to his thesis that justification and receiving the blessing promised to Abraham and his descendants is based on faith (3:6–9). The first corollary explained that justification cannot come through keeping the Mosaic law because a curse rests on all who fail to keep it perfectly (3:10–14). This second corollary provides another reason keeping the Mosaic law cannot lead to justification: the Mosaic law covenant came 430 years after the promise made to Abraham, which established that justification was by faith (3:15–18).

Structure

Now that Paul has explained why the law cannot justify, he turns to explain the relationship between the Mosaic law and the covenant promises God made to Abraham. Using a "human illustration," the apostle insists that even with human covenants, once they are ratified they cannot be altered (3:15). This assertion sets the stage for summarizing God's covenant promise to Abraham and his singular seed—Jesus Christ (3:16). Since the Mosaic law covenant came 430 years after this promise was made to Abraham and his seed, it does not in any way nullify that covenant promise to Abraham (3:17). Paul concludes this paragraph by identifying a key underlying premise: inheriting the blessing God promised to Abraham cannot be based on observing the Mosaic law covenant because then that inheritance would no longer be based on promise but rather performance (3:18).

3:15. Now that Paul has completed the first stage of his argument that those who have faith in Christ are sons of Abraham, Paul now moves to explain further the connection between the promise made to Abraham and Christ. By addressing them as "Brothers and sisters" (Ἀδελφοί), Paul both signals the beginning of a new section of his argument and reminds the Galatians of their identity as fellow members of God's family. Rather than immediately add another argument, Paul says, "I'm using a human illustration" (κατὰ ἄνθρωπον λέγω).⁴⁵¹ Like Jesus in his use of parables, the apostle seeks to illustrate and explain a spiritual reality based on his audience's everyday experience. Paul will move from the lesser (the human illustration) to the greater (the spiritual reality), in effect saying, "If this is true in the realm of human experience, how much more when it comes to God's ways?" Behind the phrase "human illustration" is a prepositional phrase that woodenly reads "according to man" (κατὰ ἄνθρωπον). It is the same prepositional phrase used in 1:11, where Paul insists that his gospel is not "based on human thought" (HCSB; κατὰ ἄνθρωπον).

Since Paul's example does not have an exact parallel in Greek, Roman, or Jewish sources, he appears to be making a general illustration that does not depend on one of these specific backgrounds.⁴⁵² In any case, the larger point of the illustration is clear enough: "No one sets aside or makes additions to a validated human will" (ὅμως ἀνθρώπου κεκυρωμένην διαθήκην οὐδεὶς ἀθετεῖ ἢ ἐπιδιατάσσεται).⁴⁵³ The focal point of this illustration is the word rendered "will" (διαθήκη), which was used for a variety of agreements. In Greek literature the term most often referred to a person's last will and testament, and some scholars prefer that sense here.⁴⁵⁴ But in Jewish literature the word regularly refers to a covenant between God and humanity, and that is probably the preferable translation here.⁴⁵⁵

---

⁴⁵¹ Paul uses this or a similar expression in 1 Cor 3:3; 9:8; Rom 3:5. In each of these examples there is an emphasis on the "the inferiority of human beings in contrast with God" (BDAG s.v. ἄνθρωπος 2.b).

⁴⁵² See the discussion of possible backgrounds in Longenecker, *Galatians*, 128–30; he summarizes: "On the basis of our present knowledge of inheritance laws in the Greco-Roman and Jewish worlds, it seems, therefore, that Paul's use of διαθήκη in 3:15 is not exactly in accord with the legal situation of the day. It may be that we lack sufficient data. Or it may be that Paul felt no compulsion to speak in precise legal parlance, and that his readers would have felt the same" (130).

⁴⁵³ Paul introduces this clause with the adverb ὅμως, which usually has the sense of "all the same, nevertheless, yet" (BDAG s.v. ὅμως). But both times Paul uses this adverb (1 Cor 14:7; Gal 3:15) it has a comparative sense (so BDF §450.2). Others, however, noting the unusual position of the adverb, see this as an example of hyperbaton (i.e., when an adverb is located in the wrong position); see, e.g., Robertson, *Grammar*, 423.

⁴⁵⁴ See, for example, Moo, *Galatians*, 227 and Das, *Galatians*, 347–49, who after a thorough discussion of the issues, opts for "last will and testament." For discussion and examples of this usage, see BDAG s.v. διαθήκη 1; LSJM s.v. διαθήκη; MM, 148–49; TDNT 2:124–25. The rabbis appear to have taken up the word and concept in their literature with this sense (*TDNT* 2:124–25).

⁴⁵⁵ In the LXX, διαθήκη consistently (270 of 286 occurrences according to Longenecker, *Galatians*, 128) translates the Hebrew בְּרִית. This noun was likely an intentional choice in contrast to συνθήκη, which tended to refer to an "agreement" and was readily available as

Paul chooses this term here to tie his "human illustration" of a "human covenant" (3:15 HCSB) to his explanation of the relationship between the Abrahamic and Mosaic covenants (3:17–18).[456] Paul further describes this human covenant as one that "has been ratified" (HCSB; κεκυρωμένην). As used here, this verb (κυρόω) has the sense of giving official sanction to something, or even to make something legally binding.[457] The related adjective κυρία often occurs in Greek literature in the expression "the will is valid" (ἡ διαθήκη κυρία).[458] By using a perfect tense participle here, Paul stresses the settled state of this ratified human covenant.

With such a human covenant that has been ratified, Paul says there are two things that are not done. First, no one "sets aside" such a covenant. Paul uses additional legal language here. In such contexts this verb (ἀθετέω) means "to reject something as invalid."[459] It is the same verb used in 2:21, where Paul asserts, "I do not set aside the grace of God."[460]

---

well. As a general rule the latter communicated a mutual agreement closer to the idea of a contract, which the various LXX translators likely thought was not analogous to the nature of biblical covenants. Philo consistently uses διαθήκη to refer to the biblical covenants (Leg. 3:85; Sacr. 1:57; Det. 1:67–68; Her. 1:313; Mut. 1:51–53, 57–58, 263; Somn. 2:223–224, 237; Spec. 2:16), reserving συνθήκη for human agreements or contracts (Congr. 1:78; Legat. 1:37); see further discussion in TDNT 2:128. By contrast, Josephus uses διαθήκη 32 times, yet always in the sense of testament or will and never in reference to a biblical covenant (Longenecker, Galatians, 128). In addition to this evidence of the LXX and Jewish usage, Schreiner (Galatians, 227) lists three reasons for translating διαθήκη as covenant here: (1) in the larger context Paul uses this same term for God's promise to Abraham; (2) wills could be altered, whereas covenants could not; (3) the use of legal terminology does not demand a reference to a will here, since legal terms are also used in connection with covenants. See further Scott Hahn, "Covenant, Oath, and the Aqedah: Διαθηκη in Galatians 3:15–18," CBQ 67 (2005): 79–100. Hahn goes beyond the evidence, however, in limiting the covenant in view here to what is promised in Genesis 22:16–18.

[456] It is perhaps somewhat surprising that Paul only uses διαθήκη nine times in his letters (Rom 9:4; 11:27; 1 Cor 11:25; 2 Cor 3:6, 14; Gal 3:15, 17; 4:24; Eph 2:12). But its importance in the structure of Paul's thought far surpasses the explicit uses of this term, as N. T. Wright has helpfully pointed out in various places; see, e.g., Paul and the Faithfulness of God, Christian Origins and the Question of God vol. 4 (Minneapolis: Fortress Press, 2013), 780–83.

[457] See BDAG s.v. κυρόω 1 and TDNT 3:1098. "In historical writings it is commonly used of ratifying political agreements and the like (e.g., Polyb. 1.17.1), and it often occurs in the pass[ive] with the sense 'to be decided, determined' (e.g., ibid. 1.11.3)" (NIDNTTE 2:778). All four LXX occurrences (Gen 23:20; Lev 25:30; Dan 6:10; 4 Macc 7:9) occur in a legal context. The only other NT occurrence (2 Cor 2:8) refers to Paul asking the Corinthians to reaffirm their love for Paul.

[458] See, e.g., P. Oxy., III, 491, 12: 493, 12; 494, 30 (noted in TDNT 3:1098).

[459] BDAG s.v. ἀθετέω 1.

[460] Interestingly, in Psalm 89:34 [LXX 88:35] ἀθετέω occurs in close connection with διαθήκη, where Yahweh says, "I will not profane my covenant [διαθήκην] and the words

Criticizing the religious leaders of his day, Jesus noted, "You have a fine way of invalidating [ἀθετεῖτε] God's command in order to set up your tradition!" (Mark 7:9). Second, no one "makes additions to" such a covenant. Using still more legal language, this verb (ἐπιδιατάσσομαι) was a legal technical term that meant to add additional or modifying instructions to an agreement.[461]

Stepping back to the big picture, Paul's point is straightforward—once a covenant has been ratified, no one is allowed to set it aside or alter the terms.[462] As we shall see, Paul is constructing this analogy to establish the priority and unchangeable nature of God's covenant with Abraham. Throughout the ages, that has been the firm foundation of God's people, as the classic hymn reminds us:

> How firm a foundation, ye saints of the Lord,
> is laid for your faith in his excellent word.
> What more can he say, than to you he hath said,
> To you who for refuge to Jesus hath fled.[463]

3:16. Paul moves from the general situation described by the illustration to the specific application.[464] He begins: "Now the promises were spoken to Abraham and to his seed" (τῷ δὲ Ἀβραὰμ ἐρρέθησαν αἱ ἐπαγγελίαι καὶ τῷ σπέρματι αὐτοῦ). In Galatians Paul has already quoted from Genesis 15:6 (Gal 3:6) and appears to have combined elements of Genesis 12:3; 18:18; and 22:18 (Gal 3:8). Later in Galatians 4:21–5:1 Paul will also summarize Genesis 16 and cite 21:10. And one should not overlook the most recent occurrence of the word promise in 3:14, where Paul spoke of "the promised Spirit" (τὴν ἐπαγγελίαν τοῦ πνεύματος) coming to believers through faith. So when Paul refers to "the promises" here in 3:16 it is

---

going out through my lips I will never set aside [ἀθετήσω]" (my translation). In this context the covenant in view is the one made with David.

[461] BDAG s.v. ἐπιδιατάσσομαι. This is the only occurrence of the word in the NT or Greek literature, for that matter. Moulton suggests that "The Pauline use of this verb in connexion [sic] with a will in Gal 3¹⁵ may be illustrated from the occurrence of διατάσσεσθαι, διάταξις, etc., in inscr[iptions] from Asia Minor with the specialized meaning of 'determine by testamentary disposition' " (MM, 238).

[462] De Boer (*Galatians*, 219) insists that the context clearly indicates no one means "no one except the testator himself should he be so inclined."

[463] K., "How firm a foundation, ye saints of the Lord," in Rippon's *A Selection of Hymns*, 1787, https://hymnary.org/text/how_firm_a_foundation_ye_saints_of.

[464] On this use of δέ, see Beale, Ross, and Brendsel, *Interpretive Lexicon*, 33.

best to see a reference to the entire complex of promises that God made to Abraham, with a particular focus on all the nations being blessed in him (Gal 3:8).[465] By stating that these promises were "spoken," Paul highlights the personal and direct nature of God's interaction with Abraham.

These promises were made "to Abraham and to his seed" (τῷ ... Ἀβραὰμ ... καὶ τῷ σπέρματι αὐτοῦ). In Greek Paul places the phrase "to Abraham" at the beginning of the sentence both for emphasis and to refocus the argument that began in 3:6 where Abraham was first introduced. Repeatedly throughout Genesis 12–25 God states that a promise is for both Abraham and his seed, but Paul may specifically have Genesis 17:7–10 in mind.[466] While we will discuss Genesis 17 and its context below, here it is important to note that five times in these verses God says to Abraham that the promises are for "you and your seed after you" (HCSB). While the noun rendered "seed" (σπέρμα) can refer to the seed of plants or even semen, in both the LXX and the New Testament it most often refers to descendants or offspring. In Genesis the notion of "seed" is central. When God announces judgment on the serpent, he says in part, "I will put hostility between you and the woman, and between your offspring and her offspring. He will strike your head, and you will strike his heel" (Gen 3:15). This conflict between the offspring of the woman and the offspring of the serpent is in fact the central conflict of the Bible, setting the trajectory for the rest of human history. This thread is picked up in Genesis 12:7, where, after promising to make Abram into a great nation (Gen 12:1–3), God says to Abram, "To your offspring I will give this land." From this point forward in Genesis, the theme of Abraham and his offspring drives the narrative forward.[467]

At this point Paul drills down deeper into the notion of seed when he notes: "He does not say 'and to seeds,' as though referring to many" (οὐ λέγει· καὶ τοῖς σπέρμασιν, ὡς ἐπὶ πολλῶν).[468] In both Hebrew (זֶרַע) and Greek (σπέρμα) the word for "seed" can be used individually or collectively;

---

[465] It is interesting that whereas Paul only uses the word "covenant" (διαθήκη) three times in Galatians (3:15, 17; 4:24), the word "promise" (ἐπαγγελία) occurs ten times (3:14, 16, 17, 18 [2x], 21, 22, 29; 4:23, 28). Witherington (Grace in Galatia, 244) suggests that the plural "promises" here stems from Gen 17:1–9, which mentions land, descendants, and God's presence. Paul's apparent allusion to Genesis 17 (see below) make this suggestion plausible.

[466] Das (Galatians, 351–52) suggests that Paul is also citing Genesis 13:15, but if so, it is in the background to the stronger connections with Genesis 17:8.

[467] On the theme of seed, see further Biblical Theology §4.0.

[468] As used here the preposition ἐπί functions as a marker of perspective, having the sense of "in consideration of, in regard to, on the basis of, concerning, about" (BDAG s.v. ἐπί 8).

only the context can determine which is intended.[469] Sometimes the context itself is ambiguous, or in some cases both may be intended. Paul insists that when God made promises to Abraham and his seed, God was "referring to one, and to your seed, who is Christ" (ἀλλ᾽ ὡς ἐφ᾽ ἑνός· καὶ τῷ σπέρματί σου, ὅς ἐστιν Χριστός). According to Paul, the promises were made to one individual descendant from Abraham—Christ.[470]

Although Paul does not explain how he reaches this conclusion, there is solid evidence for this claim within the Old Testament itself. The starting point is Genesis 17. Despite God's promise to make him into a great nation, he and his wife Sarai remained childless. God had reassured Abram that his heir would be a son who comes from his own body, not his servant Eliezer (Gen 15:1–21). Impatient with God's timetable, Sarai encourages Abram to impregnate her Egyptian maid Hagar to produce the promise heir (Gen 16:1–16). Thirteen years later God appears to Abram, where he reaffirms his covenant promises to multiply him into the father of nations and even kings (17:1–6). Yahweh continues by swearing:

> I will confirm my covenant that is between me and you and your future offspring throughout their generations. It is a permanent covenant to be your God and the God of your offspring after you. And to you and your future offspring I will give the land where you are residing—all the land of Canaan—as a permanent possession, and I will be their God. (Gen 17:7–8)

The context here clearly indicates that multiple descendants are in view.[471] The gift of circumcision as the sign of this covenant seems to confirm that

---

[469] The Hebrew noun זֶרַע never occurs in the plural in the OT. However, when an author intends זֶרַע to refer to a specific individual, he uses "singular verb inflections, adjectives and pronouns"; see C. John Collins, "A Syntactical Note (Genesis 3:15): Is the Woman's Seed Singular or Plural?," *TynBul* 48 (1997): 139–48. Throughout the LXX, זֶרַע is consistently translated with σπέρμα, which occurs in the plural just six times (Lev 26:16; 1 Sam 8:15; Ps 125:6; Isa 61:11; Dan 1:16; 11:31). In each of these occurrences σπέρμα refers to agricultural seeds. Galatians 3:16 is the only plural occurrence of σπέρμα in the NT.

[470] Although this exegetical move has troubled modern interpreters, Moo (*Galatians*, 229–30) makes four helpful observations. First, Paul's argument is in line with interpretive techniques common in the Judaism of his day. Second, Paul clearly knows that σπέρμα has a collective sense in 3:29. Third, some of the Genesis promise texts clearly do use σπέρμα to refer to a singular seed, especially Isaac. Fourth, Paul may be reflecting interpretive traditions that linked σπέρμα to a descendant of David, such as 2 Sam 7:12, where the seed in view at one level refers to Solomon while at the same time pointing forward to the Messiah.

[471] Martyn (*Galatians*, 340) claims that Paul ignores the clear plural reference of seed here in Gen 17:8 because he is so determined to hear in it a messianic prophecy. But Martyn completely ignores Gen 17:15–21, where a singular seed is clearly in view.

multiple descendants are in view (17:9–14). But a shift occurs in 17:15–21. God promises to give Abraham a son through his wife Sarah (17:15–16). Abraham laughs in light of their advanced age and pleads for God to bless Ishmael (17:17–18). But God insists:

> "No. Your wife Sarah will bear you a son, and you will name him Isaac. I will confirm my covenant with him as a permanent covenant for his future offspring ... I will confirm my covenant with Isaac, whom Sarah will bear to you at this time next year." (17:19, 21)

Here the seed/offspring in view is clearly singular. Yahweh will confirm his covenant with Isaac and his seed. It is through the singular seed Isaac that the promises will be fulfilled and the blessings of that covenant will extend to his offspring. Paul picks up on this emphasis on the singular seed Isaac as the key to the fulfillment of God's promises to Abraham.

Further confirmation is found in Genesis 22. Yahweh tests Abraham by commanding him to sacrifice Isaac (22:1–8). Just as Abraham is about to plunge the knife into his son, the angel of Yahweh stays his hand (22:9–14). The Lord reaffirms his promise to multiply Abraham's seed like the stars of heaven and the sand of the seashore (22:15–17a). But immediately after this reference to multiple seed/offspring, Yahweh says, "Your offspring shall possess the gate of his enemies" (22:17b ESV).[472] The blessing of the many offspring hinges on a singular offspring who will defeat the enemies of God's people. Through Isaac, Abraham's only son, the promises find their fulfillment and result in blessing to the nations.[473]

---

[472] Although most English versions have "their enemies," the Hebrew reads "his enemies" (אֹיְבָיו). Both T. D. Alexander ("Further Observations," 363–67) and Paul Williamson (*Abraham, Israel, and the Nations*, 248–50) have shown that the reference to seed here is singular.

[473] Further support for a possible Isaac "typology" at work here surfaces in Gal 4:28, where Paul writes, "Now you too, brothers and sisters, like Isaac, are children of promise." Romans 8:32 may also betray an underlying Isaac typology when Paul states: "He did not even spare his own Son but gave him up for us all. How will he not also with him grant us everything?" On the possible presence of Isaac typology in these texts and elsewhere in the NT, see J. Edwin Wood, "Isaac Typology in the New Testament," *NTS* 14 (1968): 583–89 and Nils Alstrup Dahl, *The Crucified Messiah and Other Essays* (Minneapolis: Augsburg, 1974), 153–57. Focus on an individual seed is also found in Pseudo-Philo (LAB 8:3) and Jub. 16:17–19. Some scholars have further suggested that Paul interprets the singular seed messianically by seeing a link to 2 Sam 7:12–14, which speaks of a descendant from David's line; see, e.g., Max Wilcox, "The Promise of the 'Seed' in the New Testament and the Targumin," *JSNT* 5 (1979): 2–20; Richard B. Hays, *Echoes of Scripture in the Letters of Paul* (New Haven: Yale University Press, 1989), 85; Matthew V. Novenson, *Christ among the Messiahs: Christ Language in Paul and Messiah Language in Ancient*

Paul may also have drawn his emphasis on the singular seed from several key texts in Isaiah.[474] Our starting point is Isaiah 41:8, where God says, "But you, Israel, my servant, Jacob, whom I have chosen, descendant of Abraham, my friend—I brought you from the ends of the earth and called you from its farthest corners. I said to you: You are my servant; I have chosen you, I haven't rejected you."[475] Notice the parallelism: Israel, my servant // Jacob, whom I have chosen // descendant of Abraham, my friend. "The progression in both the titles and the descriptive phrases works backwards chronologically. First there was the seed of Abraham upon whom God set his love, which through Isaac resulted in Jacob, whom God chose. Eventually from Jacob (whose name was changed to Israel) comes forth Israel, who was Yahweh's servant. Thus Isa 41:8 brings together the ideas of Abraham's seed and Israel as Yahweh's servant in its description of the people of God."[476]

This connection between the seed of Abraham and Yahweh's servant is further developed in the chapters that follow. The people of the nation of Israel failed to live up to their calling to be the servant of the LORD (42:1–25). But God promises a day when he will pour out his Spirit on the seed of the servant (44:3–5). In light of the Israelites' failure, God raises up a new individual servant to redeem Israel and obey where the Israelites had failed (49:1–8). The saving righteousness this servant accomplishes will fulfill the promise God made to Abraham and result in a new creation (51:1–8). As a result of the servant giving his life as an offering for sin, the servant "will see his seed, he will prolong his days, and by his hand, the LORD's pleasure will be accomplished" (53:10). Just as God gave offspring to once-barren Sarah, so too he will bring into existence the eschatological people of God to fulfill his promise to Abraham so that his seed will multiply and possess the nations (54:1–3). The merging of the themes of

---

Judaism (New York: Oxford University Press, 2012), 138–42. On a biblical-theological level it is certainly true that the singular seed of Abraham eventually leads to the singular seed of David. And Paul does use sonship language in Gal 4:4–7 to refer to both Jesus and believers, which may allude to the promise made to David. But whether this evidence is enough to see a reference to 2 Sam 7:12–14 here in Gal 3:16 remains questionable.

[474] This is a summary of what is treated at length in Harmon, *She Must and Shall Go Free*, 151–55.

[475] In Hebrew, every second person reference in 41:8–9 is singular, further suggesting an individual emphasis.

[476] Harmon, *She Must and Shall Go Free*, 152–53.

servant and seed in Isaiah 40–55 may have led Paul to move from Christ as the servant to Christ as the singular seed.

N.T. Wright takes a different view of the reference to seed here in Galatians 3:16. Since the reference to Abraham's seed later in 3:29 clearly refers to believers (regardless of ethnicity), Wright claims that the singularity of the seed "is not the singularity of a singular person contrasted with the plurality of many human beings, but the singularity of one *family* contrasted with the plurality of families which would result if the Torah were to be regarded the way Paul's opponents apparently regard it."[477] Thus the identification of the singular seed as Christ has a representative or corporative sense, in which it carries "the significance of the one 'in whom' the people of God is summed up precisely *as* the people of God."[478] But as Chris Bruno has helpfully noted, the immediate context of Galatians 3:16 "virtually demands that 'seed' be read as a reference to a single person."[479] It is far more natural to take the clause "who is Christ" that immediately follows the reference to a singular seed in 3:16 as defining the seed as the individual Christ than it is to leap to 3:29 for the plural reference of seed and read that back into 3:16.

When it comes to reading Scripture, attention to the details matters. Paul rests his argument on noting that the promise would be fulfilled in a singular seed based on his careful reading of Genesis and other key Old Testament texts. Jesus addressed the Sadducees' rejection of the resurrection based on a verb tense (Matt 22:29–32). As God's people, we need to dig into the details of God's word as a means of strengthening our faith in Christ and fueling our obedience to him.

3:17. Perhaps recognizing that his point is not yet clear to his readers, Paul writes, "My point is this" (τοῦτο δὲ λέγω).[480] Although the sentence that follows is complicated, the basic thought is straightforward: "The law ...

---

[477] See Wright, *Climax of the Covenant*, 157–74; the quote is from 163.

[478] Wright, *Climax of the Covenant*, 165.

[479] Christopher R. Bruno, *"God Is One": The Function of Eis Ho Theos as a Ground for Gentile Inclusion in Paul's Letters*, LNTS 497 (London: Bloomsbury, 2013), 172–74, quote taken from 174.

[480] Once again, Paul uses δέ to signal a new development in the argument (DeSilva, *Handbook*, 68).

does not invalidate a covenant" (διαθήκην … ὁ … νόμος οὐκ ἀκυροῖ). Each of these elements—law, revoke, and covenant—are further described.[481]

The law refers to the Mosaic law, as the following verses make clear. But Paul is not merely referring to the legal stipulations that God gave to Israel. He has in view the entirety of the Mosaic covenant that God made with Israel at Sinai.[482] Paul points out that the law "came 430 years later" (μετὰ τετρακόσια καὶ τριάκοντα ἔτη γεγονώς),[483] which Exodus 12:40–41 indicates is the number of years Israel lived in Egypt.[484] This temporal marker is important because it establishes the priority of the Abrahamic covenant over the Mosaic law. Despite the common Jewish belief that the law was eternal,[485] Paul insists that the Mosaic law had a specific beginning point, and he will go on to argue later in this chapter that it has a specific ending point as well.

The giving of the law does not "invalidate" the covenant with Abraham. Paul uses a rare verb here (ἀκυρόω) that has the sense of "make void."[486] This same verb describes how the religious leaders of Jesus' day nullified God's word by their traditions (Matt 15:6; Mark 7:13).[487] In Greek literature this word family regularly occurs in legal contexts referring to the

---

[481] In Greek Paul places the expression "a covenant previously established" at the front of the clause to further stress the priority of the Abrahamic covenant over the Mosaic law covenant.

[482] Paul likely avoids using the word covenant in connection with the Sinai event to prevent confusion, since he uses it to refer to the Abrahamic covenant.

[483] DeSilva (*Handbook*, 68) suggests the perfect tense of the verb γίνομαι "may be significant insofar as the law continued to be in effect alongside the promise many centuries after it 'came into being.' "

[484] Both Genesis 15:13 and Acts 7:6 refer to a period of 400 years, but specifically refer to this as a time of slavery and affliction. Perhaps the difference rests in the emphasis on Israel's affliction versus their total time in Egypt. Longenecker (*Galatians*, 133) notes that Josephus resolved it by concluding 430 years covers the span between Abraham entering Canaan and Moses leading the people out (*Ant.* 2:318), and 400 years covers the time of Israel's sojourn in Egypt (*Ant.* 2:204; *War* 5:382). The rabbis often connected the 430 years to the time between God's covenant with Abraham and the giving of the law at Sinai, while the 400 years covers the time Israel spent in Egypt (Tg. Ps-J. Exod. 12:40; Mek. Exod. 12:40; Gen. Rab. 44:18; Exod. Rab. 18:11).

[485] Das (*Galatians*, 354) notes the following texts: Wis 18:4; 4 Ezra 9:37; 1 En. 99:2; Jub. 3:31; 6:17; Bar 4:1; 2 Bar. 77:15; Philo, *Mos.* 2.3.14.

[486] BDAG s.v. ἀκυρόω.

[487] The only occurrences in the LXX are in the non-canonical books: 1 Esd 6:31; 4 Macc 2:1, 3, 18; 5:18; 7:14; 17:2.

voiding of agreements or contracts.[488] In this scenario the purpose/result of making the covenant void would be to "cancel the promise" (εἰς τὸ καταργῆσαι τὴν ἐπαγγελίαν).[489] "Cancel" (καταργέω) is a much more common verb in Paul; here it has the sense of "cause something to lose its power or effectiveness."[490] As is the case here, Paul regularly uses it in discussions of the relationship between faith, God's promises, the law, and God's faithfulness (Rom 3:3, 31; 4:14; 7:2, 6; Gal 5:4, 11). Although "promise" (ἐπαγγελία) is singular, it refers back to the "promises" made to Abraham mentioned in 3:16. The switch from plural to singular may simply be stylistic, or it may be an effort to more closely align the promise with the covenant as a single (albeit complex) entity.

The (Abrahamic) covenant that the Mosaic law does not revoke is further described as "previously established by God" (προκεκυρωμένην ὑπὸ τοῦ θεου). Paul adds the prefix προ- ("before") to the verb κυρόω ("ratify") used in 3:15 to make the connection with the analogy clear.[491] In speaking of God establishing the covenant, he may have in mind Genesis 15:7–21, where God "ratifies" his covenant with Abraham. To assure Abraham that he would keep his promise, God instructed him to cut several animals in half. When it became dark, God caused Abraham to fall asleep and then appeared to him in a vision as a smoking fire pot and flaming torch passing between the animal pieces. By doing so God affirmed that he would take full responsibility for fulfilling the covenant promises.

By making the simple observation that the Abrahamic promise/covenant came 430 years before the Mosaic law covenant, Paul is showing us how to read the Bible in a redemptive-historical fashion. His argument rests on reading the text chronologically and tracing the development

---

[488] See references in MM, 120; LSJM s.v. ἀκυρόω. This verb is the opposite of the verb κυρόω ("ratify") used in 3:15 and 3:17 to describe a covenant being ratified.

[489] Although in the construction εἰς + the articular infinitive usually indicates purpose (DeSilva, *Handbook*, 68), as is often the case, distinguishing between purpose and result is difficult and perhaps unnecessary (Robertson, *Grammar*, 1002–3).

[490] BDAG s.v. καταργέω 2. Of the twenty-seven NT occurrences, only two (Luke 13:7; Heb 2:14) are outside of Paul's letters. In Gal 5:4 Paul uses it to refer to being "alienated from Christ" and again in 5:11 to describe the offense of the cross being abolished. This verb has a broader meaning than ἀκυρόω, being used in many more contexts, ranging in meaning from exhaust to make powerless and points in between.

[491] The verb προκυρόω occurs nowhere else in the LXX or NT. To this point only two occurrences of this verb have been found predating its appearance here in Gal 3:17 (*NIDNTTE* 2:778).

of God's plan of redemption. By doing so Paul is able to see the priority of the Abrahamic promise covenant over the Mosaic law. By contrast, "Jewish theology generally viewed the Abrahamic covenant, with the requirement of circumcision, as the first stage of a covenant arrangement that was later expanded in the Mosaic covenant."[492] But as far as Paul is concerned, whatever the purpose of the law, it cannot be to nullify the promise with Abraham. In fairness, Paul's opponents likely would have claimed they are doing no such thing. But the fundamental difference is in Paul's conclusion that the Mosaic law was intended as a servant of the Abrahamic covenant, not something that replaced it. In contrast to the widely held view of his Jewish contemporaries that the Mosaic law was eternal in nature, Paul is setting the stage for his claim in 3:19–25 that it came with an expiration date—the arrival of the promised seed Jesus Christ. But the apostle is likely making more than a simple chronological argument, for as we have noted he sees the Abrahamic covenant operating on the principle of faith in the promise in contrast to the Mosaic law covenant, which functions on the principle of doing what is commanded.[493]

The Bible is not simply a collection of wise religious sayings or interesting moral tales. It tells an overarching story that runs from Genesis to Revelation. In that story God progressively reveals his plans and purposes. Paying attention to the sequence of events and the relationship between people, promises, and covenants is an essential part of understanding how the Bible fits together as a coherent whole. As believers, we benefit tremendously by learning to read Scripture the way that Jesus and the apostles model for us.

3:18. To further explain his point, Paul now uses an if/then statement to demonstrate that the fulfillment of the promise made to Abraham cannot come through the Mosaic law: "For if the inheritance is based on the law, it is no longer based on the promise" (εἰ γὰρ ἐκ νόμου ἡ κληρονομία, οὐκέτι ἐξ ἐπαγγελίας).[494] Paul introduces a new term into the discussion: inheritance (κληρονομία). From this point forward this word and its cognates (heir, inherit) become a shorthand for experiencing the blessings

---

[492] Moo, *Galatians*, 230.

[493] Schreiner, *Galatians*, 231.

[494] This is a first class conditional statement, which presents the "if" clause as true for the sake of argument. But, as DeSilva (*Handbook*, 68) notes, "The effect of the second half of the verse will be to turn this, essentially, into a contrary-to-fact condition by presenting evidence that shows the protasis to be impossible."

promised to Abraham (Gal 3:18, 29; 4:1, 7, 30: 5:21). As such it is closely
related to terms such as justify/justification/righteousness (2:16–17, 21;
3:6, 8, 11), bless/blessing (3:8–9, 14), and live (3:12) that have already been
used to this point. This usage is consistent with how the word family is
used elsewhere in the New Testament, often referring to experiencing
the various blessings that come to the believer through the work of Christ
(e.g., Rom 4:13–14; 8:17; Eph 1:14, 18; Heb 6:12, 17; 1 Pet 1:4).[495] As believers,
we already experience the blessings of our inheritance in Christ through
the gift of the Holy Spirit (Eph 1:14, 18), yet we still await the fullness of
that inheritance (1 Cor 15:50; Col 3:24; 1 Pet 1:4). This connection between
the believer's inheritance and the gift of the Spirit is a theme Paul will
return to in Galatians 4:1–7.

The Old Testament concept of inheritance was regularly tied to God's
promise to give the land of Canaan to Abraham and his descendants
(Gen 12:7; 15:18–21; 17:8; Num 34:1–29; Deut 12:10).[496] This inheritance is
God's gracious gift, not something Israel earned by its righteousness (Deut
9:4–7). Descriptions of the land and its fertility portray this gift as a new
Eden where God will dwell with his people (Exod 3:8, 17; Lev 20:24; Num
16:13–14; Deut 11:9–12). In some texts the language of inheritance moves
beyond the land of Canaan to an international scope. In Psalm 2:8, the
Lord's anointed king is promised the nations as his inheritance, and the
expansion of the inheritance beyond the land of Canaan to the ends of
the earth prepares the way for a similar expansion in the New Testament
(cf. Rom 4:13). As such, discussion of believers' inheritance anticipates
the summary phrase "new creation" that Paul uses to summarize his
argument in 6:15. Through the gift of the Spirit believers experience the
inauguration of this new creation promise (3:14), and through him they
continue to experience their inheritance as they await its consummation
(5:5–6; Eph 1:13–14).[497]

---

[495] See further Matthew S. Harmon, "Inheritance," in *The Baker Illustrated Bible Dictionary*,
ed. Tremper Longman (Grand Rapids: Baker, 2013), 839–40.

[496] God's relationship with Israel is also described in terms of inheritance. On the one
hand, Israel is described as the Lord's inheritance (Deut 32:9; 1 Sam 10:1; 1 Kgs 8:51–53). On
the other hand, God is Israel's inheritance (Pss 16:5; 73:26; Jer 10:16; 51:19). This mutuality
expresses the intimacy of God's relationship with Israel. Das (*Galatians*, 355) notes that in
the Jewish thought of Paul's day, inheritance was also linked to eternal life or eschatological
realities (Pss. Sol. 14:5, 9–10; 15:10–11; 17:23; 1 En. 40:9; Sib. Or. frag. 3:47).

[497] Although it is clear that the Spirit is a central aspect of the inheritance believers
receive, it is misleading to say "the Spirit appears to replace the land in Paul's thinking"

Paul insists that receiving the inheritance promised to Abraham and his seed is not "based on the law" (ἐκ νόμου), or possibly "from the law" (compare NRSV). The latter rendering would stress that the law is not the source of the inheritance, while the former would emphasize that the law is not the basis for receiving the inheritance. While both ideas are true, the larger context suggests the phrase indicates basis.[498] Paul has already stressed that no one is justified (2:16) or receives the Spirit (3:2, 5) "by the works of the law" (ἐξ ἔργων νόμου). Furthermore, all who "rely on works of the law" (ἐξ ἔργων νόμου) are under the curse (3:10). This pattern of usage in Galatians suggests that Paul has in view the basis of receiving the inheritance. Again, Paul departs from a common Jewish strain of thought that connected law and promise. For example, 2 Maccabees 2:17–18 states, "It is God who has saved all his people, and has returned the *inheritance* to all, and the kingship and priesthood and consecration, *as he promised through the law*."[499] While it is likely Paul shared a similar view in his pre-conversion days, his encounter with the risen Christ led him to see that the law was not the path to inheriting what God had promised.

If, as Paul implies his opponents contend, receiving the inheritance did come on the basis of the law, then "it is no longer based on the promise" (οὐκέτι ἐξ ἐπαγγελίας). The inheritance comes on the basis of the promise, not the Mosaic law covenant. The phrase "no longer" has more a logical than temporal force; again, Paul is noting the fundamental opposition between the law and the promise.[500] This claim is confirmed by the fact that "God has graciously given it to Abraham through the promise"

(Das, *Galatians*, 351). Central to the Abrahamic promise was both God's presence ("I will be with you") and a place where God's presence would dwell with his people (i.e., land). The promise of God's presence is fulfilled (in an inaugurated sense) through the gift of the Spirit. The promise of a "place" is fulfilled (again, in an inaugurated sense) as the Spirit dwells inside the individual believer who experiences the new creation (again, in an inaugurated sense) that one day will transform the entire created order. Thus when the promised inheritance is consummated in a new heavens and new earth, God's Spirit will indeed fill the new creation. Thus the promise of land is not replaced by the Spirit.

[498] So also DeSilva, *Handbook*, 68.

[499] Noted by Das (*Galatians*, 356), who also highlights Pss. Sol. 12:6; Sib. Or. 3:768–69; 2 Bar. 14:12–13; 57:2.

[500] Schreiner, *Galatians*, 232. Compare Moo (*Galatians*, 232): "Paul argues against imposing the law on the Galatian Christians, then, not only because it belongs to an earlier phase of salvation history. It is also not a channel of blessing or inheritance, because its nature contradicts the fundamentally gracious manner in which God bestows his blessing on his people."

(τῷ δὲ Ἀβραὰμ δι᾽ ἐπαγγελίας κεχάρισται ὁ θεός). The verb rendered "graciously given" (χαρίζομαι) was "a common term in honorific documents lauding officials and civic-minded persons for their beneficence."[501] Elsewhere Paul uses this verb to describe God giving believers his Son (Rom 8:32), the Holy Spirit (1 Cor 2:12), and the gifts of faith and suffering (Phil 1:29). By using this verb Paul highlights the gracious and undeserved nature of God's interaction with Abraham, with the perfect tense of the verb stressing the ongoing status of the gift. As such he is reinforcing his point in 3:17 that the law coming 430 years later does not nullify the covenant with Abraham. The inheritance comes to Abraham and his seed "through the promise" (δι᾽ ἐπαγγελίας), once again highlighting the promise as the means or the efficient cause of the inheritance.[502]

Paul's assertion that the inheritance comes to Abraham through the promise and not the law runs contrary to a major strain of Jewish thought, which postulated that Abraham obeyed the law and was blessed by God as a result.[503] But by insisting on reading Scripture in a redemptive-historical manner, Paul demonstrates that it was not Abraham's obedience that was the path of receiving the inheritance. Instead, it was the promise of God and the faithfulness of the God of the promise.

The same is true for believers today. We receive our spiritual inheritance not based on anything good we do, but by faith in the same God who revealed himself to Abraham. Yet despite knowing this, we are still prone to think that our performance is what earns the spiritual blessings we enjoy. Paul's words here remind us that not even a man as great as Abraham was able to earn his inheritance through his obedience to God; why should we think we are any different?

Bridge

We live in a world of broken promises. Even the best among us sometimes fail to deliver on something that we had promised to do. Yet our

---

[501] BDAG s.v. χαρίζομαι 1. In the LXX this verb only occurs in the non-canonical books (Esth 8:7; 2 Macc 1:35; 3:31, 33; 4:32; 7:22; 3 Macc 1:8; 5:11; 7:6; 4 Macc 5:8; 11:12; Sir 12:3). For examples from Greek literature, see MM, 684.

[502] Although BDAG labels the use of διά here as occasion (s.v. διά A.3.e), it seems preferable to see the stronger sense of either means/instrument (A.3.a) or efficient cause (A.3.d); see similarly DeSilva, Handbook, 69.

[503] See further Biblical Theology §1.1.2.

hope as believers is grounded in the absolute faithfulness of God to keep his promises. God has promised us an inheritance that is "imperishable, undefiled, and unfading, kept in heaven for you" (1 Pet 1:4). Since it is kept in heaven for us, it is safe from moth and rust, protected from any thief (Matt 6:20). That is where our hearts should be focused (Matt 6:21) as we, as believers, await the day when our full inheritance is given to us in a new creation. Yet in the meantime, God has given us the Holy Spirit, who is "the down payment of our inheritance, until the redemption of the possession, to the praise of his glory" (Eph 1:14).

E. THE PURPOSE OF THE LAW (3:19–25)

> [19] Why then was the law given? It was added for the sake of transgressions until the Seed to whom the promise was made would come. The law was put into effect through angels by means of a mediator. [20] Now a mediator is not just for one person alone, but God is one. [21] Is the law therefore contrary to God's promises? Absolutely not! For if the law had been granted with the ability to give life, then righteousness would certainly be on the basis of the law. [22] But the Scripture imprisoned everything under sin's power, so that the promise might be given on the basis of faith in Jesus Christ to those who believe. [23] Before this faith came, we were confined under the law, imprisoned until the coming faith was revealed. [24] The law, then, was our guardian until Christ, so that we could be justified by faith. [25] But since that faith has come, we are no longer under a guardian,

Context

In light of his thesis that justification and status as sons of Abraham who receive the promise are both based on faith (3:6–9), Paul has explained two corollaries: (1) the Mosaic law brings a curse rather than blessing because no one can keep it perfectly (3:10–14); and (2) because it came 430 years after the promise to Abraham and his seed (i.e., Christ), the Mosaic law does not nullify the promise, which is received by believing rather than doing. Given the seemingly negative statements about the Mosaic law, Paul must now explain the place of the Mosaic law in God's plan of redemption (3:19–25).[504]

---

[504] While this paragraph is certainly important for Paul's argument, Longenecker (*Galatians*, 137) goes too far when he calls it "the *crux interpretum* for Paul's response to the problems in Galatia."

Structure

Since the Mosaic law cannot bring about the covenant blessings God promised to Abraham (i.e., justification, sonship, blessing to the nations, the gift of the Spirit, inheritance, etc.), the natural question is, Why then did God give the law? Paul answers that question in three parts. First, he explains why the law was given (3:19–20). The purpose was to bring sin out into the open as a violation of God's holy will. But the Mosaic law covenant had a built-in expiration date; once the promised seed came, its role would be complete. It was never intended to bring into existence the one seed in whom the one God would bless all the nations. Second, Paul insists that the Mosaic law does not run contrary to God's promises to Abraham. The Mosaic law was never intended to bring eschatological life; instead it was God's instrument to imprison all things under sin so that Jew and gentile alike could inherit the promises made to Abraham by trusting in Christ Jesus. The third part of Paul's answer is to explain how the Mosaic law covenant functioned (3:23–25). It was a guardian for Israel until Christ the promised seed arrived, imprisoning them until Christ the promised seed arrived and Jew and gentile alike could be justified by faith in Christ. As a result, now that Christ has arrived, the supervisory role of the Mosaic law has ceased, having fulfilled its temporary purpose.

3:19. In light of Paul's prioritization of the covenant God made with Abraham over the Mosaic law (3:15–18), a natural question arises: "Why, then, was the law given?" (Τί οὖν ὁ νόμος).[505] Paul answers this question by stating: (1) the purpose of the law, (2) the timeframe for the validity of the law, and (3) the mechanism through which the law was given.

As for the purpose of the law, Paul says that "It was added for the sake of transgressions" (τῶν παραβάσεων χάριν προσετέθη).[506] The verb "added" (προστίθημι) portrays the law as something put in place alongside the already existing Abrahamic promise covenant. As such it does not nullify the promise God made to Abraham (3:15). The focus of the word "transgressions" (παράβασις) is "an act deviating from an established boundary or norm."[507] Although sometimes Paul uses this word with specific reference to the Mosaic law (Rom 2:23; 4:15), he also

---

[505] As used here the conjunction οὖν ("then") "invites further discussion of a topic made problematic by the preceding material" (DeSilva, *Handbook*, 69).

[506] Paul may be placing emphasis on the phrase "because of transgressions" by placing it first in the clause.

[507] BDAG s.v. παράβασις.

uses it to describe both Adam (Rom 5:14) and Eve (1 Tim 2:14) violating God's command not to eat from the tree of the knowledge of good and evil. Here it seems to have the broader sense of any violation of God's will, though likely with a specific emphasis on deviations from the Mosaic law. The precise force of the preposition rendered "for the sake of" (χάριν) is difficult to determine. In a general sense it means "for the sake of, on behalf of, on account of."[508] Although the specific meaning of the phrase "for the sake of transgressions" remains hotly debated, Paul likely means that the law was added to expose sin as a violation of God's revealed will (compare Rom 5:20).[509] By giving the law, sin was brought out into the open and more clearly identified so that when the promised descendant of Abraham came he could deal with it decisively.[510]

The timeframe for this role of the law was "until the Seed to whom the promise was made would come" (ἄχρις οὗ ἔλθῃ τὸ σπέρμα ᾧ ἐπήγγελται).[511] As Paul has already stated in 3:16, Christ is the seed to whom the promises were made. Paul argues here that the Mosaic law covenant came with a built-in expiration date—the arrival of Jesus Christ the promised seed.[512] Once again Paul is out of step with his Jewish contemporaries, many of whom viewed the law as eternal (Jub. 1:27; Wis 18:4; 4 Ezra 9:37).[513] One clear example is Josephus, who wrote "for though we be deprived of our wealth, of our cities, or of the other advantages we have, our law

---

[508] BDAG s.v. χάριν.

[509] See the discussion in Biblical Theology §5.2.1.

[510] Similarly Moo, *Galatians*, 234. Dunn (*Galatians*, 189–90) attempts to give this expression a positive sense, arguing that it means "in order to provide a way of dealing with, in order to provide some sort of remedy for transgressions." By this Dunn has in view the sacrificial system, but there is nothing in the context to suggest this "positive" interpretation of the reason for the law.

[511] As used here the expression rendered "until" (ἄχρις οὗ) has the sense of "until the time when" (BDAG s.v. ἄχρι 2.b.α). A few witnesses (B 0278. 33. 1175. 1962. 2464; Clement) have ἄν instead of οὗ, probably influenced by the subjunctive verb ἔλθῃ that follows. But when temporal constructions such as this refer to a time in the future when a new situation begins, they often use the aorist subjunctive; see Constantine R. Campbell, *Verbal Aspect and Non-Indicative Verbs: Further Soundings in the Greek of the New Testament*, SBG 15 (New York: Lang, 2008), 60 (cited in DeSilva, *Handbook*, 70).

[512] N.T. Wright argues that here seed refers to the one family of God, but the context clearly favors a reference to Christ the individual seed; see discussion at 3:16. As Das (*Galatians*, 364) notes, Wright's reading of 3:20 in light of 3:28–29 actually reverses the logic of the text. See further Jason S. DeRouchie and Jason C. Meyer, "Christ or Family as the 'Seed' of Promise? An Evaluation of N. T. Wright on Galatians 3:16," *SBJT* 14 (2010): 36–48.

[513] Noted in Moo, *Galatians*, 233.

continues immortal; nor can any Jew go so far from his own country, nor
be so frightened at the severest lord, as not to be more frightened at the
law than at him" (*Ag. Ap.* 2:277). Instead of the noun promise (ἐπαγγελίας)
used in 3:16–18, here Paul uses the verb "promise" (ἐπαγγέλλομαι). The
perfect tense of this verb emphasizes the ongoing validity of the promise,
while the passive voice implies that God is the one making the promise.

To further distinguish the promise made to Abraham and the Mosaic
law covenant, Paul describes the mechanism through which the latter
was given. The law was "put into effect through angels" (διαταγεὶς δι'
ἀγγέλων). The verb rendered "put in effect" (διατάσσω) usually has the
sense of "to give (detailed) instructions as to what must be done."[514] Paul
often uses this verb when giving direction or instruction, such as what
he expected Titus to do when he left him in Crete (Titus 1:5; compare
1 Cor 7:17; 9:14; 16:1). The passive voice of the verb implies that God is the
one putting into effect or giving detailed instruction through the law.[515]
The expression "through angels" (δι' ἀγγέλων) identifies the angels as
the intermediate agents through whom God put the law into effect.[516]
Although the Old Testament does not explicitly mention the role of angels
in giving the law, it was a widely held view in Second Temple Judaism. In
Deuteronomy 33:2 the LXX states that when Yahweh appeared at Sinai
there were angels with him, and Josephus also seems to indicate that the
law came "through angels [δι' ἀγγέλων]" (*Ant.* 15:136). Psalm 68:17 may
also have contributed to this belief: "God's chariots are tens of thousands,
thousands and thousands; the Lord is among them in the sanctuary as
he was at Sinai." Both Jubilees 1:27–29 and Philo (*Somn.* 1:140–44) bear
witness to the belief that angels were involved in the giving of the law.
Using language almost identical to Galatians 3:19, in Acts 7:53 Stephen
unambiguously states that the Jewish people "received the law under
the direction of angels" (ἐλάβετε τὸν νόμον εἰς διαταγὰς ἀγγέλων). So
Paul was on familiar ground with his Jewish contemporaries in positing
the involvement of the angels in the giving of the law. But whereas other
Jewish writers view this as a positive, Paul paints this as evidence of the

---

[514] BDAG s.v. διατάσσω 2.

[515] Although this seems rather clear from both the context here and the OT background,
Hans Hübner contends that Paul argues here that God did not in fact give the law; see Hans
Hübner, *Law in Paul's Thought* (Edinburgh: T&T Clark, 1984), 27–29 and similarly Martyn,
Galatians, 364–70, and de Boer, *Galatians*, 227–36.

[516] See further Wallace, *Greek Grammar*, 433–34.

Mosaic law's inferiority to the Abrahamic covenant, which God spoke directly to Abraham in the form of a promise.[517]

Not only was the law put in place through angels; it was given "by means of a mediator" (ἐν χειρὶ μεσίτου), or more woodenly, "by the hand of a mediator." Although not mentioning him by name, Paul is clearly referring to Moses. But by using the word "mediator" (μεσίτης), the apostle is further stressing the distance between God and the people of Israel at the heart of the Mosaic law covenant. In a general sense a mediator is "one who mediates between two parties to remove a disagreement or reach a common goal."[518] Paul appears to be echoing Leviticus 26:46,[519] which concludes a long chapter detailing the blessings for obedience and the curses for disobedience to the Mosaic law covenant by stating: "These are the statutes, ordinances, and laws the LORD established between himself and the Israelites through Moses on Mount Sinai." Appearing at the end of the covenant legislation that began in Exodus 20, "this verse may function as a summary of the covenant *in toto.*"[520] In both the MT (בְּיַד־מֹשֶׁה) and the LXX (ἐν χειρὶ Μωυσῆ) the expression is woodenly "by the hand of Moses."[521] The larger context of this echo coheres with his allusions

---

[517] By itself, mention of the angels' involvement in the giving of the law could be seen as evidence of the law's divine origin; see, e.g., Andrew J. Bandstra, "The Law and Angels: *Antiquities* 15.136 and Galatians 3:19," *CTJ* 24 (1989): 223–40. But the contrast between the indirect experience of God in connection with the law (through angels, by the hand of a mediator) and the direct speech of God in giving the promise to Abraham face to face strongly suggests a negative connotation; see further Terrance Callan, "Pauline Midrash: The Exegetical Background of Gal 3:19b," *JBL* 99 (1980): 549–67.

[518] BDAG s.v. μεσίτης. The only occurrence in the LXX is Job 9:33, where Job bemoans the lack of a mediator/arbiter between him and God. Of the six NT occurrences, the two here in Galatians refer to Moses (3:19–20), while the remaining four refer to Christ as the only mediator between God and man (1 Tim 2:5) by being the mediator of the new covenant (Heb 8:6; 9:15; 12:24). In Greek literature the word was widely used of neutral third parties stepping into disputes between two parties, functioning in a wide variety of ways, including "administrators or trustees for something in dispute, or as witnesses to legal business that had been settled (with the responsibility of guaranteeing that the decision would be carried out). A mediator could further be a pawnbroker and sometimes a guarantor who secured the liabilities of another with his own property" (NIDNTTE 3:284).

[519] See the helpful discussion in Bruno, *God Is One*, 180–85. Das (*Galatians*, 393–94) suggests a possible allusion to Exodus 34:29, which in the LXX uses the expression ἐπὶ τῶν χειρῶν Μωυσῆ ("by/in the hands of Moses").

[520] Bruno, *God Is One*, 183.

[521] The expression "by the hand of Moses" (ἐν χειρὶ Μωυσῆ) occurs in the LXX a total of nineteen times. With but two exceptions, where it refers to Israel being led "by the hand of Moses" (Num 33:1; Ps 76:21 [ET=77:20]), it consistently refers to the commandments of

to Deuteronomy 27:26; 28:58; 30:10 in Galatians 3:10, which announce a curse on all who fail to do everything written in the Mosaic law. Even in this seemingly "neutral" statement about the role of Moses as mediator, there is a negative hue—the prospect of exile for disobedience.

Thus the purpose of the law, the temporal limitations of the law, and the mechanism of giving the law through angels by the hand of a mediator together demonstrate that it has a subordinate role to the Abrahamic promise covenant in God's economy.

Throughout Galatians 3 to this point, Paul has stressed the continuity of God's purposes beginning as far back as the promise to Abraham. Yet here he notes a point of discontinuity in explaining that the Mosaic law covenant was given for a particular timeframe within God's plan. Being a careful reader of Scripture demands that we pay attention to elements of both continuity and discontinuity to be faithful interpreters of the Bible.

3:20. Mention of the mediator in the previous verse leads Paul to now further explain its significance in his argument.[522] He states, "Now a mediator is not just for one person alone, but God is one" (ὁ δὲ μεσίτης ἑνὸς οὐκ ἔστιν, ὁ δὲ θεὸς εἷς ἐστιν). This is one of the truly enigmatic verses in Galatians, with commentators often suggesting that several hundred different interpretations exist. While that is certainly an exaggeration, it is true that scholars are far from reaching consensus on Paul's meaning.[523] What seems like a simple statement—"Now a mediator is not just for one person"—belies the difficulty of the underlying Greek, which woodenly reads "now the mediator is not of one." Sorting out this difficult clause requires looking at four key factors: (1) who or what the "mediator" refers to in this context; (2) the force of the genitive phrase "of one" that follows

---

Yahweh given "by the hand of Moses" (Lev 26:46; Num 4:41, 45, 49; 9:23; 10:13; 15:23; 17:5; 36:13; Josh 21:2; 22:9; Judg 3:4; 1 Kgs 8:53, 56;1 Chr 16:40; 2 Chr 33:8; Neh 10:30). The same two uses are found elsewhere in Jewish literature as well: commandments (Bar 2:28) and leadership out of Egypt (T. Sim. 9:1).

[522] Thus the force of the δέ here is to signal a new development in the argument; see further Runge, *Discourse Grammar*, 31–32.

[523] Noting advocates for each view, Bruno (*God Is One*, 177–78) summarizes the major interpretations into three broad categories: (1) the presence of a mediator compromises the oneness of God, since a mediator demands two parties; (2) the presence of a mediator compromises the oneness of God because a mediator prevents each party from dealing directly with each other; (3) the presence of a mediator compromises the oneness of God because (at least in this case) a mediator represents a large group (i.e., the angels).

mediator; (3) who or what "one" refers to in the context; and (4) the significance of the clause "God is one" that follows.

At one level it seems rather obvious that the word "mediator" (μεσίτης) refers to Moses. After all, the previous verse describes how the law was given through angels "by means of a mediator," which clearly refers to Moses. The echo of Leviticus 26:46 further confirms this identification. But we must also allow for the strong possibility that Paul uses the word mediator as metonymy for the law covenant itself.[524] This conclusion fits well with the echo of Leviticus 26:46 in the previous verse, which closely linked Moses' mediatorial role with the giving of the law covenant. It also fits the contrast that Paul is drawing between the Mosaic law covenant and the Abrahamic covenant here in Galatians 3:15–29; 4:21–5:1.

When the noun μεσίτης ("mediator") is followed by a genitive noun or pronoun, it can indicate either the parties between whom the mediator does his work (Job 9:33; 1 Tim 2:5; compare T. Dan 6:2) or the content of what is mediated (Heb 8:6; 9:15; 12:24; compare T. Mos. 1:1).[525] If Paul uses it the first way, then Paul's point is that a mediator necessitates two parties, not simply one.[526] While this is the way nearly all English versions understand the clause, the second way is in fact preferable.[527] As Christopher Bruno, notes, "Although we are working with a limited database, apart from cases of a clearly possessive genitive, when μεσίτης is used with just one genitive noun in the first three centuries CE and earlier, the genitive noun refers to an object of mediation, such as a covenant."[528] Therefore the sense is "now the mediator [which here stands for the Mosaic law covenant] does not produce the one."

---

[524] See similarly Wright, *Climax of the Covenant*, 169 and Bruno, *God Is One*, 188. Metonymy is a figure of speech where "one term is used in place of another with which it is associated" (DeSilva, *Handbook*, 151). For example, in the classic statement "The pen is mightier than the sword," the word "pen" is used as metonymy for the words that a pen produces, while the word "sword" is used as metonymy for the violent force it produces.

[525] The former would thus be a genitive of association, while the latter would be an objective genitive.

[526] One of the many proponents of this view is Longenecker, *Galatians*, 142–43. He notes an interpretive tradition stemming from Isa 63:9 that stressed God's direct dealing with his people in contrast to any form of mediation, and traces it through rabbinic sources (Sifre Deut 42, 325; 'Abot R. Nat. B 2), Qumran (1QH 6:13–14), Josephus (*Ant.* 3:89), and Philo (*QG* 1:55). See also Das, *Galatians*, 365–66.

[527] Here I am following Bruno, *God Is One*, 184–89.

[528] Bruno, *God Is One*, 187.

So what then does "one" refer to here? Most interpreters see it as indicating that a mediator is not needed when there is only one party involved. Understood this way, Paul's point is to further the contrast between the Abrahamic promise covenant and the Mosaic law covenant. Whereas the Mosaic law covenant was given through angels by the hands of a mediator, God spoke the Abrahamic promise covenant directly to Abraham and took upon himself full responsibility for fulfilling its terms and conditions (see Gen 15:7–21). As true as this interpretation is, that does not seem to be what Paul is saying here. Instead, based on its use in 3:16, "one" refers to the one seed Jesus Christ.[529] Thus when Paul writes "the mediator is not of one," he is in effect saying, "the law is not able to bring into being the single seed (and all that he represents)."[530]

The final piece of the puzzle here in Galatians 3:20 is the significance of the last clause: "but God is one" (ὁ δὲ θεὸς εἷς ἐστιν). A pious Jewish person like Paul, steeped in Israel's Scriptures, could not have said these words without having Deuteronomy 6:4 (i.e., the Shema) in mind: "Listen, Israel: The Lord our God, the Lord is one." Paul introduces this assertion as a contrast to the previous clause ("now a mediator is not of one"). If that clause means that the Mosaic law covenant could not bring about the one seed Christ Jesus, then the claim "God is one" likely draws on the eschatological conviction that a day is coming when all nations will acknowledge that "God is one." The main source for this conviction is Zechariah 14:9, which Paul may be echoing here.[531] At the culmination of a vision that foresees a renewed creation, the prophet asserts that "the Lord will be king over all the earth. On that day the Lord will be one and his name one" (Zech 14:9 ESV). Paul makes a similar connection between the "oneness" of God and the unification of Jews and gentiles within the people of God in Romans 3:29–30: "Or is God the God of Jews only? Is he not the God of Gentiles too? Yes, of Gentiles too, since there is one God who will justify the circumcised by faith and the uncircumcised through

---

[529] Again, following Bruno, *God Is One*, 184–89. Bruno's view is similar to but distinct from that of N.T. Wright (*Climax of the Covenant*, 169), who contends that "one" refers to "the one family, the single 'seed', promised to Abraham and fulfilled in Christ." But Bruno (*God Is One*, 171–75) has shown that Wright's conclusion is based on a strained interpretation of the one seed in Gal 3:16 referring to a single family of God and not simply Christ individually.

[530] Bruno, *God Is One*, 188.

[531] See further Bruno, *God Is One*, 190–94.

faith." The conviction that God is one establishes why the Mosaic law covenant could not bring forth the promised seed.

Stepping back to the big picture, Paul's point in this verse is that the Mosaic law covenant (referred to in this verse by metonymy as the mediator) was not able to produce the one seed promised to Abraham (identified by Paul in 3:16 as Christ) because the fulfillment of the Abrahamic promise-covenant requires the universal and eschatological acknowledgment of the one true God by all nations (foreseen in Zech 14:9).

As Paul stated in 3:8, God's plan all along has been to redeem for himself a people from among the nations. Since this is fundamental to the Lord's purposes in human history, the church must prioritize through time, energy, and resources the spread of the good news not only in their local communities, but also to the ends of the earth. While every individual believer is not called to a far-off land to preach the good news, we are all called to participate in the spread of the gospel to the ends of the earth through prayer, giving, and encouraging those who are laboring in those fields of ministry.

3:21. To this point in his argument, Paul has claimed that the Mosaic law covenant is subordinate to the Abrahamic promise covenant because: (1) it came 430 years later; (2) it was not the basis for receiving the promised inheritance; (3) it was added because of transgressions; (4) it was unable to produce the one seed; and (5) it was unable to produce the universal and eschatological confession of the one true God by Jew and gentile alike. Based on this "negative" picture of the law, Paul anticipates another question about the law: "Is the law therefore contrary to God's promises?" (ὁ οὖν νόμος κατὰ τῶν ἐπαγγελιῶν [τοῦ θεοῦ]).[532] The promises in view are the ones God spoke to Abraham, and based on the larger context here include justification/righteousness, being a son of Abraham, the gift of the Spirit, eschatological life, and an inheritance. Does the Mosaic law covenant work against these promises?[533] Put another way,

---

[532] Some significant textual witnesses (𝔓⁴⁶ B d; Ambst) lack the phrase τοῦ θεοῦ ("of God"). But its presence is well attested in many other witnesses (ℵ A C D K L P Ψ 0278 33. 81. 365. 630. 1175. 1241. 1505. 1739. 1881. 2464 𝔐 lat sy co) and is likely original to the text. One eleventh-century witness (104) even has του Χριστου ("of Christ"). See discussion in Metzger, *Textual Commentary*, 525–26. Regardless of whether the phrase is original or not, the meaning is not significantly altered, as the promises in view are clearly the ones spoken by God to Abraham (cf. 3:16).

[533] The prepositional phrase κατὰ τῶν ἐπαγγελιῶν ("against the promises") communicates "the idea of hostile movement directed against someone or something. The opposition

does the Mosaic law covenant cut against the grain of the Abrahamic promise covenant?

Paul's answer is an emphatic "Absolutely not!" (μὴ γένοιτο).[534] For the apostle such a conclusion is unthinkable. He explains why with a conditional statement: "if the law had been granted with the ability to give life, then righteousness would certainly be on the basis of the law" (εἰ γὰρ ἐδόθη νόμος ὁ δυνάμενος ζῳοποιῆσαι, ὄντως ἐκ νόμου ἂν ἦν ἡ δικαιοσύνη). The way that Paul states the "if" clause indicates that he is effectively saying, "if a law had been given that was able to give life (and we know that's not the case)."[535] In the New Testament the verb rendered "give life" (ζῳοποιέω) consistently refers to God's power to make someone who is dead alive, whether it is Jesus Christ (1 Pet 3:18) or believers (Rom 8:11; 1 Cor 15:22). While the focus of this word is usually bodily resurrection (Rom 8:11; 1 Cor 15:22; 1 Pet 3:18), in other cases, as it does here, it refers to the present experience of resurrection life (1 Cor 15:45; 2 Cor 3:6). In some examples both present spiritual life and future bodily resurrection may be in view (John 5:21; 6:63).[536] Paul has already described his own experience as dying to the law and living for God (2:19) and that he no longer lives but Christ lives in him (2:20). He has also asserted that the righteous will live by faith (3:11) and that the law is not of faith because it is based on the premise that those who do the commandments of the law will live by them (3:12). Later in 5:25 Paul will speak of living by the Spirit in contrast to living by the flesh. Lastly, in 6:8 Paul states that "the one who sows to the Spirit will reap eternal life from the Spirit." So with the probable exception of 6:8, here in Galatians life consistently refers to the present experience of resurrection life that the believer enjoys by virtue of being joined to Jesus Christ and justified by faith in him. Paul's point here in 3:21 is that the Mosaic law covenant could not give

---

involved ranges from a simple accusation laid against someone to aggressive hostility between irreconcilable adversaries" (Harris, *Prepositions and Theology*, 154).

[534] The Greek expression μὴ γένοιτο ("absolutely not") is one of Paul's favorite ways of emphatically rejecting an argument or a conclusion (compare Rom 3:4, 6, 31; 6:2, 15, 7:7, 13; 1 Cor 6:15; Gal 2:17; 6:14).

[535] Thus it is a second class conditional statement.

[536] "In the NT and post-apostolic fathers ζῳοποιεῖν always means "to make alive" in the soteriological sense" (*TDNT* 2:874). In all but one LXX occurrences (Judg 21:14), either God or wisdom is the subject of the verb (2 Kgs 5:7; Ps 70:20 [ET=71:20]; Eccl 7:12; Job 36:6). The verb does not appear in Josephus or Philo. In Greek literature ζῳοποιέω was often used in reference to "the birth of animals or the growth of plants" (*TDNT* 2:874).

eschatological, resurrection life because it was never intended to do so. Again, Paul's claim is out of step with his Jewish contemporaries, who extolled the life-giving power of the law (Sir 17:11; 45:5; Bar 3:9; 4:1; 4 Ezra 1:17, 21; 14:30; Pss. Sol. 14:2).[537] But as far as Paul is concerned, expecting the Mosaic law to give life is like expecting a hammer to drive in a screw.

But if in fact the Mosaic law covenant had been able to give life, Paul insists under those circumstances "righteousness would certainly be on the basis of the law" (ὄντως ἐκ νόμου ἂν ἦν ἡ δικαιοσύνη). The apostle has already insisted that if righteousness came through the law, Christ died in vain (2:21); instead, it is faith that is credited to a person for righteousness (3:6). The expression translated "on the basis of the law" (ἐκ νόμου) is the same one used in 3:18 to insist that the inheritance is not "based on the law" (ἐκ νόμου). The point is that neither receiving the inheritance nor being declared righteous is based on the law.

Paul's larger point here in 3:21 is that the Mosaic law covenant is not contrary to God's promises to Abraham once you understand the purpose of each one. The law was never intended to give eschatological, resurrection life—that was the purpose of the Abrahamic promise. If the law had been intended to give spiritual life, then righteousness would have been based on obedience to the Mosaic law. So if the Mosaic law was never intended to give eschatological life, how did it serve the Abrahamic promise covenant? Paul will address that question in the next verse.

By default, we as human beings pursue what we believe will bring us life. For some that may be pleasure, status, or possessions; for others it may be performance of religious rules that we can use to build up our pride. On the night he was betrayed, Jesus made it clear where true life is found when he prayed, "This is eternal life: that they may know you, the only true God, and the one you have sent—Jesus Christ" (John 17:3). Looking for life in any other place will only disappoint and frustrate.

3:22. Instead of the law being given to bring spiritual life, Paul insists that "the Scripture imprisoned everything under sin's power" (ἀλλὰ συνέκλεισεν ἡ γραφὴ τὰ πάντα ὑπὸ ἁμαρτίαν). The shift from "law" (νόμος) to "the Scripture" (ἡ γραφὴ) is unexpected and calls for an explanation. In 3:8 "Scripture" is described as foreseeing God justifying the

---

[537] Noted in Das, *Galatians*, 366. Especially noteworthy is m. 'Aboth 2:7–8: "The more study of the Law the more life ... If [a man] has gained for himself the words of the Law he has gained for himself life in the world to come."

gentiles by faith, a claim grounded in a citation of Genesis 12:3/18:18. Later in 4:30 Paul introduces his quote of Genesis 21:10 by asking "what does the Scripture say?" Some have argued that since Scripture is described here as imprisoning everything under sin, Paul is referring back to his citation of Deuteronomy 27:26 in 3:10.[538] But it seems best to see in the word "Scripture" a reference to the entire witness of Old Testament revelation (i.e., the Law, the Prophets, and the Writings), perhaps with a focus "on how the OT as a whole, via the law, [brought] everything under sin."[539] By moving from a specific reference to the Mosaic law to the entirety of the Old Testament Scriptures, Paul is preparing the way to argue for the shared and universal experience of Jew and gentile under the bondage of the elementals (4:3, 10), a bondage from which Christ must deliver both (4:4–7).

In saying that Scripture "has imprisoned everything under sin," Paul uses a verb (συγκλείω) that means "to confine to specific limits."[540] Outside its two occurrences in Galatians 3:22–23, it appears just two other places in the New Testament.[541] In Luke 5:6 it refers to fish being caught in a net, but Paul's use of it in Romans 11:32 is similar to its use here in Galatians. Arguing that both Jews and gentiles are disobedient to God, Paul states that "God has imprisoned all in disobedience, so that he may have mercy on all." This parallel reinforces that when Paul says *Scripture* imprisoned everything under sin, it is another way of saying that *God* imprisoned everything under sin. While the expression "all things" (τὰ πάντα) includes all people (Jew and gentile alike),[542] the phrase likely refers to all of creation, which groans under the curse of humanity's sinful rebellion against God (Rom 8:19–22). "Paul pictures sin as a power that exerts its influence over the world, with particular focus in this context on the condemnation that results from sin's dominion."[543] God thus imprisoned all creation under the power of sin, an assertion that Paul hinted at when he wrote in the greeting of the letter that Christ

---

[538] See, e.g., Burton, *Galatians*, 195–96; Longenecker, *Galatians*, 144.

[539] Moo, *Galatians*, 239.

[540] BDAG s.v. συγκλείω 2.

[541] In the LXX the verb is far more common, appearing forty-four times. Perhaps the closest parallel is 1 Macc 5:5, where the sons of Baean were "confined [συνεκλείσθησαν]" by Judas Maccabeus in a tower. For the use of this verb in Greco-Roman literature with the sense of lock up or throw into prison, see Polybius, *Hist.* 38.18.2 and Plutarch, *De Deione* 30.

[542] On the use of τὰ πάντα to mean everyone, see BDF §138.1.

[543] Similarly Moo, *Galatians*, 239.

"gave himself for our sins to rescue us from this present evil age" (Gal 1:4). Just as those who rely on the works of the law are "under a curse" (ὑπὸ κατάραν), so too all creation has been imprisoned "under sin" (ὑπὸ ἁμαρτίαν).[544] As used here, the preposition "under" (ὑπό) expresses a controlling power or authority.[545] The assertion of Galatians 3:22a is similar to Romans 3:9, where Paul writes, "What then? Are we any better off? Not at all! For we have already charged that both Jews and Greeks are all under sin." What follows is a string of Old Testament citations, drawn mostly from the Psalms and Isaiah, that decisively and vividly describe human depravity (Rom 3:10–18).

The purpose of Scripture imprisoning all things under sin is "so that the promise might be given on the basis of faith in Jesus Christ to those who believe" (ἵνα ἡ ἐπαγγελία ἐκ πίστεως Ἰησοῦ Χριστοῦ δοθῇ τοῖς πιστεύουσιν). The promise refers to the promise-covenant that God made with Abraham (3:14–21). As Paul has already insisted (3:9, 14), the promise is given "on the basis of faith in Christ" (ἐκ πίστεως Ἰησοῦ Χριστοῦ), or perhaps better "on the basis of faith in Jesus Christ." Paul repeats the same prepositional phrase that he argues is the basis of being justified (2:16; 3:8), experiencing the Spirit (3:2, 5), and experiencing eschatological life (3:11–12). The promise made to Abraham is given on the basis of faith in Jesus Christ,[546] and it is given "to those who believe" (τοῖς πιστεύουσιν).[547] This last expression emphasizes the identity of those who receive the Abrahamic promises: they are identified not by their ethnicity or their obedience to the Mosaic law, but by their faith in Jesus Christ (2:16; 3:9).

Paul's point is that God imprisoned all creation under sin for a redemptive purpose. Through the Mosaic law covenant, God made the nature of sin clear and easily identifiable, as well as its awful consequences—being under the curse that comes from violating God's will (3:10). But by imprisoning all under the same sentence of condemnation for sin, God has

---

[544] This parallel further suggests that the "us" of 3:13–14 refers to all people, not merely Jews; see discussion at 3:13–14.

[545] See BDAG s.v. ὑπό B.2; Harris, *Prepositions and Theology*, 220–21.

[546] The expression translated "faith in Jesus Christ" (ἐκ πίστεως Ἰησοῦ Χριστοῦ) can also be rendered "faithfulness of Jesus Christ"; for discussion of this important phrase and the reasons for understanding it as "faith in Jesus Christ" see the discussion at 2:16 and Biblical Theology §8.2.

[547] The use of the present tense of the participle here may suggest that continual, ongoing faith is in view; see further Wallace, *Greek Grammar*, 621n22.

also made the solution available to all. Regardless of ethnicity, everyone who trusts in Jesus Christ receives the inheritance/blessing promised to Abraham: justification, the gift of the Spirit, and eschatological life. Those who believe in Christ receive these blessings because Christ is the promised offspring of Abraham (3:16) who redeemed his people from the curse of the law by becoming a curse for them (3:13).

God in his sovereignty regularly uses what Satan or people intend for evil as a means to advance his purposes in this world. Speaking to his brothers who had sold him into slavery out of envy years before, Joseph said, "You planned evil against me; God planned it for good to bring about the present result—the survival of many people" (Gen 50:20). This truth should be a great comfort to us as believers, for we know that even when people inflict evil or pain upon us, "all things work together for the good of those who love God, who are called according to his purpose" (Rom 8:28).

3:23. To this point Paul has established that the Mosaic law is not contrary to the promise-covenant God made with Abraham (3:21a). The Mosaic law was never intended to give eschatological, resurrection life (3:21b). Instead, it was the means by which God imprisoned all things under sin (3:22a). By performing this function, the law set the stage for all who believe in Jesus Christ to receive the promise made to Abraham on the basis of faith (3:22b). Here in verse 23 Paul continues the contrast between the Mosaic law covenant and the Abrahamic promise covenant from a temporal angle.[548] When Paul says, "Before this faith came" (Πρὸ τοῦ δὲ ἐλθεῖν τὴν πίστιν), he refers to the time period before Christ came as the promised offspring of Abraham. He cannot mean that before the incarnation of Christ faith in general did not exist, since he has already insisted that Abraham believed God and was counted righteous (Gal 3:6).[549] The faith Paul has in view here is the specific kind of faith described in the previous verse—faith in Jesus Christ.[550]

---

[548] The δέ that begins this clause marks a new development in the argument; see further Runge, *Discourse Grammar*, 30.

[549] Contrary to Betz (*Galatians*, 176), who claims that before Christ came "faith existed only exceptionally in Abraham and in Scripture as a promise ... faith was not generally available to mankind before Christ's coming, but was a matter for the future."

[550] The underlying Greek (τὴν πίστιν) can be woodenly rendered as "the faith." But here the definite article is anaphoric, referring back to the specific kind of faith mentioned in the previous verse. Wallace (*Greek Grammar*, 217–18) notes that the anaphoric article "has,

So Paul says that during that time period before faith in Jesus Christ came, "we were confined under the law" (ὑπὸ νόμον ἐφρουρούμεθα). While the "we" in view likely refers to the Jewish people, this specific reference must be understood against the backdrop of the claim in the previous verse that Scripture imprisoned all things under sin (3:22). As Moo notes, "the sequence of Paul's argument, as he applies this salvation-historical sequence to the situation of the Galatians (see esp. 4:4–9), reveals that he somehow views this salvation-historical sequence as relating to and even in some sense including the Galatians."[551] The verb rendered "confined" (φρουρέω) has a range of meaning from guarding something/someone for their protection to confining someone against their will.[552] The surrounding context here clearly indicates a negative sense.[553] Not only does the following clause repeat the idea of imprisonment, but also the status of being "under the law" is consistently a negative status in Galatians, requiring Christ to be born under the law so that he might redeem his people (4:4–7). Paul's use of this verb here "is consistent with the Roman use of prisons principally for holding of prisoners until disposition of their case."[554] The imperfect tense of this verb has the effect of drawing attention to the prolonged nature of the confinement. Notice also the close relationship between being "under sin" (3:22) and being "under law" (3:23), a connection confirmed by the similar interchange in Romans 6:14–15.[555]

The clause that follows further clarifies what Paul means when he says that the Jewish people were confined under the law: "imprisoned until the coming faith was revealed" (συγκλειόμενοι εἰς τὴν μέλλουσαν πίστιν

---

by nature, then, a pointing force to it, reminding the reader of who or what was mentioned previously."

[551] *Galatians*, 241. See also Das, *Galatians*, 372–73.

[552] The verb is rare, occurring only three times in the LXX (1 Esd 4:56; Jdt 3:6; Wis 17:15) and a total of four times in the NT (2 Cor 11:32; Gal 3:23; Phil 4:7; 1 Pet 1:5). Of the other six occurrences (excluding Gal 3:23), five are positive (1 Esd 4:56; Jdt 3:6; 2 Cor 11:32; Phil 4:7; 1 Pet 1:5) and one is negative (Wis 17:15). Examples from secular Greek (see MM) reveal both positive and negative senses and thus only the context can determine the sense here.

[553] Contrary to Dunn (*Galatians*, 197), who contends the law was God's way of protecting Israel during the present evil age before the coming of Christ. Israel was "like a city garrisoned by the law within a larger territory ruled by sin." But this conclusion simply does not fit the larger context, given that Paul associates being under the law with being under sin.

[554] BDAG s.v. φρουρέω 2.

[555] Schreiner, *Galatians*, 246–47.

ἀποκαλυφθῆναι).⁵⁵⁶ Paul repeats the verb from verse 22 to cement the
link between Scripture imprisoning all things under sin and the Jewish
people being confined under the law. The present tense of this verb portrays the imprisonment as something that extended over a period of
time. That state of imprisonment was in force "until the coming faith
was revealed" (εἰς τὴν μέλλουσαν πίστιν ἀποκαλυφθῆναι).⁵⁵⁷ Just as God
suddenly broke into human history to "reveal" (ἀποκαλύψαι) his Son in
Paul (1:16), so too in a more general sense faith in Jesus Christ has been
"revealed" (ἀποκαλυφθῆναι) through the preaching of the gospel.⁵⁵⁸

In effect Paul divides history into two epochs—the period of imprisonment under the law and the period of faith in Jesus Christ. Although Paul
does not make the point explicit in this section of the argument, part of
the reason that the apostle is so upset is that the Galatians do not seem
to recognize the shift from the first epoch to the second. And despite the
insistence of Paul's opponents in Galatia, one cannot simply mix together
the Mosaic law covenant and faith in Jesus Christ.

By default, every single person enters this world in a state of slavery
to sin. Try as we may, there is no way to escape this state of confinement
on our own. The only possible escape is through God revealing his Son
to us (compare 1:15–16) so that our eyes are opened to see the light of
the knowledge of the glory of God in the face of Jesus Christ (2 Cor 4:6).

3:24. Paul now draws an inference from the previous verse: "The law,
then, was our guardian until Christ" (ὥστε ὁ νόμος παιδαγωγὸς ἡμῶν
γέγονεν εἰς Χριστόν).⁵⁵⁹ Paul describes the Mosaic law as the "guardian"
(παιδαγωγός) of the Jewish people, using a word that does not have a
good English equivalent. In Greco-Roman culture the παιδαγωγός was
a man (often a slave) who was responsible for taking a boy back and

---

⁵⁵⁶ The adverbial participle that begins this clause (συγκλειόμενοι) is likely either circumstantial or perhaps indicates manner (DeSilva, *Handbook*, 74). Another option is to see
this as a participle of identical action in which the participle refers to the same action as the
verb it modifies; see Ernest De Witt Burton, *Syntax of the Moods and Tenses in New Testament
Greek* (Chicago: University of Chicago Press, 1900), 54–55.

⁵⁵⁷ Here the preposition εἰς has a temporal sense, indicating the point "up to which
something continues" (BDAG s.v. εἰς 2.a.α). Noting how rare a purely temporal use of εἰς is
in Paul, Moo (*Galatians*, 242–43) argues for a combined "temporal/telic" sense best reflected
in the English word "unto."

⁵⁵⁸ Others see "faith" (πίστις) as a reference to the faithfulness of Jesus; see, e.g.,
Witherington, *Grace in Galatia*, 267–68.

⁵⁵⁹ On this use of ὥστε, see Beale, Ross, and Brendsel, *Interpretive Lexicon*, 96. This is
preferable to seeing it as indicating result, as DeSilva (*Handbook*, 75) does.

forth to school and overseeing his conduct.[560] The responsibilities of the παιδαγωγός included "carrying books or other objects, sometimes securing an education for himself in the process. He took the child to athletic practice, oversaw his meals, made him do his homework, protected him from harm, and supervised his social engagements. Twenty-four hours a day the pedagogue accompanied the child in virtually every activity of life."[561] While the practice had its origin in Greek culture, by the first century AD it was common in Roman and even Jewish circles as well. Although Paul's use of the pedagogue as a metaphor for the law is unparalleled, the term was used in Jewish rabbinic writings to describe figures such as Moses, Aaron, Miriam, David, and Jeremiah as pedagogues for Israel.[562] Despite the fact that some in the ancient world viewed the pedagogue positively while others viewed the role negatively, here in Galatians Paul casts it in a negative light.[563] It is likened to a state of imprisonment and slavery (3:23; 4:1–3) and contrasted with the freedom of an adult son who has received his inheritance (4:4–7). The law is like a pedagogue in that it had a supervisory role over Israel during their childhood and adolescence

---

[560] See BDAG s.v. παιδαγωγός. For descriptions of the work of the παιδαγωγός in the papyri, see C. Laes, "Pedagogues in Greek Inscriptions in Hellenistic and Roman Antiquity," *ZPE* 171 (2009): 113–22. Ramsay notes that while in Greek culture the pedagogue did not have any teaching responsibilities, within Roman culture the pedagogue would offer informal instruction in the Greek language; see William Mitchell Ramsay, *A Historical Commentary on St. Paul's Epistle to the Galatians* (New York: G. P. Putnam's Sons, 1900), 382–83.

[561] For a helpful discussion of the role of the παιδαγωγός, see Michael J. Smith, "The Role of the Pedagogue in Galatians," *BSac* 163 (2006): 197–214 (quote from 201). My summary here draws substantially from Smith's article.

[562] See, e.g., Gen. Rab. 29:6; 31:7; Exod. Rab. 21:8; 42:9; Num. Rab. 1:2; Deut. Rab. 2:11. For a helpful summary, see Longenecker, *Galatians*, 146–48 and the additional detail in his earlier article "The Pedagogical Nature of the Law in Galatians 3:19–4:7," *JETS* 25 (1982): 53–61. Longenecker ("Pedagogical Nature," 55) does note that 4 Macc 1:17 and 5:34 use language from the same word family to refer to the law, but not the actual word παιδαγωγός.

[563] Dunn (*Galatians*, 198–99) argues that the role of the pedagogue is presented positively here. He claims that as a pedagogue "the law gave [Israel] the protection it needed from idolatry and the lower moral standards prevalent in the Gentile world." But, again, Dunn fails to recognize the larger context. The problem with the law is not merely that it confined Israel in a period of immaturity, but that it enslaves just like the other elements of the world (4:3, 9). Nor should the role of the pedagogue be seen as that of a teacher preparing a person for Christ. As Das (*Galatians*, 375) further notes, "If the pedagogue were fulfilling a positive educational function in leading people to Christ, it would be unclear why Paul would consider pedagogy to have ended with Christ's coming."

for a specific and limited period of time.[564] That limited period of time was "until Christ came" (εἰς Χριστόν), which is another way of saying "until the coming faith was revealed" (3:23).[565]

The purpose of the law serving as a pedagogue was "that we could be justified by faith" (ἵνα ἐκ πίστεως δικαιωθῶμεν). Yet again, Paul insists that the basis of justification is faith (compare 2:16; 3:6–9, 11, 22). The temporary, supervisory role of the Mosaic law covenant is yet another reason why no one can be justified by the law (2:16; 3:10–14). God never intended the law to serve that function.

Every child at some point needs supervision from a babysitter or care-taker. Yet the goal is for the child to one day grow up into an adult where such supervision is no longer needed. As believers, if we seek to relate to God on the basis of the Mosaic law rather than faith, we are in essence turning away from the freedom and maturity that comes from faith in Christ to return to a state of confinement and supervision befitting a child.

3:25. Whereas the previous verse focused on the epoch of the law, Paul now transitions to the epoch of faith: "But since that faith has come, we are no longer under a guardian" (ἐλθούσης δὲ τῆς πίστεως οὐκέτι ὑπὸ παιδαγωγόν ἐσμεν).[566] While most English versions translate the opening phrase with a temporal sense (so, e.g., ESV: "now that faith has come"), the causal sense fits well here.[567] It is because faith in Jesus Christ has come that "we are no longer under a guardian" (οὐκέτι ὑπὸ παιδαγωγόν ἐσμεν). The "we" here refers to the Jewish people, who are no longer under the temporary supervision of the pedagogue since Jesus Christ has come. Yet here again, in light of Paul's larger argument about the shift in

---

[564] While it is likely overstated, perhaps the closest modern equivalent would be au pair or nanny, though without the cooking and cleaning responsibilities that sometimes come with such a role.

[565] Instead of understanding the phrase εἰς Χριστόν temporally (see BDAG s.v. εἰς 2.a.α), some English translations render it along the lines of "to lead us to Christ" (compare NIV1984, NASB, NKJV, KJV). But as Das (Galatians, 375) notes, the repeated temporal references in the surrounding context clearly indicate a temporal sense here.

[566] As DeSilva (Handbook, 75) summarizes, the δέ that begins this clause "carries an adversative sense, as Paul introduces a decisive change and new stage in the unfolding history of salvation."

[567] In Greek the construction is a genitive absolute, which according to Wallace (Greek Grammar, 655) has a temporal force nearly 90 percent of the time. But it can indicate any of the relationships of circumstantial participles, such as a causal force as it does here (compare Rom 9:1); see Robert Walter Funk, A Beginning-Intermediate Grammar of Hellenistic Greek, 3rd ed. (Salem, OR: Polebridge Press, 2013), 493.

redemptive history with the coming of Christ, gentile believers may at least be indirectly in view as well.[568] Once again Paul uses the preposition "under" (ὑπό) to describe a power that wields authority over someone. As such, being under the pedagogue is in some way analogous to being "under the curse" (3:10), "under sin" (3:22), and "under the law" (3:23). Although each expression communicates a slightly different meaning, the overall picture that emerges is negative. Or perhaps better stated, it speaks of an experience that is short of God's ultimate intention for his people.

Watching someone settle for something lesser when something far greater is available can be difficult. Yet that is in essence what Paul says happens when we as believers choose to relate to God and others on the basis of the Mosaic law rather than live out the freedom that Christ has purchased for us through his death and resurrection.

Bridge

From this rich and challenging passage we should reflect on two significant dangers to our spiritual life. First, we must be careful not to misuse a good gift from God. As Paul states elsewhere, "So then, the law is holy, and the commandment is holy and just and good" (Rom 7:12). But trying to use the law as the path to eschatological life will never work because it was never intended to give that. Any of God's good gifts can become a snare to us if we seek to use them in a way that God never intended. Second, we need to understand where we are in the unfolding storyline of the Bible. As those who live after the death and resurrection of Jesus, we must not try to use the Mosaic law as a means of relating to God or others. Jesus has inaugurated the new creation and given us the Spirit to live in freedom from the captivity of the law; why would we want to return to a state of slavery?

F. SONS OF GOD IN CHRIST JESUS (3:26–29)

> [26] For through faith you are all sons of God in Christ Jesus. [27] For those of you who were baptized into Christ have been clothed with Christ. [28] There is no Jew or Greek, slave or free, male and female; since you are all one in Christ Jesus. [29] And if you belong to Christ, then you are Abraham's seed, heirs according to the promise.

---

[568] Moo, *Galatians*, 244.

Context

Paul reaches a provisional conclusion to the argument that began with
the thesis (3:6–9) that those who believe in Christ are sons of Abraham
and recipients of the blessing promised to him. This conclusion picks up
themes from the thesis (faith, sonship, promise/blessing, inclusion of
gentiles) and extends them in anticipation of their further development
in 4:1–5:1.[569]

Structure

Paul draws together an initial conclusion to his argument that all who
believe—regardless of their ethnicity—are justified sons of Abraham who
receive the blessing promised to him (3:6–9). But instead of referring to
believers as sons of Abraham, Paul makes an even grander claim. Through
faith in Christ, believers are "sons of God" (3:26), terminology that in the
Old Testament is applied to Adam, Israel, David, and the promised Davidic
descendant who would rule over an eternal kingdom. This identity as
sons of God is vividly portrayed in baptism, where believers put on Christ
like a new set of clothes (3:27). This status as sons of God is available to
all people—regardless of their ethnicity, socioeconomic status, or gender—because through faith they are made one in Christ (3:28). That leads
to Paul's punchline: those who belong to Christ by faith are Abraham's
seed who receive the inheritance based on God's promise to bless all the
nations in Abraham, a promise that finds fulfillment in Christ the promised seed (3:29). Underlying Paul's conclusion here is his conviction that
all who believe in Christ are united to Christ in such a profound way that
what is true of Christ becomes true of believers.

3:26. The reason that that "we" are no longer under a pedagogue is
that "through faith you are all sons of God in Christ Jesus" (Πάντες γὰρ
υἱοὶ θεοῦ ἐστε διὰ τῆς πίστεως ἐν Χριστῷ Ἰησου).[570] The shift from "we"

---

[569] Some scholars contend that 3:26–29 is the center of the letter; see, e.g., Das, *Galatians*,
377. It is certainly true that 3:26–29 is an important summary of the key themes of sons of
God, faith, union with Christ, and descendants of Abraham who receive the inheritance.
But given that these themes are further developed in the remaining chapters, designating
3:26–29 likely goes too far.

[570] A number of scholars contend that here in 3:26–28 Paul adapts an early pre-Pauline
baptismal formula; for a concise summary of the reasons for such a conclusion, see de Boer,
Galatians, 245–47. While this view is possible, it should be noted that: (1) there is no reason
that Paul himself could not have crafted the language here and (2) even if Paul is using a
piece of early Christian tradition, his use of it here demonstrates he has made it his own.

in the previous verse (referring to Jews) to "you" (referring to the Galatian believers, most of whom are gentile) reinforces that although, strictly speaking, the gentiles were not under the temporary supervision of the Mosaic law covenant, they were under a similar status (later described as childhood and enslavement to the elemental forces [4:1–3, 8–11]). The "all" here is emphatic. Not just Jewish believers but gentile believers as well are "sons of God." This expression connects the identity of believers with Jesus Christ, whom Paul has twice already referred to as God's Son (1:16; 2:20). It also signals a key development in Paul's argument in Galatians 3. Beginning in 3:7 Paul has been contending that those who believe in Christ are "sons of Abraham." Now he insists that those same people who believe in Christ are sons of God. While it will take 3:27–4:7 to explain the connection between being sons of Abraham and sons of God, it is important here to note that in the Old Testament, Adam, Israel, David, and the promised Davidic king were all referred to as God's son. This title expresses a combination of authority and intimacy.[571] Thus while not diminishing the significance of being a "son of Abraham," Paul stresses that believers have an even greater status—sons of God.[572]

The assertion that believers are sons of God is further explained by two prepositional phrases. First, believers have this status as sons of God "through faith" (διὰ τῆς πίστεως). One does not become a son of God by obeying the Mosaic law. Faith in the person and work of Christ is the means by which believers are not only justified (2:16) and receive the Holy Spirit (3:2, 5), but also the means by which we are made sons of God.[573] Second, believers are sons of God by virtue of being "in Christ Jesus" (ἐν Χριστῷ Ἰησοῦ). Although this phrase could indicate the object of faith,[574] it is more likely that this phrase modifies the expression "you are" (ἐστε).[575] As such,

---

[571] For the larger biblical background of sons of God, see Biblical Theology §7.2.1.1.

[572] The crucial connection between the status of believers (both male and female) as "sons of God" and the identity of Jesus as the son of God is sadly obscured when well-meaning English translations render the expression "children of God" (compare NIV). Whatever ground might be gained in communicating that the title applies to male and female alike is offset by the lost connection between Jesus the Son of God and believers as sons of God.

[573] Consistent with his larger argument, Hays (*Faith of Jesus*, 155–56) argues that "faith" (πίστις) here refers instead to the faithfulness of Christ. See discussion at 2:16.

[574] So Campbell, *Paul and Union with Christ*, 113, 18. But he does acknowledge that the phrase "also expresses the existence of a new status—that of being *sons of God*" (Campbell, *Paul and Union with Christ*, 118).

[575] So most commentators. The following points support this conclusion. First, nowhere else in Galatians does Paul use ἐν to indicate the object of either πίστις or πιστεύω. He either

the point is that believers are sons of God by virtue of being "in Christ Jesus." Just as in 3:14 where the blessing of Abraham comes to those in Christ and the promised Spirit is received through faith, so here in 3:26 believers are sons of God because they are in Christ through faith.[576] Dunn aptly notes that "As 'faith' has replaced the law as the distinctive mark of the 'sons of God', so 'Christ Jesus' has replaced ethnic Israel as the social context of this sonship."[577]

Through our union with Christ, God has adopted us into his family and made us sons. That is our true identity as believers, regardless of what our earthly family situation is. Because each individual believer is a son of God (male and female alike), we are brothers and sisters in God's family. That is our true identity, regardless of what the world says.

3:27. Paul further explains believers' status as sons of God through faith by pointing back to the public declaration of their faith: "For those of you who were baptized into Christ have been clothed with Christ" (ὅσοι γὰρ εἰς Χριστὸν ἐβαπτίσθητε, Χριστὸν ἐνεδύσασθε).[578] While the origins of baptism are not certain,[579] in the New Testament the starting

---

uses εἰς (2:16) or an objective genitive construction (2:16; 3:22). In Paul's Letters there are only four places (Eph 1:15; Col 1:4; 1 Tim 3:13; 2 Tim 3:15) where ἐν clearly introduces the object of faith (though Eph 1:1 and Rom 3:25 are also possible examples). Second, if Paul meant "faith in Christ" he could have made this clear by adding the definite article in front of the prepositional phrase (as he does in 1 Tim 3:13 and 2 Tim 3:15). Third, in the verses that follow (3:27–28), the focus is on incorporation into Christ, with 3:28 concluding that all believers are one "in Christ Jesus" (ἐν Χριστῷ Ἰησοῦ).

[576] Helpfully noted by Oakes, *Galatians*, 130.

[577] Dunn, *Galatians*, 202.

[578] The verb βαπτίζω plus the preposition εἰς is common in the NT. Although it does occur in Matt 28:19; Acts 8:16; 19:3, it is primarily a Pauline expression (Rom 6:3 [2x]; 1 Cor 1:13, 15; 10:2; 12:13). BDAG (s.v. βαπτίζω 2.c) notes that in Paul the idea is of "involvement in Christ's death and its implications for the believer." See similarly Campbell (*Paul and Union with Christ*, 207–8), who claims that the emphasis here in Gal 3:27 is "the new status that believers enjoy" through their incorporation into Christ.

[579] While it is true that gentile converts to Judaism were baptized, it is unclear when the practice began; see Scot McKnight, *A Light among the Gentiles: Jewish Missionary Activity in the Second Temple Period* (Minneapolis: Fortress Press, 1991), 82–85. There is evidence that by the beginning of the second century AD baptism was regarded by some gentiles as an act of initiation into Judaism; see Michael F. Bird, *Crossing over Sea and Land: Jewish Missionary Activity in the Second Temple Period* (Peabody, MA: Hendrickson, 2010), 37–39. For discussion of the possible precedents to Christian baptism, see J. Delorme, "The Practice of Baptism at the Beginning of the Christian Era," in *Baptism in the New Testament: A Symposium*, ed. Augustin George (Baltimore: Helicon, 1964), 25–60.

point is the ministry of John the Baptist, who baptized people with water in preparation for the coming Messiah and his kingdom (Matt 3:1–12). But John also promised that the one coming after him would baptize "with the Holy Spirit and fire" (Matt 3:11). Although he had no sin to repent of, Jesus was also baptized by John "to fulfill all righteousness" (Matt 3:15). Immediately after Jesus was baptized, the Holy Spirit descended on him, marking him off as the promised messianic servant king (Matt 3:16–17). After his resurrection, Jesus commissioned his followers to make disciples of all the nations, "baptizing them in the name of the Father and of the Son and of the Holy Spirit" (Matt 28:19). But first they were instructed to remain in Jerusalem until they were baptized with the Holy Spirit (Acts 1:5), which happened on the day of Pentecost (Acts 2:1–4). In his letters, Paul refers to both water baptism and baptism in the Spirit.[580] In 1 Corinthians 1:13–17 he appears to downplay water baptism, but that is because some in Corinth were taking pride in the person who baptized them. Later in the same letter he even draws a typological connection between Israel being "baptized into Moses in the cloud and in the sea" and believers being baptized into Christ (1 Cor 10:2).

But two particular Pauline passages are especially helpful for understanding Galatians 3:27. In discussing the unity of the body of Christ in the midst of their diverse spiritual gifts, Paul states that "we were all baptized by one Spirit into one body—whether Jews or Greeks, whether slaves or free—and we were all given one Spirit to drink" (1 Cor 12:13; compare Col 3:11). Baptism in the Holy Spirit is a defining experience for believers, one that should bring unity not division. The second key text is Romans 6:3–4, where Paul responds to the suggestion that believers should continue in sin so grace may abound by saying:

> Or are you unaware that all of us who were baptized into Christ Jesus were baptized into his death? Therefore we were buried with him by baptism into death, in order that, just as Christ was raised from the dead by the glory of the Father, so we too may walk in the newness of life.

---

[580] For a helpful discussion of baptism in Paul's letters, see Thomas R. Schreiner, "Baptism in the Epistles," in *Believer's Baptism: Sign of the New Covenant in Christ*, ed. Thomas R. Schreiner and Shawn D. Wright (Nashville: B&H Academic, 2006), 67–96.

Baptism is a picture of the believer being united with Christ in his death
to sin and his resurrection to new life.

So in baptism the believer publicly testifies that through faith he/she
has been united with Christ in his death and resurrection. In addition to
visually representing union with Christ in his death and resurrection, it
also symbolizes that the believer has been baptized with the Holy Spirit
and joined to the body of Christ. This visible act of water baptism was the
act of initiation that marked a person as part of the church. While water
baptism does not save a person, it was an expected step of obedience for
those who professed faith in Christ, so that Paul can speak of believing
in Christ and being baptized in almost interchangeable ways.[581]

With respect to how baptism was practiced in the early church, there
are only suggestive hints.[582] The Greek terms (βαπτίζω) suggest immersion, though some sources seem to allow for pouring water over the
head when immersion was not possible.[583] Because of this desire for
immersion, most early Christian baptisms took place in rivers or lakes;
few people would have had a private bath or facility large enough in their
home to facilitate this. According to at least one source, Christians were
baptized naked; taking off their clothes symbolized leaving behind their
old life and its domination by sin, demonic powers, etc. They were then
immersed into the water, symbolizing their death with Christ, and lifted
from the water to symbolize their union with Christ in resurrection to
new life. Putting on new clothes symbolized their new life of purity in
Christ. While it cannot be determined with certainty, there was likely
the recital of some type of creed or confession (perhaps "Jesus is Lord";
see Rom 10:9).

Continuing to use imagery from baptism, Paul says that the Galatians
"have been clothed with Christ" (Χριστὸν ἐνεδύσασθε).[584] Although the

---

[581] Or, as Moo (*Galatians*, 251) puts it, "Paul can appeal to baptism as 'shorthand' for the
entire conversion experience."

[582] Much of what follows is summarized and adapted from Wayne A. Meeks, *The First
Urban Christians: The Social World of the Apostle Paul*, 2nd ed. (New Haven: Yale University
Press, 2003), 150–57.

[583] See Hippolytus, *Apostolic Tradition* 21, which probably reflects late second-century
practice in the church at Rome and speaks of triple immersion. The *Didache*, which may
reflect late first-century practices, allows for pouring of water over the heard three times
when immersion is not possible (7:3).

[584] This second clause acts in effect as the apodosis ("then") of the implied condition
stated in the first clause. Paul is essentially saying, "if you have been baptized into Christ,

verb that Paul uses (ἐνδύω) regularly refers to the act of putting on clothing, it was also used metaphorically "of the taking on of characteristics, virtues, intentions, etc."[585] Just as it does today, clothing reflects the identity and social standing of the person wearing it. Clothes also communicate symbolic significance as well. When Adam and Eve realized they were naked after sinning, they covered themselves with loincloths made of fig leaves (Gen 3:9). This inadequate clothing made from their own efforts to cover their sin was replaced by God's gracious act of clothing them with garments made from skin (Gen 3:21). Israel's high priest also wore special clothing to reflect his unique role (Exod 28:1–43). The Old Testament contains a number of references to being clothed with characteristics such as righteousness (Job 29:14; Ps 132:9), salvation (2 Chr 6:41; Ps 132:16; Isa 61:10), strength (Prov 31:25; Isa 51:9; 52:1), glory (Job 40:10), or shame (Ps 132:18).[586] Among these Old Testament references, Isaiah 61:10 may be especially significant here. The promised anointed one who will bring salvation to God's people says, "I rejoice greatly in the Lord, I exult in my God; for he has clothed me with the garments of salvation and wrapped me in a robe of righteousness, as a groom wears a turban and as a bride adorns herself with her jewels."[587] Thus in baptism the believer is clothed with the garments of Christ himself, who was clothed in salvation and righteousness.

Regardless of whether Isaiah 61:10 is in view here or not, in Galatians 3:27 clothing imagery is clearly used as a picture of the believer's cleansing from sin and a transformed life. God removed the filthy garments of the high priest Joshua and gave him clean clothing to symbolize God's act of cleansing him and the people (Zech 3:1–10). Paul uses similar imagery for believers. Sometimes this imagery describes what has already happened in conversion, such as in Ephesians 4:22–24, where Paul says believers have taken off "your former way of life" and "put on [ἐνδύσασθαι] the new self, the one created according to God's likeness in righteousness and purity of the truth" (compare Col 3:9–10). Other

---

then you have put on Christ as a garment."

[585] BDAG s.v. ἐνδύω 2.b.

[586] Helpfully noted by Longenecker, *Galatians*, 156.

[587] Scholars debate whether the speaker in Isa 61:10 is the anointed deliverer or renewed Zion. Regardless, though, the point of connection still stands—God's renewed people are clothed with the garments of their redeemer. See further J. Alec Motyer, *The Prophecy of Isaiah: An Introduction & Commentary* (Downers Grove, IL: IVP, 1993), 504–5.

times Paul uses this imagery to call believers to a life of obedience to God, such as in Romans 13:12–14, where Paul commands believers to "put on [ἐνδύσασθε] the Lord Jesus Christ, and don't make plans to satisfy the fleshly desires." As Das aptly notes, "Whereas Paul's rivals were encouraging the stripping off of sinful flesh in circumcision, Paul counters with putting on Christ."[588]

While the mere act of immersing someone in water does not save a person from their sin, it is an important symbolic and public act that vividly portrays the believer's faith in Christ and the realities of what God has done for us in Christ. Paul appears to have no category for a person who claims to believe in Jesus and yet has not been baptized. And according to Jesus, baptizing converts was an essential aspect of the Great Commission (Matt 28:18–20). As believers today, we would be wise to treat it with a similar importance.

3:28. Based on the shared experience of baptism that unites a person with Christ and joins them together with fellow believers in one body, Paul now moves to remind the Galatians that their identity as followers of Christ transcends divisions and distinctions that are fundamental to this fallen world.[589] Paul uses similar language in both 1 Corinthians 12:13 and Colossians 3:11, and there are loose parallels to similar kinds of sayings in the ancient world as well.[590] But before discussing each of these distinctions, two things must be made clear. First, it is important to remember the context. In the larger argument of 3:1–5:1, Paul is explaining who the true sons of Abraham are and on what basis those people have that status. His point in raising these common distinctions is to assert that one's status as a justified son of Abraham who receives the promised Spirit as an inheritance is in no way determined by these distinctions.[591] He is *not* arguing that these distinctions no longer have any significance in other respects, as Paul makes clear in other passages

---

[588] Das, *Galatians*, 382–83.

[589] The lack of a connecting particle (asyndeton) at the beginning of this verse has the effect of making this statement stand out in the context.

[590] For a helpful comparison of the NT texts, see Moo, *Galatians*, 252–53 and Das, *Galatians*, 380–81. For similarities in ancient Greek literature, see Betz, *Galatians*, 188–92.

[591] Longenecker (*Galatians*, 157) suggests these three couplets were part of an early Christian confession intended "to counter the three běrākôt ("blessings," "benedictions") that appear at the beginning of the Jewish cycle of morning prayers." While possible, there is no clear evidence such blessings existed in the first century.

(see, e.g., 1 Cor 11:2–16; Eph 5:22–33; 1 Tim 2:8–15).[592] Instead, they have been relativized, as Dunn helpfully notes: "As distinctions marking racial, social and gender differentiation, which were thought to indicate or imply relative worth or value or privileged status before God, they no longer have that significance."[593] Second, a number of scholars have suggested that this verse contains a piece of early Christian baptismal liturgy that was cited by the convert during their baptism.[594] Regardless of whether this is the case, Paul appeals to it in such a way that he assumes it is common ground.

Before we look at each of these polarities, we should note their common structure. In Greek each one begins with the phrase "there is no" (οὐκ ἔνι) and is followed by the contrasting pair.[595] In the first two pairs the two terms are joined by "or" (οὐδὲ), whereas the third pair is joined by "and" (καὶ). These three contrasting pairs set up the climactic final clause of this verse, where the basis for their common identity is stated.

The first pair contrasted is "Jew or Greek" (Ἰουδαῖος οὐδὲ Ἕλλην). For the Jew this was arguably the most fundamental distinction of all, and it went beyond ethnicity. Being identified as a Jew was a claim to have a special relationship with God; after all, as Paul notes in Romans 3:2, the Jews "were entrusted with the very words of God." Among all the nations, God had made a covenant only with the Jewish people, and he chose them to be a blessing to the rest of the world (Gen 12:1–3; Exod 19:5–6). As used here, the term "Greek" is synonymous with gentile, though perhaps here with an emphasis on their polytheistic practices in contrast to the monotheism of the Jews.[596] Of the three pairs, this is the most pertinent to the situation in Galatians. It is this very distinction that is ultimately at the heart of the opponents' argument that gentile

---

[592] See similarly Schreiner, *Galatians*, 258–59 and Moo, *Galatians*, 254–55.

[593] Dunn, *Galatians*, 207.

[594] See, e.g., Martyn, *Galatians*, 378–83. For a survey of interpretation of this verse up to 1987, see Dennis Ronald MacDonald, *There Is No Male and Female: The Fate of a Dominical Saying in Paul and Gnosticism*, HDR 20 (Philadelphia: Fortress, 1987), 1–62. For a survey from 1990 to the present, see D. F. Tolmie, "Tendencies in the Interpretation of Galatians 3:28 since 1990," *AcT* 19 (2014): 105–29.

[595] The verb Paul uses here (ἔνι) is a shortened form of ἔνειμι and indicates existence (BDAG s.v. ἔνι). All six NT occurrences of ἔνι are negated (1 Cor 6:5; Gal 3:28 [3x]; Col 3:11; Jas 1:17).

[596] See BDAG s.v. Ἕλλην 2.a. In a more general sense it could refer to "all persons who came under the influence of Greek, as distinguished from Israel's culture."

believers must obey the Mosaic law (symbolized by being circumcised) in order to be justified before God and regarded as sons of Abraham.

The second pair contrasted is "slave or free" (δοῦλος οὐδὲ ἐλεύθερος). This contrast works on several levels within Galatians. At the most basic level within Greco-Roman society, this distinction was a central dividing line between those who had access to power, wealth, opportunity, and those who were shut out. By the first century AD nearly one-third of the population of the Roman Empire may have been slaves.[597] Unlike eighteenth and nineteenth century Western slavery, slavery in the Roman world was not based on race or ethnicity. People became slaves through a variety of means, including selling oneself into slavery as a means of providing a measure of economic and personal stability. It was even possible for slaves to eventually purchase their freedom. But at the end of the day the basic reality of the slave was being owned by another person, regarded as property. By contrast, those who were free in Greco-Roman society had a whole range of privileges and opportunities available to them that the slave did not.[598] So the distinction between "slave or free" was fundamental to Greco-Roman society, a loose ancient equivalent to the modern expression "the haves and the have nots."

But within Galatians this contrast between slave and free takes on a larger theological significance. Paul has already described humanity's state before Christ as one of being "imprisoned ... under sin's power" (3:22) and "confined under the law, imprisoned until the coming faith was revealed" (3:23). In 4:1–7 Paul will compare the pre-conversion state of the Christian to slavery (4:1–3) and the post-conversion status of freedom that comes with being an adopted son and heir of God who

---

[597] Scholars vary in their estimates of the slave population in the Roman Empire, with lower estimates around 15 percent and the higher estimates around 33 percent. For helpful surveys of slavery in the first century, see Dale B. Martin, *Slavery as Salvation: The Metaphor of Slavery in Pauline Christianity* (New Haven: Yale University Press, 1990), 1–49; I. A. H. Combes, *The Metaphor of Slavery in the Writings of the Early Church: From the New Testament to the Beginning of the Fifth Century*, JSNTSup 156 (Sheffield: Sheffield Academic, 1998); Harris, *Slave of Christ*, 25–45; Jeffers, *Greco-Roman World*, 220–36; Gregory S. Aldrete, *Daily Life in the Roman City: Rome, Pompeii, and Ostia* (Westport, CT: Greenwood Press, 2004), 65–68; Scot McKnight, *The Letter to Philemon*, NICNT (Grand Rapids: Eerdmans, 2017), 6–29. For a sampling of attitudes toward slaves and their treatment, see Jo-Ann Shelton, *As the Romans Did: A Sourcebook in Roman Social History*, 2nd ed. (New York: Oxford University Press, 1998), 163–85.

[598] Social status in the Greco-Roman world was a complex and multifaceted reality that depended on a number of factors, only one of which was slave or free; for a helpful summary see Jeffers, *Greco-Roman World*, 180–96.

has the Spirit of God's Son (4:4–7). Paul reminds the Galatians of their pre-conversion slavery to "weak and worthless elements" and marvels that they would want to return to this state of slavery (4:8–11). The contrast between slavery and freedom is at the heart of Paul's contrast between the Abrahamic covenant fulfilled in Christ and the Mosaic law covenant, represented by Abraham's two sons and their respective mothers (4:21–5:1). The gospel is a call to a freedom that empowers believers to serve others in love (5:13–15). The concepts of freedom and slavery underlie Paul's contrast between walking in the flesh and walking by the Spirit as well (5:16–26).

Here in Galatians 3:28 Paul's point with respect to "slave or free" is that one's social status has no relevance for one's status before God. What matters is being "in Christ" and "sons of God in Christ Jesus" through faith, not their status as slave or free (3:26). Indeed, one of the distinguishing features of the early church was the mingling together in close fellowship of kinds of people that in Greco-Roman society would not have had such close interaction.[599] Is such fellowship a mark of your local congregation of believers?

The final pair contrasted is "male and female" (ἄρσεν καὶ θῆλυ).[600] This phrase appears to be drawn from Genesis 1:27, where God creates humanity "in the image of God; he created them male and female." The distinction between male and female was another fundamental division within Greco-Roman society, accompanied with expectations for

---

[599] This reality did appear to create some challenges for believers outside of the church, however. In 1 Corinthians 7:20–24 Paul instructs believing slaves to gain their freedom if they are able but reminds those who cannot that they are "the Lord's freedman" (7:22). Likewise, he reminds those who are free that they are "Christ's slave" (7:22). Paul also gives instructions for both slaves and masters in the church, calling them to conduct themselves in a manner consistent with the gospel (Eph 6:5–9; Col 3:22–4:1). And, most notably, Paul writes Philemon to encourage him to receive back his runaway slave Onesimus, hinting that Philemon should grant Onesimus his freedom. While our modern sensibilities may wonder why Paul does not come out and directly call for the end of slavery, one must keep in mind the realities of Paul's day. Paul lived in the Roman Empire, not a democratic republic. Slavery was a foundational element of Greco-Roman society in his day. Slave rebellions were brutally crushed by the Romans. Openly calling for the end of slavery could have led to the brutal persecution of the church. Paul's approach appears to have been to allow the gospel to transform individuals such that eventually the foundations of slavery would be undermined.

[600] Whereas the first two pairs are joined by "or" (οὐδέ as part of an οὐκ ... οὐδέ construction), this pair is joined by "and" (καί). This is likely because Paul is borrowing this phrase from Gen 1:27 (LXX).

appropriate behavior and roles for each gender. Again, the context here is important. Paul is not asserting that there are no differences between men and women when it comes to every sphere of life. In several other texts Paul gives instruction on what roles are appropriate for men and women in both the church (1 Cor 11:2–16; 14:33–35; 1 Tim 2:8–15) and in the home (Eph 5:22–33; Col 3:18–19). Paul's point is that when it comes to an individual's status as a justified son of God and heir of the promises to Abraham, gender makes no difference.[601] Now that Christ has come, the new creation has dawned in which neither circumcision nor uncircumcision matters (Gal 6:15), and by extension then, there are no distinctions between men and women regarding the requirements for full participation in the new covenant.[602]

The reason these distinctions, which were fundamental to the present evil age, do not matter when it comes to one's status before God is that "you are all one in Christ Jesus" (πάντες γὰρ ὑμεῖς εἷς ἐστε ἐν Χριστῷ Ἰησου). Because all believers—regardless of ethnicity, social status, or gender—are united to Christ by faith and live under his power and authority, they are also united with each other within the one body of Christ. Put another way, believers are one in Christ because they are all united to the one seed of Abraham, Jesus Christ. The oneness that Paul speaks of here is not one of

> levelling and abolishing of all racial, social or gender differences, but as an integration of just such differences into a common participation 'in Christ', wherein they enhance (rather than detract from) the unity of the body, and enrich the mutual interdependence and service of its members. In other words, it is a oneness, because such differences cease to be a barrier and cause of pride or regret or embarrassment, and become rather a means to display the diverse richness of God's creation and grace, both in the acceptance of the 'all' and in the gifting of each.[603]

By pointing back to their baptism, Paul reminds the Galatians that within the very act that symbolizes their faith in Messiah and marks their initiation into the people of God is the claim that the social distinctions being pressed by the opponents are now irrelevant to one's standing

---

[601] Thus Martyn (*Galatians*, 376–77) is right to see a link to new creation here (cf. 6:15) but wrong to assert that Paul is setting aside the original order of creation.

[602] Moo, *Galatians*, 254.

[603] Dunn, *Galatians*, 208.

before God and standing within the people of God. Our tendency as fallen creatures is to divide the world based on the very distinctions Paul mentions in this verse. Sadly, such divisions are all too common in the church. But when our local congregations reflect the diversity of our communities, the beauty of the gospel is seen even more clearly.

3:29. As Paul brings this section of his argument to a close, he adds one final conclusion that flows from believers being one in Christ.[604] He uses an "if/then" statement to move from what he has already established to a twofold finale: "And if you belong to Christ, then you are Abraham's seed, heirs according to the promise" (εἰ δὲ ὑμεῖς Χριστοῦ, ἄρα τοῦ Ἀβραὰμ σπέρμα ἐστέ, κατ᾽ ἐπαγγελίαν κληρονόμοι).[605] Saying that believers belong to Christ[606] stresses that our identity is rooted in our union with him and not in ethnicity, social status, or gender.

Two things follow from belonging to Christ. First, "you are Abraham's seed" (τοῦ Ἀβραὰμ σπέρμα ἐστε). In 3:16 Paul insisted that the promise made to Abraham finds its fulfillment in the one seed, Jesus Christ. Now Paul insists that all who are joined to Christ by faith—represented by their baptism—are also Abraham's seed. As Abraham's seed through faith in Christ, believers are therefore "heirs according to the promise" (κατ᾽ ἐπαγγελίαν κληρονόμοι). As the one seed, Christ received the inheritance God had promised to Abraham (3:15–18). All who are joined to him by faith share in that inheritance. Sharing in this inheritance is not based on one's ethnicity, social status, gender, or even one's observance of the Mosaic law covenant.

Thus, in contrast to the opponents in Galatia, Paul argues that being a son of Abraham and heir to the promises made to him is based solely on faith. The good news of the gospel is that God has done everything necessary for our salvation through his Son Jesus Christ, the one promised seed of Abraham. Attempting to add anything to the work of Christ—even observing the Mosaic law—in fact subtracts from the sufficiency of the work of Christ and nullifies the grace of God shown to us through him (2:21).

---

[604] This clause is introduced with a δέ that signals a continuation of the argument by adding a new development; see Burton, *Galatians*, 208 and DeSilva, *Handbook*, 77.

[605] This is a first class conditional statement, meaning that the "if" clause is assumed true for the sake of the argument. Here the "then" clause is an inference that follows from the truth of the "if" clause. By placing the Greek particle ἄρα ("then") at the beginning of the "then" clause, Paul makes the conclusion even more forceful.

[606] In Greek the expression is simply "of Christ" (Χριστοῦ), with the genitive here indicating either relationship or possession.

Bridge

In many realms of life, what matters is who you know and who knows you. When it comes to spiritual realities, the same is true. Regardless of our performance, ethnicity, socioeconomic status, or gender, there is only one way to be justified before God—we must be united to Christ by faith. When we are united to Christ, everything that is true of him becomes true of us. That is our true identity as believers, regardless of what the world says about us. When we truly understand that reality, we are freed from the slavery of other people's expectations.

G. ADOPTED SONS SEALED WITH THE SPIRIT (4:1–7)

> [1] Now I say that as long as the heir is a child, he differs in no way from a slave, though he is the owner of everything. [2] Instead, he is under guardians and trustees until the time set by his father. [3] In the same way we also, when we were children, were in slavery under the elements of the world. [4] When the time came to completion, God sent his Son, born of a woman, born under the law, [5] to redeem those under the law, so that we might receive adoption as sons. [6] And because you are sons, God sent the Spirit of his Son into our hearts, crying, "*Abba,* Father!" [7] So you are no longer a slave but a son, and if a son, then God has made you an heir.

Context

In the previous paragraph (3:26–29), Paul states the provisional conclusion to his argument (3:1–5:1) that those who trust in Christ are justified sons of Abraham and sons of God who inherit what was promised to him through their union with Christ. Based on that conclusion, Paul now extends the argument by further explaining several key themes from that conclusion, with a particular focus on being under authorities/powers until the time of sonship and inheritance arrives.[607] The following chart shows the overlap between 3:23–29 and 4:1–7.[608]

---

[607] Noting the convergence of several major themes in the letter, Martyn (*Galatians*, 388) claims that 4:3–5 "is nothing less than the theological center of the entire letter." While this claim goes too far, Martyn is correct in highlighting the importance of this passage in Galatians.

[608] Adapted from a similar chart in Moo, *Galatians*, 257.

Table 8:

Galatians 3:23–29	Galatians 4:1–7
Before this faith came, we were confined under the law, imprisoned until the coming faith was revealed (3:23)	Now I say that as long as the heir is a child, he differs in no way from a slave, though he is the owner of everything. Instead, he is under guardians and trustees until the time set by his father. In the same way we also, when we were children, were in slavery under the elements of the world (4:1–3)
The law, then, was our guardian until Christ, so that we could be justified by faith (3:24)	he is under guardians and trustees until the time set by his father (4:2)
But since that faith has come, we are no longer under a guardian (3:25)	When the time came to completion, God sent his Son, born of a woman, born under the law, to redeem those under the law (4:4–5)
for through faith you are all sons of God in Christ Jesus (3:26)	so that we might receive adoption as sons (4:4–5) You are no longer a slave but a son (4:7)
You are Abraham's seed, heirs according to the promise (3:29)	God has made you an heir (4:7)

These parallels indicate that Paul is covering similar ground but from a slightly different perspective to drive home his point that believers (Jew and gentile alike) are in fact sons of God on the basis of faith in Jesus the Son of God.

Structure

To expand on his conclusion in 3:26–29, Paul again uses an illustration, though its precise background has been vigorously debated (see below). The paragraph falls into two broad parts.[609] In 4:1–3 Paul lays out the illustration and applies it to all humanity. When an heir is underage he is under the authority of guardians and trustees until the time appointed by his father; as such he is in reality no different than a slave (4:1–2). That was the condition of all humanity before Christ came—enslaved to the elements of this world (4:3). In 4:4–7, Paul then explains what God did to

---

[609] Schreiner (*Galatians*, 263–65) suggests a threefold structure: illustration (4:1–2), application of the illustration to the Galatians (4:3–5), and implications for the readers (4:6–7).

remedy this situation. He sent his Son to redeem those under the law so that Jew and gentile alike would be adopted as sons of God (4:4–5). Based on this status as sons, God sent the Spirit of his Son into the hearts of his people as a down payment on the fullness of the inheritance they will one day receive (4:6). Since believers are adopted sons, they are no longer slaves; instead, they are heirs of the promises God made to both Abraham and David because they are united to Christ, the seed of Abraham and the son of God.

As noted above, scholars have debated how best to understand the background of the illustration Paul uses here in 4:1–7. A number of scholars conclude that the apostle is drawing from a basic Roman legal background. The difficulty with this view is that the details do not line up exactly with any practices known from the Greco-Roman world.[610] Instead of a Greco-Roman background, other scholars have proposed that Paul is typologically describing Israel's experience in the exodus as a framework for presenting the work of Christ as the long-promised new exodus. Perhaps a mediating position is possible. Perhaps the imagery functions on two levels. The first level is the basic Roman legal backdrop suggested by many, while the second level is the theological/typological level. So instead of an either/or approach, perhaps a both/and is at work.[611]

4:1. Picking up the contrast between life before Christ came and life after Christ came in the previous section (3:23–29), Paul further explains the radical difference that the coming of Christ has inaugurated. Just as in 3:15 and 3:17, Paul introduces this explanation with a form of λέγω ("I say") to clarify what he is doing.[612] While there is a sense in which what Paul offers here in 4:1–3 is an "illustration," it is mistaken to see it

---

[610] For a robust discussion of these parallels and potential shortcomings, see the extended summary and critique in Das, *Galatians*, 427–38 and especially John K. Goodrich, "Guardians, Not Taskmasters: The Cultural Resonances of Paul's Metaphor in Galatians 4.1–2," *JSNT* 32 (2010): 251–84 and John K. Goodrich, "'As Long as the Heir Is a Child': The Rhetoric of Inheritance in Galatians 4:1–2 and P.Ryl. 2.153," *NovT* 55 (2013): 61–76.

[611] Noting that none of the suggested backgrounds tightly fits the details, Moo (*Galatians*, 259) suggests that "Paul has allowed his statement of the illustration to be affected by the intended application. Paul describes a situation with sufficient analogies to the experience of his readers in order for the illustration to be effective and meaningful, but takes liberties with some of the details of that experience in order to facilitate its application to their spiritual situation."

[612] These parallels are usually obscured in English translation: "I'm using a human illustration" (κατὰ ἄνθρωπον λέγω; 3:15); "My point is this" (τοῦτο δὲ λέγω; 3:17); "Now I say"

as only that. Instead, Paul offers a retelling of salvation history through an exodus/new exodus framework.

Paul sets the temporal framework by stating, "as long as the heir is a child" (ἐφ' ὅσον χρόνον ὁ κληρονόμος νήπιός ἐστιν).[613] By referring to "the heir" (κληρονόμος), Paul picks up the final word of 3:29, where he caps 3:15–29 by stating that believers are "Abraham's seed, heirs according to the promise" because they are in Christ. But there was a period of time when the heir did not have full possession of the inheritance, which Paul refers to as being a "child" (νήπιός). This noun can refer to infants (Matt 21:16) or children of any age (1 Cor 13:11) but also is used in a figurative sense to refer to young believers (Rom 2:20; Eph 4:14; Heb 5:13). Although this noun can be used in a neutral sense that connotes innocence or simplicity (Pss 114:6 LXX [ET= 116:6]; 118:130 LXX [ET= 119:130]), it often highlights a state or condition of immaturity, with varying degrees of negativity.[614] But most significant is the use of this noun in Hosea 11:1, where the prophet writes, "When Israel was a child, I loved him, and out of Egypt I called my son." In its original context, Hosea 11:1 looks back to Israel's exodus out of Egypt but does so in the context of recalling their repeated sinful rebellion and idolatry (11:2). Despite this repeated rebellion, Yahweh continued to lead and feed them (11:3–4). Nevertheless, Yahweh vows to send them into exile (11:5–6) since they "are bent on turning from me" (11:7).[615]

So as long as the heir in view here is a child, in practical terms "he differs in no way from a slave" (οὐδὲν διαφέρει δούλου). At one level Paul's language is hyperbole; while the heir is a child, he would still have certain privileges that a slave would not. But Paul's point is that with respect to the inheritance awaiting the child, in effect he is no different than a slave because neither have possession of the inheritance. By loosely equating the status of the heir while a child with a slave, Paul is also tapping into the larger thread of freedom and slavery that

---

(Λέγω δέ; 4:1). The δέ here in 4:1 marks the transition to a new section of the letter while maintaining a link to what has come before.

[613] The prepositional phrase "as long as" (ἐφ' ὅσον χρόνον) indicates a duration or period of time (see BDAG s.v. ἐπί 18.c.β.)

[614] See especially Eph 4:14 and Heb 5:13, where believers are exhorted to move beyond a state childhood into a state of spiritual maturity.

[615] The possibility of an echo of Hos 11:1 is strengthened by the fact that Matt 2:15 quotes Hos 11:1 to draw a typological connection between Israel and Jesus; see G. K. Beale, "The Use of Hosea 11:1 in Matthew 2:15: One More Time," *JETS* 55 (2012): 697–715.

runs throughout Galatians. This state of slavery echoes the language of 3:21–26, where Paul argued that God imprisoned all things under sin. It also looks forward to the Hagar-Sarah allegory in 4:21–5:1 and the extended instruction of 5:2–26 contrasting a life of slavery to the flesh with the freedom that comes from being led by the Spirit.

This status of being no better than a slave is true even "though he is the owner of everything" (κύριος πάντων ὤν),[616] or perhaps better, "though he is lord of all." Paul highlights the paradoxical state of the heir. As one who has been promised an inheritance, he is thus at one level in fact the owner/lord (κύριος) of everything. Yet there may be another significance to this expression "lord of all" (κύριος πάντων), as it was used in both religious and political contexts as a title ascribing universal sovereignty.[617] Understood this way, Paul would be making a larger point that the heir in view here has been promised universal sovereignty. If so, the heir would seem to be not just any heir in general, but a veiled reference to Israel, who through the Abrahamic covenant was promised universal dominion.[618]

Because we live in this fallen world, our circumstances often do not align with what is true of us spiritually. We may live in poverty, but we have been given every spiritual blessing in the heavens (Eph 1:3). We may be estranged from our earthly family, yet we have been adopted into God's family as his children and have countless siblings in the Lord (Mark 3:31–35). We may have no place to call home, but we have a Savior who has gone to prepare an eternal home for us (John 14:1–3). As a result, we can experience joy in the midst of any circumstances.

4:2. In sharp contrast to being "owner of everything" (4:1), while the heir is a minor and practically no different from a slave, "he is under guardians and trustees" (ὑπὸ ἐπιτρόπους ἐστὶν καὶ οἰκονόμους). The term rendered "guardian" (ἐπίτροπος) referred to a variety of officials

---

[616] Thus the participle here is concessive.

[617] James M. Scott, *Adoption as Sons of God: An Exegetical Investigation into the Background of Huiothesia in the Pauline Corpus,* WUNT 2/48 (Tübingen: Mohr, 1993), 130–34. Scott adduces an impressive number of examples from Greco-Roman literature, including examples in Josephus (*Ant.* 13:172; 20:90).

[618] Although not explicit in the OT, both Second Temple Jewish writings (e.g., Jubilees 22:11–14; 32:19; Sir 44:19–23) and Paul (Rom 4:13) seem to interpret the Abrahamic promise as inheriting the world; see Scott, *Adoption as Sons of God,* 134–35.

serving in different capacities in government or in the home.[619] It also commonly referred to the role of a guardian within the household who was responsible for the oversight and protection of a minor child,[620] and that would seem to be its sense here. The second term is even broader; "trustee" (οἰκονόμος) could refer to a wide range of roles within public service or within a household.[621] Within the context of a household, it often had a financial component, as it does in Luke 16:1–9. The difficulty with this term here is that it rarely seems to have included responsibilities overseeing a minor child. But it is also possible that the two terms should be understood together as referring to the supervisory role over both the minor heir and his inheritance.[622] In any case, regardless of the specifics, Paul's larger point is clear: the minor is under a state of supervision by others.

---

[619] For the wide range of roles and functions, see LSJM s.v. ἐπίτροπος. There are only two other NT occurrences. In Matt 20:8 it refers to a foreman who oversees the payment of day workers, while in Luke 8:3 it refers to Chuza being the steward or household manager for Herod Antipas. In the three LXX occurrences, it refers to Lysias, the guardian/protector of King Antiochus (2 Macc 11:1; 13:2; 14:2), which in the context means a high-ranking government official. The term is especially common in Josephus (60x) and Philo (41x)

[620] For examples from the papyri, see MM, 249.

[621] For the range of possibilities, see LSJM s.v. οἰκονόμος. This word occurs ten times in the NT, either in reference to a household steward/manager (Luke 12:42; 16:1, 3, 8) or as a metaphor for someone serving in gospel ministry (1 Cor 4:1–2; Titus 1:7; 1 Pet 4:10). In Romans 16:23 it is a title given to Erastus indicating he is the city treasurer in Corinth. All fifteen LXX occurrences (1 Kgs 4:6; 16:9; 18:3; 2 Kgs 18:18, 37; 19:2; 1 Chr 29:6; 1 Esd 4:47, 49; 8:64; Esth 1:8; 8:9; Isa 36:3, 22; 37:2) refer to a government official of some kind. The same is true of the eight occurrences in Josephus (Ant. 8:164, 308; 9:47; 11:138, 272; 12:199–200, 205). For examples in the papyri, see MM, 442.

[622] This is the argument of Goodrich, "Guardians, Not Taskmasters," 251–84. He argues that "During the Greek and Roman periods, both ἐπίτροπος and οἰκονόμος were used to identify the slave or freedmen agents and administrators who managed the estates of their principals" (265). Goodrich admits that a potential weakness for his conclusion is that it relies on a sixth-century AD source (Digest of Justinian) for the particulars of the Roman guardianship customs, but he dismisses it with the assertion that "the Digest is a compendium of laws established sometimes several centuries earlier, and that the position being advanced here is not reliant upon the codification of specific laws, but the recurrence of certain practices" (269n30). In a subsequent article Goodrich has proposed a close parallel to Gal 4:1–2 in a second-century AD Roman will discovered in Hermopolis, Egypt; see Goodrich, "'As Long as the Heir Is a Child,'" 61–76. The significant overlap in vocabulary and terminology with Gal 4:2 makes for a striking parallel and establishes a plausible background for Paul's analogy here, though Goodrich still cannot adequately account for the use of οἰκονόμος here in this context.

This state of supervision lasts "until the time set by his father" (ἄχρι τῆς προθεσμίας τοῦ πατρός). The word rendered "the time set" (προθεσμία) has the general sense of "a point of time set in advance."[623] Although this is the only New Testament occurrence, there is evidence that "while the term could be used for any number of predetermined deadlines, it could also be employed in and around contexts involving guardianship and succession."[624] In legal documents, the term referred to a specific day when the stipulations of a contract had been fulfilled or a change in status occurred.[625] While there were general customs for what age an heir would receive his inheritance, "the father also had the right to defer that date to a time more desirable either to himself or to his heir."[626] The point, then, is that the father is the one who sets the time when the heir takes possession of the inheritance.[627]

Continuing his argument that Paul is using exodus typology, James Scott contends that the guardians and stewards mentioned here in 4:2 refer to Israel's Egyptian taskmasters.[628] The time set by the father, then, is 430 years of slavery the Israelites experienced in Egypt until they were set free (compare Gal 3:17).[629] Understood this way, Paul is

---

[623] BDAG s.v. προθεσμία. For examples of this general use in the papyri, see MM, 540. The sixteen occurrences in Philo refer to various set times or periods of time (*Post.* 1:5; *Fug.* 1:87, 106, 116; *Ios.* 1:97; *Decal.* 1:100; *Spec.* 1:143–144, 161, 251; 2:142, 220; 4:196, 208; *Virt.* 1:53, 113).

[624] Goodrich, "'As Long as the Heir Is a Child,'" 75. In addition to P.Ryl. 2.153.37–39, Goodrich notes BGU 3.919 and CPR 6.78.

[625] Das, *Galatians*, 405. He notes the following examples from the papyri: P.Oxy. 485.20, 27; 491.8–10; 728.18; *IG* 5.1208.29; *OGIS* 509.22.

[626] Goodrich, "'As Long as the Heir Is a Child,'" 75. There are varying views as to the exact age an heir typically received his inheritance, which reflects diversity in the sources. See the discussion in Keener (*Galatians*, 323–24), who notes that the typical age in Roman law was fourteen while in Greek law it was closer to fifteen. However, Keener also notes that other Greek sources place the age at twenty, and apparently it was possible for an heir in his twenties to squander his inheritance.

[627] Thus the genitive τοῦ πατρός is subjective.

[628] Scott, *Adoption as Sons of God*, 135–45. He argues that ἐπίτροπος and οἰκονόμος, both together and individually, often refer to subordinate state officials. He then suggests that, since there was not set terminology for Israel's Egyptian taskmasters, the combination of these two terms is Paul's own choice in light of proposed parallels in Greco-Roman and Jewish sources. The suggestion is intriguing, but the lack of any other text where ἐπίτροπος and οἰκονόμος are used to refer to the Egyptian taskmasters makes this identification tenuous.

[629] Scott, *Adoption as Sons of God*, 140–43. Scott argues that προθεσμία is not a technical term referring to the time a father sets for the end of guardianship, but rather a general term for various kinds of dates or time limits. In light of this, he claims that the article

describing Israel the heir's 430 years of slavery in Egypt as a period of
time when they were minors awaiting the fulfillment of the Abrahamic
promise to receive their inheritance.

There is a certain kind of perceived security that comes from being
under the supervision of the law. Stringent rules and regulations can
provide a structure that leads us to think we can manage ourselves.
The result is either pride at our impressive keeping of those rules or
a despair at our inability to do so. Either way, God never intended his
people to live under the permanent supervision of the law; he has something far better for us through the gospel.

4:3. With the terms of the analogy/typology in place, Paul now transitions to its significance/antitype: "In the same way we also, when
we were children, were in slavery under the elements of the world"
(οὕτως καὶ ἡμεῖς, ὅτε ἦμεν νήπιοι, ὑπὸ τὰ στοιχεῖα τοῦ κόσμου ἤμεθα
δεδουλωμένοι). Paul uses the expression "in the same way" to draw a
correspondence between the heir described in 4:1–2 and all believers—
Jew and gentile alike.[630] The "we" (ἡμεῖς) here is emphatic, signaling
the transition to the experience of believers. There was a time when we
too were minors or "children" (νήπιοι), picking up the language of 4:1,
where it described the heir's pre-inheritance stage. Just as the heir of
4:2 was under guardians and trustees during his immaturity, believers
in their stage of immaturity "were in slavery under the elements of the
world" (ὑπὸ τὰ στοιχεῖα τοῦ κόσμου ἤμεθα δεδουλωμένοι). Paul uses
an expression that highlights the past state of slavery experienced by
believers.[631]

---

before προθεσμία likely then refers to a specific time period mentioned in the context,
which leads him to the 430 years mentioned in 3:17. Again, the possibility is intriguing, but
seeing προθεσμία as a technical term is not essential to the traditional view of the analogy,
and the weight Scott places on the article before it seems more than it can likely bear.

[630] A number of scholars see the "we" here as exclusively referring to Jews; see, e.g.,
Longenecker, *Galatians*, 164; Dunn, *Galatians*, 212; Witherington, *Grace in Galatia*, 284. But
several factors indicate "we" is inclusive, referring to Jewish and gentile believers. First,
Paul states that the slavery in view is to the "elements of the world" (τὰ στοιχεῖα τοῦ
κόσμου), which later in 4:8–9 clearly includes both the Mosaic law covenant and pagan
religions, idolatry, principles, etc. Second, Paul seems to use the first person plural "we"
interchangeably with the second person "you" in 4:5–6. See similarly Schreiner, *Galatians*,
267; de Boer, *Galatians*, 256–58; Moo, *Galatians*, 260; Das, *Galatians*, 405–6.

[631] Paul uses a periphrastic construction consisting of an imperfect tense form of εἰμί
(ἤμεθα) with a perfect tense participle (δεδουλωμένοι). Wallace (*Greek Grammar*, 585) states
that "This periphrastic construction is evidently intensive, showing the state that was

The key interpretive question, however, is the best way to interpret the expression rendered here as "the elements of the world" (τὰ στοιχεῖα τοῦ κόσμου). The noun Paul uses here (στοιχεῖον) can be understood in four primary ways: (1) the basic elements of the material world (typically understood as earth, wind, fire, and water); (2) celestial bodies such as stars, planets, etc.; (3) the basic or fundamental principles of a subject; and (4) transcendent spiritual forces that influence or control events in this world.[632] Each of these views can be found in English translations, and the scholarly literature on this expression is extensive. Although certainty is impossible, it seems most likely that Paul is referring to the basic elements of the material world.[633] But Paul uses them to represent all that is associated with this fallen world, this present evil age (1:4) that is under the curse that fell on creation as a result of Adam's rebellion.[634] Within Galatians various themes are associated with this old creation, such as sin, works of the law, being under sin, being under law, the flesh, curse, being imprisoned under sin, being confined under the law, being under a guardian, being enslaved, dividing humanity along

---

simultaneous with the main statement (ὅτε ἦμεν νήπιοι). An implication to be drawn from the context (but not from the pluperfect alone) is that the enslavement was now past. The pluperfect is thus well suited for such a notion, but it does not by itself indicate this."

[632] See BDAG s.v. στοιχεῖον. This word occurs seven times in the NT (Gal 4:3, 9; Col 2:8, 20; Heb 5:12; 2 Pet 3:10, 12), always in the plural. In Heb 5:12, τὰ στοιχεῖα refers to "the basic principles of God's revelation"; in every other occurrence the meaning is disputed. Regardless of one's interpretive conclusion, given the unusual nature of the expression, it would make sense that Paul uses the term with the same meaning all four times. All three of the LXX occurrences (4 Macc 12:13; Wis 7:17; 19:18) refer to physical matter. Perhaps the closest parallel to Gal 4:3 is Wis 7:17, where Solomon claims that God "gave me an unerring knowledge of the things that exist, to know the constitution of the world [κόσμου] and the activity of the elements [ἐνέργειαν στοιχείων]" (NETS). Dunn (Galatians, 213) argues for an "all of the above" approach, stating that "we would do better to suppose the phrase was [Paul's] way of referring to the common understanding of the time that human beings lived their lives under the influence or sway of primal and cosmic forces, however they were conceptualized."

[633] The most decisive factor is that when the expression τὰ στοιχεῖα is modified by a form of κόσμος in Greek literature, it almost always refers to the physical elements of material world; see the evidence provided in Dietrich Rusam, "Neue Belege Zu Den Stoicheia Tou Kosmou (Gal 4,3.9, Kol 2,8.20)," ZNW 83 (1992): 119–25. But as both de Boer (Galatians, 252–56) and Moo (Galatians, 260–63) note, this observation does not preclude Paul extending the meaning of the expression beyond its physical reference.

[634] Similarly Schreiner, Galatians, 267–69. Along similar lines, Das (Galatians, 442–44) helpfully notes that the ancients understood the world to be governed by opposing pairs, which would fit well with the pairs Paul lists in 3:28 as fundamental to this present age.

ethnic, socioeconomic, and gender lines, being under guardians and stewards, observing special days, circumcision, the desires and works of the flesh, biting and devouring one another, inflated self-esteem, etc. All of these are facets of the old creation, the present evil age that rests under a curse, represented here by the expression "elements of the world" (τὰ στοιχεῖα τοῦ κόσμου). As such, one could see this phrase as the opposite to the expression "new creation" (καινὴ κτίσις) Paul uses in Galatians 6:15, "For both circumcision and uncircumcision mean nothing; what matters instead is a new creation."

This then is the state of all human beings apart from Christ. Regardless of our ethnicity, socioeconomic status, or gender, we all enter this world in a state of slavery to sin and subject to the elements of this world. Paul describes this same reality in Ephesians 2:1–3, where he writes, "And you were dead in your trespasses and sins in which you previously walked according to the ways of this world, according to the ruler of the power of the air, the spirit now working in the disobedient. We too all previously lived among them in our fleshly desires, carrying out the inclinations of our flesh and thoughts, and we were by nature children under wrath as the others were also." Unless someone recognizes how disastrous their condition apart from Christ truly is, they will never see the beauty of what Christ has done.

4:4. The state of slavery to the elements described in 4:3 is not the final word. When all looked hopeless, God acted: "When the time came to completion, God sent his Son" (ὅτε δὲ ἦλθεν τὸ πλήρωμα τοῦ χρόνου, ἐξαπέστειλεν ὁ θεὸς τὸν υἱὸν αὐτοῦ).[635] Just as there was a time appointed by the father for the son to receive the inheritance, so too there was a specific point in time God had determined to act. The expression rendered "when the time came to completion" (ὅτε δὲ ἦλθεν τὸ πλήρωμα τοῦ χρόνου) could also be rendered "when the fullness of time came" (compare ESV).[636] The conviction that the arrival of Jesus

---

[635] As Paul is fond of doing, he transitions from a description of humanity's sinfulness and lostness with a strong adversative (δέ, which regrettably is not translated by the CSB); compare Eph 2:4. Paul uses this same construction (ὅτε δὲ) in Gal 1:15 to mark the decisive act of God invading his life on the Damascus Road.

[636] As used here, the Greek word πλήρωμα ("fullness") has the sense of "the state of being full" (BDAG s.v. πλήρωμα 6). Twelve of the seventeen NT occurrences are in Paul, with the closest parallel being Eph 1:10 (see above). Depending on the context, the word can also have the sense of consummation (e.g., Philo, *Spec.* 2:213), a sense which would also fit with its use here in Gal 4:4 (see *TDNT* 6:299). The cognate verb πληρόω and its cognates is used

Christ signaled the fulfillment of the Old Testament promises is pervasive in the New Testament. According to Mark 1:15, the opening words
of Jesus' public ministry were "The time is fulfilled, and the kingdom
of God has come near. Repent and believe the good news!" Elsewhere
Paul states that God's purpose in sending forth Christ was "as a plan
for the right time—to bring everything together in Christ, both things
in heaven and things on earth in him" (Eph 1:10). Paul's point here in
Galatians 4:4 is that God's act of redemption through his Son came at
a specific moment of fulfillment in human history, bringing an end to
the period of slavery to the elementals and signaling that the period
of eschatological fulfillment had begun.[637]

The hinge upon which human history turned was when "God sent his
Son" (ἐξαπέστειλεν ὁ θεὸς τὸν υἱὸν αὐτοῦ).[638] Although the language of
God sending the Son is most prominent in the Gospels (especially John),
Paul does state in Romans 8:3 that God "condemned sin in the flesh by
sending his own Son in the likeness of sinful flesh as a sin offering."
Paul further describes the Son with two participles.[639] First, the Son

---

frequently in the NT to refer to the fulfillment of OT promises, hopes, and expectations;
on the temporal use of πληρόω in extrabiblical literature, see *NIDNTTE* 3:785–86. For helpful discussion of the use and meaning of fulfillment language in the NT, see D. A. Carson,
"Mystery and Fulfillment: Toward a More Comprehensive Paradigm of Paul's Understanding
of the Old and the New," in *Justification and Variegated Nomism: The Paradoxes of Paul*, ed.
D. A. Carson, Peter T. O'Brien, and Mark A. Seifrid, 2 vols. (Grand Rapids: Baker, 2001),
393–436 and G. K. Beale, *Handbook on the New Testament Use of the Old Testament: Exegesis and
Interpretation* (Grand Rapids: Baker, 2012), 55–67. The word Paul uses here for "time" is
χρόνος, which refers to a period of time rather than a specific point or moment (see BDAG
s.v. χρόνος 1). The point then is that when the time period of bondage under the elements
had been "filled up," God sent his Son.

[637] De Boer (*Galatians*, 262) takes a slightly different approach, claiming that Paul uses
this expression in anticipation of mentioning the calendrical observances in 4:10 and to
signal that, with the arrival of Christ, a new time of faith and the Spirit (in contrast to the
law) has begun.

[638] The verb rendered "sent" (ἐξαποστέλλω) is an intensified form of the verb that he
normally uses (ἀποστέλλω). These two verbs are used interchangeably in the LXX and
Philo (*TDNT* 1:406), and in the thirteen NT occurrences of ἐξαποστέλλω it is difficult to
identify an emphatic sense in comparison to ἀποστέλλω. Since Gal 4:4, 6 are the only two
occurrences of ἐξαποστέλλω in Paul, it does raise the question as to why Paul uses it here.
The answer may lie in a possible echo of Isa 48:16 (see discussion below).

[639] While the basic sense of these participles is quite clear, the precise grammar is not.
They could be adverbial, modifying the verb "sent" (ἐξαπέστειλεν), in which case they
would indicate manner (see, e.g., DeSilva, *Handbook*, 81). But they could also be adjectival,

was "born of a woman" (γενόμενον ἐκ γυναικός). At one level this statement simply affirms the full humanity of the Son. And while the text does not explicitly affirm the preexistence of the Son, it seems to be a reasonable inference.[640] There may also be echoes of Old Testament texts that speak of prophetic callings from birth (Isa 49:1; Jer 1:5), which, as we have seen, Paul himself draws on in 1:15–16.[641] Second, the Son was "born under the law" (γενόμενον ὑπὸ νόμον). We have already seen the phrase "under the law" in 3:23, where Paul used it to describe the experience of the Jews before the coming of Christ. In reference to the Son, it means that Christ was born under the authority of the law. Considered together, the two phrases may also indicate that the work of the Son was intended for both gentiles ("born of a woman") and Jews ("born under the law").[642]

Paul's language here shows strong parallels to what he would later write in Romans 8:1–17, as the following chart shows:[643]

---

modifying "Son" (see, e.g., Burton, *Galatians*, 218–19; Longenecker, *Galatians*, 171). On the whole, the latter seems more likely, since one would have expected these participles to be in the nominative case if they were adverbial. Indeed, Martin Culy has argued that adverbial participles are never in the accusative unless they modify an infinitive; see Martin M. Culy, "The Clue Is in the Case: Distinguishing Adjectival and Adverbial Participles," *PRSt* 30 (2003): 441–53. Regardless of the grammatical specifics, the meaning is not significantly different between the two possibilities.

[640] Even though the participle "born" (γενόμενον) here is likely adjectival, modifying "his Son" (τὸν υἱὸν αὐτοῦ), the fact that Paul follows his claim about God sending the Son with a statement about him being born suggests the Son's preexistence. Paul clearly affirms the preexistence of the Son in Phil 2:6–7. For a concise summary of several arguments for seeing Christ's preexistence in view here, see Das, *Galatians*, 410–11; for an extended discussion of Christ's preexistence in Paul, see Gordon D. Fee, *Pauline Christology: An Exegetical-Theological Study* (Peabody, MA: Hendrickson, 2007), 546–52. Dunn (*Galatians*, 215–16) denies that Paul has in view Christ's preexistence, arguing instead for an Adam Christology in which Christ was "the man who retraced the course of Adam through his fallenness to death (cf. Rom. vii.3), in order by his exaltation to complete the divine purpose in creating humankind, that is to put all things under his feet (Ps. viii.6) in order that those in him might share in this completion of the divine purpose for creation." But even if there is Adam Christology present here, that does not automatically rule out a reference to Christ's preexistence.

[641] Longenecker, *Galatians*, 171.

[642] So Roy E. Ciampa, "The History of Redemption," in *Central Themes in Biblical Theology: Mapping Unity in Diversity*, ed. Scott J. Hafemann and Paul R. House (Grand Rapids: Baker, 2007), 300–1.

[643] Adapted from Moo, *Galatians*, 264.

Table 9:

Galatians 4:4–7	Romans 8:1–17
ὅτε δὲ ἦλθεν τὸ πλήρωμα τοῦ χρόνου When the time came to completion	
ἐξαπέστειλεν ὁ θεὸς τὸν υἱὸν αὐτοῦ God sent his Son	ὁ θεὸς τὸν ἑαυτοῦ υἱὸν πέμψας God did ... by sending his own Son (8:3)
γενόμενον ἐκ γυναικός, γενόμενον ὑπὸ νόμον born of a woman, born under the law	ἐν ὁμοιώματι σαρκὸς ἁμαρτίας καὶ περὶ ἁμαρτίας in the likeness of sinful flesh as a sin offering (8:3)
ἵνα τοὺς ὑπὸ νόμον ἐξαγοράσῃ to redeem those under the law	
ἵνα τὴν υἱοθεσίαν ἀπολάβωμεν so that we might receive adoption as sons	ἐλάβετε πνεῦμα υἱοθεσίας you received the Spirit of adoption (8:15)
Ὅτι δέ ἐστε υἱοί, ἐξαπέστειλεν ὁ θεὸς τὸ πνεῦμα τοῦ υἱοῦ αὐτοῦ εἰς τὰς καρδίας ἡμῶν κρᾶζον· αββα ὁ πατήρ And because you are sons, God sent the Spirit of his Son into our hearts, crying, "Abba, Father!"	οὗτοι υἱοὶ θεοῦ εἰσιν ... ἐν ᾧ κράζομεν· αββα ὁ πατήρ those ... are God's sons ... by whom we cry out, "Abba, Father!" (8:14–15)
ὥστε οὐκέτι εἶ δοῦλος ἀλλ᾽ υἱός So you are no longer a slave but a son	οὐ γὰρ ἐλάβετε πνεῦμα δουλείας you did not receive a spirit of slavery (8:15)
εἰ δὲ υἱός, καὶ κληρονόμος διὰ θεοῦ and if a son, then God has made you an heir.	εἰ δὲ τέκνα, καὶ κληρονόμοι and if children, also heirs (8:17)

The variation in order and additional content in Romans 8:1–17 indicate a more extended reflection on these issues several years after he wrote Galatians and further suggest that Paul is not drawing on a set piece of early Christian tradition.

The conviction that God sent his Son into the world in fulfillment of his promises is at the heart of the gospel message. He directed all of human history to the fullness of time when the Son would enter the world and accomplish the redemption of his people, Jew and gentile alike. Now, as his people, we "wait for the day of God and hasten its coming" (2 Pet 3:12) through our lives of holiness and faithful witness to Christ, with the confidence that his timing will be perfect and result in all creation acknowledging Jesus Christ as Lord (Phil 2:9–11).

4:5. In the previous verse Paul stated what God did (sent his Son), what his Son is like (born of a woman, born under the law), and when this action took place (when the time came to completion). Here in verse 5 Paul now states the purpose of God sending the Son: "to redeem those under the law" (ἵνα τοὺς ὑπὸ νόμον ἐξαγοράσῃ). The verb rendered "redeem" (ἐξαγοράζω) is the same one Paul used in 3:13. As noted there, the verb not only has strong commercial connotations, but it also carries the overtones of the new exodus promised in the prophets and especially Isaiah. The recipients of this redemptive act are "those under the law" (τοὺς ὑπὸ νόμον), which although it could be a reference to Jews is likely instead a reference to all believers (Jew and gentile alike).[644] In Greek this phrase is placed at the beginning of the clause, which may signal emphasis. The point then is that God's purpose in sending his Son was to redeem everyone under the law, regardless of their ethnicity. Through his death on the cross, Jesus has freed his people from their slavery to the elements of this world (4:3), from this present evil age (1:4) that remains under the curse pronounced upon creation when Adam rebelled in the garden.

The purpose of this act of redemption was "so that we might receive adoption as sons" (ἵνα τὴν υἱοθεσίαν ἀπολάβωμεν).[645] The death and resurrection of Jesus to redeem his people—Jew and gentile alike—from the penalty their sin deserved was not an end in and of itself, as glorious as that reality is. Christ's work of redemption was for the further purpose of believers receiving adoption as sons. Although not especially common in the New Testament, the verb translated "receive" (ἀπολαμβάνω) is often

---

[644] A decision here is difficult. On the one hand, Paul uses the phrase "under the law" to describe the Jewish people in 3:23 as "confined under the law, imprisoned until the coming faith was revealed." On the other, the "we" in the next clause who receive adoption as sons seems to be used interchangeably with the "you" in the first clause of 4:7 who are described as sons and the "our" in the second clause of 4:7 who have the Spirit. This apparent interchange between the first and second person seems to make the second option more likely. Two other considerations further support an inclusive reference here. First, Paul's reference to the Jews being "under the law" in 3:23 comes immediately after he has stated that "Scripture imprisoned everything under sin's power" (3:22). Thus it would seem that there is a close relationship between being "under sin's power" and being "under the law." Second, in 4:21 Paul will address the Galatians who are enticed by his opponents as "you who want to be under the law." This expression would seem to suggest that anyone, Jew or gentile, can be considered "under the law." For an explanation of how Paul can say that gentiles were "under the law," see the discussion at 3:23.

[645] Given the parallel thought and structure between 3:13–14 and 4:4–5, it is certainly possible that the two ἵνα clauses here, like their counterparts in 3:13–14, are coordinate (see discussion at 3:14). But here in 4:4–5 there seems to be a clear logical progression from the first clause ("to redeem those under the law") to the second ("so that we might receive adoption as sons"); see similarly Schreiner, *Galatians*, 271n30. Those who see them as coordinate include Betz, *Galatians*, 206; Longenecker, *Galatians*, 172. Martyn (*Galatians*, 390) suggests that the second clause functions "as an enriching explication of the first."

used to refer to receiving something from God, sometimes even in eschatological contexts.[646] Note, for example, Colossians 3:24, where Paul exhorts slaves to obey their masters, "knowing that you will receive the reward of an inheritance from the Lord." What believers receive is adoption, a practice that was common in Greek, Roman, and even Jewish culture.[647] The specific term used here for "adoption as sons" (υἱοθεσία) is uniquely Pauline in the New Testament (Rom 8:15, 23; 9:4; Gal 4:5; Eph 1:5), and in Greek literature it often has a particular emphasis on the legal status of the one adopted as an heir.[648] As a general rule, the primary purpose of adoption in the ancient world was to continue the family line, usually when there was not a natural-born son.[649] While caution must be exercised in pressing the analogy too far, Paul seems to be drawing on this general practice of adoption that was reasonably common in both the Greco-Roman and Jewish contexts of his day.

Perhaps even more significant than any particular cultural background for understanding Paul's use of adoption terminology here is the Old Testament background. Although the exact terminology of adoption is not used in the Old Testament, the concept is almost certainly present in at least two places (Gen 16:2; Exod 2:10).[650] More significantly, Paul lists "adoption" as one of Israel's blessings (Rom 9:4), likely referring to God describing the Israelites as "my firstborn son" (Exod 4:22–23). This designation is part of a larger scriptural theme of Adam, Israel, and the Davidic king all being referred to as the son of God.[651] Paul asserts that believers—regardless of ethnicity, socio-economic status, or gender—now have been designated as sons of God. Such

<hr/>

[646] Of the ten NT occurrences, eight refer to receiving something from God, whether blessing/reward (Luke 15:27; 16:25; Gal 4:5; Col 3:24; 2 John 8) or judgment (Luke 23:41; Rom 1:27). In Num 34:14 (LXX) this verb refers to the tribes of Reuben and Gad receiving their inheritance of land.

[647] For an extensive discussion of adoption practices in Greek, Roman, and Jewish cultures, see Scott, *Adoption as Sons of God*, 1–117. A more concise summary can be found in Keener, *Galatians*, 340–45.

[648] For a survey of how υἱοθεσία was used in Greek literature, see Scott, *Adoption as Sons of God*, 45–55. Although dating nearly three hundred years after Paul, an example from P. Oxy IX. 1206.8 is illuminating here: "we agree, Heracles and his wife Isarion on the one part, that we have given away to you, Horion, for adoption [υἱοθεσίαν] our son Patermouthis, aged about two years, and I Horion on the other part, that I have him as my own son so that the rights proceeding from succession to my inheritance [κληρονομίας] shall be maintained for him" (cited in MM, 648).

[649] Another (though not mutually exclusive) motivation for adoption in some cases included social and political maneuvering; see Scott, *Adoption as Sons of God*, 9.

[650] Several Second Temple Jewish texts interpreted these passages (as well as a few others) in terms of adoption; see Scott, *Adoption as Sons of God*, 75–79.

[651] See Biblical Theology §7.2.1.1.

a status does not come from keeping the Mosaic law, but rather through faith in Christ Jesus (3:26). From all eternity, God had purposed to adopt believers into his family (Eph 1:5), and because we are united to Christ by faith, we are no longer slaves to anything associated with this present evil age/old creation (Gal 4:3; compare Rom 8:15). But we still await the full realization of all that comes with being adopted sons of God, as Romans 8:23 makes clear: "Not only that, but we ourselves who have the Spirit as the firstfruits—we also groan within ourselves, eagerly waiting for adoption, the redemption of our bodies."

Now that we have worked our way through the details of Galatians 4:4–5, we are in a position to step back and note that its basic features share a similar pattern with several other key texts in Galatians. The similarities can be laid out as follows:[652]

Table 10:

	God/ Christ	Redemptive Act	Object	Realm	Means	Purpose/ Result
1:4	Christ	rescue	us	from this present evil age	gave himself for our sins	according to the will of our God and Father
2:19–20	Christ	crucified	me	the law	loved me and gave himself for me	I no longer live, but Christ lives in me
3:13–14	Christ	redeemed	us	from the curse of the law	by becoming a curse for us	that the blessing of Abraham would come to the Gentiles by Christ Jesus, so that we could receive the promised Spirit through faith
4:4–5	God sent his Son	to redeem	those under the law	(slavery under the elements of the world; 4:3)	born of a woman, born under the law	so that we might receive adoption as sons

[652] Also noting the parallels between 3:13–14 and 4:4–6, Richard Hays (*Faith of Jesus*, 74–117) argues that there is an underlying "narrative substructure" in which the faithfulness of Christ is the means by which the Jews receive redemption and the gentiles receive the blessing of Abraham, and both Jew and gentile alike receive the gift of the Spirit. But while this claim is true on a theological level, it remains unlikely in our estimation that these texts in Galatians refer to Christ's faithfulness when using the term πίστις. If indeed there is a narrative substructure present, it seems more likely to be that of Isaiah 51–54; see Harmon, *She Must and Shall Go Free*, 161–67, 250–54.

Given that each of the first three occurrences of this formula appear to have their background in Isaiah 53, it seems reasonable to conclude the same is true here. Christ is the Isaianic servant who has redeemed his people from their slavery to sin and set them free to receive their promised inheritance as adopted sons.[653]

In his classic book *Knowing God*, J. I. Packer helpfully explains how, although justification is the *primary* blessing of the gospel, it is not the *highest* blessing of the gospel:

> Justification is a *forensic* idea, conceived in terms of *law*, and viewing God as *judge*. In justification, God declares of penitent believers that they are not, and never will be, liable to the death that their sins deserve, because Jesus Christ, their substitute and sacrifice, tasted death in their place on the cross ... Adoption is a *family* idea, conceived in terms of *love*, and viewing God as *father*. In adoption, God takes us into his family and fellowship—he establishes us as his children and heirs. Closeness, affection, and generosity are at the heart of the relationship. To be right with God the Judge is a great thing, but to be loved and cared for by God the Father is a greater.[654]

4:6. With the identity of the Galatian gentile believers as adopted sons of God firmly established, Paul now highlights one particular result from this status: "because you are sons, God has sent the Spirit of his Son into our hearts" (Ὅτι δέ ἐστε υἱοί, ἐξαπέστειλεν ὁ θεὸς τὸ πνεῦμα τοῦ υἱοῦ αὐτοῦ εἰς τὰς καρδίας ἡμῶν).[655] Paul began this lengthy argument stretching from 3:1–5:1 by asking the Galatians about their reception and experience of the Holy Spirit (3:1–5). He then reintroduces the Spirit in 3:14, noting that God has given the promised Spirit to his redeemed people in fulfillment of the Abrahamic promise. Once again at a critical juncture here in 4:6, Paul asserts that God sent the Spirit, using the same rare verb (ἐξαποστέλλω) for God sending his Son in 4:4. Unlike previous references to the Spirit in Galatians, Paul refers to "the Spirit of his Son"

---

[653] On the Isaianic background here, see further Harmon, *She Must and Shall Go Free*, 163–66.

[654] J. I. Packer, *Knowing God*, 20th anniversary ed. (Downers Grove, IL: IVP, 1993), 207.

[655] Thus the δέ at the beginning of the clause introduces the result in an "action-result" relationship, on which see Beale, Ross, and Brendsel, *Interpretive Lexicon*, 33. It should be noted that while logically adoption as sons precedes the gift of the Spirit, temporally in the experience of the believer both happen simultaneously at conversion.

(τὸ πνεῦμα τοῦ υἱοῦ αὐτου). This unusual expression—found nowhere else in the New Testament—forges a close link between the work of the Son and the work of the Spirit in the life of the believer.[656] Because we are united to Christ by faith, the same Spirit who indwelled and empowered him now dwells in us.

God has sent the Spirit of his Son "into our hearts" (εἰς τὰς καρδίας ἡμῶν), the very core of our being.[657] Even in the midst of trials, believers have hope that will not disappoint "because God's love has been poured out in our hearts through the Holy Spirit who was given to us" (Rom 5:5). God had promised that as part of restoring his people from exile, he would give them a new heart and put his Spirit in them to empower their obedience (Ezek 36:26–28; compare Jer 31:33–34). Now that the Son has inaugurated that return from exile through his death and resurrection, God has sent the Spirit of his Son into the hearts of all those who are his adopted sons by faith in Christ—Jew and gentile alike. Indeed, in keeping with the larger analogy of adoption in 4:1–7, the Spirit is pictured as a central component of our inheritance. Ephesians 1:13–14 makes this connection clear when it refers to the Holy Spirit as "the down payment of our inheritance, until the redemption of the possession, to the praise of his glory" (compare 2 Cor 1:22). As the seed of Abraham and the Davidic son of God, Jesus Christ has received the promised inheritance and shares that inheritance with all who are united to him by faith and thus adopted sons of God.

As evidence that the Spirit of God's Son dwells in believers, he cries out "*Abba*, Father!" (αββα ὁ πατήρ). "*Abba*" is the Aramaic word for father, and its use here stems from Jesus' practice of referring to God the father as "*Abba*" in prayer (Mark 14:36). Although "*Abba*" is not quite equivalent to our English term "Daddy," it does communicate a sense of intimacy, warmth, trust, and affection. The fact that Greek-speaking gentile believers used this Aramaic term in their prayers shows how meaningful this term of intimacy was to the early church (compare Rom 8:15). It was an experiential way of expressing the intimacy with God that Jesus prayed

---

[656] Paul does refer elsewhere to "the Spirit of Christ" (Rom 8:9) and the "Spirit of Jesus Christ" (Phil 1:19).

[657] A few manuscripts (D² K L Ψ 33) have "your" (ὑμῶν) rather than "our" (ἡμῶν) hearts, and this is the reading preferred by Witherington, *Grace in Galatia*, 289–90. But the reading "our" is well supported (𝔓⁴⁶ A B C D* F G P) and is almost certainly original; see the discussion in Moo, *Galatians*, 271–72.

all believers would experience (John 17:20–24). The present tense participle rendered "crying" (κρᾶζον) suggests this is an ongoing experience for believers. On a regular basis the Spirit of the Son is crying out to the Father in the most intimate terms, interceding for us with groanings too deep for words (Rom 8:26–27).

The parallel language of God sending his Son (4:4) and the Spirit of his Son (4:6) may echo Isaiah 48:16, where an unnamed speaker claims, "And now the Lord God has sent me and his Spirit."[658] Beale notes that "Isaiah 48:16 refers to God's two primary agents who will carry out Israel's future restoration, which is set in a second Exodus context ... who both become the means of the Lord's 'redemption.' "[659] While one cannot be certain, such an echo would fit with the pattern of Isaianic allusions and echoes in Galatians, as well as the second exodus motif here in 4:1–7.

Also worth noting is the Trinitarian structure of redemption here in 4:4–6. The Father sends the Son in the fullness of time. The Son redeems his people through his death and resurrection. The Father sends the Spirit into the hearts of his people. The Spirit cries out, "*Abba*, Father!" All three persons of the Trinity work together in harmony and fulfill their respective roles in accomplishing the salvation of God's people.

God made us to experience community. Even in the perfection of Eden, God said that it was not good for man to be alone. This statement applies well beyond marriage; it speaks to our fundamental need as human beings to belong. Even at their best, earthly families are a shadow in comparison to the greater reality of belonging to the family of God. Not only is Christ not ashamed to call us his brothers (Heb 2:11–12), but he is willing to share his inheritance with us. We even have his Spirit dwelling in us to draw us so close to the Father that we can call out to him "*Abba*, Father!" It is in the family of God that we find our ultimate sense of belonging.

4:7. All that remains for Paul in this paragraph is to state his conclusion: "So you are no longer a slave but a son" (ὥστε οὐκέτι εἶ δοῦλος ἀλλ᾽ υἱός). Paul switches from the plural "you" in 4:6 to the singular "you" here in 4:7 to drive home his point for each individual believer. Whereas believers were once slaves to the elemental forces of the world (4:3), they are now adopted sons in God's family because of the work of Jesus the

---

[658] See G. K. Beale, "The Old Testament Background of Paul's Reference to 'the Fruit of the Spirit' in Galatians 5:22," *BBR* 15 (2005): 10–11.

[659] Beale, "The Old Testament Background," 11.

Son of God (4:4–6). The evidence that they are sons is that they possess the Spirit of God's Son, the down payment on the full realization of their inheritance that is yet to come.

Paul draws one final inference from the status of the believer as an adopted son of God: "and if a son, then God has made you an heir" (εἰ δὲ υἱός, καὶ κληρονόμος διὰ θεοῦ).[660] The logical inference to be draw from the believer's status as a son is that he is also an heir. Paul has already connected being Abraham's seed (through faith in Christ) to being "heirs according to the promise" (3:29); here he makes a similar connection between being a son of God and God making the believer an heir. Thus the emphasis falls on God alone being the one responsible for our status as heirs.[661] As human beings, we did nothing to contribute to that status, not even obeying the Mosaic law.

People tend to love a good rags-to-riches story. There is none better than the one that we as followers of Christ have experienced through the gospel. Why then are we so hesitant to share that story with others to invite them to experience that same reality?

Bridge

From minor children no better than slaves to sons with a full inheritance—that is the story of every person who trusts in Christ regardless of our ethnicity, gender, or socioeconomic status. Even those without a drop of Jewish blood in our veins can say with Joshua that "the Lᴏʀᴅ our God brought us and our ancestors out of the land of Egypt, out of the place of

---

[660] This is a first class conditional statement, which assumes that the "if" clause is true for the sake of the argument. The logical relationship between the protasis and the apodosis is cause-effect. The δέ here indicates this conditional statement is an extension of the conclusion in the previous clause.

[661] In Greek this last phrase is woodenly "an heir through God" (κληρονόμος διὰ θεοῦ). Normally διά plus the genitive expresses the efficient means or instrument through which something happens. But, as Harris (*Prepositions and Theology*, 70) notes, "Sometimes, however, διά with the genitive expresses not the efficient means but the ultimate cause, not instrumentality but sole agency" (compare Rom 11:36; 1 Cor 1:9). This unusual expression led to a variety of textual variants as scribes likely attempted to "correct" the grammar: (1) "because of God" (δια θεον; F G 1881); (2) "through Christ" (δια Χριστου; 81. 630 sa); (3) "through Jesus Christ" (δια Ιησου Χριστου; 1739ᶜ); (4) "heir of God through Jesus Christ" (κληρονομος θεου δια Χριστου; ℵ²C³ D K L 0278. 104. 365. 1175. 1241. 2464 𝔐 ar); (5) "heir of God, and fellow heir with Christ" (κληρονομος μεν θεου, συγκληρονομος δε Χριστου; Ψ). But the reading "through God" (δια θεου) is well supported in the witnesses (𝔓⁴⁶ ℵ* A B C* 33. 1739ᵛⁱᵈ lat bo; Cl) and best explains the origin of the variants; see Metzger, *Textual Commentary*, 526–27.

slavery, and performed these great signs before our eyes" (Josh 24:17). Our place of slavery was a place far more dangerous than the land of Egypt. It was the present evil age that Christ the suffering servant and Son of God delivered us from (cf. 1:4). We have an inheritance that is "imperishable, undefiled, and unfading, kept in heaven" (1 Pet 1:4) for us, and in the meantime, we have the Spirit of God's Son dwelling in us. Why not take a moment to praise God in prayer for this immeasurable gift?

H. A REMINDER FROM THEIR PAGAN PAST (4:8–11)

> [8] But in the past, since you didn't know God, you were enslaved to things that by nature are not gods. [9] But now, since you know God, or rather have become known by God, how can you turn back again to the weak and worthless elements? Do you want to be enslaved to them all over again? [10] You are observing special days, months, seasons, and years. [11] I am fearful for you, that perhaps my labor for you has been wasted.

Context

In this paragraph Paul moves from a focus on theological exposition to apply the content of 4:1–7. Since the Galatians have been changed from slaves to sons with an inheritance, Paul wonders aloud why the Galatians would even consider a return to their former status as slaves to the elements of the world.

Structure

Throughout this short paragraph Paul highlights the sharp contrast between life before Christ and life in Christ. Before Christ, the Galatians were enslaved to false gods (4:8). Paul wonders how, now that they have come to know God through faith in Christ, they can even consider returning to enslavement under the worthless elements again (4:9). Whereas, before, their enslavement to the elements took the form of pagan beliefs and worship of idols, now it would take the form of observing the Jewish calendar found in the Mosaic law (4:10). The danger is so real that Paul wonders aloud whether his gospel ministry among them may prove to be in vain, since observing the Mosaic law in an effort to be justified and receive the blessing promised to Abraham would be a rejection of the true gospel (4:11).

4:8. Paul now moves to specifically apply what he argued in 4:1–7 to the Galatians' own experience and current circumstances. He describes their pre-conversion state as "in the past, since you didn't know God" (Ἀλλὰ τότε μὲν οὐκ εἰδότες θεὸν).[662] Although it is not prominent here in Galatians, describing the believer's relationship to God in terms of knowing God or Christ is common in Paul. Perhaps the clearest example is Philippians 3:8, where Paul says, "I also consider everything to be a loss in view of the surpassing value of knowing Christ Jesus my Lord." For Paul, a relational knowledge of God through Jesus Christ is central to the gospel. Yet in emphasizing this Paul was drawing on the Old Testament, which repeatedly describes Israel as knowing God (Exod 10:2; Deut 4:35; Ps 83:18; Ezek 36:36) in contrast to the pagan nations who do not know God (Ps 79:6; Jer 10:25). As sons of God, believers know the God of the universe intimately, calling out to him "*Abba*, Father" (4:6).

Paul reminds the Galatians that before they believed the gospel and came to know God, they "were enslaved to things that by nature are not gods" (ἐδουλεύσατε τοῖς φύσει μὴ οὖσιν θεοῖς). Picking up language from 4:3, Paul returns to the Galatians' pre-conversion slavery.[663] Whereas in 4:3 the enslaving power was the "elemental forces of the world" (HCSB), here it is "things that by nature are not gods" (τοῖς φύσει μὴ οὖσιν θεοῖς).[664] This would seem to be a reference to the pagan deities that the Galatians worshiped before their conversion.[665] These pagan deities are a subcat-

---

[662] The ἀλλά that begins this sentence introduces a negative proposition that will be followed by a positive assertion in the following sentence. This construction is reinforced with the μέν ... δέ construction that unites the two sentences in 4:8–9. The participle εἰδότες ("knowing"), occurring here with the adverb τότε ("then"), is most likely temporal in force, though a causal sense would also make sense.

[663] In 4:3 Paul used the verb δουλόω ("to be a slave"), while here in 4:8–9 he uses δουλεύω ("to be a slave"). There appears to be no substantive difference in meaning between the two verbs, though Paul only uses δουλεύω from this point forward (4:25; 5:13).

[664] Although there is no exact parallel to the expression "things that by nature are not gods" (τοῖς φύσει μὴ οὖσιν θεοῖς), there is a loose parallel with Isa 37:19 (LXX). In his prayer for deliverance, King Hezekiah states that the Assyrians "have hurled their [i.e., the nations] idols into the fire, for they were no gods [οὐ γὰρ θεοὶ ἦσαν], but the works of human hands—wood and stone—and they destroyed them" (NETS). See also 2 Chr 13:9; Jer 5:7; 16:20.

[665] Witherington (*Grace in Galatia*, 297–98) suggests that the imperial cult is in view here: "Paul is drawing an analogy between going back to observing the calendrical feasts and days of the Emperor cult with going forward and accepting the calendrical observances enunciated in the Mosaic covenant." Hardin (*Galatians and the Imperial Cult*, 103–14) agrees, arguing that the opponents were urging the Galatian gentile believers to participate in the imperial cult by offering sacrifices to God on behalf of the emperor. Yet while the imperial cult appears to have been present and active in several of the cities addressed by this letter, Keener (*Galatians*, 353–55) rightly notes the wide variety of gods worshiped

egory of the "elements of the world" (4:3), part of the old creation, this
present evil age (1:4), along with the Mosaic law.

When it comes to the "gods," Paul gives his clearest insights in
1 Corinthians 8–10 when dealing with the issue of whether Christians
should eat meat that has been offered to idols.[666] Paul asserts that, on
the one hand, there is only one true God, idols have no real existence,
and that so-called "gods" and "lords" are not in fact actually gods (1 Cor
8:4–6). Yet he also acknowledges that when pagans sacrifice to so-called
gods, "they sacrifice to demons and not to God" (1 Cor 10:20). So at one
level Paul reserves the category of "god" for Yahweh the one true God,
but he acknowledges that there are lesser spiritual powers (i.e., demons)
behind the so-called gods of the pagans.

Human beings today are just as prone to worship "things that by
nature are not gods." In our Western culture these so-called gods do
not tend to be made of stone, wood, or precious metals. But the idols of
wealth, power, and sex, along with many others, are pervasive and just
as powerful at enslaving people. They too are part of the elements of this
world, the old creation, this present evil age, that Christ has rescued his
people from.

4:9. Using an emphatic "But now" (νῦν δὲ),[667] Paul transitions to the
Galatians' current state as believers as a starting point for challenging
their willingness to take on the yoke of the Mosaic law: "But now, since
you know God, or rather have become known by God" (νῦν δὲ γνόντες
θεόν, μᾶλλον δὲ γνωσθέντες ὑπὸ θεοῦ).[668] A great transition took place
when the Galatians believed the gospel; they now know God. Or, more

---

in these regions. Thus it goes beyond the evidence to single out the imperial cult as being
particularly in view here.

[666] For a helpful survey of Jewish monotheism and how the early Christians maintained
their commitment to it while at the same time recognizing Jesus as God, see Bauckham,
Jesus and the God of Israel, 1–59.

[667] Paul regularly uses this expression to signal the dramatic shift that has taken place
between the previous unconverted state of believers and their current experience as believers (Rom 11:30; Gal 4:9; Eph 5:8) or the shift in redemptive history with the coming of Christ
(Rom 16:26; Col 1:26; 2 Tim 1:10).

[668] According to Burton (*Galatians*, 230), when the expression μᾶλλον δὲ follows a positive
statement (as it does here), "it introduces an additional and more important fact or aspect
of the matter, not thereby retracting what precedes ... but so transferring the emphasis
to the added fact or aspect as being of superior significance as in effect to displace the
previous thought."

importantly, they "have become known by God" (μᾶλλον δὲ γνωσθέντες ὑπὸ θεοῦ).[669] This qualifier functions on two levels. First, it reminds the believer that as great as it is to know God, it is an even greater privilege that God knows us personally and entered into a covenant relationship with us. Second, it reminds the believer that the only reason that he or she knows God is because God has first chosen to know the believer. Paul draws on the larger biblical theme that God's knowledge of his people is not merely intellectual, but personal, covenantal, and sovereign. In Romans 8:29 Paul writes that "those he foreknew he also predestined to be conformed to the image of his Son, so that he would be the firstborn among many brothers and sisters." Believers know God because he has chosen to know them in a personal and saving way.

Since the Galatian believers know and are known by God, Paul asks them "how can you turn back again to the weak and worthless elements?" (πῶς ἐπιστρέφετε πάλιν ἐπὶ τὰ ἀσθενῆ καὶ πτωχὰ στοιχεῖα). Paul uses this verb (ἐπιστρέφω) in 1 Thessalonians 1:9 to describe how in their conversion the Thessalonians "turned to God from idols to serve the living and true God" (see also Acts 3:19; 9:35; 11:21; 14:15; 15:19; 26:18–20; 2 Cor 3:16; 1 Pet 2:25). In essence, Paul portrays the Galatians as considering a sort of backwards repentance, in which they turn from the living and true God back to "the weak and worthless elements" (τὰ ἀσθενῆ καὶ πτωχὰ στοιχεῖα).[670] In 4:3 he has already referred to the "elements of the world" (τὰ στοιχεῖα τοῦ κόσμου). There we noted this phrase refers to the basic elements of the material world, used to represent all that is associated with this fallen world, this present evil age (1:4), the "old creation" (in contrast to the "new creation"; 6:15) that is under the curse that fell on creation as a result of Adam's rebellion in the garden.[671] Here Paul fur-

---

[669] This rhetorical device was known as epanorthosis, or "self-correction" (DeSilva, *Handbook*, 84).

[670] Todd Wilson suggests a possible allusion to Israel's desire to return to Egypt while in the wilderness (e.g., Num 11:4–6, 18; 14:2–4); see Todd A. Wilson, "Wilderness Apostasy and Paul's Portrayal of the Crisis in Galatians," *NTS* 50 (2004): 560–63. The presence of the new exodus motif in the larger context makes an echo possible, but it is admittedly faint at best.

[671] In the immediate context of Gal 4:8–9, there is a clear parallel between "things that by nature are not gods" (4:8) and "the weak and worthless elements" (4:9). This has led some to argue that τὰ στοιχεῖα τοῦ κόσμου (4:3) refers to evil spirits; see, e.g., Clinton E. Arnold, "Returning to the Domain of the Powers: Stoicheia as Evil Spirits in Galatians 4:3,9," *NovT* 38 (1996): 55–76. But on the whole it is better to see the evil spiritual forces as one particular manifestation of the elements of this world, actively working in this present evil age and exploiting its fallen and cursed status.

ther describes these elemental forces in two ways. First, they are "weak" (ἀσθενής), a word that stresses their inability to produce spiritual life.[672] Using the related verb (ἀσθενέω), Paul writes in Romans 8:3, "What the law could not do since it was weakened by the flesh, God did. He condemned sin in the flesh by sending his own Son in the likeness of sinful flesh as a sin offering." Second, they are "worthless" (πτωχός). This is the same word Paul used in 2:10 to refer to those who lack money or resources and are thus in need of help. As used here this financial term could also be rendered "miserable" or "shabby" since it has the sense of "being extremely inferior in quality."[673] The elementals lack the resources necessary to produce the life, blessing, justification, or inheritance that God offers through the gospel.[674]

In light of the inferior nature of the elementals, Paul asks, "Do you want to be enslaved to them all over again?" (οἷς πάλιν ἄνωθεν δουλεύειν θέλετε).[675] By saying "again" (πάλιν ἄνωθεν) Paul indicates that if the gentile Galatian believers observe the Mosaic law, they are returning to a state of slavery to the elementals "all over again."[676] What is so stunning in this statement is the inference that Mosaic law and its requirements are classified under the category of the elementals, alongside the gentiles' worship of pagan deities. This is not to say that Paul puts them on the exact same level, for the apostle has numerous good things to say about the Mosaic law covenant and nothing good to say about pagan deities. But both are part of the old creation and as such done away with

---

[672] Half of the twenty-six NT occurrences of this adjective are in Paul's letters, with nine of those in 1 Corinthians. Paul often uses this word family to express human weakness in a moral/spiritual sense (Rom 5:6) or physical sense (Rom 8:26; 1 Cor 15:43–44); see *NIDNTTE* 1:421–22.

[673] BDAG s.v. πτωχός 4. In general, this term "denotes the complete destitution which forces the poor to seek the help of others by begging" (Friedrich Hauck, "πτωχός, πτωχεία, πτωχεύω" *TDNT* 6:886).

[674] Martyn (*Galatians*, 411) notes a parallel to Wis 13:18–19, which describes gentiles who do not have the law as follows: "for life he prays to that which is dead; for aid he supplicates that which is utterly inexperienced; for a good journey that which cannot take a step, for means of livelihood and work and success with his hands, he asks strength of that which has no strength at all in its hands."

[675] Although in Greek the entirety of 4:9 is one long question, the csb has broken it into two questions for easier readability in English.

[676] The combination of πάλιν and ἄνωθεν together occurs nowhere else in the NT and just once in the LXX (Wis 19:6). Each word individually means "again," but pairing them together intensifies the force (BDAG s.v. ἄνωθεν 4), leading DeSilva (*Handbook*, 85) to suggest translating the expression "all over again."

through Christ and the dawn of the new creation through his life, death, resurrection, and ascension.[677] Adding observance of the Mosaic law to the Christian life is not an upgrade to a better version, but a downgrade back to a previous life of slavery.[678] Dunn succinctly captures the irony of the situation: "In seeking to grasp Israel's privileges more firmly the Judaizing Gentiles were in danger of losing that very promise and blessing in which they already shared."[679]

Despite the freedom that the gospel brings, we can be tempted to return to our former ways of life that we pursued before we knew Christ. While sometimes that takes the form of returning to patterns of obvious sin, for others it may involve a performance-based approach to relating to God. Despite starting with good intentions, such a person can create a complex set of rules or structures that they think are the key to relating to God. The result is a new form of slavery to a manmade structure rather than living in the freedom that Christ purchased for us (5:1).

4:10. As an example of the Galatians' flirtation with taking on the requirements of the Mosaic law, Paul notes: "You are observing special days, months, seasons, and years" (ἡμέρας παρατηρεῖσθε καὶ μῆνας καὶ καιροὺς καὶ ἐνιαυτούς).[680] As used here, the verb rendered "observe" (παρατηρέω) has the sense of "to carefully observe custom or tradition, *observe scrupulously.*"[681] The present tense of the verb may suggest the

---

[677] Even though he rejects the conclusion that Paul equates the στοιχεῖα with the law, or that the law is a subcategory of the στοιχεῖα, Moo (*Galatians*, 263) tentatively concludes that Paul "wants to suggest that Gentiles under the στοιχεῖα share with the Jews under the law the same condition of living under a religious regimen involving rules relating to material realities—and that together these religious realities are all outmoded with the coming of Christ."

[678] By using the present tense of the verb "enslaved" (δουλεύω), Paul may be emphasizing living the life of a slave rather than the simple act of being enslaved (so also DeSilva, *Handbook,* 85).

[679] Dunn, *Galatians,* 225.

[680] In Greek there is no connecting particle to begin this sentence (asyndeton). As used here the asyndeton likely moves from the generic statement in the previous sentence to the specific example listed here. On this use of asyndeton, see Stephen H. Levinsohn, *Discourse Features of New Testament Greek: A Coursebook on the Information Structure of New Testament Greek,* 2nd ed. (Dallas: SIL International, 2000), 118–20. Less likely is the suggestion by Longenecker (*Galatians,* 182) that the asyndeton here indicates "emotion, passion, liveliness of speech."

[681] BDAG s.v. παρατηρέω 3. It occurs just six times in the NT (Mark 3:2; Luke 6:7; 14:1; 20:20; Acts 9:24), and in every other place but here it has the sense of watching someone or something carefully. Of the six LXX occurrences (Pss 36:12; 129:3; Sus. 1:12, 15–16; Dan. 6:12), all but one (Ps 129:3 [ET= 130:3]) have the sense of watch carefully. Josephus does use

Galatians have already begun observing these days, though it does not demand such a conclusion. The choice of this particular verb suggests careful and scrupulous observation; in the Gospels it describes Jesus' opponents watching him closely for an opportunity to bring a charge against him (Mark 3:2; Luke 6:7; 14:1; 20:20). But similar to Paul's use here in Galatians 4:10, Josephus uses it to describe carefully observing the Sabbath or other special days in the Jewish calendar (*Ant.* 3:91; 11:294; 13:234; 14:264). Paul may have chosen this specific verb to highlight the level of difficulty and effort necessary to keep all the requirements of the Jewish calendar under the Mosaic covenant in contrast to the freedom that the sons of God have through the gospel.

In this context it is difficult to specify what exactly each of the terms refers to in the expression "special days, months, seasons, and years" (ἡμέρας ... καὶ μῆνας καὶ καιροὺς καὶ ἐνιαυτούς).[682] But at the general level it seems most likely that this refers to observing the various elements of the Jewish religious calendar, which likely included the Sabbath and the various festivals God instituted as part of the Mosaic law covenant.[683] For the gentile Galatian believers to scrupulously observe these

the verb to refer to observing the Sabbath or special days proscribed in the law (*Ant.* 3:91; 11:294; 13:234; 14:264; *Apion* 2:282). Philo often uses the verb to call attention to something the reader should observe in a text or philosophical argument (*Leg.* 1:107; 2:50; 3:61, 147; *Sacr.* 1:98; *Sobr.* 1:22; *Conf.* 1:75; *Her.* 1:67; *Spec.* 4:155).

[682] Various attempts have been made, with none achieving consensus; for a helpful survey of the various views, see Hardin, *Galatians and the Imperial Cult*, 116–27. Paul uses the same general word for "day" (ἡμέρα) in Rom 14:5–9 to likely refer to the Sabbath, though it could have a broader sense of festival days there as well. "Months" (μήν) could refer to the celebration of the new moon that marked a new month (Num 10:10; 28:11; for a description of how this may have been practiced in NT times, see *TDNT* 4:640) or perhaps more generally to the various festival days. "Seasons" (καιρός) could also refer to periods of time for celebrating specific festivals, a possibility supported by the use of this Greek term in connection with the three festivals—Passover, Firstfruits, and Pentecost—that all Jews were required to keep (Exod 23:14, 17; Lev 23:4). "Years" (ἐνιαυτός) could refer to the Sabbatical Year prescribed in Lev 25:1–7. See further discussion in Dunn, *Galatians*, 227–29. Others conclude that Paul is simply expressing a general idea of what "religiously scrupulous people" do rather than the specifics of the Jewish calendar; see, e.g., Betz, *Galatians*, 217–18; Witherington, *Grace in Galatia*, 299; de Boer, *Galatians*, 276. Even more novel (and unlikely) is the claim that Paul refers to the Galatians returning to observance of calendar events connected to the imperial cult; see Thomas Witulski, *Die Adressaten des Galaterbriefes: Untersuchungen zur Gemeinde von Antiochia ad Pisidiam*, FRLANT 193 (Göttingen: Vandenhoeck & Ruprecht, 2000), 158–68, 83–214 and Hardin, *Galatians and the Imperial Cult*, 122–47.

[683] For a helpful discussion of pagan, Jewish, and early Christian calendars, see Troy W. Martin, "Pagan and Judeo-Christian Time-Keeping Schemes in Gal 4.10 and Col 2.16,"

special days, festivals, etc. as a part of pursuing justification was not a step forward in their spiritual life, but a return to slavery to the elementals. Paul was not opposed to Jewish believers observing the Sabbath or celebrating the various festivals (Rom 14:5–9). He himself seems to have celebrated Pentecost (Acts 21:17–26), even going so far as to participate in ritual purification and pay the vows of other Jewish believers (21:26). But what Paul could not tolerate was any effort to make these observances a necessary part of the Christian life, or especially any effort to impose them upon gentile Christians.

The combination of "seasons" (καιροὺς), "days" (ἡμέρας), and "years" (ἐνιαυτούς) may echo Genesis 1:14, where God creates the lights in the heavens to regulate the passing of time.[684] If so, Paul may be linking these calendrical observances to the old creation, an element of the present evil age that believers have been delivered from through the gospel (1:4). As Das aptly notes, "By adopting the Jewish calendar, the Galatians are losing track of what time it is."[685] The new creation has dawned through the work of Christ (6:15); therefore, the Galatians should turn away from observing these features of the Mosaic law and turn back to living in their freedom as the sons of God who have the Spirit of the Son of God dwelling in them.

Part of what is attractive about observing these special days is that it feels like something we can control. We can fall into a sense of false security because we are doing what good Christians do by attending church or participating in certain rituals such as the Lord's Supper. Approached the proper way, these are good gifts of God, given for our encouragement and spiritual growth. But when they are viewed as actions that we check off of our spiritual to-do lists, we fall into the dangerous trap of pursuing a relationship with God on the basis of doing rather than believing.

4:11. In light of this troubling development, Paul laments: "I am fearful for you, that perhaps my labor for you has been wasted" (φοβοῦμαι ὑμᾶς

NTS 42 (1996): 105–19.

[684] Schreiner, *Galatians*, 279; similarly Das, *Galatians*, 425. Moo (*Galatians*, 278) notes similar language in Jubilees 2:9: "God appointed the sun to be a great sign on the earth for days and for sabbaths and for months and for feasts and for years and for sabbaths of years and for jubilees and for all seasons of the years."

[685] Das, *Galatians*, 425.

μή πως εἰκῇ κεκοπίακα εἰς ὑμᾶς).[686] The Galatians' flirtation with taking on the Mosaic law as part of their spiritual life has put them in a perilous situation, and Paul wrestles with the possibility that his ministry efforts may prove to be fruitless if the Galatians fully embrace the Mosaic law. Just as Paul had worried that he "may have run in vain" when it comes to his ministry among the gentiles (2:2), so now he worries that he has labored in vain.[687] Paul uses a verb (κοπιάω) that stresses the difficulty of the work and the energy expended, and the perfect tense focuses on the status or results of that labor.[688] If the Galatians depart from the gospel of freedom through the work of Christ and return to slavery to the elementals (this time in the form of the Mosaic law), Paul's time among them preaching the gospel will have been in vain, as would their suffering for the sake of Christ (3:4).

Ministry is often hard work. Laboring to help people see the beauty of Christ and walk faithfully with him can be exhausting physically, mentally, emotionally, and spiritually. Having fellow believers in our lives (family, friends, ministry coworkers) with whom we can share these struggles and seek their encouragement, help, counsel, and support is vital. Pursuing such relationships should be a priority for all believers, but especially for those serving in ministry.

Bridge

Even after experiencing freedom in the gospel, we can find ourselves tempted to return to old patterns of behavior because they offer perceived comfort and security. The Israelites in the wilderness experienced

---

[686] Paul normally uses μή plus the subjunctive to express apprehension, a common construction in classical Greek; see further BDF §370. According to BDF, this is only one of two places (Heb 4:1 is the other) where the construction μή + πως + φοβέω + indicative occurs. But it is likely pushing the grammar too far to claim that the construction indicates that "the feared outcome is now out of Paul's hands (BDF §370) and entirely up to the Galatians to determine" (DeSilva, Handbook, 86). If so, Paul writing a letter trying to persuade them away from taking on the yoke of the Mosaic law seems pointless.

[687] Although the concept is very similar between 2:2 and 4:11, the specific language is slightly different. In 2:2 Paul worries that he has "run" in vain, while here in 4:11 he worries he has "labored" in vain. Paul also uses different expressions to communicate "in vain" in 2:2 (εἰς κενὸν) and in 4:11 (εἰκῇ). But the conceptual similarity may suggest that just as in 2:2, here in 4:11 there is an echo of the servant's concern that he has labored in vain (Isa 49:4); see Harmon, She Must and Shall Go Free, 168.

[688] BDAG s.v. κοπιάω 2. Paul often uses this verb in connection with gospel ministry (Rom 16:6, 12; 1 Cor 4:12; 15:10; 16:16; Phil 2:16; Col 1:29; 1 Thess 5:12; 1 Tim 4:10; 5:17; 2 Tim 2:6).

this pull, repeatedly expressing a desire to return to Egypt when things got tough, saying things like, "Who will feed us meat? We remember the free fish we ate in Egypt, along with the cucumbers, melons, leeks, onions, and garlic. But now our appetite is gone; there's nothing to look at but this manna!" (Num 11:4–6). The remedy for such foolishness is to look at what it cost to rescue us from our bondage to sin and cry out for God to change our affections so that we long for holiness more than comfort.

I. A REMINDER FROM THEIR RECEPTION OF PAUL (4:12–20)

[12] I beg you, brothers and sisters: Become like me, for I also became like you. You have not wronged me; [13] you know that previously I preached the gospel to you because of a weakness of the flesh. [14] You did not despise or reject me though my physical condition was a trial for you. On the contrary, you received me as an angel of God, as Christ Jesus himself.

[15] Where, then, is your blessing? For I testify to you that, if possible, you would have torn out your eyes and given them to me. [16] So then, have I become your enemy because I told you the truth? [17] They court you eagerly, but not for good. They want to exclude you from me, so that you would pursue them. [18] But it is always good to be pursued in a good manner—and not just when I am with you. [19] My children, I am again suffering labor pains for you until Christ is formed in you. [20] I would like to be with you right now and change my tone of voice, because I don't know what to do about you.

Context

In the previous paragraph Paul applied his theological argument to the situation in Galatia by making a personal appeal based on the fact that when they came to know God they were freed from their slavery to the elementals. In 4:12–20 he makes a second personal appeal, this time based on Paul's first arrival in Galatia to share the gospel and their reception of him despite his physical ailment.[689] These two personal appeals are

---

[689] Betz (*Galatians*, 221) suggests that this section contains "a string of *topoi* belonging to the theme of 'friendship,'" where the force of the argument rests on a contrast between true and false friendship. Along the way Betz makes a number of helpful points about the nature of true friendship in the ancient world, but he seems to overplay the significance of the friendship theme in this section. Witherington (*Grace in Galatia*, 306), while noting he thinks Betz is on the right track, suggests instead that Paul speaks in terms of family relationships.

rooted in the truths Paul explained in 3:6–4:7 and prepare the reader to hear Paul's climactic theological argument in 4:21–5:1.[690]

Structure

The opening verse provides the central thrust of the paragraph, where Paul begs the Galatians to become like him in his law-free approach to the Christian life, just as he became like them (being without the law) when he first preached the gospel to them (4:12). He then reminds the Galatians of their initial encounter with him when he first arrived (4:13–14). Paul suffered some kind of physical ailment that could have tempted the Galatians to reject him. Instead, they welcomed Paul as if he were an angel of God. From this foundation Paul challenges the Galatians to remember and rekindle the blessing they experienced and the self-sacrificial love they showed for him (4:15). But now because of the influence of the false teachers, things have changed (4:16–18). Portraying Paul as their enemy (4:16), the opponents are trying to isolate the Galatians from Paul so that the opponents alone will be able to shape their beliefs and practice (4:17–18). Paul concludes the paragraph with another personal appeal using childbirth as a metaphor (4:19–20). As he sometimes does, Paul mixes the metaphor, first portraying himself as a pregnant woman in labor trying to give birth to mature believers and then portraying the Galatians as pregnant with Christ being formed in them (4:19). Frustrated with the limitations of trying to address the problems in Galatia, Paul wishes he could be with them in person to restore his relationship with the Galatians and deal decisively with the opponents (4:20).

4:12. In this section Paul continues his personal appeal to the Galatians, but now he bases that appeal on his own personal experience with them. In some ways this is the most personal section of the letter. Again he addresses the Galatians as "brothers and sisters" (ἀδελφοί), a sign of affection and a reminder that they share an identity as adopted sons of God through faith in Christ (4:1–7). The appeal is both weighty and urgent: "I beg you" (δέομαι ὑμῶν). The content of this appeal is straightforward: "Become as I am" (Γίνεσθε ὡς ἐγώ). But in what sense does Paul want the Galatians to be like him? The larger context suggests that he refers to living the Christian life in a way that does not view the Mosaic law as

---

[690] By contrast, a number of scholars see 4:12 as the beginning of a new major section in Galatians; see, e.g., Longenecker, *Galatians*, 186–87 and Schreiner, *Galatians*, 281–82.

the means of relating to God or others. As one who has died to the law through his union with Christ, Paul does not want to see the Galatians pursue a way of life that he left behind once he came to know Christ.

Paul wants the Galatians to become like him "for I also have become as you are" (ὅτι κἀγὼ ὡς ὑμεῖς). In his life and ministry Paul displayed a situational approach to observing the tenets of the Mosaic law, summarized most clearly in 1 Corinthians 9:19–23. When seeking to reach Jews with the gospel, he willingly observed various aspects of the Mosaic law. But to "those who are without the law, like one without the law—though I am not without God's law but under the law of Christ—to win those without the law" (1 Cor 9:21). When Paul preached the gospel in Galatia he became like the gentile Galatians in the sense that he did not observe the Mosaic law. Based on that, Paul now asks the Galatians to once again join him in the non-observant camp.

Lest the Galatians think that Paul's personal appeal indicates the issue at hand is personal rather than doctrinal, Paul adds, "You have not wronged me" (οὐδέν με ἠδικήσατε). Paul uses the same expression in his defense before Festus when he claims, "I have done no wrong to the Jews" (Acts 25:10).[691] It is an assertion of innocence; Paul assures the Galatians that he does not view himself as personally wronged by the Galatians. This declaration here in Galatians 4:12 sets the stage for Paul to recount his initial arrival in Galatia and how the Galatians received him. Despite his dire concern for the spiritual condition of the Galatians, Paul's love for them has not wavered.

What a model for those who serve in ministry! When there is conflict it easy for things to become personal quickly. But Paul simultaneously maintains his commitment to the truth of the gospel and his personal love for the Galatians. Those who serve in ministry would do well to model the same approach.

---

[691] In Greek the expression consists of the verb ἀδικέω with a neuter form of οὐδείς as its object. In addition to Acts 25:10 and Gal 4:12, the expression occurs in 3 Macc 3:8; Luke 10:19; 2 Cor 7:2. There is also a moving example in *Martyrdom of Polycarp*, where in response to the invitation to renounce his faith Polycarp says, "Eighty and six years have I served Him, and He never did me any injury [καὶ οὐδέν με ἠδίκησεν]: how then can I blaspheme my King and my Savior?" (9:3). There are also a handful of examples in Josephus (*Ant.* 2:138; 5:108; 6:224) and Philo (*Spec.* 2:26; 3:158; *Flacc.* 1:115). With the presence of the personal pronoun along with this expression here in Gal 4:12, this becomes a double accusative that can be described as an accusative of person and thing (Robertson, *Grammar*, 482).

4:13. In the one Greek sentence that spans verses 13–14, Paul seeks to reassure the Galatians of his love for them by first reminding them of his initial reason for preaching the gospel in Galatia (4:13) and their response (4:14). Reflecting on his initial arrival in Galatia, Paul states: "you know that previously I preached the gospel to you because of a weakness of the flesh" (οἴδατε δὲ ὅτι δι' ἀσθένειαν τῆς σαρκὸς εὐηγγελισάμην ὑμῖν τὸ πρότερον).[692] When Paul says "previously" (τὸ πρότερον), he refers to the first time he arrived in Galatia,[693] which occurred during his first missionary journey around AD 47–48 (Acts 13–14:23). The reason Paul preached the gospel in Galatia that first time was "because of a weakness of the flesh" (δι' ἀσθένειαν τῆς σαρκὸς).[694] Acts does not mention this motivation for heading into Galatia, and scholars throughout the centuries have speculated as to the nature and severity of the weakness of the flesh, which almost certainly refers to some kind of physical illness. Perhaps the most common suggestion is some sort of eye-related malady in light of Paul's comments about eyes in 4:15 and large letters in 6:11,[695] though other reasons for these comments seem more likely. Some suggest the physical ailment may be one of several mentioned in 2 Corinthians 11:23–25.[696] Others have linked the illness to the thorn in his flesh that

---

[692] In Greek this clause is introduced with δέ, which signals that what follows is a further development of the previous clause.

[693] Because the Greek expression Paul uses here (τὸ πρότερον) can have the specific meaning of "the first of two or more," some scholars have argued that it is evidence that Paul made multiple visits to Galatia. But the more natural meaning of this expression here in Gal 4:13 is "formerly" or "the first time," with no indication of multiple visits—a meaning that is well attested in both the NT and Greco-Roman literature; see BDAG s.v. f 1.b.β; MM, 554; *EDNT* s.v. πρότερος 3; BDF §62.

[694] The exact expression Paul uses here (ἀσθένειαν τῆς σαρκὸς) occurs elsewhere in the NT only in Rom 6:19, where the apostle says, "I am using a human analogy because of the weakness of your flesh [διὰ τὴν ἀσθένειαν τῆς σαρκὸς ὑμῶν]." In that context, the phrase seems to refer to a limited understanding of spiritual matters, which leads Paul to use a "human analogy." As alternatives to the physical illness view here in Gal 4:13, scholars have suggested the phrase refers to opposition to the gospel or even the physical results of such opposition. While this view is certainly possible, the immediate context here seems to suggest physical illness is in view. For a lengthy discussion of possible interpretations of this expression, see Das, *Galatians*, 455–61, who ultimately concludes it refers to "a bodily illness or condition that he bore wherever he went that served as a visual display of the weakness of Christ's cross."

[695] For an extended discussion of this possibility, see Witherington, *Grace in Galatia*, 309–10.

[696] So Longenecker, *Galatians*, 191.

Paul mentions in 2 Corinthians 12:7–9,[697] a connection that is possible but difficult to establish with any confidence. In any case, Paul's larger point is that when he first arrived in Galatia, the Galatians showed him true friendship, providing help in his time of need.[698]

At the end of the day, the precise nature of the illness does not seem to matter; what matters is that it led Paul to head to Galatia with the gospel. Whether he believed the climate of that region would help him recover or Galatia was simply the closest populated area where he might find medical care is unclear. But what is clear is Paul's belief in the sovereign hand of God directing his path to Galatia for the advancement of the gospel. Do you have a similar trust in God directing your own life for the same purpose?

4:14. When it comes to how the Galatians responded to Paul's arrival in Galatia, the apostle first lays out what they did not do: "You did not despise or reject me though my physical condition was a trial for you" (καὶ τὸν πειρασμὸν ὑμῶν ἐν τῇ σαρκί μου οὐκ ἐξουθενήσατε οὐδὲ ἐξεπτύσατε). The verb "despise" (ἐξουθενέω) has the sense of "to show by one's attitude or manner of treatment that an entity has no merit or worth."[699] Luke 18:9 uses this same verb to explain that Jesus told the parable of the Pharisee and the tax collector to people who "looked down on everyone else." Nor did the Galatians "reject" (ἐκπτύω) Paul, a Greek verb that literally means to spit but came to have the metaphorical sense of show contempt for someone.[700] The act of spitting at or on someone was a significant insult, an expression of disgust, revulsion, and rejection, with the most noteworthy example being the soldiers who spit on Jesus during his trial (Matt 26:67; 27:30; Mark 14:65; 15:19). But perhaps even

---

[697] As Dunn (*Galatians*, 233) tentatively does. Moo (*Galatians*, 282–83) is more confident, yet still cautious.

[698] Betz (*Galatians*, 224) notes that in the ancient world "the sign of real friendship [was] to provide unlimited help at the moment of great need, in particular in illness."

[699] BDAG s.v. ἐξουθενέω 1. Eight of the eleven NT occurrences are in Paul (Rom 14:3, 10; 1 Cor 1:28; 6:4; 16:11; 2 Cor 10:10; Gal 4:14; 1 Thess 5:20), with the other three in Luke–Acts (Luke 18:9; 23:11; Acts 4:11). Of the eight LXX occurrences (1 Sam 8:7; 10:19; 2 Macc 1:27; Prov 1:7; Wis 4:18; Amos 6:1; Jer 6:14; Dan 4:31), perhaps the most noteworthy are 1 Sam 8:7 and 10:19, where it describes Israel's rejection of Yahweh in requesting a king. This verb also occurs with a compound form of the verb πτύω in Jos. *Asen.* 2:1 (where it describes Aseneth's dismissal of potential suitors) and Barn. 7:9 (where it describes the soldier's treatment of Christ).

[700] BDAG s.v. ἐκπτύω.

more relevant here was the ancient belief that spitting was a means of warding off disease, demon possession, or the evil eye.[701] Given the common response to illness in the ancient world, Paul was rightly concerned that the gentile Galatians would reject him and his message. It is in this sense that Paul's illness was a "trial" (πειρασμός) or temptation for the Galatians.[702]

Paul says the Galatians, instead of rejecting him, "received me as an angel of God, as Christ Jesus himself" (ὡς ἄγγελον θεοῦ ἐδέξασθέ με, ὡς Χριστὸν Ἰησοῦν). The verb rendered "received" (δέχομαι) has the sense of welcoming someone as a guest.[703] Since the Greek word for "angel" (ἄγγελος) can also mean messenger, it is possible that Paul is saying the Galatians received him as a messenger of God (i.e., a prophet).[704] In either case the welcome was so warm that Paul claims they received him "as Christ Jesus himself" (ὡς Χριστὸν Ἰησοῦν).[705] When Paul arrived in Galatia he experienced firsthand what Jesus had told his disciples: "The one who welcomes you welcomes me, and the one who welcomes me welcomes

---

[701] Witherington, *Grace in Galatia*, 311. For an example of the various uses of spit in the Greco-Roman world, see Pliny, *Nat. Hist.* 38.7.6, cited in Jodi Magness, *Stone and Dung, Oil and Spit: Jewish Daily Life in the Time of Jesus* (Grand Rapids: Eerdmans, 2011), 128.

[702] Strictly speaking, the Greek expression rendered "a trial for you" (τὸν πειρασμὸν ὑμῶν) is ambiguous. First, there is the slight difference between πειρασμός meaning "trial" (which would seem to focus on outward circumstances) or "temptation" (focusing on internal enticement to evil). Second, a number of manuscripts (𝔓⁴⁶ Cᵛⁱᵈ D¹ K L P Ψ 365. 630. 1175. 1505 𝔐 ar vgᵐˢ syʰ sa boᵐˢ) have μου ("my") rather than ὑμῶν ("your"). If μου is the original reading, Paul is referring to the trial his physical condition brought him. If ὑμῶν is original, the temptation/trial is what the Galatians experienced in their initial encounter with Paul. But even though μου has substantive support in several key manuscripts, on the whole ὑμῶν has even better manuscript support (ℵ* A B C² D* F G 6. 33. 1739. 1881. Bo; Origen). Based then on this textual support and the fact that this reading is better able to explain the other variants, ὑμῶν is more likely to be original (see Metzger, *Textual Commentary*, 527). Third, assuming that ὑμῶν is the original reading, the force of the genitive must be determined. If it is subjective, the sense is that Paul caused the temptation/trial, whereas if it is objective, the focus is on the Galatians' experience of trial/temptation. But at the end of the day the difference in meaning is negligible. For a helpful discussion of these various issues, see Moo, *Galatians*, 284, 90.

[703] BDAG s.v. δέχομαι 3.

[704] Although this term can refer to human messengers (e.g., Matt 11:10; Luke 9:52), there is no clear example of Paul using it this way in his letters. On the whole, then, it seems likely Paul refers to an angel here.

[705] Incidentally, Paul's claim to be received as Christ Jesus himself may indirectly reinforce the claim that Paul understood his own apostolic ministry as Christ living in and through him to fulfill the ministry of the servant as a light to the nations; see further Biblical Theology §3.0.

him who sent me" (Matt 10:40). Acts 14:8–18 records that when Paul and Barnabas arrived in Lystra, some of the people believed that the gods had come down among them. They even called Paul Hermes and Barnabas Zeus, with local priests going so far as to attempt to offer sacrifices to them! Perhaps Paul is ironically recalling this incident in describing his initial reception in Galatia, though Paul's immediate rejection of such a reaction and his subsequent stoning make this unlikely.

A distinguishing mark of the early church was the hospitality it showed to both believers and unbelievers. Such hospitality was rooted in a truth fundamental to the gospel: Christ welcomed us when we had nothing to offer him (Rom 15:7–13). Hospitality comes more naturally to some than others, but it is a biblical expectation nonetheless.[706] Who might the Lord want you to show hospitality to today?

4:15. Paul expresses wonder at how things have changed since this initial warm welcome. He asks, "Where, then, is your blessing?" (ποῦ οὖν ὁ μακαρισμὸς ὑμῶν).[707] Because the Galatians received Paul as Christ Jesus himself, they felt blessed that God had sent Paul to them.[708] The apostle laments that this sense of blessing has apparently evaporated, leaving behind suspicion and distrust. This former sense of blessing was so intense that Paul asserts, "I testify to you that, if possible, you would have torn out your eyes and given them to me" (μαρτυρῶ γὰρ ὑμῖν ὅτι εἰ δυνατὸν τοὺς ὀφθαλμοὺς ὑμῶν ἐξορύξαντες ἐδώκατέ μοι).[709] Paul portrays himself as a witness testifying to the enthusiastic welcome the

---

[706] For a helpful and engaging treatment of hospitality, see Rosaria Butterfield, *The Gospel Comes with a House Key: Practicing Radically Ordinary Hospitality in Our Post-Christian World* (Wheaton: Crossway, 2018).

[707] In Greek the conjunction οὖν ("then") seems to signal the resumption of the present circumstances after the background material supplied in 4:13–14; on this use of οὖν, see further Runge, *Discourse Grammar*, 44–45.

[708] Dunn (*Galatians*, 235) suggests the blessing in view here is the blessing of Abraham (see 3:9, 14), but the use of a different Greek word and the context make this proposal unlikely. Moo (*Galatians*, 286) goes a different direction, concluding that the expression refers to the blessing the Galatians pronounced upon Paul. Another possibility is that Paul has in mind here the work of the Holy Spirit in/among the Galatians; see Bruce W. Longenecker, "'Until Christ Is Formed in You': Suprahuman Forces and Moral Character in Galatians," *CBQ* 61 (1999): 102.

[709] The γάρ introduces this clause as an explanation of the blessing the Galatians experienced. Embedded in this ὅτι clause that introduces the content of Paul's testimony is a second class conditional statement (without ἄν in apodosis, which is not uncommon in the NT; see Nigel Turner, *Syntax*, ed. James Hope Moulton, A Grammar of New Testament Greek, 4 vols. [Edinburgh: T&T Clark, 1963], 92), which presents the statement as not true for the

Galatians gave him when he first arrived. Scholars have debated how to interpret Paul's statement that the Galatians were willing to tear out their own eyes and give them to Paul. Some have used this claim as evidence that Paul's "weakness of the flesh" (4:13) was an eye problem of some sort, but it is also possible that Paul is simply engaging in hyperbole and in no way hinting at his medical condition or thorn in the flesh. The eyes were regarded as the most precious human organ;[710] and while there are some examples in Greco-Roman literature of offering one's eyes as an expression of love and sacrifice for another, it does not appear to have been a widely used metaphor.[711] A decision is difficult, but on the whole it seems slightly more likely that Paul is simply speaking figuratively rather than hinting at the specific nature of his weakness of flesh.

Regardless of how literally we should understand Paul's language of the Galatians' willingness to gouge their eyes out for him, the larger point should not be missed. A mark of their believing response to the gospel Paul preached was a sacrificially generous desire to meet the needs of others. Those who have received the generosity of God through the gospel should be eager to show generosity to others.

4:16. The sacrificial nature of the Galatians' love and generosity toward Paul makes his question here in verse 16 all the more shocking: "So then, have I become your enemy because I told you the truth?" (ὥστε ἐχθρὸς ὑμῶν γέγονα ἀληθεύων ὑμῖν).[712] By convincing some that Paul did not preach to them the whole gospel message, the opponents have in effect portrayed Paul as their enemy.[713] With a combination of irony and sarcasm, Paul points out that he has apparently become their enemy

---

sake of the argument. Paul is acknowledging that gouging the eyes out was not actually a feasible action while affirming the genuine depth of the Galatians' affection for him.

[710] See, e.g., LSJM s.v. ὀφθαλμός.

[711] See similarly Moo, *Galatians*, 286. For examples of this metaphor/motif in Greco-Roman literature, see Betz, *Galatians*, 227–28 and Das, *Galatians*, 466.

[712] The ὥστε (here rendered "now") introduces this clause as a result (so also DeSilva, *Handbook*, 90). Instead of interpreting this as a question (there was no punctuation in the earliest manuscripts of the Greek NT), some scholars read it as an exclamation ("So I have become your enemy by telling you the truth!"); see Burton, *Galatians*, 345; Longenecker, *Galatians*, 193; Dunn, *Galatians*, 230; Witherington, *Grace in Galatia*, 313; de Boer, *Galatians*, 281–82. Either way, however, the rhetorical effect and meaning are the same.

[713] The perfect tense verb γέγονα ("I have become") highlights Paul's state of being their enemy; his status has changed from beloved messenger of God to enemy.

"because I told you the truth" (ἀληθεύων ὑμῖν).[714] Paul does not refer to truth in general, but the truth of the gospel that he has been so zealous to preserve (2:5, 14). Because the opponents have confused and deceived the Galatians, the very truth of the gospel that brings eschatological life has ironically become the means by which Paul has become their enemy.

Such a transition from being received as Christ Jesus himself to an enemy to be shunned may seem shocking, but sadly it is a reality played out all too often in churches. The beloved pastor who first shared the good news with a person suddenly becomes their enemy when the convert falls under the spell of false teaching. Those who find themselves in such situations should follow Paul's example in re-explaining the truth of the gospel and showing genuine love for those who are deceived in the hope that God will grant them repentance (2 Tim 2:24–26).

4:17. Paul now turns his sights toward the opponents, attempting to surface their motives: "They court you eagerly, but not for good" (ζηλοῦσιν ὑμᾶς οὐ καλῶς). The verb Paul uses here (ζηλόω) has the sense of "be deeply interested in someone, court someone's favor" in order to win them over to one's side.[715] It is part of the same word family as the term Paul used in 1:14 (ζηλωτής) to describe his own pre-conversion zeal for Jewish traditions. Such pursuit is not inherently bad, but the opponents' motives are not good. "They want to exclude you from me" (ἀλλ' ἐκκλεῖσαι ὑμᾶς θέλουσιν). Despite what might appear to be an interest in the truth, the opponents are motivated by a desire to cut the Galatians off from Paul and his influence over them.[716] "These teachers surely claimed

---

[714] Thus the adverbial participle here indicates either cause ("because I am telling you the truth") or means ("by telling you the truth"). The difference in meaning is negligible at best. The verb ἀληθεύω ("tell the truth") occurs only one other place in the NT (Eph 4:15) and five times in the LXX (Gen 20:16; 42:16; Prov 21:3; Sir 34:4; Isa 44:26).

[715] BDAG s.v. ζηλόω 1.b. "The verb generally speaks of admiring people with a view to imitating them and thereby acquiring the good reputation or success that they had also enjoyed ... The verb is used both to speak of men and women pursuing one another and of the relationship of teachers and students, both of the teachers' quest for followers and of followers' attachment to their teachers" (DeSilva, *Handbook*, 90–91). Witherington (*Grace in Galatia*, 313) claims the language used here is that of courtship but could also refer to the relationship between a teacher and his students.

[716] Witherington (*Grace in Galatia*, 314) thinks that, instead of referring to cutting the Galatians off from Paul, Paul refers here to the opponents' desire to "exclude the Gentile Christians from the people of God unless and until they are prepared to be circumcised and follow the Mosaic Law."

that they desired to *include* the Galatians in the true people of God, but in fact, they were *excluding* them from God's people if the Galatians followed them."[717] The verb rendered "exclude" (ἐκκλείω) is part of the same word family that Paul used in 3:23–24 to describe Scripture and the Mosaic law confining everything until Christ came.[718]

The purpose of the opponents cutting the Galatians off from Paul is "so that you would pursue them" (ἵνα αὐτοὺς ζηλοῦτε). By repeating the same verb from the first clause (ζηλόω), Paul indicates that the opponents want the Galatians to reciprocate the pursuit the opponents directed toward them. The verb and the context suggest a sense of exclusivity. The opponents want the exclusive loyalty of the Galatians so that Paul will no longer have any influence on them. Once the Galatians are cut off from Paul, the opponents will be able to complete their program of leading the gentile Galatian believers to submit themselves to the Mosaic law.

It is natural for us to enjoy when people pursue us to make much of us. It feeds our pride and makes us feel special. But Paul highlights that sometimes those pursuing us have less than pure motives. False teachers are often skilled at making people feel special, gifted, and valued when others have not. The question we must ask is whether those pursuing us and making much of us are truly interested in our spiritual well-being or their own.

4:18. Paul now clarifies his previous statement: "But it is always good to be pursued in a good manner" (καλὸν δὲ ζηλοῦσθαι ἐν καλῷ πάντοτε).[719] The issue is not with the fact that the opponents are pursuing the Galatians. After all, Paul himself pursued the Galatians through his preaching of the gospel. But that kind of pursuit is in a good manner—in

---

[717] Schreiner, *Galatians*, 288.

[718] While there are no LXX occurrences of this particular compound form (ἐκκλείω), it does occur in Rom 3:27, where Paul asserts that boasting is excluded by the law of faith. Herodotus uses the term to describe inhabitants of a city excluding their neighbors from entering into their temple (*Hist.* 1.144); for further examples in Greco-Roman literature, see LSJM s.v. ἐκκλείω. Betz (*Galatians*, 230) notes several examples of the verb with political or legal overtones that "may refer to exclusion from political activities, to conspiracies, deprivation from rights or even from philosophical teaching."

[719] The δέ that begins this verse signals a further development in the argument, in this case a qualification. In Greek the grammar of this sentence is challenging. The infinitive ζηλοῦσθαι ("to be sought") is the subject of a verbless equative clause in which καλὸν is a predicate adjective in the accusative to match the implied case of the infinitive; see Burton, *Syntax*, §385 and DeSilva, *Handbook*, 91. The present tense of the infinitive may suggest a repeated pursuit (Wallace, *Greek Grammar*, 521).

other words, with good motives.[720] Such pursuit that is rooted in good motives is "not just when I am with you" (μὴ μόνον ἐν τῷ παρεῖναί με πρὸς ὑμᾶς). Paul was not a hit-and-run evangelist who moved on to the next city, never again to concern himself with those to whom he preached the gospel. Acts 14:21–23 indicates that, after his initial founding of these churches, Paul and Barnabas passed back through these same cities to appoint elders in these congregations. Now, upon hearing of their crisis, Paul has fired off this letter to express his grave concern that the Galatians are in danger of abandoning the true gospel of grace for a syncretistic blend of faith in Jesus with obedience to the Mosaic law that ultimately leads to destruction.

4:19. At this point the depth of his love and concern for the Galatians pours forth from Paul's pen: "My children, I am again suffering labor pains for you" (τέκνα μου, οὓς πάλιν ὠδίνω). Up to this point he has called the Galatians "brothers and sisters" (1:2, 11; 3:15; 4:12), but here he changes to "my children" in light of the metaphor that follows. Paul portrays himself as a pregnant woman in labor, writhing in pain. Although Paul more frequently refers to himself as a spiritual father (1 Tim 1:2; Titus 1:4), he can also describe himself in maternal terms as well.[721] In 1 Thessalonians 2:7 Paul refers to himself as a gentle nursing mother nurturing her children. Here the imagery is even more intense. The verb rendered "suffering labor pains" (ὠδίνω) is consistently used in a metaphorical sense in the LXX/New Testament, often in eschatological contexts.[722] It occurs frequently in Isaiah, where it consistently describes Yahweh's powerful actions, whether for judgment or salvation.[723] Most noteworthy is

---

[720] In Greek the expression is simply ἐν καλῷ, which should be understood as either indicating extension toward a goal ("for a good purpose"; see BDAG s.v. ἐν 3) or perhaps more likely indicating manner ("in a good way"; see BDAG s.v. ἐν 11); so, rightly, DeSilva, *Handbook*, 91.

[721] Dunn (*Galatians*, 239) notes that similar imagery of spiritual generation "was used in hellenistic religion (*TDNT* 5.953–4; Oepke 145) and for the relationship between teacher and pupil (*TDNT* 1.665–6; cf. Philo, *Legat.* 58)."

[722] There are only two other occurrences of ὠδίνω in the NT: Gal 4:27 (on which see below) and Rev 12:2. For an extended discussion of this verb and the metaphor Paul uses here, see Martyn, *Galatians*, 426–31.

[723] Nine of the fourteen LXX occurrences of ὠδίνω are in Isaiah (23:4; 26:17–18; 45:10; 51:2; 54:1; 66:7–8), and there are an additional four occurrences of the related noun ὠδίν (13:8; 21:3; 26:17; 37:3; 66:7). "The thirteen combined occurrences of ὠδίνω and ὠδίν in Isaiah can be divided into two groups. The first group consists of those which refer to the anguish experienced on account of judgment (13:8; 21:3; 24:3; 37:3), with the emphasis resting upon

Isaiah 45:7–11 (LXX), where Yahweh describes his saving action that he will accomplish through Cyrus. In verse 10 a woe is pronounced on those who question Yahweh's saving work, asking, "What are you giving birth to?" (τί ὠδινήσεις). In Isaiah 51:2 the same verb describes Sarah's labor pains in bringing forth the promised seed. In both cases the verb is used to portray the bringing forth of the people of God, and Paul uses it in a similar sense to describe his role in bringing forth the Galatian gentile believers as the eschatological people of God.[724] As Martyn notes, the apostle "sees in the Teachers' persecuting activity an instance of the last-ditch effort by which God's enemies hope to thwart the eschatological redemption of the elect."[725] Paul's labor pains are his suffering as an apostle that must be endured during this present evil age.[726]

Paul's labor pains will continue "until Christ is formed in you" (μέχρις οὗ μορφωθῇ Χριστὸς ἐν ὑμῖν). This imagery works on two levels. On the one hand, Paul is the writhing mother who has conceived the Galatians

---

the overwhelming nature of God's action(s). The second group is far more common; in these cases, ὠδίνω and ὠδίν refer to difficulties associated with God's saving action(s) (26:17 [2x], 18; 45:10; 51:2; 54:1; 66:7 [2x], 8 [2x]). More importantly, in each case the fate of the people of God is clearly in view. Furthermore, these occurrences are found in apocalyptic contexts in which God is decisively bringing salvation to his people and judgment on his enemies. The one experiencing birth pangs or giving birth varies by context: Israel (26:17–18; 54:1; 66:7–8), Sarah (51:2), and even Yahweh himself (45:10; 66:7–8). Although the intransitive sense of the verb (i.e., "experience birth pangs") accounts for six of the eight occurrences, the two transitive uses of the verb (45:10; 51:2) are particularly important for our discussion of Gal 4:19" (Harmon, *She Must and Shall Go Free*, 169–70).

[724] Martyn (*Galatians*, 426–31) has a helpful comparison of Isa 45:7–11 and Gal 4:19. He "observes four interlocking motifs in both passages: (1) the verb is used in a metaphor; (2) the verb has a direct object; (3) Paul is the subject of the verb even though he is male; (4) the offspring are the corporate people of God (Galatian Christians). Martyn then turns to Isa 45:7–11, where ὠδίνω is also used, and notes the following correspondences to Gal 4:19: (1) within the context ὠδίνω is used metaphorically; (2) the verb has a direct object; (3) although the grammatical subject of the verb is feminine, it metaphorically represents God, who is referred to as masculine in 45:1; (4) the child born is the corporate people of God, Israel. In addition to these conceptual parallels, Martyn adds two additional considerations. First, Paul elsewhere uses the imagery of childbirth to refer to his own church planting in 1 Cor 4:14–15; this is analogous to Isaiah's use of the masculine metaphor of begetting with reference to God (e.g., Isa 42:14). Second, Paul either cites or alludes to portions of Isa 45 in Rom 9:20; 14:11; 1 Cor 14:25 and Phil 2:9–11, which reveals his knowledge of and interest in Isa 45" (Harmon, *She Must and Shall Go Free*, 171).

[725] Martyn, *Galatians*, 430.

[726] Schreiner, *Galatians*, 289. Oakes (*Galatians*, 151) is less confident of alleged apocalyptic overtones, instead suggesting that the metaphor simply communicates "acute pain involved with bringing new life."

through their faith in Christ, but they have yet to reach their full spiritual maturity. They must persevere in believing the true gospel and walk in the power of the Spirit until the last day, when they will be fully remade in the image of Christ (Rom 8:29), who himself is the image of God (Col 1:15). As such, what Paul has in view here is the complete restoration of the image of God that was marred in the garden.[727] On the other hand, the imagery portrays the Galatians as the ones who are pregnant, with Christ being formed inside of them.[728] Although the verb he uses (μορφόω) occurs nowhere else in the LXX/New Testament, the second-century Greek physician Galen used this same verb to describe the formation of an embryo.[729]

There are few better concise expressions that capture the essence of the Christian life than "Christ is formed in you."[730] God is at work in his people to mold and shape them into the image of his Son Jesus Christ so that we will be a perfect reflection of him. Although this process will not be completed until the believer dies or Christ returns, we diligently pursue a life of purity because that is our hope (1 John 3:1–3).

4:20. Paul concludes his personal appeal with a wish: "I would like to be with you right now and change my tone of voice" (ἤθελον δὲ παρεῖναι πρὸς ὑμᾶς ἄρτι καὶ ἀλλάξαι τὴν φωνήν μου).[731] The apostle bemoans the limitations of trying to deal with the crisis in Galatia through a letter. He would much prefer to look the Galatians in the eye and confront the

---

[727] Similarly Dunn, *Galatians*, 240–41.

[728] In Greek the prepositional phrase rendered "in you" (ἐν ὑμῖν) could also be translated "among you." Although the "you" (ὑμῖν) is plural, the imagery of childbirth favors "in" as the preferable rendering. It also corresponds with Paul's use of the phrase "in me" earlier in the letter (1:16, 24; 2:20). Of course, as Christ is formed "in" the individual Galatians, that will result in Christ being formed "among" the Galatians.

[729] See BDAG s.v. μορφόω. All three occurrences in the Sibylline Oracles (4:182; 8:259, 379) describe God forming resurrection bodies. Philo uses this verb nineteen times, sometimes to describe God giving shape to what he has created (*Plant.* 1:3; *Conf.* 1:63; *Fug.* 1:12, 69; *Somn.* 1:210; 2:45; *Spec.* 1:171; *Aet.* 1:41) and other times in the context of the idols and images that pagans form as part of their worship (*Deo* 1:55; *Conf.* 1:87; *Decal.* 1:7, 66, 72; *Spec.* 1:21; 2:255). The one occurrence in Josephus has this latter sense (*Ant.* 15:239). On the use of μορφόω in Greek literature, see *TDNT* 4:752–53 and R. Hermann, "Über Den Sinn Des Μορφοῦσθαι Χριστὸν Ἐν'Υμῖν in Gal. 4, 19," *TLZ* 80 (1955): 713–26.

[730] On this theme, see the helpful book by Brian G. Hedges, *Christ Formed in You: The Power of the Gospel for Personal Change* (Wapwallopen, PA: Shepherd Press, 2010).

[731] The δέ that introduces this verse signals a further development in the argument, which in this case is the final one of the paragraph and thus the conclusion; so similarly Longenecker, *Galatians*, 196 and DeSilva, *Handbook*, 93.

opponents face to face, but circumstances do not permit it.[732] Paul is confident that if he were able to get face to face with the Galatians, he would "change my tone of voice" (ἀλλάξαι τὴν φωνήν μου). The sharp tone and pointed rebukes in the letter are necessary from Paul's perspective, but his preference would be to change to a warmer tone of voice. Paul acknowledges that the reason he wants to be face to face with them is that "I don't know what to do about you" (ὅτι ἀποροῦμαι ἐν ὑμῖν). The verb Paul uses here (ἀπορέω) means "to be in a confused state of mind."[733] The combination of distance, disappointment, and uncertainty of all that is happening in Galatia produced a state of confusion for Paul that leaves him perplexed at how things have gone bad so quickly with these churches.

Life and ministry in a fallen world often present us with difficult situations. Often we may find ourselves at a loss as to how to handle them. Even though he was an apostle commissioned by the risen Christ, Paul too faced challenges in ministry that left him perplexed. Despite such uncertainty, Paul moved forward in faith based on the truths of the gospel, the revealed will of God in the Scriptures, the guidance of the Holy Spirit, and the wisdom that came from having the mind of Christ. What a comfort to know that we have the same God and the same resources when we face circumstances that perplex us!

Bridge

Spend enough time in ministry and you will inevitably experience the heights of joy and the depths of discouragement and frustration that Paul describes here. Few things in ministry are more painful than seeing a person you led to Christ go from being grateful for you to becoming suspicious of you. Yet in the midst of such personal pain we must never lose sight of the goal of ministry—to see Christ formed in the people we serve. Those of us in ministry are like pregnant mothers doing everything possible to facilitate the health and growth of the spiritual children God has entrusted to us. When those whom we serve in ministry experience

---

[732] As a general rule, Paul seems to have preferred dealing with difficult ministry situations in person, but there is at least one example where he decided a letter sent through one of his ministry teammates was preferable (2 Cor 7:12–15).

[733] BDAG s.v. ἀπορέω. In the NT this verb is used to describe the perplexity of Herod Antipas (Mark 6:20), the women at the empty tomb of Jesus (Luke 24:4), the disciples (John 13:22), Festus (Acts 25:20), and Paul (2 Cor 4:8; Gal 4:20). For examples from Greek literature, see LSJM s.v. ἀπορέω, and MM, 67.

the kind of motherly affection Paul speaks of here, they are far more likely to receive our words of correction when necessary.

J. Free Sons of the Heavenly Jerusalem (4:21–5:1)

[21] Tell me, you who want to be under the law, don't you hear the law? [22] For it is written that Abraham had two sons, one by a slave and the other by a free woman. [23] But the one by the slave was born as a result of the flesh, while the one by the free woman was born through promise. [24] These things are being taken figuratively, for the women represent two covenants. One is from Mount Sinai and bears children into slavery-- this is Hagar. [25] Now Hagar represents Mount Sinai in Arabia and corresponds to the present Jerusalem, for she is in slavery with her children. [26] But the Jerusalem above is free, and she is our mother. [27] For it is written,

> Rejoice, childless woman,
> unable to give birth.
> Burst into song and shout,
> you who are not in labor,
> for the children of the desolate woman will be many,
> more numerous than those
> of the woman who has a husband.

[28] Now you too, brothers and sisters, like Isaac, are children of promise. [29] But just as then the child born as a result of the flesh persecuted the one born as a result of the Spirit, so also now. [30] But what does the Scripture say? "Drive out the slave and her son, for the son of the slave will never be a coheir with the son of the free woman." [31] Therefore, brothers and sisters, we are not children of a slave but of the free woman.

[5:1] For freedom, Christ set us free. Stand firm then and don't submit again to a yoke of slavery.

Context

The argument that began in 3:1 reaches its climax here in 4:21–5:1,[734] with Paul drawing together a number of key threads that have run throughout: the identity of the true sons of Abraham, the contrast between slavery and freedom, the relationship between the promise to Abraham and the Mosaic law covenant, Jesus as the suffering servant who brings an end to exile, and the gift of the Spirit as the defining mark of the new creation

---

[734] Although this is a minority view, a substantive case has been made by Alicia D. Myers, "'For It Has Been Written': Paul's Use of Isa 54:1 in Gal 4:27 in Light of Gal 3:1–5:1," *PRSt* 37 (2010): 295–308. Especially helpful is her table of key concepts that unite 3:1–5:1 as a unit (303).

that has dawned with the death and resurrection of Jesus. Extending his argument that those who trust in Christ are justified sons of Abraham who receive the promised inheritance, Paul contends that the fulfillment of the Abrahamic covenant has come in Christ, the promised seed and the suffering servant. Through his resurrection the Jerusalem above is now bringing forth children (i.e., all who belong to Christ by faith) who live in freedom, something the law could never do. In this way the gospel promise made to Abraham that "all the nations will be blessed in you" (Gal 3:8 = Gen 12:3 and 18:18) is being fulfilled.

Structure

Despite the numerous interpretive challenges, the basic structure of the paragraph is reasonably clear. After an introductory challenge to hear and understand what the law says (4:21), the paragraph falls into three sections. First the apostle lays out the components of the trope in sharp contrasting terms (4:22–23).[735] On the one side of the comparison is the slave woman (Hagar, though Paul does not explicitly name her until 4:24) and her son (Ishmael, though Paul never names him), who was born in accordance with the flesh. On the other side of the comparison is the free woman (Sarah, never explicitly named by Paul) and her son (Isaac, not named until 4:28), who was born through the promise. Second, Paul explains the significance of those elements (4:24–28). The two women represent two covenants: Hagar represents the Sinai covenant while Sarah corresponds to the Abrahamic covenant (understood christologically). The point of connection between Hagar and the Sinai covenant is that both bear children into slavery, which is also their link to the present Jerusalem (a reference to all who base their relationship to God on the law, regardless of their ethnicity). In contrast to the present Jerusalem, Paul puts forward the Jerusalem above (the consummation of God's redemptive purposes that believers experience now in part in anticipation of

---

[735] As a convenience I am using the term "trope" (defined as a literary device in which the words used have a sense other than, though not necessarily in contradiction to, the literal sense) rather than "allegory" or "typology"; for a similar approach, see Karen H. Jobes, "Jerusalem, Our Mother: Metalepsis and Intertextuality in Galatians 4:21–31," *WTJ* 55 (1993): 299. As noted above, Paul's engagement with the OT here has elements of both allegory and typology, defying our modern attempts to make it one or the other; see further Matthew S. Harmon, "Allegory, Typology, or Something Else? Revisiting Galatians 4:21–5:1," in *Studies in the Pauline Epistles: Essays in Honor of Douglas J. Moo*, ed. Matthew S. Harmon and Jay E. Smith (Grand Rapids: Zondervan, 2014), 144–58.

their full experience at the consummation), which is both free and the mother of all believers regardless of their ethnicity. The citation of Isaiah 54:1 provides the grounds from which Paul draws his conclusions and leads to the concluding assertion that the Galatian believers are in fact children of promise like Isaac. Finally, the implications of the trope are laid out for the Galatians (4:29–5:1). Like Isaac (born according to the Spirit) before them, the Galatians are being persecuted by the false teachers (born according to the flesh). As a result, they should hear Sarah's words to Abraham from Genesis 21:10 as God's instructions to them to have nothing to do with those who are stuck in the present Jerusalem. Because Christ has set them free, they should not even consider a return to slavery under the law.

This passage is the most difficult in the letter and one of the most challenging in the New Testament. The primary challenge is Paul's engagement with the Old Testament; he provides an interpretation of Genesis 16–21 that is not immediately obvious from a surface-level reading of the text itself. He seems to acknowledge as much when he says, "These things are being taken figuratively" (4:24). Further complicating the picture is a citation of Isaiah 54:1, which (along with its surrounding context) Paul uses as an interpretive lens to read Genesis 16–21 in a way that supports his conviction that those who trust in Christ are the true sons of Abraham, regardless of ethnicity. Despite these challenges, the picture that emerges from careful attention to these scriptural echoes is compelling: the promised new creation has come into existence through the death and resurrection of Jesus, who is both the seed of Abraham and the suffering servant who has accomplished the promised new exodus.

4:21. With his powerful personal appeal and acknowledgment of his perplexity completed, Paul resumes the argument that began in 3:1, bringing that argument to its climax here in 4:21–5:1. He begins with a challenge: "Tell me, you who want to be under the law, don't you hear the law?" (Λέγετέ μοι, οἱ ὑπὸ νόμον θέλοντες εἶναι, τὸν νόμον οὐκ ἀκούετε).[736] This question is specifically directed at those in the Galatian churches who are considering taking on the obligations of the Mosaic law as an essential means of being justified before God on the last day. The use of the present tense for the verbs "want" (θέλω) and "to be" (εἰμί) suggests they have not yet taken the plunge. In other words, they have not yet been

---

[736] The combination of the imperative ("tell me") and the direct address ("you who want to be under the law") mark this as the beginning of a new section. Normally the vocative case is used for direct address, but here Paul uses the nominative; on this see Wallace, *Greek Grammar*, 56–59.

circumcised but are seriously contemplating it in light of the teaching of the opponents (5:2–6). Paul has already used the expression "under the law" (ὑπὸ νόμον) in a negative light as a state or condition from which Christ has redeemed his people, so its connotation here is clearly negative.[737] Paul sees the desire of some to keep the Mosaic law as an effort to return to submission to something that no longer has authority over them because they have died to the law through faith in Christ. Christ has already redeemed his people from being "under the law" (4:4–5), so a return to that condition is unthinkable to Paul.

The question Paul asks is both direct and preparatory for what follows: "don't you hear the law?" (τὸν νόμον οὐκ ἀκούετε). The verb "hear" (ἀκούω) has a range of nuances; in this context it has the sense of "to hear and understand a message."[738] Although to this point in Galatians Paul has been using the term "law" (νόμος) to refer to the Mosaic law covenant, it seems to have a broader sense here. Given that Paul introduces the story of Abraham and his two sons in the following verse, it would seem that law includes at least what we refer to as the Pentateuch. Yet since Paul also cites Isaiah 54:1 later in 4:27 as the hermeneutical key for understanding the law, he may have in mind the entirety of what we would consider the Old Testament today. Once the entire witness of Scripture is brought to bear on the issue, Paul believes the Galatians will see things his way.

The summons to truly hear and understand what the Bible says must be heeded by every Christian, or false doctrine and sinful living are sure to follow. The situation in Galatia makes it clear that it is possible to hear what Scripture says but misunderstand it in such a way that we end up disobeying it. May God grant us the humility and wisdom to grow in both our understanding of and obedience to his word.

---

[737] DeSilva (*Handbook*, 94) suggests that Paul places the prepositional phrase "under the law" at the front of the clause in Greek for emphasis. The preposition ὑπό ("under") occurs numerous times in Galatians in a negative light to describe the condition of those apart from Christ: under a curse (3:10), under sin (3:22), under law (3:23; 4:5; 5:18), under a guardian (3:25), under guardians and trustees (4:2), under the elements of the world (4:3). In all of these cases, the construction is used to refer to a controlling authority or influence, and that is definitely the usage here.

[738] BDAG s.v. ἀκούω 7. Galatians 4:21 is the only place in the NT where ἀκούω takes νόμος as its object; this construction is found in the LXX in Neh 13:3 and Isa 30:9 (in 1 Esd 9:40, 50 ἀκούω is an infinitive taking the genitive νόμου as its object; see also Isa 42:24). Hays ("Galatians," 300) suggests an ironic echo of the Shema (Deut 6:4), but this seems unlikely.

4:22. Paul begins this section of his argument with an appeal to Scripture: "For it is written that Abraham had two sons, one by a slave and the other by a free woman" (γέγραπται γὰρ ὅτι Ἀβραὰμ δύο υἱοὺς ἔσχεν, ἕνα ἐκ τῆς παιδίσκης καὶ ἕνα ἐκ τῆς ἐλευθέρας).[739] In the New Testament the expression "it is written" (γέγραπται) usually introduces an Old Testament quotation, but that is not the case here.[740] Instead, it introduces a summary of an Old Testament narrative that extends into verse 23. The Old Testament narrative in view is Genesis 16–21, which, given the importance of Abraham (and Gen 12:1–3 and 15:6 in particular) in Galatians 3–4 up to this point, should come as no surprise.[741]

That summary begins with a simple assertion: "Abraham had two sons" (Ἀβραὰμ δύο υἱοὺς ἔσχεν). Paul seems to assume the Galatians are already familiar with the basic story of Abraham, his wife Sarah, her maidservant Hagar, and his sons Ishmael and Isaac.[742] But the way he summarizes this story reveals Paul's particular interpretive perspective. Rather than identifying the sons and their respective mothers by name, he describes them based on the status of their respective mothers. Paul begins with Ishmael, who was born "by a slave" (ἐκ τῆς παιδίσκης).[743] Genesis 16–21 (LXX) uses

---

[739] The γάρ in this clause signals that the content of verse 22 further explains Paul's implied contention in 4:21 that if the Galatians would truly hear and understand the law, they would hold his viewpoint (similarly DeSilva, *Handbook*, 94).

[740] Here and Luke 24:46 are the only places in the NT where it introduces a summary of an OT passage rather than a direct quotation.

[741] A number of scholars insist that Paul's treatment of the Abraham story is prompted by the fact that his opponents have already used it to support their own Torah-observant version of the gospel; see, e.g., C. K. Barrett, "The Allegory of Abraham, Sarah, and Hagar in the Argument of Galatians," in *Essays on Paul* (Philadelphia: Westminster Press, 1982), 154–69; Dunn, *Galatians*, 243; de Boer, *Galatians*, 286–87; Das, *Galatians*, 484. But given the treatment of so many key themes from 3:1–4:20, it is far better to see Paul's exegetical argument here as at least in part prompted by his own theological purposes; see similarly Andrew C. Perriman, "The Rhetorical Strategy of Galatians 4:21–5:1," *EvQ* 65 (1993): 27–42.

[742] For a helpful summary of how the Hagar–Sarah story was understood in Second Temple Jewish literature, see Longenecker, *Galatians*, 200–6. From a completely different angle, Susan Elliott argues that the worship of the Mountain Mother of Gods in Galatia provides the key to understanding Paul's argument here; see Susan M. Elliott, "Choose Your Mother, Choose Your Master: Galatians 4:21–5:1 in the Shadow of the Anatolian Mother of the Gods," *JBL* 118 (1999): 661–83. But the fact that Elliott's argument rests on evidence that spans six centuries and cannot conclusively be dated to the first century casts doubt on how relevant such a context is for understanding Paul's argument here.

[743] Another way of translating this prepositional phrase would be "from a slave," since the preposition ἐκ is being used in an expression related to giving birth (see BDAG s.v. ἐκ 3.a). The same is true of the phrase "by a free woman" that follows.

this same word for female slave (παιδίσκη) ten times for Hagar. But Paul is doing more than simply repeating the language of Genesis 16–21. By using this term, Paul is connecting Hagar's status with the slavery that Jew and gentile alike experienced before Christ came (Gal 3:22–4:11).[744] As such he is anticipating the interpretive move he will make later in this passage.

By contrast, Isaac was born "by a free woman" (ἐκ τῆς ἐλευθέρας). Describing Sarah this way makes Paul's interpretive agenda even clearer, as nowhere in Genesis 16–21 is she described this way. On one level free woman is simply the logical opposite of slave woman, but the use of freedom language elsewhere in Galatians indicates a greater significance. When false brothers infiltrated his discussions with the Jerusalem pillars, they were there "to spy on the freedom we have in Christ Jesus" (2:4). Being justified by faith and an heir of the promises made to Abraham transcends the basic distinctions that constitute this present evil age, including "slave or free" (3:28). Within 4:21–5:1 freedom is a central theme, occurring in some form seven times (4:22–23, 26, 30–31; 5:1 [2x]), including the climactic statement of 5:1: "For freedom, Christ set us free." Indeed, the contrast between slavery and freedom is a key theme throughout Galatians that encapsulates the fundamental contrast between the present evil age/old creation and the messianic age/new creation that has dawned with the coming of Christ.[745]

Sometimes a person's significance goes well beyond his or her personal identity. Rosa Parks, who bravely refused to sit in the section of a segregated bus reserved for "colored" people, became a symbol of someone who was unjustly oppressed for standing up for what is right. Not only did her courage inspire others to resist racial injustice, but her name became a powerful symbol. As believers, a key component of the significance of our lives is that we are living, breathing symbols of the transforming grace of God that has freed us from our slavery to sin, death, the devil, and all the powers of this present evil age.

---

[744] Das (*Galatians*, 494) notes that some Jewish texts (Ps 116:6 [LXX 115:7]; Wis 9:4–5; 1QS XI.16; 4Q381 Frag. 15; 4Q381 Frag. 33) use this same or similar expressions to describe Jewish people who are faithful to God's law and thus children of the Abrahamic covenant. Thus in using it here "Paul has taken a phrase associated with Jewish privilege and turned it into a designation of bondage under the Law."

[745] See Biblical Theology §1.3.1.

4:23. There is more to the story of Abraham's two sons than the difference in status of their respective mothers.[746] There was also a significant difference in the underlying principles that led to their respective births.[747] Again, Paul begins with Ishmael: "the one by the slave was born as a result of the flesh" (ὁ μὲν ἐκ τῆς παιδίσκης κατὰ σάρκα γεγέννηται). So when it comes to the birth of Ishmael, the operating principle behind it was "the flesh."[748] As noted in 3:3, when used in this manner, flesh (σάρξ) has the negative sense of human nature under the power and control of sin and subject to the spiritual forces of evil in this fallen world. A life that is governed by the flesh leads to death because it is hostile toward God and unsubmissive to his will (Rom 8:5–8, 12–13).

So how then did the flesh serve as the operating principle behind the birth of Ishmael? Rather than trusting in God to fulfill his promise in his own timing, Abraham and Sarah took matters into their own hands by having a child through Sarah's maidservant Hagar (Gen 16:1–16). Using their own wisdom and human efforts, Abraham and Sarah tried to bring God's promise to fulfillment. The result of this flesh-based effort was the birth of Ishmael, the son of the slave woman.

In contrast to Ishmael, "the one by the free woman was born through promise" (ὁ δὲ ἐκ τῆς ἐλευθέρας δι' ἐπαγγελίας). The birth of Isaac from his mother Sarah the free woman came "through promise" (δι' ἐπαγγελίας), an expression that highlights God's promise as the instrument through which the birth of the promised seed/son came about.[749]

---

[746] In Greek this verse is introduced with ἀλλά ("but"), which normally has a strong adversative sense. But as Runge (*Discourse Grammar*, 55–58) suggests, its most basic function is to introduce a correction to a previous statement. As used here, then, it seems to signal that there is even more of a contrast between the two sons and the social status of their respective mothers.

[747] In Greek this contrast is signaled by the μέν ... δέ construction that frames the description of each son. In such constructions the emphasis usually falls on the content of the δέ clause (BDF §447.5), as it does here.

[748] In Greek the expression is κατὰ σάρκα, which woodenly translated means "according to the flesh." When followed by the accusative case, κατά often expresses the norm or principle that governs an action, event, or result (BDAG s.v. κατά B.5.a. α). For this use here in Galatians, see 1:4, 11; 2:2; 3:15, 29; 4:23, 28–29.

[749] See BDAG s.v. διά A.3.e. By writing "through promise" (δι' ἐπαγγελίας) rather than "according to promise" (κατ' ἐπαγγελίαν; compare Gal 3:29), Paul may further emphasize the work of God to fulfill the promise in contrast to the human efforts of Abraham and Sarah; see similarly Moo, *Galatians*, 298–99; Das, *Galatians*, 492–93.

In Genesis, up to the point of Ishmael's birth, God had promised to bless Abraham with seed and soil (Gen 12:1–3) and declared Abraham righteous when he expressed his faith in God's promise (Gen 15:1–6). Within Galatians the term "promise" (ἐπαγγελία) has functioned as a summary term for the various blessings that God had sworn to give Abraham and his seed, with special emphasis on justification (Gal 3:6, citing Gen 15:6), gentile inclusion in God's saving purposes (Gal 3:8–9, citing Gen 12:3 and 18:18), the gift of the Spirit (Gal 3:14, alluding to Isa 44:3–5), the birth of the promised seed Christ (Gal 3:16–18, alluding to Gen 17), and receiving the inheritance based on being identified with Christ by faith (Gal 3:29). Paul has taken what he sees in Genesis and expanded it in light of its fulfillment in Christ the promised seed.

The contrast, then, between flesh and promise is not something Paul imposes on the Genesis narrative. Instead, it is one of the fundamental structures of the Abraham story in Genesis that Paul brings to the surface by reading it through the lens of fulfillment in Christ. This contrast is also something that we as believers experience today. We are regularly faced with the choice between living on the basis of the flesh or by faith in the promises and power of God. Thankfully the apostle gives practical guidance on this issue later in Galatians 5:16–26.

4:24. With the basic summary of the Old Testament narrative of Abraham's two sons and their respective mothers now complete, Paul reveals his interpretive approach: "These things are being taken figuratively" (ἅτινά ἐστιν ἀλληγορούμενα), which could also be rendered "these things have a deeper meaning."[750] Behind this expression is the use of the verb ἀλληγορέω, which in a basic sense means "to use analogy or likeness to express something."[751] Paul uses this unusual verb—which occurs nowhere else in the New Testament—to "signal that he is reading Gen 16–21 through the lens of another textual, philosophical, or theological framework to

---

[750] On the meaning and use of this verb here, see Harmon, "Allegory, Typology, or Something Else," 144–58.

[751] BDAG s.v. ἀλληγορέω. A number of English translations render this verb with some form of the word "allegory" (e.g., ESV, NASB, KJV, NET, ASV), but this runs the risk of giving the impression that Paul's interpretation of Gen 16–21 is fanciful and not rooted in the text. Such a conclusion could not be further from the truth. Instead, Paul engages in a combination of allegory and typology. "Paul's reading is typological in that it depends on real historical and textual correspondences intended by the author(s). But it is allegorical in that those correspondences are more fully revealed through the use of a theological and textual framework provided by Isa 54:1 and its surrounding context" (Harmon, "Allegory, Typology, or Something Else," 156)

reveal a fuller meaning."[752] That textual and theological framework is the citation of Isaiah 54:1 (and its surrounding context) that Paul introduces in Galatians 4:27. But before reaching that quotation, Paul must first lay out the theological significance of the various elements of Genesis 16–21, understood through the lens of Isaiah 54:1 and the gospel.

Paul begins his theological explanation by stating: "the women represent two covenants" (αὗται γάρ εἰσιν δύο διαθῆκαι).[753] Although the word "covenant" (διαθήκη) has occurred just twice to this point in Galatians (3:15, 17), the concept has been fundamental to the entire letter. The first of the two covenants is described in three ways. First, it "is from Mount Sinai" (μία μὲν ἀπὸ ὄρους Σινᾶ). Exodus 19 identifies Mount Sinai as the place where God instituted the Mosaic law covenant with the nation of Israel. The repeated references to the law throughout Galatians refer not only to the specific legislation God gave to Israel, but the entirety of the Mosaic law covenant. Indeed, Sinai and the Mosaic law covenant were so connected that sometimes a reference to Sinai was intended to evoke remembrance of the Sinai covenant (Deut 33:2; Neh 9:13).[754]

While this first description/association would not have been controversial to Paul's opponents, the next two most certainly were. Secondly, the Mosaic law covenant "bears children into slavery" (εἰς δουλείαν γεννῶσα). At one level this assertion merely states plainly what has been implied from Galatians 3:23–4:11. The time before Christ came, when the Mosaic law covenant was in effect, was characterized by captivity, imprisonment, and enslavement to the elementals. But to state so directly that the Mosaic law covenant continues to this day to bring forth children into a state of slavery would still have been a punch to the gut of Paul's opponents.[755]

The final description of the Mosaic law covenant would have been even more scandalous to Paul's opponents. Within his theological reading of Genesis 16–21, Paul says it "is Hagar" (ἥτις ἐστὶν Ἁγάρ). The apostle

---

[752] Harmon, "Allegory, Typology, or Something Else," 154. Paul's use of ἀλληγορέω in this way has similarities to the way that Philo uses ἀλληγορέω and its cognate ἀλληγορία in *Post.* 1:1–7; *Leg.* 2:5–12; 3:1–6; see further Harmon, "Allegory, Typology, or Something Else," 150–54.

[753] The γάρ that introduces this clause has its customary explanatory force.

[754] Sometimes even when the specific term "Sinai" does not occur, the imagery associated with the giving of the Mosaic law covenant at Sinai is used to communicate the same concept (Heb 12:18–21).

[755] Both the present tense of the verb "bears" (γεννάω) and the identification with the "present Jerusalem" in the next verse suggest ongoing action. For a survey of how Second Temple Jews viewed the Mosaic law, see Biblical Theology §1.1.2.

audaciously identifies the Mosaic law covenant with the slave woman
rather than Sarah the free woman. This identification is based on two factors. First, Hagar's status as a slave woman who bore a son (Ishmael) into
slavery corresponds to the Mosaic law covenant bringing forth children
into a state of slavery. Second, Hagar's giving birth to Ishmael was the result
of attempting to receive the promised blessing of God on the basis of the
flesh. Those who are seeking to inherit the blessing promised to Abraham
through keeping the Mosaic law are operating on the same principle of
performance that is empowered by the flesh.

At one level Scripture is clear and straightforward enough that even
a young child can understand its basic message. But at the same time
Scripture is so deep and profound that not even a lifetime of intensive
study will reveal all its wonders. Paul models for us the importance of
re-reading familiar passages in light of what later passages teach to reveal
a fuller and richer understanding of Scripture. When we do so, we become
like a teacher of the law, who because he has become a disciple in God's
kingdom "is like the owner of a house who brings out of his storeroom
treasures new and old" (Matt 13:52).

4:25. The theological explanation continues into this verse, which
begins: "Now Hagar represents Mount Sinai in Arabia" (τὸ δὲ Ἁγὰρ Σινᾶ
ὄρος ἐστὶν ἐν τῇ Ἀραβίᾳ).[756] Associating Hagar with Mount Sinai simply
makes explicit what was implicit in the previous verse. More puzzling is
noting that Mount Sinai is located in Arabia. As noted in 1:17, Arabia could
refer in general to the vast area east of the Jordan River spanning Israel
from the northeast to the southeast, including the northern portion of the
Arabian Peninsula. Whereas in 1:17 Paul uses it to refer to the Nabatean
kingdom where he preached the gospel, here it refers to the region surrounding Mount Sinai in the Arabian Peninsula. So why does Paul make
this geographical reference? Perhaps the most likely reason is to set up the
reference to the "present Jerusalem" in the following clause. In effect Paul
is saying that the "Hagar-Sinai mountain" being physically located in Arabia

---

[756] There is significant diversity in the textual witnesses for this verse, making it difficult to determine the precise wording of the original text. While there are a handful of
variants, the problem can be reduced to two primary issues: (1) whether Ἁγάρ ("Hagar")
is original, and (2) whether γάρ ("for") or δέ ("and/but/now") is original. On the whole
Moo (*Galatians*, 313) is likely correct when he concludes that "the presence of the word
Ἁγάρ is by far the more difficult reading and that δέ should be read because it has much
stronger external support than γάρ." For a helpful discussion of the variants and the issues
surrounding them, see Das, *Galatians*, 479–81. Assuming that the δέ is original, it signals a
new development in the argument.

is no barrier to identifying it symbolically with the present Jerusalem.[757] Paul portrays those who are in the Hagar/Ishmael line as stuck at the foot of Mount Sinai, clinging to a covenant whose time has passed and never could deliver eschatological life.[758]

With this geographical note in place, Paul provides the final identification on the Sinai-covenant side of the comparison. This Hagar-Sinai mountain located in Arabia "corresponds to the present Jerusalem" (συστοιχεῖ δὲ τῇ νῦν Ἰερουσαλήμ). The rare verb rendered "corresponds" (συστοιχέω) likely has the sense here of aligning related items of the same category into tables.[759] Paul's choice of this verb may stem from his reference to the "elements of the world" (τὰ στοιχεῖα τοῦ κόσμου; 4:3, 9) earlier in his argument.[760] In any case, using this verb makes explicit Paul's use of "typological-allegory" to give the symbolic meaning to the two women and their respective sons. The "present Jerusalem" (νῦν Ἰερουσαλήμ) is not simply a reference to the city of Jerusalem as the center and source of Paul's opponents;[761] it refers more broadly to any and all who place the law at the center of their understanding of relating to God and others, regardless of whether they claim to be Christ-followers or not.[762]

---

[757] See similarly Moo, *Galatians*, 302–3 and Das, *Galatians*, 496–97. This view works regardless of whether the definite article τὸ goes with the neuter noun ὄρος (Moo, *Galatians*, 302–3) or with Ἀγὰρ to effectively put it in quotation marks (Das, *Galatians*, 496–97).

[758] Compare the similar conclusion of Schreiner (*Galatians*, 302): "Perhaps Paul is suggesting the Judaizers are still in the wilderness. They have never entered into the promised inheritance, but they still live in slavery as Hagar and Ishmael did."

[759] This verb occurs nowhere else in the LXX, NT, Josephus, Philo, or any other Jewish writings. The Greek historian Polybius (second century bc) used the verb to describe soldiers marching in a line (*Hist.* 10.23.7). Although the verb is not found with the meaning of placing items in parallel columns before the time of Paul, the related noun συστοιχία is used approximately twenty-five times in Aristotle (fourth century bc) with this sense (*NIDNTTE* 4:379; see also *TDNT* 7:669). For further examples of this word family in Greco-Roman texts, see LSJM s.v. συστοιχέω and MM, 612.

[760] On this connection, see especially Martyn, *Galatians*, 393–406, 49–50.

[761] So Longenecker, *Galatians*, 213, who notes that it recalls references to Jerusalem in 1:17–18 and 2:1. He further suggests that the difference in spelling between 1:17, 18; 2:1 (Ἱεροσόλυμα) and in 4:25–26 (Ἰερουσαλήμ) is that the former is a strictly a geographical reference, whereas the latter emphasizes the religious significance of the city. Bruce (*Galatians*, 220) concludes that the present Jerusalem refers to Judaism as focused on Torah observance centered in Jerusalem. Less likely is the view of Martyn (*Galatians*, 457–66), who argues that it refers to the Jerusalem church as proponents of the law-observant gentile mission.

[762] This conclusion may find further support in the historical context of Paul's day. As the apostle writes these words, Jerusalem is still under Roman occupation, a historical reality that also symbolized the plight of Jews who had not come to Christ still awaiting liberation from their spiritual slavery to sin. If in fact political and ethnic tensions were high (see discussion in Introduction, 14–21), this observation becomes even more salient.

The grounds for this connection is that the present Jerusalem "is in slavery with her children" (δουλεύει γὰρ μετὰ τῶν τέκνων αὐτῆς). On a general level the language of slavery continues the broader theme of 3:23–4:11. More specifically, by repeating the same verb used in 4:8–9 that described the Galatians' slavery to the elementals, Paul links their experience of slavery as gentiles to the slavery of those who remain devoted to the Mosaic law covenant. This state of slavery is true of all who align themselves with the present Jerusalem by relying on the Mosaic law to inherit the promise made to Abraham, regardless of whether they are Jew or gentile.

4:26. With his description of the Hagar-Ishmael side of the comparison complete, Paul now transitions to the Sarah-Isaac side (representing the Abrahamic covenant fulfilled in Christ): "But the Jerusalem above is free" (ἡ δὲ ἄνω Ἰερουσαλὴμ ἐλευθέρα ἐστίν).[763] The present Jerusalem is not the only Jerusalem; in fact, it is not even the most important one. What truly matters is the "Jerusalem above." Although this particular expression is not paralleled elsewhere in Greek Jewish writings before the time of Paul,[764] the concept is present in both Second Temple Judaism and the New Testament.[765] The idea has its roots in the Old Testament, where a heavenly Jerusalem is part of the consummation of God's redemptive purposes (Ps 87:3; Ezek 40–48); prominent among these Old Testament texts was Isaiah 54, which Paul will cite in the following verse. In the New Testament the heavenly Jerusalem plays a prominent role in Hebrews (11:10–16; 12:22–24; 13:14) and Revelation (21:10–27). While the focus of Revelation 21:10–27 is the final consummation, both here in Galatians 4:26–27 and Hebrews 11:10–16 and 12:22–24 the heavenly Jerusalem is a reality that believers experience now in anticipation of its full consummation on the last day. That Jerusalem, rather than the present Jerusalem, is free from sin, death, the curse, the law, and the present evil age.

This heavenly Jerusalem "is our mother" (ἥτις ἐστὶν μήτηρ ἡμῶν). In contrast to the present Jerusalem (representing the Mosaic law covenant

---

[763] The δέ that introduces this clause has an adversative force.

[764] The expression is found in 4 Bar. 5:35 (which likely dates to the end of the first or the beginning of the second century AD), where Abimelech pronounces a blessing upon an old man: "God will light your way into the city of Jerusalem above [τὴν ἄνω πόλιν Ἰερουσαλήμ]."

[765] For a helpful summary, see Pilchan Lee, *The New Jerusalem in the Book of Revelation: A Study of Revelation 21–22 in the Light of Its Background in Jewish Tradition*, WUNT 129 (Tübingen: Mohr Siebeck, 2001), 53–229. Within Second Temple Jewish literature, see especially 1 En. 53:6; 90:28–29; 2 En. 55:2; 4 Ezra 10:25–28; 2 Bar. 4:2–6.

and all who seek to relate to God through it), this heavenly Jerusalem bears children who are free. She is the mother of all who put their trust in Jesus Christ, regardless of their ethnicity and apart from any observance of the Mosaic law. Paul may have had Psalm 87:5 (LXX 86:5) in view, which foresees a day when gentile nations will refer to Zion as their mother.[766] Believers are citizens of God's kingdom (Phil 1:27; 3:20–21) living as strangers and exiles in this present evil age (1 Pet 1:1–2; 2:11–12) as they await the consummation of God's promises in a new heavens and earth (Rev 21–22). Through their identification with Jesus Christ they share in all that God had promised to Abraham. The work of Jesus Christ the seed of Abraham, the servant of Yahweh, the son of David has brought into existence the heavenly Jerusalem, something the Mosaic law covenant was never able to do. Through his death and resurrection Jesus Christ has brought the long-promised eschatological people of God—consisting of all who believe in Christ regardless of ethnicity, gender, or socioeconomic status—into existence at last.

At this point it will be helpful to lay out the points of comparison in Paul's argument:[767]

Table 11:

"Abraham had two sons"	
One from the slave woman [Hagar] (22)	One from the free woman [Sarah] (22)
Born according to the flesh [Ishmael] (23)	(Born) through the promise [Isaac] (23)
Covenant from Mount Sinai (24)	(Abrahamic covenant fulfilled in Christ)
Bears children into slavery (24)	(Bears children into freedom)
Hagar (24)	Jerusalem above is our mother (26)
Hagar is Mount Sinai in Arabia (25)	[Sarah is Mount Zion in heaven][768]
Present Jerusalem (25)	Jerusalem above (26)
Enslaved with her children (25)	Free (with her children) (26)

---

[766] Das, *Galatians*, 500.

[767] This chart is adapted from Harmon, *She Must and Shall Go Free*, 176. The entries in parentheses are not directly stated in the passage but seem to be reasonable inferences.

[768] Of all the elements in the comparison, this one is the most difficult for the reader to supply since there is little if any help in the immediate context. From a biblical-theological perspective, Longenecker (*Galatians*, 213–14) is probably correct that the most likely candidate would seem to be something like "Sarah is Mount Zion in heaven"; compare Heb 12:18–24, where the author contrasts Mount Sinai (12:18–20) with "Mount Zion ... the city of the living God (the heavenly Jerusalem)" (12:22).

With these comparisons in place, Paul is now ready in the next verse to reveal the Old Testament passage that is the key to unlock his understanding of the Abraham story.

It also worth noting here that verses 25–26 appear to have a chiastic structure:[769]

A   Hagar
  B   Mount Sinai
    C   slavery
      D   the present Jerusalem
      D1   the Jerusalem above
    C1   freedom
  B1   (Mount Zion)
A1   our mother

Such a structure focuses attention on the center elements: the contrast between the present Jerusalem and the Jerusalem above.

The Galatians' opponents were so focused on the present Jerusalem that they lost sight of the heavenly one. As believers we can easily fall into the trap of focusing on the things of this present evil age that we lose sight of the greater realities of the messianic age that has broken into this fallen world through Christ. In such times we would do well as believers to remember these lines from the classic hymn: "Turn your eyes upon Jesus, look full in his wonderful face; and the things of earth will grow strangely dim, in the light of his glory and grace."[770]

4:27. The grounds for this breathtaking claim comes from Isaiah 54:1, which Paul now cites.[771] To properly understand what Paul is doing with this verse, we must first explain its meaning within the Hagar-Ishmael/

---

[769] Adapted from Longenecker, *Galatians*, 213.

[770] Helen Howarth Lemmel, "Turn Your Eyes upon Jesus," *Hymnal.net*, accessed March 19, 2021, https://www.hymnal.net/en/hymn/h/645.

[771] There is debate regarding what exactly the γάρ that introduces the quote grounds. Some claim it merely grounds the claim of 4:26 that Jerusalem is our mother (e.g., Schreiner, *Galatians*, 303–4; DeSilva, *Handbook*, 98). Another possibility is that it grounds 4:24–26; see Joel Willitts, "Isa 54,1 in Gal 4,24b–27: Reading Genesis in Light of Isaiah," *ZNW* 96 (2005): 201. But it seems better to see this citation as the grounds for the entirety of 4:22–26, since Isaiah 54:1 is the lens through which Paul is reading Gen 16–21 (similarly Moo, *Galatians*, 306–7; Das, *Galatians*, 502–3). Paul's citation matches the LXX precisely, with the exception of omitting the final phrase εἶπεν γὰρ κύριος ("for the Lᴏʀᴅ has spoken"), but this omission is insignificant. The LXX is a straightforward translation of the ᴍᴛ.

Sarah-Isaac allegory. Once that has been accomplished, we can then examine what Isaiah 54:1 meant within its original context and seek to follow Paul's train of thought that led him to use it.

The verse begins with a command, followed by two parallel descriptions of a woman: "Rejoice, childless woman, unable to give birth" (εὐφράνθητι, στεῖρα ἡ οὐ τίκτουσα). Within the allegory, the childless woman is Sarah, whose barrenness was a prominent feature of the Abraham narrative in Genesis. As used in the LXX, the verb for "rejoice" (εὐφραίνω) often occurs in corporate contexts where the people of God unite to express joy at cultic celebrations or sacrificial feasts.[772] Sarah's barrenness is accentuated further when she is described as "childless" (στεῖρα) and "unable to give birth" (ἡ οὐ τίκτουσα).[773] A second and third command, along with another description of this woman, follow: "Burst into song and shout, you who are not in labor" (ῥῆξον καὶ βόησον, ἡ οὐκ ὠδίνουσα). The call to "burst into song" uses a verb (ῥήγνυμι) that has the sense of "to effect an action or intensify it by initially throwing off restraint."[774] The verb "shout" (βοάω) also carries with it a note of shouting with joy or excitement. Within Isaiah (LXX), this verb is connected with the coming salvation that God promises to bring to his people (40:3, 6; 42:11, 13; 44:23). The description of the woman as "you who are not in labor" uses the same verb (ὠδίνω) found in 4:19 to describe Paul's labor in seeing Christ formed in the Galatians. As noted there, this verb often occurs in eschatological contexts in connection with God's redemptive work (Isa 45:10; 51:2).

The reason that this woman should rejoice is given in the final two lines of the citation: "for the children of the desolate woman will be many, more numerous than those of the woman who has a husband" (ὅτι πολλὰ τὰ τέκνα τῆς ἐρήμου μᾶλλον ἢ τῆς ἐχούσης τὸν ἄνδρα). Despite Sarah's seemingly hopeless barrenness, God fulfilled his promise to Abraham through the birth of Isaac, who was part of the line that eventually led to Jesus Christ, the true singular seed of Abraham. All who are united to him by faith—regardless of their ethnicity, gender, or socioeconomic

---

[772] *NIDNTTE* 2:332. Even in its fourteen NT occurrences, there is often a corporate element to the rejoicing this verb describes (Luke 15:23–24, 29, 32; 16:9; Acts 7:41; Rom 15:10; Rev 11:10; 12:12; 18:20).

[773] The LXX uses this same word for "childless" (στεῖρα) in Gen 11:30, where Sarai is first introduced.

[774] BDAG s.v. ῥήγνυμι 2.

status—are thus children of Sarah the desolate woman (Gal 3:28–29). As a result, Sarah's children, who are the result of the promise, are in fact more numerous than those who were born to Hagar, the "woman who has a husband."[775] Although Paul does not specifically state it, it would seem that within his allegory Hagar's "husband" is the Mosaic law (compare Rom 7:2–6).[776]

In sum, Paul uses Isaiah 54:1 (and its larger context) to argue that the fulfillment of the Abrahamic covenant has come in Christ, the promised seed and servant, and through his death and resurrection the promised heavenly Jerusalem has come into existence and begun to bring forth children (all who belong to Christ by faith, regardless of ethnicity, gender, socioeconomic status, or Torah observance). In this way the promise made to Abraham that "all the nations will be blessed through you" (Gal 3:8 = Gen 12:3) is being fulfilled. But is Paul's use of Isaiah 54:1 consistent with its original context?

---

[775] At first sight it might seem strange to identify Hagar as the woman who has the husband. But the underlying Greek construction (ἔχω with a form of ἀνήρ as its object) occurs in the LXX (Tob 3:8), secular Greek (e.g., Aristotle, *Cat.* 15) and the NT (1 Cor 7:2) to refer to sexual intercourse, and perhaps that is the meaning that Paul sees in Isa 54:1 when looking back at Gen 16–21 through the lens of Isa 54:1. But it should also be noted how Gen 16:3 describes the act of Sarai giving Hagar to Abraham: "Sarai took Hagar ... and gave her to her husband, Abram, as a wife for him." So in seeing that Hagar is referred to as Abram's wife in Gen 16:3, we can understand how Paul could see a reference to Hagar in the final line of Isa 54:1. But at the same time, what distinguishes Hagar from Sarah as Abram's wife is the fact that Abram's sexual union with Hagar produced a child. So in that sense the inherent ambiguity of the construction ἔχω + ἀνήρ allows both the sexual and marital aspects to emerge regarding Hagar; see further Harmon, *She Must and Shall Go Free*, 177–80.

[776] At least four arguments suggest this. First, Paul uses the imagery of marriage to describe a person's relationship to the law in Rom 7:2–6. Second, Paul has already associated Hagar/Sinai/slavery, so adding law to that side of the column does nothing more than make explicit what is implicit in the reference to Sinai. Third, husband = law coheres with the larger argument of the passage that those who are currently without a husband/law (by which Paul refers to the church, the Israel of God in which Jew and gentile together are in Christ) are in fact the fulfillment of the promise of abundant seed from Sarah and thus have no need for a husband/law because they have already received the promised blessing of Abraham. Finally, Cosgrove argues that Paul understands the barrenness of Sarah-Jerusalem to extend until its eschatological fulfillment in Christ, and thus "the law has given Sarah no children" ("The Law Has Given Sarah No Children [Gal 4:21–30]," *NovT* 29 [1987]: 230–31). If this is correct, then it is a small step to conclude that just as Sarah's attempt in Gen 16 to have children through Hagar was attempting to accomplish an end for which God had a different means, so too is the use of the law as a husband to bring forth children into the eschatological Jerusalem by Paul's opponents; see further Harmon, *She Must and Shall Go Free*, 180–81.

The answer is a resounding yes.[777] Within Isaiah 49–54 the fulfillment of the Abrahamic promise and the restoration of Zion are merged
together. The call for the barren woman in Isaiah 54:1 to rejoice and
burst into song echoes those same verbs from Isaiah 49:13, where they
are addressed to Zion in light of the promised salvation announced in
the servant's commission (49:1–12). The salvation promised in Isaiah 49
through the individual servant is accomplished through his self-sacrificial
suffering. By rising from the dead, the servant is vindicated as innocent
and receives an inheritance (52:13–53:12). The description of the barren woman who is called to rejoice (54:1) echoes language describing
Sarah (Isa 51:1–2). There the faithful remnant is exhorted to recall the
past dealings of Yahweh with Abraham and Sarah as a means of encouragement to believe that Yahweh will in fact comfort Zion by restoring
them from exile (51:3). Isaiah 52:9 repeats the same imperatives found in
49:13 and 54:1 to summon his people to respond to Yahweh comforting
his people. That comfort comes through the work of the suffering servant. The barren woman of Isaiah 54:1 is a restored and renewed Zion/
Jerusalem,[778] whose children (including gentiles) inherit the promises
made to Abraham (54:1–3). Thus within Isaiah 49–54, the fulfillment of
the Abrahamic covenant and the restoration of Zion after exile converge
in the culmination of God's saving purposes. The result is a new covenant
(54:9–10), a new city (54:11–12), and a new people of God who dwell in
peace as vindicated servants of Yahweh (54:13–17). In sum, Isaiah foresees
a day when out of the ruins of Israel's exile the promise made to Abraham
and the restoration of Zion will be fulfilled, and the result will be children
far more numerous than Israel while under the Mosaic law covenant.

So far, from engaging in a fanciful reading of Scripture, Paul has seen
within Isaiah 49–54 the key lenses necessary to read the entire Abraham

---

[777] What follows is a brief summary of my argument in Harmon, *She Must and Shall Go
Free*, 176–82.

[778] She is referred to as the spouse of Yahweh (54:5–6; compare 50:1–3) whose descendants will be so numerous that they will overwhelm her (54:1–3; compare 49:19–21). The
Targum makes the identification explicit by inserting יְרוּשְׁלֵם ("Jerusalem") twice in 54:1,
but perhaps even more strikingly interprets the married woman as "inhabited Rome" (רוֹמִי
יְתֵיבְתָא). In traditional Jewish exegesis, the barren woman of Isa 54:1 was often identified as
post-exilic Israel and the married woman as Israel's pagan enemies. For a survey of Jewish
interpretation in Second Temple Jewish sources, see Kamila Abrahamova Blessing, "The
Background of the Barren Woman Motif in Galatians 4:27" (Ph.D. diss., Duke University,
1996), 205–305; for interpretation in the rabbinic texts, see Florian Wilk, *Die Bedeutung des
Jesajabuches für Paulus*, FRLANT 179 (Göttingen: Vandenhoeck & Ruprecht, 1998), 190–95.

story (Gen 12–21), now understood in light of its fulfillment in Jesus Christ the promised seed of Abraham, the promised son of David, and the promised suffering servant. Whereas the Mosaic law covenant could never bring about the realization of God's redemptive purposes, Jesus Christ has through his death and resurrection. As Karen Jobes helpfully summarizes:

> Paul is arguing that the nation which God promised to bring from Sarah's dead womb and the population of the new Jerusalem prophesied by Isaiah are those people who are born through the resurrection of Jesus, not those who are circumcised. Just as the birth of Isaac eventually issued in the population of earthly Jerusalem by his descendants, the resurrection of Jesus issues in the populating of the new Jerusalem. The faithful mother-city of Zion was desolate because of sin and had no inhabitants until the sinless Jesus rose from the dead. (Do I hear an echo of Gen 3:24?) When Paul cites Isa 54:1, he is metaleptically announcing to the Galatians that when Jesus rose from death, all of the elect seed of Abraham were also born. In this way Paul not only establishes Christians as rightful heirs of the Abrahamic covenant as it was fulfilled in Christ, but at the same time disinherits those who reject Christ's resurrection, though they may be circumcised.[779]

The obvious conclusion, then, is that keeping the commands of the Mosaic law covenant is not the path to eschatological life.

Joy should be a defining characteristic of our lives as believers. As those who have experienced the fulfillment of God's promises in Jesus, we of all people should be most joyful. Jesus told his disciples that a key purpose of his teaching was that we might experience the fullness of his joy in our lives (John 15:11). Because our joy is rooted in Christ and what he has done for us, we are able to rejoice in all things (Phil 4:4; 1 Thess 5:16).

4:28. With his theological argument completed, Paul now moves to apply it to the situation in Galatia: "Now you too, brothers and sisters, like Isaac, are children of promise" (Ὑμεῖς δέ, ἀδελφοί, κατὰ Ἰσαὰκ ἐπαγγελίας

---

[779] Jobes, "Jerusalem, Our Mother," 316. Compare the summary of Cosgrove ("Law," 231): "Here, then, is the argument: if Is. 54:1, in speaking of Sarah-Jerusalem, implies that her barrenness extends until the eschatological time of fulfillment, *then the law has given Sarah no children.* And with this point Paul reinforces in the strongest possible terms the repeated accent in Galatians of *life* (the Spirit, the realization of the promise, access to the inheritance, the blessing of Abraham) is not to be found in the Torah."

τέκνα ἐστε).[780] In Greek the plural pronoun "you" (Ὑμεῖς) is emphatic, stressing that the truths of 4:21–27 apply to the gentile Galatian believers as "brothers and sisters" in the one family of God. In other words, they are "children of promise" (ἐπαγγελίας τέκνα).[781] Within the framework of his allegory, the gentile Galatian believers belong to the Sarah side. Calling them children of promise is another way of saying that they are "Abraham's seed, heirs according to the promise" (3:29) and adopted sons who are heirs (4:4–7). Even though they are gentiles, they belong to the Sarah-Isaac side of the allegory. The expression "like Isaac" (κατὰ Ἰσαὰκ) more precisely has the sense of "according to Isaac" (i.e., according to the standard/pattern of Isaac).[782] Thus the point is that their status as children of the promise is consistent with the pattern established by Isaac's birth—faith in the promise rather than a work of the flesh.

In Hebrew, if you wanted to describe someone as being characterized by a particular trait, you would call them a "child of" that trait. So when Paul says we as believers are children of promise, he is saying our lives are characterized and shaped by a promise. The fulfillment of God's promise in Jesus the seed of Abraham is what characterizes us as believers. That is what defines us, not our performance or obedience. But is that how we live our everyday lives?

4:29. The gentile believers' status as children of the promise, however, comes with complications. Paul does not stop his reading of the Genesis story with the birth of Isaac, the child of promise; instead, he continues forward to the climactic and decisive break between Isaac, the child born from the promise, and Ishmael, the child born from the flesh: "But just as then the child born as a result of the flesh persecuted the one born as a result of the Spirit, so also now" (ἀλλ᾽ ὥσπερ τότε ὁ κατὰ σάρκα

---

[780] The δέ that begins this clause marks a new development in the argument, which in this case is a move to the application of what Paul has argued to this point. Some manuscripts (א A C D² K L P Ψ 062. 81. 104. 630. 1241. 1505. 2464 𝔐 lat sy bo) have "we are" (ἡμεῖς ... ἐσμέν) instead of "you are" (ὑμεῖς ... ἐστέ), but early and diverse manuscripts (𝔓⁴⁶ B D* F G 0261ᵛⁱᵈ. 0278. 6. 33. 365. 1175. 1739. 1881 b sa; Irˡᵃᵗ Ambst) support "you are." Metzger (*Textual Commentary*, 528) suggests that the variant stems from an attempt to match the first plural pronouns in 4:26 and 4:31.

[781] The genitive here is probably source (so also DeSilva, *Handbook*, 99).

[782] As it has been used several times to this point in Galatians (1:4, 11; 2:2; 3:15, 29; 4:23), the preposition κατά with the accusative indicates the standard or norm that governs an action or state (BDAG s.v. κατά 5.a.α). This makes better sense than seeing it as periphrasis to express equality, as BDAG s.v. κατά 5.b.α suggests.

γεννηθεὶς ἐδίωκεν τὸν κατὰ πνεῦμα, οὕτως καὶ νῦν).[783] Rather than identify Isaac and Ishmael by their names, Paul describes them in terms of
what each one represents within his allegory. Ishmael is "the child born
as a result of the flesh" (ὁ κατὰ σάρκα γεννηθεὶς), or perhaps better,
"according to the flesh."[784] This description uses the same expression as in
4:23 to identify Ishmael as coming into existence on the basis of the flesh
(i.e., Abraham and Sarah's efforts to accomplish God's purposes through
their own efforts by producing an heir through Hagar). Isaac is described
as "born as a result of the Spirit" (τὸν κατὰ πνεῦμα), or perhaps better,
"according to the Spirit." This description is slightly different from 4:23,
where Isaac was described as born "through promise" (δι᾽ ἐπαγγελίας).
While Paul may simply be changing things up for stylistic purposes, there
is likely a more significant reason for this shift. Paul has already closely
associated the promise made to Abraham with the gift of the Spirit (3:14;
4:6). Indeed, for Paul the gift of the Spirit is the preeminent blessing that
believers receive through their union with Christ (Eph 1:14). So by referring to the Spirit, Paul may simply be using the best aspect of the fulfilled
promise to refer to the entirety of the promise and all that it entails.[785]
The shift to "according to the Spirit" also anticipates the fundamental
contrast between the flesh and the Spirit that dominates 5:13–26.

Within Genesis Paul sees that Ishmael (the one born according to the
flesh) "persecuted" Isaac (the one born according to the Spirit). This is
the same verb (διώκω) Paul used in 1:13, 23 to describe his own efforts to
destroy the church. According to Genesis 21:9, Sarah observed Ishmael
"mocking" Isaac, though the Hebrew verb used here is somewhat ambiguous.[786] But Paul may be drawing on Jewish interpretive tradition that
argued Ishmael did in fact persecute Isaac.[787] In any case, by using the

---

[783] The ἀλλά that introduces this verse "introduces a correction of the expectation" created by the previous statement, with the result that "an incorrect expectation is cancelled
and a proper expectation is put in its place" (Runge, Discourse Grammar, 56).

[784] Just as in 4:23, Paul uses the preposition κατά with the accusative to indicate the
standard or norm that governs an action or state (BDAG s.v. κατά 5.a.α).

[785] The literary term for this is synecdoche, in which part of something is used to refer
to its whole.

[786] The Hebrew verb צחק means to laugh, and is the verbal root from which the name
Isaac (which means "he laughs") comes (Gen 21:3, 6). In the piel stem it can have the sense
of mock (Gen 39:14, 17) or even to amuse oneself (Exod 32:6), with connotations of idolatry
and immorality (HALOT s.v. צחק). The LXX renders this verb παίζω, which has a similar
range of meaning (compare its only NT use in 1 Cor 10:7, where it alludes to Exod 32:6).

[787] Although most of the evidence is from the Targums and rabbinic materials, there is
no reason why Paul could not have been familiar with such exegetical traditions; see brief

imperfect tense of the verb here in 4:29, Paul presents Ishmael's persecution of Isaac as an ongoing pattern of life. Paul sees in Ishmael's persecution of Isaac a pattern that applies to the present day when he says, "so also now" (οὕτως καὶ νῦν). True to their identity as sons of Hagar the slave woman, the opponents who are advocating the necessity of keeping the Mosaic law covenant are persecuting the Galatian believers, who are sons of Sarah the free woman. This identification sets up Paul to draw direct application from the Genesis story in the following verse.

Persecution is something we as believers should expect, and yet we are often caught off guard by it. Before he left Galatia Paul had even warned them, "It is necessary to go through many hardships to enter the kingdom of God" (Acts 14:22). Even though we have been rescued from the forces of this present evil age, they can still make our lives as believers challenging. Cultivating a continual and deepening trust in the Lord and his promises is a vital foundation for withstanding the inevitable persecution that all of us as God's people face.

4:30. Paul's instruction on how to handle the reality of those born according to the flesh persecuting those born according to the Spirit is to ask, "But what does the Scripture say?" (ἀλλὰ τί λέγει ἡ γραφή). The answer he points the Galatians toward is found in Genesis 21:10. In their original context these are the words of Sarah to Abraham, but Paul sees in them a word from God to the Galatians: "Drive out the slave and her son" (ἔκβαλε τὴν παιδίσκην καὶ τὸν υἱὸν αὐτῆς). Sarah was obviously asking Abraham to send Hagar and Ishmael away, but how does Paul expect the Galatians to apply this command? Here it is important to remember that the apostle is still working within the framework of his allegory. If the Hagar-Ishmael-Sinai-Present Jerusalem side stands for the Judaism of Paul's day, which still relies on the Mosaic law and remains in slavery and exile, then Paul is calling the Galatians to have nothing to do with this approach to relating to God. A natural corollary of this would be to avoid or have nothing to do with this law-oriented approach to inheriting God's blessing, including the opponents.

The reason for driving out the slave and her son is that "the son of the slave will never be a coheir with the son of the free woman" (οὐ γὰρ μὴ κληρονομήσει ὁ υἱὸς τῆς παιδίσκης μετὰ τοῦ υἱοῦ τῆς ἐλευθέρας).[788]

---

summary in Longenecker, *Galatians*, 202–3.

[788] In citing this portion of Gen 21:10 (LXX), Paul makes two notable, albeit minor, changes. First, he intensifies the force of the negative by adding μή to the already existing οὐ.

Regardless of whether Sarah understood the larger theological issue behind her words or was simply acting to protect the inheritance of Isaac her son, God instructed Abraham to listen to his wife's words. Because Ishmael was not part of the line of promise, he and his mother were sent away so as to no longer persecute Isaac. Paul sees within this a picture of the Galatians' situation. Returning to the language of inheritance (compare 3:15–4:7), Paul insists that no one who has aligned themselves with Hagar-Ishmael through their reliance upon the Mosaic law will ever inherit what was promised to Abraham. Only those in the line of Sarah the free woman and her promise-born son Isaac will be heirs, a status which only happens through one's union with Christ.

When faced with a difficult situation, Paul models the right question for us as believers to ask: "What does the Scripture say?" Too often we look first to our own wisdom, or the wisdom of others, for the solution. As followers of Christ, our instinctive response should be to search the Scriptures prayerfully for the wisdom we need, for God is an eager and generous giver (Jas 1:5–8). And those of us who serve in ministry should work to cultivate this kind of reflex in those whom God has called us to lead.

4:31. Paul begins to draw his argument to a close by introducing a conclusion that follows logically: "Therefore, brothers and sisters, we are not children of a slave but of the free woman" (διό, ἀδελφοί, οὐκ ἐσμὲν παιδίσκης τέκνα ἀλλὰ τῆς ἐλευθέρας).[789] By switching from second person to first person, Paul includes himself within the conclusion that all who believe in Christ (regardless of ethnicity, gender, or socioeconomic status) are part of the same spiritual family ("brothers and sisters"), children of the promise born according to the Spirit.

This move, however, appears to have resulted in later scribes trying to change the future indicative to an aorist subjunctive (on the overlap between these two constructions, see BDF §365.2). Second, Paul changes the end of the phrase from μετὰ τοῦ υἱοῦ μου Ἰσαακ ("with my son Isaac") to μετὰ τοῦ υἱοῦ τῆς ἐλευθέρας ("with the son of the free woman"). This second change ties the statement more tightly into his allegory and makes it easier for him to apply the command to the Galatian situation.

[789] Paul uses the conjunction διό, which often presents what follows as self-evident based on what precedes it. While διό has the strongest support to be the original reading (ℵ B D* H 0261. 0278. 33. 365. 1175. 1319. 1573. 1739. 1881 sa; Mcion^T), other readings include αρα (𝔓⁴⁶ D F [with ουν] G [with ουν] L 049 056 075 1. 35. 69. 76. 131. 205. 209. 424. 927. 945. 999. 1243. 1244. 1245. 1251. 1315. 1424. 1505. 1646. 1735. 1751 [with δέ]. 1874. 2495), ἡμεις (with δέ: A C P 1962; with διό: 218; alone: 1563), and omitting a conjunction altogether (Ψ).

5:1. The transitional nature of this verse makes it difficult to decide whether it is the final verse of the Hagar/Sarah allegory or the beginning of a new section.[790] On the whole, however, it seems slightly preferable to keep it with the allegory.[791] Continuing his emphasis on believers' status as children of the free woman, Paul asserts: "For freedom, Christ set us free" (Τῇ ἐλευθερίᾳ ἡμᾶς Χριστὸς ἠλευθέρωσεν). What may seem repetitious to the modern reader is Paul's way of stating the truth emphatically. The destination/goal of Christ setting his people free was a state of freedom.[792] To this point in Galatians that state of freedom includes freedom from the Mosaic law (2:18–21; 3:23–4:7), the curse that disobeying the law brings (3:10–14), sin (3:22), and the elementals (4:3, 8–11). But further describing the nature of this freedom (including what it does not mean) is a central theme of 5:2–6:10.

Although not common in the New Testament, the verb rendered "set free" (ἐλευθερόω) always refers to Christ releasing either believers (John 8:32, 36; Rom 6:18, 22; 8:2; Gal 5:1) or creation (Rom 8:21) from some form of bondage related to sin, death, or the curse. None of these powers

---

[790] Noting the transitional nature of the verse, Moo (*Galatians*, 319) calls 5:1 a "Janus" that looks both backwards and forwards before concluding that it is best taken as the beginning of a new unit that extends through 5:12.

[791] Several factors support this conclusion: (1) the lack of any connecting particle/conjunction (asyndeton) in the first clause of the verse suggests a continuation of the previous clause (though this is not by itself decisive, since asyndeton can introduce a new unit; see BDF §463); (2) the repetition of "freedom" terminology flows naturally from the last word of 4:31 ("free woman"); (3) the οὖν that introduces the final clause of 5:1 seems to be the practical action point that comes from the theological conclusion ("we are children of the free woman") in 4:31.

[792] The exact force of the dative is disputed. One possibility is an instrumental or causal sense, but this sense demands an implied ᾗ (present in D and other manuscripts, probably as a result of "correcting" the text); see Lightfoot, *St. Paul's Epistle to the Galatians. A Revised Text with Introduction, Notes, and Dissertations*, 200–202; Bruce, *Galatians*, 226. Better options, however, are available. At one level this is an example of a cognate dative (it occurs with its cognate verb ἐλευθερόω). But it most likely indicates destination or purpose, since the formula τῇ ἐλευθερίᾳ was used in manumission records to indicate destination or purpose; see Deissmann, *Light from the Ancient East*, 321–28. Regarding the importance of the first clause in Gal 5:1, Dunn (*Galatians*, 262) claims, "In these words Paul sums up the whole argument of 3:1–4:11—both the recognition (now) that the life he had previously lived 'within Judaism' (1:13–14) was an immature and unnecessarily restricted one (3:23–4), and the sense of liberation which he personally had experienced through his conversion and which he wanted his converts to experience for themselves in full measure, in contrast to their previous slavery (4:8–9)."

associated with the elements of the world—not even the pagan gods they previously worshiped—now have the authority to enslave those who trust in Christ.[793] Betz is on the right track when he claims that freedom "is the central theological concept which sums up the Christian's situation before God as well as in this world. It is the basic concept underlying Paul's argument throughout the letter."[794]

Paul's statement here also resonates with two previous claims in Galatians about the work of Christ:

Table 12:

Verse	Christ	Redemptive Act	Object	Realm
1:3–4	Our Lord Jesus Christ	[gave himself to] rescue	us	from this present evil age
3:13	Christ	redeemed	us	from the curse of the law
5:1	Christ	set ... free	us	for freedom

In each of these statements Christ performs a redemptive act for his people. But whereas 1:3–4 and 3:13 state the realm out from which Christ takes the believer, here in 5:1 Paul states the realm into which Christ places the believer. Our redemption is not merely rescue from something, but rescue for something.

In light of the twin truths that believers are children of the free woman and have been set free for freedom, Paul now exhorts the Galatians to pursue two specific actions—one stated positively, the other stated negatively—in response to their identity in Christ. The first is "Stand firm" (στήκετε). Paul often uses this verb (στήκω) in contexts where he calls believers to remain steadfast in their faith despite various kinds of opposition or resistance (1 Cor 16:13; Phil 1:27; 4:1; 1 Thess 3:8; 2 Thess 2:15).[795] Like soldiers standing firm in the face of an enemy assault, the Galatians

---

[793] For a helpful discussion of the fear and bondage these gods produced, see Arnold, "Paul and Anatolian Folk Belief," 438–44.

[794] Betz, *Galatians*, 255.

[795] The present tense of the imperative reinforces the ongoing nature of standing firm. The NT is the first place this verb is found in Greek literature, with the few possible occurrences in the LXX likely being unreliable variants supplied by later scribes (BDAG s.v. στήκω). Usually when Paul uses this verb, he provides a sphere/realm in which the believer is to stand firm, such as the faith (1 Cor 16:13), the Spirit (Phil 1:27), or the Lord (Phil 4:1; 1 Thess 3:8). Although he uses the verb without such a sphere/realm stated here in Gal 5:1, based on the context one could supply "in freedom."

must stand firm in the face of those who would deprive them of their freedom in the gospel.

The second action states what the Galatians should not do: "don't submit again to a yoke of slavery" (μὴ πάλιν ζυγῷ δουλείας ἐνέχεσθε). As used here, the rare verb translated "submit" (ἐνέχω) has the sense of "experience constraint."[796] Although this specific word is nowhere used to describe submitting to the law, that is clearly what Paul has in view when he refers to a yoke of slavery. Addressing the Jerusalem council regarding whether gentile converts should be required to keep the Mosaic law, Peter asks, "why are you testing God by putting a yoke on the disciples' necks that neither our ancestors nor we have been able to bear?" (Acts 15:10).[797] Associating the law with a yoke was common in Jewish tradition,[798] so Paul's doing so here is not surprising. What is surprising is Paul's assertion that if the gentile Galatians take up the yoke of the Mosaic law, they would be submitting to a yoke of slavery "again" (πάλιν). That claim only stands when one understands that the Mosaic law is in fact another form of the elements of the world that the gentile Galatians were enslaved to before their conversion (4:3, 9).

The life of the Christian is one of freedom. But that freedom is only possible because Jesus Christ has freed us from sin, the law, the elementals, the curse, and even death. He has adopted us into his family as sons of promise who have his Spirit dwelling inside of us. Retreating from this

---

[796] BDAG s.v. ἐνέχω 2, which suggests "have it in for someone" as a modern equivalent. This verb more commonly has the sense of holding a grudge or being hostile toward someone (Gen 49:23 Mark 6:19; Luke 11:53). But the sense here is attested in Josephus (Ant. 18:179) and Letter of Aristeas 1:16; see also Herodotus (Hist. 2.121), where it describes a thief caught in a trap, and Xenophon (Anab. 7.4.17), where it refers to shields caught in stakes.

[797] More often than not in the Bible, a yoke is used symbolically, often referring to political bondage whether domestic (2 Chr 10:1–14) or foreign (Isa 14:25). But a yoke can have positive references, such as Jesus' invitation to his followers to take his yoke upon themselves (Matt 11:29; compare the three references in the Apostolic Fathers [1 Clem. 16:17; Barn. 2:6; Did. 6:2], which are all positive in nature). See the helpful summary in Leland Ryken et al., Dictionary of Biblical Imagery (Downers Grove, IL: IVP, 1998), 975.

[798] Pointing to texts such as m. 'Aboth 3.5 and m. Ber. 2.2, Longenecker (Galatians, 224) notes that the word ζυγός ("yoke") "was current in an honorable sense for Torah study and for various kinds of governmental, social, and family responsibilities." There may also be echoes of Israel's redemption from a yoke of slavery in Egypt (Lev 26:13) as well as the promise of a new exodus (Isa 10:24–27; Ezek 34:27); see Sylvia C. Keesmaat, Paul and His Story: (Re)-Interpreting the Exodus Tradition, JSNTSup 181 (Sheffield: Sheffield Academic, 1999), 171–73.

glorious status to a yoke of slavery to the Mosaic law should therefore be unthinkable.

Bridge

Satan loves to make believers forget or doubt their true identity. He even tried this tactic with Jesus in the wilderness when he began his temptation with the phrase, "If you are the Son of God" (Matt 4:3). Satan knows that if we lose sight of our identity as sons of Abraham, sons of God, children of promise, and children of the heavenly Jerusalem, we will inevitably live in ways that are inconsistent with those spiritual realities. That is one of many reasons why immersing ourselves in God's word is so vital, because that is where we are reminded of who we are and how that identity should shape our everyday lives. Otherwise we risk the very real possibility of turning away from our freedom in Christ back to some form of slavery.

IV. Living in the Freedom of Sonship (5:2–6:10)

With the central argument of the letter now completed, Paul turns to apply the message of freedom through the gospel of Jesus Christ. The central theme of this section is learning to live out the freedom that Christ has purchased for his people through his death and resurrection as the seed of Abraham, the suffering servant, and the son of David. As sons and daughters of the Jerusalem above who have been redeemed from their exile away from God's presence and now participate in the new creation, believers' lives should be characterized by freedom from anything associated with the elements of the world.

Paul's first step of application is to make clear the implications of the freedom believers have because of Christ, which means he must emphasize that circumcision has no value when it comes to being justified before God; instead, what matters is faith working through love (5:2–6). At this point Paul sets his sights directly on the effect the opponents are having on the Galatians (5:7–12). Like yeast that permeates a lump of dough, the teaching of the opponents has begun to spread among the Galatians and hinder them from remaining on the path of faithfulness to the true gospel; no wonder Paul wishes they would emasculate themselves! In the paragraph that follows, Paul returns explicitly to the theme of freedom, stating that its true purpose is to serve one another in fulfillment of the command to love one's neighbor as oneself (5:13–15). But God has not left believers on their own to live out their freedom; he has given them the Spirit to empower them to walk in obedience (5:16–26). The Spirit leads believers to resist the desires and works of the flesh, while at the same time producing fruit that reflects the character of Jesus himself. The freedom to serve one another through love in the power of the Spirit comes to expression when believers bear one another's burdens, and in doing so they fulfill the law of Christ (6:1–5). Despite the very real temptation of growing weary in doing good, believers are called to persevere in being a conduit of blessing to others, especially fellow believers (6:6–10).

As this extended section demonstrates, understanding and believing the true gospel that leads to freedom through Jesus Christ matters. It matters not merely for what will happen on the last day, but for how we live our everyday lives in anticipation of that last day. Believers do not need the Mosaic Law covenant to regulate their relationship with God or others. God has given his people the Spirit and the law of Christ to govern their lives as the eschatological people of God.

A. Faith Working through Love (5:2–6)

> [2] Take note! I, Paul, am telling you that if you get yourselves circumcised, Christ will not benefit you at all. [3] Again I testify to every man who gets himself circumcised that he is obligated to do the entire law. [4] You who are trying to be justified by the law are alienated from Christ; you have fallen from grace. [5] For we eagerly await through the Spirit, by faith, the hope of righteousness. [6] For in Christ Jesus neither circumcision nor uncircumcision accomplishes anything; what matters is faith working through love.

Context

With the central theological argument of the epistle now completed, Paul turns to the practical outworking of the freedom that Christ the suffering servant has accomplished for those who by faith in him are sons of Abraham. Paul now returns to the specific issue of circumcision, describing its relationship to the Mosaic law covenant and justification. Believers have something far greater than circumcision: Spirit-empowered faith that produces love motivated by eschatological hope.

Structure

The paragraph divides into three parts. First, Paul warns that circumcision is not only of no benefit to the believer, but in fact separates one from Christ (5:2-3). Far from being something that is necessary to add to faith in Christ for a right status with God, circumcision has no value in God's economy now that Christ has come (5:2). Nor is circumcision something that can be separated from the Mosaic law covenant as a stand-alone requirement; those who are circumcised are required to keep the entire Mosaic law (5:3), which as Paul has already stated results in a curse when it cannot be kept perfectly (3:10-14). Second, Paul contrasts the outcome of the two different paths to justification (5:4-5). Those who seek justification through obeying the Mosaic law are cut off from Christ and the grace of the true gospel (5:4). By contrast, that true gospel produces people who are empowered by God's Spirit to trust in Christ alone for their righteousness and eagerly await their vindication before God on the last day (5:5). Paul concludes the paragraph with a summary statement that highlights what truly matters (5:6). It is not the presence or lack of one's foreskin but faith in Christ that produces a life of love.

5:2. The interjection "Take note!" (Ἴδε) signals the start of a new section in the epistle. Similar to what he did in 4:12, Paul makes a personal appeal: "I, Paul, am telling you that if you get yourselves circumcised, Christ will not benefit you at all" (ἐγὼ Παῦλος λέγω ὑμῖν ὅτι ἐὰν περιτέμνησθε, Χριστὸς ὑμᾶς οὐδὲν ὠφελήσει).[799] With his lengthy theological argument (2:14-5:1) in place, the apostle cuts to the bottom line. If the Galatians take on the yoke of the Mosaic law covenant by getting circumcised,[800] they will not get what they want. This is the first mention of circumcision since 2:12, where Paul referred to the "circumcision party." Before that, however, circumcision took center stage in 2:1-10,

---

[799] The combination of the first person pronoun, Paul's name, and the interjection "Take note!" (Ἴδε) draw particular attention to this statement such that Paul "mobilizes his whole authority as an apostle" (Betz, *Galatians*, 258). Paul uses a third class conditional statement here, which presents the "if" clause as hypothetical in nature. Burton (*Syntax*, §250) classifies this as a "Future Supposition with More Probability" in which "The protasis states a supposition which refers to the future, suggesting some probability of its fulfilment." The force of the future tense is not so much temporal but logical certainty.

[800] The present tense of the verb περιτέμνω, along with the force of the conditional statement, suggests that the Galatians have not yet been circumcised. Regardless of whether this verb is middle or passive voice, there may be a permissive sense (i.e., "let yourselves be circumcised"); see BDF §314 and §317 (noted in DeSilva, *Handbook*, 103).

where Paul refused to have his Greek ministry partner Titus circumcised despite pressure from "false brothers" (2:4). Yet that account, along with the dispute over observing food laws (2:11–14), served as the launching point for Paul's lengthy theological argument regarding the place of the law within God's redemptive purposes. Since the decisive step in taking up the yoke of the Mosaic law was circumcision, Paul focuses his efforts here in an effort to stop the Galatians from this disastrous path.

The opponents appear to have been arguing that the gentile Galatians should simply add observing the Mosaic law to their Christian experience.[801] But Paul insists that circumcision (and thus by extension the Mosaic law) is not something that can be added to Christ. Instead, if they are circumcised, "Christ will not benefit you at all" (Χριστὸς ὑμᾶς οὐδὲν ὠφελήσει). The verb translated "benefit" (ὠφελέω) was sometimes used to describe "the activity of a benefactor toward a beneficiary."[802] Rather than being something that supplements what Christ has done for believers through his death and resurrection, circumcision is a repudiation of it. "If they were to seek to secure God's favor for themselves on the basis of works of Torah, this would now amount to a vote of no confidence in Jesus' mediation, to which they had previously committed themselves."[803] When it comes to relating to God and others, the relationship between the Mosaic law and faith in Christ is either/or, not both/and.

Syncretism has always been a danger faced by God's people. The Israelites fell victim to this deadly danger, often trying to incorporate beliefs and practices from their pagan neighbors into their own worship of Yahweh. The opponents were trying to lead the Galatians to mix the Mosaic law covenant with the new covenant. Believers today can fall prey to the same impulse by trying to add to their standing before God through the good works they do. Therefore, we need the constant reminder that Jesus has done everything necessary for our salvation and that our efforts to add to that work only subtract from it.

5:3. Stressing the gravity of the situation and the seriousness of the error, Paul puts himself on the witness stand: "Again I testify to every man

---

[801] De Boer (*Galatians*, 311–12) helpfully notes the communal and familial ramifications of these gentile believers adopting circumcision as a distinguishing mark of their religious identity, but in doing so minimizes the individual ramifications.

[802] DeSilva, *Handbook*, 103.

[803] David A. DeSilva, *Honor, Patronage, Kinship & Purity: Unlocking New Testament Culture* (Downers Grove, IL: IVP, 2000), 145.

who gets himself circumcised" (μαρτύρομαι δὲ πάλιν παντὶ ἀνθρώπῳ περιτεμνομένῳ).[804] Whether Paul refers to earlier in the letter or to a previous occasion by saying "again" (πάλιν) is unclear. Given the parallels to 3:10–14, it seems likely Paul is linking what he is saying about the law with his statements there. Regardless, the present tense of the verb "testify" presents the action as ongoing. His strong words are directed toward "every man who gets himself circumcised" (παντὶ ἀνθρώπῳ περιτεμνομένῳ). Such a reference indicates that Paul expected this letter to be read to the entire congregation in each of the Galatian cities, not merely the leadership or the opponents. The apostle is taking his case directly to the people.

The content of his testimony to every man who gets circumcised is direct: "he is obligated to do the entire law" (ὅτι ὀφειλέτης ἐστὶν ὅλον τὸν νόμον ποιῆσαι). The word rendered "obligated" (ὀφειλέτης) stresses the solemnity that comes from placing oneself willingly under the Mosaic law.[805] The expression "do the entire law" (ὅλον τὸν νόμον ποιῆσαι) picks up language from 3:10, 12. In 3:10 (citing Deut 27:26) a curse was pronounced on everyone who "does not do everything written in the book of the law" (ἐν τῷ βιβλίῳ τοῦ νόμου τοῦ ποιῆσαι αὐτά), while in 3:12 (citing Lev 18:5) Paul supported his claim that the law is not of faith by stating "the one who does these things (i.e., the law) will live by them" (ὁ ποιήσας αὐτὰ ζήσεται ἐν αὐτοῖς). By echoing this language Paul wants his readers to realize not only that the Mosaic law is an entire package that one must keep, but that the inevitable failure to keep it results in a curse.

While first-century Jews may have differed on their understanding of what keeping the Mosaic law entailed, Paul was not alone in his conviction that the Mosaic law was a package deal. James wrote that "whoever keeps the entire law, and yet stumbles at one point, is guilty of breaking it all" (Jas 2:10). A number of Jewish texts make a similar point about the responsibility to keep the entire Mosaic law.[806] In making this point Paul

---

[804] The δέ that begins this clause marks a new development in the argument.

[805] Paul uses this same word to describe the divine obligation he has to preach the gospel (Rom 1:14) as well as the believer's obligation to put sin to death (Rom 8:12). Although ὀφειλέτης occurs just seven times in the NT (Matt 6:12; 18:24; Luke 13:4; Rom 1:14; 8:12; 15:27; Gal 5:3), the broader word family is somewhat common: ὀφείλω (35x); ὀφειλή (3x), ὀφείλημα (2x). This word family often has a financial sense; see NIDNTTE 3:573–78. Although from different word families, there may be a subtle wordplay between "benefit" (ὠφελέω) in 5:2 and "obligated" (ὀφειλέτης) in 5:3 (so DeSilva, Handbook, 104).

[806] Das (Galatians, 524) notes m. 'Aboth 2.1; 4.2; 4 Macc 5:20–21; Sir 7:8; 1QS 1.13–14. Moo (Galatians, 323) notes the claim of Justin Martyr (second century AD), who summarized the

is likely not disagreeing with the opponents; they too probably shared the view that the Mosaic law should be kept in its entirety. Paul "reminds his would-be Gentile judaizers that what was being demanded of them was not simply a matter of a single act of circumcision, but a whole way of life, a complete assimilation and absorption of any distinctively Gentile identity into the status of a Jewish proselyte."[807] Paul's point in reminding the Galatians of the necessity to keep the law further serves to remind them of the impossibility of doing so, which he stressed in 3:10–14. Furthermore, now that the animal sacrifices prescribed in the law have been invalidated with the coming of Christ, the final and perfect sacrifice, there is no longer any provision within the Mosaic law covenant to cover sin.

Paul's assertion that getting circumcised obligates one to keep the entire law also suggests that dividing the law into moral, civil, and ceremonial categories is inadequate. Within such an approach it is claimed that Christians are required to keep the moral laws, while being able to safely disregard the civil and ceremonial laws. Besides being extremely difficult to divide the Mosaic law neatly into these three categories, nowhere does the New Testament establish these particular categories. Instead, Paul will put forward the "law of Christ" (Gal 6:2) as the standard by which believers should regulate their behavior as God's people (see discussion there).

5:4. That Paul sees being justified by faith in Christ and keeping the Mosaic law as mutually exclusive paths rather than complementary becomes even more evident when the apostle asserts: "You who are trying to be justified by the law are alienated from Christ" (κατηργήθητε ἀπὸ Χριστοῦ, οἵτινες ἐν νόμῳ δικαιοῦσθε). In Greek the phrase "you are alienated from Christ" comes first, likely for a shocking rhetorical effect. The verb rendered "alienate" (καταργέω) is a Pauline favorite, often used with the sense of nullify or abolish (e.g., Gal 3:17).[808] But here in the passive voice it means to be separated from something or someone, as it does

---

standard Jewish view of his day: "first be circumcised, then observe the precepts concerning the Sabbath, the feasts, and God's new moons; in brief, fulfill the whole written law, and then, probably, you will experience the mercy of God" (*Dial.* 8.4).

[807] Dunn, *Galatians,* 267.

[808] Of the twenty-seven NT occurrences, all but two (Luke 13:7; Heb 2:14) are in Paul's letters. All four LXX occurrences appear in Ezra (4:21, 23; 5:5; 6:8). Silva (*NIDNTTE* 2:641–42) divides Paul's use of this verb into three categories: (1) God eliminates the destructive powers that threaten our spiritual well-being through the cross of Christ and his second coming; (2) God replaces what is passing away to make way for better things; (3) humanity attempts to cancel out what God has done.

in Romans 7:2, 6. There Paul claims that just as a married woman whose husband has died "is released [κατήργηται] from the law regarding the husband" (7:2), so too believers "have been released [κατηργήθημεν] from the law" (7:6) by dying to it and being joined to Christ. The imagery of divorce is apt here in Galatians 5:4, as Paul has in view a decisive break away from Christ. In promoting circumcision (the cutting away of the foreskin), the opponents are ultimately leading people to cut themselves off from Christ.

The apostle says this startling state applies to "you who are trying to be justified by the law" (οἵτινες ἐν νόμῳ δικαιοῦσθε). In Greek the expression makes it clear that it applies to any and all who pursue this path.[809] For the first time since 3:24, Paul returns to the language of justification/righteousness.[810] By getting circumcised and placing oneself under obligation to keep the entire Mosaic law, the Galatians would be trying to secure a right standing before God on the last day by doing the law rather than by trusting in the finished work of Christ.[811] Implied here is the basic contrast from 2:16, where being justified by the works of the law is set against being justified by faith in Christ.

To make his point crystal clear, Paul adds: "you have fallen from grace" (τῆς χάριτος ἐξεπέσατε). To fall away from grace means to depart from the one true gospel,[812] which proclaims that a person's standing before God is not based on what a person does but on receiving the free gift of what Christ has done through his death and resurrection. By definition, those who pursue the path of justification by the law are not on the path of faith, since "the law is not based on faith" (3:12). Those who try to be justified by the law in effect "set aside the grace of God, for if righteousness comes through the law, then Christ died for nothing" (2:21). As Moo

---

[809] The use of the relative pronoun οἵτινες has the sense of "as many as" and extends the force of this statement beyond the situation in Galatia to any and all who pursue this course of action.

[810] The larger context suggests that Paul's use of the present tense of the verb δικαιόω here has a conative force (i.e., the action is being attempted but not accomplished); see BDF §319 and Wallace, *Greek Grammar*, 535.

[811] While the phrase ἐν νόμῳ likely has an instrumental sense ("by the law"), another possibility is to understand it as indicating sphere/realm ("in the law"). But the parallel expression "justified by Christ" (δικαιωθῆναι ἐν Χριστῷ) in 2:17 suggests the instrumental sense here. DeSilva (*Handbook*, 105) proposes reference/respect as another possibility.

[812] The NT often uses the language of falling (usually from the πίπτω word family, such as here in Gal 5:4 with the compound ἐκπίπτω) to describe a person's spiritual downfall (e.g., Matt 7:24–27; Rom 9:32–33; 1 Cor 10:12; Heb 4:11; 1 Pet 2:8); for a helpful summary see *NIDNTTE* 3:758–59.

aptly states, "pursuit of the law as a means of justification involves an attempt to find security with God by means of human effort, a 'doing' of the law (cf. v. 2) that, with whatever attitude it is pursued, introduces into the divine-human relationship a nexus of obligation that is incompatible with the nature of our gracious God."[813]

Paul's language here often raises the question of whether believers can "lose" their salvation, but that issue does not appear to be in view.[814] Despite the severe warnings throughout the letter, Paul seems confident that the Galatians will ultimately reject the teaching of the opponents and remain faithful to the true gospel (3:2–5; 4:28; 5:10). At the same time, however, Paul also insists that those who depart from the true gospel subject themselves again to slavery to the elementals (4:9–11) and the curse that comes from failing to perfectly obey God (3:10). Whether such a person was genuinely born again by God's Spirit and then fell away into condemnation or was never truly converted is a question Paul does not seem interested in answering here. Either way the solution is the same— abandon any efforts to be right with God based on what we do and trust completely in the finished work of Christ, received as a gift of God's grace.

5:5. In contrast to those who alienate themselves from Christ and fall from grace by trying to be justified by the law, Paul explains that as children of promise who have been freed by the work of Christ, "we eagerly await through the Spirit, by faith, the hope of righteousness" (ἡμεῖς γὰρ πνεύματι ἐκ πίστεως ἐλπίδα δικαιοσύνης ἀπεκδεχόμεθα).[815] The switch from second person plural pronouns in verse 4 to the first person plural intensifies the contrast, and placing the first person plural pronoun "we" (ἡμεῖς) at the beginning of the clause in Greek draws even more attention to it. As used in the New Testament, the verb rendered "eagerly await" (ἀπεκδέχομαι) has strong eschatological overtones, with an emphasis on anticipating the culmination of God's redemptive purposes.[816] Both

---

[813] Moo, *Galatians*, 326–27.

[814] For a helpful discussion of this complex issue, see Thomas R. Schreiner and Ardel B. Caneday, *The Race Set before Us: A Biblical Theology of Perseverance & Assurance* (Downers Grove, IL: IVP, 2001).

[815] Although admittedly a rare usage (Beale, Ross, and Brendsel, *Interpretive Lexicon*, 33; Zerwick, *Biblical Greek*, 159), the γάρ that introduces this clause seems to have a contrasting force to the previous clause. Yet this contrast also "introduces explanatory material that strengthens or supports what precedes" (Runge, *Discourse Grammar*, 54).

[816] All but two (Heb 9:28; 1 Pet 3:20) of the eight NT occurrences are in Paul (Rom 8:19, 23, 25; 1 Cor 1:7; Gal 5:5; Phil 3:20). The only "non-eschatological" use is 1 Pet 3:20, where the patience of God is described as eagerly waiting during the days of Noah. Yet even in

creation and believers eagerly wait patiently with hope for "God's sons to be revealed" and the consummation of their adoption when God raises their bodies from the dead (Rom 8:19, 23, 25). Of course, these realities will be the result of eagerly awaiting the return of Jesus Christ himself, who will make these hopes a reality (1 Cor 1:7; Phil 3:20–21). By using this particular verb, Paul stresses the eagerness with which believers await the full realization of all God's promises.

This eager anticipation is directed toward "the hope of righteousness" (ἐλπίδα δικαιοσύνης), by which Paul means that our hope as believers is being declared righteous on the last day.[817] Whereas in English the word hope often has an element of uncertainty attached to it (e.g., "I hope my favorite team wins"), as used in the Bible it regularly refers to realities that are certain to happen (e.g., Rom 8:24–25; Heb 11:1; 1 Pet 1:3). As we have noted before, there is an already/not-yet dynamic to righteousness/justification. On the one hand, believers are justified the moment they believe in Jesus (compare Rom 5:1). But consistent with what we have seen throughout Galatians, here Paul has in view future/final justification, when God vindicates his people before all creation on the last day.[818] That is the certain reality that believers fix their hope on as they live in this fallen world.

How believers wait for this hope of righteousness is described from both a divine and a human angle. From a divine angle, believers eagerly wait "through the Spirit" (πνεύματι).[819] The Spirit is the definitive evidence that a person is an adopted son (4:4–6) and an heir of the promise

---

1 Pet 3:20 there is still an anticipation of a significant moment in redemptive history, which one could argue is an eschatological use.

[817] The genitive construction here is thus epexegetical/appositional, in which hope = righteousness (so also Zerwick, *Biblical Greek*, 17). Another possibility is objective, in which righteousness would be the object of the believer's hope. The difference in meaning is negligible.

[818] See discussion in Biblical Theology §6.3.3.

[819] Thus this dative expresses agency. Wallace (*Greek Grammar*, 163–66) prefers means, arguing that calling datives such as these agency rather than means reveals an assumption by commentators that the author has in view the divine personhood of the Spirit. But Wallace's definition of the dative agency is unnecessarily restrictive; see the helpful counterpoints in Andreas J. Köstenberger, Benjamin L. Merkle, and Robert L. Plummer, *Going Deeper with New Testament Greek: An Intermediate Study of the Grammar and Syntax of the New Testament* (Nashville: B&H Academic, 2016), 132–33. Porter (*Idioms of the Greek New Testament*, 98–99) argues that making distinctions between instrument, agency, cause, means, and manner is often so difficult as to be unhelpful.

to Abraham (3:14). As children of promise, believers have been "born as a result of the Spirit" (4:29), so it should come as no surprise that the Spirit is also the one who empowers our hope that we will in fact be declared righteous on the last day. By mentioning the Spirit here, Paul is also setting the stage for his explanation of what the Spirit does in and through the life of the believer (5:16–26). From a human angle, believers eagerly wait "by faith" (ἐκ πίστεως). The same faith in Christ that justifies believers (2:16; 3:8, 11, 24) also sustains hope in the full realization of that justification on the last day. In Greek these two phrases "through the Spirit" and "by faith" are placed at the beginning of the sentence for emphasis.

As believers, our entire experience of the Christian life is based on faith and the work of the Spirit. It was through our initial faith in Jesus Christ that we received the Spirit (3:2, 14). It is through faith that we continue to experience the work of the Spirit and grow in Christlikeness (3:5). It is by faith that we are sons of God (3:26), and because we are sons, we have the Spirit of God's Son dwelling in us (4:6). And it is by faith and through the Spirit that we eagerly await the hope of righteousness (5:5). From beginning to end, the Christian life is experienced by faith and through the Spirit.[820]

5:6. Paul now provides a final explanatory point to support his argument in 5:2–5 that those who take on circumcision to pursue justification by the law are alienated from Christ: "For in Christ Jesus neither circumcision nor uncircumcision accomplishes anything" (ἐν γὰρ Χριστῷ Ἰησοῦ οὔτε περιτομή τι ἰσχύει οὔτε ἀκροβυστία).[821] The expression "in Christ" (ἐν ... Χριστῷ) establishes the context in which the statement that follows is true. By faith believers are placed within the realm/sphere that Christ rules over.[822] In Christ believers have freedom from the law's demands (2:4), are justified (2:17), receive the blessing promised to Abraham (3:14), are sons of God (3:26), and are united across ethnicity, socioeconomic

---

[820] Longenecker (*Galatians*, 228–29) contends that 5:5–6a provides a concise summary of what Paul has argued in 2:15–4:11 with the emphasis on the Spirit, faith, eager expectation of righteousness on the last day, being in Christ, and the irrelevance of circumcision; see similarly de Boer, *Galatians*, 315.

[821] The γάρ that introduces this clause could explain the claim of 5:5 or 5:4–5. But since 5:6 seems to have a summarizing force, it seems best to see it referring all the way back to 5:2. As such it provides the gospel alternative to taking up the yoke of the law and pursuing justification through obedience to it.

[822] So also Campbell, *Paul and Union with Christ*, 145–46.

status, and gender (3:28).[823] So also in Christ "neither circumcision nor uncircumcision accomplishes anything" (οὔτε περιτομή τι ἰσχύει οὔτε ἀκροβυστία). The verb rendered "accomplish" (ἰσχύω) has the sense of having "requisite personal resources to accomplish something."[824] The opponents were in effect claiming that circumcision (understood as the first step in keeping the Mosaic law) could accomplish justification before God on the last day. Not only does Paul deny the efficacy of circumcision; he rejects the entire framework within which circumcision and uncircumcision matter. As he will note later in a very similar vein: "For both circumcision and uncircumcision mean nothing; what matters instead is a new creation" (6:15). The categories of circumcision and uncircumcision are part of the present evil age, a relic of the elementals that have been done away with through the coming of Christ.

What does have the power, then, to empower the believer's eager expectation as they wait for the hope of righteousness? The answer is "faith working through love" (πίστις δι' ἀγάπης ἐνεργουμένη).[825] The faith in Christ that results in the initial justification of the believer at conversion does not remain dormant, as if its job were finished. Genuine saving faith continues to "work" (ἐνεργέω) in the life of the believer.[826] This is the same verb Paul uses in Philippians 2:13, where he writes that "it is God who is working in you both to will and to work according to his good

---

[823] DeSilva (Handbook, 106) notes that Paul's rationale here "draws an inference on the basis of premises established in 2:15–16 (Jewish Christians agree that trusting Jesus is necessary to attain righteousness before God); 2:21 (works of the Torah are, in fact, antithetical to trusting in the efficacy of Jesus' death); 3:1–5 (the Holy Spirit was granted to those who trust regardless of the condition of their foreskin); 3:14 (Christ died specifically to make this grant possible); 3:23–4:11 (circumcision along with the rest of the Torah's statutes, belongs to a time that has come to a decisive end); and 3:28 (in Christ there is neither Jew nor Greek, a distinction upheld by the rite of circumcision)."

[824] BDAG s.v. ἰσχύω 2. This classification makes better sense than BDAG's own assessment, which places Gal 5:6 under the category "have meaning, be valid, be in force" (4). While it is no doubt true that Paul believes that neither circumcision nor uncircumcision are in force when it comes to relating to God, his point goes beyond that to insist that neither of those states has the power/ability to accomplish justification. The use of the verb ἐνεργέω in the contrasting clause that follows confirms this sense.

[825] The ἀλλά that introduces this clause signals the sharp contrast between relying on the inability of circumcision or uncircumcision and the gospel alternative: faith working through love.

[826] The present tense of the participle here portrays the work as ongoing/continuous in nature.

purpose."[827] Through the Holy Spirit God uses the gifts he has given to his people (1 Cor 12:6, 11). In fact, God is able to do far more than we can ask or imagine "according to the power that works in us" (Eph 3:20). Faith in Christ works in the life of the believer "through love" (δι' ἀγάπης),[828] which likely encompasses both love for God and love for others. Of course, such love is only possible because Christ loved us and gave himself for us (2:20). That we are on the right track is suggested by the parallel expression in 1 Corinthians 7:19, where Paul writes, "Circumcision does not matter and uncircumcision does not matter. Keeping God's commands is what matters." Faith working through love expresses itself in obedience to God's will. In 5:13–15 Paul will further unpack what it looks like for faith to express itself through love.

The power to obey God was one of the great promises of the new covenant (Ezek 36:26–27). As we trust in Christ and rely on the power of his Spirit, we are empowered to love others in self-sacrificial ways that resemble Christ's own love for us. Knowing and believing this enables us to love even those who are difficult to love. After all, we follow a Savior who loved us even when we were his enemies (Rom 5:8).

Bridge

In this paragraph we see one of the great Pauline triads at work: faith, hope, and love. As believers it is our faith that justifies us before a holy God and our faith that sustains us as we live in this present evil age. Our hope is fixed on the day when God will set every wrong thing right in a new creation. In the meantime, it is the combination of faith and hope that the Spirit uses to empower us to love others as Christ loved us and gave himself for us (cf. 2:20).

B. JUDGMENT WILL COME ON THE TROUBLEMAKERS (5:7–12)

> [7] You were running well. Who prevented you from being persuaded regarding the truth? [8] This persuasion does not come from the one who calls you. [9] A little leaven leavens the whole batch of dough. [10] I myself

---

[827] Within the NT ἐνεργέω is predominantly a Pauline word; all but three (Matt 14:2; Mark 6:14; Jas 5:16) of the twenty-one occurrences are in his letters. He regularly uses this verb in connection with supernatural activity.

[828] As used here the preposition διά indicates that love is the efficient cause (BDAG s.v. A.3.d) or the means by which faith accomplishes its work (DeSilva, *Handbook*, 107).

am persuaded in the Lord you will not accept any other view. But whoever it is that is confusing you will pay the penalty. [11] Now brothers and sisters, if I still preach circumcision, why am I still persecuted? In that case the offense of the cross has been abolished. [12] I wish those who are disturbing you might also let themselves be mutilated!

Context

Now that Paul has explained that circumcision and the Mosaic law cannot compare to the Spirit-empowered faith, hope, and love experienced through the gospel (5:2–6), the apostle reminds them of their initial experience with the true gospel of grace as the grounds for calling them to remain true to it (5:7–12). In the midst of his intense frustration with the opponents, Paul expresses his confidence that the Galatians will come to their senses.

Structure

Paul's style reflects the intensity of his concern, as 5:7–10a has a string of clauses that lack a connecting particle (asyndeton), creating a rapid-fire staccato effect. Despite not being a tightly argued paragraph, broadly speaking it falls into two sections. In the first half of the paragraph Paul focuses on the Galatians (5:7–10a). While affirming their strong start in the gospel, Paul marvels that the opponents have steered the Galatians away from the truth (5:7). Echoing what he said in 1:6–10, Paul insists that these opponents have not been sent by the God who called them into his grace (5:8). Instead they are like yeast that starts small but eventually can infect the entire congregation (5:9). Yet despite his concern about the situation in Galatia, Paul is confident that the Galatians will remain true to the gospel and ultimately reject the views of the opponents (5:10a). In the second half of the paragraph Paul turns his attention to the false teachers (5:10b–12). Paul begins by expressing his confidence that regardless of who the opponents are they will one day face God's judgment (5:10b). In response to the opponents' claim that in other contexts Paul does preach circumcision, the apostle insists that if that were the case, he would not experience the persecution that he does (5:11). At this point Paul's frustration boils to the surface in a wish that the opponents would mutilate themselves (5:12).

5:7. Paul shifts again from theological argumentation to personally address the Galatians. Just as he did in 4:12–14, he refers to their past as a means of motivating them to remain faithful in the present and the future: "You were running well" (Ἐτρέχετε καλῶς). Paul has already used running as a metaphor for gospel ministry in 2:2 (compare Phil 2:16), but here it is a metaphor for the Christian life.[829] Paul uses this same imagery in 1 Corinthians 9:24–27, where he calls believers to run the race of the Christian life with self-control so that they may win the imperishable prize of eternal life. The imperfect tense of the verb here portrays the running as an ongoing action in the past. The Galatians had gotten off to a good start in living the Christian life on the basis of faith in Christ and empowered by the Holy Spirit.

But in light of the influence of the opponents and the growing threat that their false teaching poses to the Galatians, Paul asks, "Who prevented you from being persuaded regarding the truth?" (τίς ὑμᾶς ἐνέκοψεν [τῇ] ἀληθείᾳ μὴ πείθεσθαι). The apostle engages in a play on words, as the verb translated "prevented" (ἐγκόπτω) comes from a word family that can have the sense of cut into something.[830] Thus the false teachers are portrayed as outsiders who have jumped into the race and cut the Galatians off through their promotion of circumcision (i.e., the cutting off of the foreskin). But the use of this same verb in 1 Thessalonians 2:18 in connection with Satan preventing Paul from visiting the Thessalonians may hint that Satan himself is behind the efforts of the false teachers in Galatia.[831]

By cutting in on the Galatians, the opponents have tried to prevent them "from being persuaded regarding the truth" ([τῇ] ἀληθείᾳ μὴ πείθεσθαι).[832] Another way to translate this clause is "from obeying the

---

[829] The classic study of this theme is V. C. Pfitzner, *Paul and the Agon Motif. Traditional Athletic Imagery in the Pauline Literature*, NovTSup 16 (Leiden: Brill, 1967).

[830] See the entry for ἐγκόπτω in *NIDNTTE* 2:81–82. Although all five NT occurrences (Acts 24:4; Rom 15:22; Gal 5:7; 1 Thess 2:18; 1 Pet 3:7) have the sense of hinder or prevent (BDAG s.v. ἐγκόπτω), the reference to running and the discussion of circumcision in the surrounding context of Gal 5:7 suggest Paul is engaging in wordplay. Recognizing this wordplay, the NIV renders this clause "who cut in on you?" This word does not occur in the LXX, Philo, the OT Pseudepigrapha, or the Apostolic Fathers. The two occurrences in Josephus (*War* 1:629; *Ant.* 6:111) refer to conversation being interrupted. For use in Greco-Roman literature, see the entries in BDAG and LSJM.

[831] Similarly Das, *Galatians*, 533.

[832] After this clause, a few witnesses (F G ar b vg^s; Lcf Pel) have μηδενι πειθεσθε, which when taken in conjunction with what follows in 5:8 results in the following translation: "obey no one in such a way as to disobey the truth; such obedience/persuasion is not from him who calls you" (see discussion in BDF §488.1). But this additional phrase is best understood as a later scribal attempt to smooth over the difficulty of the text.

truth" (compare ESV, NIV, NASB). At issue is how best to render the verb πείθω, which in the passive voice can either mean "be persuaded, believe" or "obey, follow."[833] The difficulty, however, rests in English rather than Greek. Whereas in English we tend to think of persuade or believe as intellectual acts/states that do not necessarily lead to action, that distinction is rarely present in Greek. To be persuaded or to believe was to act accordingly in light of that persuasion/belief, and that is likely the sense here.[834] A helpful example is the use of this verb in Acts 5:36, where Gamaliel, describing the movement led by Theudas, notes that after his death "all his followers [ἐπείθοντο] were dispersed." As his followers, they were both persuaded by what Theudas said and thus obeyed by following him. The use of the verb here in Galatians 5:7 likely has a similar sense. Paul's question, then, is addressing both the change of mind the opponents are seeking to produce through their teaching and the practical actions that flow from it. The "truth" (ἀλήθεια) in view here is the one true gospel that God revealed to Paul and he faithfully preached to the Galatians, in contrast to the "other" gospel that his opponents were propagating (1:6–9, 11–17; 2:5, 14; 4:12–20).

Hindrances to believing and obeying the truth of the gospel are just as present today as in the first century. Whether the hindrance is false teaching or the pleasures of this world, believers must be vigilant and diligent to run the race of the Christian life by faith in Christ and in the power of the Holy Spirit.

5:8. Paul does not hold back what he thinks of this development: "This persuasion does not come from the one who calls you" (ἡ πεισμονὴ οὐκ ἐκ τοῦ καλοῦντος ὑμᾶς). The rare word "persuasion" (πεισμονή) comes from the same word family as the verb "persuaded" (πείθω) in the previous verse.[835] The "persuasion" that keeping the Mosaic law is necessary for justification on the last day did not come from God, who is described as

---

[833] See BDAG s.v. πείθω 3. The present tense of the infinitive here suggests that Paul has in view continuing in their persuasion/obedience. The Galatians have begun down the path of persuasion/obedience, but that is now in question.

[834] Although BDAG classifies the use of πείθω here in Gal 5:7 under "obey, follow" (3.b), it acknowledges a third possibility that "some passages stand between a and b and permit either translation" (3.c). Given the context it seems Gal 5:7 fits better in this third hybrid category.

[835] This is the earliest known use of the noun πεισμονή in Greek literature. Witherington (*Grace in Galatia*, 371) notes that Epiphanius, a bishop writing in the fourth century, uses this term in connection with empty rhetoric (*Adv. Haer.* 30.21.2).

"the one who calls you" (τοῦ καλοῦντος ὑμᾶς). In 1:6 Paul used similar language to describe the Galatians' conversion as a result of God calling them by the grace of Christ; here Paul uses the language to describe the ongoing call of God to persevere in the faith until the end.[836] Paul describes this same reality in Philippians 3:14 when he writes, "I pursue as my goal the prize promised by God's heavenly call in Christ Jesus." Paul insists that God does not call his people to their final reward on the last day through keeping the Mosaic law; instead, they must continue to put their faith into action through love, empowered by the Spirit.

False teachers often use smooth sounding words and elements of the truth to persuade people. Behind these efforts are the work of Satan himself, who "disguises himself as an angel of light" (2 Cor 11:14). Recognizing that spiritual powers of evil are behind false teaching should motivate us to pray for the Spirit of God to expose falsehood and confirm the truth of God's word.

5:9. Lest the Galatians think the efforts of the opponents are inconsequential, Paul reminds them "A little leaven leavens the whole batch of dough" (μικρὰ ζύμη ὅλον τὸ φύραμα ζυμοῖ). In the Old Testament, leaven is always mentioned in connection with the Passover and the Festival of Unleavened Bread (e.g., Exod 12:15–20; 13:3–10) or with the sacrificial system (e.g., Lev 2:11; 6:14–18). "The physical phenomenon of infiltration, as the yeast fungus multiplies throughout its medium, provides the basis for a symbolic use of leaven or yeast."[837] This symbolic use is prominent in the New Testament.[838] The kingdom of heaven is likened to leaven that is placed in flour and eventually leavens the entire batch of flour (Matt 13:33). Jesus refers to the teaching of the Pharisees as leaven that his disciples should avoid (Matt 16:11–12), and Paul seems to use the imagery in a similar fashion here in Galatians 5:6.[839] The teaching and influence of

---

[836] Whereas in 1:6 Paul uses the aorist participle (καλέσαντος) to refer to God's initial call in conversion, here in 5:8 he uses the present participle (καλοῦντος) to describe God's ongoing call to finish the race of the Christian life (so also DeSilva, *Handbook*, 109).

[837] Ryken et al., *Dictionary of Biblical Imagery*, 499.

[838] The symbolic use of leaven is also found in Jewish literature outside of the New Testament. Philo uses the imagery in a variety of ways, including as a symbol of luxury (*Cong.* 1:161), pride (*Spec.* 1:293), and lust (*QE* 2:14); see the summary in *TDNT* 2:904–5. Silva (*NIDNTTE* 2:363–64) notes that in the rabbinic literature it symbolized human restraints on obeying God or the Torah's power to lead observant Israelites back to God.

[839] Although one cannot be sure, it certainly seems possible that Paul's use of the imagery here reflects his knowledge of Jesus' use of the imagery, though likely in oral form since

the opponents may have started small, but if left unchecked it threatens to spread to the point where it infests the entire church. The imagery here may also work on a second level as well. In 1 Corinthians 5:6–8 Paul uses this same proverbial statement to warn about the dangers of sin, which may start small but if left unaddressed can expand in its severity and scope. As a result, believers should live out their identity as those who have been redeemed by Christ the Passover lamb and put away the sinful leaven that threatens their individual and corporate spiritual lives.

False teaching often starts with a seemingly small departure from biblical truth. Left unchecked, however, it regularly leads down the path of greater and greater lies and deception. While each believer is responsible to evaluate what they hear against what the Bible says, God has appointed elders within the church to identify, confront, and correct false teaching in the church (Titus 1:9–16).

5:10. Despite the serious threat that the opponents pose to the spiritual health of the Galatians, Paul again expresses optimism that the Galatians will come to their senses: "I myself am persuaded in the Lord you will not accept any other view" (ἐγὼ πέποιθα εἰς ὑμᾶς ἐν κυρίῳ ὅτι οὐδὲν ἄλλο φρονήσετε).[840] Whereas the Galatians are in danger of being persuaded (πείθεσθαι) to abandon the truth of the gospel (5:7) by a persuasion (πεισμονή) that does not come from God, Paul is "persuaded" (πέποιθα) otherwise. Such a translation preserves the wordplay, but another way of rendering this verb is with the stronger sense of "I have confidence" (cf. ESV). This confidence is "in the Lord" (ἐν κυρίῳ) rather than in the Galatians themselves.[841] Based on the work of the Spirit in

---

the Gospels were likely not yet written at the time he wrote Galatians. For a helpful treatment of possible allusions/echoes of Jesus tradition in Paul's letters (though he does not mention Gal 5:9), see Craig Blomberg, "Quotations, Allusions, and Echoes of Jesus in Paul," in *Studies in the Pauline Epistles: Essays in Honor of Douglas J. Moo*, ed. Matthew S. Harmon and Jay E. Smith (Grand Rapids: Zondervan, 2014), 129–43.

[840] To signal this shift to his own perspective, Paul uses the emphatic pronoun ἐγώ. Woodenly this clause could be rendered "I myself have confidence toward you in the Lord." The CSB, along with most English versions, simply omits translating the phrase "toward you" (εἰς ὑμᾶς), though the NASB and KJV do include it. In effect Paul is saying that he has confidence directed toward/with respect to the Galatians that is rooted in the Lord and his character as faithful to his promises and his people.

[841] Paul uses a similar construction (a form of πείθω with the prepositional phrase ἐν κυρίῳ) in Rom 14:14; Phil 1:14; 2:24; 2 Thess 3:4 to express confidence in the Lord about a situation.

their midst as evidence of their conversion, Paul seems confident that "he who started a good work in you will carry it on to completion until the day of Christ Jesus" (Phil 1:6).[842] The content of that confidence is that "you will not accept any other view" (ὅτι οὐδὲν ἄλλο φρονήσετε). The force of what Paul says here is likely stronger than what this translation suggests. The apostle uses the verb φρονέω, which, although it can have the sense of hold a view, often has the stronger sense of having a mind-set or what we might refer to today as a worldview.[843] Paul uses similar language in Philippians 3:15, where after explaining the proper mindset of the believer he expresses confidence that "if you think differently about anything, God will reveal this also to you."[844] Undergoing circum-cision and taking on the yoke of the Mosaic law is not a minor tweak or a slightly different view, but in effect a completely different approach to relating to God.

Paul's confidence extends beyond the fate of the Galatians to that of the opponents as well: "But whoever it is that is confusing you will pay the penalty" (ὁ δὲ ταράσσων ὑμᾶς βαστάσει τὸ κρίμα, ὅστις ἐὰν ᾖ).[845] The verb rendered "confusing" (ταράσσω) is the same one translated "troubling" in 1:7, where it refers to the actions of the opponents. As noted there, the verb refers to causing a state of inner turmoil and may be a subtle echo of Achan bringing trouble on Israel by wrongfully taking items God had set apart for destruction during the conquest of Jericho (1 Chr 2:7). But whereas in 1:7 he refers to plural "troublers," here in 5:10 he speaks of an individual "troubler." The switch seems to narrow Paul's focus here to the leader of the opponents in Galatia, though by adding the expression "whoever it is" (ὅστις ἐὰν ᾖ) he may be indicating a measure of uncertainty as to who this leader is. Alternatively, Paul could be indi-cating that the identity of the leader is ultimately irrelevant.[846]

---

[842] In Phil 1:6 Paul uses a form of the same verb (πείθω) as is here in Gal 5:10.

[843] See BDAG s.v. φρονέω. The future tense of the verb here could have a temporal force (i.e., the Galatians will eventually come around to the right mindset) or instead commu-nicate certainty.

[844] Paul uses the verb φρονέω but uses a form of ἕτερος rather than ἄλλος, a variation which makes little difference.

[845] The δέ that introduces this clause signals a further development in the argument; see similarly DeSilva, Handbook, 110.

[846] Also possible is the view of Schreiner (Galatians, 325), who concludes that the singular form is simply generic and thus refers to the adversaries as a whole.

In either case, the apostle singles out the leader to indicate that he "will pay the penalty" (βαστάσει τὸ κρίμα), or perhaps more precisely, "will bear the judgment." The verb in question (βαστάζω) has the sense of "sustain a burden" and is used in this very sense later in the letter (6:2, 5, 17).[847] By trying to persuade others to take upon themselves the burden of the yoke of the Mosaic law (compare Acts 15:10; Sir 6:24–25), the leader of the opponents will one day bear the weight/burden of "judgment" (κρίμα). Although some have suggested that this simply refers to some form of discipline or excommunication from the church, the parallels to 1:6–9 indicate that eternal condemnation is in view. Although Paul does use this same word for human judgment (1 Cor 6:7), his predominant use of the word refers to divine judgment on the last day (Rom 2:2–3; 3:8; 5:16; 11:33; 1 Tim 5:12). By preaching a different gospel, all of the opponents—including their leader—will be eternally condemned (1:6–9).

In the midst of troubling circumstances in the church, it can be easy to become pessimistic. Yet Paul models for us a deep and abiding confidence in God's power to preserve his people and bring judgment on his enemies. All who are in ministry, regardless of their natural temperament, need to cultivate a similar perspective in ministry.

5:11. In what amounts to a surprising twist in the argument, Paul appears to address a charge that the opponents were making about him by asking a question: "Now brothers and sisters, if I still preach circumcision, why am I still persecuted?" (Ἐγὼ δέ, ἀδελφοί, εἰ περιτομὴν ἔτι κηρύσσω, τί ἔτι διώκομαι).[848] Although we cannot be certain, it seems that Paul's opponents claimed that at least in other contexts besides Galatia Paul in fact preached circumcision.[849] Perhaps they argued that Paul held back preaching circumcision out of fear that gentiles would turn away from the gospel. Or perhaps the opponents simply presented themselves and their message as the completion of what Paul himself would have preached if

---

[847] See BDAG s.v. βαστάζω 2.

[848] The δέ that introduces this question marks it off as a new development in the argument. The personal pronoun ἐγώ is emphatic, drawing the contrast between Paul and his opponents.

[849] Paul's word choice here is pointed; the verb "preach" (κηρύσσω) is the same one he used in 2:2 to describe his own preaching of the true gospel. Based on dating the letter after the Jerusalem Council, Dunn (*Galatians*, 279–80) suggests the possibility that the opponents knew of Paul's decision to circumcise Timothy (Acts 16:1–5) and are pointing out what they perceive to be an obvious inconsistency in Paul's message and practice. But this later date is unlikely; see Introduction 2–14.

he had remained in Galatia. While the word "still" (ἔτι) could suggest that Paul acknowledges at one time preaching a message of circumcision plus the gospel like his opponents, it seems more likely that Paul is referring to his pre-conversion promotion of obedience to the Mosaic law (cf. 1:14).[850]

Regardless of the precise circumstances, Paul highlights two inconsistencies that follow if this were in fact true.[851] The first is in the form of a question: "why am I still persecuted" (τί ἔτι διώκομαι). This is the same verb (διώκω) Paul used in 1:13, 23 to describe his own efforts to destroy the church and the gospel it proclaimed. But Paul insists that the consistent persecution he faces should make it evident that under no circumstances does he advocate circumcision and observing the Mosaic law for followers of Jesus.

The second inconsistency that follows if Paul were in fact preaching circumcision is that "In that case the offense of the cross has been abolished" (ἄρα κατήργηται τὸ σκάνδαλον τοῦ σταυρου).[852] The word rendered "offense" (σκάνδαλον) is common in the New Testament, used in the sense of "that which causes offense or revulsion and results in opposition, disapproval, or hostility."[853] Paul consistently uses this word to refer to realities that cause people to reject the truth of the gospel, usually in reference to Jews (Rom 9:33; 11:9) but sometimes broadened out to include gentiles as well (Rom 16:17; 1 Cor 1:23).[854] Here the source of the offense is the cross (σταυρός), a shorthand way of referring to the death of Jesus as the means by which redemption is accomplished.[855] The cross is an offense or stumbling block because it requires one to humbly acknowledge the insufficiency of all other means of being justified,

---

[850] See similarly DeSilva, *Handbook*, 111; Moo, *Galatians*, 336–37; for a helpful summary of the various views, see Das (*Galatians*, 536–40), who ultimately concludes Paul refers to his pre-conversion preaching.

[851] Paul uses a first class conditional statement, in which the "if" clause is assumed true for the sake of the argument.

[852] The particle ἄρα introduces the apodosis (the "then" clause") of the conditional statement; on this use see Beale, Ross, and Brendsel, *Interpretive Lexicon*, 31.

[853] BDAG s.v. σκάνδαλον 3. The expression "offense of the cross" is likely a genitive of apposition, in which the offense = the cross; see similarly Moo, *Galatians*, 337.

[854] Six of the fifteen NT occurrences are in Paul. The prominence of this word family in the NT likely stems from its occurrence in Isa 28:16 (LXX), which is cited by both Paul (Rom 9:33) and Peter (1 Pet 2:6).

[855] Thus the genitive indicates origin. Another possibility is an epexegetical genitive, where the offense is the cross (so DeSilva, *Handbook*, 111). The difference in meaning is insignificant.

including observing the Mosaic law. If Paul were in fact preaching circumcision then the offense of the cross would be abolished (καταργέω), done away with. Paul's point is that the centrality of the cross for a right standing before God is nullified when it is combined with circumcision because part of the scandal of the cross is that it proclaims the insufficiency of the law to justify or bring life.

Knowing when and how to respond to false charges against you can be challenging. We serve a Savior who was falsely charged and never defended himself. But when the charges go to the core of the gospel message, we are often left with no choice but to respond.

5:12. Paul's anger and frustration toward the opponents comes to a head as he exclaims: "I wish those who are disturbing you might also let themselves be mutilated!" (Ὄφελον καὶ ἀποκόψονται οἱ ἀναστατοῦντες ὑμᾶς).[856] Instead of describing the opponents as those troubling the Galatians, here he refers to them as "those who are disturbing you" (οἱ ἀναστατοῦντες ὑμᾶς). Paul uses a verb (ἀναστατόω) that has the sense of upsetting the stability of a person or group.[857] The rioting crowds in Thessalonica use this verb to describe the early Christians as the "men who have turned the world upside down" (Acts 17:6).[858] While it is unlikely Paul is indicating there were physical riots that the opponents had provoked, his word choice here does highlight the severity of the turmoil the opponents are creating by advocating obedience to the Mosaic law.

The verb translated "let themselves be mutilated" (ἀποκόψονται) could also be rendered "cut themselves off."[859] In essence Paul is wishing

---

[856] By using the particle ὄφελον with a future indicative verb, Paul introduces this as a wish that is attainable (BDF §384).

[857] BDAG s.v. ἀναστατόω.

[858] The only other NT occurrence is Acts 21:38, where a Roman soldier inquires whether Paul is the Egyptian who "started a revolt some time ago." The single LXX occurrence is Dan 7:23, where it describes the fourth beast in the vision upsetting/disturbing the whole earth. It is absent from Josephus and Philo, though used in Greco-Roman literature with the sense of disturb, destroy, or even drive out; see examples listed in LSJM s.v. ἀναστατόω and MM, 38.

[859] Wallace (*Greek Grammar*, 423–24) describes Paul's use of the middle voice as a causative middle, in which "the subject has something done for or to himself or herself ... The difference between the causative active and causative middle is that the causative active simply implies the source behind an action, while the causative middle implies both source and results: The action was caused by someone who also was the recipient of its outcome in some sense. The causative middle is thus an indirect middle or occasionally a direct middle as well."

his opponents would castrate themselves. The apostle is saying that if the opponents are so committed to circumcision, why stop with cutting off the foreskin? If removing the foreskin is so valuable, why not go all the way and cut off the entire male sexual organ?[860] This same verb is used in Deuteronomy 23:1 (23:2 LXX) to prohibit a man whose genitalia has been mutilated or crushed from entering the assembly of the Lord.[861] For a man who grew up as a devout Jew, Paul's words are shocking, given the importance of circumcision for Jewish identity. But in light of the Christ event, Paul now realizes that when circumcision is promoted as essential to justification, it in fact becomes mutilation (compare Phil 3:2–3). And by promoting circumcision the opponents are actually putting themselves outside the eschatological assembly of the Lord—the church, composed of Jew and gentile alike.

Paul's words may be shocking to us in an age that promotes "tolerance" as the highest virtue, but when matters of eternity were at stake, Paul was not afraid to use cutting language to drive home the severity of his opponents' error.

Bridge

Jesus promised that during the period between his first and second coming there would be false teachers (Matt 24:24–26). In a culture that prizes

---

[860] Castration was practiced in the ancient world in connection with the worship of various deities, including Cybele. As a general rule the practice was considered abhorrent by Jew and gentile alike. Jesus himself refers to eunuchs who make themselves such for the kingdom of God (Matt 19:12) but does not seem to make a value judgment on the practice. Jewish thought on this practice was rather clear, however; it was widely condemned and even compared to murdering one's own children (1QSa 2:5–6; 4QmmT B.39–44; Josephus, *Ant.* 4:290–91, Philo, *Spec.* 1:325; m. Yebam. 8:2; Gen. Rab. 34:8). For a helpful and concise summary of castration in the ancient world with respect to its practice in both secular and religious contexts, see Keener, *Galatians*, 471–75. Several commentators note that in Galatia every spring there was a festival celebrating Attis, the consort of Cybele, who after being unfaithful castrated himself to demonstrate his desire never to be unfaithful again; see, e.g., Das, *Galatians*, 542–43.

[861] Four of the remaining five LXX occurrences of the verb refer to cutting off body parts or clothes (Deut 25:12; Judg 1:6–7; 2 Sam 10:4) while one refers to God cutting off his steadfast love forever (Ps 76:9). Four of the other NT occurrences refer to cutting off body parts (Mark 9:43, 45; John 18:10, 26), while one refers to cutting ropes from a ship (Acts 27:32). Eleven of the twenty-five occurrences in Josephus refer to cutting off body parts (*Ant.* 14:464; *Wars* 1:507; 2:246, 642, 644; 3:378, 527; 6:164; *Life* 1:147, 177). Although Philo's use of the verb is usually figurative, he does use this verb in his discussion of Num 5:2 and Deut 23:2 to explain the prohibition against mutilated men entering God's assembly (*Leg.* 3:8).

tolerance above all else, it can be tempting to avoid confronting false teaching. Since doctrine divides, why not just love Jesus? But without doctrine, who is the Jesus that we claim to love? It may not be easy or pleasant, but one of the key roles of elders in the church is to identify, confront, and correct false teaching in the church. The ongoing perseverance of God's people in the true gospel is at stake.

C. FREEDOM TO SERVE OTHERS IN LOVE (5:13–15)

> [13] For you were called to be free, brothers and sisters; only don't use this freedom as an opportunity for the flesh, but serve one another through love. [14] For the whole law is fulfilled in one statement: Love your neighbor as yourself. [15] But if you bite and devour one another, watch out, or you will be consumed by one another.

Context

The γάρ that begins this paragraph resumes the train of thought from 5:1, where Paul concluded his lengthy theological argument (3:1–5:1) with the assertion that Christ freed his people to live in freedom. But what is the nature of that freedom? And how should it shape the Christian life? Those are the questions Paul addresses in this paragraph.

Structure

After restating the call to freedom (5:13a), Paul uses a chiasm to contrast what true gospel freedom is and is not (5:13b–15):

5:13b		What freedom is not: an opportunity to indulge the flesh
	5:13c	What freedom produces: serving others through love
	5:14	What freedom produces: fulfillment of the law through love for neighbor
5:15		What freedom is not: an opportunity to indulge the flesh, which leads to destruction in the body

Stated negatively, freedom is not a pretense to indulge the flesh and engage in activities that destroy the body of Christ (5:13b, 15). Instead, true biblical freedom enables God's people to serve others through love and in so doing fulfill the ultimate goal of the law itself (5:13c–14). To support this claim Paul quotes Leviticus 19:18 as a summary of the whole Mosaic law, which Jesus also quotes as one of the two commandments that summarize the law (Matt 22:38–42).

5:13. Resuming the theme of freedom (5:1) after his personal appeal to the Galatians (5:2–12), Paul reminds them, "For you were called to be free, brothers and sisters" (Ὑμεῖς γὰρ ἐπ᾽ ἐλευθερίᾳ ἐκλήθητε, ἀδελφοί).⁸⁶² Whereas in 5:1 Paul speaks of freedom as a reality that believers experience, here in 5:13 it is an ideal that believers are called to live out. The use of the pronoun "you" (Ὑμεῖς) shifts the discussion from the false teachers and highlights the contrast between the opponents and the Galatians. He again returns to the fact that God called the Galatians, a term that stresses God's sovereign summons to be part of his people (1:6, 15; 5:8). The freedom in view is that which comes from the work of Jesus, the seed of Abraham and servant of the Lord, who through his death and resurrection has brought the eschatological people of God into existence (4:21–5:1).

But since the concept of freedom could easily be misunderstood, Paul first clarifies what freedom does not entail: "only don't use this freedom as an opportunity for the flesh" (μόνον μὴ τὴν ἐλευθερίαν εἰς ἀφορμὴν τῇ σαρκί).⁸⁶³ Just as today, in the ancient world there were a variety of different ways that the concept of freedom was understood.⁸⁶⁴ In political contexts the concept was connected with rights and benefits accorded to citizens of the *polis* (city). In philosophical discussions, the Cynics emphasized freedom from any human authority, being subject only to the gods. The Stoics used the term to describe a state of detachment from the world such that one's passions and external circumstances have no effect upon oneself. Still other philosophers (e.g., Epictetus) described freedom in terms of self-determination based on self-knowledge and rational insight.

---

⁸⁶² The γάρ that begins this clause seems to resume the assertion of 5:1 and introduce further explanation of that claim; see similarly DeSilva, *Handbook*, 113; Longenecker, *Galatians*, 238–39. Less likely is Burton's claim that it provides a reason for the content of verse 12 (*Galatians*, 291). The expression "to freedom" (ἐπ᾽ ἐλευθερίᾳ) could indicate destination but more likely communicates purpose ("you were called for the purpose of freedom"); see similarly Schreiner, *Galatians*, 333.

⁸⁶³ In Greek this clause does not have a verb, requiring the reader to supply one such as "use" (found in nearly all English translations). When used with the negative particle μή, the adverb μόνον that introduces this clause signals a limitation on the previous clause (BDAG s.v. μόνος 2.c.α).

⁸⁶⁴ For a discussion of these various kinds of freedom in the Greco-Roman world, see Heinrich Schlier, "ἐλεύθερος, ἐλευθερόω, ἐλευθερία, ἀπελεύθερος," in *TDNT* 2:487–96. The brief summary that follows depends in large part on this discussion.

And for still others at the popular level, freedom was perceived as a life free from any moral, ethical, or political restraints.

It is this last approach to freedom that Paul seeks to correct here. Having stressed that believers are not under the authority of the Mosaic law, the apostle must now make sure the Galatians understand that they are not free from any and all moral restraints. The freedom the gospel brings must not be considered "an opportunity for the flesh" (ἀφορμὴν τῇ σαρκί). By introducing this clause with the word "only" (μόνον), Paul signals the importance of this command, as if indicating that by simply doing this one thing other things will fall into place.[865] The word rendered "opportunity" (ἀφορμή) refers to "a base or circumstance from which other action becomes possible, such as the starting-point or base of operations for an expedition."[866] Paul uses this same word to describe sin seizing an opportunity through the commandment to bring death (Rom 7:8, 11). If the nature of the freedom that the gospel brings is misunderstood, it might be used as a base of operations for the flesh to produce a life of unrestrained immorality.[867] As used here, "flesh" (σάρξ) refers to humanity in its fallen state, with an emphasis on weakness and propensity toward sin and rebellion against God. It is personified as an enemy power, looking to establish a beachhead for its campaign to incite and encourage rebellion against God and his ways.

Instead of understanding freedom as an opportunity for the flesh, Paul exhorts the Galatians that true gospel freedom is the starting point to "serve one another through love" (ἀλλὰ διὰ τῆς ἀγάπης δουλεύετε ἀλλήλοις).[868] The present tense of the verb "serve" (δουλεύω) suggests an ongoing pattern of life; it is the same one Paul used earlier in Galatians to describe the state of slavery to the elements of this world/the law people experience before they are united to Christ by faith (4:8–9, 25).

---

[865] On the use of the adverb μόνον with negatives, see BDAG s.v. μόνος 2.c. Moo (*Galatians*, 343) rightly notes it has an adversative sense here in this context. Paul makes similar use of this adverb in Phil 1:27 to signal the importance of living as citizens of God's kingdom in a manner worthy of the gospel.

[866] BDAG s.v. ἀφορμή. All seven NT occurrences are found in Paul's letters (Rom 7:8, 11; 2 Cor 5:12; 11:12; Gal 5:13; 1 Tim 5:14). There are just three LXX occurrences (3 Macc 3:2; Prov 9:9; Ezek 5:7). The word is common in both Philo (39x) and Josephus (62x); for examples of usage in Greco-Roman literature, see LSJM s.v. ἀφορμή and MM, 292.

[867] Thus the expression τῇ σαρκί is a dative of advantage.

[868] The ἀλλά that introduces this clause signals the contrast between this clause and the previous one.

This wordplay makes it clear that gospel freedom is not the absence of obligation to live a certain way, but the power to live a certain way. True gospel freedom provides the opportunity and the power to live a life of ongoing service to others, with a specific focus on fellow believers.[869] This life of service to others is done not out of grim-faced duty, but rather "through love" (διὰ τῆς ἀγάπης). Because Christ loved us and gave himself for us (2:20), we are able to serve others through love, which itself is an outworking of our faith in Christ (5:6).

By using "serve" language, Paul may also be linking his exhortation here with his conviction that Christ is the Isaianic servant of the Lord who has set his people free from their slavery to sin/elementals/law through his sacrificial death and resurrection (see 1:4; 2:20; 3:13; 4:1-7; 4:21–5:1).[870] After describing the freedom that those redeemed by the servant will experience, Isaiah 54:17 states, "This is the heritage of the LORD's servants, and their vindication is from me."[871] The work of the suffering servant produces servants who are empowered by the same self-sacrificial love to serve others.[872] One of the great paradoxes of the Christian faith is that true freedom is only found in service to Christ and others.

Satan is a master at turning good gifts of God into weapons that lead to self-destruction. He did it with Adam and Eve in the garden, offering them freedom from the restraints that God had placed on them. The enemy does the same thing with us today, tempting us with freedom from God masked as Christian liberty to do as we please. But the gospel offers a better and truer kind of freedom—the freedom to live as God's image bearers.

5:14. Paul now moves to explain why serving one another through love is foundational to the Christian life: "For the whole law is fulfilled in

---

[869] Paul's use of the present tense of this verb here in 5:13 highlights the ongoing nature of the service. The word for "one another" (ἀλλήλων) consistently refers to fellow believers in the NT.

[870] See further Harmon, *She Must and Shall Go Free*, 205–9. What follows is a brief summary of the larger argument provided there. This connection is also noted by Oakes, *Galatians*, 170.

[871] In Isaiah 54:17 the word rendered "heritage" (נַחֲלָה) from the MT is translated in the LXX as "inheritance" (κληρονομία) to describe this reality, suggesting a further link to Paul's argument in Galatians. So too does the use of righteousness language (which the CSB renders "vindication"), which plays a prominent role here in Galatians.

[872] There may also be parallels to the original exodus, in which God's people were freed from their Egyptian bondage to serve Yahweh (Exod 4:23; 19:4–6; 20:1–6; Lev 25:42); see Wilson, "Wilderness Apostasy," 565–68.

one statement" (ὁ γὰρ πᾶς νόμος ἐν ἑνὶ λόγῳ πεπλήρωται).[873] Given Paul's argument that believers are not bound by the requirements of the Mosaic law, one might conclude that there is no foundation or are no constraints left for the Christian life. In response to such a concern, Paul gets to the heart of the Mosaic law by offering a summary of the entire law in one statement.[874] In offering this one statement, however, Paul goes beyond a simple summary. He insists that the law is "fulfilled" (πληρόω), a word that has the sense of something reaching its complete significance or full realization.[875] The perfect tense of this verb highlights that the law is in a state of fulfillment.[876] The point, then, is that the entire law finds its ultimate realization and fullest significance in the statement that follows.

That one statement is a citation of Leviticus 19:18, "Love your neighbor as yourself" (ἀγαπήσεις τὸν πλησίον σου ὡς σεαυτόν).[877] In its original context, Leviticus 19:18 concludes a section of various laws that prescribe how the Israelites were to treat one another, covering subjects such as caring for the poor, theft, conduct in legal disputes, and harboring hatred

---

[873] The γάρ that begins this clause has an explanatory force, further explaining why serving one another through love is so vital (similarly DeSilva, *Handbook*, 115).

[874] Whereas in 5:3 Paul uses the expression "the entire law" (ὅλον τὸν νόμον), here in 5:14 he uses the phrase "the whole law" (ὁ ... πᾶς νόμος). The difference between these two verses is less the exact phrase than it is the immediate context. In 5:3 Paul speaks of "doing" the entire law as an obligation for those who are circumcised, while here Paul speaks of "fulfilling" the whole law as an expression of the freedom the gospel brings; see further Schreiner, *Galatians*, 334–35.

[875] See the full range of meaning in BDAG s.v. πληρόω. Paul's use of fulfillment language is varied and complex; for a helpful overview, see Carson, "Mystery and Fulfillment," 393–436.

[876] Some manuscripts (D F G Ψ 0122. 630. 1505. 1881. 2464. 𝔐) have the present tense πληροῦται, which would portray the fulfillment as on ongoing process. But the perfect tense has strong and early support (𝔓⁴⁶ ℵ A B C 062ᵛⁱᵈ. 0254. 0278. 33. 81. 104. 326. 1175. 1241. 1739) and should be considered original.

[877] In Greek the syntax that introduces this citation is slightly unusual. The previous clause states the law is fulfilled "in one word" (ἐν ἑνὶ λόγῳ), and the citation is then woodenly introduced with the expression, "in this" (ἐν τῷ), with the definite article both referring back to the "one word" and at the same time referring forward to the OT citation that follows. Indeed, the article was sometimes used to introduce citations (see BDF §267; Robertson, *Grammar*, 766; Wallace, *Greek Grammar*, 238). It appears some scribes, likely misreading the syntax here, corrected the future indicative "love" to an infinitive, so that the resulting expression reads "when you love" (see, e.g., 𝔓⁴⁶). But the reading of NA28 matches the LXX and has strong and early textual support (ℵ A Bᶜ D L Ψ 1. 33. 1739, among many others). Instead of the reflexive pronoun σεαυτόν ("yourself"), some witnesses (e.g., 𝔓⁴⁶ F G H Ψ 1881) have εαυτόν ("himself"). Here too, however, the NA28 matches the LXX and has strong and early textual support (ℵ A B C D 1739, among many others).

or grudges (19:9–18). It functions as a basic summary of one's obligations to others, indicating that keeping the regulations that precede it is an expression of love. Love for neighbor is then further grounded in the statement "I am the LORD" (Lev 19:18), a reminder that love for one's neighbor is rooted in understanding who God is and what he has done for his people. Based on the fact that in the original context the "neighbor" in view is one's fellow Israelites, some have suggested that Paul is primarily concerned with Christians' love for fellow believers.[878] But in light of Paul's call in 6:10 for believers to "work for the good of all, especially for those who belong to the household of faith," it seems a broader reference is intended here in 5:14.[879] Paul cites this same verse in Romans 13:9 to support his claim that "the one who loves has fulfilled the law" (Rom 13:8). James also cites Leviticus 19:18 to condemn showing partiality within the body on the basis of status (Jas 2:8–9). Both likely are dependent on Jesus' own repeated use of this text to summarize the law (Matt 5:43–48; 19:19; 22:34–39; Mark 12:28–33; Luke 10:25–28).[880]

In addition to his familiarity with Jesus' teaching on love as the fulfillment of the law, Paul's viewpoint may also have been shaped by the promise of restoration in Deuteronomy 30. God had promised that when he restored his people from exile, he would circumcise their hearts so that they would love God with a whole heart (30:6), which would lead to them obeying the Lord and experiencing his blessing (30:16, 20).[881] In their conversion, believers have experienced a circumcision far more important than the removal of the foreskin; they have had their hearts

---

[878] See, e.g., de Boer, *Galatians*, 350.

[879] Moo, *Galatians*, 346.

[880] Philo also summarized the basic requirements of the law as loving God and loving others (*Decal.* 1:109–10); for a summary of similar Jewish summaries of the law, see W. D. Davies and Dale C. Allison, *A Critical and Exegetical Commentary on the Gospel According to Saint Matthew*, 3 vols.; ICC (New York: T&T Clark International, 2004), 243–45. Das (*Galatians*, 552) notes that with the exception of CD 9:2.7–8 there is little discussion of Lev 19:18 in Second Temple Jewish texts, though in the rabbinic literature there are a number of discussions of it, perhaps in response to Christian use of the text. He notes that the rabbis "employed Lev. 19:18 as a means of summarizing the main point of obeying the Law in its entirety; the various laws of Moses show how love expresses itself in concrete action." The lack of discussion about Lev 19:18 in Jewish texts that pre-date the time of Jesus further suggests that its prominence in the NT stems from a significant emphasis on it by Jesus himself.

[881] Given the prominence of sin, exile, and return from exile motifs here in Galatians, such a link is at least plausible; see Biblical Theology §1.2.3.

circumcised (Rom 2:29; Phil 3:3). As a result, they are able to fulfill the righteous requirement of the law by walking in the Spirit (Rom 8:4).[882] What the Mosaic law aimed for but could never produce, believers are able to experience because Christ has fulfilled the law on our behalf and now lives in us by his Spirit to empower us to love others with the love that he has first shown to us.[883]

At this point it is important to note that Paul here does not speak of doing or keeping the law, but rather fulfilling it. The apostle has been clear throughout the letter that believers are not under the obligation to do or keep the Mosaic law and its requirements. He has further insisted that the Mosaic law covenant works on a different principle (doing) from the Abrahamic promise (believing). Paul's point here is that by serving others through love, believers are able to live out the kind of life devoted to God that the Mosaic law commanded but could never produce in a person's life. Paul will return to this subject in 6:2 when he refers to the law of Christ. Furthermore, the Spirit plays a key role in this life of love that fulfills the intent of the law, which is why Paul deals extensively with the Spirit in the paragraph that follows (5:16–26).

Love is regularly misunderstood in our surrounding culture. It is considered a feeling that comes and goes, beyond our ability to control. But the Bible shows us that love is first and foremost a disposition of the will, an outworking of God's own love for us shown preeminently in the cross. No wonder Jesus said, "By this everyone will know that you are my disciples, if you love one another" (John 13:35).

5:15. The alternative to loving your neighbor as yourself is laid out in vivid terms, framed in the form of a conditional statement: "But if you bite and devour one another, watch out, or you will be consumed by one another" (εἰ δὲ ἀλλήλους δάκνετε καὶ κατεσθίετε, βλέπετε μὴ

---

[882] Das (*Galatians*, 553) claims that Paul's citation of Lev 19:18 here "functions not as a command but as a promise." But given the frequency with which the future indicative is used as a command and the original context of Lev 19:18 (which is clearly a command), it is difficult to eliminate any sense of a command here. Yet at the same time, Das is correct that the empowerment of the Spirit in the believer's life makes this statement in effect a promise that is fulfilled in the experience of the Christian.

[883] Moo (*Galatians*, 348) argues that rather than Paul referring here to believers fulfilling the law through their love for neighbor, Paul instead has in view Christ as the one who fulfills the law through his sacrificial love shown in both his life and death. Perhaps a both/and rather than an either/or approach makes the best sense.

ὑπ' ἀλλήλων ἀναλωθῆτε).[884] Although the verb rendered "bite" (δάκνω) occurs nowhere else in the New Testament, it is used a number of times in the LXX, almost always in reference to snakes.[885] Perhaps the closest parallel to Galatians 5:15 is Sirach 21:2, where the author warns, "Flee from sin as from a snake; for if you approach sin, it will bite you. Its teeth are lion's teeth, and destroy the souls of men" (RSV). Philo vividly describes drunken men at pagan parties who are driven from their natural reason as those who "rage about and tear things to pieces like so many ferocious dogs, and rise up and attack one another, biting and gnawing each other's noses, and ears, and fingers, and other parts of their body" (*Contempl.* 1:40).[886] The verb "devour" (Κατεσθίω) is consistently used in both the New Testament and the LXX in the sense of destroy or tear apart.[887] Like the prodigal son who devoured his inheritance until there was nothing left (Luke 15:30), using one's freedom as an opportunity for the flesh leads to the sinful and self-centered destruction of those around us. Paul has in view both actions and words that tear down others or bring division within the body, leaving hurt and frustration in their wake and undermining the corporate life and witness of the body. Those who bite

---

[884] The δέ that introduces this clause signals a contrast with the previous verse. DeSilva (*Handbook*, 117) prefers to see the δέ as indicating a new step in the argument, but even so that new step is introduced as the contrast to fulfilling the law by loving one's neighbor. By using a first class conditional statement, Paul presents the "if" clause as true for the sake of argument.

[885] Of the fifteen LXX occurrences, all but three (Tob 11:8; Mic 3:5; Hab 2:7) refer to snakes biting. There are three basic categories of usage: (1) to portray someone as dangerous and devious (Gen 49:17; Mic 3:5; Tob 11:8); (2) as a form of judgment, whether in a literal or figurative sense (Num 21:6–9; Amos 5:19; 9:3; Hab 2:7; Jer 8:17); and (3) to express danger whether in a literal or figurative sense (Deut 8:15; Eccl 10:8, 11; Sir 21:2). All but four of the twenty-eight occurrences in Philo are used in connection with snakes, and all four of those refer to the passions, which Philo elsewhere compares to serpents. The one occurrence in Josephus (*War* 1:208) is used figuratively of envy biting someone.

[886] Betz (*Galatians*, 277) notes that it was common in the ancient world to compare bad behavior to that of animals. Witherington (*Grace in Galatia*, 385) notes that Plutarch (*Phil.* 486B) uses similar language to describe how blood-brothers should not behave; how much more those who are brothers and sisters through the blood of Christ!

[887] The word often occurs in contexts of judgment, where God is judging his enemies (Deut 32:42; Rev 20:9), the enemies of his people (1 Kgs 16:4; Isa 29:6; Rev 11:5), or even his own people (Num 11:1; 16:35; 26:10; Hos 2:12). In other contexts, it describes the actions of evil people, nations, or forces bringing destruction (2 Sam 18:8; Isa 1:7). The Gospels use this word to describe the actions of the religious leaders who devour the houses of widows (Matt 12:40; Luke 20:47).

and devour their fellow believers rather than serve one another through love are following in the path of the great serpent who is the enemy of God's people.

If the Galatians proceed down the path of biting and devouring each other, Paul has a stern warning for them: "watch out, or you will be consumed by one another" (βλέπετε μὴ ὑπ᾽ ἀλλήλων ἀναλωθῆτε). The command "watch out" is regularly used in the New Testament to warn of serious danger to one's spiritual life, such as false teachers (Mark 13:5; Phil 3:2; Col 2:8), persecution (Mark 13:9), failing to recognize coming judgment (Acts 13:40), or causing other believers to stumble (1 Cor 8:9).[888] Here the danger is that believers will be "consumed" by each other, a verb (ἀναλίσκω) that describes the complete destruction of something to the point where it is completely used up or exhausted.[889] The only other New Testament occurrence is the request by the sons of Zebedee to call down fire from heaven to consume a Samaritan village that refused to welcome Jesus (Luke 9:54). In using this verb here, perhaps Paul had Proverbs 30:14 in mind: "There is a generation whose teeth are swords, whose fangs are knives, devouring the oppressed from the land and the needy from among mankind." Using one's freedom as an opportunity for the flesh rather than serving one another through love leads to people turning against each other within the body, resulting in the destruction of the community.

The opposite of divine love working itself out through our love for others is a calculating selfishness that is only interested in what's in it for me. A local church where everyone is out for themselves will not last long. Inevitably those who promote division in the body through their self-serving actions will fall victim to the same tactics unless the Spirit intervenes to produce repentance and lasting change.

Bridge

When we truly grasp that Christ has freed us from the iron chains of slavery to the elementals (in all their various forms), we cannot help but

---

[888] Paul uses the imperative form of the verb βλέπω, which, as used here, has the sense of "be ready to learn about something that is needed or is hazardous" (BDAG s.v. βλέπω 5). When used this way, it is often followed by μή, μήποτε, μήπως and the aorist subjunctive, which is the case here.

[889] BDAG s.v. ἀναλίσκω. In the twenty LXX occurrences, it refers to the destruction of something such as land or people (Gen 41:30; Num 14:33; Prov 23:28; 24:22; 30:14; Isa 32:10; 66:17; Ezek 5:12; 15:4–5; Joel 1:19; 2:3), the consumption of food, sacrifices, or resources (1 Esd 6:29; 2 Macc 1:31; 2:10–11; Wis 13:12).

live changed lives. The freedom we experience in the gospel empowers us to follow in the steps of Jesus, who said, "For even the Son of Man did not come to be served, but to serve, and to give his life as a ransom for many" (Mark 10:45). By loving others with the love Christ has shown us, we make him visible to those around us.

D. WALK IN THE SPIRIT NOT THE FLESH (5:16–26)

[16] I say then, walk by the Spirit and you will certainly not carry out the desire of the flesh. [17] For the flesh desires what is against the Spirit, and the Spirit desires what is against the flesh; these are opposed to each other, so that you don't do what you want. [18] But if you are led by the Spirit, you are not under the law.

[19] Now the works of the flesh are obvious: sexual immorality, moral impurity, promiscuity, [20] idolatry, sorcery, hatreds, strife, jealousy, outbursts of anger, selfish ambitions, dissensions, factions, [21] envy, drunkenness, carousing, and anything similar. I am warning you about these things—as I warned you before—that those who practice such things will not inherit the kingdom of God.

[22] But the fruit of the Spirit is love, joy, peace, patience, kindness, goodness, faithfulness, [23] gentleness, and self-control. The law is not against such things. [24] Now those who belong to Christ Jesus have crucified the flesh with its passions and desires. [25] If we live by the Spirit, let us also keep in step with the Spirit. [26] Let us not become conceited, provoking one another, envying one another.

Context

In the previous paragraph Paul contrasted using freedom as an opportunity to serve one another through love with using freedom as opportunity for the flesh, the result of which is biting and devouring one another. This basic contrast sets the stage for the contrast between the Spirit and the flesh that dominates 5:16–26. Yet this contrast was anticipated as early as 3:3, where the question was the basis on which the Christian life is lived. It also appears in 4:29, where Paul describes believers as "born as a result of the Spirit" in contrast to unbelievers who are "born as a result of the flesh." In response to those who might question how the Christian life is to be governed without the Mosaic law, Paul offers the eschatological Spirit—who empowers an obedience that fulfills the intent of the Mosaic law—as the answer.

Structure

The paragraph can be broken down into four smaller units. First, Paul explains the conflict between the Spirit and the flesh (5:16–18). Believers must walk by the Spirit to avoid indulging the desires of the flesh (5:16). This requires intentional effort because the flesh and the Spirit are in a state of constant warfare with each other (5:17). As those who are led by the Spirit, believers are no longer under the authority of the law (5:18). The reality of the conflict between the flesh and the Spirit leads Paul in the second subsection to describe the works of the flesh (5:19–21). Although far from an exhaustive list, the apostle focuses on examples drawn from the realms of sex, forms of idolatry, and divisions within the community of believers. Third, by contrast to the works of the flesh, Paul describes the fruit of the Spirit (5:22–23). These various character qualities, virtues, and inclinations are a multifaceted expression of the Spirit's work in the life of the believer, marking them off as the eschatological people of God. As such they transcend what the Mosaic law could produce. Finally, Paul concludes this paragraph by explaining how life in the Spirit overcomes the flesh (5:24–26). As those who have already crucified the flesh because of their union with Christ (5:24) and been made alive by the Spirit (5:25a), believers are called to keep in step with the Spirit on a continual basis (5:25b). By doing so believers will avoid the arrogance that leads to division within the body of believers (5:26).

As with the previous paragraph (5:13–15), this section has a basic chiastic structure:

A   Conflict between the Spirit and the flesh (5:16–18)
  B   Works of the flesh described (5:19–21)
  B′   Fruit of the Spirit described (5:22–23)
A′   Life in the Spirit overcomes the flesh (5:24–26)

5:16. Functioning as a summary of the entire paragraph (5:16–26), this verse introduces the central conflict in the Christian life: "I say, then, walk by the Spirit and you will certainly not carry out the desire of the flesh" (Λέγω δέ, πνεύματι περιπατεῖτε καὶ ἐπιθυμίαν σαρκὸς οὐ μὴ τελέσητε).[890] The contrast between the flesh and the Spirit and its relationship to the

---

[890] The δέ that introduces this clause signals a new development in the argument, and its use with the expression "I say" (Λέγω) signals the beginning of a new unit.

Christian life that was first introduced in 3:3 now takes center stage. It is important to stress that Paul does not envision the flesh and the spirit as two aspects of a person. Both the flesh and the Spirit are powerful agents who act upon the believer, locked in a battle to shape the lives of believers. Thus the cosmic battle between the flesh and the Spirit plays out within the scope of the believer's individual life, as well as within the body of believers. Indeed, the conflict between the flesh and the Spirit is another way of talking about the conflict between the present evil age that is dominated by sin, the curse, and the elementals and the new creation that has dawned in Christ, bringing righteousness, freedom, and the Spirit. What may seem to us in our experience as an equal fight between the flesh and the Spirit in reality is no such thing, as the Spirit overcomes the flesh just as light overcomes darkness.[891]

Jettisoning the Mosaic law as the governing structure of the Christian life does not leave believers on their own when it comes to how to live. Paul commands them to "walk by the Spirit" (πνεύματι περιπατεῖτε). The Bible regularly uses the verb "walk" (περιπατέω) to refer to a person's way of life, encompassing beliefs, attitudes, desires, and actions.[892] This metaphor is especially prominent in wisdom contexts, which often present a contrast between two different ways of walking/living (e.g., Ps 1:1–6; Prov 4:10–19). Paul regularly uses this language to describe the Christian life. Because of Jesus' resurrection, believers "walk in newness of life" (Rom 6:4), in the good works that God prepared beforehand (Eph 2:10), and in wisdom (Col 4:5). Christians are called to walk in a manner worthy of the Lord (Col 1:10; 1 Thess 2:12; 4:1) and the calling he has placed on our lives (Eph 4:1). Here the command is to walk "by the Spirit," which means living a life that is empowered and controlled by the Spirit.[893]

---

[891] For a helpful summary of the contrast between the flesh and the Spirit, see Das, *Galatians*, 591–94.

[892] See BDAG s.v. περιπατέω 2 for the various nuances on this basic idea. For a helpful summary of ways walking language is used, see Ryken et al., *Dictionary of Biblical Imagery*, 922–23. In the Dead Sea Scrolls, walking as a metaphor for how one lives is common, especially in presenting a choice between the path of good/light and evil/darkness (e.g., 1 QS 3:13–4:26).

[893] In Greek this phrase is the simple dative πνεύματι, which can be understood several ways: (1) association (BDF §198.5); (2) instrumental/means (Wallace, *Greek Grammar*, 165–66; Fee, *God's Empowering Presence*, 430; DeSilva, *Handbook*, 117); (3) agency; (4) sphere (suggested but not preferred by Fee, *God's Empowering Presence*, 430); (5) rule/standard (suggested but not preferred by DeSilva, *Handbook*, 117); (5) origin (Longenecker, *Galatians*, 244). On the

Given the ambiguity of the phrase in Greek, Paul may also have in view the ideas of walking in the realm/sphere of the Spirit, as well as walking in accordance with Spirit (compare Rom 8:4). The empowerment of the Spirit to walk in obedience that was promised by the prophets is a reality for all who have the Spirit of the Son (Jer 31:31–34; Ezek 36:26–27).

Although this verse is not a formal conditional statement, it has that force.[894] Paul insists that if/when believers walk by the Spirit, they "will certainly not carry out the desire of the flesh" (ἐπιθυμίαν σαρκὸς οὐ μὴ τελέσητε). Paul uses the strongest form of negation to emphasize the incompatibility of carrying out the desire of the flesh with walking by the Spirit.[895] The verb "carry out" (τελέω) could also be translated "fulfill"; as used here it has the sense of bringing something to realization. Paul uses this same verb in 2 Timothy 4:7 when he describes the imminent end of his life by writing "I have finished the race." What cannot be carried out when walking by the Spirit is the "desire of the flesh" (ἐπιθυμίαν σαρκὸς). As noted before, the flesh refers to humanity in its weakness and proclivity toward sin.[896] The flesh is portrayed as a hostile power that works in humanity to produce sinful desires that lead to disobeying God.[897] Although he does not use the term flesh, James 1:14–15 describes this same process: "But each person is tempted when he is drawn away and enticed by his own evil desire. Then after desire has conceived, it gives birth to sin, and when sin is fully grown, it gives birth to death." Paul's Jewish contemporaries often referred to the "evil inclination" and some even argued that circumcision was the answer to curbing it (perhaps

---

whole it seems best to see the Spirit as the agent by whom believers are empowered to live a life that is pleasing to God.

[894] This is an example of an informal implied condition, which uses an imperative with καί rather than the formal conditional clause structures; see William G. MacDonald, *Greek Enchiridion: A Concise Handbook of Grammar for Translation and Exegesis* (n.p.: Bibleworks, 2005), 130. The first clause ("walk by the Spirit") expresses a cause while the second ("you will certainly not carry out the desire of the flesh") communicates the effect.

[895] In Greek the construction is the double negative οὐ μή with the subjunctive, which BDF §365 describes as "the most definite form of negation regarding the future." Wallace (*Greek Grammar*, 468) notes that "while οὐ + the indicative denies a *certainty*, οὐ μή + the subjunctive denies a *potentiality* ... οὐ μή rules out even the idea as being a possibility."

[896] See Biblical Theology §1.3.6.

[897] Thus the genitive here is best understood as subjective, indicating the flesh produces the desire (e.g., DeSilva, *Handbook*, 118), or what Wallace (*Greek Grammar*, 104–6) would categorize as a genitive of producer. A related possibility is origin, but 5:17–18 portrays the flesh as an active agent rather than an impersonal source.

even the opponents in Galatia?).[898] Thus Paul may be reframing that evil inclination as the desire of the flesh, but making it clear that only the Spirit can overcome it.

Paul's wording here is quite purposeful. Walking by the Spirit does not guarantee the absence of the desires of the flesh. Those will be with us as long as we live in this fallen world. But what walking by the Spirit does do is prevent us from acting on and bring to realization those desires such that we disobey God. These desires of the flesh come from within us and are enflamed by our circumstances, tempting us to disobey God. Likely alluding to Adam and Eve's own rebellion in the garden, John notes, "For everything in the world—the lust of the flesh, the lust of the eyes, and the pride in one's possessions—is not from the Father, but is from the world" (1 John 2:16). When we as believers stop living by the power of the Spirit, we will inevitably put into action the sinful desires that the flesh produces in us.

5:17. Paul now provides further explanation of the antithesis between walking by the Spirit and carrying out the desires of the flesh.[899] He begins with a direct contrast between the two that is crafted in parallel language: "For the flesh desires what is against the Spirit, and the Spirit desires what is against the flesh" (ἡ γὰρ σὰρξ ἐπιθυμεῖ κατὰ τοῦ πνεύματος, τὸ δὲ πνεῦμα κατὰ τῆς σαρκός). The flesh and the Spirit are portrayed as mortal enemies, locked in a heated battle. In saying that the flesh "desires" what is against the Spirit, Paul uses the cognate verb (ἐπιθυμέω) of the noun desire (ἐπιθυμία) from the previous verse.[900] Paul uses this same verb in Romans 7:7, where he asserts, "I would not have known what it is to covet [ἐπιθυμίαν] if the law had not said, Do not covet [ἐπιθυμήσεις]." Quoting from Exodus 20:17, Paul identifies coveting/desiring as central to our bent toward sin. As Silva notes, "Paul sees ἐπιθυμία as an expression of the sin that rules humanity. He sees in it the driving power of the σάρξ ("flesh") ... When all is said and done, it expresses the deeply rooted tendency we have to find the focus of our life in ourselves, to trust

---

[898] See further de Boer, *Galatians*, 335–39.

[899] Thus the γάρ that begins this verse has an explanatory sense.

[900] Paul uses the noun ἐπιθυμία (19x) more often than the verb ἐπιθυμέω (5x). Four of the five verb occurrences are negative (1 Tim 3:1 is the exception). All but two (Phil 1:23; 1 Thess 2:17) of the nineteen occurrences of the noun are negative as well. Although the predominant connotation of these words is negative, note that the following line in Gal 5:17 assumes a positive use.

ourselves, and to love ourselves more than others."[901] Here in Galatians
5:17 Paul uses the present tense of the verb to portray the flesh's desiring
as a constant reality. The flesh desires "what is against the Spirit" (κατὰ
τοῦ πνεύματος), meaning anything that the Spirit prompts the believer
to be, think, feel, believe, or do.

In the same way that the flesh desires what is against the Spirit, so
too "the Spirit desires what is against the flesh" (τὸ δὲ πνεῦμα κατὰ
τῆς σαρκός).[902] In announcing the coming of a new covenant, God had
promised, "I will give you a new heart and put a new spirit within you; I
will remove your heart of stone and give you a heart of flesh. I will place
my Spirit within you and cause you to follow my statutes and carefully
observe my ordinances" (Ezek 36:26–27). That is what Paul describes
here—the Spirit gives the believer the desire and the ability to obey God
in a way that transcends what God's people under the Mosaic law covenant experienced.

Paul further explains that "these are opposed to each other" (ταῦτα
γὰρ ἀλλήλοις ἀντίκειται). The verb "opposed" (ἀντίκειμαι) vividly portrays the conflict between the flesh and the Spirit as open warfare.[903] The
purpose of this warfare is "that you don't do what you want" (ἵνα μὴ ἃ
ἐὰν θέλητε ταῦτα ποιῆτε).[904] Paul's precise meaning is not clear, and as
a result, commentators have offered a variety of interpretations. While
acknowledging the difficulty,[905] on the whole it seems best to under-

---

[901] Moises Silva, "ἐπιθυμία," *NIDNTTE* 2:243.

[902] In Greek Paul elides the verb "desire" (ἐπιθυμέω), expecting the reader to carry it
over from the previous clause.

[903] Paul uses this verb six times (1 Cor 16:9; Gal 5:17; Phil 1:28; 2 Thess 2:4; 1 Tim 1:10;
2 Tim 5:14), always in reference to forces or people that oppose Christ or his gospel. The
substantival participle of this verb is used in both Luke (13:17; 21:15) and the LXX (Exod
23:22; Isa 41:11) to refer to enemies.

[904] The exact force of the ἵνα with the subjunctive here is debated, and one's decision
largely rests on what one concludes Paul means by this clause. The three main options
are result (e.g., Wallace, *Greek Grammar*, 473), purpose (e.g., Schreiner, *Galatians*, 344), or
consecutive (e.g., Moo, *Galatians*, 356). As the discussion above indicates, purpose makes
the best sense.

[905] Two main grammatical issues are in play here. The first is the force of the ἵνα (see
previous note) and the nature of the wanting/willing (is it the Spirit, the flesh, both of them,
or the individual doing the wanting/willing?). In addition, the interpreter's theological
assumptions/beliefs/convictions about the nature of the Christian life influence one's
decision here as well. In light of these factors, Das (*Galatians*, 563–66) lists and discusses
six main views: (1) "what you want" refers to both what the Spirit wants and what the
flesh wants, resulting in the believer's inability to do what he or she wants; (2) "what you

stand Paul as saying that the purpose of the flesh opposing the Spirit is to prevent the believer empowered by the Spirit from accomplishing what he/she desires, and that the purpose of the Spirit opposing the flesh is to prevent the believer tempted by the desires of the flesh from accomplishing what he/she desires. "With the coming of the Spirit, a new eschatological reality has dawned. A conflict between the flesh and the Spirit has ensued, explaining why it is so vital for believers to walk in and to be led by the Spirit. Therefore, walking in the Spirit is not the same thing as coasting along in a fair breeze, for the flesh wars against the Spirit and the Spirit wars against the flesh."[906] Whereas before they are in Christ people are slaves to the flesh and what it desires, now believers are able to walk in the power of the Spirit. Similar to what Paul says in Romans 6:17–18, unredeemed human beings are slaves to sin, while believers are slaves of righteousness. As Moo summarizes, "Christians should not think that they have the choice to do 'whatever they want'; whether conscious of it or not, their actions at every point are governed by the flesh or the Spirit."[907]

Although we often live oblivious to this reality, believers live every moment of their lives in the midst of the all-out war between the flesh and the Spirit. While it is true that as believers we have been freed from our slavery to sin and the tyranny of the flesh, that does not mean we are no longer tempted by the desires of the flesh. But the battle between the Spirit and the flesh is not one of two equally matched opponents. As long as we are walking by the Spirit, we will not fulfill the desires of the flesh, no matter how powerful they may seem.

---

want" refers only to what the Spirit desires, resulting in an inability to do what the Spirit wants; (3) "what you want" refers only to what the flesh desires, meaning that the Spirit prevents the believer from doing what the flesh desires; (4) taking a corporate approach, Martyn (*Galatians*, 525–32) argues that those who walk by the Spirit are those in Galatia who are faithful to the true gospel, while the "you" here in 5:17 who do what they want are those following the opponents; (5) Ronald Lutjens ("'You Do Not Do What You Want': What Does Galatians 5:17 Really Mean?," *Presb* 16 [1990]: 103–17) proposes that 5:17 contains a parenthetical comment, such that it should read as follows: "For what the flesh desires is opposed to the Spirit (and what the Spirit desires is opposed to the flesh; for these are opposed to each other) to prevent you from doing what you want"; according to this view, Paul can hardly mention the work of the flesh without immediately diminishing it in light of the Spirit; (6) the Spirit and flesh are not equal antagonists; the Spirit prevents the flesh from producing what it desires (e.g., Barclay, *Obeying the Truth*, 112).

[906] Schreiner, *Galatians*, 344–45.
[907] Moo, *Galatians*, 356.

5:18. By describing the intense warfare between the Spirit and the flesh in the previous verse, one might conclude Paul views the Christian life as one of hopeless struggle. To show that is not the case, Paul uses a conditional statement that highlights the superiority of the Spirit: "But if you are led by the Spirit, you are not under the law" (εἰ δὲ πνεύματι ἄγεσθε, οὐκ ἐστὲ ὑπὸ νόμον).[908] The present tense of the verb portrays the leading as ongoing. To be led by the Spirit is another way of describing walking by the Spirit, though with more of an emphasis on the authority and guidance of the Spirit.[909] Paul also may have chosen this specific language to echo at least two specific Old Testament passages. The first is Isaiah 63:11–14.[910] Recalling how God led his people in the wilderness in the original exodus, Isaiah writes, "Like cattle that go down into the valley, the Spirit of the Lord gave them rest. You led your people this way to make a glorious name for yourself" (63:14). Such an echo resonates with other Isaianic texts that supply the backdrop for the fruit of the Spirit (see below) and reinforces Paul's conviction that the outpouring of the Spirit is definitive evidence that the age to come has broken into this present evil age through the work of Christ.

A second possible echo resounds from Psalm 143:10, where, after crying out for deliverance from his enemies, David prays, "Teach me to do your will, for you are my God. May your gracious Spirit lead me on level ground." Just as here in Galatians, the leading of the Spirit is connected to God providing guidance for how to live based on a covenant relationship. Together, Isaiah 63:14 and Psalm 143:10 ground the leading of the Holy Spirit in providing guidance for a life that pleases God, which in turn is grounded in a covenant relationship that has been established by the work of Christ and sealed by the gift of the eschatological Spirit. Thus, being led by the Spirit is yet another way of describing the blessings that come to the believer through union with Christ, the promised seed of Abraham. This language also picks up the theme of the new exodus that

---

[908] The δέ that introduces this verse signals a development in the argument with an adversative sense. By using a first class conditional statement, Paul presents the "if" clause as true for the sake of the argument. The relationship between the protasis and the apodosis is most likely evidence-inference.

[909] Thus the dative πνεύματι expresses agency (though Wallace, *Greek Grammar*, 165–66 prefers means), just as it does in 5:16 (see DeSilva, *Handbook*, 120 for a helpful explanation).

[910] See Harmon, *She Must and Shall Go Free*, 221-25; Beale, "Fruit of the Spirit," 10-12; William N. Wilder, *Echoes of the Exodus Narrative in the Context and Background of Galatians 5:18*, SBL 23 (New York: Lang, 2001), 130-38.

Christ has accomplished through his death and his leading of his people as they make their way to their new creation inheritance.

As those who are led by the Spirit, believers "are not under the law" (οὐκ ἐστὲ ὑπὸ νόμον). Given that Paul has been contrasting the Spirit with the flesh, this expression is at first surprising. Paul used it in 3:23, where he described the period before Christ came as one of captivity under the law. Indeed, God sent Christ as one born under the law to redeem those who were under the law (4:4–5). These references (along with 4:21 as well) indicate that Paul has in view here being under the authority of the Mosaic law covenant. By equating being under the law with life controlled by the desires of the flesh, Paul reveals that the flesh can manifest itself in a self-directed life that seeks to earn favor before God through doing what the law commands, or through a life that completely disregards God's moral will and pursues its own selfish pleasure.

In the most basic sense, the Spirit of God leads us to obey what God has said in his word. While the Spirit can and does prompt believers to do or say things that are not specifically or explicitly commanded in Scripture, often we cannot be sure of the Spirit's leading in such situations until after the fact. How kind of God to lead us by his Spirit and not leave us to our own abilities or wisdom to live as his people!

5:19–21. To clarify the sharp difference between the flesh and the Spirit,[911] Paul now describes the works of the flesh (vv. 19–21) and the fruit of the Spirit (vv. 22–23). Although in one sense quite different from the works of the law, the works of the flesh ultimately put a person in a similar predicament as objects of God's judgment. Thus the flesh can manifest itself in both a self-righteousness that strives to earn favor or standing before God based on performance of his requirements, or in a self-focused pursuit of a life that completely disregards God and his moral requirements. From Paul's perspective, "the works of the flesh are obvious" (φανερὰ δέ ἐστιν τὰ ἔργα τῆς σαρκός). There is no mystery involved in what kind of works the flesh produces;[912] they are in fact quite "obvious" (φανερός), a word that refers to "being evident so as to be readily known."[913] Paul uses this same adjective in Romans 1:19 to explain

---

[911] This verse is introduced with δέ, which here signals a new development in the argument. Moo (*Galatians*, 358) tags it as resumptive.

[912] Thus in the expression τὰ ἔργα τῆς σαρκός ("works of the flesh") the genitive is subjective, or what Wallace (*Greek Grammar*, 104–6) refers to as a genitive of production.

[913] BDAG s.v. φανερός 1.

that "what can be known about God is evident" to all human beings. Yet despite their obvious nature, Paul goes on to list fifteen representative examples before concluding with a warning.[914]

The first three works of the flesh are associated with sex.[915] First is "sexual immorality" (πορνεία), a term that encompasses sexual activity outside of God's appointed context of marriage.[916] Here it has the most general meaning just mentioned, though elsewhere it can refer to more specific forms of sexual immorality (cf. 1 Cor 5:1).[917] In a Greco-Roman world that was saturated with sexual activity, the sexual ethic of Judaism and Christianity stood out. Sexual immorality is especially wicked because it distorts God's good gift of marriage and the picture of God's relationship to his people that it is supposed to portray. The phrase "moral impurity" (ἀκαθαρσία) renders a word that refers to anything that is unclean, whether in a literal, spiritual, or moral sense.[918] Paul often uses this word

---

[914] There is a striking parallel between Paul's list of works of the flesh and what the Qumran community attributes to the spirit of deceit: "greed, sluggishness in the service of justice, wickedness, falsehood, pride, haughtiness of heart, dishonesty, trickery, cruelty, much insincerity, impatience, much foolishness, impudent enthusiasm for appalling acts performed in a lustful passion, filthy paths in the service of impurity, blasphemous tongue, blindness of eyes, hardness of hearing, stiffness of neck, hardness of heart in order to walk in all the paths of darkness and evil cunning" (1 QS 4:22–26). For a helpful and concise comparison/contrast between this text and Paul's thought, see de Boer, *Galatians*, 353–54. For another example in Jewish literature, see Jubilees 4:15–16; on such lists in Greco-Roman literature, see Betz, *Galatians*, 281–83; Witherington, *Grace in Galatia*, 403–6. After an extended discussion of vice and virtue lists, Longenecker (*Galatians*, 249–52) concludes that Paul's use here is more indebted to the Hellenistic rather than Jewish tradition. Martyn (*Galatians*, 496), however, objects to calling these virtue and vice lists, preferring to see them as "marks of a community under the influence of the Flesh and marks of a community led by the Spirit."

[915] Witherington (*Grace in Galatia*, 398–99) argues that the first and last vices listed deal with sin connected to the Galatians' pagan past, while the vices in between focus on sins against the Christian community. But this proposal assumes too much knowledge of the Galatians' background and appears to force a distinction not evident in the context. More common is dividing the list into four categories: (1) three works related to sex; (2) two works related to worship of false gods; (3) eight dealing with interpersonal relationships; and (4) two connected to a life of debauchery; see, e.g., Moo, *Galatians*, 358.

[916] For a helpful summary of extramarital sexual activity in the Greco-Roman world, see Friedrich Hauck, "πόρνη, πόρνος, πορνεία, πορνεύω, ἐκπορνεύω," in *TDNT* 6:581–84.

[917] Paul regularly criticizes πορνεία, giving it particular attention in 1 Corinthians (5:1; 6:13, 18; 7:2).

[918] In the ancient world the concept of purity and impurity was one of the major cultural values; for a helpful discussion and overview, see DeSilva, *Honor, Patronage, Kinship, and Purity*, 241–315. Not surprisingly, most (34 of 63) of the LXX occurrences of ἀκαθαρσία are in Leviticus (23x) and Ezekiel (11x), both books with strong priestly interests.

in connection with sexual immorality (e.g., Rom 1:24) and in particular when discussing πορνεία as he does here (compare 2 Cor 12:21; Col 3:8; Eph 5:3).[919] According to 1 Thessalonians 4:7, its opposite is sanctification/holiness (ἁγιασμός). Next is "promiscuity" (ἀσέλγεια), which in Greek has the broader sense of a "lack of self-constraint which involves one in conduct that violates all bounds of what is socially acceptable."[920] Both Paul and Peter list this as a distinctive characteristic of unbelievers (Eph 4:19; 1 Pet 4:3). The connotation here is of unrestrained sexual expression.

Switching gears slightly, the next two works of the flesh describe a failure to worship the one true God.[921] When we hear the word "idolatry" (εἰδωλολατρία),[922] we tend to think first of ancient people bowing down to statues made of wood, stone, or precious metals, but at the most basic level idolatry is simply placing anything or anyone in the place rightly reserved for God.[923] Understood from another angle, idolatry is often taking a good thing and trying to make it an ultimate thing. That is why Paul can refer to greed as idolatry (Col 3:5). Living in a Greco-Roman culture that was saturated with gods everywhere one looked, early gentile converts often struggled to know how best to relate to their culture and the people in their community (cf. 1 Cor 8–10). "Sorcery" (φαρμακεία) was an attempt to control or manipulate one's circumstances to one's advantage through the use of magic, a common practice in the ancient world but out of step with obedient trust in the Lord.[924] It was explicitly forbidden for the Israelites in the Old Testament (Deut 18:10), and the prohibition continues for the church. As the gospel spread throughout the

---

[919] BDAG s.v. ἀκαθαρσία 2.

[920] BDAG s.v. ἀσέλγεια. While there are only two LXX occurrences (3 Macc 2:26; Wis 14:26), there are ten in the NT (Mark 7:22; Rom 13:13; 2 Cor 12:21; Gal 5:19; Eph 4:19; 1 Pet 4:3; 2 Pet 2:2, 7, 18; Jude 4). The sexual nature of this term is evident in both Jewish (e.g., Philo, Mos. 1:3, 305; Josephus, War 2:121; Jub. 4:15; Sib. Or. 2:279) and Greco-Roman (Polybius, Hist. 25.3.7; 36.15.4) literature.

[921] Schreiner, Galatians, 346.

[922] Three of the four NT occurrences are in Paul (1 Cor 10:14; Gal 5:20; Col 3:5; 1 Pet 4:3), and the noun does not appear in the LXX at all. Yet the concept is prevalent in both testaments; for a helpful biblical-theological treatment of idolatry, see G. K. Beale, We Become What We Worship: A Biblical Theology of Idolatry (Downers Grove, IL: IVP, 2008).

[923] On this see especially Timothy J. Keller, Counterfeit Gods: The Empty Promises of Money, Sex, and Power, and the Only Hope That Matters (New York: Dutton, 2009).

[924] The only other NT occurrence of this noun is Rev 18:23, where it refers to the magical spell that Babylon has over all who participate in her wickedness. In the LXX the word occurs in Exod 7:11, 22; 8:3, 14 to refer to the magical powers of Pharaoh's magicians.

Greco-Roman world, conflict with those who practiced magic was inevitable (Acts 8:19–24; 13:4–12; 19:18–19).[925] This particular word "generally refers to the use of drugs as medicines, with two major negative connotations: poisoning and using drugs in the context of practicing sorcery."[926]

The next several works of the flesh focus on the disruption of life within the community of believers. "Hatreds" (ἔχθρα) has the sense of hostility or enmity toward God (Rom 8:7; Jas 4:4) or others (Luke 23:12; Eph 2:14, 16). The LXX uses this word for the "hostility" that God promises between the serpent and the woman along with their respective offspring (Gen 3:15). "Strife" (ἔρις) refers to "engagement in rivalry, especially with reference to positions taken in a matter."[927] Although it is characteristic of life as an unbeliever (Rom 1:29; 13:13), strife was a constant danger in the early church (1 Cor 1:11; 3:3; 2 Cor 12:20; Phil 1:15; 1 Tim 6:4; Titus 3:9). Given the activity of the opponents in the Galatian churches, strife was likely a very real threat. While the word rendered "jealousy" (ζῆλος) can have the positive sense of zeal or dedication (cf. 2 Cor 9:2; 11:2; Phil 3:6), here it clearly has the negative sense of envy toward what someone is, has, or has done. James warns that "where envy [ζῆλος] and selfish ambition exist, there is disorder and every kind of evil" (Jas 3:16). The word rendered "outbursts of anger" (θυμός) often refers to God's righteous wrath as an expression of his holiness and justice (e.g., Rom 2:8; Rev 14:10, 19; 15:1, 7; 16:1, 19), but when referring to human beings it describes "a state of intense anger, with the implication of passionate outbursts."[928] These outbursts of anger are something the believer must set aside in pursuit of godliness (Eph 4:31; Col 3:8). "Selfish ambitions" (ἐριθεία) translates a term that outside the New Testament referred to "a self-seeking pursuit

---

[925] On the practice of magic in the Greco-Roman world, see C. Brown and J. Stafford Wright, "Magic, Sorcery, Magi," in NDNTT 2:556–62 and C.E. Arnold, "Magical Papyri," in DNTB 666–70.

[926] DeSilva, Handbook, 121.

[927] BDAG s.v. ἔρις. There are just three LXX occurrences (Sir 28:11; 40:4, 9), and all nine NT examples are found in Paul's letters (Rom 1:29; 13:13; 1 Cor 1:11; 3:3; 2 Cor 12:20; Gal 5:20; Phil 1:15; 1 Tim 6:4; Titus 3:9). DeSilva (Handbook, 122) notes that ἔρις "was so prominent a vice as to be personified in Greek mythology as the goddess Eris, who famously began the Trojan War by stirring up a contest between the three goddesses Aphrodite, Athena, and Hera by offering a golden apple to the one who would be deemed most desirable. The mythic story well captures the vice: self-centered competition that leads to the erosion of community (even the destruction of empires)."

[928] L&N s.v. θυμός 88.178.

of political office by unfair means."[929] While the political connotations are not present here, the idea of pursuing one's ambitions while disregarding others and its effects on them certainly is a concern Paul noted in the churches in Corinth (2 Cor 12:20) and Philippi (Phil 1:17; 2:3). The note of disunity continues with the next work of the flesh: "dissensions" (διχοστασία). The only other New Testament use of this term is related to dissension stemming from false teaching (Rom 16:17), and that sense seems likely here as well.[930] The next term—"factions" (αἵρεσις)—has an even stronger association with differences in belief or practice that lead to division. In Acts this term regularly refers to different sects within Judaism, including Christianity (Acts 5:17; 15:5; 24:5, 14; 25:5; 28:22). Paul warns the Corinthians about the dangers of forming such sects within the church (1 Cor 11:19).[931]

The final three works of the flesh seem to return to a transition from sins related to factions within the body to more general departures from God's will. In the most basic sense, "envy" (φθόνος) is "a state of ill will toward someone because of some real or presumed advantage experienced by such a person."[932] It is characteristic of the unbeliever (Rom 1:29; Titus 3:3) but something that believers can fall prey to as well (Phil 1:15). Next is "drunkenness" (μέθη),[933] consuming alcohol to the point where one's capacities become so diminished as to lose control of oneself. In

---

[929] BDAG s.v. ἐριθεία, which notes several occurrences in Aristotle (*Pol.* 1303a.13). All but two (Jas 3:14, 16) of the seven NT occurrences are in Paul (Rom 2:8; 2 Cor 12:20; Gal 5:20; Phil 1:17; 2:3).

[930] In Greek literature this term was often used in the context of political dissension between rival parties (see Heinrich Schlier, "ἀφίστημι, ἀποστασία, διχοστασία," in *TDNT* 1:514).

[931] In the only other NT occurrence, 2 Peter 2:1 refers to "destructive heresies" (αἱρέσεις ἀπωλείας) that false teachers will introduce, which would be the earliest occurrence of this word with the sense of heresy, from which our English word comes (see further *NIDNTTE* 1:176–77).

[932] L&N s.v. φθόνος 88.160. There are just four LXX occurrences (1 Macc 8:16; 3 Macc 6:7; Wis 2:24; 6:23), and five of the nine NT uses are in Paul (Rom 1:29; Gal 5:21; Phil 1:15; 1 Tim 6:4; Titus 3:3). According to DeSilva (*Handbook*, 123), it refers to "that desire, born of bitterness, to see a person deprived of the rewards his or her virtues and efforts have justly won (see Aristotle, *Rhet.* 2.10)."

[933] Some manuscripts (A C D F G Ψ 0122. 0278. 1739. 1881 𝔐 lat sy^(p) bo) list φόνοι ("murder, killing") between φθόνος and μέθαι. But its absence has strong support, including early witnesses (𝔓^46 ℵ B 33. 81. 323. 945 vg^mss sa), and Metzger (*Textual Commentary*, 529) is likely correct when he concludes that scribes familiar with Rom 1:29 (where φθόνοι and φόνοι occur next to each other in a vice list) inserted it from memory.

Ephesians 5:18 Paul contrasts this with being filled with the Spirit. The final named work of the flesh is closely related; "carousing" (κῶμος) refers to "excessive feasting," often in association with celebratory meals or banquets.[934] Moo notes that "the word always has the negative sense of 'excessive feasting,' always involving too much drinking and often sexual liberties."[935] And just to be sure no one considers the list of works of the flesh exhaustive, Paul adds "and anything similar" (τὰ ὅμοια τούτοις).

Based on the threat these works of the flesh pose to the believer on both an individual and corporate level, Paul states, "I am warning you about these things" (ἃ προλέγω ὑμῖν), and then he reminds them this is not the first time he has addressed the issue: "as I warned you before" (καθὼς προεῖπον).[936] The content of the warning now follows: "those who practice such things will not inherit the kingdom of God" (οἱ τὰ τοιαῦτα πράσσοντες βασιλείαν θεοῦ οὐ κληρονομήσουσιν). The first thing to note about this remarkable warning is that it is directed to "those who practice such things." By using the present tense of the verb rendered "practice" (πράσσω), Paul makes it clear he has in mind those whose lives display a pattern of works of the flesh.[937] He does not have in view the believer who is tempted and occasionally gives in to sin, but people who have given themselves over to a life that is controlled by the flesh and its desires.

Thus, people whose lives are characterized by the works of the flesh "will not inherit the kingdom of God" (βασιλείαν θεοῦ οὐ κληρονομήσουσιν). As often is the case in the New Testament, a list of vices is followed by a warning (Rom 1:32a; 1 Cor 6:9–11; Eph 5:5; Col 3:6;

---

[934] BDAG s.v. κῶμος. DeSilva (Handbook, 123) further describes it as "eating beyond the needs of the body to the detriment of the body, and to the neglect of those who are hungry and lack even the necessities." For a helpful summary of banquets in the Greco-Roman world, see W. L. Willis, "Banquets," in DNTB 143–46. In drawing a sharp contrast between observing the Sabbath/Jewish festivals and Greco-Roman festivals, Philo describes in detail the debauchery and immorality at such Greco-Roman festivals, including among the list κῶμοι (Cher. 1:91–93).

[935] Moo, Galatians, 361.

[936] Another way of translating the Greek is "which things I am telling you beforehand, just as I told you before." Based on the context, the csb translates the two occurrences (the first is present tense while the second is aorist) of the verb προλέγω ("tell beforehand") as "warn." Martyn (Galatians, 497) notes that similar to here, 1QS 4:12–14 has an eschatological warning that follows a vice list.

[937] This conclusion is borne out by how Paul uses the verb πράσσω in other passages such as Rom 2:1–3; 13:4; 2 Cor 5:10; 12:21. Thus, instead of these works of the flesh, Paul exhorts believers, "Do [πράσσετε] what you have learned and received and heard from me, and seen in me, and the God of peace will be with you" (Phil 4:9).

Rev 21:8).[938] We have already seen inheritance language throughout Galatians. The inheritance promised to Abraham comes through God's grace received by faith, not obeying the Mosaic law covenant (3:18). All who belong to Christ by faith are heirs of this promise (3:29) since they have been made sons of God through the work of Christ the Son of God (4:1–7). As sons of the promise, believers—Jews and gentiles alike—will not share this inheritance with those who base their relationship with God on the Mosaic law covenant (4:30). Thus, to this point in Galatians a variety of blessings have been tied to the theme of inheritance: justification, removal of the curse, the gift of the Spirit, freedom from the Mosaic law, sonship, adoption, freedom from the elementals, the hope of righteousness, and freedom to serve another through love. The future tense of the verb here points forward to the consummation of these blessings.

In light of the connection between inheritance language and the various blessings listed above, we should probably understand the phrase "kingdom of God" as a shorthand summary of those blessings. Jewish expectations of the coming kingdom of God revolved around the hope of a Davidic king who would defeat Israel's enemies and reestablish Israel as an independent nation, ushering in a golden age of peace and security. Jesus, however, had a different perspective on the kingdom, calling people to repent and believe in the good news to experience forgiveness of sins and the gift of the Spirit. Although not as prominent as in the Synoptic Gospels, Paul does use kingdom language with the same already/not-yet dynamic. The kingdom is a present reality that believers currently experience (Rom 14:17; Col 1:13) while at the same awaiting its future consummation (1 Cor 15:20–28). Here in Galatians 5:21 the focus is on experiencing the consummation of the kingdom, a reality which those whose lives are marked by the works of the flesh will not inherit (compare 1 Cor 6:9–10; Eph 5:5). As sons who have the Spirit of the Son, believers will inherit the kingdom of God in the consummated new creation (Gal 4:4–7; 6:15).

Thus, while it is true that honest believers can see examples of the works of flesh in their lives, what Paul has in view here is the overall character and shape of a person's life. John makes a similar point that the life of the believer is not marked by pervasive sin (1 John 3:4–10). The Christian life is one of putting to death the deeds of the body by the power

---

[938] Moo, *Galatians*, 362.

of the Spirit (Rom 8:12–13). While sinless perfection is unattainable in this life (1 John 1:5–2:2), the follower of Christ is called to "work out your own salvation with fear and trembling. For it is God who is working in you both to will and to work according to his good purpose" (Phil 2:12–13).

5:22–23. In sharp contrast to the works of the flesh that characterize the life of the unbeliever, Paul now presents what characterizes the life of the believer: "the fruit of the Spirit" (ὁ δὲ καρπὸς τοῦ πνεύματός).[939] As the foils to the plural works of the flesh, Paul puts forward the singular fruit of the Spirit.[940] Thus, while different expressions of the fruit of the Spirit can be identified, they are deeply interconnected. They are like a multifaceted diamond with distinctive sides that look different depending on the light yet are still part of the same diamond. This fruit is what the Spirit produces in the lives of believers,[941] marking them off as the eschatological people of God who have received the blessing of Abraham because of their union with Christ.

Before working through the individual expressions of the fruit of the Spirit, we should note that Paul likely draws this concept from at least two texts in Isaiah.[942] As part of God saving his people, Isaiah 32:15–20 foresees a day when Yahweh will pour out his Spirit, producing fruit such as justice, righteousness, and peace. In a similar vein, in Isaiah 57:15–20 (LXX) God promises that "the Spirit will go forth from me" (57:16) to heal, lead, and comfort his people, resulting in the fruit of lips and peace for God's people (57:17–19). Together these two texts foresee a time "when the Spirit will come from on high as part of God's eschatological salvation, producing fruit that is both physical in its transformation of the land and spiritual/moral in the transformation of his people. This pouring out of the Spirit is connected to the restoration of Israel and even more specifically that of Jerusalem."[943] By drawing on these two texts, Paul provides further evidence that the promised restoration of Israel and the fulfillment of the promise to Abraham have both been accomplished

---

[939] The δέ that introduces this clause highlights the contrast between the works of the flesh and the fruit of the Spirit.

[940] Moo (*Galatians*, 363) disagrees, noting that Paul regularly uses the singular in his letters (compare Eph 5:9).

[941] Thus the genitive expression here is subjective, or perhaps more specifically what Wallace (*Greek Grammar*, 105–6) would call a genitive of producer.

[942] See Beale, "Fruit of the Spirit," 1–38 and Harmon, *She Must and Shall Go Free*, 215–21.

[943] Harmon, *She Must and Shall Go Free*, 217.

through the work of Christ.[944] The fruit that Israel was called to bear but never could (Isa 5:1–7) is now being manifested in the church, composed of Jew and gentile together.

With that foundation in place, we are ready now to briefly discuss each expression of the fruit of the Spirit.[945] The first is "love" (ἀγάπη), which refers to a self-sacrificial concern for others that manifests itself in action. Paul has already highlighted love as the means by which faith works to serve others (5:6, 13). Such love is rooted in the reality that the Son of God has loved us and given himself for us (2:20). Paul treats the supremacy of love in the well-known 1 Corinthians 13, where its preeminence is rooted in the fact that, whereas faith and hope will cease when the perfect comes, love will remain. "Joy" (χαρά) refers to something much deeper than happiness rooted in circumstances; instead it speaks of a deep sense of contentment and pleasure in God and his ways. Paul prays that believers will experience it (Rom 15:13) and even describes fellow believers as a source of great joy in his life (Phil 4:1; 1 Thess 2:19–20). But ultimately biblical joy is rooted in the Lord himself (Phil 3:1; 4:4, 10). "Peace" (εἰρήνη) should be understood in its loaded sense of the cessation of hostilities with God (and others). As we noted at 1:3, the background to this term is the eschatological promise of God setting things right in the world and establishing his dominion. Because we are justified by faith, we have peace with God, meaning we are no longer his enemies but his sons (Rom 5:1–10). Such peace with God transcends human understanding and guards our hearts and minds (Phil 4:7). "All that the world can offer

---

[944] Just as there was a striking parallel to the works of the flesh in the writing of the Qumran community, there is a parallel to the fruit of the Spirit, where they refer to the "spirit of meekness, of patience, generous compassion, eternal goodness, intelligence, understanding, potent wisdom which trusts in all the deeds of God and depends on his abundant mercy; a spirit of knowledge in all the plans of action, of enthusiasm for the decrees of justice, of holy plans with firm purpose, of generous compassion with all the sons of truth, of magnificent purity which detests all unclean idols, of careful behaviour in wisdom concerning everything, of concealment concerning the truth of the mysteries of knowledge. ... These are the foundations of the spirit of the sons of truth (in) the world. And the reward of all those who walk in it will be healing, plentiful peace in a long life, fruitful offspring with all everlasting blessings, eternal enjoyment with endless life, and a crown of glory with majestic raiment in eternal light" (1 QS 4:2–8).

[945] Some scholars have argued that there is some kind of ordering principle at work in the list; see, e.g., Betz, *Galatians*, 286–89; Martyn, *Galatians*, 498–99. None of these proposals have proved persuasive, especially in light of the loose parallels in other Pauline texts such as 2 Cor 6:6; 1 Tim 4:12; 6:11; 2 Tim 2:22 and also 2 Pet 1:5–7 (on these parallels see further Dunn, *Galatians*, 309–10).

is a peace that is based on circumstances that are favorable; the peace of God, by contrast, is rooted in the character of our God, who is a loving and sovereign Father who works for His glory and our good."[946]

As a fruit of the Spirit, "patience" (μακροθυμία) could refer to either remaining calm while waiting for something or enduring in the face of opposition or hardship.[947] Since the context does not point in a specific direction, it is best to understand the term broadly. God's patience toward us is shown in his not immediately judging sin to allow time for repentance (Rom 2:4; 9:22; 1 Tim 1:16; compare Exod 34:6 LXX). Because God has shown us patience, we are empowered by the Spirit to show patience as we wait for the consummation of God's promises and face opposition from others and the world around us. "Kindness" (χρηστότης) has the sense of being helpful or beneficial to others, often with the connotation of generosity.[948] God shows his kindness in both not immediately bringing judgment on sin (Rom 2:4) and electing his people despite their sinfulness (Rom 11:22; Eph 2:7; Titus 3:4). Closely related to kindness is "goodness" (ἀγαθωσύνη), which can be defined as a "positive moral quality characterized especially by interest in the welfare of others."[949] In 2 Thessalonians 1:11 Paul prays that by his power God will "fulfill your every desire to do good and your work produced by faith."

The next fruit of the Spirit could be translated either "faithfulness" or "faith" (πίστις). Throughout the letter Paul has emphasized the central role of faith as the means by which individuals experience the blessing of Abraham and all that is associated with it. But as we have also noted, in several places scholars have argued that instead of referring to the believer's faith/trust, πίστις refers to the faithfulness of Jesus in fulfilling the terms of the covenant as the basis of our salvation.[950] Given that it occurs here in a list of character qualities that the Spirit produces, it seems

---

[946] Matthew S. Harmon, *Philippians*, Mentor Commentary (Fearn, Ross-shire, Scotland: Christian Focus, 2015), 414.

[947] BDAG s.v. μακροθυμία.

[948] BDAG s.v. χρηστότης 2. Although somewhat common in the LXX (28x), there are only eight NT occurrences, all of which are in Paul (Rom 2:4; 3:12; 11:22; 2 Cor 6:6; Gal 5:22; Eph 2:7; Col 3:12; Titus 3:4).

[949] BDAG s.v. ἀγαθωσύνη. All four NT occurrences are in Paul (Rom 15:14; Gal 5:22; Eph 5:9; 2 Thess 1:11). In Jewish literature this term often describes an attribute of God (T. Judah 18:4; T. Abr. 1:5; Pr. Man. 1:7, 14).

[950] See Biblical Theology §8.2.

more likely that faithfulness is in view.[951] As the Spirit works in the life of the Christian, he empowers us to remain faithful to Christ and others.

As a fruit of the Spirit, "gentleness" (πραΰτης) refers to "the quality of not being overly impressed by a sense of one's self-importance," thus bringing together the ideas of humility, meekness, and considerateness.[952] In 2 Corinthians 10:1 Paul bases his appeal to the Corinthians on "the meekness and gentleness of Christ"; thus the gentleness that we show to others rests on the gentleness that Christ has first shown to us. Gentleness should be characteristic of all believers (Eph 4:2; Col 3:12) but is essential for leaders within the church (2 Tim 2:25; Titus 3:12). "Self-control" (ἐγκράτεια) refers to the ability to restrain one's emotions, desires, and actions. Acts 24:25 summarizes Paul's preaching before Felix as centering on "righteousness, self-control, and the judgment to come." Although rare in the LXX/New Testament,[953] the term was common in Greek moral writers. Socrates is alleged to have claimed that self-control was the foundation of virtue (Xenophon, *Mem.* 1.5.4), and Plato emphasizes its role in controlling the sensual desires.[954] Self-control is a fitting conclusion to the list of the fruit of the Spirit, as it is in one sense the fundamental thing lacking when the works of the flesh are evident.

Although Paul has regularly drawn a sharp contrast between the Mosaic law and work of the Spirit throughout Galatians, here he notes that "the law is not against such things" (κατὰ τῶν τοιούτων οὐκ ἔστιν νόμος).[955] Once the Mosaic law is removed as the structure that determines how God's people relate to him and others, one might worry that

---

[951] See similarly Witherington, *Grace in Galatia*, 410; Schreiner, *Galatians*, 350; Das, *Galatians*, 582.

[952] BDAG s.v. πραΰτης. It occurs five times in Sirach, where it describes how one should: (1) do good works (3:17); (2) answer the poor (4:8); (3) glorify oneself (10:28); (4) speak (36:23); and (5) imitate Moses (45:4). As used in Greek literature it is the opposite of roughness, bad temper, sudden anger, and brusqueness (see Friedrich Hauck and Seigfried Schulz, "πραΰς, πραΰτης" in *TDNT* 6:646).

[953] Just one occurrence in the LXX (4 Macc 5:34), and three in the NT (Acts 24:25; Gal 5:23; 2 Pet 1:6).

[954] Noted in *NIDNTTE* 2:83. Silva goes on to note that "Among the Stoics, ἐγκράτεια was taken as a sign of human freedom; it was part of being truly human to moderate one's desires, particularly one's sexual drive and enjoyment of food and drink."

[955] Noting a close parallel to this phrase in Aristotle (*Pol.* 3.13.1294a), Witherington (*Grace in Galatia*, 411) argues that Paul is here attempting to connect his paraenesis with ethical exhortations his audience would have been familiar with.

believers are left to do whatever they want. But as Paul has already stated in 5:13-14, what the law was intended to produce but could not because of human sinfulness comes to fulfillment in the fruit that the Spirit produces in and through the believer.

Jesus promised that his disciples would bear fruit by abiding in him (John 15:4-5). That fruit is produced by the Spirit who dwells inside of us as he transforms us more and more into the image of Christ (2 Cor 3:17-4:6). A farmer cannot make a tree produce fruit, but he can do everything in his power to create an environment where fruit grows by watering the tree, using fertilizer, and pruning away dead branches. In a similar way, as believers we cannot produce the fruit but we can cultivate that fruit production through the means of grace God has given us, such as his word, prayer, and fellowship with other believers.

5:24. With his contrast between the works of the flesh and the fruit of the Spirit complete, Paul now moves the argument forward by stating what is true of believers: "Now those who belong to Christ Jesus have crucified the flesh with its passions and desires" (οἱ δὲ τοῦ Χριστοῦ ['Ἰησοῦ] τὴν σάρκα ἐσταύρωσαν σὺν τοῖς παθήμασιν καὶ ταῖς ἐπιθυμίαις).[956] By referring to believers as those who belong to Christ, Paul recalls his statement in 3:29 that those who belong to Christ "are Abraham's seed, heirs according to the promise."[957] In saying that believers "have crucified the flesh," Paul describes the decisive break with the old life that takes place at conversion.[958] It may seem surprising that Paul describes believers as crucifying the flesh when he normally refers to believers as being crucified (compare Gal 2:20), but he may do so here to emphasize the

---

[956] The δέ that begins this verse marks the development in Paul's argument.

[957] In both places Paul uses a genitive form of the word Χριστός ("Christ") to express the idea of belonging to Christ. It is difficult to determine whether the word Ἰησοῦ ("Jesus") following Χριστοῦ ("Christ") is part of the original text or not. The external evidence is evenly split between witnesses that have it (א A B C P Ψ 0122¹. 0278. 33. 104*. 1175. 1241. 1739. 1881) and those that do not (𝔓⁴⁶ D F G K L 0122*.². 81. 104ᶜ. 365. 630. 1505. 2464 𝔐). The presence of the definite article before the phrase Χριστοῦ Ἰησοῦ is unusual (Eph 3:1 is the only other example), leading Dunn (*Galatians*, 294 n.6) to suggest that "The absence of 'Jesus' from 𝔓⁴⁶ and other manuscripts and versions, strengthens the possibility that the definite article was intended to retain its earlier titular significance—'the Messiah, Jesus.'"

[958] Paul's use of the aorist tense of the verb σταυρόω here portrays this crucifixion as a simple act, which may seem surprising since crucifixion is a process. Yet even in the accounts of Jesus' crucifixion the aorist tense is used repeatedly while Jesus was still alive on the cross (compare Mark 15:24-27). Moo (*Galatians*, 367) suggests that the aorist refers to Christ's own crucifixion, but this may be placing too much weight on the aorist.

believers' active role in aligning themselves with Christ at their con-version.[959] Paul's thought here is similar to that of Romans 6:6: "For we know that our old self was crucified with him so that the body ruled by sin might be rendered powerless so that we may no longer be enslaved to sin." Because believers are united to Christ by faith, we share in his crucifixion and resurrection (Rom 6:3–11). Paul is not saying that the flesh no longer can have any influence on the believer. After all, crucifixion was in fact a gradual death; in the same way, one might say that upon our conversion the flesh is nailed to the cross and during the remainder of the believer's life the flesh is dying a slow death.

To ensure the Galatians understand the decisive nature of the break with the flesh that happened at conversion, Paul notes that believers have crucified the flesh "with its passions and desires" (σὺν τοῖς παθήμασιν καὶ ταῖς ἐπιθυμίαις). These two words are essentially synonyms and together highlight the total scope of the crucifixion. The flesh uses the passions and the desires to entice people and lead them away from obeying God (Rom 7:5; Gal 5:17), but Paul insists that even these powerful passions and desires have been crucified with Christ.

What a liberating truth to understand and believe! Far too many believers fail to live in the freedom that comes from believing that the flesh along with its passions and desires have no authority over us. No matter how strong the desire to sin may feel in our experience, the flesh can only entice, never command.

5:25. With the basic contrast between the flesh and the Spirit estab-lished, Paul now moves in verses 25–26 to some concluding exhortations. Even though believers have crucified the flesh along with its passions and desires, they must still take proactive measures to align their lives with the Spirit and not the flesh. To call believers to pursue this lofty calling, Paul uses a conditional statement to invite the readers to consider their spiritual condition: "If we live by the Spirit, let us also keep in step with the Spirit" (Εἰ ζῶμεν πνεύματι, πνεύματι καὶ στοιχῶμεν).[960] By using the

---

[959] Schreiner, *Galatians*, 351.

[960] Paul uses a first class conditional statement, which assumes that the "if" clause is true for the sake of the argument. As a rhetorical flourish, Paul structures this verse as a chiasm:

Εἰ ζῶμεν (if we live)
    πνεύματι, (by the Spirit)
    πνεύματι (with the Spirit)
καὶ στοιχῶμεν (let us also keep in step)

first person plural, Paul includes himself along with the readers in this assertion. Throughout Galatians the verb "live" (ζάω) has referred to a person's way of life or conduct (2:14, 19–20; 3:11–12), and that is probably the sense here.[961] Paul is in effect saying that if a person claims to experience eschatological life by/in the Spirit, he or she must prove that claim by keeping in step with the Spirit. The Greek expression rendered "by the Spirit" (πνεύματι) is the same one found in 5:16 and 5:18, and as noted there it most likely expresses agency.[962] Again the Spirit is portrayed as the agent who empowers the Christian life.

To those who claim to live by the Spirit, Paul exhorts, "let us also keep in step with the Spirit" (πνεύματι καὶ στοιχῶμεν). The apostle is not asking for permission; the force of what he says is a command, and the present tense presents the action as ongoing.[963] The verb rendered "keep in step" (στοιχέω) has the sense of "to be in line with a person or thing considered as [a] standard for one's conduct."[964] In all five New Testament occurrences, the standard of conduct is expressed in the context: the Mosaic law (Acts 21:24), Abraham's pattern of life (Rom 4:12), the Spirit (Gal 5:25), the rule of new creation (Gal 6:16), or the standard that Paul previously taught (Phil 3:16).[965] In Greco-Roman literature the word could be used to describe soldiers marching in line (Xenophon, *Cyr.* 6.3.34).[966] Thus, like soldiers marching in formation under the direction of their commanding officer, believers are to keep in step with the Spirit as he guides and directs his people to produce fruit and serve another through love. Given that this verb is part of the same family as the noun rendered

---

The effect of this chiasm is to emphasize the central role of the Spirit in living the Christian life.

[961] A second possibility is that Paul uses the verb "live" here with the sense of "make alive." If so, the point is that those who claim to have been made spiritually alive by/in the Spirit must demonstrate that claim by keeping in step with the Spirit.

[962] See the discussion at 5:16.

[963] Paul uses the hortatory subjunctive, which has the force of an imperative; see discussion in Wallace, *Greek Grammar*, 464–65.

[964] BDAG s.v. στοιχέω.

[965] The only LXX occurrence (Eccl 11:6) seems to have the sense of "fit" or "prosper" in the context of seeds planted in the ground.

[966] See the helpful summaries in NIDNTTE 4:377–78 and Gerhard Delling, "στοιχέω, συστοιχέω, στοιχεῖον" in *TDNT* 7:666–67. Note that this verb is part of the same word family as "elements" (στοιχεῖον) in 4:3, 9, with a compound of this verb (συστοιχέω) also occurring in 4:25 with the sense of "correspond to." Betz (*Galatians*, 294) notes that this verb was used in Hellenistic philosophy to refer to following a person's philosophical views.

"elements" (στοιχεῖον) in 4:3, 9, Paul may also be highlighting the contrast between the old life before Christ under slavery to the elementals and the new creation life in the Spirit that believers have because of Christ.

Anyone can claim to have been born again by the Spirit or to be living by the power of the Spirit. The proof comes in keeping in step with the Spirit as he guides and directs the believer, producing fruit that reflects God's own character. And it must not be missed that the act of keeping in step with the Spirit is a corporate activity. Not only are we responsible as individuals to keep in step with the Spirit, but as we do so we will keep in step with other believers.

5:26. As a particular example of keeping in step with the Spirit, Paul warns, "Let us not become conceited" (μὴ γινώμεθα κενόδοξοι).[967] The rare word rendered "conceited" (κενόδοξος) has the sense of having an inflated self-perception, or perhaps more vividly, "One who is able or who tries to establish an unfounded opinion (κενὴ δόξα), one who talks big, who is boastful and vainglorious."[968] In the ancient world the pursuit of honor and the avoidance of shame could easily lead people to think more highly of themselves than they ought (note Paul's warnings in Rom 12:3; Phil 2:3). The same is true today, as the temptation to talk a big game is a common feature of life in the realms of work, athletics, and sadly even the church sometimes.

Left unchecked, being conceited leads to two further sinful results that threaten genuine Christian community.[969] By using the Greek word for "one another" (ἀλλήλων) in both results and placing it at the front of the clause each time, Paul focuses attention on the effects of conceit within the church. The first is "provoking one another" (ἀλλήλους

---

[967] The apostle uses another hortatory subjunctive, this time negated to make it a prohibition.

[968] Albrecht Oepke, "κενός, κενόω, κενόδοξος, κενοδοξία" in *TDNT* 3:662. This is the only occurrence of the word in the LXX/NT (though the related noun κενοδοξία does occur in Phil 2:3). Philo uses the term to describe the dreamer as one who entangles himself in "vain imaginations" (*Somn.* 2:105), while in the *Letter of Aristeas* it refers to those who have vain minds fixed on possessions (1:8). In the Didache, the author includes this term in a list of vices to be avoided, including lying, stealing, and greed (3:5). The word also occurs in various Greco-Roman authors, including Polybius (*Hist.* 27.7.12) and Epictetus (*Diss.* 3.24.43); see further examples in LSJM s.v. κενοδοξέω.

[969] In Greek the command to not become conceited is followed by two adverbial participles. These two participles could express means/manner (e.g., Schreiner, *Galatians*, 355; Moo, *Galatians*, 373) or more generally attendant circumstances (e.g., DeSilva, *Handbook*, 128–29). But on the whole it seems preferable to see them communicating result.

προκαλούμενοι), a verb that was sometimes used of instigating a fight or challenge.[970] In the ancient world a common way to increase one's honor at another's expense was to publicly pose a challenge that was difficult or impossible to answer, leading to the one challenged losing honor and the challenger gaining it.[971] Yet provoking and challenging others can take far more subtle forms, and Paul warns that becoming conceited leads to provocations both large and small.

The second result of becoming conceited is "envying one another" (ἀλλήλοις φθονοῦντες). Paul uses a verb (φθονέω) related to the noun "envy" (φθόνος) in 5:21.[972] The present tense of the verb presents the envying as an ongoing experience. The envy that the flesh produces is a result of thinking more highly of oneself than one ought to. We begin to think that we deserve things that others have, forgetting what Paul says in 1 Corinthians 4:7: "What do you have that you didn't receive? If, in fact, you did receive it, why do you boast as if you hadn't received it?"

Arrogance is a grave threat to unity within the body of Christ. If left unchecked by keeping in step with the Spirit, it prompts people to provoke and envy. When that happens, the unity that the Spirit works so hard to produce and preserve (Eph 4:3) is undermined, and instead of serving one another through love, we give opportunity for the flesh to unleash division and destruction within the church.

Bridge

The Christian life can often feel like a struggle. That's because we are engaged in a constant war between our own sinful desires and the work of God's Spirit in our lives. We have an enemy who uses our sinful desires to lure us away from following the leadership of God's Spirit in our lives.

---

[970] BDAG s.v. προκαλέω notes examples from Diodorus (*Hist.* 4.17.4), Arrian (*Cyn.* 16.1), and Lucius (*Conv.* 20); see further examples from Greco-Roman literature in LSJM s.v. προκάλεσμα. This is the only NT occurrence of the verb, and it appears just once in the LXX (2 Macc 8:11). Both Philo (*Agr.* 1:110; *Migr.* 1:75; *Spec.* 4:45; *Flacc.* 1:30) and Josephus (*Ant.* 6:174, 178; 7:315; *War* 1:381; 2:464; 4:44; 6:169; *Life* 1:120, 400, 405) also occasionally use this verb with the stronger sense of provoke or challenge.

[971] This is referred to as a "challenge-riposte"; see the helpful summary in DeSilva, *Honor, Patronage, Kinship, and Purity*, 29–31. It was left to the bystanders to assess who "won" such challenges.

[972] While the noun φθόνος occurs nine times in the NT, this is the only NT occurrence of the verb φθονέω (the only two lxx occurrences are in Tob 4:7, 16). The verb is common in Josephus (29x), Philo (16x), and the OT Pseudepigrapha (18x).

But thanks be to God that the one who dwells in us is greater than Satan or our sinful desires (1 John 4:4)! Because we have been crucified with Christ, our sinful desires can no longer command us; they can only entice. As we keep in step with the Spirit of God, our lives produce more fruit that reflects the beauty of Jesus Christ, so that people see him at work in and through us. This fruit grows in the rich soil of time in God's word, prayer, and living in community with fellow believers. As we submit ourselves to the Spirit's leading, we will increasingly turn away from the arrogant selfishness that destroys biblical community.

E. Bear One Another's Burdens (6:1–5)

> [1] Brothers and sisters, if someone is overtaken in any wrongdoing, you who are spiritual, restore such a person with a gentle spirit, watching out for yourselves so that you also won't be tempted. [2] Carry one another's burdens; in this way you will fulfill the law of Christ. [3] For if anyone considers himself to be something when he is nothing, he deceives himself. [4] Let each person examine his own work, and then he can take pride in himself alone, and not compare himself with someone else. [5] For each person will have to carry his own load.

Context

With the basic conflict between the flesh and Spirit explained (5:16–26), Paul transitions to several practical outworkings of a life lived in the power of the Spirit (6:1–10). The central exhortation of this section is found in the command to "Carry one another's burdens; in this way you will fulfill the law of Christ" (6:2). Although hotly debated, the law of Christ likely refers to the moral requirements that come from Christ as expressed in his own teaching and example that are communicated to God's new covenant people through his apostles.[973] This initial paragraph (6:1–5) focuses on fulfilling the law of Christ by caring for those caught in sin.

Structure

The central idea of this paragraph is found in verse 2, where Paul exhorts believers to fulfill the law of Christ by bearing one another's burdens. Verse 1 gives a specific context for this general command: restoring those

---

[973] See the discussion in Biblical Theology §5.4.

caught in sin. The goal should be restoration, with those caring for the sinner being careful to avoid falling into temptation themselves (6:1). In particular, they must avoid pridefully thinking they are better than the one caught in sin (6:3). Instead, believers should examine themselves before God rather than compare themselves to others in order to ensure they have an accurate understanding of their own lives (6:4). For on the last day, each believer will stand before the Lord and give an account of their lives (6:5).

As a whole, 6:1–10 appears to alternate between individual accountability and corporate responsibility:[974]

Table 13:

6:1a	corporate responsibility	you (plural) restore
6:1b	individual accountability	watch yourself (singular)
6:2	corporate responsibility	bear one another's burdens (plural)
6:3–5	individual accountability	each must examine his own work and bear his own load (singular)
6:6	corporate responsibility	congregants support the teacher (plural)
6:7–8	individual accountability	how a person sows determine how that person reaps (singular)
6:9–10	corporate responsibility	we believers should do good to all, especially fellow believers (plural)

6:1. Paul signals the beginning of a new paragraph by addressing the Galatians as "Brothers and sisters" (Ἀδελφοί). After a stern warning about the dangers of not keeping in step with the Spirit, this direct address reminds them of their shared identity as members of the same spiritual family who have the same Spirit dwelling in them (4:4–7). Given the threat that the flesh poses to life in the church, it is inevitable that sin will need to be confronted: "if someone is overtaken in any wrongdoing, you who are spiritual, restore such a person" (ἐὰν καὶ προλημφθῇ ἄνθρωπος ἔν τινι παραπτώματι, ὑμεῖς οἱ πνευματικοὶ καταρτίζετε τὸν τοιοῦτον). Paul presents this as a general possibility, though no doubt one that he expects will inevitably occur within the life of the church.[975]

---

[974] Adapted from Das, *Galatians*, 598, who in turn has adapted Barclay, *Obeying the Truth*, 149–50.

[975] Paul uses a third class conditional statement, which presents the "if" clause for hypothetical consideration; in such cases only the context can indicate how likely such a

The verb "overtaken" (προλαμβάνω) portrays sin as a predator that has chased down and ensnared the believer.[976] In Wisdom of Solomon 17:16 it describes how the Egyptians overtook the fleeing Israelites in the wilderness, while in Testament of Judah 2:5 it refers to chasing down a wild boar. The noun "wrongdoing" (παράπτωμα) is an intentionally broad term that refers to any violation of God's will, whether in thought, attitude, feeling, speech, or action. The word portrays violating God's will as "making a false step so as to lose footing."[977] Paul uses this same word to describe Adam's sin several times in Romans 5:15–20 (rendered there as trespass or transgression in most English versions). At one level every transgression we commit is following in the footsteps of our forefather Adam, yet through the gospel our old Adam has been put to death and we have put on the new Adam—Jesus Christ (Eph 4:20–24).

The necessary response to someone overtaken by sin is to "restore such a person" (καταρτίζετε τὸν τοιοῦτον). As used here this verb (καταρτίζω) has the sense of returning something to its former condition, such as fishing nets after an evening's work (Matt 4:21; Mark 1:19) or a physician setting a dislocated limb.[978] The goal of such restoration is to bring the believer back to a place of wholeness and usefulness. The

---

possibility is. Additionally, he uses ἄνθρωπος in the general sense of "person" and the indefinite adjective τὶς ("some, any") to modify παράπτωμα ("wrongdoing"). Martyn (*Galatians*, 546) notes an interesting parallel in 1QS 5:24–6:1, where the Qumran sectarians describe a process for rebuking a brother caught in sin with truth, humility, and charity.

[976] The only other NT occurrences (Mark 14:8; 1 Cor 11:21) have the sense of doing something beforehand. While this is how the verb is predominantly used in Josephus, he does use it to refer to seizing government power (*Ant.* 17:233), being overcome in battle (*War* 4:637), and being caught unexpectedly in battle (*War* 5:79). Philo describes how people who worship idols are subject to all kinds of instability which suddenly overtakes them (*Spec.* 1:26). An excellent illustration of this verb with this sense occurs in P. Oxy VI. 928[8], which says in part "that if you think fit you may act before she is entrapped" (*MM*, 542). Although some suggest this verb communicates an element of surprise (e.g., Gerhard Delling, "προλαμβάνω," *TDNT* 4:14), that is a connotation supplied by the context. Thus it is going too far to claim that "Paul has in view a fault into which the brother is betrayed 'unawares,' so that it is not intentionally wrong." DeSilva (*Handbook*, 129) is more cautious when he claims that this verb "carries the suggestion of falling into sin through error, neglect, lack of vigilance, or sheer weakness rather than willful transgression."

[977] BDAG s.v. παράπτωμα. All but three (Matt 6:14–15; Mark 11:25) of the nineteen NT occurrences are in Paul. In Ps 18:13 LXX (ET=19:13) David asks, "Who will understand transgressions?" (my translation).

[978] See BDAG s.v. καταρτίζω 1.a and LSJM s.v. καταρτάω. Herodotus (*Hist.* 5.28) uses the word to describe the Parthians restoring the city of Miletus, which before had been racked by factional strife (BrillDAG s.v. καταρτίζω 1.b). In 1 Thess 3:10 Paul uses this verb with the sense of completing what is lacking in someone's faith.

present tense portrays this restoration as a process rather than a simple act, and anyone who has pursued restoring a brother or sister in sin knows that to be true from experience. The task of restoration falls to "you who are spiritual" (ὑμεῖς οἱ πνευματικοί), an expression that likely refers to believers who are keeping in step with the Spirit and therefore in a position to guide the wayward back to the path of being led by the Spirit and serving others through love. Such restoration is to be done "with a gentle spirit" (ἐν πνεύματι πραΰτητος), which is a fruit of the Spirit (5:23).[979] Restoration must be approached with a humility and gentleness that pursues what is best for the wayward believer, yet with a firmness that confronts the ugly reality of the sin and its consequences.

When pursuing the restoration of those overtaken by sin, there is no place for pride. So Paul issues a warning: "watching out for yourselves so you also won't be tempted" (σκοπῶν σεαυτὸν μὴ καὶ σὺ πειρασθῇς).[980] The verb rendered "watching out" (σκοπέω) has the sense of "to be ready to learn about future dangers or needs, with the implication of preparedness to respond appropriately."[981] Paul uses this very same verb in Philippians 2:4 to call believers to humbly be alert to the needs of others; here it sounds a note of warning. The danger in view is being tempted to join the wayward believer in the sin that has overtaken him or her, or perhaps a self-righteous pride that concludes one is better than the person caught in sin.[982] In this final clause Paul switches from the plural to the singular, which both emphasizes the individual responsibility to pursue the wayward believer as well the danger of being drawn in to the same sin.

The work of restoration is not for a chosen few in the body, but it is the responsibility of each individual believer. We are to live as our brother's keeper, intervening when necessary to help a wayward fellow believer back onto the path of obedience and keeping in step with the Spirit. And

---

[979] It is also possible that spirit (πνεῦμα) here refers to the Holy Spirit; Fee (God's Empowering Presence, 462) opts for a both/and view. But since πνεῦμα is followed by a character trait in the genitive, it is preferable to see a reference to the human spirit (so also Moo, Galatians, 375).

[980] The participle that introduces this clause (σκοπῶν) could be either temporal or attendant circumstances.

[981] L&N s.v. σκοπέω 27.58. All but one (Luke 11:35) of the six NT occurrences are in Paul. Betz (Galatians, 298) contends that Paul here draws this warning from Hellenistic philosophy originating with Socrates, but the alleged parallel is not convincing.

[982] Moo (Galatians, 375) suggests another possibility—anger toward the offender—but opts for self-righteousness.

to those who think they are beyond such temptations themselves, Paul's words in 1 Corinthians 10:12 are an apt warning: "So, whoever thinks he stands must be careful not to fall."

6:2. In this verse Paul moves from the specific command of 6:1 to the more general principle behind it. This principle is in fact the organizing center of 6:1–5, and it begins with a command: "Carry one another's burdens" (Ἀλλήλων τὰ βάρη βαστάζετε).[983] Continuing his focus on life within the body, Paul places the Greek word for "one another" at the beginning of the clause for emphasis. Although the verb "bear" (βαστάζω) can have the general sense of carrying something, in this context it has the stronger sense of bearing something burdensome.[984] Thus in Luke 14:27 Jesus calls those who wish to follow him to bear their own cross. Peter describes the Mosaic law as a yoke "that neither our ancestors nor we have been able to bear" (Acts 15:10). The word "burden" (βάρος) refers to anything that weighs down or oppresses a person.[985] It occurs in conjunction with the verb "bear" (βαστάζω) in Matthew 20:12, where workers complain about bearing the burden of hard labor in the sun. Here it refers to anything that makes following Christ difficult, whether it is sin, suffering, hardship, or something else. Believers are called to come alongside each other to shoulder whatever weighs us down and makes following Jesus difficult.

Carrying one another's burdens is not an end to itself. Paul further explains that "in this way you will fulfill the law of Christ" (καὶ οὕτως ἀναπληρώσετε τὸν νόμον τοῦ Χριστοῦ).[986] In 5:14 Paul stated that the

---

[983] Although there is no connecting particle or conjunction (asyndeton), the logical relationship between 6:1 and 6:2 seems clear enough.

[984] BDAG s.v. βαστάζω 2.b.α.

[985] J. G. Strelan argues at length that the use of βάρος plus numerous other terms in 6:1–10 with financial overtones indicates that the burdens in view are primarily financial; see John G. Strelan, "Burden-Bearing and the Law of Christ: A Re-Examination of Galatians 6:2," *JBL* 94 (1975): 266–76. But this seems overly reductionistic given the general nature of the command.

[986] The adverb οὕτως indicates the manner in which the believer fulfills the law of Christ, though without asserting this is the only way the believer does so. Instead of the future indicative ἀναπληρώσετε, a number of witnesses have the aorist imperative ἀναπληρώσατε (e.g., ℵ A C D L Ψ 1739. 1881). But the future indicative has substantive support (B; F and G read the future middle [ἀναπληρώσεται], while 𝔓⁴⁶ has [ἀποπληρώσετε]), and it seems more likely that a scribe would "correct" a future indicative to an aorist imperative (thus matching the imperatives in 6:1) rather than vice versa (so similarly Metzger, *Textual Commentary*, 530).

whole law is fulfilled in the command to love your neighbor as yourself. Here he uses an intensified compound (ἀναπληρόω) of that same verb (πληρόω), which has the sense of fill completely.[987] Instead of claiming that believers fulfill the Mosaic law, Paul says that by bearing one another's burdens, believers fulfill the "the law of Christ" (τὸν νόμον τοῦ Χριστοῦ). Given Paul's persistent claims throughout the letter that believers are not under the authority of the Mosaic law, it seems very unlikely that the law of Christ refers to a modified form of the Mosaic law. Instead, it refers to the moral requirements that come from Christ as expressed in his own teaching and example that are communicated to God's new covenant people through his apostles.[988] As believers live out the law of Christ, they embody the kind of self-sacrificial love that fulfills what the Mosaic law aimed for but could never produce (compare Gal 5:14). By faith the believer is joined to Christ such that the believer no longer lives, but Christ lives in the believer (Gal 2:20). Through the Spirit of the Son of God dwelling in the believer, the believer is empowered to self-sacrificially love others. This conclusion is consistent with Paul's only other use of this expression in 1 Corinthians 9:21, where he explains his approach to sharing the gospel with those who keep the Mosaic law (Jews) and those who do not (gentiles). When Paul is trying to reach gentiles he lives "like one without the law." Yet he quickly qualifies that statement: "though I am not without God's law but under the law of Christ."

Paul may have drawn the idea of the law of Christ rooted in bearing one another's burdens from several key texts in Isaiah.[989] According to Isaiah 42:4 the work of the servant of Yahweh will result in justice being established on earth and "the coastlands wait for his law" (ESV).[990] When God manifests his saving righteousness that results in the redemption of his people and the transformation of creation, he promises that "a law will go out from me, and I will set my justice for a light to the peoples" (Isa 51:4 ESV). That redemption is accomplished by the suffering servant, who "bore our sicknesses, and he carried our pains" through

---

[987] Gerhard Delling, "ἀναπληρόω," *TDNT* 6:305–6.

[988] Thus the genitive indicates that Christ is the source of this law and also the one who commands it (subjective). See further the discussion in Biblical Theology §5.4.

[989] See similarly Otfried Hofius, "Das Gesetz Des Mose Und Das Gesetz Christi," *ZTK* 80 (1983): 284–86.

[990] The CSB renders תּוֹרָה (LXX: νόμος) as "instruction" in Isa 42:4 and again in Isa 51:4, so I have used the ESV to make the connection clearer.

his substitutionary and sacrificial death for his people (Isa 53:4–6). It is this law of Christ that orders the life of the eschatological people of God and embodies God's love revealed in the sacrificial death of Christ on the cross for our sins.[991]

As believers we follow a Savior who bore our greatest burden—our sin and guilt before a holy God. He bore that burden by dying on the cross so that the burden of our sin and guilt would be lifted from us. He calls all who want to follow him to take up their cross (Mark 8:34–38), and one very tangible way that we do so is by seeking to restore those who have been captured by sin's wiles. Christ, as the firstborn son of the heavenly Jerusalem, perfectly embodied the fruit of the Spirit in his own life and has sent his Spirit to dwell in his people to produce the same eschatological fruit that tangibly demonstrates the self-sacrificial love of Christ. The Christian life is not intended to be lived alone or in isolation. As believers, we need others to help us bear the burdens in our lives, and other believers need us to join in bearing their burdens.

6:3. To further explain the call to bear one another's burdens and thus fulfill the law of Christ, Paul approaches it from several angles in verses 3–5, though with an emphasis on self-examination. He begins with a conditional statement: "For if anyone considers himself to be something when he is nothing, he deceives himself" (εἰ γὰρ δοκεῖ τις εἶναί τι μηδὲν ὤν, φρεναπατᾷ ἑαυτόν).[992] The pride described here in verse 3 is a major barrier to living in a way that fulfills the law of Christ.[993] The verb "think" (δοκέω) has the sense of considering something likely and is commonly used of subjective opinions.[994] This is the same verb Paul used to describe those regarded as pillar apostles (2:2, 6, 9), where it emphasized their reputation. A significant barrier to bearing each other's burdens is thinking we are a big deal or better than others. Such a view is especially damaging when in fact we are nothing.[995] Some of the most difficult people to live with in community are those whose self-perception

---

[991] Hofius, "Gesetz Christi," 286.

[992] Thus the γάρ here is explanatory (similarly, Longenecker, *Galatians*, 276; less likely is taking it as expressing reason as does Burton, *Galatians*, 330). By using a first class conditional statement Paul presents the "if" clause as true for the sake of the argument.

[993] Schreiner, *Galatians*, 361.

[994] BDAG s.v. δοκέω 1.b. Elsewhere Paul also uses this verb in conditional statements to introduce a belief or conclusion that he subsequently dismisses (1 Cor 3:18; 8:2; 11:16; 14:37; Phil 3:4).

[995] In Greek the expression is μηδὲν ὤν, in which the participle ὤν has a concessive force.

and reality are separated by a significant gap. Such people are deceiving themselves, with the present tense of this verb (φρεναπατάω) portraying the deception as ongoing.[996] A superiority complex often prevents us from appropriately sympathizing with a person in need; as a result we fail to help shoulder the load of others. But as followers of Christ we have no warrant for a superiority complex, since "all have sinned and fall short of the glory of God" (Rom 3:23). In a first-century culture that was steeped in the pursuit of honor and the avoidance of shame—usually at the expense of others—Paul's instructions make it clear how the community life of the eschatological people of God should be distinct from the present evil age. After all, even at the end of his life Paul could say of himself, "Christ Jesus came into this world to save sinners—and I am the worst of them" (1 Tim 1:15). By God's grace we as believers must strive to view ourselves exactly as God sees us, nothing more, nothing less. Moo is likely correct that Paul is also addressing "the tendency for believers to take credit for their own accomplishments without recognizing their absolute dependence on God's grace and Spirit for anything useful that is done for the Lord."[997]

6:4. Paul continues his train of thought regarding the bearing of burdens and fulfilling the law of Christ by reminding the Galatians how to think more correctly about themselves: "Let each person examine his own work" (τὸ δὲ ἔργον ἑαυτοῦ δοκιμαζέτω ἕκαστος).[998] Despite sounding like an invitation in English, this is in fact a command. The verb "examine" (δοκιμάζω) has the sense of critically examining something to determine its genuineness, usually through testing.[999] By using the term "work" (ἔργον) Paul makes it clear that he does not reject works in

---

[996] This is the only occurrence of φρεναπατάω in the NT or LXX, though the related noun φρεναπάτης occurs in 1 Tim 1:10. It is unclear why he uses this rare compound form rather than the simple ἀπατάω (Eph 5:6; 1 Tim 2:14a) or the compound ἐξαπατάω (Rom 7:11; 16:18; 1 Cor 3:18; 2 Cor 11:3; 2 Thess 2:3; 1 Tim 2:14b). Burton (*Galatians*, 331–32) notes that this is the first occurrence of the verb φρεναπατάω in extant Greek literature, and argues that the φρεν- prefix intensifies the notion of deceiving one's own mind.

[997] Moo, *Galatians*, 379.

[998] Instead of seeing the δέ as marking a step forward in the argument, DeSilva (*Handbook*, 133) argues it has an adversative force, drawing a contrast between the self-deceived person and the one who accurately examines himself.

[999] BDAG s.v. δοκιμάζω 1. Seventeen of the twenty-two NT occurrences are in Paul's letters. In some contexts, this verb can refer to proving the genuineness of something by testing it in fire (1 Cor 3:13; 1 Pet 1:7). In Greek literature this verb was sometimes used as a technical term for official testing (Walter Grundmann, "δοκιμάζω," *TDNT* 2:260).

general, but specifically those works that are performed as a means to earn favor before God.[1000] Paul makes a similar call for self-examination in preparation for the Lord's Supper (1 Cor 11:28), as well as a general self-examination to see if one is genuinely a believer (2 Cor 13:5). Here this command is in response to those who think they are something when they are in fact nothing. The emphasis falls on examining one's own work, not that of others. The present tense of the verb suggests an ongoing process of examining one's life. Honest self-examination provides a necessary check against the common human tendency toward an inflated self-perception.

As a result of examining one's own work, "then he can take pride in himself alone, and not compare himself with someone else" (καὶ τότε εἰς ἑαυτὸν μόνον τὸ καύχημα ἔξει καὶ οὐκ εἰς τὸν ἕτερον).[1001] Translated as "boasting" in many English translations, this Greek word (καύχημα) refers to the grounds or source of pride. Boasting or pride can have a negative connotation, such as when it is rooted in an effort to establish one's standing before God (Rom 4:2), in sinful actions (1 Cor 5:6), or in the flesh (Gal 6:13). But there is a positive kind of pride or boasting that is grounded in who God is and what he has done. Thus Paul, quoting Jeremiah 9:24, reminds the Corinthians, "Let the one who boasts, boast in the Lord" (1 Cor 1:31).[1002] Here in Galatians 6:4, Paul uses this word in a neutral sense of the grounds one has for one's self-perception. The grounds must be rooted in the believer himself and not based on a comparison with others.

As sinful human beings, we are prone to compare ourselves to others. Immediately after Jesus tells Peter that one day he will be executed for following him, Peter sees the apostle John and asks, "Lord, what about him?" (John 21:21). Jesus responds, "If I want him to remain until I come

---

[1000] Moo, *Galatians*, 379.

[1001] In Greek the prepositional phrase εἰς ἑαυτὸν ("in himself") occurs at the front of the clause, likely for emphasis. The precise sense of the preposition εἰς is unclear. If it expresses reference/respect, the idea is that the grounds for pride/boasting are determined in reference to oneself and not others (e.g., Harris, *Prepositions and Theology*, 91). These others could be those entrapped by sin or even the opponents. A second possibility is that εἰς indicates direction, meaning that the grounds for boasting should be kept to oneself rather than expressed before others (Martyn, *Galatians*, 550). On the whole, reference/respect makes the best sense in the context; for a helpful discussion of the options see DeSilva, *Handbook*, 133–34.

[1002] For a helpful treatment of the concept of boasting in Paul, see Simon J. Gathercole, *Where Is Boasting? Early Jewish Soteriology and Paul's Response in Romans 1–5* (Grand Rapids: Eerdmans, 2002).

... what is that to you? As for you, follow me" (John 21:22). Comparing ourselves to others leads to either arrogance because we think we are better or discouragement because we think we are worse. In both cases it hinders us from keeping in step with the Spirit and bearing the burdens of others as a way of fulfilling the law of Christ. After all, we follow a Messiah "who, existing in the form of God, did not consider equality with God as something to be exploited. Instead he emptied himself by assuming the form of a servant, taking on the likeness of humanity. And when he had come as a man, he humbled himself by becoming obedient to the point of death—even to death on a cross" (Phil 2:6–8).

6:5. The rationale for self-examination is that "each person will have to carry his own load" (ἕκαστος γὰρ τὸ ἴδιον φορτίον βαστάσει).[1003] On the surface this statement seems like a contradiction to Paul's command for believers to carry one another's burdens (6:2). But to help show he is making a different point here, instead of referring to a burden (βάρος) he speaks of a "load" (φορτίον). This word can have the general sense of something that is transported, such as cargo on a ship (Acts 27:10; compare T. Job 18:7; Philo, *Deo* 1:98; Josephus, *Ant.* 14:377).[1004] But in the New Testament it is also used figuratively of a non-physical object such as the traditions of the Jewish teachers (Matt 23:4; Luke 11:46).[1005] Jesus says that, in contrast to the loads that all human beings carry as part of living in a fallen world, "my yoke is easy and my burden [φορτίον] is light" (Matt 11:30).

Paul here has in view the final judgment, when each person must appear before God to give an account of his life (Rom 14:12). Critical and reflective self-evaluation is necessary when assessing where one stands before the Lord, and the criteria for assessment are not based on

---

[1003] The γάρ that introduces this clause could either provide the reason or further explanation of the need for self-examination. The difference in meaning here is negligible. There may, however, be emphasis in Paul's choice of ἴδιον rather than ἑαυτοῦ to express that the load is "his own" (Robertson, *Grammar*, 692).

[1004] Five of the six occurrences of φορτίον in Josephus are in the story of Joseph being sold into slavery (*Ant.* 2:32, 110, 124, 126, 134), where it refers to goods being transported. This physical sense is the most common usage in Greek literature; see examples in LSJM s.v. φορτίζω and MM, 674.

[1005] This non-physical sense of φορτίον is the predominant use in the LXX (though exceptions are Judg 9:48–49; Sir 33:25), where it can refer to a person's life (Job 7:20; 2 Sam 19:36) or sin (Ps 37:5 [ET=38:4]). In Isaiah 46:1 (LXX) the prophet says with respect to the idols for Bel and Nebo, "you carry them bound as a burden for the weary." Although not as common, this figurative sense is found in Greek literature as well; see examples in BrillDAG s.v. φορτίον and Konrad Weis, "φορτίον," *TDNT* 9:84–85.

a comparison with others but on what God has entrusted to each person (1 Cor 3:1–4:5). Like the Pharisee who thanked God he was not like the sinners around him (Luke 18:11), we can be tempted to think more highly of ourselves when we think our own sin is not as bad as those around us. Paul reminds believers that in the midst of bearing the burdens of others, we are still responsible before him for our load. As Dunn notes, one mark of spiritual maturity and discriminating self-evaluation is "the recognition that there are responsibilities that cannot be shelved or passed on to others. The mature spiritual community (and political society) is one which is able to distinguish those loads which individuals must bear for themselves, and those burdens where help is needed."[1006]

Bridge

Paul's words here address the biblical path between two harmful extremes. On the one hand, we can become so selfish that we fail to look out for the spiritual well-being of those around us. Our own problems and struggles blind us to those around us whose burdens we need to help bear. On the other hand, we can become so consumed by helping others that we fail to cultivate our own spiritual growth. As a result, we can fall into patterns of sin or overestimate our own spiritual health. The way forward is fixing our eyes on our burden-bearing Savior and keeping in step with his Holy Spirit living inside of us.

F. SHARING GOODS AND DOING WHAT IS GOOD (6:6–10)

[6] Let the one who is taught the word share all his good things with the teacher. [7] Don't be deceived: God is not mocked. For whatever a person sows he will also reap, [8] because the one who sows to his flesh will reap destruction from the flesh, but the one who sows to the Spirit will reap eternal life from the Spirit. [9] Let us not get tired of doing good, for we will reap at the proper time if we don't give up. [10] Therefore, as we have opportunity, let us work for the good of all, especially for those who belong to the household of faith.

Context

Continuing his effort to explain what living in the freedom of the gospel looks like, Paul pens a second paragraph in a longer section (6:1–10) that gives practical expressions of a life lived in the power of the Spirit.

[1006] Dunn, *Galatians*, 326.

Whereas the previous paragraph focused on caring for those caught in sin (6:1–5), the instruction here is broader. Yet it is still rooted in the call to "Carry one another's burdens; in this way you will fulfill the law of Christ" (6:2).

Structure

In this paragraph Paul focuses his attention on two subjects. The first is investing in the work of the ministry with a particular emphasis on those who preach/teach the word (6:6–8). After the command for those benefitting from the teaching ministry of the church to support those who teach (6:6), the apostle uses the analogy of sowing and reaping to make a larger point: how one uses and invests one's resources reveals the true orientation of the person's heart (6:7) and has eternal ramifications (6:8). The second subject is an exhortation to persevere in doing good (6:9–10). Paul reminds the Galatians that, despite the temptation to grow weary in doing good, in God's appointed timing they will reap an eternal harvest (6:9). Therefore, as believers have opportunity, they should pursue doing good to everyone, but should especially prioritize doing good to their fellow believers (6:10). As noted in the introduction to 6:1–5, Paul continues alternating in this section between individual accountability and community responsibility.

6:6. Moving forward in his explanation of what it looks like to keep in step with the Spirit and fulfill the law of Christ, Paul commands: "Let the one who is taught the word share all his good things with the teacher" (Κοινωνείτω δὲ ὁ κατηχούμενος τὸν λόγον τῷ κατηχοῦντι ἐν πᾶσιν ἀγαθοῖς).[1007] By using a singular rather than plural form of the imperative, Paul highlights the responsibility of each individual believer. The verb rendered "share" (κοινωνέω) can have the general sense of common participation in something (e.g., Rom 15:27; Heb 2:14), but here that sharing likely has a financial component.[1008] It is the same verb Paul uses in Philippians 4:15, where he states that "no church shared with me in the matter of giving and receiving except you alone." Sharing financial

---

[1007] The δέ that begins this verse marks a new development in the argument, which in this case is the beginning of a new subsection.

[1008] Paul is especially fond of this word family, using one of its various members twenty-nine times (there are only thirteen occurrences in the rest of the NT). It is especially important in Philippians (6x), where Paul roots financial partnership in mission in the larger category of a shared experience of the gospel and all its benefits.

resources is a tangible expression of the fellowship we have in the gospel. Central to true, biblical fellowship is a shared experience of God's grace produced by the Holy Spirit. As those who share in the benefits that Christ has procured for us as his people, we must be ready to share our resources with others as needs arise and opportunities present themselves. In doing so we bear each other's burdens and fulfill the law of Christ.

The specific kind of financial sharing Paul has in view is between "the one who is taught" and "the teacher." Both these phrases render a form of the same verb (κατηχέω), which is consistently used in the New Testament for the teaching of doctrine and its practical implications for life.[1009] The present tense of this verb portrays both the learning and the teaching as an ongoing experience. From the earliest days of the church, the teaching of Scripture and the apostolic message and traditions was central to the community life of believers (Acts 2:42), and Paul consistently emphasizes its importance (Eph 4:20–24; Phil 4:9; Col 2:6–7; 1 Tim 4:13; Titus 1:7–9). Yet in these earliest churches those who taught earned a living by some other means; as a result, devoting time to preparing to teach came at a cost to their entire household. "The general effect of Paul's instruction would be to share the cost of teaching among all the households in the house church, rather than letting it devolve solely on the household to which the teacher belongs."[1010] Despite the responsibilities of earning a living to provide for themselves and their families, these men labored to feed their flocks. Paul insists that those who benefit from their labors should share "all good things" with their teachers. Thus although the focus here is certainly financial (compare 1 Tim 4:17), the expression is intentionally broad to cover things beyond finances as well.[1011] Jesus himself taught that financial support for those ministering

---

[1009] With the exception of Rom 2:18, Paul uses this verb for instruction given within the context of the church (1 Cor 14:19; Gal 6:6; compare Luke 1:4; Acts 18:25). The two occurrences in Acts 21:21, 24 have the sense of being informed, though the content of that information is what Paul allegedly teaches! The verb is absent from the LXX, and in Greek literature it usually has the sense of inform rather than instruct, though the related noun κατήχησις was occasionally used in Stoic circles with the sense of teaching (see Hermann W. Beyer, "κατηχέω," *TDNT* 3:638). In the post-NT period, this word family took on a more formal and technical use (e.g., 2 Clem. 17:1), referring to instruction in the faith (Beyer, "κατηχέω," *TDNT* 3:639). Our English word "catechism" eventually comes from this word.

[1010] Oakes, *Galatians*, 182.

[1011] Based on the larger Greco-Roman background of student-teacher relationships, Betz (*Galatians*, 305–6) suggests Paul's language here "may indicate some kind of educational institution as part of the life of the Galatian churches." But this goes well beyond the evidence.

the gospel was necessary (Luke 10:7). Writing to the Romans about his collection for the Jerusalem saints, Paul notes that "if the Gentiles have shared in their spiritual benefits, then they are obligated to minister to them in material needs" (Rom 15:27). Given the dangerous teaching of the opponents, it is especially important that the Galatian churches provide support for those teachers who remain faithful to the true gospel preached by Paul.[1012]

The responsibility for believers to provide support for those who teach them God's word is just as binding on God's people today. The dangers of false teaching and cultural values that undermine the gospel are just as real today as they were in the first century. Faithfully communicating the truth of God's word and applying it skillfully to God's people takes time, energy, and effort. Financial support of those who labor in the teaching ministry enables them to invest the time necessary to prepare to preach and teach. Precisely what that looks like will vary from context to context. But God's people should be constantly looking for ways to support and encourage those who put in the long hours necessary to feed the flock their spiritual food. In doing so, believers help bear the burdens that teachers of the word bear, as they invest time and resources to prepare to teach.

6:7. The command to provide support for those who teach the word is rooted in a larger biblical principle: "Don't be deceived: God is not mocked" (Μὴ πλανᾶσθε, θεὸς οὐ μυκτηρίζεται).[1013] False teaching is not the only form of deception that believers must be diligent to avoid; deception can also occur in the realm of practical Christian living.[1014] To "mock" (μυκτηρίζω) God is to act in a way that not only rejects his ways, but does so openly and with a dismissive attitude of superiority. A noteworthy example of this verb in the LXX is 2 Chronicles 36:16, where the unfaithful priests and people "kept ridiculing God's messengers, despising his words, and scoffing at his prophets, until the Lord's wrath was so stirred up against his people that there was no remedy."[1015] This verb has the sense of "turn

---

[1012] Given when we believe Galatians was written, Paul cannot have the collection for the saints in Jerusalem in view here as argued by Larry W. Hurtado, "The Jerusalem Collection and the Book of Galatians," *JSNT* 5 (1979): 46–62.

[1013] There is no connecting particle that introduces this verse, but the flow of the passage suggests Paul is moving from a specific command in 6:6 to the general underlying principle from which the specific command stems.

[1014] Paul uses this exact command two other places, both in connection with sinful living that is inconsistent with the claim to be a follower of Christ (1 Cor 6:9; 15:33).

[1015] Noted by Moo, *Galatians*, 384.

up the nose, treat with contempt."[1016] As Witherington notes, "In a culture where face and honor and shame was very important, to turn up one's nose at someone was to shame them, it was to treat them as someone weak, as someone beneath one's own dignity, and as unworthy of one's respect."[1017] Paul's point here is not that people cannot mock God; sinners do so all the time. His point, rather, is that no one can do it and ultimately get away with it. Even when people seem to get away with openly and flagrantly defying God and his ways, they should know a day is coming when they will answer to God for it (Rom 2:6–11).

The assertion that God is not mocked is grounded in the fundamental biblical principle that "whatever a person sows he will also reap" (ὃ γὰρ ἐὰν σπείρῃ ἄνθρωπος, τοῦτο καὶ θερίσει).[1018] This proverbial statement appears in a variety of forms and contexts in Scripture, sometimes in reference to physical crops (Eccl 11:4) but more often in connection with how a person lives. Thus Job 4:8 warns that "those who plow injustice and those who sow trouble reap the same" (compare Prov 22:8).[1019] Sometimes, however, what is reaped from what is sown is unexpected, such as joy from mourning (Ps 125:5), thorns from wheat (Jer 12:13), or material things from spiritual things (1 Cor 9:11). Paul uses this imagery in calling the Corinthians to give to his collection for poor saints in Jerusalem: "The person who sows sparingly will also reap sparingly, and the person who sows generously will also reap generously" (2 Cor 9:6). Likewise, here in Galatians 6:7 Paul uses the imagery for a financial purpose, reminding his readers of the need to provide for the needs of those who teach them the word.

Because we often do not see this principle happen immediately, we can fool ourselves into thinking that we are somehow exempt from reaping what we sow. It is true that for a season it may appear that we do not

---

[1016] BDAG s.v. μυκτηρίζω. While this is the only NT occurrence, the compound ἐκμυκτηρίζω does occur twice in Luke to describe people mocking Jesus (Luke 16:14; 23:35). In the LXX μυκτηρίζω occurs fifteen times, most frequently in Proverbs portraying the actions of the fool (Prov 1:30; 11:12; 12:8; 15:5, 20; 23:9). In his letter to the Philippians (c. AD 125), Polycarp appears to quote Gal 6:7 when he says, "Knowing, then, that 'God is not mocked,' we ought to walk worthy of His commandment and glory" (Pol. Phil. 5:1).

[1017] Witherington, Grace in Galatia, 431.

[1018] Instead of indicating grounds (see similarly Schreiner, Galatians, 366), the γάρ that introduces this clause could express the evidence for the previous claim (DeSilva, Handbook, 135).

[1019] Similar statements can also be found in non-canonical Jewish literature (Sir 7:3; T. Levi 13:6) and Philo (Deo 1:166; Conf. 1:21, 152; Mut. 1:269; Somn. 2:76; Legat. 1:293).

reap what we sow, but on the last day, when God settles every account, each one of us will reap what we have sown. That reality should shape how we live today and every day.

6:8. Seeking to explain further the principle of reaping and sowing, Paul describes two alternative "fields" into which one can sow,[1020] and the corresponding harvest that one reaps. To highlight the contrast, Paul structures the two clauses in parallel form:

Table 14:

ὅτι	ὁ	σπείρων	εἰς τὴν σάρκα ἑαυτοῦ	ἐκ τῆς σαρκὸς	θερίσει	φθοράν
because	the one who	sows	to his own flesh	from the flesh	will reap	destruction
	ὁ δὲ	σπείρων	εἰς τὸ πνεῦμα	ἐκ τοῦ πνεύματος	θερίσει	αἰώνιον ζωὴν
	but the one who	sows	to the Spirit	from the Spirit	will reap	eternal life

He begins with the wrong choice: "the one who sows to his flesh will reap destruction from the flesh" (ὁ σπείρων εἰς τὴν σάρκα ἑαυτοῦ ἐκ τῆς σαρκὸς θερίσει φθοράν). The expression "the one who sows" (ὁ σπείρων) portrays a continuous action, representing a way of life. Sowing to the flesh refers generally to investing time, energy, and resources into activities or practices that are associated with the flesh, such as the works of the flesh described in 5:19–21. But here there is a particular emphasis on how one spends money. Instead of sharing "all good things with the teacher" (6:6), this person invests their money and resources in opportunities to indulge the flesh. The result of such sowing is "destruction" or possibly "corruption"; the underlying Greek word (φθορά) can have either sense.[1021] While a decision is difficult, on the whole "destruction"

[1020] In both clauses Paul uses the preposition εἰς to indicate the direction of the sowing (BDAG s.v. 1.a.ε).

[1021] Within the NT both senses of deterioration/corruption/perishable (Rom 8:21; Col 2:22; 1 Cor 15:42, 50) and destruction (2 Pet 2:12b) are found. In addition to the general sense of physical deterioration or destruction, this word was used in a moral sense as well by Greek philosophers such as Aristotle (*Rhet.* 1372a34). Philo regularly used the contrast between perishable (φθαρτός) and imperishable (ἄφθαρτος) to contrast the mortal with the immortal, a move that Paul himself makes in 1 Cor 15:42, 50. For further discussion, see *NIDNTTE* 4:597–602.

seems slightly preferable in light of the parallel with "eternal life" in the next clause. Yet, just as eternal life has an already/not-yet dynamic, so too does this destruction. Those who sow to the flesh reap destruction from the corruption that results in the present as they await their final destruction on the last day.

By contrast, "the one who sows to the Spirit will reap eternal life from the Spirit" (ὁ δὲ σπείρων εἰς τὸ πνεῦμα ἐκ τοῦ πνεύματος θερίσει ζωὴν αἰώνιον). Sowing to the Spirit means investing time, energy, and resources in activities and attitudes that originate from the Spirit. The result is a life that bears the fruit of the Spirit (5:22–23). Thus when it comes to how such a person spends their money and resources, they are oriented toward people and opportunities that advance the spread of the gospel. The result is "eternal life" (ζωὴν αἰώνιον). Although more common in John's writings, Paul does use this phrase occasionally to describe the believer's experience of God's saving work (Rom 2:7; 5:21; 6:22–23; 1 Tim 1:16; 6:12; Titus 1:2; 3:7). For Paul eternal life is both something that the believer receives on the last day (Rom 6:22–23) and experiences in the present (1 Tim 6:12). As such it is closely linked to the new creation (Gal 6:15) that has dawned with the coming of Christ.[1022]

Perhaps Paul worries that the Galatians will go down the path trod by the eighth-century Israelites, who violated God's covenant by pursuing false gods and establishing their own rulers (Hos 8:1–6). As a result, "they sow the wind and reap the whirlwind" (8:7). As part of his message calling the Israelites to repent, Hosea commands: "Sow righteousness for yourselves and reap faithful love; break up your unplowed ground. It is time to seek the LORD until he comes and sends righteousness on you like the rain. You have plowed wickedness and reaped injustice; you have eaten the fruit of lies" (10:12–13). The spiritual principle is quite clear: how you invest your time, energy, and resources will produce an eternal harvest, either destruction or eternal life. As believers, we should regularly evaluate how we are living in light of these realities.

6:9. The constant struggle to sow to the Spirit rather than sowing to the flesh can be wearisome. Like the hardworking farmer who rises early

---

[1022] Rather than seeing a general principle specifically applied to one's resources, Hays ("Galatians," 337) sees in this verse a recapitulation of the message of the letter as a whole: "it is a warning against placing confidence in anything that belongs to the realm of the merely human—particularly circumcision. Paul insists that only the Spirit of God has the power to confer life."

in the morning and retires late at night, believers can grow weary and wonder if their efforts are in vain (compare Gal 2:4; 4:19). So Paul exhorts the Galatians to persevere despite the weariness it brings: "Let us not get tired of doing good" (τὸ δὲ καλὸν ποιοῦντες μὴ ἐγκακῶμεν).[1023] Although in the immediate context the specific good in mind likely remains the financial support of those who faithfully teach the word, the general principle applies to any and all things done in service to the Lord (as 6:10 will go on to make clear). The verb rendered "get tired" (ἐγκακέω) means "to lose one's motivation in continuing a desirable pattern of conduct or activity."[1024] Luke 18:1 uses this same verb to describe how believers should "pray always and not give up." Paul uses it to describe how he himself does not lose heart in ministry despite hardships (2 Cor 4:1, 16) and to exhort believers to follow in his example (Eph 3:13). In 2 Thessalonians 3:13 Paul gives essentially the same exhortation as here in Galatians 6:9 when he writes, "But as for you, brothers and sisters, do not grow weary in doing good." The apostle knows from personal experience that doing good to others can be exhausting, and the temptation to simply stop can be powerful.

Paul gives the reason to persevere in doing good in the following clause: "for we will reap at the proper time if we don't give up" (καιρῷ γὰρ ἰδίῳ θερίσομεν μὴ ἐκλυόμενοι). The expression "at the proper time" (καιρῷ ... ἰδίῳ) refers to a specific point in time, likely with the sense of "at just the right moment."[1025] The proper time in view is the last day, when "we must all appear before the judgment seat of Christ, so that

---

[1023] This clause is introduced with δέ, which marks a progression in the argument (what DeSilva [Handbook, 137] calls a continuative sense). Another possibility would be to see this clause as providing the response to the situation described in 6:7–8; on this use of δέ, see Beale, Ross, and Brendsel, Interpretive Lexicon, 33–34. Although the participle ποιοῦντες ("doing") could be temporal ("while doing good"), it is more likely complementary (cf. Wallace, Greek Grammar, 646), since the verb ἐγκακέω is often followed by a participle that completes the idea of the verb (BDF §414.2).

[1024] BDAG s.v. ἐγκακέω 1. The verb occurs just six times in the NT and never in the LXX. In Greek literature the word usually had the sense of "act badly" but came to have the extended meaning of failing or growing weary (Walter Grundmann, "ἐγκακέω," TDNT 3:486; BrillDAG s.v. ἐγκακέω).

[1025] Wallace, Greek Grammar, 157. He goes on to note that while this is the only NT occurrence of this expression in the singular, there are several examples in the plural (1 Tim 2:6; 6:15; Titus 1:3). As a general rule, when time is expressed in the dative case it refers to a point in time rather than a duration, and the noun καιρός often has that very sense (BDAG s.v. καιρός 1). The addition of the adjective ἴδιος intensifies that sense here. In Greek this phrase is placed at the front of the clause, likely for emphasis.

each may be repaid for what he has done in the body, whether good or evil" (2 Cor 5:10; compare Rom 2:6; Ps 62:12).[1026] Only then will we "reap" what we have sown in the fullest sense. Yet there is a sense in which the harvest in view has already begun with the gift of the Spirit and the dawn of the new creation. "The first buds that embody the promise of the future are already found in the true community that is marked by the patient perseverance necessary for genuine service to others."[1027] The reaping of a good eternal harvest only happens "if we don't give up" (μὴ ἐκλυόμενοι).[1028] The verb translated "give up" (ἐκλύω) has the sense of having one's strength exhausted; it is often used in connection with hunger (Matt 15:32; Mark 8:32).[1029] In Hebrews 12:5 this verb describes losing heart in the midst of experiencing the Lord's discipline.

The temptation to give up in the midst of trying to serve one another through love (cf. 5:13) is often strong and persistent. We experience the frustrations that come when people do not respond well to our efforts, or the disappointment when our efforts do not bring about the results we had hoped. Paul reminds us that the key is to keep our eyes fixed on the last day, when we will indeed reap what we have sown. In this life there are no guarantees our efforts will succeed, but on the last day God will reward his faithful servants (Matt 25:14–30). Thus no matter what the results of our efforts to do good are in this life, we can continue to serve others in the power of the Holy Spirit, knowing that in the Lord our labor is not in vain (1 Cor 15:58).

6:10. Paul now draws this section (6:6–10) to a close with a conclusion that expresses a summary command: "Therefore ... let us work for the good of all" (Ἄρα οὖν ... ἐργαζώμεθα τὸ ἀγαθὸν πρὸς πάντας).[1030] Instead

---

[1026] The future tense verb θερίσομεν ("will reap") confirms that Paul has the last day in view here.

[1027] Martyn, *Galatians*, 554.

[1028] Thus the participle ἐκλυόμενοι is conditional (Robertson, *Grammar*, 1023; Wallace, *Greek Grammar*, 633). The present tense portrays the action as continuous.

[1029] Although rare in the NT (just five occurrences), ἐκλύω is common in the LXX (44x), often with the sense of fainting or failing, whether in a physical (Judg 8:15; 1 Sam 14:28; 30:21; 2 Sam 16:2) or moral (Prov 6:3) sense. It can also refer to lacking courage in battle (Deut 20:3; Josh 10:6). Josephus (12x) regularly uses the verb in the context of weakness or failing in the face of battle, usually in an emotional sense (e.g., *Ant.* 13:233). In Philo (18x), the verb usually has the sense of losing strength (*Sacr.* 1:86; *Post.* 1:112) or having restraints loosed (*Legat.* 3:193; *Ios.* 1:61).

[1030] Paul introduces this verse with Ἄρα οὖν ("so then"), an expression he often uses to conclude a section with a summary assertion or exhortation (Rom 5:18; 7:25; 14:12, 19;

of repeating the expression "doing good" (καλὸν ποιοῦντες) from 6:9, Paul uses a verb for "work" (ἐργάζομαι) that emphasizes the effort necessary to accomplish good. Pursuing good for others requires intentional effort and often comes at a cost to us. But as believers, we follow a Savior who laid down his life for us, bearing our ultimate burden upon himself (3:13). He empowers us by his Spirit to bear the burdens of others and thus fulfill the law of Christ (6:2).

Paul qualifies this command with two clauses. The first gives the temporal framework: "as we have opportunity" (ὡς καιρὸν ἔχομεν). The word rendered "opportunity" (καιρός) is the same Greek word translated "time" in the previous verse. God has divine appointments for his people on a regular basis, opportunities to show the love of Christ to others by pursuing their good. As believers, "we are his workmanship, created in Christ Jesus for good works, which God prepared ahead of time for us to do" (Eph 2:10).

While believers are to work for the good of all people, Paul says we should do so "especially for those who belong to the household of faith" (μάλιστα δὲ πρὸς τοὺς οἰκείους τῆς πίστεως). This description may be a modification of the expression "house of Israel" (e.g., Num 20:29; 2 Sam 1:12; Ezek 3:4) from the Old Testament; if so, notice the shift in the defining characteristic of this household from being ethnic descent to trust in Christ.[1031] As a result of their union with Christ, believers are adopted into God's family and share in Christ's inheritance (4:4–7).[1032] Paul expands on this in Ephesians 2:19–21, where he describes Christians as "no longer foreigners and strangers, but fellow citizens with the saints, and members of God's household, built on the foundation of the apostles and prophets, with Christ Jesus himself as the cornerstone. In him the whole building, being put together, grows into a holy temple in the Lord." Instead of biology or law, the defining characteristic of this new household is faith in Christ. This identity as the household of God transcends human family (Mark 3:31–35), though believers remain responsible to care for our earthly family (1 Tim 5:8). Because believers

---

Eph 2:19; 2 Thess 2:15), though he can also use it to begin a new section that is built on the argument of a previous section (Rom 8:12).

[1031] Dunn, *Galatians*, 333. He notes several similar expressions in the Dead Sea Scrolls describing the Qumran community: house of truth in Israel (1QS 5:6), house of holiness for Israel (1QS 8:5), house of perfection and truth in Israel (1QS 8:9), the sure house in Israel (CD 3:19), and house of the law (CD 22:10, 13).

[1032] On the theme of believers as members of God's family, see Biblical Theology §7.2.1.

are part of the same family, they must prioritize working for the good of fellow believers.

One of the earliest demonstrations of the power of the gospel in the early church was the way that fellow believers loved and cared for each other (Acts 2:42–47). As present-day followers of Jesus, our local congregations should be characterized by self-sacrificial love for each other that helps to meet tangible needs when necessary. In doing so we bear each other's burdens and fulfill the law of Christ.

Bridge

How we live our lives today matters. Every decision we make about how to spend our time, energy, and resources reflects who and/or what we truly value. Jesus made this point clear when he said, "For where your treasure is, there your heart will be also" (Matt 6:21). When we understand that we are stewards of everything God has given to us, we are freed from slavery to our possessions. As those freed by the gospel, we are able to use those resources to advance his kingdom and care for his people in self-sacrificial ways to bear one another's burdens.

V. Conclusion (6:11–18)

[11] Look at what large letters I use as I write to you in my own handwriting. [12] Those who want to make a good impression in the flesh are the ones who would compel you to be circumcised—but only to avoid being persecuted for the cross of Christ. [13] For even the circumcised don't keep the law themselves, and yet they want you to be circumcised in order to boast about your flesh. [14] But as for me, I will never boast about anything except the cross of our Lord Jesus Christ. The world has been crucified to me through the cross, and I to the world. [15] For both circumcision and uncircumcision mean nothing; what matters instead is a new creation. [16] May peace come to all those who follow this standard, and mercy even to the Israel of God! [17] From now on, let no one cause me trouble, because I bear on my body the marks of Jesus. [18] Brothers and sisters, the grace of our Lord Jesus Christ be with your spirit. Amen.

Context

Far from being an afterthought, the postscripts of ancient letters often provide an important summary of the key points and themes in the letter.[1033]

[1033] See especially Jeffrey A. D. Weima, "Gal. 6:11–18: A Hermeneutical Key to the Galatian Letter," *CTJ* 28 (1993): 90–107 and Jeffrey A. D. Weima, *Neglected Endings: The Significance of the Pauline Letter Closings*, JSNTSup 101 (Sheffield: JSOT Press, 1994), 157–73. While it is

Galatians is no exception to this general rule, even though a number of common elements in such postscripts are missing from Galatians.[1034] Like the absence of common features in the introduction, their omission likely reflects the tense situation in Galatia. Paul returns to the key issues of circumcision and the flesh as a contrast to the sufficiency of what Christ accomplished on the cross. He also highlights the radical disjunction between the present evil age and the new creation that Christ's death and resurrection has inaugurated. Yet his pronouncement of peace and mercy on the "Israel of God" reminds the reader that the work of Christ is the fulfillment of salvation-historical promises from the Old Testament.

Structure

After indicating the authenticity of this letter (6:11), Paul draws a basic contrast between the opponents and himself (6:12-14).[1035] The opponents promote circumcision: (1) to make a good impression in the flesh (6:12a); (2) to avoid persecution for the cross (6:12b); and (3) to be able to boast in the flesh of the Galatians (6:13).[1036] Furthermore, they do not even keep the entire Mosaic law themselves (6:13). By contrast, Paul refuses to boast in anything except the cross of Christ; through it this fallen world has been crucified to Paul and Paul to this fallen world (6:14). This personal testimony is grounded in a series of summary statements on what truly matters (6:15-16). It is not the absence or the presence of the foreskin that matters, but the new creation that has been inaugurated through the death and resurrection of Jesus (6:15). Paul continues by pronouncing

---

perhaps going too far to call Gal 6:11-18 the hermeneutical key to the entire letter, Weima notes several ways that Paul draws together the key themes of the letter in this postscript.

[1034] For a helpful chart of these features, see Moo, *Galatians*, 405-6. He notes the following common features: (1) statement of travel plans; (2) request for prayer; (3) prayer wish for peace; (4) mention of his associates; (5) call to greet one another; (6) the "holy kiss"; (7) the signature/autograph; (8) warning/exhortation; (9) eschatological wish/promise; (10) concluding wish of grace; (11) greetings from associates; and (12) doxology. Moo notes that (1), (2), (4), (5), (6), (11), and (12) are not found in Galatians.

[1035] Weima ("Gal. 6:11-18," 93-106) notes four key contrasts between Paul and his opponents in the closing: (1) the opponents boast in the flesh, while Paul boasts in the cross; (2) the opponents seek to avoid persecution for the cross, while Paul bears the marks of persecution for the cross; (3) the opponents try to compel circumcision, while Paul argues against the value of circumcision; and (4) the opponents are still living in the old age/world, whereas Paul lives in the new creation. Central to each of these contrasts is the cross of Christ.

[1036] Adapted from Martyn, *Galatians*, 561.

a blessing of peace and mercy on all who walk by this new creation rule and calls them the Israel of God, a title that identifies believers (regardless of their ethnicity, gender, or socioeconomic status) as the eschatological people of God (6:16). He then concludes the letter with a wish to be done with such troublesome opponents (6:17) and a final blessing of grace to be upon the Galatians (6:18).[1037]

6:11. Paul begins the closing section of the letter with what at first might seem like a strange statement: "Look at what large letters I use as I write to you in my own handwriting" (Ἴδετε πηλίκοις ὑμῖν γράμμασιν ἔγραψα τῇ ἐμῇ χειρί).[1038] In Paul's time it was common, even for those capable of writing themselves, to dictate a letter to an amanuensis (i.e., a scribe or secretary) who would actually write out the letter.[1039] But it was also common for the author of the letter to write out the conclusion in his own handwriting, both to add a personal touch to the letter and to demonstrate its authenticity as having come from the author.[1040] Paul himself identifies this feature as a distinguishing mark of his letters: "I, Paul, am writing this greeting with my own hand, which is an authenticating mark in every letter; this is how I write" (2 Thess 3:17).

Because of the reference to "large letters," some have suggested this confirms that Paul's physical weakness was related to his eyes (see

---

[1037] Moo (*Galatians*, 391) proposes a concentric structure, with the signature (6:11) and the grace wish (6:18) forming a frame. The rebuke of the opponents (6:12–13) is matched by the plea for no one to trouble him (6:17). At the center (6:14–16) are the key theological themes: crucifixion to the world, new creation, and believers as the Israel of God.

[1038] The adjective πηλίκος ("what large") occurs elsewhere only in Heb 7:4, where it refers to the importance/greatness of Melchizedek. Both dative expressions πηλίκοις … γράμμασιν ("what large letters") and τῇ ἐμῇ χειρί ("in my own handwriting") express means or instrument (Wallace [*Greek Grammar*, 170] tags these as dative of material, but this seems overly specific).

[1039] For helpful summary of the role of an amanuensis and Paul's use of them, see Richards, *Paul and First-Century Letter Writing*, 59–93. For an extensive treatment of the reference to large letters in light of the larger Greco-Roman context, see now Steve Reece, *Paul's Large Letters: Paul's Autographic Subscriptions in the Light of Ancient Epistolary Conventions*, LNTS (London: T&T Clark, 2017); for a concise summary of the different interpretations of this verse, see William C. Varner, "Can Papyri Correspondence Help Us to Understand Paul's 'Large Letters' in Galatians?," in *Paratextual Features of New Testament Papyrology and Early Christian Manuscripts*, ed. Stanley E. Porter, David I. Yoon, and Chris S. Stevens (Leiden: Brill, 2021), forthcoming. Jerome suggests Paul is not drawing attention to the size of the letters themselves, but rather the importance of the content; see Edwards, *Galatians, Ephesians, Philippians*, 95.

[1040] For examples from Greco-Roman letters, see Richards, *Paul and First-Century Letter Writing*, 172–74 and Deissmann, *Light from the Ancient East*, 170–72.

4:12–15). But this is likely reading too much into the text. Paul's writing in a large "font" was likely to ensure his own handwriting stood out from that of the amanuensis, assuring the Galatians that this letter did indeed come from him.[1041] Based on the context, William Varner suggests a possible additional purpose—in contrast to the opponents, who like to make a good outward show, Paul draws attention to his untrained penmanship as a visible expression of his refusal to boast in anything but the cross of Christ.[1042]

6:12. Once again Paul sets his sights on the troublemakers in Galatia: "Those who want to make a good impression in the flesh are the ones who would compel you to be circumcised" (Ὅσοι θέλουσιν εὐπροσωπῆσαι ἐν σαρκί, οὗτοι ἀναγκάζουσιν ὑμᾶς περιτέμνεσθαι). The verb rendered "make a good impression" (εὐπροσωπέω) occurs nowhere else in the LXX or New Testament. It has the sense of preserving or enhancing one's reputation through outward appearances.[1043] The realm in which the opponents want to make a good showing is the flesh, which here likely has a double sense. On the one hand, flesh refers to the sinful inclinations and desires that act as a hostile power in this present evil age, working in conjunction with sin and the elementals to oppose God (in particular the Spirit) and his purposes in the world. But when mentioned in connection with circumcision, flesh also evokes connections with the physical removal of the foreskin. Through advocating for the necessity of circumcision, the opponents demonstrate they are more concerned with outward appearances than inward transformation of the heart, something the Mosaic law could never produce. These opponents are persistent in their efforts to force the gentile believers in Galatia to be circumcised.[1044]

[1041] DeSilva (*Handbook*, 139) suggests that the large handwriting is "perhaps a reflection of his anxiety and emotional agitation" over the situation in Galatia, but this seems excessively speculative. Although he does not specify, it seems most likely that Paul only wrote 6:11–18 in his own hand, given the common practice of his day.

[1042] Varner, "Papyri Correspondence," forthcoming. Reece (*Paul's Large Letters*, 201) proposes that Paul writes in large letters to prove the letter is authentic and invite the audience to see it as having the authority of a legal document.

[1043] The only extant use of this word before its use here in Galatians is in a papyrus letter written in 114 bc, where a man named Polemon encourages Menches his brother not to diminish a report in comparison to a previous one "in order that we may make a good show" (ὅπως εὐπροσωπῶμεν); see P. Tebt I.19.12, cited in M–M 264.

[1044] The present tense of the participle ἀναγκάζουσιν ("compel") and the infinitive περιτέμνεσθαι ("to be circumcised") portrays these actions as continuous.

As a result, they are like the false brothers in Jerusalem who tried (but failed) to compel Titus to be circumcised (2:3–5).

Behind the zeal of the opponents to compel the Galatians to be circumcised, Paul sees a pragmatic rather than theological conviction. They want the Galatians to be circumcised "only to avoid being persecuted for the cross of Christ" (μόνον ἵνα τῷ σταυρῷ τοῦ Χριστοῦ μὴ διώκωνται). Indeed, Paul seems to suggest that this pragmatic reason was the "only" (μόνον) reason the opponents were promoting Torah observance.[1045] As we have suggested, the opponents may have been promoting Torah observance to minimize the persecution of Jewish believers (primarily in Judea). It appears that with the rise of Jewish nationalism around this time period, zealous Jews were persecuting Jewish believers because they believed this new sect known as the Way was compromising the purity of the Jewish people through their close association with gentiles.[1046] Thus by persuading the gentile believers to be circumcised and keep the Mosaic law, these opponents hoped to avoid persecution.

But behind this pragmatic reason, Paul sees a deeper theological issue. The troublemakers do not want to be persecuted "for the cross of Christ" (τῷ σταυρῷ τοῦ Χριστοῦ).[1047] As the apostle notes elsewhere, the idea of a crucified Messiah is "a stumbling block to the Jews and foolishness to the Gentiles" (1 Cor 1:23). As a means of execution, crucifixion was intended not merely to kill but to shame.[1048] For the Jewish people, being crucified was a mark of being cursed (Deut 21:23; see Acts 5:30), but Paul had come to see that in dying on the cross Jesus was taking upon himself the curse that his people deserved for their disobedience to God (Gal 3:13). Among some gentiles, crucifixion was so repulsive that it was not discussed in polite company.[1049] Yet despite these realities Paul and the

---

[1045] Another possibility is that μόνον acts "as a linking word that adds a qualification to what Paul has just said" (Moo, *Galatians*, 393).

[1046] See further Introduction, 14–21 and the discussion at 2:11–14.

[1047] The dative phrase τῷ σταυρῷ ("for the cross") expresses cause (cf. BDF §196; Wallace, *Greek Grammar*, 168). The genitive τοῦ Χριστοῦ ("of Christ") expresses possession. By putting this phrase at the beginning of the clause, Paul may be placing particular emphasis on it.

[1048] For a helpful summary, see Martin Hengel, *Crucifixion in the Ancient World and the Folly of the Message of the Cross* (Philadelphia: Fortress, 1977), 46–63.

[1049] The first-century Roman orator Cicero wrote: "Let the very name of the cross be far away not only from the body of a Roman citizen, but even from his thoughts, his eyes, his ears" (*Rab. Perd.* 5.10.16).

early Christians boldly proclaimed the crucifixion of Jesus as the means by which our sin was forgiven by God and new life could be experienced. To avoid persecution because of the cross is to deny the most fundamental reality of the gospel.

Even as believers, we face the temptation to make much of ourselves. It can be in obvious ways that draw attention to our accomplishments or subtler forms such as making every conversation ultimately about us. Yet as those who follow a Savior who humbled himself even to the point of death on the cross, we must turn away from even the subtle ways that we make much of ourselves toward making much of Christ and what he has done for us.

6:13. As further evidence that the opponents are less than sincere in promoting circumcision and Torah observance, Paul adds: "For even the circumcised don't keep the law themselves" (οὐδὲ γὰρ οἱ περιτεμνόμενοι αὐτοὶ νόμον φυλάσσουσιν).[1050] As Paul has noted already, the Mosaic law covenant is a package deal; becoming circumcised brings an obligation to keep the entire law (5:3). The verb rendered "keep" (φυλάσσω) is regularly used in the New Testament to refer to observing a commandment or ensuring that it is not broken. Although it is predominantly used in reference to the Mosaic law (e.g., Matt 19:20; Acts 7:53; 21:24; Rom 2:26), it can also refer to keeping the commandments of the apostles (Acts 16:4; 1 Tim 5:21) or the words of Jesus (John 12:47). The present tense of the verb portrays the keeping as continuous, highlighting that the opponents advocating circumcision fail to keep the Mosaic law as a pattern of life. It is not clear whether Paul means that the opponents do not keep the whole law because they are selective in which laws they observe, or whether the opponents are unable to keep the entire law because no sinful human being is able to do so (cf. 3:10). In either case, Paul highlights their hypocrisy and sets up the real reason the opponents are pressuring the Galatians to be circumcised, which is stated in the next clause.

The real reason the opponents advocate circumcision is that "they want you to be circumcised in order to boast about your flesh" (ἀλλὰ θέλουσιν ὑμᾶς περιτέμνεσθαι, ἵνα ἐν τῇ ὑμετέρᾳ σαρκὶ καυχήσωνται).[1051] To "boast" (καυχάομαι) is not merely to brag, but has the sense of putting

---

[1050] Thus the γάρ that introduces this verse provides information that strengthens the claim of verse 12; on this function of γάρ, see Runge, *Discourse Grammar*, 51–54.

[1051] This clause is introduced with the strong adversative ἀλλά to highlight the contrast between what the opponents do and why they are actually doing it.

one's trust or confidence in something. Examining boasting within the first-century Jewish context, Simon Gathercole helpfully summarizes boasting as "Israel's confidence before God, and distinctiveness in relation to other nations ... Obedience, as well as election, is the basis of Israel's confidence before God. This confidence is directed toward both God and the Gentiles; it is a confidence in the fact that God vindicates Israel in the face of the Gentiles, either by destroying the Gentiles or by not allowing the Gentiles to harm Israel."[1052] The opponents view the circumcision of these gentile believers as notches in their belt, trophies in their efforts to bring them under the authority of the Mosaic law covenant. In an honor-shame culture such as the first century, the opponents believed the path to maximizing their own honor was the circumcision of the Galatian gentile believers.[1053]

For those in ministry, the enemy loves to tempt us to boast in the spiritual progress of those whom we lead and influence. Such fruit becomes a sort of spiritual scorecard that we think validates our own spirituality and becomes grounds for boasting or comparing ourselves to others. But when we realize that any fruit that comes through our ministry is the work of the Spirit, all such boasting is immediately excluded.

6:14. In no uncertain terms Paul rejects such boasting in the flesh; instead he insists, "But as for me, I will never boast about anything except the cross of our Lord Jesus Christ" (Ἐμοὶ δὲ μὴ γένοιτο καυχᾶσθαι εἰ μὴ ἐν τῷ σταυρῷ τοῦ κυρίου ἡμῶν Ἰησοῦ Χριστοῦ).[1054] In contrast to the opponents, who ground their confidence in the flesh, Paul emphatically insists that his hope is built on a far more stable foundation.[1055] That foundation is "the cross of our Lord Jesus Christ" (ἐν τῷ σταυρῷ τοῦ κυρίου ἡμῶν Ἰησοῦ Χριστοῦ).[1056] As he often does, Paul uses the word cross as

---

[1052] Gathercole, *Where Is Boasting*, 194.

[1053] Witherington (*Grace in Galatia*, 448–49) ties this pursuit of honor to the opponents' desire to maintain esteem in the eyes of the local Jewish communities as well as the most conservative of the Jewish believers in Jerusalem, but this seems overly specific in light of the evidence (or lack thereof).

[1054] Paul highlights the contrast between the opponents and himself by placing the pronoun Ἐμοὶ ("as for me") at the beginning of the clause and using δέ ("but") with an adversative force.

[1055] The Greek of this clause could also be rendered "But with respect to me, may it never be to boast except in the cross of our Lord Jesus Christ." The expression "may it never be" translates the phrase μὴ γένοιτο, a Pauline favorite for dismissing something as unthinkable (see notes at 2:17).

[1056] As he does here, Paul often uses the preposition ἐν to express the object of the verb καυχάομαι ("boast"); see Harris, *Prepositions and Theology*, 132–33.

shorthand for the totality of what Christ did to redeem his people, though with a particular emphasis on his sacrificial death (compare 1 Cor 1:17–25). It is as the Lord incarnate that Jesus of Nazareth went to the cross as the Messiah, the suffering servant who became a curse for us so that the curse we deserved for disobeying God might be exhausted (Gal 3:13–14). The contrast between boasting in the flesh (6:13) and boasting in the cross of Christ (6:14) parallels what Paul would later write to the Philippians. From a worldly perspective, Paul had grounds for boasting in the flesh based on his ethnicity and zeal for the Mosaic law (Phil 3:2–6), but he counted all those things as dung in comparison to knowing Christ and experiencing the power of his resurrection (Phil 3:7–11).

The cross is no mere historical event for Paul; it has profoundly changed him: "The world has been crucified to me through the cross, and I to the world" (δι᾽ οὗ ἐμοὶ κόσμος ἐσταύρωται κἀγὼ κόσμῳ).[1057] As used here, the "world" (κόσμος) refers to the entirety of forces in this universe that are "hostile to God, i.e., lost in sin, wholly at odds with anything divine, ruined and depraved."[1058] Thus it is another way of speaking about the present evil age that believers have been delivered from (1:4), where the "elements of the world" (4:3, 9) and their allies sin, the flesh, and Satan himself wreak their havoc. But through the work of Jesus on the cross, the new creation has broken into this fallen world (6:15), and because Paul has been crucified with Christ (2:19–20) he is no longer under the powers of this fallen world. As someone who belongs to Christ, he has "crucified the flesh with its passion and desires" (5:24).

Paul's testimony is ultimately the story of every believer. Rather than boasting in the flesh, we are those who boast in the Lord and what he has

---

[1057] As in the first clause of this verse, Paul places the pronoun ἐμοί ("to me") at the front for emphasis. In Greek there is ambiguity whether the world is crucified to Paul through the cross or through the Lord Jesus Christ. The Greek text uses the preposition διά plus the masculine relative pronoun οὗ, which could refer back to either σταυρῷ ("cross") or τοῦ κυρίου ἡμῶν Ἰησοῦ Χριστοῦ ("our Lord Jesus Christ"), since both are masculine. In favor of cross is the parallel in Eph 2:16, where Paul refers to God reconciling to himself Jew and gentile into one body "through the cross." But Paul far more often speaks of experiencing various aspects of salvation "through Jesus Christ" (or some variant of that phrase); see, e.g., Rom 1:8; 2:16; 5:1, 11; 7:25; 15:30; 16:27; 1 Cor 15:57; 2 Cor 3:4; 5:18; Eph 1:1, 5; Phil 1:11; 1 Thess 5:9; Titus 3:6. So on the whole it seems more likely that Paul means "the world has been crucified to me through him [i.e., Christ]"; see similarly Dunn, *Galatians*, 334n2; Campbell, *Paul and Union with Christ*, 260–62. For a contrary argument that the pronoun refers to the cross, see Schreiner, *Galatians*, 379; DeSilva, *Handbook*, 142. But since Christ accomplishes this crucifixion through the cross, the difference in meaning is ultimately negligible at best.

[1058] BDAG s.v. κόσμος 7.b.

done for us on the cross (Jer 9:24; 1 Cor 1:31). By definition we have turned our backs on the values and powers of this world and put our trust in the crucified and risen Jesus Christ. As a result, we have been adopted as sons and daughters into God's family, the new humanity composed of Jew and gentile alike united in Christ.

6:15. Paul now gives further explanation for his claim that he has been crucified to the world: "For both circumcision and uncircumcision mean nothing; what matters instead is a new creation" (οὔτε γὰρ περιτομή τί ἐστιν οὔτε ἀκροβυστία ἀλλὰ καινὴ κτίσις).[1059] The first part of this verse echoes the language of 5:6, where Paul insisted that circumcision and uncircumcision do not matter; instead, it is "faith working through love" that matters to God.[1060] Ironically, the defining mark (circumcision) that Jews thought set them apart from the world is here categorized as something belonging to the world (i.e., the present evil age).[1061] Here the contrast to one's circumcision status is "new creation" (καινὴ κτίσις), an expression that acts as a summary phrase capturing many, if not all, the major themes in Galatians.[1062] Through the work of Jesus on the cross, the new age of redemption has broken into this fallen world, breaking the power of this present evil age, transforming all who have been crucified and resurrected with Christ through faith, and incorporating them into the eschatological people of God—the church.[1063] In light of that reality, the former categories

---

[1059] Thus the γάρ that introduces this verse has an explanatory force. DeSilva (*Handbook*, 143–44) notes that it "also, less directly, provides the premise that should lead to the inference that the rival teachers' (alleged) claim to honor (6:13) is empty, since that of which they allegedly boast (circumcising Gentile Christians, valuing their own circumcision as a sign of inclusion in the covenant people) 'is nothing' in God's sight." The terse syntax of the last clause (woodenly: "but new creation") reflects the sudden inbreaking of God's new creation into this fallen world (so Hays, "Galatians," 344).

[1060] Some textual witnesses (א A C D F G 1739ᶜ 1881) read ἐν γὰρ Χριστῷ Ἰησοῦ οὔτε περιτομή ("for in Christ Jesus both circumcision ... "). Despite the substantive support for this reading, a number of early witnesses lack the phrase ἐν ... Χριστῷ Ἰησοῦ (𝔓⁴⁶ B Ψ 33. 1175. 1739*), and it seems likely that scribes borrowed the phrase from the parallel in 5:6 (see similarly Metzger, *Textual Commentary*, 530).

[1061] Dunn, *Galatians*, 342.

[1062] See discussion in Biblical Theology §1.3.1. Longenecker (*Galatians*, 295–96) comes to a similar conclusion, though basing it in the claim that this verse reflects a "maxim that circulated in certain Christian circles before Paul wrote Galatians" seems tenuous based on the minimal evidence he puts forth.

[1063] For a lengthy discussion of this phrase here in Gal 6:15, see Moyer V. Hubbard, *New Creation in Paul's Letters and Thought*, SNTSMS 119 (Cambridge: Cambridge University Press, 2002), 188–232. He identifies three broad ways the phrase "new creation" has been understood: (1) ecclesiological, referring to the formation and life of the church through

that were foundational to the present evil age—including one's status with respect to circumcision—are no longer important.

Paul draws the concept of new creation—though not the exact phrase—from Isaiah.[1064] In numerous places Isaiah connects the coming redemption of God's people with the transformation of creation (e.g., 41:17–20; 43:16–21; 51:9–11), and the book culminates with two separate descriptions of a new heavens and new earth as the consummation of God's purposes (65:17–25; 66:22–24). Through the work of Jesus, God has accomplished the promised Isaianic new exodus and inaugurated the new creation, resulting in the redemption of believers from the elements of the world into the family of God as sons with an inheritance (Gal 1:4; 3:13–14; 4:1–7). It is this work of new creation that ultimately transcends the categories of this present evil age such as circumcised or uncircumcised, Jew or Greek, slave or free, male and female (3:28). As Paul succinctly states elsewhere, "Therefore, if anyone is in Christ, he is a new creation; the old has passed away, and see, the new has come!" (2 Cor 5:17).[1065]

At the heart of the gospel is the promise that in Christ we can have a new beginning, a fresh start where we have been freed from our slavery to sin and adopted into the family of God. No matter what we have done or how badly we have sinned against God and others, we can experience the new creation power of God, the same power that he will one day use to transform all of creation into a new heavens and new earth for his people to dwell in with him forever. In that day a loud voice from the throne of God will shout, "Look! God's dwelling is with humanity, and he will live with them. They will be his peoples, and God himself will be with them and will be their God. He will wipe away every tear from their eyes. Death will be no more; grief, crying, and pain will be no more, because the previous things have passed away" (Rev 21:3–4).

6:16. With the centrality of new creation through the gospel reaffirmed, Paul now pronounces a blessing on those who embrace this true gospel:

Christ; (2) soteriological-cosmological, referring to the age to come in contrast to the old age that has passed away at the cross; (3) soteriological-anthropological, referring to the new human existence possible in Christ. In my view Paul appears to have all three of these elements in view.

[1064] See the extended discussion in Harmon, *She Must and Shall Go Free*, 228–36. On this theme in Isaiah 40–66, see especially Carroll Stuhlmueller, *Creative Redemption in Deutero-Isaiah*, AnBib 43 (Rome: Biblical Institute Press, 1970), 59–237.

[1065] The fact that Paul quotes from Isa 49:8 just a few verses later in 2 Cor 6:2 confirms the Isaianic roots of the expression "new creation."

"May peace come to all those who follow this standard, and mercy even to the Israel of God!" (καὶ ὅσοι τῷ κανόνι τούτῳ στοιχήσουσιν, εἰρήνη ἐπ' αὐτοὺς καὶ ἔλεος, καὶ ἐπὶ τὸν Ἰσραὴλ τοῦ θεοῦ). This blessing is not limited to only a certain group of believers but is for all who follow the standard of new creation experienced through the true gospel.[1066] The word "standard" (κανών) originally referred to a reed, and later a measuring rod used by craftsmen in construction; by extension it came to refer to a standard or rule against which beliefs or actions were evaluated.[1067] The verb "follow" (στοιχέω) is the same verb rendered "keep in step with" in 5:26; it is also related to the noun translated "elements" (στοιχεῖον) in 4:3, 9. Whereas in 5:25 believers are called to "keep in step with the Spirit," here in 6:16 they are to "keep in step with" the new creation canon/standard articulated in Paul's gospel. The parallel further suggests an important connection between the work of the Spirit and the content of the gospel. The Spirit works in conjunction with the truth of the gospel to produce the new creation transformation that believers experience because of the work of Jesus on the cross.

For those who live by this new creation standard, Paul prays for two things: peace and mercy. As noted at 1:3, peace is more than the cessation of hostility; it is shorthand for the final state of well-being that will result from Yahweh's promised salvation, with its roots in Isaiah 40–66. "Mercy" (ἔλεος) refers to God withholding the condemnation we rightly deserve for our sin and instead showing us his kindness and favor because of what Christ has done for us on the cross. Because God is rich in mercy, he designed our salvation to magnify his mercy in saving people from among the nations (Eph 2:4; Rom 9:23; 15:9). The combination of peace and mercy appears to come from Isaiah 54:10.[1068] As a result of the new covenant that

---

[1066] The Greek expression rendered "all" (ὅσοι) could also be translated "as many as," stressing that this group is open to anyone who meets the condition that follows.

[1067] See NIDNTTE 2:620. In the LXX it refers to a bedpost (Jud 13:6), a rod (Mic 7:4), and to a philosophical rule (4 Macc 7:21). In the three other NT occurrences (2 Cor 10:13–16) besides Gal 6:16, this noun refers to "the mission assignment given to Paul, which included directions about geographical area" (BDAG s.v. κανών 2). The two occurrences in Josephus refer to a rule/standard, once referring to the life of David (Ant. 10:49) and once to the Mosaic law (Apion 2:174). Philo uses the word frequently (27x) for the rules or standards of truth, reason, philosophy, or Scripture (e.g., Legat. 3:233; Sacr. 1:59; Gig. 1:49; Agr. 1:130). The word is used similarly in 1 Clement (late first-century) referring to the rule/standard of belief or holy living (1:3; 7:2; 41:1). By the second century it took on a more technical sense, referring to the rule of faith expressed in the apostolic gospel (BDAG s.v. κανών 3); on the use of the term in reference to an authoritative list of divinely inspired writings, see NIDNTTE 2:622.

[1068] See G. K. Beale, "Peace and Mercy Upon the Israel of God: The Old Testament Background of Galatians 6,16b," Bib 80 (1999): 204–23 and discussion in Harmon, She Must

the suffering servant will inaugurate through his death and vindication, Yahweh insists that his mercy will not fail, nor will the "covenant of peace" be shaken (LXX). By pronouncing a blessing on God's people in the language of a restoration promise, Paul prays that believers would experience the powerful new creation restoration that Christ the Isaianic servant accomplished for his people on the cross.

One final matter in this verse remains to be addressed, and it is arguably the most controversial. Paul identifies the recipients of this prayer of benediction as "the Israel of God" (τὸν Ἰσραὴλ τοῦ θεοῦ). The expression is unparalleled anywhere else in the New Testament. There are grammatical, theological, and contextual issues to consider, and ultimately they are interconnected. Grammatically, the issue is the force of the καί in front of the phrase "Israel of God." An essentially word-for-word translation helps surface the difficulty:

> And as many as walk according to this standard, peace upon them and mercy also/even [καί] upon the Israel of God.

As this translation shows, the question is whether the final καί indicates that "them" and "Israel of God" refer to the same entity ("even") or whether "them" and "Israel of God" refer to two distinct entities ("also"). Theologically the issue is whether Paul would refer to believers (Jew and gentile alike—the "them") as the Israel of God, or whether such a moniker would only be reserved for Jews (or possibly Jewish believers in distinction from gentile believers). Thus "Israel of God" has three possible referents: (1) the church, consisting of Jewish and gentile believers;[1069] (2) the Jewish people in general;[1070] or (3) Jewish believers.[1071] Contextually the issue is

---

and Shall Go Free, 236–38. The only other place where the words ἔλεος and εἰρήνη occur in the same verse is Ps 85:10 (84:11 LXX), where the psalmist foresees peace and mercy as part of the eschatological fruit that will come when God restores his people. But while a collective allusion to both Isa 54:10 and Ps 85:10 may be possible, the frequent allusions to Isaiah throughout Galatians and the mention of new creation makes it more likely that Isa 54:10 is primarily in view. Others have noted the similarity with the Birkat ha-Shalom ("Blessing of Peace") found in the Shemoneh Esreh (e.g., Betz, Galatians, 321–22), but the difficulty in dating this Jewish prayer makes the parallel tenuous; see further Beale, "Peace and Mercy," 207–8.

[1069] Martyn, Galatians, 574–77; Witherington, Grace in Galatia, 453; Schreiner, Galatians, 381–83; Moo, Galatians, 400–3.

[1070] Dunn, Galatians, 344–46; Oakes, Galatians, 191–92.

[1071] Burton, Galatians, 357–58. De Boer (Galatians, 405–8) has a twist on this view, arguing that the "Israel of God" refers to "the churches of the Petrine mission, consisting of Jews

which of these possibilities makes the most sense within both the immediate paragraph and the entirety of the letter.

On the whole, it seems most likely that the expression "Israel of God" refers to the church, consisting of Jewish and gentile believers united together in Christ.[1072] "Referring to believers as the Israel of God signals that Paul has redefined the people of God around the Christ-event, which inaugurated the new creation and unleashed the eschatological Spirit. Since the redemption accomplished by Christ is at once the restoration of Jerusalem (Gal 4:26–28) and the inauguration of the new creation (Gal 6:15), it is only appropriate that Paul prays for God's redeemed people, the Israel of God, to experience the eschatological peace brought about by God's mercy (Gal 6:16)."[1073]

Regardless of how one interprets the phrase "Israel of God," the larger point should not be missed. All of us who are in Christ—regardless of ethnicity, gender, or socioeconomic status—are at peace with God because of the mercy he has shown. Such peace and mercy are not limited to our initial conversion, but are an ongoing experience as the Spirit produces such fruit in our lives. If we fail to experience such peace and mercy in our daily lives it is because we fail to keep in step with the Spirit.

6:17. As an outgrowth of his benediction of peace and mercy on the Israel of God, Paul pleads to experience a measure of that peace now: "From now on, let no one cause me trouble" (Τοῦ λοιποῦ κόπους μοι μηδεὶς παρεχέτω). With his letter nearly complete, Paul hopes it has decisively

---

who continue to practice circumcision and to observe the law, especially the mother church in Jerusalem now under the leadership of James (cf. 2:7–9)."

[1072] See Biblical Theology §7.2.2. On grammatical grounds it is true that the epexegetic use of καί is rare, but it is not unprecedented (e.g., Rom 1:5; 1 Cor 2:2; see further examples in BDAG s.v. καί 1.c). Theologically it is true that the NT nowhere explicitly and unambiguously refers to the church as Israel, but there are at least three examples where the term Israel may have a non-ethnic referent (Rom 9:6b; 11:26; 1 Cor 10:18). More importantly, there are countless places where the NT applies to the church language that in the OT referred to Israel (e.g., Rom 9:25–26; 1 Pet 2:9–11). Of course, the church is only the Israel of God because Jesus himself is the true Israel, the one who embodies everything Israel was called to be and obeyed where the Israelites failed. But most decisive here in Gal 6:16 is the context. Paul's central argument throughout has been that in Christ both Jew and gentile alike are the seed of Abraham, adopted sons and heirs in God's family, children of the heavenly Jerusalem, and recipients of the eschatological Spirit who experience the new creation. So in this final section that summarizes the main themes of the letter, it seems highly unlikely that Paul would suddenly introduce a new development—a distinction between Jew and gentile within the one people of God.

[1073] Harmon, *She Must and Shall Go Free*, 238.

turned the tide in Galatia. The phrase "from now on" (Τοῦ λοιποῦ) signals what Paul hopes will be a new period of peace between him and the Galatian churches.[1074] While Paul has focused on the trouble that the opponents have caused the Galatians (1:7; 5:10), here he gives us a window into the toll this controversy has taken on him personally.[1075] Paul admits elsewhere that he carries with him the "daily pressure" of his "concern for all the churches" (2 Cor 11:28). The situation in Galatia is but one example of the weight of responsibility Paul felt for the spiritual health of the congregations he planted.

Paul states the reason for wanting to be free from such trouble: "I bear on my body the marks of Jesus" (ἐγὼ γὰρ τὰ στίγματα τοῦ Ἰησοῦ ἐν τῷ σώματί μου βαστάζω).[1076] The apostle has already spoken of the opponents bearing the coming judgment (5:10), as well as believers bearing the burdens of others (6:2) while remaining responsible to bear their own load (6:5). Now he refers to what he bears on his body: "the marks of Jesus" (τὰ στίγματα τοῦ Ἰησοῦ). In the Greco-Roman world it was common for slaves, soldiers, and even criminals to have a mark branded on them to indicate their status and to serve as a mark of dishonor.[1077] Slaves were marked on their forehead, while soldiers bore a tattoo in the shape of the emperor's name on their hand.[1078] Given that Paul regularly refers to himself as a slave of Christ, he likely has in view the physical marks on his body earned in the service of the gospel.[1079] Elsewhere he catalogs a

[1074] On this Greek expression, see BDAG s.v. d 3.a.β and BDF §186.2. It is also possible that the expression has the sense "finally" and marks a transition to the final sentences of the letter (Witherington, *Grace in Galatia*, 453). Schreiner (*Galatians*, 383) sees a temporal sense that introduces a concluding statement.

[1075] Paul uses an idiom (παρέχω + κόπος) that occurs four other times in the NT (Matt 26:10; Mark 14:6; Luke 11:7; 18:5) and once in the LXX (Sir 29:4). For examples outside of Scripture, see BDAG s.v. παρέχω 3.a and Moulton and Milligan, *Vocabulary of the Greek Testament*, 355.

[1076] Thus the γάρ here in this clause expresses the rationale for the statement in the previous clause (similarly DeSilva, *Handbook*, 146).

[1077] See the summary in Otto Betz, "στίγμα," TDNT 7:657–60. Others have suggested that Paul alludes here to the practice of dedicating oneself to a particular god for protection and receiving a physical mark to represent this; see, e.g., Witherington, *Grace in Galatia*, 454. Understood this way, the scars of Paul's suffering for Christ are a talisman of sorts that warns others not to trouble him.

[1078] NIDNTTE 4:375. This is the only NT occurrence of στίγμα and it occurs just once in the LXX, where it refers to an ornament (Song 1:11). In the Jewish text Pseudo-Phocylides (200 BC–AD 200), the author uses the word to warn against branding slaves (1:225).

[1079] Citing similar language from a third-century AD papyrus, Deissman argues that the στίγματα refer to sacred protective marks that in the ancient world were believed to protect

sample of the kind of physical suffering he endured: "as God's ministers, we commend ourselves in everything: by great endurance, by afflictions, by hardships, by difficulties, by beatings, by imprisonments, by riots, by labors, by sleepless nights, by times of hunger, by purity, by knowledge, by patience, by kindness, by the Holy Spirit, by sincere love, by the word of truth, by the power of God; through weapons of righteousness for the right hand and the left, through glory and dishonor, through slander and good report; regarded as deceivers, yet true; as unknown, yet recognized; as dying, yet see—we live; as being disciplined, yet not killed; as grieving, yet always rejoicing; as poor yet enriching many; as having nothing yet possessing everything" (2 Cor 6:4–10). Acts further testifies to the physical toll gospel ministry inflicted on his body. Indeed, those in Lystra had seen Paul stoned by an angry crowd, dragged out of the city, and left for dead (Acts 14:19). Thus on the one hand, Paul is a new creation because he has been crucified with Christ (2:19–20); yet at the same time, his body bears the marks of suffering brought about by living as a new creation in this present evil age (compare 2 Cor 4:7–10).

Whereas his opponents focused on the marks of circumcision, Paul draws attention to another kind of mark—the marks of suffering for the sake of the gospel. "The physical marks of circumcision belong to the old world and have no saving significance ... The marks on Paul's body, however, belong to him because of the proclamation of the cross (5:11), and the opponents had no such marks since they avoided persecution because of their refusal to proclaim the scandal of the cross (5:11)."[1080] As those who follow a Lord whose risen body still retained the scars of his suffering (John 20:20), we can take courage that the scars (whether physical, emotional, or spiritual) we acquire in his service remind us of God's faithful and sovereign purposes in our suffering, marking us off as his beloved servants.

---

one from magical charms or curses, functioning similarly to an amulet; see Adolf Deissmann, *Bible Studies: Contributions, Chiefly from Papyri and Inscriptions, to the History of the Language, the Literature, and the Religion of Hellenistic Judaism and Primitive Christianity*, trans. A. J. Grieve (Edinburgh: T&T Clark, 1901), 349–60. Another possibility (noted in Moulton and Milligan, *Vocabulary of the Greek Testament*, 590) is that Paul refers to a practice similar to the one mentioned in Herodotus, who recounts that in an Egyptian temple for Heracles runaway slaves can be branded with certain sacred marks (στίγματα) as a sign they have delivered themselves to the god for protection (*Hist.* 2.113.2). But the prominence of the custom in connection with slaves, along with Paul's frequent self-identification as a slave/servant of Christ, makes these two views unlikely.

[1080] Schreiner, *Galatians*, 384.

6:18. As he does with all his letters, Paul concludes with a final wish for his readers to continue to experience God's grace: "Brothers and sisters, the grace of our Lord Jesus Christ be with your spirit. Amen" (Ἡ χάρις τοῦ κυρίου ἡμῶν Ἰησοῦ Χριστοῦ μετὰ τοῦ πνεύματος ὑμῶν, ἀδελφοί ἀμήν). For one final time Paul refers to the Galatians as "brothers and sisters, reminding them that despite his pointed letter and strong language they are part of the same spiritual family, the household of God (6:10)."[1081] By wishing for such grace to be "with your spirit" (μετὰ τοῦ πνεύματος ὑμῶν) Paul wants to see God's grace penetrate to the core of our being, taking up residence and establishing ever-deepening roots that bear fruit in every area of our lives.

By beginning (1:3) and ending (6:18) the letter with grace, Paul encompasses everything in between as an expression of God's undeserved favor to us. The opponents emphasize works of the law; Paul trumpets the grace of God. It is by grace that God sent Christ to rescue us from this present evil age (1:4). It is by grace that God called Paul to take the good news to the gentiles (1:15–16). It is by grace that we are justified through faith and not works of the law (2:15–16). It is by grace that we are crucified with Christ and raised to new life with him, a new life that we live by faith in him (2:19–20). It is by grace that we are sons and seed of Abraham through Jesus Christ the singular seed of Abraham (3:6–18). It is by grace that Christ redeems us from the curse of the law and gives us the Spirit (3:10–14). It is by grace that we have been freed from the elements of this world and adopted into God's family as sons with an inheritance (4:1–7). It is by grace that we are children of the heavenly Jerusalem, sons and daughters who have been redeemed from our exile in the great new exodus that Christ has accomplished (4:21–5:1). It is by grace that we are free to serve one another in the power of the Spirit, bearing his fruit in our lives (5:13–26). It is by grace that we are able to bear each other's burdens and thus fulfill the law of Christ (6:1–5). It is by grace that we are empowered to persevere in doing good so that one day we will reap an eternal harvest (6:6–10). It is by grace that we have experienced the new creation that will one day transform all things into a perfect and glorious reflection of Jesus (6:14–15). And it is by grace that we experience peace and mercy through the Abrahamic covenant fulfilled in Christ, marking us off as the Israel of God (6:16). Such

---

[1081] Dunn, *Galatians*, 347–48.

grace comes from the Lord Jesus Christ, who loved us and gave himself for us as the Isaianic suffering servant (1:4; 2:20; 3:13–14; 4:4–6).

After praying that as believers we will experience in fresh ways this staggering grace that God has shown us through Jesus Christ, all that remains is to say "amen"—so be it. May all who read Paul's words in this letter treasure above all else this grace and the one who gave it.

Bridge

The cross of Jesus Christ is central to every aspect of the gospel and the Christian life. The death and resurrection of Jesus are more than the foundation of our individual salvation from the curse of sin and the means by which we are justified before God and adopted into his family. The death and resurrection of Jesus are the central turning point in all of human history, for through them the present evil age has been decisively nullified and God's new creational kingdom has broken into this fallen world. Therefore the cross should be at the center of our lives as Christians. The nineteenth-century hymn "In the Cross of Christ I Glory" captures this reality well:[1082]

> In the cross of Christ I glory,
> Tow'ring o'er the wrecks of time;
> All the light of sacred story
> Gathers round its head sublime.
>
> When the woes of life o'ertake me,
> Hopes deceive, and fears annoy,
> Never shall the cross forsake me,
> Lo! it glows with peace and joy.
>
> When the sun of bliss is beaming
> Light and love upon my way,
> From the cross the radiance streaming
> Adds more luster to the day.
>
> Bane and blessing, pain and pleasure,
> By the cross are sanctified;
> Peace is there that knows no measure,
> Joys that through all time abide.

[1082] John Bowring, "In the Cross of Christ I Glory," *Timeless Truths: Free Online Library*, accessed March 19, 2021, http://library.timelesstruths.org/music/In_the_Cross_of_Christ_I_Glory/.

BIBLICAL AND
THEOLOGICAL THEMES

§1 Salvation History and/or Apocalypticism

One of the most pressing issues in scholarship on Galatians has been the dispute over whether Paul's approach in Galatians is best described as salvation-historical or apocalyptic.[1] In this context, salvation-historical refers to the gradual unfolding of God's plan within human history that culminates in Christ. Apocalyptic, by contrast, stresses the sudden inbreaking of God into human history through Christ that produces a sharp set of antitheses between "before Christ" and "after Christ."[2] Although these two views have been set in opposition to each other, a growing number of scholars have recognized that such an approach establishes a false dichotomy, and have instead argued for an approach that attempts to integrate the two in a more holistic reading of Galatians.[3]

---

[1] For a recent and helpful survey of the discussion, see Michael F. Bird, *An Anomalous Jew: Paul among Jews, Greeks, and Romans* (Grand Rapids: Eerdmans, 2016), 108–23.

[2] For a concise summary of the two strands of apocalyptic thought in Second Temple Judaism, see de Boer, *Galatians*, 31–35. J. Louis Martyn has offered the most thorough attempt to interpret Galatians from an apocalyptic perspective. In addition to the excursus in his commentary (*Galatians*, 97–105), see J. Louis Martyn, *Theological Issues in the Letters of Paul* (Edinburgh: T&T Clark, 1997), 111–24.

[3] See, e.g., N. T. Wright (*Paul and His Recent Interpreters: Some Contemporary Debates* [London: SPCK, 2015], 216–18), who after acknowledging a number of "apocalyptic" elements in Paul's gospel, insists that such elements do not exclude a salvation-historical approach but in fact necessitate it. Of course, it is one thing to argue they can be integrated, and quite another

That will be our approach here. Galatians gives one of the most sustained expositions of salvation history in the New Testament. Indeed, this exposition of salvation history is central to the letter, for it forms the basis of Paul's response to his opponents. Yet at the same time Galatians does highlight the decisive and "epoch-changing" nature of the work of Christ, resulting in a series of sharp contrasts between the present evil age and the new creation that Christ has inaugurated. So in this section we will first look at the shape of Paul's salvation-historical argument through the lenses of the Abrahamic covenant and the sin-exile-restoration motif, and then identify some of the key antitheses that the apocalyptic inbreaking of God's kingdom in Christ has produced.

§1.1 THE ABRAHAMIC COVENANT

The framework for Paul's argument in Galatians is the Abrahamic covenant fulfilled in Jesus Christ and interpreted through sustained engagement with Isaiah. Several other key biblical-theological threads are integrated into this framework along the way. The starting point for our discussion is a brief survey of the Abrahamic covenant in the Old Testament, with a special focus on those passages that are especially relevant for Paul's discussion of Abraham in Galatians.

§1.1.1 *The Abrahamic Covenant in the Old Testament*

Within the Old Testament, Genesis 1–11 sets the necessary stage for understanding the Abrahamic covenant. God made Adam and Eve in his image to reflect his beauty (Gen 1:26–27) and gave them a commission: "Be fruitful, multiply, fill the earth, and subdue it. Rule the fish of the sea, the birds of the sky, and every creature that crawls on the earth" (Gen 1:28). Humanity was to rule over creation under the authority of God himself, reflecting his beauty and wisdom as they filled the earth. God placed them in Eden, his garden sanctuary, to serve as priests who mediated God's presence to the world and protected the purity of God's garden sanctuary (Gen 2:4–24). But when Adam and Eve rebelled against God by listening to the serpent rather than the word of God (Gen 3:1–7), sin and death entered the world. Judgment falls on Adam and Eve (Gen 3:14–24), and they are expelled from Eden. God's plan of his image-bearers

to do so in a way that produces consensus. For a recent attempt at an integrated reading of Galatians, see Bird, *Anomalous Jew*, 124–69.

ruling over creation appears to be in serious jeopardy. Yet in the midst of God's judgment there are notes of hope. God promises that a descendant of the woman will crush the serpent, though it will come at the cost of being crushed himself (Gen 3:15). Instead of executing Adam and Eve for their rebellion, God takes the life of animals to provide garments of skin for them (Gen 3:21). God also sets angelic guards at the entrance to the garden to prevent Adam and Eve from being consumed by his holiness (Gen 3:22–24).

As Adam and Eve's descendants multiply on the earth, sin and wickedness intensify (Gen 4:1–6:7), becoming so bad that God "de-creates" the world through a cataclysmic flood (Gen 6:8–8:19), sparing only Noah and his family. When they emerge from the ark, God commands them to be fruitful, multiply, and fill the earth and establishes a covenant with Noah and his descendants never to destroy the earth with a flood again (Gen 9:1–17). But just like Adam before them, Noah and his descendants disobey God's command. This disobedience culminates in the attempt to make a name for themselves by building a tower into the heavens and avoiding being scattered across the earth (Gen 11:1–9). Again it appears that God's purpose of ruling over creation through image-bearers who reflect his radiant beauty is in trouble.

That is where Abraham (originally known as Abram) steps onto the stage of redemptive history. God says to him: "Go out from your land, your relatives, and your father's house to the land that I will show you. I will make you into a great nation, I will bless you, I will make your name great, and you will be a blessing. I will bless those who bless you, I will curse anyone who treats you with contempt, and all the peoples on earth will be blessed through you" (Gen 12:1–3). This staggering promise can be organized around the three themes of people, place, and presence.[4] As such God's promise to Abraham is presented as the means by which God will fulfill his purposes for creation. God will multiply Abraham's descendants into a great nation (people), give them a land to dwell in (place), and dwell among his people (presence). God's blessing on them will be so great that all the families of the earth will be blessed in Abraham. And as later expansions of the promise suggest, the promised serpent-crusher will come through Abraham's line.

---

[4] Harmon, *Rebels and Exiles*, 19-24.

Whereas Genesis 1–11 summarizes thousands of years, Genesis 12–22 covers less than thirty years; "it is as if the world has been waiting for the arrival of Abram."[5] These chapters focus on the themes of people, place, and presence, with God progressively expanding the scope of the promise. Yet nearly a decade after this initial promise, Abraham remains childless. God restates his commitment to multiply his descendants to such a degree that their number will rival the stars in the sky (Gen 15:4–5). In response Abraham "believed the LORD, and he credited it to him as righteousness" (Gen 15:6). God makes a covenant with Abraham, placing himself under an oath to fulfill his promises of people, place, and presence (Gen 15:7–21).

All is not smooth sailing from that point forward, however. Rather than trust in God's timing to fulfill the promise, Abraham and Sarah try to make the promise happen according to the flesh. Sarah persuades Abraham to have a child through her Egyptian servant Hagar (Gen 16:1–3). But when Hagar conceives a child, Sarah changes her mind and sends the pregnant Hagar away (Gen 16:4–7). When God meets Hagar in the wilderness, he promises to bless her son Ishmael and sends them back to Abraham and Sarah (Gen 16:8–16).

Thirteen years later God appears to Abraham again, reaffirming his promise to multiply his offspring and give him the land of promise (Gen 17:1–8). As a sign of the covenant God has made with Abraham, God instructs him to circumcise every male in his household (Gen 17:9–14). God then makes a stunning announcement. Sarah, even though she is ninety years old, will bear Abraham a son named Isaac (Gen 17:15–21). He, not Ishmael, will be the son of Abraham who will receive the covenant promises. It is through Isaac, the singular seed, that the promise of many descendants will be fulfilled.

When Isaac is born a year later, Abraham circumcises him just as God commanded (Gen 21:1–7). But during the celebration of Isaac being weaned, Sarah sees Ishmael mocking Isaac and is incensed (Gen 21:8–9). She insists that Abraham cast out Hagar the slave woman and her son Ishmael because they will not share in Isaac's inheritance (Gen 21:10). God instructs Abraham to do what Sarah says, affirming that Isaac is indeed the son who receives the covenant promises (Gen 21:11–12). Ishmael will also be multiplied into a nation but will not receive the covenant promises made to Abraham and his descendants (Gen 21:13).

---

[5] Dempster, *Dominion and Dynasty*, 76.

Abraham is put to the ultimate test about a decade later when God commands him to sacrifice Isaac as a burnt offering on Mount Moriah (Gen 22:1–8). He expresses his trust in the Lord by telling Isaac that God will provide the sacrificial lamb (Gen 21:8), and his faith is confirmed when an angel of the Lord stops Abraham seconds before he plunges the knife into Isaac (Gen 22:9–14). Once again the Lord reaffirms his promise to multiply Abraham's offspring, give the gates of their enemies to a singular descendant, and bless all the nations in Abraham's offspring (Gen 22:15–18).

The rest of Genesis traces the line of promise from Isaac to Jacob to his twelve sons, concluding with Jacob and his family—seventy people in all—living as sojourners in the land of Egypt because of a severe famine in the land of Canaan. As the book of Exodus opens, those seventy people have been fruitful, multiplied, and begun to fill the land (Exod 1:7) to such a degree that the Egyptians enslave them out of fear. As the generations pass and Abraham's descendants languish in slavery, God remembers "his covenant with Abraham, with Isaac, and with Jacob" (Exod 2:24). He raises up Moses to deliver them from their Egyptian slavery, all throughout reminding them that he is "the God of Abraham, the God of Isaac, and the God of Jacob" (Exod 3:6, 15–16; 4:5; 6:3, 8). God brings them out of Egypt "to relocate Israel in the land of promise in fulfillment of the Abrahamic covenant."[6] Israel arrives at Mount Sinai, where God makes a conditional covenant with the nation of Israel: "Now if you will carefully listen to me and keep my covenant, you will be my own possession out of all the peoples, although the whole earth is mine, and you will be my kingdom of priests and my holy nation." (Exod 19:5–6). As the nation of Israel, these descendants of Abraham were to be a new Adam, priest-kings who rule over a new Eden and mediate God's presence to the nations around them. This covenant was the means by which God would govern the nation of Israel while they lived in the land that God had promised to Abraham.

Forty years later, with Israel finally on the verge of entering Canaan after their wilderness wandering, God repeatedly reminds Israel that the land was promised to Abraham (Deut 1:8; 6:10; 9:5; 30:20; 34:4). Under Joshua's leadership Israel takes possession of this new Eden as an initial fulfillment of God's promise to Abraham. As Joshua comes to the end of his life, he reminds Israel of their roots as Abraham's descendants, heirs

---

[6] Dempster, *Dominion and Dynasty*, 100.

to the promise made to him (Josh 24:1–13). But for the next three centuries Israel enters a seemingly endless cycle of rebellion and subjection to foreign powers under the sporadic leadership of the judges. After the disappointing reign of Israel's first king Saul, God raises up a king after his own heart—David. Once David has established his reign, God makes a staggering promise to him: "When your time comes and you rest with your ancestors, I will raise up after you your descendant, who will come from your body, and I will establish his kingdom. He is the one who will build a house for my name, and I will establish the throne of his kingdom forever" (2 Sam 7:12–13). This covenant with David picks up the themes of people, place, and presence from the Abrahamic covenant, yet particularizes them as finding fulfillment in a royal descendant of David who will rule over an eternal kingdom.[7]

God's promise to Abraham also surfaces repeatedly throughout the writings of the Old Testament prophets, most notably in Isaiah. Israel is referred to as "my servant, Jacob, whom I have chosen, descendant of Abraham, my friend" (Isa 41:8). Similar language is used to describe Israel as the servant of Yahweh (Isa 42:1), whose mission was to be a light of salvation to the nations (Isa 42:6–7). Yet because Israel as a nation failed in this calling (Isa 42:18–25), God promises to raise up an individual servant who will obey where the nation failed, restore the people of Israel, and be a light of salvation to the nations (Isa 49:1–7). Through this servant Yahweh will fulfill his promise to Abraham and Sarah by transforming creation itself when he manifests his saving righteousness in the sight of all the nations (Isa 51:1–8).[8] He will accomplish this through the death and vindication of the suffering servant (Isa 52:13–53:12), which will produce the numerous descendants promised to Abraham and Sarah, inaugurate a new covenant that cannot be broken, and result in a transformed creation where God's people will dwell securely in peace (Isa 54:1–17).

Although not as frequently mentioned explicitly in the Writings, the Abrahamic covenant remains the basic framework for understanding Israel's relationship with God. Similar to Isaiah 41:8, Psalm 105 addresses Israel as "offspring of Abraham his servant, Jacob's descendants—his

---

[7] For a helpful summary of how the Davidic covenant builds on the promises to Abraham, see Peter J. Gentry and Stephen J. Wellum, *Kingdom through Covenant: A Biblical-Theological Understanding of the Covenants* (Wheaton: Crossway, 2012), 423–27.

[8] Isaiah 51:2 is the only place in the OT outside of Genesis where Sarah is mentioned by name.

chosen ones" (Ps 105:6). Their possession of the land is rooted in God's covenant with Abraham (Ps 105:8–11), as was God's provision for Israel in the wilderness (Ps 105:39–42). The first fifteen verses of this same Psalm are also found in 1 Chronicles 16:8–22, where David celebrates the return of the ark to Jerusalem. Thus God's presence dwelling in the land of promise is framed as a fulfillment of God's promise to Abraham (2 Chr 16:15–18). This connection is later confirmed when David prays over the offerings made for the temple, addressing God as the "Lord God of Abraham, Isaac, and Israel, our ancestors" (1 Chr 29:18). Centuries later, after the Jews have returned from exile, Nehemiah begins his prayer of confession with God's covenant with Abraham to give him the land of Canaan (Neh 9:7–8).

Far more can be said about the Abrahamic covenant in the Old Testament, but this brief survey is sufficient to show its significance. In short, the Abrahamic covenant forms the substructure of the entire Old Testament, moving the plot forward and giving significance to the various characters and key events that unfold. God's promise to Abraham is presented as God's solution to Adam and Eve's rebellion and the devastation of sin and death that it unleashed on creation. It is through this promise to Abraham that God will bring the promised serpent-crusher who will obey where Adam failed and lead God's people to a new Eden where he will dwell with his people in peace and security forever.

§1.1.2 The Abrahamic Covenant in Second Temple Judaism[9]

Writings from the Second Temple period extensively discussed Abraham and the promises made to him, so all that can be done here is to briefly summarize three primary points of emphasis. First, Abraham is regularly described as being declared righteous for his faithfulness under testing. In 1 Maccabees 2:52 (NETS) the author asks, "Was not Abraam found faithful in temptation, and it was accounted to him as righteousness?" Sirach 44:19–21 (NETS) expands this line of thinking by connecting Abraham's faithfulness with obedience to God's law: "Abraam was a great father of a multitude of nations, and no blemish was found on his glory, who kept the law of the Most High, and he entered in a covenant with him; in his flesh he established a covenant, and in a trial he was found faithful. Therefore he established by means of an oath with him that nations would

---

[9] This survey is adapted from Harmon, *She Must and Shall Go Free*, 133–34n35.

be blessed by his seed, that he would multiply him as the dust of the earth and like the stars to exalt his seed and to give them an inheritance from sea to sea and from the river to the end of the earth."[10] Notice the connections made between Abraham's blamelessness, his obedience to the Mosaic law, circumcision ("in his flesh he established a covenant"), and his faithfulness under trial. All of these together led to God establishing his covenant with Abraham. Over time this tradition grew to the point that ten specific trials were listed in which Abraham was faithful, and while the specific trials included in such lists might vary, they always ended with the binding of Isaac (Gen 22:1–19).[11] In contrast to Paul's use of Genesis 15:6 as the key text for understanding the Abraham narrative, the author of Jubilees seems to read Abraham's life through Genesis 22.[12] As a result, Jubilees stresses Abraham's faithfulness under God's testing even in places where Genesis does not appear to stress it.

A second line of emphasis is connecting Abraham's declaration of faith (Gen 15:6) with being circumcised (Gen 17:4–14). Jubilees 15:25–34 is especially clear on this connection.[13] After closely recounting the account in Genesis 17, the author gives an extended explanation of the importance of circumcision. It is an eternal law for all generations (17:25, 28), and those who are not circumcised are children of destruction (17:26). Even though Ishmael and his descendants were sons of Abraham, God did not choose them (17:30–31). The author goes on to warn of a day when the sons of Israel will deny this ordinance of circumcision (17:33), leading to God's wrath coming upon them "because they have made themselves

---

[10] A number of additional Second Temple Jewish texts assert that Abraham obeyed various requirements of the Mosaic law. Jubilees 16:20–31 claims that Abraham was actually celebrating the Feast of Booths when he held a feast marking the weaning of Isaac (Gen 21:8). According to 2 Baruch 57:2, during the time of Abraham and his descendants "the unwritten law was in force among them, and the works of the commandments were accomplished at that time." In his introduction to the life of Abraham, Philo states that "the written laws are nothing more than a memorial of the life of the ancients, tracing back in an antiquarian spirit, the actions and reasonings which they adopted" (*Abr.* 1:5). At the end of this work, Philo adapts Genesis 26:5 ("Abraham listened to me and kept my mandate, my commands, my statutes, and my instructions") to say Abraham "fulfilled the divine law, and all the commandments of God" (*Abr.* 1:275). Similar statements can be found in the rabbinic literature as well (e.g., b. Yom. 286; m. Kid. 4:14).

[11] Longenecker, *Galatians*, 110–11.

[12] For the development of this point, along with a helpful contrast between Paul's argument in Gal 3–4 and that of Jubilees 11–23, see Watson, *Paul and the Hermeneutics of Faith*, 222–36.

[13] Helpfully pointed out by Watson, *Paul and the Hermeneutics of Faith*, 231.

like Gentiles to be removed and be uprooted from the land. And there is therefore for them no forgiveness or pardon so that they might be pardoned and forgiven from all of the sins of this eternal error" (17:34). The point could not be clearer—one's status as a son of Abraham who inherits the covenant promises depends on observing the eternal commandment of circumcision. Without it there is no pardon of sin.

The third line of emphasis falls on Abraham as one who rejected idolatry to worship the true God.[14] Philo presents Abram's departure from Ur of the Chaldeans as motivated by his rejection of Chaldean idolatry and his desire to worship the true living God (*Abr.* 1:68–80). The same theme can be found in Josephus, who states that Abram "began to have higher notions of virtue than others had, and he determined to renew and to change the opinion all men happened then to have concerning God, for he was the first that ventured to publish this notion, 'That there was but one God, the Creator of the universe'" (*Ant.* 1:155). As such, Abraham became a model for all converts to the true God.

Like Paul, Philo highlights the importance of Genesis 15:6 in the Abrahamic narrative when he notes that "There is also another praise of him recorded in his honor and testified to in the holy scriptures, which Moses has written, in which it is related of him that he believed in God; which is a statement brief indeed in words, but of great magnitude and importance to be confirmed in fact" (*Abr.* 1:262). But the difference between Paul's use of Genesis 15:6 and that of Philo is helpfully summarized by Francis Watson: "Philo finds in Genesis 15:6 a general statement about Abraham's entire life. ... But Paul claims that Genesis 15:6 speaks only of a single defining moment in Abraham's life. ... In opposition to all eloquent eulogizing of his virtues, Abraham is understood as an unremarkable figure, who becomes remarkable only as the object of a divine promise that insistently reshapes his life by setting it in the light of the world's eschatological future."[15]

These various interpretive traditions within Second Temple Judaism remind us that Paul's argument about Abraham, faith, and being declared righteous did not take place in a vacuum. His opponents had their own interpretation of these matters that likely linked Abraham's faith(fulness),

---

[14] See Nancy Calvert-Koyzis, *Paul, Monotheism and the People of God: The Significance of Abraham Traditions for Early Judaism and Christianity*, JSNTSup 273 (New York: T&T Clark International, 2004), 1–84.

[15] Watson, *Paul and the Hermeneutics of Faith*, 252.

righteousness/justification, and obedience to the law (especially circumcision). Understanding these interpretive traditions sheds light on the likely contours of the opponents' arguments and helps illuminate the significance of Paul's response in Galatians 3:6–5:1.

§1.1.3 The Abrahamic Covenant in Galatians

Paul begins his discussion of the Abrahamic covenant by citing Genesis 15:6: "Abraham ... believed God, and it was credited to him for righteousness" (Gal 3:6). From this citation Paul states the thesis that drives his argument: "You know, then, that those who have faith, these are Abraham's sons" (Gal 3:7). The remainder of the argument that runs until 5:1 centers on the question of who the legitimate sons of Abraham are and on what basis they are identified as such. To his citation of Genesis 15:6 Paul then adds a quote from Genesis 12:3: "All the nations will be blessed through you" (Gal 3:8). Paul sees in these two key passages the same gospel that he preached. Together these passages communicate the good news that God justifies those who have faith (regardless of their ethnicity) and blesses them along with Abraham (Gal 3:9). In bringing together this nexus of faith, justification/righteousness, blessing to the gentiles, advance proclamation of the gospel to Abraham, and the promise to Abraham, Paul was likely drawing from Isaiah 51:1–8, where the revelation of God's saving righteousness in the sight of all the nations is the fulfillment of the promise to Abraham.[16]

In order for this blessing to be unleashed, however, the curse of the law for disobedience must be dealt with. So as the suffering servant of Yahweh (Isa 52:13–53:12), Christ redeems his people from the curse of the law by becoming a curse for them (3:10–13). As a result of his sacrificial death, the blessing of Abraham can now come to the gentiles, a blessing that Paul closely connects with the gift of the Holy Spirit (3:14). This connection between the blessing of Abraham and the gift of the Spirit is likely mediated through Isaiah 44:3–5, where the gift of the Spirit on descendants (זֶרַע/σπέρμα) is parallel to blessing on offspring (צֶאֱצָא/τέκνον),[17] The promises that God made to Abraham were made to him and his seed. Paul insists that this promise was not made "to seeds" plural but rather to the one seed: Jesus Christ (Gal 3:16). This insistence of

---

[16] See further Harmon, *She Must and Shall Go Free*, 133–40.

[17] See further the notes at 3:14 and Harmon, *She Must and Shall Go Free*, 146–50.

fulfillment of the promises coming in a singular seed likely has its roots in both Genesis 17 and several texts in Isaiah.[18] While in Genesis 17:7–10 God stresses that his covenant is with Abraham's offspring (plural), later in that same chapter he makes it clear that it is through the singular seed Isaac that the promise will be fulfilled (17:15–19). Isaiah 41:8 brings together the themes of the seed of Abraham and the servant of Yahweh, while Isaiah 54:1–10 describes the fulfillment of the promise to Abraham through the work of the suffering servant resulting in an inheritance and a covenant of peace.[19]

The addition of the Mosaic law 430 years later in no way nullified the promise to Abraham (Gal 3:17); receiving the inheritance was still predicated on the promise and not the law (Gal 3:18). But if the Mosaic law covenant did not replace the Abrahamic covenant, the natural question is why the Mosaic law covenant was given in the first place. God gave the Mosaic law to bring sin out into the open, exposing it as a violation of God's will until the seed of Abraham would come and deal with it decisively (Gal 3:19); it was never intended to bring about the promised seed of Abraham (Gal 3:20). Far from working against the Abrahamic promise, the Mosaic law covenant had a specific role for a specific time in salvation history: to imprison all of creation under sin and serve as a guardian until the promised seed of Abraham would come (Gal 3:22–24). Thus the Mosaic law covenant was never intended to give eschatological life (Gal 3:21); that was the role of Abraham's promised seed.

But now that Christ the promised seed of Abraham has come, the temporary purpose of the Mosaic law covenant has been fulfilled and is no longer needed (Gal 3:25). All who trust in Christ the promised seed of Abraham are not merely sons of Abraham; they are sons of God (Gal 3:26) who are clothed with Christ through their baptism (Gal 3:27). All those who have put on Christ through their baptism are united into one body; the distinctions that this present evil age are based on—ethnicity, socioeconomic status, gender—make no difference when it comes to one's status as a son of God (Gal 3:28). All who by faith belong to Christ the seed

---

[18] See further Harmon, *She Must and Shall Go Free*, 150–61.

[19] Isaiah 61:1–11 may be another background, as it brings together a Spirit-anointed figure who proclaims the gospel, which results in God's people experiencing forgiveness of sin, an inheritance, an eternal covenant, and seed known among the nations as blessed by Yahweh.

of Abraham are therefore also seed of Abraham and heirs of the promise that God made to Abraham (Gal 3:29).

Building on the status of believers as heirs of the Abrahamic promise through faith in Christ, Paul re-explains how believers came to have that status using the framework of the promised second exodus (Gal 4:1–7). Echoing language from Hosea 11:1, Paul presents the Israelites as recipients of the promise of universal sovereignty through the Abrahamic covenant (Gal 4:1). Yet they languished under the authority of their Egyptian taskmasters until the time appointed by God for them to receive their inheritance (Gal 4:2). This state of slavery, however, was not unique to Israel; all of humanity was enslaved to the elements of this world, the old creation that is under the curse that came because of Adam's sin and is now subject to the powers of this present evil age (Gal 4:3).

So when it came time for the Abrahamic promises to be fulfilled, God sent forth his own son, who came to rescue both gentiles ("born of a woman") and Jews ("born under the law") from this wretched state of slavery to the elements of the world (Gal 4:4). As the son of God, Christ is the promised descendant of David who rules over an eternal kingdom in fulfillment of God's promise to Abraham. He is also the Isaianic suffering servant, sent to redeem his people through a new exodus that makes them adopted sons (Gal 4:5). As sons they are freed from their slavery to the elements of this world and now experience the Isaianic new creation kingdom that Christ the son has inaugurated through his death and resurrection. To mark these adopted sons as the eschatological people of God, the Father has sent the Spirit of his Son into their hearts (Gal 4:6).[20] As sons of God, believers receive the inheritance that God had promised to Abraham through the work of God sending his Son (the seed of Abraham, the promised king from David's line, the Isaianic suffering servant) to redeem them (Gal 4:7).

After a personal appeal to not return to slavery under the elements of the world by observing the Mosaic law (Gal 4:8–20), Paul brings his discussion of the Abrahamic covenant to a stunning climax (Gal 4:21–5:1). By reading the Abraham story allegorically (by which he means reading it through the lens of Isaiah 54:1 and its surrounding context), Paul sees two covenants represented by two women and their respective sons.

---

[20] Paul may echo Isa 48:16 in speaking of God sending the Son and the Spirit; if so it further enhances the Isaianic framing of this new exodus.

Hagar the slave woman represents the Mosaic law covenant, and her son Ishmael, born according to the flesh, denotes all who try to relate to God and others on the basis of the Mosaic law. She corresponds to the present Jerusalem, a way of referring to any and all who place the Mosaic law at the center of relating to God and others. As such, they remain enslaved under the elements of the world. By contrast, Sarah the free woman refers to the Abrahamic covenant fulfilled in Christ, and her son Isaac, born according to the promise, denotes all who relate to God on the basis of faith in the promise of God. She corresponds to the Jerusalem above, who is free from slavery and the mother of all who trust in Christ as the fulfillment of the promise to Abraham. Paul grounds the typological significance of these identifications with a citation of Isaiah 54:1, which the apostle uses to argue that the fulfillment of the Abrahamic covenant has come in Christ the promised seed and servant, and through his death and resurrection the promised heavenly Jerusalem has come into existence and begun to bring forth children (all who belong to Christ by faith, regardless of ethnicity, gender, socioeconomic status, or Torah observance). In this way the promise made to Abraham that "all the nations will be blessed through you" (Gal 3:8 = Gen 12:3) is being fulfilled.

Because they are in Christ the Galatian believers are children of promise like Isaac, born according to the Spirit. So it should come as no surprise they are being persecuted by those who are born according to the flesh (Gal 4:28–29). Alluding to Genesis 21:9, Paul reminds the Galatians that Isaac the child of promise was persecuted by Ishmael the child of the flesh. Paul cites the words of Genesis 21:10 to insist that no one who has aligned themselves with Hagar-Ishmael through their reliance upon the Mosaic law will ever inherit what was promised to Abraham (Gal 4:30–31). Only those in the line of Sarah the free woman and her promise-born son Isaac will be heirs, a status which only happens through one's union with Christ. Rather than returning to a yoke of slavery under the Mosaic law, believers must stand firm in the freedom that Christ has freed them to enjoy (Gal 5:1).

With his explanation of the Abrahamic covenant fulfilled in Christ now complete, the apostle transitions to apply the significance of this to the threat posed by the opponents and everyday life in the body of Christ. Believers do not need circumcision or any other element of the Mosaic law covenant because they are in Christ, where what matters is not circumcision or uncircumcision, but faith working through love

(Gal 5:6). The Spirit that God gives in fulfillment of the Abrahamic promise empowers believers to eagerly wait for the hope of righteousness (Gal 5:5). Because they are freed from the powers of this present evil age, believers are able to serve one another through love (Gal 5:13). By loving their neighbor as themselves (a citation of Lev 19:18), believers fulfill the intent of the Mosaic law covenant (Gal 5:14). Because believers have the eschatological Spirit as part of their inheritance in Christ the seed of Abraham, they are able to overcome the desires of the flesh (Gal 5:16–18). Instead of producing the works of the flesh, believers bear the fruit of the Spirit and walk in his power to reflect Christ in their lives (Gal 5:19–26). As they do so they fulfill the law of Christ by bearing one another's burdens and doing good to others in practical ways (Gal 6:1–10). In the conclusion to Galatians Paul draws together several motifs from the Abrahamic covenant (Gal 6:11–18). The crucifixion and resurrection of Jesus has launched the new creation, the messianic age in which the old distinctions of the Mosaic law and the other elements of the world are done away with (Gal 6:14–16).

§1.1.4 Conclusion

Although the importance of the Abrahamic covenant was widely recognized within the Judaism of Paul's day, the way to interpret and apply it was hotly disputed. Given its prominence in Galatians, it seems likely that disagreement over the relationship between the work of Christ and the Abrahamic covenant was central to the conflict in Galatia. Paul argues that the promise to bless all the nations through the seed of Abraham was an announcement of the good news that all—regardless of ethnicity —who trust in Christ are justified before God. By virtue of being in Christ the seed of Abraham, they inherit the blessing God had promised to Abraham. They are sons of God who have been redeemed from slavery to the elements of the world through a new exodus accomplished by Christ the suffering servant. As sons they have been given the Spirit as part of their inheritance, marking them off as children of promise like Isaac, sons of the free woman and citizens of the heavenly Jerusalem. As such they have no reason to pursue the Mosaic law, which God gave as a temporary covenant to expose and restrain sin until the promised seed of Abraham came.

§1.2 Exile and Return from Exile

Although not as prominent as the Abrahamic covenant, exile and return from exile is an important motif in Galatians. It serves a supporting role in Paul's effort to explain the significance of the work of Christ. Paul's use of this motif in Galatians has its roots in Deuteronomy 27–30 but has been mediated through how this theme was developed and expanded in Isaiah.

§1.2.1 Sin, Exile, and Return in Deuteronomy

The starting point for understanding the exile theme in Galatians is Deuteronomy 27–30. Chapters 27–28 focus on the ceremony that Israel is to perform once they enter the land. Half of the tribes are to stand on Mount Ebal to announce the curses that will come on Israel if they break the covenant (27:15–26; 28:15–68), while the other half stand on Mount Gerizim to proclaim the blessings Israel will experience if they obey (28:1–14). Moses then intertwines a retelling of Israel's history with warnings about the judgment God will bring upon them when they disobey (29:2–29). Judgment, however, will not be the final word; when exiled Israel repents and whole-heartedly returns to Yahweh, he will bring them back from where he has scattered them (30:1–10). The choice between obedience and rebellion, life and death, good and evil now rests in Israel's hands (30:11–20).

Our entry point into this complex passage is Deuteronomy 27:26, since this is the verse that Paul quotes in Galatians 3:10. Paul's choice is far from haphazard. Deuteronomy 27:26 is the culminating curse in the initial section of curses. It encompasses all of the previous curses when it states: "'Anyone who does not put the words of this law into practice is cursed.' And all the people will say, 'Amen!'" The LXX makes the summarizing nature of this verse even clearer by adding a form of πᾶς in two key places: "Cursed is every person [πᾶς ἄνθρωπος] who does not remain in all the words of this law [ἐν πᾶσιν τοῖς λόγοις τοῦ νόμου τούτου] to do them" (my translation).

This combination of curse, all, and doing the law occurs at three key points in Deuteronomy 28:15–68, functioning as a structuring device at key points (28:15, 45, 58). The curses appear to intensify as the passage continues, and in each cycle the culminating curse is exile (28:36–44, 46–57, 64–68). In a stunning reversal of the promise to Abraham, God warns that he will reduce them from being as numerous as the stars of heaven (Gen 15:5) to being few in number (Deut 28:62). Just as God had delighted to do them good and multiply them (Deut 6:3), he will now delight to destroy them (28:63). This destruction culminates in Yahweh scattering his people among the nations, where they will worship gods of wood and stone (28:64). Instead of finding rest in the land of promise, Yahweh will give them "a trembling heart and failing eyes and a languishing soul" (28:65 ESV) in the land of exile. Life will be uncertain and full of dread (28:66–67). They won't even be able to find a buyer when they offer themselves for sale (28:68).

At this point Moses reminds the Israelites of what they have seen God do for them in bringing them out of Egypt and sustaining them for forty years in the wilderness (29:1–17). At the heart of this section is a reminder of the promise that God "swore to your fathers, to Abraham, to Isaac, and to Jacob" (29:13 ESV). But Moses also warns Israel that if anyone serves other gods, all the curses of this covenant will rest upon him (29:20–21). When future generations see Yahweh's devastating judgment, they will understand that it was the result of Israel abandoning the covenant by serving other gods (29:22–26). These generations will conclude that God has brought upon the land all the curses written in this book of the covenant and cast the people out of the land because of his great wrath (29:27–28). Once again, exile is the culminating curse written in the book of the law that comes upon God's people for their covenant unfaithfulness.

But exile is not the final word. When the people in exile return to Yahweh with their whole heart and soul to obey him, he will restore their fortunes and have mercy on them (30:1–10). Yahweh will circumcise their hearts and the hearts of their offspring so they will love Yahweh with their whole heart and soul (30:6). Yahweh will take delight in prospering them again, "when you obey the LORD your God by keeping his commands and statutes that are written in this book of the law and return to him with all your heart and all your soul" (30:10). Based on this promise Moses calls the people to choose obedience, life, and blessing rather than disobedience, death, and curse so that their offspring may live and receive the blessings God promised to Abraham, Isaac, and Jacob (30:11–20).

From this brief and selective survey of exile and return in Deuteronomy 27–30, three key insights emerge. First, the "curse, all, doing the law" formula (in its various forms) is an important thread that runs throughout these chapters, functioning as a structuring device. Its repetition reminds the hearer/reader that failure to keep the entire law covenant subjects the people to God's judgment. Second, the repeated mention of the curses "written in the/this (book of) the law" specifies the curses as a result of breaking the Mosaic covenant. This covenant is an outworking of the promise that God made to Abraham, though the exact relationship between the two is not specified. Third, exile is repeatedly singled out at as the culminating curse that comes on the people for breaking the covenant. As such, reversing that exile is the centerpiece of Yahweh restoring his people. That restoration from exile is predicated on Israel returning to Yahweh by loving him with a whole heart and whole soul. Such love will be only possible because God will circumcise the hearts of the people and their offspring. This heart circumcision will result in the people obeying what is written in the law.

§1.2.2 Sin, Exile, and Return in Isaiah

Exile and return from exile are two of the key themes that run throughout Isaiah 40–66. These chapters are set up by the account of Babylonian envoys visiting King Hezekiah, after which Isaiah announces that days are coming when his house and the people will be taken into exile in Babylon (39:1–8). While Isaiah 40–55 focuses on the redemption that Yahweh will bring to his people, that redemption is frequently linked to Israel's sin and the resulting exile. While each element of the sin-exile-return motif is informed and shaped by the Deuteronomic background, Isaiah develops and expands this motif beyond what is in Deuteronomy itself. So first we must look at how the Deuteronomic background shapes Isaiah's presentation of the sin-exile-return motif, before later turning to note how Isaiah develops it further.

Throughout Isaiah 40–55 the prophet describes the people's sin and resulting exile, often in Deuteronomic terms.[21] Although called to be the servant of Yahweh lighting the way for the nations and opening blind eyes (42:1–7), Israel as a nation is instead blind and deaf (42:18–20; compare Deut 28:28–29). They are a people "plundered and looted; they are all of them trapped in holes and hidden in prisons; they have become plunder with none to rescue, spoil with none to say, 'Restore!'" (42:22 ESV; compare Deut 28:29–34). They refused to walk in the ways of Yahweh or obey his law (42:24; compare Deut 27:26; 28:15, 45, 58).

---

[21] This section is adapted and expanded from Harmon, *She Must and Shall Go Free*, 207–8.

This Deuteronomic framing of sin-exile-return is seen even more clearly in the climactic fourth Servant Song (Isa 52:12–53:12), where the woeful condition Israel finds itself in is experiencing the curses promised in Deuteronomy 27–29, which culminate in exile.[22] Isaiah's description of this suffering servant makes it clear that this servant is experiencing Israel's curses as a substitute.[23] Isaiah says that the servant "will be successful" (יַשְׂכִּיל; Isa 52:13), just as God had promised Israel would "succeed" (תַּשְׂכִּילוּ) if they "observe the words of this covenant and follow them" (Deut 29:9 [MT 29:8]).[24] The horrible disfigurement of the servant and resulting astonishment of the nations and kings (Isa 52:14–15) may find a parallel in the astonishment of the nations at the desolation of the land God had promised to bring on rebellious Israel (Deut 29:22–27). Mention

---

[22] This section is adapted and expanded from Harmon, *She Must and Shall Go Free*, 144–45. See similarly, e.g., Anthony R. Ceresko, "The Rhetorical Strategy of the Fourth Servant Song (Isaiah 52:13–53:12): Poetry and the Exodus-New Exodus," *CBQ* 56 (1994): 42–55 (esp. 47–50); G. P. Hugenberger, "The Servant of the Lord in the 'Servant Songs' of Isaiah: A Second Moses Figure," in *The Lord's Anointed: Interpretation of Old Testament Messianic Texts*, ed. P. E. Satterthwaite, Richard S. Hess, and Gordon J. Wenham (Grand Rapids: Baker, 1995), 129–39; Rikki E. Watts, "Jesus' Death, Isaiah 53, and Mark 10:45: A Crux Revisited," in *Jesus and the Suffering Servant: Isaiah 53 and Christian Origins*, ed. W. H. Bellinger and William Reuben Farmer (Harrisburg, PA: Trinity Press, 1998), 125–51. Although he does not draw connections between the specific sufferings of the servant and Deut 28–30, Clements does link the vicarious suffering of the servant to restoration from exile; see Ronald E. Clements, "Isaiah 53 and the Restoration of Israel," in *Jesus and the Suffering Servant: Isaiah 53 and Christian Origins*, ed. W. H. Bellinger and William Reuben Farmer (Harrisburg, PA: Trinity Press, 1998), 39–54.

[23] On the vicarious suffering of the servant, see Daniel P. Bailey, "Concepts of *Stellvertretung* in the Interpretation of Isaiah 53," in *Jesus and the Suffering Servant: Isaiah 53 and Christian Origins*, ed. W. H. Bellinger and William Reuben Farmer (Harrisburg, PA: Trinity Press, 1998), 223–50; Hermann Spieckerman, "The Conception and Prehistory of the Idea of Vicarious Suffering in the Old Testament," in *The Suffering Servant: Isaiah 53 in Jewish and Christian Sources*, ed. Bernd Janowski and Peter Stuhlmacher (Grand Rapids: Eerdmans, 2004), 1–15; David L. Allen, "Substitutionary Atonement and Cultic Terminology in Isaiah 53," in *The Gospel According to Isaiah 53: Encountering the Suffering Servant in Jewish and Christian Theology*, ed. Darrell L. Bock and Mitch Glaser (Grand Rapids: Kregel, 2012), 171–89. These connections lend weight to those who see the servant here as a Moses figure (compare Deut 34:5); see, e.g., Hugenberger, "Servant of the Lord," 129–39.

[24] The verb שָׂכַל has a range of meanings. It is a verb associated with wisdom, which in Hebrew moves beyond intellectual knowledge to a right application of it. With this verb "There is the process of thinking through a complex arrangement of thoughts resulting in a wise dealing and use of good practical common sense. Another end result is the emphasis upon being successful"; see Louis Goldberg, "שָׂכַל," in *TWOT* 877. A good example of this is the use of the verb in Joshua 1:7–8, where God commands Joshua to observe the law of Moses so that he can "have success/act wisely" (תַּשְׂכִּיל) in everything. Thus the difference between "prosper" and "act wisely" in English translations of Isa 52:13 is not as significant as it might initially seem.

of the "arm of the Lᴏʀᴅ" (וּזְרֹעַ יְהֹוָה; Isa 53:1) evokes imagery from the first exodus, when "the Lᴏʀᴅ brought us out of Egypt with a strong hand and an outstretched arm (וּבִזְרֹעַ נְטוּיָה), with terrifying power, and with signs and wonders" (Deut 26:8). The sicknesses (חֳלִי) which the servant bears (Isa 53:4) are the sicknesses that Yahweh had promised to bring upon Israel if they broke the covenant (Deut 28:59–61). The servant is "struck down by God (מֻכֵּה אֱלֹהִים; Isa 53:4) just as God had vowed to strike rebellious Israel for her covenant unfaithfulness (Deut 28:22, 27–28, 35). Isaiah says of the servant that "we are healed by his wounds (וּבַחֲבֻרָתוֹ נִרְפָּא־לָנוּ; Isa 53:5), perhaps echoing Yahweh's claims in the Song of Moses: "See now that I alone am he; there is no God but me. I bring death and I give life; I wound and I heal (מָחַצְתִּי וַאֲנִי אֶרְפָּא). No one can rescue anyone from my power" (Deut 32:39). Isaiah asserts that everyone has turned "to our own way" (לְדַרְכּוֹ; Isa 53:6), a charge that resonates with the consistent description of the rebellious as failing to walk in the ways of Yahweh (Deut 28:9, 29; 30:16; 31:29). Just as God had warned that he would expel Israel from the land for their disobedience (Deut 28:64; 29:26–27), the servant is "cut off from the land of the living" (Isa 53:8). Through his vicarious death (Isa 53:8–9), the servant experiences the culminating curse of death that God promised Israel for breaking the covenant (Deut 28:19).

But the suffering servant does not merely experience the curses for sinful Israel; he also experiences their restoration and the blessings promised in connection with that restoration. When the servant makes his soul an offering for guilt, "he will see his seed, he will prolong his days, and by his hand, the Lord's pleasure will be accomplished" (53:10).[25] The expression "see his seed" surely refers to what is stated more clearly in Isaiah 54:1–3—a multitude of children in an expanded land and offspring so numerous that they possess/inherit the nations. Such language picks up elements from restoration promises in Deuteronomy 30. God had promised to circumcise the hearts of the people and their offspring to love Yahweh wholeheartedly and live (30:6). The key themes of offspring,

---

[25] Although the text does not explicitly say the servant rises from the dead, that seems to be a reasonable inference. Otherwise it is difficult to understand how someone who "gives his life as a guilt offering" will receive "a portion with the many." This inference seems to be confirmed by the echo of Isa 53:11 in Dan 12:3, which speaks of the resurrection of the righteous on the last day. Of course, the connection between resurrection and return from exile is seen most clearly in Ezek 37, where the vision of the valley of the dry bones (37:1–14) is directly tied to Israel's return from exile (37:15–28).

prolonged days, the will of Yahweh, and prospering are all present in Deuteronomy 30:8–10, which stresses that when Israel returns to the Lord in repentance, he will take delight in abundantly prospering them.

Further connections to Deuteronomy 30 can be seen in the connection between the work of the servant and the fulfillment of the promises to Abraham. The call to sing in response to the servant's suffering, death, and vindication (Isa 54:1) picks up the language of Isaiah 51:2, which uses similar language to remind God's people of his promise to Abraham: "Look to Abraham your father, and to Sarah who gave birth to you. When I called him, he was only one; I blessed him and made him many."[26] The numerous descendants promised to Abraham have come into existence through the work of the servant, resulting in them possessing the nations. In Deuteronomy 30:18–20 God had warned Israel that they would not live long in the land and possess it if they disobeyed, so he calls them to choose life by obeying Yahweh so they may dwell in the land he promised "to Abraham, to Isaac, and to Jacob."

One key result of the suffering servant's work is that it produces servants. Throughout Isaiah 40–53 the term servant (עֶבֶד) only occurs in the singular, even when it refers to the nation of Israel. But in Isaiah 54:17 a shift takes place. After promising that no weapon or charge would succeed against the people his servant has redeemed, Yahweh states: "This is the heritage of the LORD's servants [עַבְדֵי יְהוָה], and their vindication is from me" (Isa 54:17). The assertion that Yahweh would vindicate his servants echoes Deuteronomy 32:36: "The LORD will indeed vindicate his people and have compassion on his servants [עֲבָדָיו] when he sees that their strength is gone and no one is left—slave or free."

These numerous examples make it clear that Isaiah frames the sin-exile-restoration motif in chapters 40–55 against a Deuteronomic backdrop. But Isaiah does more than simply use the Deuteronomic framework; he expands upon it in five key areas.

First, Isaiah goes beyond Deuteronomy in the extent to which return from exile fulfills the promises made to Abraham and his seed.[27] As we have already noted, Deuteronomy 30:20 does tie the return from exile to God's people dwelling in the land that Yahweh promised to Abraham.

---

[26] Note that Isa 51:2 seems to echo the language of Deut 32:18, where Moses says to Israel, "You ignored the Rock who gave you birth; you forgot the God who gave birth to you (מְחֹלְלֶךָ)."

[27] This paragraph is adapted from Harmon, *She Must and Shall Go Free*, 166.

But Isaiah goes well beyond this basic assertion. He calls the people to look back to Abraham and Sarah, reminding them of Yahweh's promise to bless and multiply him (51:2). The grounds for looking to the Abrahamic promise is that Yahweh will "comfort Zion" (51:3), an expression that includes (though is not limited to) return from exile (40:1–3; 49:8–13; 52:9). The fulfillment of the promise to Abraham results in Yahweh revealing his righteousness and salvation (51:5–8). When this revelation takes place God will lead his ransomed people back to Zion with singing and joy, just as he led Israel in the original exodus (51:9–11). Once this return from exile is accomplished by the servant (52:13–53:12), the descendants promised to Abraham will be so numerous that the land will be unable to contain them (54:1–3).

Second, Isaiah places the servant at the center of God bringing his people back from exile.[28] Although called to be Yahweh's servant (42:1–9), Israel as a nation failed, becoming blind and deaf (42:18–19). As a result, Yahweh sent them into exile (42:22–25). So Yahweh raises up a new servant named "Israel" who is in fact an individual who will not only return the people from exile, but be what Israel as a nation was supposed to be: a light of salvation to the nations (49:1–12). Isaiah 52:1–6 compares Israel's captivity under both the Assyrians and the Babylonians to their sojourn in Egypt before announcing in 52:7–10 Israel's return. That new exodus is described in 52:11–12, with Yahweh both going before and acting as rear guard. What follows is the fourth Servant Song (52:13–53:12), in which the servant redeems his people from their transgression by taking on the covenant curses and justifying the many. The called-for response found in Isaiah 54:1 and following is a call to shout for joy at this redemption. Thus within Isaiah 49–54, the servant is portrayed as Yahweh's agent in bringing about the promised new exodus, accomplished through his vicarious suffering.[29]

Third, Isaiah consistently connects the promise of return from exile with the transformation of creation.[30] In the first exodus Yahweh brought

---

[28] This paragraph is adapted from Harmon, *She Must and Shall Go Free*, 163.

[29] See similarly Hans Eberhard von Waldow, "The Message of Deutero-Isaiah," *Int* 22 (1968): 259–87; Watts, "Consolation or Confrontation? Isaiah 40–55 and the Delay of the New Exodus," 49–56; Hugenberger, "Servant of the Lord," 122–39.

[30] This paragraph is adapted from Harmon, *She Must and Shall Go Free*, 162–63. On the relationship between new creation and the second exodus, see especially Stuhlmueller, *Creative Redemption*, 66–98 and Meira Polliack, "Deutero-Isaiah's Typological Use of Jacob

water out of a rock when his people thirsted in the wilderness (Exod 17:1–7); in this new exodus Yahweh will turn the desert into an abundance of rivers, springs, and pools so that his people will know that Yahweh has done this (Isa 41:17–20). In this new exodus Yahweh will make a path through the sea for his returning exiles, and in doing so he will transform the wilderness and animal kingdom (Isa 43:16–21). In response to the announcement that Yahweh will reveal his saving righteousness in fulfillment of his promise to Abraham (Isa 51:1–8), Yahweh is called upon to awake as in the days when he cut up Rahab and pierced the dragon (51:9), language which speaks of his triumph over chaos at creation.[31] Just as the original exodus was an act of Yahweh triumphing over creation, so too in this return from exile Yahweh will triumph over creation and lead his people to their promised inheritance with abundant joy (51:10–11).

Fourth, Isaiah connects return from exile with the gift of the Spirit. Shortly after promising to bring his people back from exile (43:16–21), Yahweh promises to pour out his Spirit upon his people (44:1–5). Immediately after Yahweh swears that he will accomplish his purpose of redeeming his people from Babylon, the servant interjects, "now the Lord GOD has sent me and his Spirit" (48:16).[32] Somehow the servant and the Spirit will work together to bring about God's people's return from exile. The role of the Spirit in this second exodus parallels his work in the first exodus, when the Spirit dwelled in the midst of the people and led them in the wilderness (63:7–14).

Fifth, Isaiah links Israel's return from exile to blessing for the nations. Whereas at best there is a mere hint of this in the Song of Moses,[33] there

---

in the Portrayal of Israel's National Renewal," in *Creation in Jewish and Christian Tradition*, ed. Henning Reventlow and Yair Graf. Hoffman (London: Sheffield Academic, 2002), 72–110.

[31] See Stuhlmueller, *Creative Redemption*, 88–91.

[32] While the identity of the speaker in 48:16 is unclear, several scholars, based on parallels with 49:1–6 and 61:1, have suggested it is the servant of Yahweh; see, e.g., Claus Westermann, *Isaiah 40–66: A Commentary* (Philadelphia: Westminster, 1969), 233; Motyer, *The Prophecy of Isaiah: An Introduction & Commentary*, 381; Brevard S. Childs, *Isaiah*, OTL (Louisville: Westminster John Knox Press, 2001), 377–78.

[33] In response to Israel making him jealous through their pursuit of other gods, Yahweh swears, "I will make them jealous with those who are no people; I will provoke them to anger with a foolish nation" (Deut 32:21 ESV). Paul quotes this verse in Rom 10:19 to defend his claim that Israel did not understand that God's redemptive purposes would include the gentiles. Immediately after quoting Deut 32:21, Paul cites Isa 65:1—"I was ready to be sought by those who did not ask for me; I was ready to be found by those who did not seek

are several places in Isaiah that link Israel's restoration with blessing to the nations. One of the clearest examples of this is Isaiah 49:6, where part of the mission of the individual servant is to be "a light for the nations, to be my salvation to the ends of the earth." Being a light of salvation to the ends of the earth happens in conjunction with Israel's return from exile (49:8–12), resulting in joyous praise (48:13). Because he will fulfill his promises to Abraham, redeem his people, and transform creation (51:1–3), Yahweh promises that when his saving righteousness is revealed, he will set his "justice for a light to the nations" (51:4) and "the coasts and islands will put their hope in me, and they will look to my strength" (51:5). When Yahweh bares his holy arm it will be "in the sight of all the nations; all the ends of the earth will see the salvation of our God" (52:10). In conjunction with this, Israel will return from exile, with Yahweh himself leading them (52:11–12). Thus the work of the suffering servant is not limited to Israel. The servant will "sprinkle many nations. Kings will shut their mouths because of him, for they will see what had not been told them, and they will understand what they had not heard" (52:15). While the meaning of this verse is disputed,[34] the apostle Paul sees in this verse a prefiguration of the gospel being announced to the gentiles.[35] Once the servant has accomplished his work, the people of Israel will be so numerous that the boundaries of the land will need to be expanded (54:1–2); as a result their offspring "will dispossess the nations" (וְזַרְעֲךָ גּוֹיִם יִירָשׁ) or as the LXX puts it, "inherit the nations" (τὸ σπέρμα σου ἔθνη κληρονομήσει; 54:3).[36] The same redemptive act that restores Israel from exile will also bring blessing to the nations.

---

me" (ESV). So it would seem that Paul sees Deut 32:21 anticipating a gentile inclusion that is made more explicit in Isa 65:1. See further the discussion in J. Ross Wagner, *Heralds of the Good News: Isaiah and Paul in Concert in the Letter to the Romans* (Leiden: Brill, 2003), 187–217.

[34] For a helpful discussion of the difficulties, see Jan L. Koole, *Isaiah III* (Leuven: Peeters, 1998), 271–75.

[35] See the discussion in Wagner, *Heralds of the Good News*, 329–36.

[36] The exact force of the Hebrew clause וְזַרְעֲךָ גּוֹיִם יִירָשׁ is disputed. The construction יָרַשׁ with a form of גּוֹי as its object can mean to drive out the nations, a meaning attested in places such as Exod 34:24; Deut 4:38; 9:1; Josh 23:13. In the context of Isa 54:3, however, it makes better sense to understand the MT in the way that the LXX clearly understood the Hebrew and conclude that the nations are being included within the restoration described in 54:1–10; see Edward J. Young, *The Book of Isaiah*, NICOT (Grand Rapids: Eerdmans, 1972), 3:362–63; George A. F. Knight, *Servant Theology: A Commentary on the Book of Isaiah 40–55* (Grand Rapids: Eerdmans, 1984), 182; Koole, *Isaiah III*, 2:356–57. For a dissenting opinion, see John N.

So although Isaiah bases his presentation of sin-exile-return on the Deuteronomic framework, he develops it in several significant ways. As we shall see, Paul draws on this Isaianic adaptation of the Deuteronomic sin-exile-return paradigm in Galatians.

§1.2.3 Sin, Exile, and Return in Galatians

The sin-exile-return motif first surfaces in 3:10–14.[37] Paul begins by contending that "all who rely on the works of the law are under a curse" (3:10). He grounds this claim by citing a combination of Deuteronomy 27:26 and 28:58: "Everyone who does not do everything written in the book of the law is cursed." As we noted above, this combination of "curse, all, doing the law" is a formula that runs throughout Deuteronomy 27–30 as a structuring device that frames the discourse. The phrase acts in a summative fashion, stressing the violation of the Mosaic covenant, not merely individual commandments. Paul alludes to Israel's failure to keep the Mosaic law covenant as a grounds for his larger point that relying on the Mosaic law for one's standing before God results in a curse. For Israel as a nation, the ultimate curse was exile from the land, which was a physical representation of the greater reality of their separation from God. For the gentile it refers to being under God's righteous judgment for their rebellion against him. Paul's point here in Galatians 3:10 seems to be at least twofold. First, if Israel was unable to keep the requirements of the Mosaic law covenant, why should gentile believers think they would fare any better? Second, relying upon works of the law is a step backwards in redemptive history, as the temporary supervisory role of the law has now come to an end.

After contrasting the fundamental difference between doing the law and believing in the promises of God (3:11–12), Paul explains God's solution to the curse that comes from failing to keep the Mosaic law covenant: "Christ redeemed us from the curse of the law by becoming a curse for us" (3:13). Redemption language evokes the deliverance of slaves, and thus

---

Oswalt, *The Book of Isaiah: Chapters 40–66*, NICOT (Grand Rapids: Eerdmans, 1998), 417–18n30; Joseph Blenkinsopp, *Isaiah 40–55: A New Translation with Introduction and Commentary*, AB 19 (New York: Doubleday, 2002), 362.

[37] Dunn (*Galatians*, 180) sees in 3:10–14 a "midrash on Deuteronomy's three-stage schema of salvation-history" that begins with God's covenant with Israel, followed by Israel's failure and subsequent curse of being sent into exile, and culminating in restoration through the gospel of Christ and the promise of the Spirit.

it hints at Christ accomplishing the new exodus that the prophets had promised would bring Israel's exile to an end. The curse of the law is the curse that comes from failing to keep all that is written in the Mosaic law covenant, and it falls on all who rely on the law—Jew and gentile alike. Therefore, the "us" whom Christ redeems from the curse of the law is not limited to Israel, but includes gentiles as well.

Christ accomplishes this new exodus redemption "by becoming a curse for us" (3:13), language which echoes the work of the suffering servant in Isaiah 53. Christ the suffering servant has not only experienced the curse that came upon Israel for breaking the Mosaic law covenant but also upon gentiles who have disobeyed God and stand under his righteous judgment. Paul grounds this assertion by citing Deuteronomy 21:23: "Cursed is everyone who is hung on a tree." In its original context, Deuteronomy 21:22–23 explains what to do with a man convicted of murder who is executed by being hung on a tree. His body must be taken down and buried, lest the dead body defile the land. Paul's use of this text may have been prompted by Numbers 25:4, where God instructs Moses what to do with those leaders who led the people into sexual immorality and idolatry: "Take all the leaders of the people and execute them in broad daylight before the LORD so that his burning anger may turn away from Israel."[38] The death of these covenant-breakers by hanging them turns away God's wrath, and perhaps it is this connection that underlies Paul's use of Deuteronomy 21:23.[39] The purpose/result of Christ redeeming "us" from the law is stated in two ἵνα clauses. Regardless of how these two ἵνα clauses are related, the results of Christ the suffering servant bearing the curse of exile for his people are: (1) the blessing of Abraham coming to the gentiles, and (2) believers receiving the promised Spirit.

---

[38] See Caneday, "Curse of the Law," 321–25.

[39] Regardless of whether this is the case or not, by the time of the NT period, at least some Jews applied this verse to crucifixion, and there are several allusions to Deut 21:23 in the NT that do so as well (Acts 5:30; 10:39; 1 Pet 2:24). For a helpful survey, see Chapman, *Ancient Jewish and Christian Perceptions of Crucifixion*, 117–49. Note especially 4QpNah (4Q169) frags. 3–4 and 1.5–8 (which alludes to Deut 21:23 in connection with Alexander Jannaeus crucifying thousands of Pharisees) and 11QTemple (11Q19) 64.6–13 (where it is clear that hanging a person on the tree is the means of execution). After the NT period, the second-century church father Justin Martyr, in his *Dialogue with Trypho*, quotes the Jewish writer Trypho as citing Deut 21:23 to "prove" that Jesus cannot be the Messiah. What is especially noteworthy is that in his response, he draws on Isa 53; see Bailey, "'Our Suffering and Crucified Messiah' (*Dial*, 111.2): Justin Martyr's Allusions to Isaiah 53 in His *Dialogue with Trypho* with Special Reference to the New Edition of M. Markovich," 389–406.

The second passage where the sin-exile-restoration motif surfaces is
4:1–7. As a number of scholars have noted, Paul uses new exodus typology
to describe the work of Christ.[40] Rather than give a general illustration,
Paul employs a typological reading of Israel's experience leading up to
and including their exodus from Egypt (4:1–2) and then portrays the
redemption of believers (Jew and gentile alike) in terms of the promised
new exodus (4:3–7). Taking a closer look at the type and the antitype will
reveal not only the sin-exile-restoration motif, but even more specifically
its Isaianic shape.

When Paul refers to "the heir" (ὁ κληρονόμος) who as a "child"
(νήπιός) is no better than a "slave" (δούλου) even though he is "owner
of everything" (ESV) (κύριος πάντων ὤν), he describes Israel's experience in Egypt (4:1). The expression rendered "guardians and trustees"
(ἐπιτρόπους … καὶ οἰκονόμους) refers to Israel's Egyptian taskmasters, who ruled over Israel "until the time set by his father" (ἄχρι τῆς
προθεσμίας τοῦ πατρός), a reference to the end of Israel's 430 years of
bondage in Egypt (4:2; compare 3:17). With Israel's experience in the first
exodus as the type (4:1–2), Paul now moves to the antitype in 4:3–7. He
states that as believers "we also, when we were children [νήπιοι], were in
slavery under the elements of the world" (4:3). Israel's Egyptian slavery
is portrayed as a type of the greater slavery that humanity experienced
under the elementals. Whereas for Israel the turning point was "the time
set by his Father" (4:2), for believers it was "when the time came to completion" (4:4). To accomplish this new exodus, "God sent his Son, born
of a woman, born under the law" (4:4). The Son of God came to redeem
both gentiles ("born of a woman") and Jews ("born under the law"). He
willingly placed himself in the position of those enslaved to the elementals "to redeem those under the law, so that we might receive adoption as
sons" (4:5). By entering into their slavery to the elementals, the Son was
able to rescue his people from that slavery and grant them the status of
adult sons. Because of this status as adult sons, "God sent the Spirit of his
Son into our hearts, crying, 'Abba! Father!' " (4:6). The evidence that the
transition from "children" (νήπιοι) to adult "sons" (υἱοί) has taken place

---

[40] See, e.g., Scott, *Adoption as Sons of God*, 121–86; Scott J. Hafemann, "Paul and the Exile of
Israel in Galatians 3–4," in *Exile: Old Testament, Jewish, and Christian Conceptions*, ed. James M.
Scott (Leiden: Brill, 1997), 329–71; Keesmaat, *Paul and His Story*, 155–88; Wilson, "Wilderness
Apostasy," 550–71; Harmon, *She Must and Shall Go Free*, 161–67. The brief summary here
largely follows Scott, *Adoption as Sons of God*, 145–86.

is the gift of the Spirit of the Son who accomplished their redemption. All that remains for Paul is to summarize: "So you are no longer a slave but a son, and if a son, then God has made you an heir" (4:7). Since the movement from slave to son is complete, the logical inference is that the sons have received their inheritance, which in the context of Galatians refers to what was promised to Abraham (compare 3:15–29).

At this point a chart summarizing the parallels proves helpful:

Table 15:

First Exodus (Gal 4:1–2) "Israel's Redemption to Sonship"	New Exodus (Gal 4:3–7) "Believers' Redemption to Sonship"
Israel was the heir (ὁ κληρονόμος) promised universal sovereignty (κύριος πάντων ὤν) through Abraham (4:1)	Believers are no longer slaves but sons of God and heirs of the Abrahamic promise through Christ, evidenced by the gift of the Spirit (4:6-7)
Israel was a "slave" (δοῦλος), living under taskmasters (ἐπιτρόπους ... καὶ οἰκονόμους) in Egypt (4:1-2)	Humanity was enslaved to the elements of this world (ὑπὸ τὰ στοιχεῖα τοῦ κόσμου ἤμεθα δεδουλωμένοι) (4:3)
God redeemed Israel from slavery when it was a "child" (νήπιός) at the time appointed by the Father (ἄχρι τῆς προθεσμίας τοῦ πατρός) according to the Abrahamic promise (4:1-2)	The Father sent his Son to redeem believers from their slavery when they were children (νήπιοι) when the fullness of time came (ὅτε δὲ ἦλθεν τὸ πλήρωμα τοῦ χρόνου) according to the Abrahamic promise fulfilled in Christ.[41] (4:4-5)

The second exodus that God had promised would bring an end to Israel's slavery in exile has done more than that—it has freed humanity from its slavery to the elementals.

The third passage where the sin-exile-restoration motif surfaces in Galatians is the well-known "allegory" of 4:21–5:1. In his summary of Genesis 16–21 Paul sees a deeper meaning that at least in part is mediated by his reading of Isaiah 51–54. Hagar represents the Sinai covenant, which operates on the basis of the flesh and produces sons who are enslaved; this corresponds to the present Jerusalem. Sarah represents the Abrahamic covenant fulfilled in Christ, which operates on the basis of the promise

---

[41] Based on the sonship language, Scott (*Adoption as Sons of God*, 178–85) roots the redemption described here in the Davidic promise (2 Sam 7:14). But he goes on to note that the Davidic promise was the means by which the Abrahamic promise would find its fulfillment. Both the Abrahamic and Davidic promises find their fulfillment in Christ, who is the seed of Abraham and the son of God.

and produces sons who are free; this corresponds to the Jerusalem above. This last assertion is grounded in a citation of Isaiah 54:1, which in its original context invites God's people to celebrate the redemption of the servant in fulfillment of the Abrahamic promise. The Jerusalem above is Paul's way of referring to the eschatological state that results from God fulfilling his promises to redeem his people from their sin, bring them out of their exile, and transform creation itself. Paul's point, then, is that through his death on the cross and resurrection from the dead, the servant Jesus Christ has brought into existence the eschatological people of God and inaugurated the promised new creation.

A fourth passage where sin-exile-restoration may be in the background is Galatians 5:16–26. In contrast to a life that is controlled by the desires of the flesh, Paul insists: "if you are led by the Spirit, you are not under the law" (5:18). This language of being led by the Spirit may be drawn from Isaiah 63:11–14, where the prophet invokes Yahweh's gracious presence among his people in the exodus as a type for God's future presence among his people when he once again leads them in a second exodus. The description of the fruit of the Spirit (5:22–23) also appears to draw upon two Isaianic texts (32:15–18; 57:15–19) that foretell a time when the Spirit will come from on high as part of God's eschatological salvation, producing fruit that is both physical in its transformation of the land and spiritual/moral in the transformation of his people. This pouring out of the Spirit is connected to the restoration of Israel and even more specifically that of Jerusalem. The fact that believers—Jew and gentile alike—are led by and produce the fruit of the Spirit confirms that that era of eschatological fulfillment has begun.

A final place where the sin-exile-restoration motif lurks in the background is Galatians 6:15, where Paul states that "both circumcision and uncircumcision mean nothing; what matters instead is a new creation." The expression "new creation" (καινὴ κτίσις), although not found in Isaiah, appears to be a summary phrase coined by Paul to capture the cosmic transformation promised in connection with the Isaianic new exodus (see, e.g., Isa 41:17–20; 43:16–21: 51:9–11; 65:17–25; 66:22–24). All of the various blessings and benefits that come from the work of Christ are encompassed under this phrase "new creation." Further evidence for this link is found in the following verse. When Paul prays for "peace and mercy" upon all who walk by the rule of new creation, he further describes this group of people as "the Israel of God" (6:16). Paul borrows the language of "peace and mercy" (εἰρήνη ... καὶ ἔλεος) from Isaiah 54:10, where the covenant that God makes with his redeemed people is described. What follows is a poetic description of the new Jerusalem (Isa 54:11–15), which Paul has already referenced in Galatians 4:26–27. The use of imagery from Isaiah 54:11–15 in Revelation 21:15–21 to describe the new Jerusalem descending from heaven confirms the link with Isaianic new creation motifs.

While each of these passages in Galatians varies with respect to the depth of engagement with the sin-exile-restoration motif, one unifying feature is that their use of this motif is mediated through Isaianic lenses. We see this in five ways.

First, the sin-exile-restoration motif is linked with the fulfillment of the promise to Abraham. The question that drives the argument of Galatians 3:1–5:1 is who are the true sons of Abraham, and the sin-exile-restoration motif is a major tool in his arsenal. It is only because Christ has redeemed believers from the curse of the law (which, as we have seen, exile is the ultimate curse for sin) that the blessing of Abraham can come to the gentiles (3:10–14). Immediately after explaining that all who are in Christ—regardless of their ethnicity—are "Abraham's offspring, heirs according to the promise" (3:15–29), Paul transitions to a section that describes Israel's original exodus as a type of the even greater exodus that believers—Jew and gentile alike—have experienced from their exile in slavery to sin to adoption as sons who inherit the promise to Abraham (4:1–7). In the climactic section of his argument Paul uses Isaiah 51–54 to reread Genesis 16–21 and demonstrate that the promise to Abraham and the promised return from exile have taken place through the work of Christ (4:21–5:1). While, as we noted above, there is a passing reference to the return from exile in connection with the promise made to Abraham in Deuteronomy 30:20, in Isaiah fulfilling the promise to Abraham and return from exile are inseparably linked such that one will not happen without the other.

Second, the sin-exile-restoration motif is rooted in the work of the Isaianic servant. As the promised seed, Jesus Christ inherits the promises made to Abraham. But in order for that promise to be fulfilled, Christ also had to be the servant who redeemed his people from their bondage to sin. So at two key points (3:13–14 and 4:4–6) in his argument Paul describes the work of Christ in language borrowed from Isaiah 53. In both passages Christ redeems people from their exile of slavery to sin so that they may inherit the promise made to Abraham, of which the Spirit is singled out as the preeminent element. The central role of the Spirit is a distinctively Isaianic element of the sin-exile-restoration motif, missing entirely from Deuteronomy.

The third distinctively Isaianic element of Paul's use of the sin-exile-restoration motif is the link to new creation. When Paul says that "both circumcision and uncircumcision mean nothing; what matters instead is a new creation" (6:15), he uses the phrase new creation as a summary phrase for the various blessings that believers experience because of Christ: justification, righteousness, faith, promise, inheritance, freedom, the Spirit, and sonship.[42] The death and resurrection of Jesus Christ the servant has inaugurated the new creation promised in Isaiah in connection with the return from exile through a new exodus. As Beale puts it, the phrase "new creation" and allusion to Isaiah 54:10 in 6:16 are "a way of speaking not only of the effects of Christ's death but also of the resurrection life mentioned in 5:25, both of which underlie Paul's comprehension of how both the Isa. 54:1 prophecy and the Isa. 65:17 'new creation' prophecy began fulfillment."[43]

Fourth, the sin-exile-restoration motif is linked to the gift of the Spirit. The result of Christ taking upon himself the curse of sin and exile to redeem his people is the gift of the promised Spirit to those who believe (3:10–14). Because Jesus the Son of God redeemed his people from their slavery to the elementals, they have been adopted as sons who are given the Spirit of the Son as a down payment on their inheritance (4:1–7). Believers are sons of the free woman, born according to the promise, born according to the Spirit. Through the death and resurrection of Jesus, God has fulfilled the promise to Abraham and accomplished the restoration of Jerusalem promised in Isaiah 51–54 (Gal 4:21–5:1). As a result, believers are led by the eschatological Spirit of God and display his fruit in their lives (5:16–26).

The final way the sin-exile-restoration motif shows its Isaianic flavor is the inclusion of the gentiles. Paul is trying to reassure the largely gentile congregations in Galatia that they are full-blooded sons of Abraham. They too are included in the servant's death to exhaust the curse that comes

---

[42] See Harmon, *She Must and Shall Go Free*, 245–47. For a helpful unpacking of the phrase "new creation" within Galatians, see G. K. Beale, *A New Testament Biblical Theology: The Unfolding of the Old Testament in the New* (Grand Rapids: Baker, 2011), 304–14.

[43] Beale, *New Testament Biblical Theology*, 310.

on all who rely on works of the law (3:10–14). They too were led in a new exodus from their enslavement to the elementals through Christ the servant and Son of God, resulting in their adoption as sons who receive the Spirit as a mark of their inheritance (4:1–7). They too, "like Isaac, are children of promise" who were "born as a result of the Spirit" (4:28–29) because the servant has accomplished the restoration of Zion (4:21–5:1). They too are being led by the Spirit (5:16–26) and experience the blessings of the new creation that Jesus Christ has inaugurated (6:15–16).

§1.2.4 Conclusion

Paul uses the sin-exile-restoration theme as a supplement to the larger framework of the Abrahamic covenant fulfilled in Christ. Through his death on the cross, Jesus the suffering servant experienced the culminating curse of exile that the Mosaic law covenant had threatened for failure to obey. Through his resurrection he has experienced the promised restoration that God had promised through a new exodus and inaugurated the new creation kingdom of God.

§1.3 APOCALYPTIC ANTITHESES

Throughout Galatians Paul draws a number of contrasts that highlight the stark difference between reality before/apart from Christ and reality after/in Christ. These antitheses form a major substructure within the letter and emphasize the cosmic shift that took place with the death and resurrection of Jesus.[44] Although there is overlap between the antitheses that follow, treating them individually draws attention to distinct features in Galatians.

§1.3.1 Present Evil Age and the New Creation[45]

Arguably the most fundamental antithesis in Galatians is the contrast between the present evil age and the new creation/messianic age that has dawned through the work of Christ. Paul appears to have shared a modified version of the common Second Temple Jewish view that history was divided into two ages: the present evil age (characterized by sin, death, and evil spiritual forces) and the messianic age (marked by

---

[44] John Barclay goes so far as to argue that "every reading [of Galatians] is determined by the way it construes and organizes the polarities of the letter"; see Barclay, *Paul and the Gift*, 337–39.

[45] This section is adapted from Harmon, *She Must and Shall Go Free*, 228–36, 45–47.

the reign of the Messiah, the gift of the Spirit, and the transformation of creation itself).

In the letter opening Paul refers to the present evil age as a realm from which Christ delivers his people (1:4). Yet the remainder of the letter makes it clear that believers still live within this fallen world and are in danger of being influenced by the various powers associated with the present evil age. These powers include the flesh (4:23; 5:13, 16–17, 19, 24; 6:8), the elements of this world (4:3, 9), and even the Mosaic law (4:1–11). The present evil age is characterized by slavery to these various powers, whose authority over sinful humanity at best is likened to a minor child living under some form of adult supervision (3:23–4:7) and at worst is described as an oppressive slavery that cannot be escaped except through Christ (3:22; 4:3, 9–11, 24–25, 29–30). A surprising manifestation of this present evil age is the present Jerusalem (4:25), which refers to not merely the city of Jerusalem as the center and source of Paul's opponents but more broadly to any and all who place the law at the center of their understanding of relating to God and others, regardless of whether they claim to be Christ-followers or not. The final destiny of those who remain captives in the present evil age and subject to its hostile powers is destruction (6:8).

By contrast, those who trust in Christ have been delivered from the oppressive slavery of the present evil age into the freedom of the messianic age/new creation (6:15). Instead of being enslaved to the elements of this world, they walk according to the standard of the new creation which has dawned through the death and resurrection of Christ (6:14–16). They live as free sons who have received the Spirit as the firstfruits of the inheritance that is rightfully theirs because of their union with Christ, the Son of God who loved them and gave himself for them (2:20; 4:4–7). They are citizens of the Jerusalem above, children born according to the promise (4:21–5:1). Their final destiny is eternal life (6:8).

Even though 6:15 is the only explicit mention of "new creation" (καινὴ κτίσις) in Galatians, there is a very real sense in which the phrase functions as a shorthand summary for the major themes in the letter. The starting point for understanding this important phrase is Isaiah 40–66. In announcing the coming redemption of his people, God repeatedly connects this act of new exodus with the transformation of creation itself (Isa 41:17–20; 43:16–21; 51:9–11). God's saving act will do more than free the Jewish people from their Babylonian exile; it will overturn the curse that fell on creation when Adam rebelled in the garden. Isaiah culminates in a vision of a new heavens and new earth that draws on various restoration motifs from earlier in the book. The former things will be no more and Jerusalem will be filled with joy (Isa 65:17–19). God's people will experience abundance and fruitful labor because "they will be a people blessed by the Lord along with their descendants" (Isa 65:20–23). God's promise to Abraham of descendants more numerous than the stars of the sky will at last be consummated. God will answer the prayers of his people before they are even uttered (Isa 65:24), and peace will be established even among the animal kingdom (Isa 65:25). In the final verses of the book, the Lord insists that not only will the new heavens and new earth endure forever, but also "your offspring and your name will remain" (Isa 66:22). All humankind will come to worship Yahweh and witness the destruction of his enemies (Isa 66:23–24). The Isaianic background of Paul's use of the phrase "new creation" is further confirmed by the context of its only other occurrence. In 2 Corinthians 5:17 the apostle asserts, "if anyone is in Christ, he is a new creation; the old has passed away, and see, the new has come!" Just a few verses later he quotes from Isaiah 49:8 to support this argument that the salvation he announces brings the promised new creation.

Against this backdrop, several key themes come into sharper focus. At the beginning of the letter Paul states that the self-sacrificial death of Jesus rescues his people from the present evil age (Gal 1:4), but it is not until the end of the letter that he explicitly states that it ushers in the new creation as well (Gal 6:14–15). The crucifixion of Jesus has dealt the decisive blow to this fallen world and its powers. The resurrection of Jesus is the inauguration of the new creation; as the firstfruits from the dead (1 Cor 15:20) he is the embodiment of the transformation that will one day encompass the entire universe. The resurrection of Jesus has ushered in a new era in redemptive history where God sends out his apostles as heralds of the good news (Gal 1:1). The connection between the death and resurrection of Jesus and new creation is rooted in Paul's reading of Isaiah, where the work of the servant (Isa 52:13–53:12) ushers in the transformation of creation itself (54:1–17).

Paul's emphasis on righteousness and justification is rooted in his understanding of the new creation. As noted above, justification is God's verdict of not-guilty on the last day announced in the present for all who believe in Christ. As Beale helpfully summarizes,

Therefore justification is related to new creation in that the last judgment paves the way for new creation; the last judgment is not merely the punishment of the wicked, but it is also inextricably linked to God's judgment of the old cosmos by which he destroys the sin-tainted and corrupted world. Therefore in that the last judgment has been pushed back to the cross and has begun there, so also the destruction of the cosmos has begun there (so Gal 6:14–15).[46]

Thus Paul's already/not-yet understanding of justification/righteousness is inseparably connected to the broader theme of new creation.

The restoration of Jerusalem through a new exodus out of exile is also an outworking of the broader motif of new creation. The connection is implied in Isaiah 54:1–17, where the death of the suffering servant brings Israel's exile to an end and the new Jerusalem comes into existence. Paul makes the same point in Galatians 4:21–5:1, where he cites Isaiah 54:1. The point becomes explicit in Isaiah 65:17–25, where prophet writes, "For I will create new heaven and a new earth ... for I will create Jerusalem to be a joy and its people to be a delight" (vv. 17–18). The description of the new heaven and earth in Isaiah 65:17–25 uses language that parallels the description of restored Jerusalem in Isaiah 54.[47] By using this parallel language, Isaiah invites the reader to interpret the earlier references to the new Jerusalem through the lens of the climactic vision of a new creation. Paul appears to have followed Isaiah's cues once again.

A final important theme in Galatians that stems from Paul's understanding of the Isaianic new creation is the gift of the Holy Spirit. In Isaiah 32:15–20 the outpouring of the Spirit results in the wilderness being transformed into a fertile field, which then becomes a lush forest. This transformed land is the place where God's people dwell in peace. The Spirit thus is the agent of bringing this promised new creation life that is experienced by God's people and even the universe itself. "The picture that emerges is that the Spirit endues the believer with the new life that flows from the crucifixion and resurrection of Jesus, resulting in a spiritual transformation that anticipates God making all things new."[48]

---

[46] G. K. Beale, "The Eschatological Conception of New Testament Theology," in *Eschatology in Bible and Theology: Evangelical Essays at the Dawn of a New Millennium*, ed. K. E. Brower and M. W. Elliott (Downers Grove, IL: IVP, 1997), 33–34.

[47] Those parallels include rejoicing, lack of weeping, long life, building of houses, and planting of vineyards.

[48] Harmon, *She Must and Shall Go Free*, 235.

§1.3.2 Slavery and Freedom

The antithesis between slavery and freedom runs throughout Galatians, and its presence goes beyond the explicit occurrences of those two word families.[49] Jesus is the one who gave himself to "rescue" (ἐξαιρέω) believers from the present evil age (1:4), using second exodus imagery to portray salvation as deliverance from bondage to sin (compare the use of this same verb in Isa 42:22; 43:13; 44:17, 20; 47:14; 48:10; 50:2; 57:13; 60:16). The false brothers who infiltrated Paul's discussions with the leaders of the Jerusalem church did so "to spy on the freedom we have in Christ Jesus in order to enslave us" (2:4). Again in 3:13, Paul asserts that Christ "redeemed" (ἐξαγοράζω) believers from the curse of the law; he is the suffering servant who frees his people from their bondage to sin, death, and the elements of this world.

The contrast between slavery and freedom takes center stage in 3:23–4:11. Before faith in Christ came, "we were confined under the law, imprisoned until the coming faith was revealed" (3:23). The Mosaic law functioned as a guardian (παιδαγωγός) who supervised and restricted people until the coming of Christ (3:23–25).[50] Now those who are in Christ are adult sons of God who receive an inheritance, regardless of their ethnicity, socioeconomic status (i.e., "slave or free"), or gender (3:28–29). Paul further develops this contrast in 4:1–11. Before Christ came, humanity was like a minor child under the supervision of "guardians and stewards" and, even more significantly, enslaved to the elements of the world (4:1–3). Into this state of bondage God sent his Son to redeem (ἐξαγοράζω, compare 3:13) his people through a second exodus as the suffering servant and Davidic king who is also the promised seed of Abraham. As a result, believers are adopted as sons into God's family and marked off as such by the Spirit of God's Son indwelling them (4:4–6). The summary "punch line" of 4:1–7 makes the contrast between slavery and freedom clear: "So you are no longer a slave but a son, and if a son, then God has made you an heir" (4:7). Paul uses this conclusion as the basis for appealing to the

---

[49] Words related to slavery include: δοῦλος (4x; 1:10; 3:28; 4:1, 7); δουλεύω (4x; 4:8, 9, 25; 5:13); παιδίσκη (5x; 4:22, 23, 30, 31); δουλόω (4:3); καταδουλόω (2:4). Words related to freedom include: ἐλεύθερος (6x; 3:28; 4:22, 23, 26, 30, 31); ἐλευθερία (4x; 2:4; 5:1, 13); ἐλευθερόω (5:1). One could also include verbs related to deliver or rescue such as ἐξαιρέω (1:4) and ἐξαγοράζω (3:13; 4:5). For additional language associated with slavery, see the discussion of Paul's use of "under" language (ὑπό + the accusative) in Biblical Theology §7.1.

[50] Even if one views the role of the παιδαγωγός in a neutral light, at best it still describes a state of immaturity that must be somehow overcome.

Galatians not to return to slavery to the elements of this world (4:8–11). Since life before Christ was a state of slavery to "things that by nature are not gods" (4:8), it makes no sense to return to another form of slavery to the "weak and worthless elements" by taking upon themselves the Mosaic law requirements (4:9–11).

After another personal appeal to the Galatians based on his initial visit (4:12–20), Paul returns to the slavery/freedom contrast in the climax of his argument (4:21–5:1). He links each concept to a specific son and his mother, as well as a specific covenant and its city:

Table 16:

SLAVERY	FREEDOM
Slave woman (Hagar)	Free woman (Sarah)
One born by the flesh (Ishmael)	One born through the promise (Isaac)
Mosaic law covenant	Abrahamic covenant fulfilled in Christ
Present Jerusalem	Jerusalem above

The climactic statement of the paragraph shows that the fundamental contrast remains the distinction between slavery and freedom when Paul emphatically writes: "For freedom, Christ set us free. Stand firm, then, and don't submit again to a yoke of slavery" (5:1). Given the staggering nature of the freedom that Christ has purchased for believers, returning to any form of slavery should be unthinkable.[51]

Although the specific language of slavery and freedom is less prominent in 5:2–6:10, this entire section describes what it looks like to live as free sons who have the Spirit as the down payment of their future full inheritance. The freedom that Christ purchased for his people enables believers to serve others through love so that they fulfill the ultimate intention of the law (5:13–14). The ongoing battle between the flesh and the Spirit is waged between living in the freedom that the Spirit gives and turning away from patterns of sinful behavior that once enslaved the believer (5:16–26). Having been freed from the bondage of the law, believers are now free to bear each other's burdens and fulfill the law of Christ (6:1–10).

---

[51] See further Harmon, *She Must and Shall Go Free*, 199–200.

§1.3.3 Human and Divine

At various points in Galatians Paul makes a sharp contrast between the human and the divine. This contrast takes center stage at the beginning of the letter, where Paul asserts that his status as an apostle is "not from men or by man, but by Jesus Christ and God the Father who raised him from the dead" (1:1). As a result, he seeks to please God rather than people, portraying those two options as mutually exclusive (1:10). The gospel that Paul preaches is not of human origin, but came from God revealing his Son in Paul (1:12–16). This divine gospel transcended what Paul had expected as a zealous Pharisee who dedicated his life to scrupulous observance of the Mosaic law and the numerous human traditions associated with it.[52] This divine gospel is not dependent on the authority or reputation of the Jerusalem church or its pillar apostles (1:18–2:10).

This fundamental contrast between the human and the divine informs other key motifs in Galatians as well.[53] As those enslaved to the various powers of the present evil age, human beings view the world through lenses that divide the world on the basis of ethnicity, gender, and socio-economic status (3:28). But through union with Christ believers are able to see the world through God's promise to bless the nations through the seed of Abraham (3:7–29). Rather than relate to God and others based on one's performance of the Mosaic law, believers are to believe in Christ and his promises (3:10–14). Believers are also called to walk by God's Spirit to avoid carrying out the desires of the flesh (5:16–26).

§1.3.4 Doing and Believing

The antithesis between doing and believing is central to Paul's response to his opponents' advocacy of combining faith in Christ with observing the Mosaic law. The contrast is seen most clearly in 3:11–12, where Paul explains that the Mosaic law operates on the principle of doing while

---

[52] Given Paul's extensive engagement with Isaiah throughout Galatians (including the use of Isaianic language to describe his sudden conversion), the apostle would likely have seen his own experience in these words from Isaiah: "'For my thoughts are not your thoughts, and your ways are not my ways.' This is the Lord's declaration. 'For as heaven is higher than earth, so my ways are higher than your ways, and my thoughts than your thoughts'" (55:8–9).

[53] The extent of this antithesis between the human and the divine is widely debated. Such debate typically runs along the "salvation-historical" versus "apocalyptic" fault lines, though it often transcends it.

justification operates on the principle of believing. Thus the repeated contrast between works of the law and (hearing with) faith is simply an extension of this fundamental antithesis between doing and believing applied to justification (2:16), receiving the Spirit at conversion (3:2), experiencing the ongoing work of the Spirit after conversion (3:5), and experiencing the blessing/inheritance promised to Abraham (3:6–18).

The antithesis between doing and believing is also the foundation of the various contrasts that Paul draws with the Mosaic law. Receiving the inheritance does not come through doing the Mosaic law but rather through believing the promise that God made to Abraham as fulfilled in Christ the seed of Abraham (3:15–18).[54] Since the Mosaic law and salvation in Christ operate on the fundamentally different principles of doing versus believing, the two cannot be combined in order to bring about justification (5:2–6). Similarly, the Mosaic law is contrasted with the Spirit when it comes to living the Christian life. Those who are led by the Spirit are not under the authority of the Mosaic law (5:18), and as believers serve others through love in the power of the Spirit, they are fulfilling the ultimate intent of the Mosaic law (5:13–14). Indeed, the Mosaic law in no way opposes the kind of fruit the Spirit produces in the lives of believers (5:23).

§1.3.5 Curse and Blessing

The contrast between blessing and curse runs from the beginning of the Bible to the end. After creating human beings in his image, God blessed Adam and Eve by commissioning them to be fruitful, multiply, and rule over creation under his authority (Gen 1:28). Yet God also warned them that if they disobeyed, they would experience the curse of death (Gen 2:16–17), which is what came to pass when they ate from the tree of the knowledge of good and evil and were exiled from Eden (Gen 3:14–19, 22–24). When God makes his original promise to Abraham, he promises, "I will bless those who bless you, I will curse anyone who treats you with contempt" (Gen 12:3). This dynamic is played out regularly in Abraham's life, as those who are associated with him are blessed (Gen 13:1–6; 16:10–12; 17:20; 21:15–34) while those who oppose him experience

---

[54] Though Paul is quick to note that the Mosaic law is not contrary to the Abrahamic promise; it served as a temporary guardian over God's people until Christ the promised seed came (3:19–25).

some measure of curse (Gen 12:10–20; 14:1–16). The same blessing/curse dynamic is passed down as the Abrahamic promise from Abraham to Isaac (Gen 22:17–18), Isaac to Jacob (Gen 27:29), and Jacob to his twelve sons (Gen 49:1–27).

The antithesis between blessing and curse plays a prominent role in Israel's history. In the initial giving of the Mosaic law covenant, God laid out both the blessings for obedience (Lev 26:3–13) and the curses for disobedience (Lev 26:14–45). Balak king of Moab tried to convince the prophet Balaam to curse Israel during their forty years of wilderness wandering, saying to him, "I know that those you bless are blessed and those you curse are cursed" (Num 22:6). Not only does God warn Balaam not to curse the people because they are blessed (Num 22:12), but eventually through Balaam he repeats the promise, "Those who bless you will be blessed, and those who curse you will be cursed" (Num 24:9). Nations and kings who opposed Israel during their time in the wilderness regularly met with God's judgment (e.g., Num 21:21–35).

As Moses stood before Israel on the edge of the promised land and taught the people God's law, he instructed them, "Look, today I set before you a blessing and a curse" (Deut 11:26). Blessing would come by obeying Yahweh's commandments, while cursing would come if they disobeyed. He then commanded the people that when they entered the land, they were to have half the people stand on Mount Gerizim and recite the blessings for obeying the covenant while the other half stood on Mount Ebal to recite the curses for disobeying the covenant (Deut 11:29). That scene takes place in Deuteronomy 27–28, where two extended sections of curses (27:9–26; 28:15–68) surround a section of blessing (28:1–14). Paul cites the final curse of that section—"Everyone who does not do everything written in the book of the law is cursed" (Deut 27:26)—to support his contention that those who rely on works of the law are under a curse (Gal 3:10). The scene culminates in 30:11–30, where Moses states that he has set before the people "life and death, blessing and curse. Choose life so that you and your descendants may live" (30:19). If they obey, Yahweh "will prolong your days as you live in the land the Lord swore to give to your fathers Abraham, Isaac, and Jacob" (30:20).

Throughout their history Israel experienced both blessing and curse, though on the whole they experienced more curse than blessing. The peak of blessing occurred during the reigns of David and Solomon, who led Israel to an extended period in which God's promises to Abraham and

Israel found their fullest realization. During David's reign, God made a covenant with him that he would establish the throne of his kingdom forever through his offspring (2 Sam 7:12–16). When David's offspring sin, God will discipline him, but he will bring blessing through the offspring's obedience. This promise finds initial and partial fulfillment in Solomon, but David (Pss 2; 8; 110) and later biblical writers foresaw that its ultimate fulfillment awaited someone greater (Ps 89). It was this hope of eschatological blessing through the fulfillment of God's promises to Abraham and David that sustained God's people even in the midst of their exile (e.g., Ezek 34:23–24), which was the culminating curse God had promised for breaking the covenant (Deut 28:64–68).

In Galatians, Paul sees the antithesis of blessing and curse through the person and work of Christ. Those who believe in Christ receive the blessing that God promised to Abraham, who received the blessing of justification through his faith in God and his promises (3:6–9). But those who rely on works of the law to relate to God and others are under a curse because no one can obey God's law perfectly (3:10). Through his death on the cross Jesus redeemed his people from the curse that his people deserved for their disobedience by taking the curse upon himself (3:13). The curse that Christ bore for his people included both the curse that Israel deserved for breaking the Mosaic covenant and the curse that fell upon all humanity and creation itself when Adam rebelled in the garden. As a result of his bearing this curse, Jew and gentile alike receive the blessing promised to Abraham through the gift of the Spirit (3:14). The blessing of the inheritance promised to Abraham comes to God's people through faith in that promise (3:15–18) and not through the Mosaic law, which was a temporary custodian of God's people until Christ the promised seed came (3:19–25). Now that Christ—the promised seed of Abraham, the suffering servant, the son of David, the son of God—has come, all who are united to him by faith share in his inheritance and are sealed by his Spirit (3:26–4:7). Like Isaac, they are sons of promise who are free citizens of the Jerusalem above and not in slavery under the Mosaic law like those who identify themselves with the present Jerusalem (4:21–5:1).

Believers' experience of the Abrahamic blessing through faith in Christ is mediated through the Holy Spirit. They experience his presence and power in their lives now as the Spirit produces fruit that reflects the character of Christ himself (5:16–6:10). Despite being freed from the power and authority of this present evil age (1:4), believers still live in a fallen world that remains under the curse and must therefore fight against sin, the flesh, and the elements of this world (4:8–11; 5:16–26; 6:8). But when the blessing of new creation reaches its final and complete realization in a new heavens and earth (6:15), believers will live in the unfettered joy that comes from experiencing the fullness of God's peace and mercy (6:16), finally free from every last effect of the curse from the garden.

§1.3.6 Flesh and Promise/Spirit[55]

The antithesis between the flesh and the promise/Spirit is in a very real sense a sub-category of the contrast between the present evil age and the new creation, since the flesh is a primary agent in the realm of the present evil age and the Spirit is the primary agent in the new creation. The Greek term (σάρξ) rendered flesh is difficult to translate into English. Although it can refer to the physical body (Gal 1:16; 2:20), in many places it refers to weak and frail human nature under the power and control of sin and subject to the spiritual forces of evil in this fallen world. That is the sense we will explore in this section, as it plays a key role in Galatians as a foil to the promise/Spirit.

The contrast between the flesh and the promise/Spirit first occurs in 3:3, where Paul rhetorically asks if the Christian life begins with the Spirit but is completed by/in the flesh, clearly indicating the answer is an emphatic no. The point is that the Christian life both begins and continues in the basis of the Spirit and not the flesh. The apostle makes a similar point with this antithesis in 4:23 and 4:29, where the close relationship between promise and Spirit comes out especially clearly:

> But the one by the slave was born as a result of the flesh, while the one by the free woman was born through promise. (4:23)

> But just as then the child born as a result of the flesh persecuted the one born as a result of the Spirit, so also now. (4:29)

Thus the antithesis between the flesh and the promise/Spirit is a contrast between human effort and divine action as a means of experiencing eschatological life, regardless of whether one refers to its beginning or its continuation.

---

[55] In Galatians the Spirit is so closely associated with the term promise that at times they are almost interchangeable (3:14; 4:23, 29). Therefore I have treated them together in this section.

The mention of this contrast at the beginning and the end of the main argument in 3:1–5:1 sets the stage for the more sustained development of this contrast in 5:2–6:10. The freedom that Christ freed believers to experience must not be distorted into an opportunity to indulge the flesh; instead it should empower serving others through love as a fulfillment of the law's intent (5:13–14). The power to do so comes from the Spirit who enables believers to walk in obedience to the Lord and resist gratifying the desires of the flesh (5:16). This work of the Spirit was promised in Ezekiel 36:26–27 as part of the new covenant. Indeed, the war between the flesh and the Spirit is one particular manifestation of the antithesis between the present evil age and the new creation (5:17). The Spirit leads believers in a way that transcends the limitations of the Mosaic law (5:18). Just as the Holy Spirit led Israel in the wilderness after their exodus from slavery in Egypt, so now the Spirit leads God's people in the wilderness period between the second exodus from slavery to the unholy trinity of sin, death, and the flesh as they anticipate the consummation of the new creation (Isa 63:11–15).

Since the flesh and the Spirit are opposing forces in the conflict between the present evil age and the new creation, the results they produce are radically different. The works of the flesh are expressions of a self-centered life that leads to behavior that destroys both the individual and the larger community (5:19–21a). Those whose lives are characterized by these works of the flesh demonstrate that they are not Abraham's offspring or sons of God and therefore will not inherit the eschatological new creational kingdom (5:21b). By contrast, in fulfillment of Isaiah 32:15–20, the eschatological Spirit lives inside of God's people to produce fruit that reflects the character of Christ and builds a community that transcends anything the Mosaic law could ever produce (5:22–23). The triumph of the Spirit over the flesh is rooted in the cross, where the flesh—along with its passions and desires—was crucified (5:24). Thus the Spirit not only gives initial spiritual life to believers but sustains and nourishes their ongoing experience of it (5:25).

Although the contrast between the flesh and the Spirit occurs explicitly just in 6:1–10, conceptually it underlies the entire section. It is only as believers walk and are led by the Spirit that they are able to bear one another's burdens and thus fulfill the law of Christ (6:2). Paul returns to the contrast in 6:8, where he describes one's pattern of life as either sowing to the flesh (which leads to destruction) or sowing to the Spirit (which leads to eternal life). The apostle likely draws this language from Hosea, where the prophet describes Israel's plunge into idolatry as sowing to the wind and reaping the whirlwind (8:1–7) and calls them instead to sow righteousness so they will reap faithful love (10:12–13).

In summary, the antithesis between the flesh and the Spirit has both individual and cosmic levels. The flesh is one of the active powers of the present evil age that enslaves people in their sin and subjects them to the elements of this world. The Spirit is the active agent of the new creation, empowering God's people to live in obedience to God by serving others through love.

§1.4 CONCLUSION

The death and resurrection of Jesus was the dramatic turning point in history that inaugurated the end of the present evil age and the beginning of the new creation. At the same time his death and resurrection were the fulfillment of God's promise to Abraham through a singular seed who was the suffering servant, the promised Davidic king, and the incarnate Son of God. Only when both the salvation-historical and apocalyptic elements in Galatians are recognized can a holistic understanding of Galatians emerge.

§2 God

Since God is the central character of the Bible, it makes sense to summarize what Galatians teaches about him. In addition to the number of general references to God, all three persons of the Trinity play a key role in Paul's argument in the letter.

§2.1 GOD THE FATHER

The importance of God the Father in Galatians goes beyond the four explicit references (1:1, 3, 4; 4:6). He called Paul to be an apostle (1:1) by delighting to reveal his Son Jesus Christ in Paul (1:15–16). The Father also calls all believers to himself through the grace of Christ (1:6), of which he, along with the Son, is the source and giver (1:3). Every aspect of salvation happens according to the will of the Father (1:4), who, when the time of fulfillment came, sent his Son to redeem his people from their slavery (4:1–7). Because of what his Son has done, the Father has adopted his people as sons and sent the Spirit of his Son to dwell inside of them. As a result, his adopted sons cry out to him, "*Abba*, Father" (4:6).

§2.2 JESUS CHRIST

Jesus Christ is at the heart of Paul's defense of the gospel in Galatians. Three times Paul uses the full title "Lord Jesus Christ" (1:3; 6:14, 18), with the first and the last forming an inclusio for the entire letter. Each element of that full title has its own significance that is enriched by its combination with the others. The most common way Paul refers to him is with the title Christ (38x), which in the most basic sense meant someone who was anointed. It was the Greek equivalent of the Hebrew term Messiah, which in the Second Temple period came to refer to the promised descendant of David who would defeat Israel's enemies and reestablish Israel's independence (compare Ps 2:2). By the time Paul wrote Galatians the term Christ had become a shorthand title that referred to Jesus as the fulfillment of the Old Testament hope, while retaining its royal overtones. Although less common, Lord (κύριος) is also an important title ascribed to Jesus in Galatians (1:3, 19; 5:10; 6:14, 18). At one level the title portrays Jesus as the master and ruler of his people with sovereign authority over them. But more significantly, κύριος was frequently used in the LXX to translate the divine name Yahweh (יהוה). While it is not always easy to determine when Paul uses κύριος with this full divine significance, he does so in enough places to indicate that he firmly believed that Jesus was in fact Yahweh in the flesh. As such Jesus is the sovereign Lord, the creator of the universe, and the one true God to whom every knee will bow in heaven and on earth and under the earth (compare Phil 2:10–11). And we must not overlook the name Jesus, which in Hebrew meant "Yahweh saves." All but once in Galatians (6:17) it occurs in tandem with Christ, though the order varies.[56] Additionally, Jesus Christ is identified as the servant of the Lord, seed of Abraham, and the son of David, all of which are treated elsewhere.

The bulk, however, of what Paul says about Jesus Christ occurs in describing what he has done, with a particular focus on his death and resurrection.[57] We can summarize what Galatians teaches about the death

---

[56] Both "Jesus Christ" (1:1, 3, 12; 2:16; 3:1, 22; 6:14, 18) and "Christ Jesus" (2:4, 16; 3:14, 26, 28; 4:14; 5:6, 24) appear eight times in Galatians. It is difficult to discern any consistent reason for the choice of one order rather than the other; note, for example the use of both in 2:16.

[57] Without question Jesus' death receives far more explicit attention than his resurrection, with only one direct reference to the latter (1:1). But Christ's resurrection nonetheless plays an important role throughout Galatians, supporting key points in Paul's argument; see Bryant, *The Risen Crucified Christ in Galatians*, 143–61. Furthermore, although the Bible

and resurrection of Jesus by explaining what he did, why he did it, and what happened as a result. Jesus' death was a sacrificial act of giving himself for sins and for his people (1:4; 2:20), language that has its roots in Isaiah 53. Christ died and rose again for at least two reasons: (1) to rescue his people from the present evil age (1:4) and their enslavement to the elements of the world (4:3, 9) and (2) to redeem his people from the curse that the law brings upon all who fail to obey it perfectly (3:10–14; 4:4–5). Paul identifies several distinct (albeit overlapping) results of Jesus' death and resurrection: (1) it gives freedom (2:4, 19; 3:25; 4:26, 31; 5:1, 13); (2) it unleashes the blessing of Abraham to Jew and gentile alike and qualifies them as heirs (3:13, 16–18, 23–29; 4:1–7, 21–31; 5:21); (3) it unleashes the gift of the Spirit to all God's people (3:14; 4:6; 5:16–26); (4) it enables a new kind of life for God's people (2:19–20; 5:6, 16–26; 6:14–16); (5) it makes God's people adopted sons of God (3:25–29; 4:4–7); and (6) it inaugurates the new creation (6:14–16). As a result, Jesus Christ is both the content and the source of the gospel (1:7, 12, 15–16). He is the object of the Christian's faith (2:15–16, 20; 3:22).

Jesus Christ is also at the center of the believer's ongoing experience of the Christian life. He is the giver of grace that sustains the believer (1:3, 6; 6:18) and the one who dwells in believers through his Spirit to empower them to live a life pleasing to God (2:20; 4:6). Although believers are not under the authority of the Mosaic law covenant, they are subject to the law of Christ (6:2), which refers to both the teaching and example of Jesus as a paradigm for a life that fulfills the purpose of the Mosaic law (5:13–14). Believers belong to Christ (3:29; 5:24) and live their lives "in Christ" (3:14, 28; 5:6). In their baptism believers have also "put on Christ" (3:27), which vividly portrays the old life of sin as filthy clothing that the believers take off to put on the new life of holiness that is possible because they are now united to Christ. Paul even describes the goal of his ministry as seeing Christ formed in believers (4:19), a way of portraying the progressive growth in Christlikeness that believers experience through the work of the Holy Spirit.

Jesus Christ is also the hinge point of human history. Before he came the world was subject to the powers of this present evil age (1:4), enslaved

---

often highlights one particular aspect of Christ's work, the life, ministry, death, resurrection, and ascension of Jesus Christ are best regarded as one complex redemptive act, with each aspect playing a necessary role in the salvation of God's people.

under the elements of this world (1:4; 4:1–3, 8–11), and subject to the curse of the law for failing to keep it (3:10). But when the time of fulfillment came, God sent his Son to invade this fallen world and inaugurate the new creation kingdom of God (6:15), the long-promised messianic age in which the Spirit dwells in God's people (5:16–26).

§2.3 THE HOLY SPIRIT

With all of the attention in Galatians devoted to justification, the law, grace, works, and faith, the person and work of the Holy Spirit has sometimes been overlooked.[58] At several points in the Old Testament the gift of the Spirit for all of God's people was anticipated as one of the definitive blessings of the messianic age when God would fulfill his promises and establish his kingdom (Isa 32:15–20; Ezek 36:27; Joel 2:28–32). That conviction is evident in Galatians, where the Spirit is the definitive blessing of the new creation kingdom that God has inaugurated through his Son Jesus Christ. In fulfillment of the promise to Abraham, the Spirit is given to all who believe regardless of their ethnicity (3:14). As sons of God through the work of Jesus the Son of God, believers are given the Spirit of God's Son, who prompts them to cry out "*Abba*, Father" (4:6). The Mosaic law covenant is no longer the means by which God's people relate to him and others; with the coming of Christ, the Spirit is now at the focal point of how to love God with their whole lives and their neighbor as themselves (5:13–14, 18). The Holy Spirit is central to Paul's understanding of salvation history in Galatians.

From this foundation Paul presents the Spirit as the one who begins, sustains, and completes the Christian life. Believers are "born as a result of the Spirit" (4:29) and receive the Spirit when they first believe the gospel message (3:2). Indeed, Paul uses this truth as a starting point for convincing the Galatians that works of the law are not a necessary component of the Christian life (3:2–5). As part of their ongoing Christian lives, believers receive fresh supplies of the Spirit as they continue to trust in Christ and his promises (3:5). The Spirit is the one who not only initiates the Christian life, but sustains and nurtures it to produce spiritual maturity and holiness in the believer (3:3). To accomplish this goal, the Spirit wages war against the desires of the flesh (5:16–17) and produces fruit in

---

[58] A notable exception to this is Charles H. Cosgrove, *The Cross and the Spirit: A Study in the Argument and Theology of Galatians* (Macon, GA: Mercer University Press, 1988).

the life of the believer (5:22–23). The believer is responsible to walk by (5:16), submit to the leadership of it (5:18), and keep in step with the Spirit (5:25). As believers do so, the Spirit produces an eager anticipation for the culmination of all God's promises on the last day (5:6) and motivates them to live in a way that sows to the Spirit in anticipation of reaping eternal life on that day (6:8).

§3 The Servant of the Lord[59]

At several points in Galatians, Paul draws language from the Servant Songs of Isaiah to describe his own self-understanding as well as his understanding of the identity and work of Christ. So it is necessary to look at both separately before synthesizing these two strands.

§3.1 PAUL AS THE SERVANT OF THE LORD

Several times in Galatians Paul echoes the language of Isaiah 49 to explain his conversion and commission to preach the gospel to the gentiles. His claim that God set him apart from the womb to preach the gospel to the gentiles (1:15–16) echoes the description of the servant of Yahweh in Isaiah 49:1–6. Residual echoes of this same text are found in Paul's claim that the Judean churches were glorifying God in him (1:24) and his concern about running or laboring in vain (2:2; 4:11). Isaiah 49:1–6 also seems to inform Paul's statements about the scope of his mission focusing on the gentiles (2:2, 8–9). Additionally, the use of the terms εὐαγγέλιον ("gospel"), εὐαγγελίζομαι ("preach the gospel"), and εἰρηνή ("peace") have as their background Isaiah 52:5–7, 10, where the good news of Yahweh's redemption is announced to all the nations. These allusions, echoes, and thematic parallels strongly suggest that Paul understands his identity as an apostle to the gentiles prefigured in the mission of the servant described in Isaiah 49:1–6, with other passages from the larger Isaianic context providing additional support for this conviction.

This conclusion is confirmed by several other New Testament texts. In Romans 10:14–16 Paul brings together his apostolic self-understanding, the content of the gospel, and the work of Christ as the suffering servant.

---

[59] This section summarizes a much longer discussion in Harmon, *She Must and Shall Go Free*, 103–21, which has now been expanded in Matthew S. Harmon, *The Servant of the Lord and His Servant People: Tracing a Biblical Theme through the Canon*, NSBT 54 (Downers Grove, IL: IVP, 2021).

Later in that same letter, the apostle cites Isaiah 52:15 to explain his focus on preaching the gospel in areas where the gospel has not yet been proclaimed rather than build on the work of other missionaries (Rom 15:22). Near the end of his lengthiest explanation of his apostolic ministry (2 Cor 2:14–6:13), Paul cites Isaiah 49:8 as the message that God speaks through him as an ambassador of Christ (2 Cor 5:20–6:2). In Philippians 2:16 Paul expresses his goal that on the last day he will be able to say that he did not run or labor in vain, language that is borrowed from Isaiah 49:4. Luke's account of Paul and Barnabas' ministry in Pisidian Antioch provides additional confirmation of Paul's testimony in his letters. Defending the shift in ministry focus to the gentiles, Luke records Paul citing Isaiah 49:6 as God's command to Barnabas and him (Acts 13:47).

Thus the evidence in Galatians and the rest of the New Testament makes it clear that Paul saw his ministry in some way fulfilling the mission of the Isaianic servant bringing salvation to the nations.

§3.2 Jesus as the Servant of the Lord

At the same time, Paul describes the work of Christ in language borrowed from the Isaianic Servant Songs at several points in Galatians. The apostle describes the self-sacrificial death of Jesus as delivering his people from this present evil age according to the Father's will (1:4), placing the servant's work within an apocalyptic framework. The key turning point in human history has occurred at the cross; the long-awaited messianic age has dawned and God's work of new creation has begun as a result of Christ the suffering servant. Paul again uses Isaiah 53 language when he insists, "The life I now live in the body, I live by faith in the Son of God, who loved me and gave himself for me" (2:20). When it comes to explaining how Christ takes upon himself the curse that humanity deserves for failing to keep the law, Paul alludes to Isaiah 53 in asserting that "Christ redeemed us from the curse of the law by becoming a curse for us" (3:13). In Isaiah 53 the servant suffers the curse that God's people deserve for their rebellion and idolatry, and Paul appears to have a similar framework in mind here in Galatians. Just as the death and resurrection of the servant in Isaiah 53 ushers in the fulfillment of the promise to Abraham (Isa 54:1–17), so the curse-bearing death of Christ results in the blessing of Abraham coming to the gentiles, epitomized by the gift of the Spirit (Gal 3:13–14). The death of the servant also redeemed his people from the law and all the other elements of this world that enslaved humanity, leading the eschatological people of God in a new exodus that results in them being adopted as sons of God who are sealed with God's Spirit (4:1–7). This new exodus fulfills the promise to Abraham and inaugurates the new creation that God had promised (Isa 41:17–20; 43:16–21; 51:1–10).

Within Galatians, then, the death of Jesus is presented as the fulfillment of the suffering servant offering himself as a sacrifice for the sins of his people, fulfilling the promise to Abraham and inaugurating the new creation reign of God over the nations.

§3.3 SYNTHESIS: JESUS AS THE SERVANT OF THE LORD WHO
DWELLS IN PAUL

So how do we integrate these two streams—Paul as the servant in Isaiah 49 and Jesus as the servant from Isaiah 53? The key is Galatians 2:20, where Paul states, "I have been crucified with Christ, and I no longer live, but Christ lives in me. The life I now live in the body, I live by faith in the Son of God, who loved me and gave himself for me." The phrase "in me" (ἐν ἐμοί) picks up the previous uses of this phrase in 1:16, 24 that echo Isaiah 49:3, thus reaffirming his self-understanding as the servant from Isaiah 49. Yet in speaking of Christ as the one who loved Paul and gave himself for him, Paul reaffirms Christ as the suffering servant of Isaiah 53. The apostle, then, believes that "Jesus Christ the suffering Servant of Isa 53, who gave himself for Paul, now lives in Paul to carry out the mission of the Servant portrayed in Isa 49 to be a light to the nations. Because of this truth, Paul can refer to his own apostolic mission as the fulfillment of the Servant's commission in Isa 49 to be a light to the nations, since it is ultimately Christ who fulfills that mission through him. As a result, God's intention of revealing his Son 'in' Paul (Gal 1:16) reaches its intended goal of God being glorified 'in' Paul (Gal 1:24), because Christ lives 'in' Paul (Gal 2:20) to fulfill the Servant's commission to be a light to the nations."[60]

§4 Seed/Offspring

Central to the argument of Galatians is Paul's claim that Jesus Christ is the promised seed/offspring of Abraham (3:16). Just as is true with the English terms seed and offspring, the Hebrew noun rendered "offspring" (זֶרַע) can refer to an individual or a group of people depending on the context.

---

[60] Harmon, *She Must and Shall Go Free*, 119.

This ambiguity can sometimes lead to a dual reference where the term has in view both a singular individual as well as the group of people that comes from that individual. Paul is well aware of that ambiguity and uses it to make his point that Jesus is the singular seed of Abraham in whom the promises are fulfilled. Tracing this theme through the Old Testament sheds light on Paul's interpretive conclusions in Galatians.

The starting point is Genesis 3:15. In the context of judging the serpent for deceiving Eve into eating from the tree of the knowledge of good and evil, God announces, "I will put hostility between you and the woman, and between your offspring and her offspring. He will strike your head, and you will strike his heel." Embedded within this judgment is a promise that an individual offspring will defeat the serpent, though not without suffering.[61] In one sense the rest of the Old Testament storyline is rooted in the anticipation of this suffering serpent-crusher. When Seth is born to replace the murdered Abel, Eve identifies him as "another offspring instead of Abel" (4:25 ESV), perhaps hoping he was the singular serpent-crushing seed. After the flood God renews his covenant with Noah and his offspring after him, commanding him to be fruitful, multiply, and fill the earth (Gen 9:1–17; compare 1:28).

But the promise of offspring comes into sharper focus with God's promise to Abram to make him into a great nation so that in him all the nations of the earth will be blessed (Gen 12:1–3). As part of that plan God promises to give Abram and his offspring land (Gen 12:1, 7). Thus through the line of Abraham will come a multitude of descendants, one of whom will be the promised serpent-crusher. The interplay between a singular offspring and multiple offspring from Abraham appears again at two critical points. In Genesis 17, God renews his promise to make Abram the father of a multitude of nations and establish his covenant with his many offspring in the land he promised to give them (17:1–8). Circumcision will be the sign of this covenant throughout their generations (17:9–14). The fulfillment of this promise of countless offspring, however, hinges on the birth of a singular offspring—Isaac, who will be born from Abraham's barren wife Sarah (17:15–21). It is in and through this singular offspring that God's promises will find fulfillment (17:19). Similarly, the same dynamic between singular and plural offspring occurs in Genesis 22:15–18. In the

---

[61] For a defense of seeing the offspring here as singular, see Collins, "Syntactical Note," 139–48.

aftermath of nearly sacrificing Isaac, God swears to bless and multiply Abraham's offspring (22:17a), a clear reference to multiple descendants. Yet the very next line promises that Abraham's offspring "shall possess the gate of his enemies" (22:17b ESV).[62] The fulfillment of the promise to Abraham hinges on a singular offspring, and all those who are "in" this singular offspring will be blessed (22:18).

This interplay between singular and multiple offspring continues throughout the rest of the Old Testament. Despite beginning as a family of seventy when they entered Egypt, Abraham's offspring multiplied to such an extent that the land was filled with them (Exod 1:7; compare Gen 1:28; 12:1–3). In the wake of Israel's idolatry with the golden calf, Moses reminds Yahweh of his promise to Abraham, Isaac, and Jacob of a multitude of offspring (Exod 32:12; 33:1). Yet even with the consistent emphasis on multiple offspring from Abraham, there are hints of a singular offspring in whom the promises find their fulfillment. In his third oracle, Balaam describes the camp of Israel in Edenic terms (Num 24:5–6) before noting that "Water will flow from his buckets, and his seed will be by abundant water. His king will be greater than Agag, and his kingdom will be exalted" (Num 24:7). Here "his" refers to the people of Israel, whose multiple offspring will live by abundant water. Yet also in view is a singular offspring, a king whose kingdom will be exalted. This king is further described as a star that comes out of Jacob and a scepter from within Israel who will crush the enemies of God's people and exercise dominion (Num 24:17–19).[63]

The interplay between singular and multiple offspring is further seen in God's covenant with David. God promises, "When your time comes and you rest with your ancestors, I will raise up after you your descendant, who will come from your body, and I will establish his kingdom" (2 Sam 7:12). So the promise finds its fulfillment in a singular offspring. Yet God also promises, "Your house and kingdom will endure before me forever, and your throne will be established forever" (2 Sam 7:16); the mention of a house seems to imply multiple descendants coming from David. The

---

[62] For a helpful explanation and defense of reading this as a reference to a singular offspring, see Alexander, "Further Observations," 363–67 and Williamson, *Abraham, Israel, and the Nations*, 248–50.

[63] On the numerous connections between Gen 1–3 and Num 24:6–9, see especially James M. Hamilton, Jr., "The Seed of the Woman and the Blessing of Abraham," *TynBul* 58 (2007): 263–66.

point seems to be that the line of descendants will culminate in a single offspring in whom the promises find their fulfillment. That David himself understood this may be implied by some of David's own psalms, where he seems to have in view a future descendant of his who will rule as Yahweh's anointed (מָשִׁיחַ / Χριστός) over all the nations (Pss 2:1–12; 18:50).[64] The Davidic covenant, then, is an extension of the Abrahamic covenant in that God will use the singular offspring of David to give God's people rest in the land and bring blessing to the nations.[65]

This hope of a singular descendant from David's line becomes a focal point of the Old Testament hope in the centuries that followed. In the wake of a national disaster (perhaps exile?), Psalm 89 recalls God's covenant with David and his singular offspring as the grounds for hope, applying to this future Davidic king language from Genesis 1–3 describing Adam's commission and the serpent crusher and language from Genesis 12:1–3 describing God's promise to Abraham (Ps 89:20–29).[66] Hosea foresees a day when God will multiply his people in fulfillment of his promise to Abraham and appoint a Davidic king to rule over them (Hos 1:10–11). Through this righteous Branch from David's line God's people will be fruitful and multiply, living at peace in the land (Jer 23:1–8; compare 33:19–22; Ezek 34:23–24).

Isaiah 40–55 places particular emphasis on the theme of offspring in relationship to the fulfillment of God's promises to both Abraham and David. Isaiah 41:8 brings together the themes of servant and the offspring of Abraham when it describes the people of God as "Israel, my servant, Jacob, whom I have chosen, descendant of Abraham, my friend." This connection between the seed of Abraham and Yahweh's servant is further developed in the chapters that follow. The nation of Israel failed

---

[64] Although Psalms itself does not attribute Psalm 2 to David, Acts 4:25 does.

[65] See the helpful summary of these two points in Gentry and Wellum, *Kingdom through Covenant*, 423–27.

[66] It appears that the targum of Ps 89 also saw a strong connection between the promises to Abraham and the Davidic covenant, as it changes the superscription from "Ethan the Ezrahite" (אֵיתָן הָאֶזְרָחִי) to "Abraham who came from the east" (דאברהם דאתא מן מדינחא); see David M. Stec, *The Targum of Psalms*, The Aramaic Bible 16 (Collegeville, MN: Liturgical Press, 2004), 187 as noted in John Goldingay, *Psalms*, 3 vols. (Grand Rapids: Baker Academic, 2006), 2:666. Goldingay goes on to note that this is strikingly similar to the phrase "from the east" (מִמְּזְרָח) in Isa 41:2, where a few verses later the servant and offspring of Abraham are parallel to each other (41:8). As noted below, Isaiah 40–55 makes a strong connection between the fulfillment of the Abrahamic and Davidic promises.

to live up to their calling to be the servant of the Lord (42:1–25). But God promises a day when he will pour out his Spirit on the seed of the servant (44:3–5). In light of Israel's failure, God raises up a new individual servant to redeem Israel and obey where Israel had failed (49:1–8). The salvation/righteousness this servant accomplishes will fulfill the promise God made to Abraham and result in a new creation (51:1–8). As a result of the servant giving his life as an offering for sin, the servant "will see his seed, he will prolong his days, and by his hand, the LORD's pleasure will be accomplished" (53:10). Just as God gave offspring to once barren Sarah, so too he will bring into existence the eschatological people of God to fulfill his promise to Abraham so that his seed will multiply and possess the nations (54:1–3). The merging of the themes of servant and seed in Isaiah 40–55 may have led Paul to move from Christ as the servant to Christ as the singular seed.

The New Testament opens by identifying Jesus as the offspring of Abraham and David (Matt 1:1), signaling that Jesus is the fulfillment of the two covenants that God made with them. John the Baptist warned the Jewish leaders not to believe that their biological descent from Abraham guaranteed a right standing with God (Matt 3:9). When the Jewish crowds debate whether Jesus is the Messiah, they rightly note that the Messiah must be the offspring of David (John 7:42). Paul also explicitly identifies Jesus as the offspring of David (Rom 1:3; 2 Tim 2:8). Hebrews 2:16 asserts that God does not give help to the angels but to the offspring of Abraham (Heb 2:16). Paul devotes significant attention to Abraham's offspring in Romans 4:1–25 and again in Romans 9–11. The issue in the latter passage is who are the true offspring of Abraham, and Paul's basic point is that one's identity as an offspring of Abraham is not based on ethnicity but on faith in Christ.

Paul's argument here in Galatians that Christ is the singular offspring in whom the promises are fulfilled fits within this larger biblical trajectory. Far from being a desperate and questionable exegetical move, identifying Christ as Abraham's singular seed is rooted in a careful reading of the biblical storyline.

§5 The Law

Without question one of the most challenging biblical-theological issues in Galatians is Paul's understanding of the law. At the heart of Paul's disagreement with his opponents in Galatia was what role (if any) the Mosaic law should play in the life of the Christian.

While Galatians is not the only place where Paul deals with this issue, our discussion here will necessarily focus on what Paul writes in this letter, while drawing in relevant insights from his other letters when helpful and/or necessary.

§5.1 TERMINOLOGY

The starting point for discussing the law in Galatians must be clarifying terminology. The vast majority of the thirty-two occurrences of the word "law" (νόμος) refer to the Mosaic law; in fact, the only clear exception is 6:2, where Paul refers to the law of Christ.[67] This observation is important. Paul is not against "law" in the sense of commands that express the moral will of God. He is more than willing to state commands that believers are obligated before God to observe. So how do we make sense of this apparent tension?

The starting point is to recognize that the concept of law as an expression of God's moral will goes back to the garden. God commanded Adam not to eat from the tree of the knowledge of good and evil, warning that if he did, he would surely die (Gen 2:16–17). In the period between the fall and the giving of the Mosaic law covenant at Sinai, God issues a number of commands that express his moral will. All of these are expressions of God's law, given centuries before the Mosaic law covenant was instituted. Many of them were incorporated into the Mosaic law covenant (compare Gen 9:5–6 and Exod 20:13). Yet the important point to observe is that law as an expression of God's moral will existed before the Mosaic law covenant, and according to the New Testament, exists after the Mosaic covenant has served its purpose and is no longer valid. Thus, although the Mosaic law covenant does not have authority over believers, they remain under the obligation to obey the revealed will of God as expressed in the law of Christ (see below).

---

[67] There are two other possible exceptions. The first comes in 3:21, where the second occurrence of νόμος could be understood as a general reference to law: "For if the law had been granted with the ability to give life, then righteousness would certainly be on the basis of the law." But even if this is a generic reference to law, the context makes it clear the Mosaic law is in view. The second possible exception is in 5:23, where at the end of describing the fruit of the Spirit Paul states, "against such things there is no law" (ESV). But again the larger context clearly indicates Paul has the Mosaic law in view here; hence the CSB translates: "The law is not against such things."

Thus it is important to stress that when Paul says believers are not "under the law," he is *not* saying that Christians are under no obligation to obey God. His letters, including Galatians, are filled with commands that he expects believers to obey as an expression of God's will (1 Cor 7:19). The goal of his apostolic ministry was "to bring about the obedience of faith for the sake of his name among all the Gentiles" (Rom 1:5). In fact, the new covenant had promised a greater degree of obedience among God's people as a result of God's indwelling Spirit (Jer 31:31–34; Ezek 36:26–27). Such obedience is never presented as a means to earning God's favor, but rather an expression of love for God, joy in our salvation, and gratitude for what he has done for us.

§5.2 THE MOSAIC LAW COVENANT IN GALATIANS

Before Paul encountered the risen Christ on the road to Damascus, his life was characterized by a zealous pursuit of the traditions of his fathers (1:14), by which he means the various traditions connected with the observance of the Mosaic law. By the time of Jesus, the Pharisees had developed an extensive set of traditions and interpretations designed to ensure that none of the Mosaic law requirements was violated. Yet all that changed when God revealed his Son in Paul to commission him to preach the gospel to the gentiles (1:15–17). From that encounter Paul realized not only that Jesus was in fact the Messiah, but also that a new era in redemptive history had dawned. Whereas the Mosaic law had once been the focal point of God's relationship to his people, now that role was filled by the crucified and risen Christ. So what then becomes of the Mosaic law?

In the most basic sense, Paul argues that the Mosaic law covenant was a temporary administration, given as a servant of God's larger covenant promises with Abraham for a specific period of time. Now that its expiration date has come with the arrival of Christ the promised seed of Abraham, it is no longer a binding authority over God's people. To unpack this concise summary, we will briefly explore the purpose of the law, the timeframe during which it was valid, and the means by which it was given.

§5.2.1 *The Purpose of the Law*

Paul states four purposes for the giving of the law. First, it was "added for the sake of transgressions" (3:19). Unfortunately, this phrase is not immediately self-explanatory. There are at least six different ways to interpret the claim that the law "was added for the sake of transgressions" (3:19).[68] Within these various views the law is seen to have either a negative or a positive function.

1. The law was added to limit or restrain transgression.[69] Understood this way, the law keeps sin in check. It acts as a disciplinarian that restrains the human tendency toward disobedience to God.

2. The law was added to provide a means of dealing with sin.[70] Through the sacrificial system God gave Israel a way of taking care of sin. Atonement (albeit provisional until the coming of Christ) was available through the ministry of priests in the tabernacle/temple.

3. The law was added because of Israel's sin with the golden calf (Exod 32).[71] The law was given to help Israel in their role as those entrusted with the revelation of God's redemptive purposes as they awaited the arrival of the Messiah.

4. The law was added to restrain Israel to keep them distinct from the rest of the world for a particular period of time.[72] Since God's redemptive purposes depended on preserving the line through which Messiah would come, he gave Israel the law to keep them distinct from the gentiles.

5. The law was added to provoke transgression.[73] According to this view, the law actively incites people to sin. When combined with the work of the flesh in the sinful human heart, the very presence of the law leads human beings to assert their autonomy from God's will.

6. The law was added to expose sin by making it an obvious violation of a known law, or to convert sin into a transgression of God's

---

[68] This summary is adapted from Das, *Galatians*, 358–61. For convenience I have combined his sixth and seventh categories.

[69] E.g., David J. Lull, "'The Law Was Our Pedagogue': A Study in Galatians 3:19–25," *JBL* 105 (1986): 481–98; Bruce W. Longenecker, *The Triumph of Abraham's God: The Transformation of Identity in Galatians* (Nashville: Abingdon Press, 1998), 122–28.

[70] E.g., Dunn, *Galatians*, 189–90.

[71] E.g., Don B. Garlington, *An Exposition of Galatians: A Reading from the New Perspective*, 3rd ed. (Eugene, OR: Wipf and Stock, 2007), 218–19.

[72] E.g., Hays, "Galatians," 266.

[73] E.g., Betz, *Galatians*, 165; Martyn, *Galatians*, 354–55; Schreiner, *Galatians*, 240.

revealed will.[74] Understood this way, the law convicts people of specific violations of God's will, enabling God to decisively deal with it through the work of Jesus.

The first key to understanding this phrase is to note that the very next clause qualifies it temporally. In other words, whatever function of the law is in view, it seems to be limited to the time period "until the Seed to whom the promise was made would come" (3:19). Second, the larger context of Galatians strongly suggests that whatever this phrase means, it is predominantly negative in nature. Rather than be given directly to God's people it was given by angels through a mediator (3:19–20). The law could not give life and was not intended to be the means by which righteousness/justification comes (3:21). If Scripture can be equated with law, then it is the agent that imprisoned all things under sin (3:22). This state of being under the law until the faith came is likened to confinement and imprisonment (3:23). The law was a guardian whose role was finished once Christ came (3:24–25). This status of being under the law is further compared to being a slave under the bondage of the "elemental forces of the world" (4:1, 3, 8–11). It is equivalent to being "under guardians and trustees until the time set by his father" (4:2). This state of slavery under the law is one that requires redemption (4:4–6) and is sharply contrasted with the status of being a son and an heir who has the indwelling Spirit of God's Son (3:26, 29; 4:6–7). The Mosaic law covenant is associated with Hagar, bearing children for slavery, and operating on the premise of the flesh rather than the promise or the Spirit (4:21–5:1). Pursuing obedience to the Mosaic law results in being alienated from Christ (5:2–6). Life under the law is the opposite of being led by the Spirit (5:16–26).

On the whole some combination of views 5–6 seems most likely. God gave the law to expose sin as a violation of God's revealed will, and in that sense, "The law came along to multiply the trespass" (Rom 5:20). Through the Mosaic law sin was brought out into the open and made clearly identifiable so that its true nature could be seen. As Romans 7:13 states, "Therefore, did what is good become death to me? Absolutely not! But, sin, in order to be recognized as sin, was producing death in me through what is good, so that through the commandment, sin might become sinful beyond measure."

---

[74] E.g., Witherington, *Grace in Galatia*, 256; Moo, *Galatians*, 234; Das, *Galatians*, 360–61.

A second purpose of the law is stated negatively: the law was not intended to give eschatological life (3:21). On the surface such a statement may seem out of step with texts like Leviticus 18:5: "Keep my statutes and ordinances; a person will live if he does them. I am the Lord." But since no one is able to keep the law perfectly, the inevitable result of trying to gain eschatological life through keeping the law is the curse that comes for disobeying the law (Gal 3:10–12). Furthermore, if the law were in fact able to give eschatological life, the death and resurrection of Christ would be unnecessary since righteousness/justification (δικαιοσύνη) could come through the law (2:21; 3:21). Receiving eschatological life and the promised inheritance comes through the fulfillment of the promise to Abraham in his seed Jesus Christ (3:15–18); by faith in him believers share in his death and resurrection as well as his inheritance (3:26–4:7).

A third purpose of the law was to imprison everything under sin. In 3:22 Paul asserts that "the Scripture imprisoned everything under sin's power." Here the term "Scripture" (γραφή) draws in the entirety of the Old Testament revelation, which through the law brought everything under the power of sin. Paul may also use the broader term Scripture to widen the scope of his claim, making this statement similar to what the apostle says in Romans 3:9: "What then? Are we any better off? Not at all! For we have already charged that both Jews and Gentiles are all under sin." Both Jew and gentile are subject to the universal experience of bondage under sin's power through the law. Paul makes a similar point in Romans 11:32: "For God has imprisoned all in disobedience so that he may have mercy on all." This state of bondage extends beyond humanity to creation itself, which groans under its present captivity in anticipation of its redemption (Rom 8:20–22).

A fourth purpose of the law was to confine God's people. According to 3:23, before faith in Christ came, "we were confined under the law, imprisoned until the coming faith was revealed." Although Paul has in particular view the experience of the Jewish people under the Mosaic law, given the remainder of the argument (3:23–4:7) he also envisions the gentiles being included within the captivity of the Mosaic law. In a sense this is a specific application of the previous point, but one that is important enough for Paul to explicitly highlight. Despite the efforts of some to paint the confinement here as merely one of protection, the context will not allow this. The phrase "under the law" in Galatians consistently has a negative connotation, and the repetition of the verb "imprison" (συγκλείω) from the previous verse makes the negative sense clear. Thus while the law did serve to protect God's people so that the Abrahamic promise would come to fulfillment in Christ the singular seed, the focus here is one of confining God's people under the power of sin to make their need for redemption crystal clear.

§5.2.2 The Timeframe of the Law

According to Paul, the Mosaic law covenant came with a built-in expiration date; it was valid "until the Seed to whom the promise was made would come" (3:19). Although the Old Testament does not make this expiration date explicit, there are strong hints. In promising a new covenant, God asserts, "This one will not be like the covenant I made with their ancestors on the day I took them by the hand to lead them out of the land of Egypt" (Jer 31:32). In contrast to the Mosaic law, which was written on breakable stone tablets (Exod 31:18; 32:19), God promised to write his law on the hearts of his people (Jer 31:33). He would put his Spirit in his people to cause them to walk in his ways (Ezek 36:26–27). What these and many other Old Testament passages envision goes beyond the internalization of the Mosaic law, as the New Testament—at a minimum—makes it clear that at least some elements of the Mosaic law are abrogated, even elements that a surface reading of the Old Testament might suggest were intended to be eternal (compare Exod 40:15 with Heb 7:1–10:18).

A second line of evidence from the Old Testament that the Mosaic law was not intended to be permanent are the numerous references to a "law" or "instruction" (תּוֹרָה / νόμος) that would go forth in the last days when God fulfills his promises. These references are especially prominent in Isaiah.[75] In the latter days people will stream to the mountain of Lord and "instruction [תּוֹרָה / νόμος] will go out of Zion" (Isa 2:3; compare Mic 4:2). The Servant of Yahweh will establish justice on the earth and "The coasts and islands will wait for his instruction" (תּוֹרָה / νόμος; Isa 42:4). Along similar lines is the claim that when God reveals his saving righteousness

---

[75] In the passages that follow, the csb consistently translates תּוֹרָה as instruction to help the reader see that it refers more generally to instruction rather than torah in the sense of the Mosaic law. All but one of the twelve occurrences of תּוֹרָה in Isaiah are rendered as νόμος; the lone exception is 42:21, where the LXX does not translate תּוֹרָה at all. Although some of these references in their immediate context may refer to specific stipulations of the Mosaic law (e.g., 24:5), all of them make good sense as generalized references to instruction or teaching from the Lord.

to comfort his people and transform creation itself, "instruction [תּוֹרָה /
νόμος] will come from me, and my justice for a light to the nations" (Isa
51:4). Texts such as these suggest the possibility that the instruction in
view may extend beyond the specific requirements of the Mosaic law. Moo
summarizes the point well: "This 'Zion torah,' perhaps to be understood
as a fresh publication of God's will for his people, in continuity with but
not identical to the 'Sinai torah,' may be what is envisaged in Jeremiah
31:31–34 and the Ezekiel texts."[76]

Yet even if one rejects this interpretation of the so-called Zion torah
texts, the fact remains that the New Testament itself asserts in no uncertain terms that at least some elements of the Mosaic law are done away
with now that Christ has come. Paul insists in no uncertain terms that
the Mosaic law was only intended to govern God's people for a particular
period of time—until the arrival of the promised seed Jesus Christ. Now
that Christ has indeed come, the Mosaic law exits the stage of redemptive
history, its role fulfilled and its purpose met.

§5.2.3 The Means by which the Law was Given

An additional way that Paul indicates that the Mosaic law played a subordinate role to the Abrahamic promise is by describing how the law
was given to God's people. He uses two expressions to do so. First, the
law was given "through angels" (δι' ἀγγέλων), which was a common
belief in Second Temple Judaism. But rather than see this as a positive,
Paul portrays this as a negative feature. Second, the law was "put into
effect through angels by means of a mediator" (ἐν χειρὶ μεσίτου), a clear
reference to Moses. Together these phrases stress the distance between
God and his people. Under the Mosaic law covenant God and his people
are at least two steps removed from each other. By contrast, God spoke
the promise directly to Abraham (Gen 15:1; 17:1).

§5.2.4 Paul's Use of the Law

Paul interacts with the Mosaic law in a variety of ways. Brian Rosner has
helpfully identified three broad ways that Paul engages the Mosaic law.[77]

---

[76] Douglas J. Moo, "The Law of Christ as the Fulfillment of the Law of Moses : A Modified
Lutheran View," in *Five Views on Law and Gospel*, ed. Wayne G. Strickland (Grand Rapids:
Zondervan, 1993), 346.

[77] Brian S. Rosner, *Paul and the Law: Keeping the Commandments of God*, NSBT 31 (Downers
Grove, IL: IVP, 2013).

The first is repudiation, in which Paul rejects the law as a "law-covenant." This is a prominent theme in Galatians, where Paul rejects both specific requirements of the Mosaic law covenant and the covenant as a whole. Both circumcision (2:3–6; 5:2–6) and the food laws (2:11–14) are set aside in light of the truth of the gospel. Indeed, neither these nor any other works of the law are able to justify a person before God (2:15–16), nor are they the means by which one grows in the Christian life (3:2–5). Paul's rejection of these works of the law flows from his rejection of the Mosaic law as a covenant. The law is something that Paul died to in order that he might live to God (2:18–19). In sharp contrast to many of his Jewish contemporaries, Paul rejected the Mosaic law as a path to eschatological life (3:21) because it brings a curse upon all who fail to obey it perfectly (3:10–14). An additional reason that Paul repudiated the Mosaic law covenant is that it is no longer in force now that Christ has come (3:25–26; 4:1–7). It was a temporary covenant put in place until Christ the promised seed of Abraham came (3:15–29). God gave it to expose sin as a violation of God's will, bringing it out into the open so that the seed of Abraham (3:15–18) and the servant of the Lord (3:13–14) could decisively deal with it once and for all (3:19). The Mosaic law covenant served to constrain the people of God until Christ came and all who believed in him would receive their inheritance as sons (3:23–4:7). As a result, believers are not under the authority of the Mosaic law covenant (5:18).

The second is replacement; Paul replaces the Mosaic law with a substitute that guides the life of the believer. Within Galatians Paul works within this category on both a general and more specific level. On a general level, the truth of the gospel produces a pattern of life that replaces the distinctive practices of the Mosaic law such as circumcision and the food laws (2:5, 14). The period of imprisonment under the guardianship of the law has not been replaced with the full inheritance of adopted sons (3:23–4:7). On the more specific level of governing the behavior of God's people, the Mosaic law has been replaced by the leading of the Holy Spirit (5:18) and the law of Christ (6:2). This appears to be in fulfillment of the prophetic promises that when the new covenant was inaugurated, God would write his law on the hearts of his people and put his Spirit inside of them to cause them to obey (Jer 31:31–34; Ezek 36:26–27). With respect to circumcision in particular, Paul offers two replacements. In 5:6, the dichotomy of circumcision or uncircumcision is replaced with "faith working through love." At the close of the letter, Paul offers a second replacement for this dichotomy: "a new creation" (6:15).

The third is reappropriation. Paul takes up the Mosaic law and puts it to use as either prophecy or wisdom. Although this kind of engagement with the law is less frequent in Galatians, there are at least two examples. Paul sees within the story of Abraham and his two sons a prophetic anticipation of the contrast between the Abrahamic covenant fulfilled in Christ and the Mosaic covenant (4:21–5:1). The apostle also reappropriates a key passage from the law (Lev 19:18) as wisdom that summarizes the intent and goal of the law being realized in the lives of believers (5:14). In both cases, Paul takes up the law and uses it in a fresh way to further his doctrinal and/or ethical purposes.

§5.3 WORKS OF THE LAW

No discussion of the law in Galatians would be complete without arguably the most controversial expression in Galatians—works of the law (ἔργων νόμου). In the most basic sense this expression refers to doing what the Mosaic law requires. Many advocates of the New Perspective have focused on the specific requirements that distinguished the Jews from gentiles (sometimes called "boundary markers"), such as circumcision, food laws, and Sabbath observance. But while these specific requirements of the Mosaic law were clearly flashpoints of controversy, one cannot limit the works of the law to just those requirements that distinguished Jew from gentile. Paul insists that those who are circumcised are obligated to keep the entire Mosaic law, not merely these distinguishing requirements (Gal 5:3).

Having stressed this point, however, it is still helpful to briefly discuss the key works of the law that were particular sources of controversy and how Paul addresses them here in Galatians and in his other epistles.

§5.3.1 Circumcision

By the first century, circumcision had become one of the defining markers of Jewish identity, so it is not surprising that it is at the heart of the dispute in Galatia. During the prelude to the Maccabean rebellion, the Seleucids "put to death the women who had their children circumcised, and their families and those who circumcised them; and they hung the infants from their mothers' necks" (1 Macc 1:60–61). As a result, in the decades following the Maccabean rebellion, many Jews tenaciously clung to circumcision (as well as the food laws and Sabbath observance) as practices which distinguished them from gentiles. Indeed, the contrast between circumcised and uncircumcised became synonymous with the contrast between Jew and gentile (see 2:8–9; compare Rom 4:9–12). Even though not all Jews believed that gentile converts to Judaism were required to be circumcised, this appears to have been a minority view, and the general expectation was that male converts should in fact be circumcised to complete their conversion.[78] As Betz notes, "The internal Jewish debate became an internal Christian conflict"[79] as the early church wrestled with how to handle the growing number of gentiles who believed in Jesus.

The dawn of the Galatian crisis was not the first time Paul was forced to confront the issue of whether gentile converts needed to be circumcised. Several years earlier Paul had forcefully rejected this view when false brothers attempted to compel Titus—a gentile convert—to be circumcised (Gal 2:1–10 //Acts 11:27–30). Paul insists that circumcision is of no benefit to the believer because it is inseparable from taking on the obligations of the entire Mosaic law (5:2–3). One cannot simply add circumcision to faith in Jesus; they are mutually exclusive approaches to relating to God and others. To choose circumcision and the Mosaic law is to cut oneself off from Christ and his grace (5:4–5). What matters is the circumcision of the heart accomplished by the Spirit in the new covenant inaugurated through Jesus (Rom 2:29; Phil 3:3).

§5.3.2 Table Fellowship and Food Laws

In the ancient world meals were more than just an opportunity to consume food and drink; they were expressions of kinship and friendship that communicated "honor, social rank in the family and community, belonging and purity, or holiness."[80] Jewish convictions about clean and unclean foods, along with concerns about purity and contact with gentiles, meant that many Jews avoided eating with gentiles altogether.[81] Yet there appears to have been significant debate over the specifics of what obedience to the Mosaic law entailed, including whether one could ever eat

---

[78] Keener, *Acts*, 3:2215–22.
[79] Betz, *Galatians*, 89.
[80] See "Meal," *DBI* 544–45, quote from 544.
[81] For a helpful summary of the issues involved, see Dunn, *Galatians*, 118–21.

with gentiles, and if so, under what circumstances and/or restrictions.[82] Given this broader context, it is not surprising that this issue was a flashpoint in the early church. Paul himself even addresses a similar subject at length in 1 Corinthians 8–10, where he explains how believers should handle eating with unbelievers when the meat they are served has been first sacrificed to idols.

As part of his personal narrative defending his status as an apostle and the divine origins of the gospel he preached, Paul recounts an incident in (Syrian) Antioch where observing the food laws created division within the church there (Gal 2:11–14). While Paul had no problem with Jewish believers doing this of their own volition, he was adamant that gentiles not be compelled to keep the dietary restrictions of the Mosaic law (Rom 14:1–23; Col 2:16–19; 1 Tim 4:1–5). The example of Jesus himself eating with sinners (e.g., Matt 9:10–13) provided the groundwork for the early church to recognize that all of God's people, regardless of their ethnicity, should eat together as a demonstration of their unity in Christ.

§5.3.3 The Sabbath and Jewish Festivals

As part of the Mosaic covenant, God commanded the Israelites to observe the seventh day of the week as the Sabbath, a day of rest patterned after God's rest after the six days of creation (Exod 20:8–11; 23:12).[83] It was intended as a sign of God's covenant with Israel; failure to observe the Sabbath was grounds for death (Exod 31:12–17). Despite this stiff penalty, Israel's failure to observe the Sabbath was a frequent element of the prophets' message (e.g., Isa 1:13; Jer 17:19–27; Ezek 20:12–26; Amos 8:5). By the first century, there was a wide diversity of opinions on the specific details of observing the Sabbath.[84] In some Jewish sects that appear to

---

[82] See the discussion in Markus N. A. Bockmuehl, *Jewish Law in Gentile Churches: Halakhah and the Beginning of Christian Public Ethics*, 1st pbk. ed. (Grand Rapids: Baker, 2003), 58–61. While it was not technically forbidden in the Torah to eat with a gentile, it was strongly frowned upon out of fear that such close fellowship could easily violate Jewish purity laws (the food might be offered to idols, it might not be kosher, it may be prepared with unclean hands, etc.). In fact, following on the heels of the Maccabean era, table fellowship with gentiles became even more frowned upon in many quarters.

[83] For a helpful overview of the Sabbath in the OT, see Harold H. P. Dressler, "The Sabbath in the Old Testament," in *From Sabbath to Lord's Day: A Biblical, Historical, and Theological Investigation*, ed. D. A. Carson (Grand Rapids: Zondervan, 1982), 21–41.

[84] See Chris Rowland, "A Summary of Sabbath Observance in Judaism at the Beginning of the Christian Era," in *From Sabbath to Lord's Day: A Biblical, Historical, and Theological Investigation*, ed. D. A. Carson (Grand Rapids: Zondervan, 1982), 43–55.

have had limited interaction with gentiles, strict and detailed restrictions were laid out that even regulated eating and sex (Jub. 50:6–11; CD 11:1–12:23).[85] Other Jewish groups who had more regular interaction with gentiles developed extensive restrictions along with mitigating circumstances to provide direction on how to observe the Sabbath. Such restrictions and mitigating circumstances are regularly reflected in rabbinic texts that likely reflect first-century debates between different schools of thought.[86] Yet what was not in dispute was the necessity of observing the Sabbath as an expression of faithfulness to God's covenant.

Under the Mosaic law covenant, the Israelites were commanded to celebrate several feasts/festivals, three of which were of particular importance: Unleavened Bread/Passover (Exod 23:14–15; Lev 23:4–8), Harvest/Weeks/Pentecost (Exod 23:16; Lev 23:15–22), and Ingathering/Booths/Tabernacles (Exod 23:16; Lev 23:33–44). By the Second Temple period, with a substantial portion of the Jewish population living outside of Judea, it was difficult for many devout Jews to meet this expectation. Nevertheless, large numbers of Jews would make the pilgrimage to Jerusalem for these feasts—especially Passover, when according to some estimates the population of Jerusalem would swell from 50,000 to 200,000. Yet even those who were unable to make such a trek would develop alternative means for celebrating these festivals. In Paul's day they remained an important feature of Jewish piety.

Although observing the Sabbath or the Jewish festivals is not specifically mentioned in Galatians, Paul may hint at it in 4:10, where he laments, "You are observing special days, months, seasons, and years." Apparently some of the Galatians, with the encouragement of the opponents, has begun observing the Jewish calendar. Although not a major issue Paul addresses in his letters, he does indicate that gentile believers are under no obligation to observe the Sabbath or other elements of the Jewish calendar (Rom 14:1–23; Col 2:16). Paul himself was willing to observe Jewish festivals (Acts 21:17–26) and likely observed the Sabbath at least when evangelizing Jews (1 Cor 9:20). Yet his insistence that under

---

[85] Rowland, "A Summary of Sabbath Observance," 45–47. Rowland highlights several texts in Jubilees and the Damascus Document, as well as Josephus and Philo's descriptions of how the Essenes observed the Sabbath.

[86] For a sampling of such rabbinic discussions, see David Instone-Brewer, *Traditions of the Rabbis from the Era of the New Testament. Volume 2a, Feasts and Sabbaths - Passover and Atonement*, TRENT 2A (Grand Rapids: Eerdmans, 2011), 1–114.

the new covenant believers are no longer obligated to observe these elements of the Jewish calendar was out of step with most of his Jewish contemporaries.

§5.3.4 The Necessity and Impossibility of Perfect Obedience

Despite the objections of some scholars, there is good reason to conclude that the Mosaic law demanded perfect obedience. Andrew Das notes discussions in several Second Temple Jewish texts that discuss the near impossibility of perfect obedience.[87] The authors of the Dead Sea Scrolls call their members to walk in perfection (CD 2:15–16; 1QS 1:8; III.9; IX.18–19) while noting that human beings will not be cleansed of the tendency to sin until the eschaton (1QS III.21–23; IV.18–22; XI.14–15' 1QH VII[=XV].15–17; XIV [=VI].8–10). According to Jubilees, only a handful of figures such as Noah (5:19), Abraham (15:3; 23:10), and Jacob, Leah, and Joseph (27:17; 36:23; 40:8) were regarded as perfect or righteous. Philo regarded Noah as perfect relative to his generation, though not in an absolute sense (Abr. 6:34; 7:36–39; 9:47; Deo 25:117; 26:122; 30:140). By contrast Moses was in fact sinless (Mos. 1:28; 2:1–11; Legat. 3:134; 3:140; Ebr. 23:94; Sacr. 3:8). Das summarizes: "The concession in such texts that only very rare, exceptional individuals perfectly obeyed God's Law explains how a Jew of this period, such as the apostle Paul, could assume that his coreligionists simply do not obey God's Law without sin."[88] Thus Paul insists that those who are circumcised are obligated to keep the entire Mosaic law, not merely these distinguishing requirements (Gal 5:3), with the underlying assumption that such perfect obedience is impossible. James 2:10 makes a very similar point: "For whoever keeps the entire law, and yet stumbles at one point, is guilty of breaking it all."

§5.4 THE LAW OF CHRIST

Even though believers are under the guidance of the Holy Spirit and no longer under Mosaic law covenant, they are still governed by God's moral will as expressed in the law of Christ. Paul exhorts believers to "Carry one another's burdens; in this way you will fulfill the law of Christ" (Gal 6:2). Although the law of Christ has been understood in a variety of different

---

[87] For an extended discussion, see A. Andrew Das, *Paul, the Law, and the Covenant* (Peabody, MA: Hendrickson, 2001), 145–70; for a concise summary see Das, *Galatians*, 314–15.

[88] Das, *Galatians*, 315.

ways,[89] it most likely refers to the teaching and example of Jesus communicated through the apostles which the Holy Spirit empowers believers to fulfill through loving self-sacrificial service to God and others.[90] As such it fulfills what the Mosaic law aimed for (Gal 5:14) but could never truly produce because of human weakness and sinfulness (Rom 7:7-25; 8:3). Paul's only other explicit reference to the law of Christ is 1 Corinthians 9:21. Describing his efforts to reach different kinds of people with the gospel, Paul says that "To those who are without that law, [I become] like one without the law—though I am not without God's law but under the law of Christ—to win those without the law."[91] In this revealing statement, the apostle indicates that one can be no longer under the authority of

---

[89] The literature discussing the meaning of this clause is substantial. Martyn (*Galatians*, 587) helpfully organizes the various views into five large categories. (1) The law of Christ is linked to the Jewish belief in a messianic torah; see, e.g., W. D. Davies, *Torah in the Messianic Age and/or the Age to Come*, JBLMS VII (Philadelphia: Society of Biblical Literature, 1952), 85-95; Peter Schäfer, "Die Torah Der Messianischen Zeit," ZNW 65 (1974): 27-42; Hofius, "Gesetz Christi," 262-86. (2) The law of Christ refers to Jesus' teaching, sometimes expanded to include the apostolic instruction; see, e.g., C. H. Dodd, *More New Testament Studies* (Grand Rapids: Eerdmans, 1968), 134-48; Richard Longenecker, *Paul, Apostle of Liberty: The Origin and Nature of Paul's Christianity* (Grand Rapids: Baker, 1976), 183-90; Moo, "Law of Christ," 319-76. (3) The law of Christ was a phrase used by Paul's opponents which he transforms; see, e.g., Betz, *Galatians*, 300-1; Victor Paul Furnish, *Theology and Ethics in Paul* (Nashville: Abingdon Press, 1968), 64-65. (4) Fulfilling the law of Christ means fulfilling Torah through love for others just as Christ did; see, e.g., Barclay, *Obeying the Truth*, 134-41; Bruce W. Longenecker, "Defining the Faithful Character of the Covenant Community: Galatians 2:15-21 and Beyond: A Response to Jan Lambrecht," in *Paul and the Mosaic Law* (Tubingen: J. C. B. Mohr, 1996), 75-97; Longenecker, *The Triumph of Abraham's God: The Transformation of Identity in Galatians*, 82-88. (5) The noun νόμος here means "principle" and not the Mosaic law, and thus the focus is on the principle of love with Christ as the paradigmatic example; see, e.g., Heikki Räisänen, *Paul and the Law*, WUNT (Tübingen: J. C. B. Mohr, 1983), 79-80; Richard B. Hays, "Christology and Ethics in Galatians: The Law of Christ," CBQ 49 (1987): 268-90. As the discussion shows, view (2) seems most likely to me, with perhaps a combination of view (1) as well.

[90] See the similar definition in Richard N. Longenecker, *New Testament Social Ethics for Today* (Grand Rapids: Eerdmans, 1984), 15. Moo ("Law of Christ," 368), after offering a similar definition, notes that "there is strong continuity with the law of Moses, for many specifically Mosaic commandments are taken up and included within this 'law of Christ.' "

[91] Whereas in Gal 6:2 the Greek expression is τὸν νόμον τοῦ Χριστοῦ, in 1 Cor 9:21 Paul writes ἔννομος Χριστοῦ. The adjective ἔννομος has the sense of "pertaining to being in accordance with law" (BDAG s.v. ἔννομος). BDAG goes on to offer a helpful paraphrase of this verse that clarifies the sense of ἔννομος here: "I identified as one outside Mosaic jurisdiction with those outside it; not, of course, being outside God's jurisdiction, but inside Christ's." Its only other NT occurrence is Acts 19:39, where the city clerk warns the rioting mob in Ephesus that their complaint against Paul must be settled "in a legal assembly" (ἐν τῇ ἐννόμῳ ἐκκλησίᾳ); in other words, in an assembly that is governed and regulated by the laws of the city. This unusual word choice in 1 Cor 9:21 is likely driven by the contrast

the Mosaic law while still remaining under God's law. Under the new covenant, "God's law" is expressed in the law of Christ.

Paul nowhere explicitly lays out the content of the law of Christ. The immediate context in Galatians 6:2 portrays fulfilling this law as bearing one another's burdens. This echo of the suffering servant from Isaiah 53 embodies the self-sacrificial love that expresses itself in specific ways, such as humbly restoring those who are caught in sin (6:1–5), generously supporting those who teach God's word (6:6–8), and doing good to all as opportunity arises, especially fellow believers (6:9–10). Believers fulfill the law of Christ as the Spirit produces fruit in their lives that embodies the love that Christ showed in his life, ministry, death, and resurrection. As believers today we have the law of Christ expressed in the apostolic writings of the New Testament, where both the teaching and the example of Jesus is expressed in written form for us to believe and obey in the power of the Spirit.

§5.5 CONCLUSION

Despite the complexities of Paul's discussion of the Mosaic law in Galatians, the apostle leaves no doubt that it can no longer be the basis for how believers relate to God or others. The Mosaic law was a temporary institution, given by God to supervise his people until Jesus Christ the promised seed of Abraham came. Now that he has come and the Mosaic law has served its purpose, it is no longer binding for God's people. Those who walk in the power of the Spirit fulfill the law of Christ through their loving self-sacrificial service to God and others. Yet Paul is no Marcionite jettisoning the Mosaic law altogether. He eagerly reappropriates the law as a source of wisdom reflecting God's moral will for his people and as a source of prophecy that anticipates key elements of Christ's work and God's redemptive plan for the nations. Now that Christ has come, Paul cannot fathom why anyone would prefer the shadow of the law to the reality of Christ and his life-giving Spirit.

§6 Justification and Righteousness

Central to the dispute Paul addresses in Galatians is the issue of justification and righteousness. When recounting his rebuke to Peter in Antioch,

---

with "without God's law" (ἄνομος θεοῦ) in the previous line, and therefore is unlikely to indicate any difference in meaning from the expression in Gal 6:2.

Paul stresses that the common ground of the gospel is rooted in being justified by faith and not works of the law (2:16), and from that foundation he draws out several implications (2:17–21). The thesis of the long argument that stretches from 3:1–5:1 takes its starting point from Paul's citation of Genesis 15:6, which centers on righteousness: "Abraham ... believed God, and it was credited to him for righteousness" (Gal 3:6). It is apparent, then, that understanding what Paul refers to when he speaks of justification and righteousness is crucial for rightly understanding Galatians.

Yet doing so is no simple task, as the scholarly discussion on this issue has been robust. While these debates will inform our overview, the focus will center on the biblical text itself, with special emphasis on the Old Testament and Jewish background for understanding justification/righteousness in Galatians.

§6.1 TERMINOLOGY

The words translated justification, justify, righteousness, and righteous come from the same root in both Greek (δικ-) and Hebrew (צדק).[92] Yet the use of two very distinct (albeit related conceptually) word groups in English complicates the discussion.[93] All that can be done in this brief discussion is to provide a short overview of the terms to situate how they are used in Galatians.

As used in the LXX, the verb δικαιόω (43x) has the sense of being in the right or declaring someone to be in the right.[94] It regularly has a forensic sense, especially when it renders a form of the Hebrew verb

---

[92] For helpful surveys of the lexical data, see David Hill, *Greek Words and Hebrew Meanings: Studies in the Semantics of Soteriological Terms*, SNTSMS 5 (Cambridge: Cambridge University Press, 1967), 82–98 and John A. Ziesler, *The Meaning of Righteousness in Paul: A Linguistic and Theological Enquiry*, SNTSMS 20 (Cambridge: Cambridge University Press, 1972), 17–67; Mark A. Seifrid, "Righteousness Language in the Hebrew Scriptures and Early Judaism," in *Justification and Variegated Nomism Volume 1—the Complexities of Second Temple Judaism*, ed. D. A. Carson, Peter T. O'Brien, and Mark A. Seifrid (Grand Rapids: Baker, 2001), 415–42; Mark A. Seifrid, "Paul's Use of Righteousness Language against Its Hellenistic Background," in *Justification and Variegated Nomism Volume 2—the Paradoxes of Paul*, ed. D. A. Carson, Peter T. O'Brien, and Mark A. Seifrid (Grand Rapids: Baker, 2004), 39–74. Our focus will be on the Greek word family, only drawing on the Hebrew when helpful.

[93] In an attempt to bypass this difficulty, some scholars have coined their own terms; see, e.g., Martyn, *Galatians*, 263–75, who uses rectify/rectification, and Stephen Westerholm, *Perspectives Old and New on Paul: The "Lutheran" Paul and His Critics* (Grand Rapids: Eerdmans, 2004), 261–96, who uses dikaios/dikaiosness/dikaiosify.

[94] This summary largely follows Moises Silva, "δικαιοσύνη," in *NIDNTTE*, 705. In most of these occurrences it renders a form of the Hebrew verb צדק.

צדק. The noun δικαιοσύνη (320x) is far more common in the LXX, most frequently rendering a form of either צְדָקָה or צֶדֶק. It has the general sense of that which is right/just or doing what is right and is especially prominent in the Psalms (80x) and Isaiah (50x). In contrast to its usage outside of Jewish literature, frequently the standard by which doing right is judged is Yahweh's covenant with Israel. Yet it must also be noted that sometimes the standard is God's very own character (e.g., Ps 98:9). Also worth noting is the unusual expression "to do righteousness" (ποιεῖν δικαιοσύνην), which, although unparalleled in Greek literature outside of Jewish literature, is common in the LXX to express actions that conform to what is right (e.g., Gen 18:19). The adjective δίκαιος describes someone who either is or does what is right or just, again with the sense of conforming to some kind of norm or standard. Although he is analyzing Paul's use of righteousness language, Westerholm's summary is helpful for the LXX usage as well: the verb δικαιόω refers to declaring someone to be innocent of wrongdoing, the noun δικαιοσύνη refers to doing what someone ought to do, and the adjective δίκαιος refers to one who does δικαιοσύνη.[95]

This brief summary raises two issues that are frequently discussed when addressing righteousness language. The first is the relationship between the forensic and ethical uses of these terms. In Galatians, righteousness language has a clear forensic sense. Yet it must be stressed that this forensic sense of righteousness language is the foundation from which the believer pursues a life of obedience that is pleasing to God. Paul simply uses terminology other than righteousness language to express this reality, such as faith working through love (5:6), serving one another through love (5:13), loving one's neighbor (5:14), walking/being led by the Spirit (5:16–26), bearing one another's burdens (6:2), fulfilling the law of Christ (6:2), sowing to the Spirit (6:8), and doing good to others (6:9–10). Thus it is the believers' status as righteous before God that enables them to conform their lives to his revealed standards.

A second issue is how to explain the relationship between the relational/covenantal use of righteousness language and its sense of accordance with a norm.[96] Too often these have been pitted against each other when

---

[95] Westerholm, *Perspectives Old and New*, 265.

[96] For a helpful discussion, see Westerholm, *Perspectives Old and New*, 286–96 and Thomas R. Schreiner, *New Testament Theology: Magnifying God in Christ* (Grand Rapids: Baker, 2008), 353–62.

in reality they complement each other. The starting point is to recognize that righteousness does in fact refer to being in accordance with a norm, but for God that norm is his own holy character. Abraham bases his intercession for the people of Sodom on this reality when he prays, "Won't the Judge of the whole earth do what is just?" (Gen 18:25). Yet God has also chosen to enter into a covenant with his people, thus binding himself to the covenant as the standard by which he interacts with his people. To enter that covenant relationship, however, one must be declared righteous—that is, in the right before God. Once in the covenant, there is absolutely a relational element to righteousness created by the covenant relationship. God binds himself to fulfill certain promises, and the believer bases his/her life on God's faithfulness to those promises.

§6.2 THE ISAIANIC BACKGROUND OF RIGHTEOUSNESS LANGUAGE
IN GALATIANS

Although righteousness language occurs throughout the Old Testament, the occurrences in Isaiah appear to be the most significant for Paul's understanding.[97] A brief survey of how Isaiah uses this language will shed some light on Paul's use here in Galatians.

Righteousness language occurs in all three major sections of Isaiah.[98] In Isaiah 1–39, righteousness language is primarily used in an ethical sense; in other words, it refers to doing what is right (as defined by God).[99]

---

[97] For a helpful discussion, see Seifrid, "Righteousness Language in the Hebrew Scriptures and Early Judaism," 415–42. See also his follow-up essay, Seifrid, "Paul's Use of Righteousness Language against Its Hellenistic Background," 39–74. On righteousness language in Isaiah, see John J. Scullion, "Sedeq-Sedeqah in Isaiah Cc 40–66 with Special Reference to the Continuity in Meaning between Second and Third Isaiah," *UF* 3 (1971): 335–48; C. F. Whitley, "Deutero-Isaiah's Interpretation of Sedeq," *VT* 22 (1972): 469–75; John W. Olley, *"Righteousness" in the Septuagint of Isaiah: A Contextual Study* (Missoula: Scholars, 1979); John N. Oswalt, "Righteousness in Isaiah: A Study of the Function of Chapters 56–66 in the Present Structure of the Book," in *Writing and Reading the Scroll of Isaiah: Studies of an Interpretive Tradition*, ed. Craig C. Broyles and Craig A. Evans (Leiden: Brill, 1997), 177–91.

[98] This section is adapted from Harmon, *She Must and Shall Go Free*, 93–99. In the Hebrew text there are eighty-one occurrences of the צדק family, and all but ten (1:27; 11:4; 28:17; 41:26; 49:13, 24; 51:7; 56:1; 59:16; 61:10) are rendered with a word from the δικ- family in the LXX. Of the seventy-nine occurrences of the δικ- family in the LXX, all but seven (1:17; 33:6; 38:19; 39:8; 47:3; 57:1; 63:7) render a word from the צדק family. This substantial overlap allows us to treat them together.

[99] One confirmation of this conclusion is the thirteen times that righteousness language occurs in the same verse as a form of the noun מִשְׁפָּט or the verb שָׁפַט in Isa 1–39; see 1:21, 26, 27; 5:7, 16; 9:6; 11:4; 16:5; 26:9; 28:17; 32:1, 16; 33:5.

It is applied to a variety of different situations: the reign of the promised Davidic king (9:6; 11:4–5; 16:5; 32:1), the ethical behavior of those redeemed by Yahweh (26:2, 7–10; 32:16–17; 33:5, 15), and even Yahweh's standard of judgment (28:17). A notable exception to this trend is 10:22, where God promises that the coming destruction will be "overflowing with righteousness" (שׁוֹטֵף צְדָקָה, ESV; CSB: "justice overflows"). Although the idea of God executing justice is in accordance with his own righteous character, the connection between God's future judgment and righteousness anticipates a common theme in Isa 40–55.

In Isaiah 40–55, an important shift takes place. Righteousness language is consistently placed in parallelism with salvation language; look, for example, at Isaiah 51:5–6:

> My **righteousness** is near,
> my **salvation** appears,
> and my arms will bring justice to the nations.
> The coasts and islands will put their hope in me,
> and they will look to my strength.
> Look up to the heavens,
> and look at the earth beneath;
> for the heavens will vanish like smoke,
> the earth will wear out like a garment,
> and its inhabitants will die like gnats.
> But my **salvation** will last forever,
> and my **righteousness** will never be shattered.

In passages such as these (see also 45:21; 46:12–13; 51:8), Yahweh's righteousness refers to his action(s) in bringing about a state of well-being for his people, resulting in rescue from their unrighteousness and judgment upon their enemies. This "saving righteousness" is pervasively eschatological; God's people in Isaiah's day did not possess it but are told to eagerly wait for the time when God will bring it near. This saving righteousness also is forensic, as it refers to God as judge and ruler of all creation granting a status to a person (and by extension even creation itself) as a result of God's judgment.[100]

---

[100] For cases where the status or result is emphasized, see Isa 45:8; 46:13; 48:18; 51:5, 6, 8; 54:17; for the act of judgment itself, see Isa 43:9, 26; 45:25; 50:8; 53:11; for God acting in accordance with his character, see Isa 41:2, 10, 26; 42:6, 21; 45:13, 19, 21, 23, 24; 54:14. Again it should be stressed that these uses cannot be rigidly distinguished.

The opening verse of Isaiah 56–66 lays out the relationship between ethical righteousness and eschatological/forensic: "This is what the Lord says: Preserve justice and do what is right [וַעֲשׂוּ צְדָקָה], for my salvation is coming soon, and my righteousness will be revealed [וְצִדְקָתִי לְהִגָּלוֹת]." This combination of ethical and eschatological/forensic righteousness anticipates the dual use of righteousness language in these chapters. God's people are to live righteous lives as they await the revelation of Yahweh's saving righteousness.

In addition to these Isaianic texts, Psalm 143:1–2 is also relevant since Paul cites it in Galatians 2:16. David asks God to respond to his heartfelt prayer based on Yahweh's faithfulness and "righteousness" (בְּצִדְקָתֶךָ / δικαιοσύνῃ). He then pleads that God would not bring him into judgment, since no one is "righteous" (יִצְדַּק / δικαιωθήσεται) in God's sight. This last clause could also be rendered "since no one will be justified in your sight," and that seems to be how Paul understood the clause given how he uses it in Galatians 2:16. Regardless, note that David's assertion that no one is righteous/will be justified comes in the context of standing before God in judgment, and he pleads that God would shield him from judgment on the basis of Yahweh's own righteousness. The forensic overtones of David's request are clear.

This brief survey of righteousness in Isaiah (with an assist from Ps 143:1–2) highlights several features of righteousness. In several texts righteousness has strong eschatological overtones; in other words, it is linked to God acting to fulfill his promises and set things right in this world. As such it is closely linked with God saving his people from their sins and bringing judgment on his enemies. Thus this righteousness is primarily forensic in nature, dealing with a person's status before a holy and just God in his court of law. Yet the revelation of this forensic righteousness should lead to ethical righteousness that permeates the life of God's people in response.

§6.3 Justification/Righteousness in Galatians

In Galatians Paul uses words from δικ- family thirteen times: the verb δικαιόω (2:16 [3x], 17; 3:8, 11, 24; 5:4), the noun δικαιοσύνη (2:21; 3:6, 21; 5:5), and the adjective δίκαιος (3:11).[101] First, we will look briefly at each

---

[101] Strictly speaking there is also the verb ἀδικέω (4:11), which means to treat someone unjustly. But this verb occurs in the context of Paul reminding the Galatians of their initial

of these occurrences in the flow of the argument to determine how they are being used. Second, we will examine the means by which a person is justified. Finally, we will explore when justification occurs.[102]

§6.3.1 Occurrences of Justification/Righteousness Language in Galatians

The first appearance of righteousness language occurs in 2:16–21, where Paul uses the verb δικαιόω four times in 2:16–17 and the noun δικαιοσύνη once (2:21). He contrasts two possible means of a person being justified: works of the law and faith in Jesus Christ. Those who believe in Jesus Christ are justified by Christ: his death and resurrection are the means by which a person is justified. Through faith in Christ the believer is joined to Christ in such a way that he/she shares in Christ's death and resurrection. In this context, to be justified is to be declared "in the right" before God. Put another way, it means to be not guilty before God, vindicated in the face of any charges laid against a person. In the summary statement of this same paragraph Paul insists that δικαιοσύνη (righteousness/justification) cannot come through the Mosaic law but must come through the grace of God manifested through the death of Christ (2:21). Thus righteousness/justification is the status given to the one who is justified by faith in Jesus Christ.

From the foundation established in 2:16–21, Paul draws on righteousness language five more times in the lengthy argument that runs from 3:1–5:1. Its importance is seen in the two occurrences in the thesis statement of 3:6–9. Bringing forward Abraham as his star witness, Paul quotes Genesis 15:6, which states that "Abraham ... believed God, and it was credited to him for righteousness." The result of Abraham believing God was δικαιοσύνη; i.e., a status of being in the right, not guilty before the Lord.[103] In saying that faith was "credited to him" (ἐλογίσθη αὐτῷ), Paul is further confirming that δικαιοσύνη is a status that God grants to someone. From this foundational premise that righteousness/justification is based on faith in God and his promises, Paul insists that "Scripture

---

reception of him, and is thus not relevant for our discussion of justification/righteousness.

[102] For a very helpful discussion of righteousness and justification in Galatians, see Moo, *Galatians*, 48–62.

[103] While not denying the forensic sense of righteousness language here, N. T. Wright argues that justification language here has the sense of being declared part of God's family; see N. T. Wright, *Justification: God's Plan & Paul's Vision* (Downers Grove, IL: IVP, 2009), 111–22. But Moo (*Galatians*, 60) is correct that when Wright privileges "the dinner table over the law court" he "illegitimately privileges context over semantics."

saw in advance that God would justify the Gentiles by faith" (3:8). Here again the verb δικαιόω has the same sense as in 2:16–17—to declare to be in the right, not guilty before God. As far as Paul is concerned, this act of God to justify gentiles who believe is embedded in the original promise to Abraham that in him all the nations will be blessed (Gen 12:3). Several verses later Paul returns to the contrast between pursuing justification through the law and pursuing it through faith. Paul insists that it is evident that "no one is justified before God by the law." As in the previous examples, the verb δικαιόω means to declare to be in the right, not guilty before God. This confident assertion is grounded in a citation of Habakkuk 2:4: "the righteous will live by faith." The adjective δίκαιος describes a person who is in the right, someone who is in line with God's standard (which is rooted in God's own righteous character). Thus the person who is righteous experiences eschatological life on the basis of faith in God and his promises, not by doing what the Mosaic law demands. Indeed, the law was never intended to give eschatological life. If it had been able to do so, "then righteousness would certainly be on the basis of the law" (3:21). From the beginning God's intention was to demonstrate that the status of being right before God could never come through one's own effort to do what God commands, even through the Mosaic law. Instead, the law acted as a "guardian until Christ, so that we could be justified by faith" (3:24). God's declaration that a person is in the right rests on faith in Christ and his work on the believer's behalf, not one's efforts to obey God's commands.

After the argument of 3:1–5:1 climaxes with the bold assertion of the freedom the believer has in Christ, there is only one more occurrence of righteousness language in the letter. Describing the posture of the believer, Paul writes, "For we eagerly await through the Spirit, by faith, the hope of righteousness" (5:5). Here again the focus is on the status of being in the right as determined by God. Yet this status is something the believer eagerly awaits and hopes for, indicating that in some sense this status is a future reality. Through the empowerment of the Spirit and ongoing trust in Christ and his promises, the believer longs for the revelation of his/her status as "in the right" before God.

§6.3.2 The Agent and Means of Justification/Righteousness in Galatians

When we speak of the agent of justification, we are asking the question of who does what is necessary to meet the required standards for a person to be declared not guilty before God. One of the fundamental contrasts Paul draws in Galatians is between a human being's effort to achieve that status through obeying what God commands in the Mosaic law versus God's actions in and through the person of Christ to accomplish that status. Paul takes great pains to emphasize that God is the one who accomplishes the justification of his people through the work of his Son Jesus Christ.

Christ as the agent of the believer's justification is expressed at several points in Galatians. In 2:17 Paul speaks of believers being justified "by Christ" (ἐν Χριστῷ), identifying him as the agent of justification.[104] More specifically, it is the death of Christ that accomplishes the believer's justification. In 2:21 Paul insists that if justification (δικαιοσύνη) comes through the Mosaic law, "then Christ died for nothing." The clear implication is that Christ accomplished our justification through his death. The logic of that claim is teased out further in 3:10–14. Although a curse rests upon all who rely on works of the law to be justified, Christ redeemed his people from the curse that the law brings for disobedience by becoming a curse for us—that is, experiencing and receiving the curse that we deserved. He took that curse on himself through his death on the cross. By raising Jesus from the dead (1:4), God the Father vindicated Jesus—that is, declared that he was in fact not guilty and therefore not deserving of the punishment of death. As Paul summarizes in Romans 4:25, Jesus "was delivered up for our trespasses and raised for our justification."[105]

The means by which believers receive this status of righteousness is clear throughout Galatians—faith in Jesus Christ (2:16–17). This faith in Christ is contrasted with the dead-end path of justification through works of the law. Abraham was also declared righteous on the basis of his faith (Gen 15:6 // Gal 3:6); he believed that God would fulfill his promises to him, even in the face of difficult circumstances (Gen 15:1–21; compare Rom 4:13–25). Although Paul does not spell this out, the believer is justified in a similar way: through faith in Christ, who has promised that all who believe in him have eternal life and will be raised to life on the last

---

[104] Admittedly, this expression could also be rendered "in Christ" as is the case in most English translations besides the CSB. For further discussion, see the notes at 2:17.

[105] It should be further noted that if one interprets the ambiguous genitive expression πίστεως Χριστοῦ ("faith of Christ") in 2:16 and 3:22 as a subjective genitive ("Christ's faithfulness"), there is even more emphasis on Christ as the agent of the believer's justification. But in the end the objective genitive seems more likely; see the discussion in Biblical Theology §8.2.

day (compare John 5:19–29). Faith is the means by which believers are justified because faith unites the believer to Christ in such a complete and intimate way that what is true of Christ is now true of the believer. Through faith the believer shares in the death, burial, and resurrection of Jesus. In other words, believers share in God's justification/vindication of Jesus Christ and are thus assured to be declared righteous on the last day.

§6.3.3 The Timing of Justification/Righteousness in Galatians

Within the Protestant tradition, justification has consistently been discussed as a present reality that the believer experiences the moment one trusts in Christ. Only more recently have the future aspects of justification received attention. So before addressing where the emphasis falls in Galatians, it will be helpful to lay out the already/not-yet nature of justification.[106]

Since justification refers to God's verdict on the last day that a person is in the right (i.e., not guilty before him), it is inherently future oriented. When justification was discussed in Second Temple Judaism, the emphasis was consistently on God rendering this verdict in the great judgment at the end of human history as part of consummating his promises.[107] Understandably this future focus led to a measure of uncertainty when it came to whether a person could know in the present that one would in fact be justified or vindicated on the last day. Yet part of what set the early Christians apart was their insistence that one could know now, in the present, that he or she was justified by God. How was that possible? The early Christians boldly proclaimed that by trusting in Jesus Christ, one could know now that a verdict of righteous would be rendered on the last day because it has in effect already been rendered through the death and resurrection of Christ. As Ladd helpfully summarizes, "Justification, which primarily means acquittal at the final judgment, has already taken place in the present. The eschatological judgment is no longer alone future; it has become a verdict in history. Justification, which belongs to the Age to Come and issues in the future salvation, has become a present reality inasmuch as the Age to Come has reached back into the present evil age to bring its soteric blessings to human beings ... Justification is

---

[106] For a broadly similar view, see Moo, *Galatians*, 60–62.

[107] For discussion of the Second Temple Jewish texts, see Chris VanLandingham, *Judgment & Justification in Early Judaism and the Apostle Paul* (Peabody, MA: Hendrickson, 2006), 66–174.

one of the blessings of the inbreaking of the new age into the old. In Christ the future has become the present."[108]

So in Galatians where does the emphasis fall? Present or future justification? Although both aspects are present, more often than not Paul has in view future justification. In other words, Paul most often uses justification and righteousness language to refer to what happens on the last day rather than the present status of those who trust in Christ. One helpful way to see the timing of justification in Galatians is to explore the verb tenses used when discussing justification and righteousness.[109] In 2:16–17 the first occurrence of the verb δικαιόω is in the present tense and seems to have a gnomic quality, while the second is an aorist subjunctive that is part of a purpose/result clause. But most significant is the third occurrence, which is a future indicative. While it is possible that this future tense could also have a gnomic sense, it seems far more likely that it refers to justification as a future reality.[110] If so this would seem to shed light on the previous two uses, as well as the one in 2:17. There Paul refers to "seeking to be justified by Christ"; here δικαιόω is an aorist infinitive completing the present participle ζητοῦντες. The very idea of seeking to be justified suggests the focus is on the future and not the present. In 3:8 δικαιόω is again a present tense (likely with a gnomic sense), but the context suggests a future reference, since Paul asserts that Scripture "saw in advance that God would justify the Gentiles by faith." This claim is grounded in a combined citation of Genesis 12:3 and 18:18: "All the nations will be blessed through you." Note again the future perspective,

---

[108] George Eldon Ladd, *A Theology of the New Testament* (Grand Rapids: Eerdmans, 1993), 483–84.

[109] The relationship between Greek verb tenses and their temporal reference is a longstanding debate within NT scholarship which cannot be settled here; for a helpful introduction to the subject see Constantine R. Campbell, *Basics of Verbal Aspect in Biblical Greek* (Grand Rapids: Zondervan, 2008). Key for the discussion that follows is understanding that the tense of a Greek verb does not automatically indicate when an action happens; determining that is based primarily on deictic markers (i.e., elements in the surrounding context such as adverbs, adjectives, prepositions, conjunctions, and particles); see further Rodney J. Decker, *Temporal Deixis of the Greek Verb in the Gospel of Mark with Reference to Verbal Aspect*, SBG 10 (New York: Lang, 2001), 29–59.

[110] It is true that Paul is citing Ps 143:2, so he could simply be using the form borrowed from there. But given that his opponents are arguing that one must keep the Mosaic law in order to be justified, it seems the primary issue is God's verdict on the last day. Thus the future tense borrowed from Ps 143:2 furthers the argument that no one will be justified on the last day based on works of the law.

though admittedly it could simply be future from the perspective of the Old Testament passage, not necessarily the Galatians' current perspective. In 3:11 Paul uses the present tense of δικαιόω to make a gnomic statement that no one is justified by the law, yet in the very next clause cites Habakkuk 2:4, "the righteous will live by faith." Again, the future tense could simply be from the perspective of the Old Testament audience, but the use of future verbs in the immediate context of justification language is beginning to accumulate. Like the second occurrence in 2:16, Paul uses the aorist subjunctive as part of a purpose/result clause in 3:24, so not much can be gleaned from the timing of justification.

Perhaps most significant is the use of righteousness language in 5:4–5. Those who are "trying to be justified by the law" have fallen away from grace. The present tense of δικαιόω suggests an ongoing effort by the opponents. By contrast, Paul provides the proper perspective in the following verse: "For we eagerly await through the Spirit, by faith, the hope of righteousness." Here it seems clear that righteousness is a future reality. It is something believers eagerly await (a word loaded with eschatological significance; see the notes at 5:5). Furthermore, if one's current status of justification is in view, why does the believer await the hope of righteousness? Thus Paul's statement here in 5:5 only makes sense if future justification is in view.

This focus on the future aspect of justification seems to be necessary in light of what the opponents are arguing. They seem to claiming that God will not declare gentile Christians to be "in the right" on the basis of faith alone; they must be circumcised and observe the Mosaic law as well. In response, Paul insists that faith in Christ is sufficient for a person to be vindicated in the final judgment on the last day. Yet despite this emphasis on future justification here in Galatians, Paul does not see this as a distant reality disconnected from the present. The future justification of the believer is a reality that should shape everyday life. Furthermore, the faith that future justification rests on is the mark of how one knows in the present who will in fact be justified on the last day.

§6.4 CONCLUSION

For Paul, justification refers to God's declaration that a person has a right standing before him in his court of law. In making this declaration, God is acting in accordance with his own character as the one who is righteous and rules over creation in righteousness. The status that God grants in this declaration is righteousness. Believers receive this status of righteousness on the basis of faith, which unites the believer to Christ. Through this union with Christ the believer shares in his death, burial, and resurrection, which was God the Father's vindication of Jesus as the righteous one. Justification has an already/not-yet dynamic. The final vindication and revelation of the verdict of justification await the last day when God administers final justice and sets all things aright. But all who trust in Jesus have the assurance in the present that they will be declared "not guilty/righteous" before God on the last day. This forensic and positional reality provides the foundation for the believer's pursuit of Spirit-produced righteous living in the present.

§7 Humanity

Paul has two general categories for humanity—those who are apart from Christ and those who are in Christ. Although in one sense this fundamental contrast is a subcategory of the antithesis between the present evil age and the new creation, discussing this contrast here highlights its importance in Galatians.

§7.1 HUMANITY APART FROM CHRIST

Paul paints a dark portrait of humanity apart from Christ. At the most basic level, humanity apart from Christ is in a state of slavery/bondage. Although the language describing this state of bondage varies, the basic idea of confinement endures.

§7.1.1 Bondage

Humanity's bondage is seen in the way that Christ's redemptive work is described. Christ gave himself for our sins to rescue people out of this present evil age (1:4). Through his death on the cross Christ redeemed people from the curse of the law by becoming a curse for us (3:13). God sent his Son to redeem those who were under the law (4:4–5). Paul (using himself as a representative example) also describes his own experience before Christ as one of bondage. It was through the law that he died to the law when he was crucified with Christ (2:19–20). Through the cross of Christ, the world has been crucified to Paul and Paul to the world.

Another common way Paul communicates the bondage of humanity apart from Christ is by describing them as being under the power or authority of something.[111] Relying on the works of the law results in being under a curse, since it is impossible to do everything written in the law (3:10; compare 3:13). Scripture has imprisoned all things under sin's power (3:22). But the two most consistent powers that humanity apart from Christ are under are the law and guardians/trustees. Regarding the former, the entire period before faith in Christ came is categorized as "under the law" (3:23). Christ was born under the law to redeem those who were under the law (4:4–5). Those who are considering taking on circumcision are described as those who want to be under the law (4:21). The opposite of being led by the Spirit is being under the law (5:18). The other common power that enslaves humanity is guardians/trustees (3:25; 4:2–3). Although their custodial role could be understood in a more benign fashion, at a minimum these guardians/trustees restrict the freedom of those whom they oversee until they reach a state of maturity/adulthood. These guardians/trustees include the Mosaic law (3:23) and the elements of this world (4:3, 9).

It should be stressed that these various enslaving powers work together, like an axis of evil coordinating their efforts for the ultimate goal of keeping humanity enslaved. Yet given the importance of these different enslaving powers, looking at each of them separately can shed light on their nefarious ways.

§7.1.2 The Elementals

Despite being mentioned just twice (4:3, 9), the elements of the world (τὰ στοιχεῖα τοῦ κόσμου) are the master category under which every other enslaving power should be understood. The elements refer to the basic elements of the material world (earth, wind, fire, water), used representatively to refer to everything associated with this fallen world. As such these elements are foundational to this present evil age (1:4), which lies under the curse that came from Adam's rebellion in the garden (Gen 3). By extension these elements encompass the way things work in this fallen world, such as the fundamental distinctions of ethnicity, socioeconomic background, and gender. For the gentiles, the elementals include the worship of pagan deities and the basic principles of life as gleaned from

---

[111] In Greek it is the use of the preposition ὑπό + the accusative, where the word in the accusative indicates the controlling power over someone or something (BDAG s.v. ὑπό B.2); for a helpful summary of the expression ὑπὸ νόμον, see Harris, *Prepositions and Theology*, 220–21.

various forms of religion and/or philosophy. More shocking is that Paul considers the Mosaic law covenant as the form of elementals to which the Jewish people were enslaved. This does not put pagan religion and practices on the same level as the Mosaic law covenant; as Paul says elsewhere, "So then, the law is holy, and the commandment is holy and just and good" (Rom 7:12). But it does mean that the Mosaic law, like its pagan counterparts, has no place in the new creation that is defined by Christ and his redemptive work on the cross.

Of the various expressions of the elementals, three are particularly prominent in Galatians: the flesh, sin, and the law.

§7.1.2.1 The Flesh

Paul uses the Greek word σάρξ eighteen times in Galatians. In several of these instances, the term refers to bodily existence as a human being (1:16; 2:16, 20; 4:13–14), though even with this "neutral" sense there is usually a connotation of weakness and/or frailty. But more frequently σάρξ refers to human existence under the power and control of sin, subject to the various evil spiritual forces in this fallen world. Paul regularly portrays the flesh as a hostile power. It is engaged in open warfare against the Holy Spirit, opposing his work in the lives of believers (5:16–18). The flesh is so cunning that it can even take the freedom the gospel provides and turn it into an opportunity to indulge its desires (5:13).

The flesh manifests itself in various ways. The most obvious ways are the works of the flesh that characterize a life of open rebellion against God and his ways: "sexual immorality, moral impurity, promiscuity, idolatry, sorcery, hatreds, strife, jealousy, outbursts of anger, selfish ambitions, dissensions, factions, envy, drunkenness, carousing, and anything similar" (5:19–21). But the flesh can also manifest itself in the self-driven striving to earn or maintain a right standing with God through attempts to obey God's law (3:3). This desire to pursue the fulfillment of God's promises through their own efforts rather than faith is what led to the birth of Ishmael (4:23), and by extension is the motivating principle behind those who desire to be under the Mosaic law. Those whose lives are characterized by the flesh persecute those who live according to the promise (4:29). Ironically, those who are promoting circumcision are motivated by a desire "to make a good impression in the flesh" and avoid persecution for the cross of Christ (6:12–13). All who sow to the flesh by pursuing the desires and works of the flesh will one day reap destruction (6:8). Only through union with Christ by faith is slavery to the flesh broken and the flesh along with its desires crucified (5:24).

§7.1.2.2 Sin

An additional ally of the elementals is sin. In its most basic sense sin (ἁμαρτία) is missing the mark of God's perfection in thought, belief, feeling, attitude, speech, or action. As a result, it was necessary for Christ to give himself "for our sins" (ὑπὲρ τῶν ἁμαρτιῶν ἡμῶν), with the plural here emphasizing the specific acts of sin committed (1:4). Yet perhaps even more fundamental to Paul's thinking is sin as a power that actively enslaves a person. In this sense Paul can say in 3:22 that "the Scripture imprisoned everything under sin's power" (συνέκλεισεν ἡ γραφὴ τὰ πάντα ὑπὸ ἁμαρτίαν).[112] Paul expands on sin's enslaving power in Romans 6:1–23. Apart from Christ, people are slaves to sin (Rom 6:16–20), but once they are united to Christ by faith, they are freed to become slaves of God and slaves of righteousness (Rom 6:1–11, 15–19). As a result, believers must choose to present themselves to God as those who have been freed from sin's power and offer every aspect of their lives as instruments for righteousness (Rom 6:12–14).

Paul also uses the term "sinners" (ἁμαρτωλός) in Galatians, though he does so with a slightly different sense than described above.[113] It was common for first-century Jews to use this term in the more specific sense of anyone who did not keep the specific requirements of the Mosaic law covenant, with a particular emphasis on circumcision, food laws, and Sabbath observance. Those who fail to observe these defining marks of Jewish identity, even if they were ethnically Jewish, were considered no better than gentiles (Gal 2:15, 17), who by definition were sinners in this sense.

A related family of terms Paul uses in Galatians is lawbreaker (παραβάτης; 2:18), transgressions (παράβασις; 3:19), and wrongdoing (παράπτωμα; 6:1). Each of these words has the sense of violating a specific command of God. The first two are used in direct connection with the Mosaic law. In 2:18 it refers to a person who violates the requirements of the Mosaic law to remain distinct from the gentiles, whereas in 3:19

---

[112] In Greek the final phrase simply reads "under sin"; by rendering it "under sin's power" the csb has made the force of the prepositional phrase more explicit for the English reader.

[113] To show the polemical force of Paul's use of this term, the csb helpfully puts the term sinners in quotation marks.

transgressions are the reason God gave the Mosaic law in the first place.[114] The third use is different, however; it refers to a violation of the law of Christ committed by a professing believer (6:1). So even though believers are no longer under the Mosaic law, they are still capable of transgressing the law of Christ.

§7.1.2.3 The Law

The final prominent expression of the elementals that enslave humanity is the Mosaic law. Coming from the pen of a devout Jewish man like Paul, such a conclusion is shocking. Even though Paul does not come out and explicitly state this conclusion, it seems to be a reasonably clear inference based on 4:1–11. Paul describes the state of humanity apart from Christ as a form of slavery to the elements of the world under the control of guardians and trustees (4:1–3), language that clearly echoes how the law functioned in God's redemptive plan before Christ came (3:23–25). After explaining that God sent his Son to redeem his people from this slavery into adoption as sons who have the Spirit of the Son as the firstfruits of their inheritance (4:4–7), Paul wonders why they would return to slavery under the elements (4:8–11). Before they were known by God, the Galatians were enslaved "to things that by nature are not gods" (4:8). In light of their emancipation, Paul wonders how they can "turn back again to the weak and worthless elements" to which they were once enslaved (4:9). The form of slavery to the elements the Galatians are contemplating is stated in 4:10: "You are observing special days, months, seasons, and years." In the larger context of Galatians this almost certainly refers to observing the Jewish calendar. Paul's opponents are seeking to make the Galatian gentile believers observe the requirements of the Mosaic law, and Paul concludes that this would be a return to enslavement under the elements of this world.

The Mosaic law as an enslaving power is seen elsewhere in Galatians as well. The law brings a curse on all who fail to do everything written in it (3:10); the only escape from this curse is the redemptive work of Christ (3:13). The Mosaic law holds sinful humanity captive, imprisoning them under its curse (3:23). It is a guardian who holds humanity under custody

---

[114] This difficult expression "for the sake of transgressions" in 3:19 probably means that God gave the Mosaic law to bring the violation of his holy will out into the open and expose it for what it was (compare Rom 7:13); see further the discussion at 3:19 and Biblical Theology §5.2.1.

in a state equivalent to slavery until the arrival of Christ (3:24–25; 4:1–3). So awful was this bondage to the Mosaic law that it required the Son of God being born under the law to redeem those languishing under the law (4:4–5). Paul describes those enticed by his opponents' teaching as those "who want to be under the law" (4:21). By contrast, those who are led by the Spirit are no longer under the enslaving power of the law (5:18).

§7.2 HUMANITY IN CHRIST

For those who are in Christ, the fundamental category Paul uses for them in Galatians is being members of God's family. This status as members has both vertical and horizontal dimensions.

§7.2.1 The Family of God

Throughout Galatians Paul uses family terminology to describe believers, a practice that has its roots in the Old Testament.[115] God commands the Israelites to act or not act in certain ways toward each other because they are brothers (Lev 19:17; 25:17; Deut 15:12; 17:15), and the people of Israel are often referred to as a house/household (e.g., Exod 16:31; 40:38; Lev 10:6; Num 12:7; Ps 114:1; Hos 8:1). At the same time, the terminology of house/household can refer to a place where God dwells (Gen 28:17, 19; Judg 18:31; 2 Sam 12:20; Mic 3:12; Hag 1:8) as well as a dynasty of kings (2 Sam 7:11; 1 Kgs 2:24).[116] To explore how these concepts inform the use of familial language for believers in Galatians, we will first look at sonship and then brother/sister.

§7.2.1.1 Sonship and Adoption

Sonship is a significant theme in Galatians. Paul roots his understanding of the gospel in the fact that God "was pleased to reveal his Son in me" (1:15–16). As a result of this revelation, Paul can assert that "I no longer live, but Christ lives in me. The life I now live in the body, I live by faith

---

[115] For a helpful discussion and overview of the background and significance of kinship language in the NT, see DeSilva, *Honor, Patronage, Kinship, and Purity,* 157–240. The use of family language for people not related to each other by blood or marriage is often referred to as "fictive kinship."

[116] While the two concepts of brother/sister and house/household are closely related, they each make a distinctive contribution to our understanding of the people of God; see David G. Horrell, "From Ἀδελφοί to Οἶκος Θεοῦ: Social Transformation in Pauline Christianity," *JBL* 120 (2001): 293–311.

in the Son of God, who loved me and gave himself for me" (2:20). But Paul
was not the only recipient of the self-sacrificial love of Jesus the Son of
God. In a passage that is central to the letter, Paul asserts that "When
the time came to completion, God sent his Son, born of a woman, born
under the law, to redeem those under the law, so that we might receive
adoption as sons. And because you are sons, God has sent the Spirit of his
Son into our hearts, crying, 'Abba , Father!' So you are no longer a slave
but a son, and if a son, then an heir through God" (4:4–7) The redemptive
work of Jesus the Son of God enables believers to be adopted into God's
family as sons who have the Spirit of God's Son dwelling in them as they
await the day when they receive their inheritance.[117] Believers receive
this status as sons of God as a result of their union with Christ, which
comes on the basis of faith (3:26).

Along with this emphasis on being sons of God, Galatians also places
significant importance on being sons of Abraham. Immediately after noting that Abraham was justified by faith (3:6), Paul insists that "those who
have faith are Abraham's sons" (3:7). This assertion helps set the stage for
the lengthy argument that runs through 5:1. In the allegory at the climax
of this argument, Paul reminds his readers that "Abraham had two sons,
one by a slave and the other by a free woman" (4:22). Not only does each
woman represent a covenant, but their respective sons represent two
different ways of relating to God (according to the flesh vs. believing in
the promise). Just like Isaac, believers (regardless of their ethnicity) are
children of promise who are born according to the Spirit and live in the
freedom that Christ has purchased for them (4:28–5:1).

How are these two themes of sons of God and sons of Abraham related?
The answer lies in tracing the theme of sonship in the Old Testament,
with special attention to the relationship between the Abrahamic and
Davidic covenants.

The starting point for the sonship theme in the Old Testament is
Adam. Adam "fathered a son in his likeness, according to his image, and
named him Seth" (Gen 5:3); this language echoes the assertion in 5:1 that

---

[117] As we noted in our exposition of 3:7, in an effort to make clear that sonship language
refers to male and female believers alike, some translations (e.g., NIV, NLT) render such expressions as "children." But while this is well-intentioned, it obscures the "sonship" theme that
runs throughout Galatians and prevents the English reader from connecting the believers'
status as sons of Abraham (3:7; 4:21–5:1) and sons of God (3:26; 4:6–7) with Jesus' identity
as the Son of God (1:16; 2:20; 4:4–6).

"On the day that God created man, he made him in the likeness of God."
Although the Old Testament nowhere explicitly calls Adam a son of God,
it is a natural inference that Luke 3:38 confirms when it explicitly refers
to Adam as "son of God."

Central to God's covenant with Abraham is the promise of descendants more numerous than the stars in the sky (Gen 15:5). That promise
will be fulfilled through the birth of a particular son: Isaac. God says to
Abraham, "I will bless [Sarah]; indeed, I will give you a son by her. I will
bless her, and she will produce nations; kings of peoples will come from
her" (Gen 17:16). Through the birth of this particular son will eventually
come kings, a link that anticipates the covenant that God will make with
David centuries later. The line of promise passes from Isaac to Jacob to
his twelve sons, whose descendants eventually form the people of Israel.
It is in the context of God sending Moses to deliver them that God calls
Israel "my firstborn son" (Exod 4:22). From this point forward the people
of Israel are often referred to as God's son (e.g., Jer 31:9; Hos 11:1).

A notable development takes place when God makes his covenant
with David in 2 Samuel 7. This covenant builds upon the promises God
made to Abraham. In addition to promising to make David's name great
and establish Israel in the land, Yahweh promises David a descendant
from his own body (compare Gen 15:4!) whose kingdom he will establish
forever (2 Sam 7:12–16). This descendant will build a house (i.e., temple)
for Yahweh to dwell among his people in the land of promise, and they
will dwell in security and peace in the presence of God. These promises
are rooted in the Abrahamic covenant, which in addition to promising
land and a line had promised that kings would come forth from him (Gen
17:5–7). The Davidic covenant develops these themes of a covenant being
established with offspring, resulting in kings coming forth, with dominion
over territory, and God being their God (2 Sam 7:12–16). God says that he
will be a father to the promised king from the line of David and he will be
a son to God (2 Sam 7:14). In other words, this descendant of David will
obey where Adam, Israel, and all humanity had failed. He will defeat the
enemies of God's people (including the serpent, the archenemy) and lead
them into an Edenic type of experience of God's presence. The promise
of people, place, and presence that God made Abraham as the means by
which he would reverse the effects of the fall will be fulfilled through
a Davidic king, a son of God who would rule over an eternal kingdom.

Several Psalms build upon these connections and themes. The anointed king of Psalm 2 is referred to as Yahweh's son whose inheritance is a dominion over the nations that extends to the ends of the earth (2:4–8).[118] The warning of a curse upon those who rebel against him and the promise of blessing to those who surrender to him (2:9–12) echo God's promise to bless those who bless Abraham and curse those who curse him (Gen 12:3). In Psalm 8, David seems to implicitly understand God's promise to him as the means by which God will fulfill his commission to Adam to exercise dominion over creation itself. Psalm 89 is an extended reflection on God's promise to David that emphasizes the eternal reign of David's offspring rooted in Yahweh's faithful covenant love (89:1–4). Unlike Adam, he will not be outwitted by the enemy but crush and strike him down (89:20–24). His reign will be such that it will extend to the sea and rivers; he will call God his Father and be designated as the firstborn son, the highest of the kings of the earth (89:25–29). In Psalm 110 David sees Yahweh instructing his Lord to sit at his right hand until all his enemies are made a footstool, and goes on to assert the universal reign of David's descendant.

Numerous texts in the Prophets highlight the connection between the Abrahamic promise and the Davidic covenant. According to Isaiah 55:3, the new covenant that the death and vindication of the servant inaugurates in fulfillment of God's promise to Abraham is a "permanent covenant with you on the basis of the faithful kindnesses of David." When God gathers the remnant of his people from exile, they will be fruitful and multiply, with a Davidic shepherd king ruling over them as they live in peace and security in the land (Jer 23:1–6). Ezekiel 37:24–28 foresees a similar reality, promising an eternal covenant of peace in which God's people are fruitful and multiply in the land, where they will dwell securely and experience God's presence.

The Abrahamic and Davidic covenants are brought together in the opening line of the New Testament, where Matthew introduces his Gospel as "An account of the genealogy of Jesus Christ, the Son of David, the Son of Abraham" (1:1). The genealogy that follows presents Jesus as the fulfillment of both covenants. The very end of Matthew also brings the

---

[118] Although Psalm 2 does not identify its author, Acts 4:25 attributes it to David. It would seem, then, that David understood God's promise to him as an extension of God's promise to Abraham.

promises to Abraham and David together. As the risen Davidic king, Jesus has universal authority over all creation, and he sends out his disciples to be fruitful and multiply the number of disciples through preaching the gospel to all the nations (28:18–20).

In light of this biblical-theological pattern, it should be no surprise that here in Galatians Paul brings together the promise to Abraham and the Davidic covenant. Even though Paul does not explicitly mention David in Galatians 4:1–7, elsewhere he clearly connects Jesus' identity as the Son of God with his descent from David's line (Rom 1:3–4). Because Jesus is the Son of God from David's line who redeems his people from their exile through a new exodus, his redeemed people are adopted as sons of God and given the Holy Spirit.[119] As adopted sons they experience the presence of God's Spirit in their lives and receive the inheritance promised to Abraham's seed.

Thus, believers are not only sons of Abraham, but they are sons of God because Jesus is the Son of God (in both the Davidic and ontological sense). Through faith in Christ they share in his identity as a son and also in his inheritance, which here in Galatians includes the gift of the Holy Spirit.

§7.2.1.2 Brothers and Sisters in the Household of God

Despite Paul's concern over and frustration with the Galatians, he repeatedly refers to them as brothers and sisters (1:11; 3:15; 4:12, 28, 31; 5:11, 13; 6:1, 18). Although a common feature in Paul's letters,[120] it is especially noteworthy in a letter where Paul addresses the very real possibility that his readers will abandon the true gospel for the so-called other gospel propagated by the false teachers (1:6–9). Paul goes out of his way to mention the brothers who are with him as he writes the letter (1:2), reminding the Galatian believers of their membership in the same spiritual family. At key turning points in his argument Paul addresses the Galatians as brothers and sisters to remind them of their shared identity in the family of God (1:11; 3:15; 5:13; 6:1), while at other times he uses sibling language to apply the truth of his argument directly to the Galatians (4:28, 31; 5:13). Paul also addresses the Galatians as brothers and sisters to remind them of their shared experience of the gospel when he first arrived in Galatia

---

[119] On the connection between adoption and God's promise to David in 2 Sam 7, see Scott, *Adoption as Sons of God*, 178–82.

[120] Indeed, one can argue it is the most common title for Christians in Paul's letters.

and to call them to return to that sense of blessing they had (4:12). And when it comes time to call the Galatians to restore those caught in sin, he reminds them that they are brothers and sisters (6:1). It would seem, then, that Paul calls the Galatians brothers and sisters throughout the letter to reassure the Galatians that, despite the efforts of his opponents, he still believes they are part of the family of God through the work of Jesus the Son of God.[121]

§7.2.1.3 Conclusion

Paul's use of familial language serves his larger purpose of reinforcing the Galatians' status as full members of God's family, sons who do not need to observe the Mosaic law covenant in order to experience the inheritance promised to Abraham. The convergence of family, God's presence, and participation in a royal line with a promised inheritance comes to their clearest expression in Galatians 4:1–7, where Paul brings together the fulfillment of the Davidic covenant with receiving the inheritance promised to Abraham through their union with Christ the seed of Abraham and son of God. They are adopted sons of God (Jew and gentile alike, male and female alike) who are indwelt by the Spirit of God's Son, a house for God's powerful presence to inhabit. As sons they are no longer slaves to the elementals but now live in the freedom that Christ has purchased for them.

§7.2.2 The Israel of God

This expression may be the most disputed in the entirety of the letter. The basic question is who Paul has in mind when he refers to the Israel of God. Does Paul have in view: (1) Jewish believers in distinction from gentile believers; (2) a future remnant of Jews who will be saved prior to Christ's return; or (3) the church, composed of Jew and gentile alike? A decision must be based on grammar, context, and broader theological considerations.[122]

---

[121] Compare the conclusion of Horrell ("From Ἀδελφοί to Οἶκος Θεοῦ," 302–3): "Paul uses sibling language to promote the solidarity and mutual regard among members of the congregations. His emphatic use of such language when confronting situations in which there is currently a lack of such concern indicates that he sees sibling bonds as implying precisely that mutualism which he seeks to foster."

[122] For helpful overviews of the issues involved, see Ole Jakob Filtvedt, "'God's Israel' in Galatians 6:16: An Overview and Assessment," *CurBR* 15 (2016): 123–40 and Das, *Galatians*, 644–52.

Grammatically, the issue is whether the "them" (αὐτοὺς) who follow the new creation rule and "Israel of God" (τὸν Ἰσραὴλ τοῦ θεοῦ) refer to the same or different entities. If the καί that joins these two expressions has its usual continuative or copulative sense ("and"), then Paul has in view two distinct entities. But if instead the καί has an explicative or appositional force ("even"), then the "them" and the "Israel of God" are one and the same. While it is certainly true that the explicative sense of καί is not common, there are in fact several clear and unambiguous examples in the New Testament.[123] But even granting the explicative καί as a possibility, it is admittedly rare. Furthermore, if Paul wanted to equate the two entities, there were more obvious ways to do it.[124] Indeed, the word order may suggest that Paul issues two distinct blessings on two distinct groups.[125] A further indication that two groups may be in view is the repetition of the preposition ἐπί, which when repeated "normally distinguishes a *second* group from those serving as the object of the first instance of the preposition."[126] Thus while not decisive, on the whole the grammar seems to favor the view that Paul refers to two distinct groups.

The context is similarly debated.[127] Those who argue for one group highlight the repeated emphasis in Galatians on the unity of Jew and gentile within the church. Jew and gentile alike are justified by faith in Christ (2:15–16). In Christ all believers, regardless of ethnicity, are sons of God through faith (3:26), sons who are adopted into God's family and have the Spirit of his Son (4:1–7). In Christ "there is no Jew or Greek ... since you are all one in Christ" (3:28). The Jerusalem above is the mother of all who are born according to the promise made to Abraham (4:21–5:1). In Christ neither circumcision nor uncircumcision matters (5:6; 6:15). Since, then,

---

[123] Some scholars claim that Paul nowhere uses καί with an explicative sense; see, e.g., S. Lewis Johnson, "Paul and 'the Israel of God': An Exegetical and Eschatological Case-Study," in *Essays in Honor of J. Dwight Pentecost* (Chicago: Moody Press, 1986), 181–96 and Das, *Galatians*, 648. But as others note, there are examples not only in the NT but even in Paul's letters; see, e.g., BDAG s.v. καί 1.c; Turner, *Syntax*, 335; Beale, "Peace and Mercy," 206–7; Moo, *Galatians*, 401–2.

[124] Johnson ("Paul and 'the Israel of God,'" 124) suggests that Paul could have simply eliminated the καί after ἔλεος. Das (*Galatians*, 648) notes that there are far more common ways of indicating apposition.

[125] Suggested by Moo (*Galatians*, 402), who nonetheless sees one group of people in view.

[126] Das, *Galatians*, 648.

[127] For a helpful survey of the context leading up to Galatians 6:16, see Andreas J. Köstenberger, "The Identity of the Ἰσραηλ Του Θεου (Israel of God) in Galatians 6:16," *Faith and Mission* 19 (2001): 3–24.

the whole tenor of the letter has stressed the unity of believers despite ethnicity, introducing a distinction between gentile and Jew (whether believers or unbelievers) seems to run counter to the rest of the letter. Those who argue for two distinct groups respond by noting that in light of the strong and repeated attacks on the Jewish opponents, Paul could be using the expression Israel of God to affirm that the believing remnant of Jews are under God's blessing of peace. The expression Israel of God would thus assure these Jewish believers who remain faithful to the true gospel that they have God's blessing upon them. And while it is true that when it comes to being in Christ "there is no Jew or Greek" (3:28), Paul does distinguish his ministry from Peter's by noting his focus is on the gentiles while Peter's is on the Jews (2:8–9). Yet despite these counter-arguments, the larger context of the letter seems to favor the view that there is only one entity in view.

When it comes to theology, the evidence is even more disputed. Proponents of the two-groups view contend that in Scripture the term Israel always refers to Jews and never refers to the church; indeed, explicitly referring to the church as Israel does not occur until Justin Martyr in the second century (*Dial.* 11:1–5). Given that Paul refers to "Israel according to the flesh" (1 Cor 10:18, my translation), the expression Israel of God could be understood as a way of contrasting believing Israelites from ethnic Jews who do not believe. As such it would connect with Paul's train of thought in Romans 9–11, where Paul argues that "not all who are descended from Israel are Israel" (Rom 9:6). Furthermore, if Paul's statement that "there is no ... male and female" does not eliminate gender distinctions, then the claim that "there is no Jew or Greek" does not automatically mean all distinctions between the two are eliminated. A final line of evidence is a possible parallel with the Jewish Benediction *Shemoneh 'Esreh*, which, like Galatians 6:16, has the unusual order of peace and mercy. In such Jewish benedictions, there are always two distinct groups in view—one that receives peace and another that receives mercy.

On the other hand, advocates of the one-group view note that claiming Paul never refers to the church as Israel simply begs the question, and Justin Martyr's explicit statement should not be dismissed lightly, even if it does come nearly a century later. The central thrust of Galatians is the argument that Jew and gentile alike are sons of Abraham, united to each other and to Christ by faith in one body of believers. When it comes to Paul's use of the term Israel, there are at least two places where Paul's use may not in fact refer to an ethnic entity (Rom 9:6b; 11:26). And instead of finding a parallel with the Jewish Benediction *Shemoneh 'Esreh*, a more likely parallel is Isaiah 54:10.[128] Along with its surrounding context, this echo points toward one people of God—Jew and gentile alike—experiencing the redemption accomplished by the suffering servant.

As this survey of evidence shows, a decision is difficult, and no view is without its problems. The grammar leans slightly toward the two-group view, while the context of the letter favors the one-group view. When it comes to theology, it is inevitable that one's larger theological framework and convictions come into play. But on the whole, it seems slightly more likely that Paul uses the phrase "Israel of God" to refer to the church, composed of Jew and gentile alike, who follow the new creation rule that flows from the true gospel.

§8 Faith

The centrality of faith for the Christian is at the heart of Paul's response to the situation in Galatians. Although he only uses the adjective πιστός once and the verb πιστεύω four times, the noun πίστις appears twenty-two times. Seventeen of these occurrences are in chapter 3, where faith takes center stage. So gaining a good grasp of how faith language is used in this letter is an important step toward understanding the message of Galatians.

§8.1 A SURVEY OF FAITH LANGUAGE IN GALATIANS

The very first occurrence of faith language occurs in 1:23, where Paul refers to preaching "the faith he once tried to destroy." Here faith (πίστις) refers to the set of beliefs that comprise the gospel message, a use that is not unheard of in Paul's writings yet nonetheless is not especially common (compare 1 Tim 4:1; 6:21). Yet as the rest of Galatians unfolds, we can organize the use of faith language under five broad and often overlapping categories.

First, faith is active trust in either God or Jesus Christ. Although Christ Jesus as the object of faith is assumed repeatedly in Galatians, in several places Paul makes this explicit. In 2:16 Paul uses faith in this way twice. He begins by contrasting works of the law with "faith in Jesus Christ"

---

[128] See Beale, "Peace and Mercy," 204–23.

(διὰ πίστεως Ἰησοῦ Χριστοῦ) as alternative means of justification.[129] He
then clarifies this potentially ambiguous expression in the next clause
when he states, "even we ourselves have believed in Christ Jesus" (καὶ
ἡμεῖς εἰς Χριστὸν Ἰησοῦν ἐπιστεύσαμεν). Paul then reemphasizes the
point later in the next clause when he says that the purpose of believing in Christ Jesus is "so that we might be justified by faith in Christ"
(ἵνα δικαιωθῶμεν ἐκ πίστεως Χριστοῦ). To drive home his point about
faith in Christ, the apostle presents as his star witness Abraham, who,
according to Genesis 15:6, "believed God, and it was credited to him for
righteousness" (ἐπίστευσεν τῷ θεῷ, καὶ ἐλογίσθη αὐτῷ εἰς δικαιοσύνην).
Just as Abraham trusted in God and believed that he would fulfill his
promises, so too followers of Jesus trust in him and are therefore considered righteous before God. Like Abraham before them, Christians
experience God's promises "on the basis of faith in Jesus Christ" (ἐκ
πίστεως Ἰησοῦ Χριστοῦ; 3:22).

Second, faith is the grounds or means by which a person initially
receives various good gifts of God.[130] The primary one is justification,
which Paul insists takes place by or on the basis of faith (2:16 [2x]; 3:6,
8, 11, 24). This is in contrast to an effort to be justified by or on the
basis of (works of) the law (2:16; 3:11). Faith is also the means by which
Christians experience the blessing/promise of Abraham (3:8, 22 [2x]),
which appears to be Paul's umbrella expression for all that believers
receive through their union with Christ, the singular seed of Abraham
(3:16). Believers also receive the Holy Spirit on the basis of faith, as
they believe what they heard proclaimed in the gospel message (3:2, 14).

---

[129] See Biblical Theology §8.2 below for discussion of this debated phrase.

[130] Paul uses two different prepositional phrases to express this idea of grounds or means.
Most frequently he uses ἐκ πίστεως (2:16; 3:8, 11, 22, 24; 5:5), though he also uses διὰ πίστεως
(2:16; 3:14, 26). Some scholars have attempted to identify subtle distinctions in meaning
between these two phrases; see, e.g., Garlington, "Paul's 'Partisan ἐκ,' " 567–89. But none
of these proposals are persuasive, and it seems best to regard these two phrases as merely
stylistic variation. In Gal 2:16 Paul asserts that justification is διὰ πίστεως Ἰησοῦ Χριστοῦ,
then two clauses later states that it is ἐκ πίστεως Χριστοῦ. Nothing in the context indicates
any shift in meaning. Romans 3:30 seems to confirm this conclusion when it describes God
as the one "who will justify the circumcised by faith [ἐκ πίστεως] and the uncircumcised
through faith [διὰ τῆς πίστεως]." Nothing in the context of Rom 3:30 indicates a difference
in meaning. In fact, Paul's larger point that both Jew and gentile alike are justified on the
same basis virtually demands the two phrases mean essentially the same thing; see further
Harris, *Prepositions and Theology*, 112–13.

Eschatological life is not based on doing what the law demands but instead comes through faith just as Habakkuk 2:4 had promised (Gal 3:11–12). All of these various good gifts of God come to the Christian by or on the basis of faith in Jesus Christ, the singular seed of Abraham and the risen Son of God.

Third, faith is not only what begins the Christian life; it is also the means by which followers of Jesus continue to live the Christian life and experience God's blessings. By faith believers share in the death and resurrection of Jesus, and the new life they continue to experience is lived by faith in Jesus Christ the Son of God (2:20). The believer's ongoing experience of the Holy Spirit is also experienced by faith; as the good news of the gospel is proclaimed and Christians believe and trust in that good news, they continue to experience the work of the Spirit in their lives, both individually and corporately (3:5). The eschatological life that began by faith at conversion is an ongoing reality that continues by faith, not works of the law (3:11–12). The believer's faith and the Holy Spirit work together to fuel hope/anticipation for final justification on the last day (5:5). In the meantime, faith works itself out through love in the everyday actions of the Christian as a fruit of God's Spirit at work in their lives (5:6, 22).

Given than faith is what begins and sustains the Christian life, it is no wonder that, fourth, faith is the defining mark/characteristic of the Christian experience. Paul even coins a phrase to describe Christians as "those of faith" (οἱ ἐκ πίστεως; 3:7, 9), or perhaps more woodenly "the by-faithers."[131] It is these "by-faithers"—in contrast to those whose identity is determined by the works of the law—that are the true sons of Abraham (3:7–9), the true sons of God (3:26; 4:5–7), and members of God's household (6:10). In fact, faith in Jesus Christ is the defining mark of the new era of salvation history that began with the life, death, and resurrection of Jesus (3:23–25). In this new creation what matters is faith in Christ working itself out through love for God and love for neighbor in fulfillment of the law of Christ, not distinctions such as circumcised/

---

[131] Paul may have created this expression based on Hab 2:4 (cited in Gal 3:11), which states that "the righteous shall live by faith" (ὁ δίκαιος ἐκ πίστεως ζήσεται). Indeed, it seems likely that the repeated used of ἐκ πίστεως (2:16 [2x] 3:7, 8, 9, 12, 22, 24; 5:5) in Galatians may have its origins in Hab 2:4.

uncircumcised, Jew/Greek, slave/free, or male/female that characterize this present evil age and the elementals that hold humanity in bondage (1:4; 3:28; 4:1–3, 8–11; 5:5–6, 13–14; 6:2, 15).

§8.2 FAITH IN CHRIST OR THE FAITHFULNESS OF CHRIST?

One of the most debated issues in scholarship on Galatians is the translation and interpretation of the phrase πίστις (Ἰησοῦ) Χριστοῦ. Traditionally, this phrase has been understood as an objective genitive referring to "faith in Christ"; in other words, the phrase refers to the believer's faith in Christ. But over the past forty years a growing number of scholars have instead interpreted the phrase as a subjective genitive referring to Christ's faithfulness, i.e., his faithful obedience to the Father as the grounds for salvation.[132] As is often the case, one's interpretive decision on this phrase is shaped by various theological factors as well as one's reconstruction of the opponents' teaching. So we will look briefly at the arguments for these two views.

§8.2.1 Arguments Supporting "Faithfulness of Christ"

A number of arguments are offered by advocates of the subjective genitive interpretation.[133] First, when πίστις is followed by a reference to a person, the construction regularly refers to the faith/faithfulness of that person, such as in Romans 3:3 (the faithfulness of God) and Romans 4:12 (faith of Abraham our forefather). Second, the normal meaning of πίστις in ordinary Greek was reliability or fidelity rather than faith or trust. Third,

---

[132] As one might expect, other views besides the objective and subjective genitive readings have been proposed, such as source/origin; see, e.g., Jae Hyun Lee, "Against Richard Hays's 'Faith of Jesus Christ,'" *JGRChJ* 5 (2008): 51–80 and Mark Seifrid, "The Faith of Christ," in *The Faith of Jesus Christ: Exegetical, Biblical, and Theological Studies*, ed. Michael F. Bird and Preston M. Sprinkle (Peabody, MA: Hendrickson, 2009), 129–46. Another alternative is to see the phrase indicating "Christ-faith" that is understood in various ways; see Preston M. Sprinkle, "Πίστις Χριστοῦ as an Eschatological Event," in *The Faith of Jesus Christ: Exegetical, Biblical, and Theological Studies*, ed. Michael F. Bird and Preston M. Sprinkle (Peabody, MA: Hendrickson, 2009), 165–84.

[133] Commentators who hold this view include Longenecker, *Galatians*, 87–88; Martyn, *Galatians*, 263–75; Witherington, *Grace in Galatia*, 179–82; de Boer, *Galatians*, 148–50. Among the most notable defenses of the subjective genitive are Hays, *Faith of Jesus*, 139–91; Sam K. Williams, "Again Pistis Christou," *CBQ* 49 (1987): 431–47; Ian G. Wallis, *The Faith of Jesus Christ in Early Christian Traditions*, SNTMS 84 (Cambridge: Cambridge University Press, 1995); Douglas A. Campbell, "The Faithfulness of Jesus Christ in Romans 3:22," in *The Faith of Jesus Christ: Exegetical, Biblical, and Theological Studies*, ed. Michael F. Bird and Preston M. Sprinkle (Peabody, MA: Hendrickson, 2009), 57–71.

this expression is a shorthand way of referring to the obedience of Jesus, something emphasized in Paul (albeit with different terminology). Fourth, the focus in Galatians 2:16 and 3:22 is on a contrast between human and divine action, not two forms of human action. Fifth, the objective genitive makes the next clause tautologous, since in the immediate context Paul speaks of believing in Christ using the verb πιστεύω.

§8.2.2 Arguments Supporting "Faith in Christ"

There are a number of arguments used to support the traditional understanding of faith in Christ.[134] First, while it is true (as advocates of the subjective genitive argue) that the general pattern of usage when πίστις is followed by a reference to a person refers to the faith of that person, there are clear exceptions (e.g., Mark 11:22; Jas 2:1).[135] Second, by far the normal meaning of πίστις in the New Testament is clearly faith/trust, not faithfulness or fidelity. Especially significant here in Galatians is the fact that Paul unambiguously cites Abraham's faith as the grounds for God reckoning him as righteous (Gen 15:6, cited in 3:6). That key text sheds light on the repeated mentions of faith throughout the letter.[136] Third, while Paul does speak of Christ's obedience as foundational to our salvation (Rom 5:12–21; Phil 2:8), nowhere does he unambiguously do so using the noun πίστις or the verb πιστεύω, and it does not appear to be what Paul is referring to in these texts. Indeed, there is no clear evidence in the context of these passages that signals to the reader a shift from the believer's faith in Christ to Christ's faithfulness. Fourth, the contrast

---

[134] Commentators who hold this view include Burton, *Galatians*, 121–23; Schreiner, *Galatians*, 163–66; Moo, *Galatians*, 38–48; DeSilva, *Handbook*, 43; Oakes, *Galatians*, 87–90; Das, *Galatians*, 250–53; see also Barclay, *Paul and the Gift*, 378–84. Among the most notable defenses of the objective genitive are Moisés Silva, "Faith Versus Works of Law in Galatians," in *Justification and Variegated Nomism: Volume 2: The Paradoxes of Paul*, ed. D. A. Carson, Peter T. O'Brien, and Mark Seifrid (Grand Rapids: Baker, 2004), 217–48; R. Barry Matlock, "Detheologizing the Pistis Christou Debate: Cautionary Remarks from a Lexical Semantic Perspective," *NovT* 42 (2000): 1–23; R. Barry Matlock, "'Even the Demons Believe': Paul and Πίστις Χριστοῦ," *CBQ* 64 (2002): 300–18; R. Barry Matlock, "Πίστις in Galatians 3.26: Neglected Evidence for 'Faith in Christ'?," *NTS* 49 (2003): 433–39; Stanley E. Porter and Andrew W. Pitts, "Πίστις with a Preposition and Genitive Modifier: Lexical, Semantic and Syntactic Considerations in the Πίστις Χριστοῦ Discussion," in *The Faith of Jesus Christ: Exegetical, Biblical, and Theological Studies*, ed. Michael F. Bird and Preston M. Sprinkle (Peabody, MA: Hendrickson, 2009), 33–53.

[135] For examples in broader Greek literature, see Roy A. Harrisville III, "Before Πίστις Χριστου: The Objective Genitive as Good Greek," *NovT* 48 (2006): 353–58.

[136] On this point see especially Silva, "Faith Versus Works," 234–36.

in texts such as Galatians 2:16 can just as easily be understood as a contrast between two different forms of action (doing vs. believing) rather than a contrast between human and divine action. Efforts to downplay the importance of human faith in Christ—often in an effort to safeguard God's sovereignty in salvation—are driven more by theological presuppositions than the text itself. Fifth, the specific mention of "believing in Christ" using the verb πιστεύω in the same or next clause (see 2:16 and 3:22) helps to clarify the use of the ambiguous "faith of Christ" expression in the immediate context and is used for emphasis, not a distinction in meaning.[137] Sixth, the early church fathers on the whole understand this phrase as an objective genitive.

§8.2.3 Summary

As the summaries above and the comments on each key verse suggest, I am persuaded that the objective genitive makes the best sense. The phrase in question refers to the believers' faith in Jesus Christ. While there is no doubt that Paul places significant weight on the role that Jesus' obedience/faithfulness plays in redemption, that is not what Paul refers to with the expression πίστις (Ἰησοῦ) Χριστοῦ.

§9 Paul's Use of the Old Testament in Galatians

The influence of the Old Testament Scriptures on Paul's argument, theology, and even structure in Galatians is pervasive.[138] This influence happens at both the conscious/explicit level (i.e., Paul specifically cites and alludes to key Old Testament passages that further his argument) and the subconscious/implicit level (i.e., various Old Testament texts, themes, and motifs shape his thinking in ways that he is not always consciously aware of while writing the letter). The Old Testament forms the very

---

[137] On the rhetorical features in the context supporting an objective reading, see R. Barry Matlock, "The Rhetoric of Πίστις in Paul: Galatians 2.16, 3.22, Romans 3.22, and Philippians 3.9," *JSNT* 30 (2007): 173–203.

[138] While there is no comprehensive study of Paul's use of the OT in Galatians, there have been a number of specialized studies. In addition to my own *She Must and Shall Go Free*, the following are among the most noteworthy monographs: Hays, *Faith of Jesus*; Ciampa, *Presence and Function*; Wilder, *Echoes of the Exodus*; Wakefield, *Where to Live*; A. Andrew Das, *Paul and the Stories of Israel: Grand Thematic Narratives in Galatians* (Minneapolis: Fortress Press, 2016); Dunne, *Persecution and Participation*. For an expanded version of what is found here (including additional bibliography), see Matthew S. Harmon, "Galatians," in *DNTUOT*, forthcoming.

substructure of how Paul thinks, argues, and communicates his message. Or, stated another way, the Old Testament Scriptures are one of the lenses (the other being the gospel of Jesus Christ) through which Paul views all of life. In one sense, Paul's fundamental disagreement with the opponents in Galatians is hermeneutical, rooted in a different understanding of the relationship between the Old Testament Scriptures and what Christ has accomplished through his life, death, and resurrection.

In this brief section we will look at the level to which Paul engages the Old Testament and which portions of the Old Testament he interacts with most frequently.

§9.1 PAUL'S LEVEL OF ENGAGEMENT WITH THE OLD TESTAMENT SCRIPTURES

In general terms, the different forms of Old Testament influence range from direct citations to thematic parallels, with allusions and echoes falling on the spectrum between them.[139] For our purposes it is unnecessary to sharply distinguish between citations, allusions, echoes, and thematic parallels; instead it is better to see them as part of a spectrum of Old Testament engagement. Nevertheless, all of the direct citations of Scripture occur in chapters 3–4 (with the exception of Ps 143:2 in Gal 2:16 and Lev 19:18 in Gal 5:14). This concentration of citations makes sense in light of the complex theological argument that Paul makes in these chapters. Allusions and echoes are more widely spread throughout the letter, though again chapters 3–4 have the highest number. Thematic parallels pervade the letter, forming the conceptual background for countless terms, concepts, and ideas.[140]

Paul does more than engage isolated scriptural texts throughout the letter, as if he is merely interested in citing an authoritative text to enhance the rhetorical force of his argument. While his citations and allusions are understandable on their own terms within the immediate context of Galatians, they regularly take on far greater depth of meaning when their original Old Testament contexts are considered. Those in Galatia who were familiar with these Old Testament passages and their

---

[139] On the distinctions between these categories as well as criteria for determining their presence, see further Harmon, *She Must and Shall Go Free*, 26–39.

[140] The pervasive influence of Scripture in Gal 1–2 has been convincingly demonstrated by Ciampa, *Presence and Function*.

larger contexts would have grasped Paul's argument at an even deeper level.

Paul's engagement with Old Testament Scripture in Galatians can be broken down into four broad categories.[141] The first is the use of an Old Testament segment as the framework for a New Testament passage. When the various citations, allusions, echoes, and thematic parallels are analyzed in their totality, a pattern emerges.[142] As I have argued elsewhere, Isaiah 40–66 provides a broad structural framework for Paul's argument, theology, and structure in Galatians.[143] More specifically, Isaiah 49–54 appears to form a broad conceptual substructure to Galatians 1–4. The allusions to Isaiah 49 in Galatians 1:15–16, 24 and the citation of Isaiah 54:1 in Galatians 4:27 form a set of bookends for this substructure. At points in between Paul draws on other Isaianic texts from within Isaiah 49–54 (as well as numerous other Old Testament texts) to move the argument along. Yet even these other Old Testament texts seem to be understood through the framework of Isaiah 49–54. Although this Isaianic substructure does not seem to continue through Galatians 5–6, those chapters do contain a number of allusions, echoes, and thematic parallels to Isaiah 40–66. Furthermore, there are a number of similarities between Galatians and Isaiah 40–66 on the thematic level, including: (1) the restoration of Jerusalem; (2) forgiveness of sins; (3) return from exile through a new exodus that transforms creation itself; (4) salvation extending to the nations; and (5) the enigmatic servant figure. Each of these themes is linked to Yahweh fulfilling his promises, with special emphasis on his covenant with Abraham. The significance of this Isaianic narrative substructure is to support Paul's larger argument in Galatians that God has fulfilled the promises to Abraham in and through Jesus Christ, who as the Isaianic suffering servant has inaugurated the return from exile through a new exodus that culminates in a new creation in

---

[141] For a helpful survey of the different ways the NT authors engage the OT, see Beale, *Handbook on the New Testament Use of the Old Testament*, 55–93.

[142] Perhaps the most well-known proposal for a narrative substructure in Galatians is that of Hays, *Faith of Jesus*. For a helpful summary of various thematic narratives in Galatians, see Das, *Paul and the Stories of Israel*.

[143] See the summary in Harmon, *She Must and Shall Go Free*, 250–58. Others who have affirmed this proposal to various degrees include Beale, *Handbook on the New Testament Use of the Old Testament*, 86–87; Wright, *Paul and the Faithfulness of God*, 2:1137; Das, *Paul and the Stories of Israel*, 225–36.

which all who believe in Christ participate, regardless of their ethnicity, gender, or socioeconomic status.

The second broad category of Paul's engagement with the Old Testament is to assert or imply fulfillment of Old Testament promises and types/patterns. Although he only uses explicit fulfillment language in 5:14 (where the whole law is said to be fulfilled in living out Lev 19:18) and 6:2 (where it is not linked to an Old Testament text), Paul clearly presents Scripture as being fulfilled at various points in the letter. He sees his own life and ministry in some sense as the fulfillment of the mission of the servant in Isaiah 49 (Gal 1:10, 15–16, 24; 2:2). The death of Jesus fulfills the description of the suffering servant of Isaiah 53 (Gal 1:4; 2:20; 3:13; 4:4–6). Believers experience the Spirit in fulfillment of God's Old Testament promises (Gal 3:2, 5, 14; 5:16–24 // Isa 32:15–20; 44:1–5; Ezek 36:26–27). The nations are being blessed through the gospel in fulfillment of God's promise to Abraham (Gal 3:8–9 // Gen 12:3; 18:18; 22:18). As the singular seed of Abraham, Jesus receives the inheritance promised to Abraham (Gal 3:16–18 // Gen 17:7–10, 19–21; 22:18; Isa 41:8; 53:10; 54:3) and shares it with all who are united to him by faith (Gal 3:26–4:7). Through him the hope of Jew and gentile together acknowledging the universal reign of the one true God has come to pass (Gal 3:19 // Zech 14:9). The prophetic promise of a new exodus through a suffering servant that results in a new creation has been fulfilled in Christ (Gal 4:1–7; 6:15 // Isa 41:17–20; 51:9–10; 52:13–53:12), as has the promise of a new Jerusalem that produces children free from their slavery to sin (Gal 4:27 // Isa 54:1). Paul concludes the letter by praying for God's people to experience the peace and mercy that was promised through the new covenant (Gal 6:16 // Isa 54:10).

A third category of Paul's use of the Old Testament is to provide authoritative support for a claim. Thus he can assert that no flesh will be justified by works of the law (Gal 2:16) on the basis of Psalm 143:2. Since Abraham was justified by faith (Gen 15:6), it naturally follows that believers are also (Gal 3:6). Those who rely on the law fall under a curse (Gal 3:10), as Deuteronomy 27:26; 28:58 make clear. Since Habakkuk 2:4 clearly establishes that the righteous shall live by faith, it is evident that no one can be justified by the law (Gal 3:11). Indeed, Leviticus 18:5 makes it clear that the law is not of faith (Gal 3:12). That Jesus took our curse upon himself (Gal 3:13) is supported by citing the curse that rests on those hanged on a tree (Deut 21:23). Paul knows that those who sow to the flesh will reap destruction because Hosea 8:1–6; 10:12–13 make a similar assertion.

A final category is the numerous places where Paul illustrates a point through the use of an Old Testament example. Referring to the opponents as those troubling the Galatians (Gal 1:7–9) echoes the story of Achan troubling Israel. Paul's own pre-conversion zeal for the law (Gal 1:13–14) echoes Phinehas' zeal to preserve the purity of Israel (Num 25:1–13). The story of Abraham's two sons from two different women (Gen 16–21) illustrates the relationship between flesh and spirit (Gal 4:21–5:1), while Sarah's command to Abraham to cast out Hagar and her son Ishmael (Gen 21:10) is a picture of what God commands the Galatians to do to the opponents (Gal 4:29).

§9.2 THE OLD TESTAMENT PASSAGES PAUL USES IN GALATIANS

Paul draws from a number of different Old Testament books (see the chart below), but he most frequently uses texts from Genesis, Deuteronomy, Psalms, and Isaiah. This pattern aligns with the Pauline corpus as a whole, where these books also take pride of place. What follows is a chart of the various citations (c), allusions (a), echoes (e), and thematic parallels (tp) proposed in this commentary, though it must be stressed that distinguishing between allusions and echoes, and echoes and thematic parallels is not a precise science:

Table 17:

Galatians	Subject	OT Background
1:1	Apostleship	Isa 52:7; 61:1 (tp)
1:1	God as Father	2 Sam 7:12–17; Pss 2:7–9; 89:26 (tp)
1:1	Resurrection of Christ (return from exile; second exodus)	Jer 16:14–15; Ezek 37:1–14 (tp)
1:2, 13	Churches as the people of God assembled for worship	Deut 4:10; 23:2–9; 2 Chr 1:2–5; 6:3–13 (tp)
1:2	Grace and peace	Num 6:25–26 (e)
1:2	Peace	Isa 40–66 (tp) [52:7; 53:5; 54:10, 13; 66:12]
1:2	From God our Father and the Lord Jesus Christ	Deut 6:4 (tp)

1:4	Christ's death	Isa 53:10 (a) [plus surrounding context of 54:1–10]; Lev 16 (tp)
1:4	Rescue, deliverance from sin a defining mark of Yahweh's identity as God	Exod 3:8; 18:4–10; Judg 6:9; Isa 31:5; 60:16; Ezek 34:27 (tp); Isa 42:22: 43:13; 44:17, 20; 47:14; 48:10; 50:2; 57:13; 60:16 (tp)
1:4	God as Father linked to the second exodus	Jer 31:9 (tp); see also Exod 4:22; Deut 32:5–20, 36–43; Isa 1:2; 63:16; 64:4–12; Jer 3:12–19; Hos 11:1–11
1:5	God's unique glory tied to forgiving sins	Exod 34:6–7 (tp)
1:6	Called	Isa 40–66 (tp); Hos 11:1–2
1:6	So quickly turning away	Exod 32–34; Deut 9:16 (e); Judg 2:17 (tp)
1:6, 8–9	Gospel	Isa 52:7; 60:1–3; 61:1 (tp)
1:7	Troublers	Josh 7:1–26 (e); 1 Chr 2:7 (e)
1:8–9	Curse/accursed	Josh 7:1–26 (e); Deut 13:1–18
1:10	Slave/servant of Christ	Isa 42:1–8; 49:1–8; 52:13–53:12 (tp)
1:13	Persecution motivated by a curse for those hung on a tree	Deut 21:23 (tp)
1:14	Zeal for the purity of God's people	Num 25:1–13 (a); Ps 105:31 (tp)
1:15	Called from the womb	Isa 49:1 (a); Jer 1:5 (tp)
1:16	Reveal his son	Isa 49:3 (e); 49:6; 52:5, 7 (tp); 52:10; 53:1 (e)
1:16	Preach the gospel to the gentiles	Isa 42:6; 49:6, 8; 52:5, 7, 10; 53:1 (tp)
1:17	Travel to Arabia	Isa 42:11; 60:6–7, 17 (tp); 1 Kgs 18:14–15 (e)
1:21	Ministry in Cilicia (Tarsus)	Isa 66:18–19 (tp)
1:23–24	Glorifying God "in me"	Isa 49:3 (e)
2:2	Running in vain	Isa 49:4 (e); Hab 2:2–3 (e)
2:7–8	Division of ministry spheres (Jew/gentile)	Isa 49:6 (e/tp)
2:2, 8–9	Ministry to the gentiles	Isa 42:6; 49:6–8; 52:5–7 (tp)
2:5	Yield in submission	Deut 13:8 (e/tp)
2:16	No flesh will be justified	Ps 143:2 (c)
2:16–21	Righteousness language	Isa 40–66 (tp)

2:18	Build up and tear down	Jer 1:10; 24:6–7; 31:27–28 (e/tp)
2:20	Christ lives in me	Isa 49:3 (e)
2:20	Live by faith	Hab 2:4 (e)
2:20	Gave himself for me	Isa 53 (a)
3:2, 5	Hearing of faith	Isa 53:1 (a)
3:2, 5	The Spirit	Isa 53:1 (a); Isa 32:15–20; 44:3–5; Ezek 36:26–27 (tp)
3:6	Abraham believed and was counted righteous	Gen 15:6 (c); Isa 53:1(e)
3:8	All the nations blessed in Abraham	Gen 12:3 (c); 18:18 (c); 22:18 (c)
3:8	Gospel preached	Isa 52:7–10 (tp)
3:6–9	Look to Abraham	Isa 51:1–8 (a); 52:7–10 (e)
3:10	Cursed are those who rely on the law	Deut 27:26 (c); 28:58 (a)
3:11	Righteous will live by faith	Hab 2:4 (c); Ps 143:2 (e); Gen 15:6 (tp)
3:12	The one doing the law will live	Lev 18:5 (c)
3:13	Christ as a curse for us	Isa 41:17–20 (tp); 43:14–21 (tp); 51:9–11 (tp); 52:10, 15; 54:3; 55:4–5 (tp) 53 (a)
3:13	Cursed is everyone hung on a tree	Num 25:4 (a); Deut 21:23 (c)
3:14	Blessing of Abraham = promised Spirit	Isa 44:1–5
3:14, 16	Blessing, seed of Abraham, Spirit	Isa 44:3–5 (a)
3:16	Singular seed → plural seed	Gen 17:7–10, 19–21 (a); 22:18 (a); Isa 41:8; 53:10; 54:3 (tp)
3:17	430 years between promise and law	Exod 12:40–41 (e)
3:17	Ratifying a covenant	Gen 15:7–21 (e)
3:18	Inheritance	Gen 12:7; 15:18–21; 17:8; Num 34:1–29; 12:10; Ps 2:8 (tp)
3:15–18	Covenant, promise, seed, inheritance	Isa 54:3–10 (e); 61:7–10 (tp)
3:19	Law given through angels	Deut 33:2 LXX (tp)
3:19	By the hand of a mediator	Lev 26:46 (e)
3:20	God is one	Deut 6:4 (a); Zech 14:9 (a)

3:27	Clothed with Christ	Isa 61:10 (tp)
4:1	Heir is a child	Hos 11:1
4:4	God sent his Son	Isa 48:16 (e); 49:1 (e/tp); Jer 1:5 (e/tp)
4:5	Adoption	Exod 4:22–23; 2 Sam 7:12–16; Pss 2:1–12; 89:25–29; Hos 11:1 (tp)
4:6	God sent the Spirit of his Son	Isa 48:16 (e); Ezek 36:26–28 (tp); Jer 31:33–34 (tp)
4:1–7	New exodus 1. new creation 2. Servant 3. Abraham/seed	Isa 41:17–20; 43:16–21; 51:9–10 (new creation) Isa 52:11–12; 52:13–53:12 (Servant) Isa 41:8, 17–20; 51:1–8 (Abraham/seed) Collective allusion or echo
4:8	Knowing God	Exod 10:2 (tp); Deut 4:35 (tp); Ps 83:18 (tp); Ezek 36:36 (tp)
4:8	Things that by nature are not gods	Isa 37:19 (tp)
4:10	Days, months, seasons, years	Exod 23:14, 17 (tp); Lev 23:4 (tp); 25:1–7 (tp); Num 10:10 (tp); 28:11 (tp);
4:11	Labor in vain	Isa 49:4 (e)
4:19	Paul's birth pangs	Isa 45:7–11 (a); 51:1–2 (e); 54:1 (tp)
4:22–23	Abraham had two sons	Gen 16–21 (a)
4:26	Jerusalem above is our mother	Isa 54:1 (tp); Ps 87:3 (tp), 5 (e); Ezek 40–48 (tp)
4:27	Rejoice barren one	Isa 54:1 (c)
4:29	One born of the flesh persecuting one born of the Spirit	Gen 21:9 (a)
4:30	Cast out the slave woman and her son	Gen 21:10 (c)
5:1	Christ freed us to freedom	Lev 26:13 (tp); Isa 10:24–27 (tp); Ezek 34:27 (tp)
5:3	Do the entire law	Deut 27:26 (e); Lev 18:5 (e)
5:5	Waiting for righteousness in the Spirit	Isa 32:15–17 (tp)
5:9	Unleavened bread	Exod 12:15–20; 13:3–10 (tp); Lev 2:11; 6:14–18 (tp)
5:13	Freedom	Isa 40–55 (tp)

5:13	Serve one another through love	Isa 40–66 (tp); 54:17 (e); Exod 4:23; 19:4–6; 20:1–6; Lev 25:42 (tp)
5:14	Love your neighbor as yourself	Lev 19:18 (c); Deut 30:6, 16, 20 (tp)
5:15	Bite and devour one another	Prov 30:14 (e)
5:16–17	Walk by the Spirit	Jer 31:31–34; Ezek 36:26–27 (tp)
5:18	Led by the Spirit	Isa 63:11–15 (e); Ps 143:10 (e)
5:22–23	Fruit of the Spirit	Isa 32:15–20; 57:15–21 (a/e)
6:2	Law of Christ	Isa 42:4; 51:4; 53:4–6 (tp)
6:7	God is not mocked	2 Chr 36:16 (tp)
6:7	Whatever a man sows he will also reap	Eccl 11:4; Job 4:8; Prov 22:8 (tp)
6:8	Sowing to the flesh and reaping destruction	Hos 8:1–6; 10:12–13 (e)
6:10	Household of faith	Num 20:29; 2 Sam 1:12; Ezek 3:4 (tp)
6:15	New creation	Isa 41:17–20; 43:16–21; 51:9–11; 65:17–25; 66:22–24 (a)
6:16	Peace and mercy on the Israel of God	Isa 54:10 (a); Ps 85:10 [84:11 LXX] (e)

BIBLIOGRAPHY

Aldrete, Gregory S. *Daily Life in the Roman City: Rome, Pompeii, and Ostia*. Westport, CT: Greenwood Press, 2004.

Alexander, T. Desmond. "Further Observations on the Term 'Seed' in Genesis." *Tyndale Bulletin* 48 (1997): 363–67.

Allen, David L. "Substitutionary Atonement and Cultic Terminology in Isaiah 53." Pages 171–89 in *The Gospel According to Isaiah 53: Encountering the Suffering Servant in Jewish and Christian Theology*. Edited by Darrell L. Bock and Mitch Glaser. Grand Rapids: Kregel, 2012.

Armitage, D. J. "An Exploration of Conditional Clause Exegesis with Reference to Galatians 1,8–9." *Biblica* 88 no. 3 (2007): 365–92.

Arnold, Clinton E. "'I Am Astonished That You Are So Quickly Turning Away' (Gal 1.6): Paul and Anatolian Folk Belief." *New Testament Studies* 51 (2005): 429–49.

———. "Returning to the Domain of the Powers: Stoicheia as Evil Spirits in Galatians 4:3,9." *Novum Testamentum* 38 (1996): 55–76.

Aune, David Edward. *The New Testament in Its Literary Environment*. Library of Early Christianity. Philadelphia: Westminster, 1987.

Bailey, Daniel P. "Concepts of *Stellvertretung* in the Interpretation of Isaiah 53." Pages 223–50 in *Jesus and the Suffering Servant: Isaiah 53 and Christian Origins*. Edited by W. H. Bellinger and William Reuben Farmer. Harrisburg, PA: Trinity Press, 1998.

———. "'Our Suffering and Crucified Messiah' (*Dial*, 111.2): Justin Martyr's Allusions to Isaiah 53 in His *Dialogue with Trypho* with Special Reference to the New Edition of M. Markovich." Pages 324–417 in *The Suffering Servant: Isaiah 53 in Jewish and Christian Sources*. Edited by Bernd Janowski and Peter Stuhlmacher. Grand Rapids: Eerdmans, 2004.

Bandstra, Andrew J. "The Law and Angels: *Antiquities* 15.136 and Galatians 3:19." *Calvin Theological Journal* 24 no. 2 (1989): 223–40.

Barclay, John M. G. "Mirror-Reading a Polemical Letter: Galatians as a Test Case." *Journal for the Study of the New Testament* 31 (1987): 73–93.

———. *Obeying the Truth: Paul's Ethics in Galatians*. Minneapolis: Fortress, 1991.

———. *Paul and the Gift*. Grand Rapids: Eerdmans, 2015.

Barrett, C. K. "The Allegory of Abraham, Sarah, and Hagar in the Argument of Galatians." Pages 154–69 in *Essays on Paul*. Philadelphia: Westminster, 1982.

Bauckham, Richard. "Barnabas in Galatians." *Journal for the Study of the New Testament* 2 (1979): 61–70.

———. *Jesus and the God of Israel: God Crucified and Other Studies on the New Testament's Christology of Divine Identity*. Grand Rapids: Eerdmans, 2008.

Beale, G. K. "The Eschatological Conception of New Testament Theology." Pages 11–52 in *Eschatology in Bible and Theology: Evangelical Essays at the Dawn of a New Millennium*. Edited by K. E. Brower and M. W. Elliott. Downers Grove, IL: InterVarsity Press, 1997.

———. *Handbook on the New Testament Use of the Old Testament: Exegesis and Interpretation*. Grand Rapids: Baker, 2012.

———. *A New Testament Biblical Theology: The Unfolding of the Old Testament in the New*. Grand Rapids: Baker, 2011.

———. "The Old Testament Background of Paul's Reference to 'the Fruit of the Spirit' in Galatians 5:22." *Bulletin for Biblical Research* 15 no. 1 (2005): 1–38.

———. "Peace and Mercy Upon the Israel of God: The Old Testament Background of Galatians 6,16b." *Biblica* 80 (1999): 204–23.

———. "The Use of Hosea 11:1 in Matthew 2:15: One More Time." *Journal of the Evangelical Theological Society* 55 (2012): 697–715.

———. *We Become What We Worship: A Biblical Theology of Idolatry*. Downers Grove, IL: InterVarsity Press, 2008.

Betz, Hans Dieter. *Galatians: A Commentary on Paul's Letter to the Churches in Galatia*. Hermeneia. Philadelphia: Fortress, 1979.

Bird, Michael F. *An Anomalous Jew: Paul among Jews, Greeks, and Romans*. Grand Rapids: Eerdmans, 2016.

———. *Crossing over Sea and Land: Jewish Missionary Activity in the Second Temple Period*. Peabody, MA: Hendrickson, 2010.

Blenkinsopp, Joseph. *Isaiah 40-55: A New Translation with Introduction and Commentary*. The Anchor Yale Bible Commentaries. New York: Doubleday, 2002.

Blessing, Kamila Abrahamova. "The Background of the Barren Woman Motif in Galatians 4:27." Ph. D. Diss., Duke University, 1996.

Blomberg, Craig. "Quotations, Allusions, and Echoes of Jesus in Paul." Pages 129–43 in *Studies in the Pauline Epistles: Essays in Honor of Douglas J. Moo*. Edited by Matthew S. Harmon and Jay E. Smith. Grand Rapids: Zondervan, 2014.

Bockmuehl, Markus N. A. *Jewish Law in Gentile Churches: Halakhah and the Beginning of Christian Public Ethics*. 1st pbk. ed. Grand Rapids: Baker, 2003.

Bovon, François. "Une formule prépaulinienne dans l'épître aux Galates (Ga 1, 4–5)." Pages 91–107 in *Paganisme, judaïsme, christianisme: Influences et affrontements dans le monde antique: Mélanges offerts à Marcel Simon.* Edited by F. F. Bruce. Paris: de Boccard, 1978.

Breytenbach, Cilliers. "Probable Reasons for Paul's Unfruitful Missionary Attempts in Asia Minor (a Note on Acts 16:6–7)." Pages 157–69 in *Die Apostelgeschichte und die hellenistiche Geschichtsschreibung: Festschrift für Eckhard Plümacher zu seinem 65. Geburtstag.* Edited by Cilliers Breytenbach and Jens Schroter. Leiden: Brill, 2004.

Brown, Raymond E. *An Introduction to the New Testament.* Anchor Bible Reference Library. New York: Doubleday, 1997.

Bruce, F. F. *The Epistle to the Galatians: A Commentary on the Greek Text.* New International Greek Testament Commentary. Grand Rapids: Eerdmans, 1982.

———. "Galatian Problems. 2. North or South Galatians?" 52 (1970): 243–66.

Bruno, Christopher R. *'God Is One': The Function of 'Eis Ho Theos' as a Ground for Gentile Inclusion in Paul's Letters.* Library of New Testament Studies. London: Bloomsbury, 2013.

Bryant, Robert A. *The Risen Crucified Christ in Galatians.* Society of Biblical Literature Dissertation Series. Atlanta: Society of Biblical Literature, 2001.

Burton, Ernest DeWitt. *A Critical and Exegetical Commentary on the Epistle to the Galatians.* International Critical Commentary. Edinburgh: T&T Clark, 1920.

———. *Syntax of the Moods and Tenses in New Testament Greek.* Chicago: University of Chicago Press, 1900.

Butterfield, Rosaria. *The Gospel Comes with a House Key: Practicing Radically Ordinary Hospitality in Our Post-Christian World.* Wheaton: Crossway, 2018.

Callan, Terrance. "Pauline Midrash: The Exegetical Background of Gal 3:19b." *Journal of Biblical Literature* 99 (1980): 549–67.

Campbell, Constantine R. *Basics of Verbal Aspect in Biblical Greek.* Grand Rapids: Zondervan, 2008.

———. *Paul and Union with Christ: An Exegetical and Theological Study.* Grand Rapids: Zondervan, 2012.

———. *Verbal Aspect and Non-Indicative Verbs: Further Soundings in the Greek of the New Testament.* Vol. 15. Studies in Biblical Greek. New York: Lang, 2008.

Campbell, Douglas A. "The Faithfulness of Jesus Christ in Romans 3:22." Pages 57–72 in *The Faith of Jesus Christ: Exegetical, Biblical, and Theological Studies.* Edited by Michael F. Bird and Preston M. Sprinkle. Peabody, MA: Hendrickson, 2009.

Caneday, Ardel B. "The Curse of the Law and the Cross: Works of the Law and Faith in Galatians 3:1–14." Ph.D. Dissertation, Trinity Evangelical Divinity School, 1992.

Carson, D. A. "Mystery and Fulfillment: Toward a More Comprehensive Paradigm of Paul's Understanding of the Old and the New." Pages 393–436 in *Justification and Variegated Nomism: The Paradoxes of Paul.*

Edited by D. A. Carson, Peter T. O'Brien, and Mark A. Seifrid. Grand Rapids: Baker, 2001.

Ceresko, Anthony R. "The Rhetorical Strategy of the Fourth Servant Song (Isaiah 52:13–53:12): Poetry and the Exodus-New Exodus." *Catholic Biblical Quarterly* 56 (1994): 42–55.

Chapman, David W. *Ancient Jewish and Christian Perceptions of Crucifixion.* Wissenschaftliche Untersuchungen Zum Neuen Testament 2 Reihe. Tübingen: Mohr Siebeck, 2008.

Childs, Brevard S. *Isaiah.* Old Testament Library. Louisville: Westminster John Knox, 2001.

Ciampa, Roy E. "The History of Redemption." Pages 254–308 in *Central Themes in Biblical Theology: Mapping Unity in Diversity.* Edited by Scott J. Hafemann and Paul R. House. Grand Rapids: Baker, 2007.

———. *The Presence and Function of Scripture in Galatians 1 and 2.* WUNT. Tübingen: Mohr Siebeck, 1998.

Clements, Ronald E. "Isaiah 53 and the Restoration of Israel." Pages 39–54 in *Jesus and the Suffering Servant: Isaiah 53 and Christian Origins.* Edited by W. H. Bellinger and William Reuben Farmer. Harrisburg, PA: Trinity Press, 1998.

Collins, C. John. "A Syntactical Note (Genesis 3:15): Is the Woman's Seed Singular or Plural?" *Tyndale Bulletin* 48 no. 1 (1997): 139–48.

Combes, I. A. H. *The Metaphor of Slavery in the Writings of the Early Church: From the New Testament to the Beginning of the Fifth Century.* Journal for the Study of the New Testament Supplement Series. Sheffield: Sheffield Academic, 1998.

Cosgrove, Charles H. "The Law Has Given Sarah No Children (Gal 4:21–30)." *Novum Testamentum* 29 (1987): 219–35.

Culy, Martin M. "The Clue Is in the Case: Distinguishing Adjectival and Adverbial Participles." *Perspectives in Religious Studies* 30 no. 4 (2003): 441–53.

Dahl, Nils Alstrup. *The Crucified Messiah and Other Essays.* Minneapolis: Augsburg, 1974.

———. "Paul's Letter to the Galatians: Epistolary Genre, Content, and Structure." Pages 117–42 in *The Galatians Debate: Contemporary Issues in Rhetorical and Historical Interpretation.* Edited by Mark D. Nanos. Peabody, MA: Hendrickson, 2002.

Das, A. Andrew. *Galatians.* Concordia Commentary. St. Louis: Concordia, 2014.

———. *Paul and the Stories of Israel: Grand Thematic Narratives in Galatians.* Minneapolis: Fortress, 2016.

———. *Paul, the Law, and the Covenant.* Peabody, MA: Hendrickson, 2001.

Davies, W. D. *Torah in the Messianic Age and/or the Age to Come.* Journal of Biblical Literature: Monograph Series. Philadelphia: Society of Biblical Literature, 1952.

Davies, W. D., and Dale C. Allison. *A Critical and Exegetical Commentary on the Gospel According to Saint Matthew.* 3 vols. The International Critical

Commentary on the Holy Scriptures of the Old and New Testaments. New York: T&T Clark, 2004.

de Boer, Martinus C. *Galatians: A Commentary.* New Testament Library. Louisville: Westminster John Knox, 2011.

Decker, Rodney J. *Temporal Deixis of the Greek Verb in the Gospel of Mark with Reference to Verbal Aspect.* Studies in Biblical Greek. New York: Lang, 2001.

Deissmann, Adolf. *Bible Studies: Contributions, Chiefly from Papyri and Inscriptions, to the History of the Language, the Literature, and the Religion of Hellenistic Judaism and Primitive Christianity.* Translated by A. J. Grieve. Edinburgh: T&T Clark, 1901.

———. *Light from the Ancient East; the New Testament Illustrated by Recently Discovered Texts of the Graeco-Roman World.* Translated by Lionel Richard Mortimer Strachan. London: Hodder & Stoughton, 1910.

Delorme, J. "The Practice of Baptism at the Beginning of the Christian Era." Pages 25–60 in *Baptism in the New Testament: A Symposium.* Edited by Augustin George. Baltimore: Helicon, 1964.

Dempster, Stephen G. *Dominion and Dynasty: A Biblical Theology of the Hebrew Bible.* New Studies in Biblical Theology. Downers Grove, IL: InterVarsity Press, 2003.

DeRouchie, Jason S., and Jason C. Meyer. "Christ or Family as the 'Seed' of Promise? An Evaluation of N. T. Wright on Galatians 3:16." *Southern Baptist Journal of Theology* 14 no. 3 (2010): 36–48.

DeSilva, David Arthur. *Galatians: A Handbook on the Greek Text.* Baylor Handbook on the Greek New Testament. Waco, TX: Baylor University Press, 2014.

———. *Honor, Patronage, Kinship & Purity: Unlocking New Testament Culture.* Downers Grove, IL: InterVarsity Press, 2000.

———. *The Letter to the Galatians.* New International Commentary on the New Testament. Grand Rapids: Eerdmans, 2018.

Dodd, C. H. *The Apostolic Preaching and Its Developments.* London: Hodder & Stoughton, 1936.

———. *More New Testament Studies.* Grand Rapids: Eerdmans, 1968.

Doty, William G. *Letters in Primitive Christianity.* Guides to Biblical Scholarship. Philadelphia: Fortress, 1973.

Dressler, Harold H. P. "The Sabbath in the Old Testament." Pages 21–41 in *From Sabbath to Lord's Day: A Biblical, Historical, and Theological Investigation.* Edited by D. A. Carson. Grand Rapids: Zondervan, 1982.

Dunn, James D. G. *The Epistle to the Galatians.* Black's New Testament Commentary. Peabody, MA: Hendrickson, 1993.

———. *The Epistle to the Galatians.* Black's New Testament Commentary. Peabody, MA: Hendrickson, 1993.

———. "Paul's Conversion—a Light to Twentieth Century Disputes." Pages 77–93 in *Evangelium, Schriftauslegung, Kirche.* Edited by Jostein Adna, Scott J. Hafemann, and Otfried Hofius. Göttingen: Vandenhoeck & Ruprecht, 1997.

Dunne, John Anthony. *Persecution and Participation in Galatians.* Wissenschaftliche Untersuchungen Zum Neuen Testament 2 Reihe. Tübingen: Mohr Siebeck, 2017.

Edwards, Mark J. *Galatians, Ephesians, Philippians.* Ancient Christian Commentary on Scripture. Downers Grove, IL: InterVarsity Press, 2005.

Elliott, Susan M. "Choose Your Mother, Choose Your Master: Galatians 4:21–5:1 in the Shadow of the Anatolian Mother of the Gods." *Journal of Biblical Literature* 118 (1999): 661–83.

Fee, Gordon D. *God's Empowering Presence: The Holy Spirit in the Letters of Paul.* Peabody, MA: Hendrickson, 1994.

———. *Pauline Christology: An Exegetical-Theological Study.* Peabody, MA: Hendrickson, 2007.

Filtvedt, Ole Jakob. "'God's Israel' in Galatians 6.16: An Overview and Assessment." *Currents in Biblical Research* 15 no. 1 (2016): 123–40.

Finegan, Jack. *Handbook of Biblical Chronology: Principles of Time Reckoning in the Ancient World and Problems of Chronology in the Bible.* Rev. ed. Peabody, MA: Hendrickson, 1998.

Fung, Ronald Y. K. *The Epistle to the Galatians.* New International Commentary on the New Testament. Grand Rapids: Eerdmans, 1988.

Funk, Robert Walter. *A Beginning-Intermediate Grammar of Hellenistic Greek.* 3rd ed. Salem, OR: Polebridge, 2013.

Furnish, Victor Paul. *Theology and Ethics in Paul.* Nashville: Abingdon, 1968.

Garlington, Donald B. "'Even We Have Believed': Galatians 2:15–16 Revisited." *Criswell Theological Review* 7 (2009): 3–28.

Garlington, Don B. *An Exposition of Galatians: A Reading from the New Perspective.* 3rd ed. Eugene, OR: Wipf and Stock, 2007.

———. "Paul's 'Partisan ἐκ' and the Question of Justification in Galatians." *Journal of Biblical Literature* 127 no. 3 (2008): 567–89.

Gathercole, Simon J. "Torah, Life, and Salvation: Leviticus 18:5 in Early Judaism and the New Testament." Pages 126–45 in *From Prophecy to Testament: The Function of the Old Testament in the New.* Edited by Craig A. Evans. Peabody, MA: Hendrickson, 2004.

———. *Where Is Boasting? Early Jewish Soteriology and Paul's Response in Romans 1–5.* Grand Rapids: Eerdmans, 2002.

Gentry, Peter J., and Stephen J. Wellum. *Kingdom through Covenant: A Biblical-Theological Understanding of the Covenants.* Wheaton: Crossway, 2012.

Goldingay, John. *Psalms.* 3 vols. Baker Commentary on the Old Testament Wisdom and Psalms. Grand Rapids: Baker Academic, 2006.

Goodrich, John K. "'As Long as the Heir Is a Child': The Rhetoric of Inheritance in Galatians 4:1–2 and P.Ryl. 2.153." *Novum Testamentum* 55 no. 1 (2013): 61–76.

———. "Guardians, Not Taskmasters: The Cultural Resonances of Paul's Metaphor in Galatians 4.1–2." *Journal for the Study of the New Testament* 32 no. 3 (2010): 251–84.

Gupta, N. K. "Mirror-Reading Moral Issues in Paul's Letters." *Journal for the Study of the New Testament* 34 no. 4 (2012): 361–81.

Hafemann, Scott J. "Paul and the Exile of Israel in Galatians 3–4." Pages 329–71 in *Exile: Old Testament, Jewish, and Christian Conceptions.* Edited by James M. Scott. Leiden: Brill, 1997.

Hahn, Scott. "Covenant, Oath, and the Aqedah: Διαθηκη in Galatians 3:15–18." *The Catholic Biblical Quarterly* 67 no. 1 (2005): 79–100.

Hamilton, James M. Jr. *God's Indwelling Presence: The Holy Spirit in the Old & New Testaments.* NAC Studies in Bible & Theology. Nashville: B&H, 2006.

———. "The Seed of the Woman and the Blessing of Abraham." *Tyndale Bulletin* 58 no. 2 (2007): 253–73.

Hansen, G. Walter. *Abraham in Galatians: Epistolary and Rhetorical Contexts.* Journal for the Study of the New Testament Supplement Series. Sheffield: JSOT, 1989.

———. "A Paradigm of the Apocalypse: The Gospel in Light of Epistolary Analysis." Pages 143–54 in *The Galatians Debate: Contemporary Issues in Rhetorical and Historical Interpretation.* Edited by Mark D. Nanos. Peabody, MA: Hendrickson, 2002.

Hardin, Justin K. "Galatians 1–2 without a Mirror: Reflections on Paul's Conflict with the Agitators." *Tyndale Bulletin* 65 no. 2 (2014): 275–303.

———. *Galatians and the Imperial Cult: A Critical Analysis of the First-Century Social Context of Paul's Letter.* Wissenschaftliche Untersuchungen Zum Neuen Testament. Tübingen: Mohr Siebeck, 2008.

Harmon, Matthew S. "Allegory, Typology, or Something Else? Revisiting Galatians 4:21–5:1." Pages 144–58 in *Studies in the Pauline Epistles: Essays in Honor of Douglas J. Moo.* Edited by Matthew S. Harmon and Jay E. Smith. Grand Rapids: Zondervan, 2014.

———. "Inheritance." Pages 839–40 in *The Baker Illustrated Bible Dictionary.* Edited by Tremper Longman. Grand Rapids: Baker, 2013.

———. *Philippians.* Mentor Commentary. Fearn, Ross-shire, Scotland: Christian Focus, 2015.

———. *Rebels and Exiles: A Biblical Theology of Sin and Restoration.* Essential Studies in Biblical Theology. Downers Grove, IL: InterVarsity Press, 2020.

———. *The Servant of the Lord and His Servant People: Tracing a Biblical Theme through the Canon.* New Studies in Biblical Theology. Downers Grove, IL: InterVarsity Press, 2020.

———. *She Must and Shall Go Free: Paul's Isaianic Gospel in Galatians.* Beihefte Zur Zeitschrift Für Die Neutestamentliche Wissenschaft Und Die Kunde Der Älteren Kirche. Berlin: de Gruyter, 2010.

———. *She Must and Shall Go Free: Paul's Isaianic Gospel in Galatians.* Beihefte Zur Zeitschrift Für Die Neutestamentliche Wissenschaft Und Die Kunde Der Älteren Kirche. Berlin: de Gruyter, 2010.

Harris, Murray J. *Prepositions and Theology in the Greek New Testament.* Grand Rapids: Zondervan, 2011.

——. *Slave of Christ: A New Testament Metaphor for Total Devotion to Christ*. New Studies in Biblical Theology. Downers Grove, IL: InterVarsity Press, 2001.

Harrisville, Roy A. III. "Before Πίστις Χριστοῦ: The Objective Genitive as Good Greek." *Novum Testamentum* 48 no. 4 (2006): 353–58.

Hays, Richard B. "Christology and Ethics in Galatians: The Law of Christ." *Catholic Biblical Quarterly* 49 (1987): 268–90.

——. *Echoes of Scripture in the Letters of Paul*. New Haven: Yale University Press, 1989.

——. *The Faith of Jesus Christ: The Narrative Substructure of Galatians 3:1–4:11*. 2nd ed. Biblical Resource Series. Grand Rapids: Eerdmans, 2002.

——. *The Faith of Jesus Christ: The Narrative Substructure of Galatians 3:1–4:11*. 2nd ed. Biblical Resource Series. Grand Rapids: Eerdmans, 2002.

——. "Galatians." Pages 181–348 in *New Interpreters Bible*. Nashville: Abingdon, 2000.

——. "The Letter to the Galatians: Introduction, Commentary, and Reflection." Pages 181–348 in *The New Interpreters Bible*. Edited by Leander E. Keck. Nashville: Abingdon, 2000.

Hedges, Brian G. *Christ Formed in You: The Power of the Gospel for Personal Change*. Wapwallopen, PA: Shepherd Press, 2010.

Hemer, Colin J. *The Book of Acts in the Setting of Hellenistic History*. Winona Lake, IN: Eisenbrauns, 1990.

Hengel, Martin. *Crucifixion in the Ancient World and the Folly of the Message of the Cross*. Philadelphia: Fortress, 1977.

Hengel, Martin, and Anna Maria Schwemer. *Paul between Damascus and Antioch: The Unknown Years*. Louisville: Westminster John Knox, 1997.

Hermann, R. "Über Den Sinn Des Μορφοῦσθαι Χριστὸν Ἐν Ὑμῖν in Gal. 4, 19." *Theologische Literaturzeitung* 80 (1955): 713–26.

Hill, David. *Greek Words and Hebrew Meanings: Studies in the Semantics of Soteriological Terms*. Society for New Testament Studies Monograph Series. Cambridge: Cambridge University Press, 1967.

Hodge, Caroline E. Johnson. *If Sons, Then Heirs: A Study of Kinship and Ethnicity in the Letters of Paul*. Oxford: Oxford University Press, 2007.

Hofius, Otfried. "Das Gesetz des Mose und das Gesetz Christi." *Zeitschrift für Theologie und Kirche* 80 (1983): 262–86.

Horrell, David G. "From Ἀδελφοί to Οἶκος Θεοῦ: Social Transformation in Pauline Christianity." *Journal of Biblical Literature* 120 no. 2 (2001): 293–311.

Hubbard, Moyer V. *New Creation in Paul's Letters and Thought*. Society for New Testament Studies Monograph Series. Cambridge: Cambridge University Press, 2002.

Hübner, Hans. *Law in Paul's Thought*. Studies of the New Testament and Its World. Edinburgh: T&T Clark, 1984.

Hugenberger, G. P. "The Servant of the Lord in the 'Servant Songs' of Isaiah: A Second Moses Figure." Pages 105–39 in *The Lord's Anointed: Interpretation of Old Testament Messianic Texts.* Edited by P. E. Satterthwaite, Richard S. Hess, and Gordon J. Wenham. Grand Rapids: Baker, 1995.

Hurtado, Larry W. "The Jerusalem Collection and the Book of Galatians." *Journal for the Study of the New Testament* 5 (1979): 46–62.

Instone-Brewer, David. *Traditions of the Rabbis from the Era of the New Testament. Volume 2a, Feasts and Sabbaths—Passover and Atonement.* Traditions of the Rabbis from the Era of the New Testament. Grand Rapids: Eerdmans, 2011.

Jeffers, James S. *The Greco-Roman World of the New Testament Era: Exploring the Background of Early Christianity.* Downers Grove, IL: InterVarsity Press, 1999.

Jobes, Karen H. "Jerusalem, Our Mother: Metalepsis and Intertextuality in Galatians 4:21–31." *Westminster Theological Journal* 55 no. 2 (1993): 299–320.

Johnson, S. Lewis. "Paul and 'the Israel of God': An Exegetical and Eschatological Case-Study." Pages 181–96 in *Essays in Honor of J. Dwight Pentecost.* Chicago: Moody Press, 1986.

Keener, Craig S. *Acts: An Exegetical Commentary.* 4 vols. Grand Rapids: Baker Academic, 2012–2015.

———. *Galatians: A Commentary.* Grand Rapids: Baker, 2019.

Keesmaat, Sylvia C. *Paul and His Story: (Re)-Interpreting the Exodus Tradition.* Sheffield: Sheffield Academic, 1999.

Keller, Timothy J. *Counterfeit Gods: The Empty Promises of Money, Sex, and Power, and the Only Hope That Matters.* New York: Dutton, 2009.

Kern, Philip H. *Rhetoric and Galatians: Assessing an Approach to Paul's Epistle.* Society for New Testament Studies Monograph Series. Cambridge: Cambridge University Press, 1998.

Kim, Seyoon. *The Origin of Paul's Gospel.* Grand Rapids: Eerdmans, 1982.

Klauck, Hans-Josef. *Ancient Letters and the New Testament: A Guide to Context and Exegesis.* Translated by Daniel P. Bailey. Waco, TX: Baylor University Press, 2006.

Knight, George A. F. *Servant Theology: A Commentary on the Book of Isaiah 40–55.* International Theological Commentary. Grand Rapids: Eerdmans, 1984.

Koch, Dietrich-Alex. *Die Schrift als Zeuge des Evangeliums: Untersuchungen zur Verwendung und zum Verständnis der Schrift bei Paulus.* Beiträge zur historischen Theologie. Tübingen: Mohr, 1986.

Koole, Jan L. *Isaiah III.* Historical Commentary on the Old Testament. Leuven: Peeters, 1998.

Köstenberger, Andreas J. "The Identity of the Ἰσραηλ Του Θεου (Israel of God) in Galatians 6:16." *Faith and Mission* 19 no. 1 (2001): 3–24.

Köstenberger, Andreas J., Benjamin L. Merkle, and Robert L. Plummer. *Going Deeper with New Testament Greek: An Intermediate Study of the Grammar and Syntax of the New Testament.* Nashville: B&H Academic, 2016.

Kruse, Colin G. *Paul, the Law, and Justification.* Peabody, MA: Hendrickson, 1997.

Ladd, George Eldon. *A Theology of the New Testament*. Grand Rapids: Eerdmans, 1993.

Laes, C. "Pedagogues in Greek Inscriptions in Hellenistic and Roman Antiquity." *Zeitschrift für Papyrologie und Epigraphik* 171 (2009): 113–22.

Lee, Chee-Chiew. *Blessing of Abraham, the Spirit, and Justification in Galatians: Their Relationship and Significance for Understanding Paul's Theology*. Eugene, OR: Wipf & Stock, 2013.

Lee, Jae Hyun. "Against Richard Hays's 'Faith of Jesus Christ.'" *Journal of Greco-Roman Christianity and Judaism* 5 (2008): 51–80.

Lee, Pilchan. *The New Jerusalem in the Book of Revelation: A Study of Revelation 21–22 in the Light of Its Background in Jewish Tradition*. Wissenschaftliche Untersuchungen zum Neuen Testament. Tübingen: Mohr Siebeck, 2001.

Légasse, Simon. *L'épître De Paul Aux Galates*. Lectio Divina. Paris: Cerf, 2000.

Levinsohn, Stephen H. *Discourse Features of New Testament Greek: A Coursebook on the Information Structure of New Testament Greek*. 2nd ed. Dallas: SIL International, 2000.

Lightfoot, Joseph Barber. *St. Paul's Epistle to the Galatians. A Revised Text with Introduction, Notes, and Dissertations*. 4th ed. Grand Rapids: Zondervan, 1957.

Longenecker, Bruce W. "Defining the Faithful Character of the Covenant Community: Galatians 2:15–21 and Beyond; A Response to Jan Lambrecht." Pages 75–97 in *Paul and the Mosaic Law*. Tubingen: J. C. B. Mohr, 1996.

———. *Remember the Poor: Paul, Poverty, and the Greco-Roman World*. Grand Rapids: Eerdmans, 2010.

———. *The Triumph of Abraham's God: The Transformation of Identity in Galatians*. Nashville: Abingdon Press, 1998.

———. "'Until Christ Is Formed in You': Suprahuman Forces and Moral Character in Galatians." *Catholic Biblical Quarterly* 61 no. 1 (1999): 92.

Longenecker, Richard. *Paul, Apostle of Liberty: The Origin and Nature of Paul's Christianity*. Grand Rapids: Baker, 1976.

Longenecker, Richard N. *Galatians*. Word Biblical Commentary. Dallas: Word, 1990.

———. *New Testament Social Ethics for Today*. Grand Rapids: Eerdmans, 1984.

———. "The Pedagogical Nature of the Law in Galatians 3:19–4:7." *Journal of the Evangelical Theological Society* 25 (1982): 53–61.

Lull, David J. "'The Law Was Our Pedagogue': A Study in Galatians 3:19–25." *Journal of Biblical Literature* 105 (1986): 481–98.

Luther, Martin. *Off the Record with Martin Luther: An Original Translation of the Table Talks*. Translated by Charles Daudert. Kalamazoo, MI: Hansa-Hewlett, 2009.

Lutjens, Ronald. "'You Do Not Do What You Want': What Does Galatians 5:17 Really Mean?" *Presbyterion* 16 (1990): 103–17.

MacDonald, Dennis Ronald. *There Is No Male and Female: The Fate of a Dominical Saying in Paul and Gnosticism*. Harvard Dissertations in Religion. Philadelphia: Fortress, 1987.

MacDonald, William G. *Greek Enchiridion: A Concise Handbook of Grammar for Translation and Exegesis*. n.p.: Bibleworks, 2005.

Magness, Jodi. *Stone and Dung, Oil and Spit: Jewish Daily Life in the Time of Jesus*. Grand Rapids: Eerdmans, 2011.

Martin, Dale B. *Slavery as Salvation: The Metaphor of Slavery in Pauline Christianity*. New Haven: Yale University Press, 1990.

Martin, Troy W. "Pagan and Judeo-Christian Time-Keeping Schemes in Gal 4.10 and Col 2.16." *New Testament Studies* 42 (1996): 105–19.

Martyn, J. Louis. *Galatians: A New Translation with Introduction and Commentary*. Anchor Bible. New York: Doubleday, 1997.

———. "A Law-Observant Mission to Gentiles." Pages 348–61 in *The Galatians Debate: Contemporary Issues in Rhetorical and Historical Interpretation*. Edited by Mark D. Nanos. Peabody, MA: Hendrickson, 2002.

———. *Theological Issues in the Letters of Paul*. Edinburgh: T&T Clark, 1997.

Matlock, R. Barry. "Detheologizing the Pistis Christou Debate: Cautionary Remarks from a Lexical Semantic Perspective." *Novum Testamentum* 42 (2000): 1–23.

———. "'Even the Demons Believe': Paul and Πίστις Χριστοῦ." *Catholic Biblical Quarterly* 64 no. 2 (2002): 300–18.

———. "The Rhetoric of Πίστις in Paul: Galatians 2.16, 3.22, Romans 3.22, and Philippians 3.9." *Journal for the Study of the New Testament* 30 no. 2 (2007): 173–203.

———. "Πίστις in Galatians 3.26: Neglected Evidence for 'Faith in Christ'?" *New Testament Studies* 49 (2003): 433–39.

McKnight, Scot. *The Letter to Philemon*. The New Testament Commentary on the New Testament. Grand Rapids: Eerdmans, 2017.

———. *A Light among the Gentiles: Jewish Missionary Activity in the Second Temple Period*. Minneapolis: Fortress, 1991.

Meeks, Wayne A. *The First Urban Christians: The Social World of the Apostle Paul*. 2nd ed. New Haven: Yale University Press, 2003.

Metzger, Bruce M. *A Textual Commentary on the Greek New Testament*. 2nd ed. Stuttgart: Deutsche Bibelgesellschaft, 2002.

Mitchell, Stephen. *Anatolia: Land, Men, and Gods in Asia Minor*. 2 vols. Oxford: Clarendon, 1993.

Moffatt, James. *An Introduction to the Literature of the New Testament*. 3rd ed. The International Theological Library. Edited by Chas. A. Briggs and S. D. F. Salmond. New York: Scribner's Sons, 1915.

Mohrmann, Douglas C. "Of 'Doing' and 'Living': The Intertextual Semantics of Leviticus 18:5 in Galatians and Romans." Pages 151–172 in *Jesus and Paul: Global Perspectives in Honor of James D.G. Dunn for His 70th Birthday*. Edited by B. J. Oropeza, C. K. Robertson, and Douglas C. Mohrmann. New York: T&T Clark, 2009.

Moo, Douglas J. *Galatians*. Baker Exegetical Commentary on the New Testament. Grand Rapids: Baker, 2013.

———. "The Law of Christ as the Fulfillment of the Law of Moses: A Modified Lutheran View." Pages 319–76 in *Five Views on Law and Gospel*. Edited by Wayne G. Strickland. Grand Rapids: Zondervan, 1993.

Morales, Rodrigo Jose. "The Words of the Luminaries, the Curse of the Law, and the Outpouring of the Spirit in Gal 3,10–14." *Zeitschrift für die neutestamentliche Wissenschaft und die Kunde der älteren Kirche* 100 no. 2 (2009): 269–77.

Morland, Kjell Arne. *The Rhetoric of Curse in Galatians: Paul Confronts Another Gospel.* Emory Studies in Early Christianity. Atlanta: Scholars Press, 1995.

Motyer, J. Alec. *The Prophecy of Isaiah: An Introduction & Commentary.* Downers Grove, IL: InterVarsity Press, 1993.

Moulton, J. H., and G. Milligan. *Vocabulary of the Greek Testament.* London: Hodder & Stoughton, 1930.

Myers, Alicia D. "'For It Has Been Written': Paul's Use of Isa 54:1 in Gal 4:27 in Light of Gal 3:1–5:1." *Perspectives in Religious Studies* 37 no. 3 (2010): 295–308.

Nanos, Mark D., ed. *The Galatians Debate: Contemporary Issues in Rhetorical and Historical Interpretation.* Peabody, MA: Hendrickson, 2002.

Naselli, Andrew David. *How to Understand and Apply the New Testament: Twelve Steps from Exegesis to Theology.* Phillipsburg: P&R Publishing, 2017.

Novenson, Matthew V. *Christ among the Messiahs: Christ Language in Paul and Messiah Language in Ancient Judaism.* New York: Oxford University Press, 2012.

Oakes, Peter. *Galatians.* Paideia: Commentaries on the New Testament. Grand Rapids: Baker, 2015.

O'Brien, Peter T. "Was Paul Converted?" Pages 361–392 in *Justification and Variegated Nomism: Volume 2: The Paradoxes of Paul*. Edited by D. A. Carson, Peter T. O'Brien, and Mark Seifrid. Grand Rapids: Baker, 2004.

Olley, John W. *"Righteousness" in the Septuagint of Isaiah: A Contextual Study.* SBLSCS. Missoula, MT: Scholars, 1979.

O'Neill, J. C. *The Recovery of Paul's Letter to the Galatians.* London: SPCK, 1972.

Ortlund, Dane C. *Zeal without Knowledge: The Concept of Zeal in Romans 10, Galatians 1, and Philippians 3.* Library of New Testament Studies. London: T&T Clark, 2012.

Oswalt, John N. *The Book of Isaiah: Chapters 40-66.* New International Commentary on the Old Testament. Grand Rapids: Eerdmans, 1998.

———. "Righteousness in Isaiah: A Study of the Function of Chapters 56-66 in the Present Structure of the Book." Pages 177–91 in *Writing and Reading the Scroll of Isaiah: Studies of an Interpretive Tradition*. Edited by Craig C. Broyles and Craig A. Evans. Leiden: Brill, 1997.

Packer, J. I. *Knowing God.* 20th anniversary ed. Downers Grove, IL: InterVarsity Press, 1993.

Perriman, Andrew C. "The Rhetorical Strategy of Galatians 4:21–5:1." *Evangelical Quarterly* 65 (1993): 27–42.

Pfitzner, V. C. *Paul and the Agon Motif. Traditional Athletic Imagery in the Pauline Literature*. Vol. 16. Supplements to Novum Testamentum. Leiden: E.J. Brill, 1967.

Polliack, Meira. "Deutero-Isaiah's Typological Use of Jacob in the Portrayal of Israel's National Renewal." Pages 72–110 in *Creation in Jewish and Christian Tradition*. Edited by Henning Graf Reventlow and Yair Hoffman. London: Sheffield Academic, 2002.

Porter, Stanley E. *Idioms of the Greek New Testament*. Biblical Languages: Greek. Sheffield: JSOT Press, 1992.

Porter, Stanley E., and Andrew W. Pitts. "Πίστις with a Preposition and Genitive Modifier: Lexical, Semantic and Syntactic Considerations in the Πίστις Χριστοῦ Discussion." Pages 33–56 in *The Faith of Jesus Christ: Exegetical, Biblical, and Theological Studies*. Edited by Michael F. Bird and Preston M. Sprinkle. Peabody, MA: Hendrickson, 2009.

Räisänen, Heikki. *Paul and the Law*. Wissenschaftliche Untersuchungen Zum Neuen Testament. Tübingen: J. C. B. Mohr, 1983.

Ramsay, William Mitchell. *A Historical Commentary on St. Paul's Epistle to the Galatians*. New York: G. P. Putnam's Sons, 1900.

Reece, Steve. *Paul's Large Letters: Paul's Autographic Subscriptions in the Light of Ancient Epistolary Conventions*. Library of New Testament Studies 561. London: T&T Clark, 2017.

Richards, E. Randolph. *Paul and First-Century Letter Writing: Secretaries, Composition, and Collection*. Downers Grove, IL: InterVarsity Press, 2004.

Riesner, Rainer. *Paul's Early Period: Chronology, Mission Strategy, Theology*. Grand Rapids: Eerdmans, 1998.

Robertson, A. T. *A Grammar of the Greek New Testament in the Light of Historical Research*. New York: Hodder & Stoughton, 1915.

Rosner, Brian S. *Paul and the Law: Keeping the Commandments of God*. New Studies in Biblical Theology. Downers Grove, IL: InterVarsity Press, 2013.

Rowland, Chris. "A Summary of Sabbath Observance in Judaism at the Beginning of the Christian Era." Pages 43–55 in *From Sabbath to Lord's Day: A Biblical, Historical, and Theological Investigation*. Edited by D. A. Carson. Grand Rapids: Zondervan, 1982.

Rusam, Dietrich. "Neue Belege Zu Den Stoicheia Tou Kosmou (Gal 4,3.9, Kol 2,8.20)." *Zeitschrift für die neutestamentliche Wissenschaft und die Kunde der Älteren Kirche* 83 (1992): 119–25.

Ryken, Leland, Jim Wilhoit, Tremper Longman, Colin Duriez, Douglas Penney, and Daniel G. Reid. *Dictionary of Biblical Imagery*. Downers Grove, IL: InterVarsity Press, 1998.

Sandnes, Karl Olav. *Paul—One of the Prophets? A Contribution to the Apostle's Self-Understanding*. Wissenschaftliche Untersuchungen zum Neuen Testament. Tübingen: J. C. B. Mohr, 1991.

Schäfer, Peter. "Die Torah der messianischen Zeit." *Zeitschrift für die neu-testamentliche Wissenschaft und die Kunde der Älteren Kirche* 65 no. 1–2 (1974): 27–42.

Schnabel, Eckhard J. *Early Christian Mission*. 2 vols. Downers Grove, IL: InterVarsity Press, 2004.

Schreiner, Thomas R. "Baptism in the Epistles." Pages 67–96 in *Believer's Baptism: Sign of the New Covenant in Christ*. Edited by Thomas R. Schreiner and Shawn D. Wright. Nashville: B&H Academic, 2006.

———. *Galatians*. Zondervan Exegetical Commentary the New Testament. Grand Rapids: Zondervan, 2010.

———. *Interpreting the Pauline Epistles*. Guides to New Testament Exegesis. Grand Rapids: Baker, 1990.

———. *The Law and Its Fulfillment: A Pauline Theology of Law*. Grand Rapids: Baker, 1993.

———. *New Testament Theology: Magnifying God in Christ*. Grand Rapids: Baker, 2008.

Schreiner, Thomas R., and Ardel B. Caneday. *The Race Set before Us: A Biblical Theology of Perseverance & Assurance*. Downers Grove, IL: InterVarsity Press, 2001.

Scott, James M. *Adoption as Sons of God: An Exegetical Investigation into the Background of Huiothesia in the Pauline Corpus*. Wissenschaftliche Untersuchungen zum Neuen Testament 2/48. Tübingen: Mohr, 1993.

Scott, James M. *Adoption as Sons of God: An Exegetical Investigation into the Background of Υιοθεσια in the Pauline Corpus*. Wissenschaftliche Untersuchungen zum Neuen Testament. Tübingen: J. C. B. Mohr, 1992.

———. *Paul and the Nations: The Old Testament and Jewish Background of Paul's Mission to the Nations with Special Reference to the Destination of Galatians*. Wissenschaftliche Untersuchungen zum Neuen Testament. Tübingen: J. C. B. Mohr, 1995.

Scullion, John J. "Sedeq-Sedeqah in Isaiah Cc 40–66 with Special Reference to the Continuity in Meaning between Second and Third Isaiah." *Ugarit-Forschungen* 3 (1971): 335–48.

Seifrid, Mark A. "The Faith of Christ." Pages 129–146 in *The Faith of Jesus Christ: Exegetical, Biblical, and Theological Studies*. Edited by Michael F. Bird and Preston M. Sprinkle. Peabody, MA: Hendrickson, 2009.

———. "Paul's Use of Righteousness Language against Its Hellenistic Background." Pages 39–74 in *Justification and Variegated Nomism Volume 2—the Paradoxes of Paul*. Edited by D. A. Carson, Peter T. O'Brien, and Mark A. Seifrid. Grand Rapids: Baker, 2004.

———. "Righteousness Language in the Hebrew Scriptures and Early Judaism." Pages 415–42 in *Justification and Variegated Nomism Volume 1—the Complexities of Second Temple Judaism*. Edited by D. A. Carson, Peter T. O'Brien, and Mark A. Seifrid. Grand Rapids: Baker, 2001.

Shelton, Jo-Ann. *As the Romans Did: A Sourcebook in Roman Social History*. 2nd ed. New York: Oxford University Press, 1998.

Silva, Moisés. "Faith Versus Works of Law in Galatians." Pages 217–48 in *Justification and Variegated Nomism: Volume 2: The Paradoxes of Paul*. Edited by D. A. Carson, Peter T. O'Brien, and Mark Seifrid. Grand Rapids: Baker, 2004.

———. *Interpreting Galatians: Explorations in Exegetical Method*. 2nd ed. Grand Rapids: Baker, 2001.

Smith, Michael J. "The Role of the Pedagogue in Galatians." *Bibliotheca Sacra* 163 no. 650 (2006): 197–214.

Spieckerman, Hermann. "The Conception and Prehistory of the Idea of Vicarious Suffering in the Old Testament." Pages 1–15 in *The Suffering Servant: Isaiah 53 in Jewish and Christian Sources*. Edited by Bernd Janowski and Peter Stuhlmacher. Grand Rapids: Eerdmans, 2004.

Sprinkle, Preston M. *Law and Life: The Interpretation of Leviticus 18:5 in Early Judaism and in Paul*. Wissenschaftliche Untersuchungen Zum Neuen Testament. 2. Reihe. Tübingen: Mohr Siebeck, 2007.

———. "Πίστις Χριστοῦ as an Eschatological Event." Pages 165–184 in *The Faith of Jesus Christ: Exegetical, Biblical, and Theological Studies*. Edited by Michael F. Bird and Preston M. Sprinkle. Peabody, MA: Hendrickson, 2009.

Stec, David M. *The Targum of Psalms*. The Aramaic Bible. Collegeville, MN: Liturgical Press, 2004.

Steinmann, Andrew. *From Abraham to Paul: A Biblical Chronology*. St. Louis: Concordia, 2011.

Strelan, John G. "Burden-Bearing and the Law of Christ: A Re-Examination of Galatians 6:2." *Journal of Biblical Literature* 94 (1975): 266–76.

Stuhlmacher, Peter. *Biblische Theologie des Neuen Testaments*. 2 vols. Göttingen: Vandenhoeck & Ruprecht, 1992.

Stuhlmueller, Carroll. *Creative Redemption in Deutero-Isaiah*. Analecta Biblica. Rome: Biblical Institute Press, 1970.

Thielman, Frank. *Paul and the Law: A Contextual Approach*. Downers Grove, IL: InterVarsity Press, 1994.

Tolmie, D. F. *Persuading the Galatians: A Text-Centred Rhetorical Analysis of a Pauline Letter*. Wissenschaftliche Untersuchungen zum Neuen Testament. Tübingen: Mohr Siebeck, 2005.

———. "Tendencies in the Interpretation of Galatians 3:28 since 1990." *Acta Theologica* 19 (2014): 105–29.

Turner, Nigel. *Syntax*. Vol. 3 of A Grammar of New Testament Greek. Edited by James Hope Moulton. Edinburgh: T&T Clark, 1963.

VanLandingham, Chris. *Judgment & Justification in Early Judaism and the Apostle Paul*. Peabody, MA: Hendrickson, 2006.

Varner, William C. "Can Papyri Correspondence Help Us to Understand Paul's 'Large Letters' in Galatians?" In *Paratextual Features of New Testament Papyrology and Early Christian Manuscripts*. Edited by Stanley E. Porter, David I. Yoon, and Chris S. Stevens. Leiden: Brill, 2021.

Wagner, J. Ross. *Heralds of the Good News: Isaiah and Paul in Concert in the Letter to the Romans*. Leiden: Brill, 2003.

Wakefield, Andrew H. *Where to Live: The Hermeneutical Significance of Paul's Citations from Scripture in Galatians 3:1–14*. Academia Biblica. Boston: Brill, 2003.

Waldow, Hans Eberhard von. "The Message of Deutero-Isaiah." *Interpretation* 22 no. 3 (1968): 259–87.

Wallace, Daniel B. *Greek Grammar Beyond the Basics: An Exegetical Syntax of the New Testament.* Grand Rapids: Zondervan, 1996.

Wallis, Ian G. *The Faith of Jesus Christ in Early Christian Traditions.* Society for New Testament Studies Monograph Series. Cambridge: Cambridge University Press, 1995.

Watson, Francis. *Paul and the Hermeneutics of Faith.* New York: T&T Clark, 2004.

Watts, Rikki E. "Consolation or Confrontation? Isaiah 40–55 and the Delay of the New Exodus." *Tyndale Bulletin* 41 (1990): 31–48.

———. "Jesus' Death, Isaiah 53, and Mark 10:45: A Crux Revisited." Pages 125–51 in *Jesus and the Suffering Servant: Isaiah 53 and Christian Origins.* Edited by W. H. Bellinger and William Reuben Farmer. Harrisburg, PA: Trinity Press, 1998.

Weima, Jeffrey A. D. "Gal. 6:11–18: A Hermeneutical Key to the Galatian Letter." *Calvin Theological Journal* 28 (1993): 90–107.

———. *Neglected Endings: The Significance of the Pauline Letter Closings.* Journal for the Study of the New Testament Supplement Series. Sheffield: JSOT Press, 1994.

———. *Paul the Ancient Letter Writer: An Introduction to Epistolary Analysis.* Grand Rapids: Baker Academic, 2016.

Westerholm, Stephen. *Perspectives Old and New on Paul: The "Lutheran" Paul and His Critics.* Grand Rapids: Eerdmans, 2004.

Westermann, Claus. *Isaiah 40–66: A Commentary.* OTL. Philadelphia: Westminster, 1969.

Whitley, C. F. "Deutero-Isaiah's Interpretation of Sedeq." *Vetus Testamentum* 22 (1972): 469–75.

Wilcox, Max. "The Promise of the 'Seed' in the New Testament and the Targumin." *Journal for the Study of the New Testament* 5 (1979): 2–20.

Wilder, William N. *Echoes of the Exodus Narrative in the Context and Background of Galatians 5:18.* Studies in Biblical Literature. New York: Lang, 2001.

———. "'To Whom Has the Arm of the Lord Been Revealed?' Signs and Wonders in Paul's Isaianic Mission to the Gentiles (Romans 15:18–21 and Galatians 3:1–5)." Pages 225–44 in *The Crucified Apostle: Essays on Peter and Paul.* Edited by Todd A. Wilson and Paul R. House. Tübingen: Mohr Siebeck, 2017.

Wilk, Florian. *Die Bedeutung des Jesajabuches für Paulus.* Forschungen zur Religion und Literatur des Alten und Neuen Testaments. Göttingen: Vandenhoeck & Ruprecht, 1998.

Williams, Sam K. "Again Pistis Christou." *The Catholic Biblical Quarterly* 49 no. 3 (1987): 431–47.

Williamson, Paul R. *Abraham, Israel, and the Nations: The Patriarchal Promise and Its Covenantal Development in Genesis.* Journal for the Study of the Old Testament. Supplement Series 315. Sheffield: Sheffield Academic, 2000.

Willitts, Joel. "Isa 54,1 in Gal 4,24b–27: Reading Genesis in Light of Isaiah." *Zeitschrift für die Neutestamentliche Wissenschaft* 96 no. 3 (2005): 188–210.

Wilson, Mark. "Galatia." Pages 522–31 in *The World of the New Testament: Cultural, Social, and Historical Contexts*. Edited by Joel B. Green and Lee Martin McDonald. Grand Rapids: Baker, 2013.

Wilson, Todd A. "Wilderness Apostasy and Paul's Portrayal of the Crisis in Galatians." *New Testament Studies* 50 (2004): 550–71.

Winter, Bruce W. "Civic Obligations: Galatians 6.11–18." Pages 123–44 in *Seek the Welfare of the City: Christians as Benefactors and Citizens*. Edited by Bruce W. Winter. Grand Rapids: Eerdmans, 1994.

Witherington, Ben. *Grace in Galatia: A Commentary on St. Paul's Letter to the Galatians*. Grand Rapids: Eerdmans, 1998.

Witulski, Thomas. *Die Adressaten des Galaterbriefes: Untersuchungen zur Gemeinde von Antiochia ad Pisidiam*. Forschungen zur Religion und Literatur des Alten und Neuen Testaments. Göttingen: Vandenhoeck & Ruprecht, 2000.

Wood, J. Edwin. "Isaac Typology in the New Testament." *New Testament Studies* 14 no. 4 (1968): 583–89.

Wright, N. T. *The Climax of the Covenant: Christ and the Law in Pauline Theology*. Minneapolis: Fortress, 1992.

———. *Justification: God's Plan & Paul's Vision*. Downers Grove, IL: InterVarsity Press, 2009.

———. *Paul and His Recent Interpreters: Some Contemporary Debates*. London: SPCK, 2015.

———. *Paul and the Faithfulness of God*. Christian Origins and the Question of God. Minneapolis: Fortress, 2013.

Young, Edward J. *The Book of Isaiah*. Grand Rapids: Eerdmans, 1972.

Zerwick, Maximilian. *Biblical Greek: Illustrated by Examples*. Roma: Editrice Pontificio Intituto Biblico, 1963.

Ziesler, John A. *The Meaning of Righteousness in Paul: A Linguistic and Theological Enquiry*. Society for New Testament Studies Monograph Series. Cambridge: Cambridge University Press, 1972.

SCRIPTURE INDEX

EXTRABIBLICAL SOURCES INDEX